*Character Disorders
and Adaptative Mechanisms*

Peter L. Giovacchini, M.D.

Character Disorders and Adaptative Mechanisms

Jason Aronson, Inc.
New York and London

Library of Congress Cataloging in Publication Data

Giovacchini, Peter L.
  Character disorders and adaptative mechanisms.

  Rev. ed. of: Psychoanalysis of character disorders.
c1975.
  Bibliography: p. 509
  Includes index.
  1. Personality, Disorders of. 2. Psychoanalysis.
I. Title. [DNLM: 1. Personality disorders—Therapy.
2. Psychoanalytic therapy. 3. Adaptation, Psychological.
WM 460.6 G512p]
RC554.G56 1983   616.8′917   83-11957
ISBN 0-87668-641-2

Manufactured in the United States of America.

Contents

Foreword

This volume represents an important and representative cross section of Peter L. Giovacchini's work as a psychoanalyst and a psychiatrist, as a clinical teacher, and as a researcher, over a period of almost two decades. It represents a wide spectrum of clinical interests in the study of psychopathology, in the exploration of developmental and ego-psychological problems, and in the investigation of a variety of object relationships, of clinical and technical issues in psychoanalysis and psychotherapy. It also touches on the exploration of psychosomatics.

The author does not make it easy for us, since he offers no final answers or definite and well-defined techniques. He has no complete textbook for us, but rather invites us to follow him into areas not yet well explored. He poses many open-ended questions without the usual ready-made, much-demanded generalizations. Thus, he follows a great tradition, since Freud himself never offered us a complete textbook on psychoanalytic technique, preferring to describe his work as "the patchwork of my labors." In 1913, he wrote a paper on technique concerning the beginning of treatment in which he suggested that:

> Anyone who hopes to learn the noble game of chess from books will soon discover that only the opening and end-games admit of an exhaustive, systematic presentation and that the infinite variety of moves which develop after the opening defy any such description. This gap in instruction can only be filled by a diligent study of games fought out by masters. The rules which can be laid down for the practice of psychoanalytic treatment are subject to similar limitations.

I do not know whether Giovacchini could or should try to sum up the experiences laid down in his volume in the form of a complete technique. I rather think that he would not. He would prefer to see himself as a teacher who wants colleagues and students to follow him into these different "games," the description of segments of difficult treatment situations. In this way they could then acquire the necessary sensitivity to go beyond some of the simple beginning and ending moves and achieve the skill "of games fought out by masters."

I believe that this is the only route leading to new and lesser-known areas of psychoanalytic treatment. However, I also know how one might react with dissatisfaction to an invitation to follow an author into the jungle of clinical experience without a safe and clear map of a well-built city allowing for a clear grid, like certain parts of Chicago or Manhattan; or the kind of old-world city map which looks like concentric circles leading from the center of the city to the periphery.

Giovacchini has followed the uncertain path along which many of us travelled when we attempted to discover whether psychoanalytic thinking and psychoanalytic technique could be applied to cases other than those to which we applied the classical technique. The cases he discusses are not primarily neurotics, but are borderline cases, prepsychotics, and schizophrenics—adults as well as adolescents. He applies psychoanalysis, psychoanalytic thinking, and psychoanalytic technique to all these cases, which would not have been considered in the past, and thus he joins those who speak about that "widening scope of psychoanalysis." This is not an easy path to travel. One would need to move out of clearly mapped areas and venture into uncharted territory. The unmarked path often leads into unknown regions, into other countries, into borderline regions; we find ourselves in situations where ordinary and simple conceptualizations are not always possible.

It is exactly that kind of clinical and scientific courage Giovacchini displays which makes him attractive to us. At the same time, however, he becomes suspect since he must deviate from the more comfortable assumptions usually expressed within the framework of classical psychoanalysis. It is not the first time that he has presented us with this dilemma: he wrote a book with L. Bryce Boyer on the *Psychoanalytic Treatment of Characterological and Schizophrenic Disorders* and he edited another on *Tactics and Techniques in Psychoanalytic Therapy*. Both these volumes are written in the same spirit as Freud's when he refused a demand to prepare a finished and definitive technique. He feared, of course, that such a "definitive" technique, while meeting an understandable desire on the part of his students and followers, might also close the door to further investigations.

In order to treat special cases of anxiety, patients with serious ego defects, subtle or overt identity problems, patients suffering from especially regressed states, symbiotic involvements, and special pathologies in the capacity to form object relations, and patients involved with serious psychosomatic disorders, Giovacchini had to borrow from theory and clinical experience wherever he could. Consequently, he does not satisfy those who would put him into their preferred pigeonhole, and make him belong to one clear and well-defined school of thought.

The reader who wants from Giovacchini a clear-cut commitment to a specific school of thought among the analytic schools will find himself deprived. The reader, however, who is satisfied with a more tentative approach, a willingness to identify with Freud's comment that: "We have never prided ourselves on the completeness and finality of our knowledge and capacity. We are just as ready now as we were earlier to meet the imperfections of our understanding, to learn new things and to alter our methods in any way that can improve them," will find this volume full of rich material, full of new openings, refreshing observations, and useful technical innovations.

This is a psychoanalytic book and describes both psychoanalytic treatment and psychoanalytically oriented psychotherapy in the spirit of Freud. It takes, perhaps, most of its nourishment from modern ego psychology in terms of adaptation and identity, but it is also heavily influenced by the different English schools of psychoanalysis.

He who borrows from different approaches, whether they are clinical or theoretical, will suffer from a certain kind of fragmentation and incompleteness, but that is exactly the fate of him who ventures out into the jungle, into virgin territory, and tries to open up a new path. It is difficult to follow him and to feel safe in these new areas. It creates a special problem for the reader who has not as yet made this journey. But that is true for all ventures which are to help us conquer the unknown or lesser known and to improve on our techniques. Giovacchini wants us to remain eternal learners. I think we learn best if we believe our teachers, too, are learners, rather than masters with final answers.

Giovacchini constantly refers to the therapeutic self, to countertransference problems, and to the task of turning countertransference obstacles into treatment opportunities, thus strengthening the therapeutic self as well as our theoretical armamentarium.

There is something highly personal about Giovacchini's contribution and his way of teaching. He once invited me to participate in teaching his students at the University of Illinois through a two- or three-hour lunch period. It was quite a meal. His volume is quite a meal; rich, challenging, and full of clinical inspiration. Having read such a volume, one feels the need to sit down with Giovacchini to talk about it for a long time, to digest it. That is what a book should do. Its reading should not be the end, but rather the means to further study, of continued work, of self-challenge, and challenge of the author. I suspect that Giovacchini might well deem that this should be the accepted function of his volume. And I want it to fulfill that task, a responsibility for the author and the readers alike.

RUDOLF EKSTEIN, PH.D.

Preface to the Second Edition

The first edition of this book, *Psychoanalysis of Character Disorders*, focused on patients whose psychopathology derived from structural defects rather than intrapsychic conflict. Although there is still controversy about the indications and contraindications for psychoanalytic treatment, many psychoanalysts have revised their previous standards and have successfully treated patients whose orientation is much more primitive than one based upon an oedipal configuration. Rather than accepting Freud's dictums about nosology (the transference and narcissistic neuroses) and treatability, therapists are now thinking in terms of the process and the interaction between patient and analyst in transference and countertransference. This is now a generally acceptable approach in contrast to the rigidly held classical attitude that prevailed in psychoanalytic circles when some of the chapters in this book were first published.

With the expansion of our clinical endeavors, the concept of psychic structure becomes increasingly dominant. Developmental stages are more important in defining the treatment process. In view of the psychopathology now encountered, many therapists no longer focus on drives, as Freud did when he postulated the sequence of psychosexual development. Instead, they concentrate on the structural characteristics of early stages of development within the context of individuation and object relations. This in no way minimizes the importance of drives and inner needs; rather, it places them in a different, preoedipal perspective. In the treatment of patients with structural defects, the transference regression is to extremely primitive ego states.

Freud placed autoerotism at the primitive end of his developmental spectrum, followed by primary and then secondary narcissism. He next described psychosexual stages that seemed to exemplify what we now call "part-object relationships." He postulated a developmental hierarchy progressing from the oral phase to the phallic phase and, finally, to the whole object-oriented genital phase, which is achieved through the resolution of the oedipal complex. He restricted the psychoanalytic method to patients whose fixation points and regression did not go further back than the oral phase. In his view, more primitively fixated patients belonged in the category of narcissistic neuroses (which included the psychoses) and were psychoanalytically untreatable. Many of the chapters in this volume represent attempts to prove otherwise.

This book deals with patients whose treatment regression goes back to the beginning of the formation of object relationships. These severely regressed patients are commonly seen by therapists today. To understand these patients, it is necessary to make the shift in conceptual perspective from Freud's id psychology to a comprehensive ego psychology.

Patients suffering from fixations at primitive mental states test our therapeutic acumen and analytic dedication to the limit. Although they certainly create technical problems that lead to therapeutic impasses, the greatest difficulties clinicians experience with such patients stem from disruptive countertransference reactions. These patients have an uncanny ability to discover and exploit our personal vulnerabilities, which may cause us to abandon our analytic perspective. We may feel so anxious, angry, and disturbed that we do not want to continue with their treatment. Sometimes their demands are so unreasonable that we cannot maintain them in an outpatient setting. However, if we can understand them in terms of primitive adaptations and their attempts to recreate the infantile environment in the treatment setting, analytic therapy may be possible.

Reaching the primitive depths of the psyche teaches us about the extensive range of mental functioning which encompasses reflex activities and primary-process operations at the earliest developmental levels, and sophisticated logic and secondary process orientations at later stages of development. This book includes chapters that deal with the higher-level processes and how they are influenced by psychopathology and structural defects. Secondary-process perceptions and actions become part of the ego's executive system and, as the ego relates to the outer world, they represent adaptive techniques that contribute to the psyche's autonomy. The ultimate adaptation leads to creative accomplishment.

Regression and progression are intimately related. The psychoanalytic understanding of character disorders deepens our insights about human nature, the depths of misery and despair, and the sublime moments of creative accomplishment. This second edition represents an extension of the previous volume in that it includes chapters that focus upon progressive factors.

As Freud repeatedly demonstrated, the understanding of psychopathology gives us insights about nonpathological mental operations. Defects in character structure, with accompanying pathological defenses such as splitting, projective identification, and overcompensatory megalomania, are related to creativity. This does not mean that creativity is the outcome of psychopathology; in fact, the chapters in Part VII demonstrate that creativity occurs despite psychopathology. However, the primitive mental mechanisms operating in psychopathological processes are also significant in creative achievement.

Preface to the First Edition

This book represents a substantial segment of my life's work. The reader will find the same clinical episodes and the same descriptions of theoretical formulations in different contexts. Each time that I refer to a specific case I do so from a different viewpoint. This allows the reader to follow me as I move from formulations based on id content to formulations based on ego development and ego structure, particularly as it is reflected in the sense of identity, and into discussions of ego operations as they affect the clinical therapeutic relationship. A general survey of the topics represented here demonstrates a pattern, one which developed without any conscious or deliberate intent, but which I believe is fairly common among those who finally choose psychoanalysis as their principal endeavor. I shall elaborate upon the pattern since it is reflected in these chapters, but more importantly, because it may tell us something significant about aspects of a psychoanalyst's character structure, at least as it pertains to his or her professional self-representation. In consequence, it may have some bearing upon the frames of reference that each psychoanalyst creates and that contribute to each analyst's particular mode of scientific thinking.

Insofar as I am going to make a comparison with Sigmund Freud, a note of apology and explanation is in order. As readers grasp what I believe to be my particular professional evolution, they will note some parallels to Freud. At worst, this could be pretentious but harmless, and simply indicate an identification with the master. The latter is a fairly common phenomenon among psychoanalysts. Still, I must point out that my acquaintance with psychoanalysis occurred at the very end of my medical training and I knew very little, if anything, about Freud's personal development and had only a sparse and confused contact with his writings. Jones's biography was still far ahead of me, for I was already a candidate in psychoanalytic training when it first appeared in print. Further, open reflections on the theme of my development have revealed similar backgrounds among many colleagues.

My first interest was science, principally the physical sciences. In this regard I differ from some colleagues whose main interest in the biological sciences led them to enroll in a premedical program in college. These students emphasized that they were interested in both science and people; therefore, medicine represented an ideal professional choice. I began with what I considered pure science—physics, chemistry, and mathematics—

and then noted that the laboratory was a lonely place. Adolescence was too restless a period to isolate oneself from the world.

Adolescence is also a period where one's perceptions of the external world, of people, are heightened. Being dedicated to science, it would be natural to focus one's interest on a scientific understanding of people. I believe this transition from science, whether biological or physical, to clinical studies is a fairly common sequence among those who choose to become physicians. The shift of interest from the body to the mind is not as frequent a phenomenon but, of course, it must occur in those medical students or physicians who choose to specialize in psychiatry.

Again referring to my personal experience, I was very skeptical as an undergraduate science student of the existence of an unconscious mind, and in my amateurish fashion insisted that anything could and should be explained in physico-chemical concepts. However, I must have been extremely ambivalent, because my conversion was sudden and complete.

One evening a fraternity brother offered to demonstrate hypnosis to me, probably in response to my sophomoric, materialistic approach. I was converted from a scoffing skeptic to a devout believer and was fascinated with the data that hypnosis provided pointing to the existence of an unconscious mind, that is, to a dynamic unconscious. From then until I began psychiatric training, I became a promiscuous practitioner of hypnosis. When I started actually learning something about it, I became more reserved and, as a psychiatrist, I have seldom used it. Following my personal analysis, I have had no inclination to practice this method, either investigatively or therapeutically, and I attribute its previous fascination for me to its omnipotent and melodramatic features.

Still, the existence of the unconscious had been, in my mind, proved and it continued to have a pressing and decisive influence, particularly so since the majority of the patients seen in medical outpatient clinics seldom demonstrated clear-cut organic pathology. Therefore, it was natural to become interested in psychosomatic medicine, an obvious transition from an initial medical orientation to a psychologically minded approach. This interest was further implemented because of the prevailing psychosomatic atmosphere in Chicago under Franz Alexander's charismatic leadership.

I have not included in this volume some of my first published efforts in this direction since they were written under the influence of Alexander's specificity hypothesis, which states that certain psychosomatic entities, originally seven, can be associated with certain psychodynamic constellations (Alexander was careful not to speak in terms of linear or singular etiologies). Instead, the chapters presented here have departed from the orientation of what has sometimes been referred to as the "Chicago

School" and represent efforts to view psychosomatic conditions in an ego-psychological frame of reference.

In any case, my thinking throughout the years, influenced by the type of patients that consulted me, wandered further away from the medical model and found itself immersed in psychoanalysis. My preoccupations with the unconscious mind became crucial and stood alone without leaning upon the principles of organic medicine.

Freud, after having written his "Project" (Breuer and Freud, 1895), constructed psychoanalysis purely on psychological grounds and elaborated an id-oriented metapsychology. In a similar manner, many of us had to undergo the same detachment from previous orientations and embrace wholly the psychoanalytic viewpoint. Many psychiatrists have not chosen such complete detachment, but others have found the psychoanalytic model the most useful both for understanding and treating patients in what might be called a scientific manner, that is, treatment based upon an understanding of psychic processes and etiological factors. Such an approach has been the most comfortable one for me and is in accord with my earlier scientific orientation.

This volume reflects the clinical problems that I and my colleagues have faced in attempting to apply standard psychodynamic formulations to our patients who very seldom resemble the classical neurotic cases Freud described so thoroughly. We have had to understand our patients from another perspective, in terms of characterological modalities and psychopathology—that is, in structural terms—in contrast to Freud's earlier psychodynamic approach. The theoretical perspective has shifted from an exclusively id-oriented metapsychology to one that embraces ego psychology. Freud himself paved the way for the understanding of these cases in his study of what he initially labeled "narcissistic psychoneuroses."

One would expect that, since the technique of psychoanalysis was elaborated from the treatment of patients suffering from transference neuroses, the so-called classical psychoneuroses, the clinician might have to modify the orthodox analytic approach in dealing with different types of patients. Many believe that such revisions are necessary and Freud himself often asserted that psychoanalysis was not an effective method for the treatment of such patients. To some extent, this viewpoint was emphasized in my training. Alexander and his co-workers introduced a variety of techniques to treat a wide range of patients under a variety of circumstances, techniques that were based upon psychoanalytic principles but that emphasized manipulation and management rather than analysis. Unfortunately, many of us believed that what we were being taught was analysis. This volume, on the contrary, represents a return to the analytic viewpoint and also indicates the belief that our patients are not fundamentally different, even though they may appear to be so from a phenomenological viewpoint, from those that Freud saw. It also emphasizes that modifications of technique, whether they are accepted as modifications or as analysis proper, are not only unnecessary but, in many instances, detrimental.

The latter opinion evolved gradually. For myself and several close colleagues, it was related to our dissatisfaction with the results of our nonanalytic, so-called supportive approaches, approaches we believed were based upon psychoanalytic principles and understanding. Working within what was the prevalent frame of reference, I recall instituting parameters and setting up conditions for treatment in order to support a weak ego or to control the acting out of aberrant, disruptive impulses. Sometimes these methods were effective, but most of the time they failed, and often the patient left treatment after a futile struggle. Besides therapeutic failure, I experienced further frustration, because I had not really succeeded in understanding what had occurred between the patient and myself. This latter point was particularly disturbing.

The patient reported in Chapter 2 was very influential in convincing me that one has to understand patients from a perspective that transcends the id-ego psychodynamic model. She taught me the value of focusing upon the psychopathology of ego subsystems, the self-representation in particular, which meant relating most of her symptoms and behavior to the poor amorphous integration of her identity sense. Today, this is a fairly familiar formulation with patients suffering from character disorders but, at the time, the application of the ego-psychological frame of reference to clinical situations was a fairly new approach. I perceived that attempting supportive psychotherapy with such patients could be disastrous. Many patients had been trying to tell me this, but because of my commitment to what I had been taught I had been unable to hear them.

These were exciting times. The application of psychoanalysis to patients that previously had been considered inaccessible created tremendous enthusiasm and caused me and a small group of colleagues and students to feel optimistic, perhaps not without some grandiosity, about our work with patients. Rather than feeling oppressed because we were bewildered, we began discovering patterns of transference responses, similarities and levels of ego development, and points of fixation as well as particular types of adaptations or failures of adaptation. These events and ideas are found in Part I of this book.

With the passage of time, and the acquisition of professional maturity and experience, there was some dampening of the attitude of therapeutic omnipotence, accompanied by further understanding of structural pathology and vicissitudes of transference relationships. In fact, the concept of therapeutic ambition underwent radical revision, and the words of Freud once again were imprinted on us: neither therapeutic nor educative ambition should have a part in psychoanalytic treatment. I am referring primarily to therapeutic ambition, since my developing reserve about using supporting psychotherapy, which I am willing to attribute to some personal characteristics, had caused me to relinquish any educational goals I might have harbored. These goals, however, undoubtedly remained with me to some extent when treating fellow professionals or students-in-training, and may represent an urge which, at times, is difficult to control. In spite of our efforts, our point of view makes itself felt for better or for worse.

The diminishing of therapeutic ambition occurred within the context of what has frequently been referred to as the analytic impasse. Paradoxically, with patients with characterological disorders, our desire to cure them frequently becomes the chief obstacle to analytic progress. Their early development was hindered by a series of traumas and impasses, and these very impasses have to be experienced within the analysis. As long as the analyst hovers over the patient with expectations, the analyst is really repeating the narcissistic demands of archaic infantile object relations and the patient will react adversely to what is felt to be an intrusion. Thus, the impasse is an intrinsic aspect of the analytic process.

Difficulties in treatment stem mainly from three sources: (1) the nature of the patient's psychopathology, (2) countertransference phenomena, and (3) ignorance on the part of the therapist. After discussing patients from an ego-psychological perspective and specifically emphasizing certain types of object relations, this volume turns to the treatment process and technical difficulties. Surprisingly, it seems that the nature of the psychopathology is not as significant as one might anticipate in creating situations where psychoanalytic treatment is not feasible; rather, countertransference difficulties and ignorance about both the patient's personality structure and the interaction between patient and therapist seem to play a predominant role in producing treatment complications. It also becomes increasingly obvious that countertransference difficulties almost always lead to some ignorance and, conversely, that ignorance often leads to countertransference difficulties.

The achievement of relaxation in a psychoanalytic ambience frequently allows the patient to attempt to dispel our ignorance. Patients do not feel threatened by our not knowing; they find it intolerable, however, to have an analyst who, consciously or unconsciously, pretends to know because he or she cannot stand to be left in a state of ambiguity and suspension.

Analysands are quite tolerant of ignorance and will with great forbearance repeatedly present us with explanatory material and correct our mistakes. It is our countertransference difficulties that stand in the way of our learning from the patient.

On the one hand, the analyst's ignorance is responsible for some of the greatest difficulties in analysis; on the other hand, it represents one of the greatest attractions inherent in conducting psychoanalysis. A major difference between psychoanalysis and other forms of psychotherapy is the therapist's attitude about *sustained ignorance*. Analysts are aware of their not knowing because in time they hope to know. Nonanalytic psychotherapists, by contrast, are not necessarily aware of being ignorant, because their aim is principally symptom remission through some manipulation of the patient's life. Since psychiatrists do not direct their attention to the workings of the patient's mind, they do not have to tolerate sustained ignorance and they become actively involved with external events rather than having to bear the discomfort of frustrated curiosity.

Psychoanalysis has often been accused of being unscientific, even by psychoanalysts. *I believe that such an assertion may have some wish-fulfillment elements, especially when made by a psychoanalyst.*

The scientific attitude is based upon tolerating ambiguity and avoiding premature closure; in other words, as it occurs in psychoanalytic treatment, it depends upon the ability to experience sustained ignorance. As the treatment unfolds, the psychoanalyst becomes a servant of a process, as Masud Khan so aptly put it (personal communication). In this respect, the psychoanalytic attitude and the scientific viewpoint are similar; it is understandable that those who are attracted to psychoanalysis are also basically dedicated to a scientific frame of reference. Adherence to the scientific and analytic viewpoint requires, among other things, a personality that is able to accept not knowing. Many might find this particularly tedious and perhaps sufficiently unbearable that *they strip the treatment of patients suffering from emotional problems of its scientific status and protect themselves from not knowing by behaving as if there were nothing to know.* One's social role then becomes predominantly relevant.

In psychoanalysis, ignorance is sustained but eventually dispelled, and it is the analysand who patiently instructs us. Thus psychoanalysts have two tasks: (1) they have to know that they do not know; and (2) they have to put themselves in a position where they are capable of learning.

This volume reflects these viewpoints. Throughout the years, I and several colleagues have been aware of how little we knew about certain clinical situations. This should not be construed as humbling ourselves or as a sign of false or exhibitionistic modesty. On the contrary, we felt that we had read extensively, had had excellent training, and that all in all we had been rather good and enthusiastic students. We also felt we knew a great deal, probably as much as any of our contemporaries. Still, the application of our knowledge to the treatment of certain patients made us realize how fundamentally ignorant we really were.

This revelation brings me to my final point. The chapters in this volume were not written to demonstrate how much this author knows. *Quite to the contrary, they were written out of ignorance because I knew so little.* They are in one sense an admission of ignorance, but they also indicate receptivity. These chapters represent my patients' attempts to fill lacunae of understanding. I myself have felt enriched, and I believe that my patients have also benefited.

Part I

IDENTITY AND PSYCHOPATHOLOGY

As stated in the preface, my dilemma during my beginning years of practice was predominantly related to understanding the basic structure of the patient's psyche. This became a particularly baffling task because I and my colleagues were formulating clinical data in terms of an id-oriented psychodynamic model. Patients with clearcut symptoms could often be made to fit into one of the standard psychoneurotic categories characterized by specific levels of psychosexual development and corresponding defenses. Frequently, however, the transference did not unfold in a manner that would have been consistent with such formulations, nor did one, throughout the treatment, detect the underlying typical (oedipal) conflict. The problem of understanding the patient in traditional terms became compounded when patients presented clinical pictures where there were no discrete symptoms; instead, they complained of vague, diffuse dissatisfactions with life and felt their amorphous existence to be futile and purposeless.

These papers reflect my clinical experience and represent attempts to make some sense out of how the minds operate in the majority of patients seeking psychotherapeutic help. One can easily note a movement away from a predominantly id-oriented psychology to a clinical approach based primarily upon an understanding of the ego and its subsystems.

Clinical necessity, in my experience, required such a theoretical shift.

1

As with any conceptual scaffold, one is dealing with a method of organizing and understanding data. Here, in contrast to Hartmann's approach, which focuses upon the ego and the interplay of instinctual forces, the adherence to a dual instinct theory is not uppermost. Instead, the psyche is conceptualized in terms of a hierarchy of various adaptations without a separate energic hypothesis. This model emphasizes structural and characterological factors in psychopathology and the role of ego defects, although intrapsychic conflicts are not at all excluded.

I believe the types of patients described in these papers are fairly typical of those seen in clinical practice. Definitively stating the clinical picture often helps us define what otherwise would be an obscure and enigmatic problem. Colleagues, upon learning that one is perplexed by the same situations, become eager to share experiences. These papers are the outcome of endless private conversations, seminars, workshops and discussion groups, as well as countless hours of listening to patients. Many of these formulations will require extensions and revisions but for the moment, and especially at the moment when I felt compelled to construct them, I find them useful in providing some organization and guideline to what otherwise would appear to be a chaotic psychic morass. Any clarification will be reflected in our therapeutic stance and provide us with an increment of security.

Chapter 1

Psychopathologic Aspects of the Identity Sense

In contrast to cases with definitive symptoms reported in the early psychiatric and psychoanalytic literature, the psychiatrist finds that the majority of his patients now do not present well-defined clinical pictures. Whether the classical case descriptions written at the beginning of this century were about disorders fundamentally different from those seen today is a moot question and the differences may be more apparent than real. Nevertheless, many patients seek treatment because they are dissatisfied with their adjustment and are in a quandary as to where they fit in the general scheme of things. Oftentimes these patients are diagnosed as having character disorders or as being borderline cases with a defective identity sense.

Clinically, the patient with a character disorder experiences a multiplicity of affective states and symptoms that are most economically explained by assuming some disturbance in the way the patient views himself. This "view of oneself" has alternately been referred to as "the identity sense," "the self-image," and "the self-concept." Despite the ubiquity of this concept there appears to be no uniform theoretical formulation regarding this particular ego function or its relationship to other ego systems.

The phenomenon of a disturbed identity has been noted in a variety of behavioral states. Patients who regress because of disruption of defenses or the upsurge of conflictual impulses often experience difficulty in retaining a consistent picture of themselves. Adolescence is characterized by doubts and obsessional ruminations about the meaning and purpose of life. Changes in the ego state, whether pathologic, nonpathologic, or as part of psychic development, are reflected in the self-image.

In order to illustrate this type of identity disturbance, the following case vignettes are presented.

Clinical Examples

The patient, a young man in his middle twenties, sought psychotherapy because of general unhappiness with his life. Although there was

First published in *Psychiat. Digest* 26 (1965), 31–41. Reprinted by permission.

nothing specific about his complaints, he felt a vague dissatisfaction in all areas: social, professional and sexual. He sought therapy following the loss of a girlfriend who, tired of his passive, clinging demandingness, left him for another man who was apparently more aggressive and masculine.

Most of the patient's complaints, although seemingly vague at first, began to reveal characteristic patterns. It became more and more apparent that he was concerned with fundamental questions about his existence. He was literally in doubt as to whether he existed and, if he did exist, as to who he was. This was not brought forth openly and directly as in the nihilistic delusion of a psychotic; rather, the patient spoke of his inability to master problems. He described how gauche he felt relating to people simply because he didn't know how. He complained vociferously about not knowing his purpose in life. Although superficially this sounded like sophomoric philosophizing, an undertone of desperation was evident. From his dreams and the development of the transference neurosis it was possible to infer that he was unconsciously concerned with the basic question as to whether he was alive.

Concerning his development, he described his mother as an extremely aggressive woman who never allowed him to do anything for himself, managing his life completely, and by whom he felt "smothered." There were, however, certain comforts and gratifications that he derived from this intensive relationship; she caused him to feel as if he were the center of the universe. On the other hand any attempt to be autonomous, to achieve a degree of separateness was quickly and effectively "squelched" by her. Although the patient was living away from home he had dinner at his mother's house every night and spoke to her on the telephone at least half a dozen times a day.

Insofar as she had picked his girlfriend, both he and his mother were upset at his being jilted. His mother's concern seemed to center upon her feeling that if he married this girl she would still be able to "keep her baby" whereas with another girl this might not be possible. The patient's feelings about his girlfriend were mixed. He liked the idea of having a girl approved of by his mother but he also felt a yearning to try to free himself from her "tentacles" by finding his "own girl." When he contemplated freedom from his mother he would feel exhilaration but the feeling would soon turn into panic.

The most significant and outstanding clinical feature in this case was the feeling this patient had concerning his inability to experience himself as a discrete, autonomous human being. He had a poorly developed concept as to who and what he was. Although there were many aspects to his development that accounted for these vaguely defined psychic boundaries, discussion of them would be tangential to the thesis of this chapter. What I wish to emphasize is the defective development of this patient's identity sense.

The mother's contribution to his emotional difficulties was, of course, crucial. She responded only to her narcissistic needs, a conjecture made from both the patient's material and from the formulation of a psychiatrist who saw her for several interviews when she was afraid of losing her "baby."

It becomes apparent, then, that in order more fully to understand cases like this one, and such cases are by no means uncommon, a more complete elaboration of the concept of the identity sense is necessary. Before attempting to elaborate this concept I will present another case vignette which I believe will highlight other clinical characteristics of the problem.

Identity Diffusion Syndrome

The second patient, also a young man in his middle twenties, revealed that he felt at a complete loss in the handling of routine tasks. The simplest situations had become inordinately complex for him. He described how driving his car two or three blocks was an agonizing and an overwhelmingly complicated experience. Getting up in the morning, brushing his teeth, having breakfast and other daily routines seemed beyond his capacity of organization. He was placed on academic probation when he was not able to complete several term papers that were required in order to remain in school. He pointed out that he had never been able to finish anything. Similar clinical phenomena have been described under the heading of identity diffusion syndrome (Erikson, 1959).

During the course of his therapy he told of innumerable incidents that illustrated his ineptness in social situations and his unfamiliarity with the standards of his social-cultural milieu. For example, he would come to the downtown section of the city in shorts. He was painfully aware that everyone was staring at him but it would take him days before he discovered why he was so conspicuous. He was aggressively nonconformist; this had become one of the main themes of his existence. He could not and would not do things in the same way others did.

If others ate turkey on Thanksgiving he had to have lobster. He would not drive an American car but had to have some unknown, comparatively rare make. His dress, sometimes bizarre, illustrated his need to be different; suit coats and pants never matched. From his description, the furniture in his apartment also showed an unconventional arrangement in that he did not seem to recognize the usual divisions of rooms. He would put living room furniture in the kitchen, kitchen furniture in the bedroom and even refused to sleep in a bed, feeling that a mattress on the floor should be sufficient. In spite of the bizarreness and disordered nature of his daily life, he had many rational arguments to justify his position and these were mainly concerned with ideas of freedom of self-expression and creativity. He recognized, however, the emptiness and futility of his existence and lamented the tragic and dismal fact that he had never been able to produce anything.

He described his mother as a harsh, cruel person. He saw her as a stony, cold and distant woman who treated him as if he were a delicate and sickly child without any capabilities or judgment regarding what was best for himself. His father was killed in an accident before he was born and, although his mother remarried when he was two, he felt his stepfather was a weak and inconsequential person from whom it was impossible to receive any support. He was brought up in a fairly wealthy, aristocratic, upper-class setting where conformity was always stressed.

Despite many economic advantages he had no sense of belonging and saw himself only as a hopelessly inadequate, vulnerable person.

He had never felt alive in any wholesome, healthy fashion and he was very much in doubt as to whether he was capable of feeling anything. He knew the routine expressions and postures that went along with various emotions, such as joy or sadness, but he never really knew whether he had experienced these affects as others did. As with the first patient, he had very little concept of himself as a person, who and what he was and his function in life. The only picture he could conjure of himself was the one he felt his mother had implanted in him, that of a weak, inept child. He found this painful but even pain had a vague quality to it. He felt it incumbent upon himself to combat this feeling of vague disillusion with the types of defenses that have been mentioned, those attempting to establish an autonomous identity, based on nonconformity. To conform was equivalent to being dissolved by his milieu. When he could not feel different he felt like "an atom among an infinite number of atoms," inconspicuous and nonexistent. He had to stand out in some manner, but as has been seen, he failed in that he only reinforced the helpless self-image that he was trying to defend himself against.

Discussion

Both these cases highlight psychopathology that involves ego defects. Their identity disturbances were explicit, and it is my impression that their distress about self feeling was not due to repression resulting from intrapsychic conflict, but was due to faulty development and structural inadequacies.

These patients had, at one time or another, suffered from feelings of depersonalization and derealization. What one feels and how one reacts to inner feelings varies in different circumstances, and there is a gradient from psychopathologic disturbance to better integrated ego states that affects the identity sense. Very often disturbances of the identity equilibrium, so to speak, are found in instances where there has been a precipitous change of environment. One is reminded of Jacobson's (1959) description of political prisoners and their experiences in a concentration camp. Eissler (1953b) speaks about a similar phenomenon when a stranger moves to a foreign country. It is also found in less drastic circumstances, such as leaving work to begin a vacation or returning from a vacation to resume work. At such times of transition there is often a momentary confusion and often some slight degree of depersonalization. In these instances, it is quite apparent that the usual adaptive techniques are no longer effective in the changed environment and that the person, in order to adjust, has to undergo some degree of reorientation.

Adaptive techniques, therefore, as part of the ego's executive system, have to be included in the concept of an identity sense. The ego's reaction to an id impulse, an affect or disturbed homeostasis, is not sufficient, by and of itself, to explain identity and disturbances of identity. The techniques that the ego has to reestablish homeostasis are what distinguish the individual from others and give him the conviction that he exists and of his own identity. It will be recalled that both of these patients felt gauche and inept and did not know how to function in a variety of settings. They complained that they had never "learned" the techniques that would be needed to handle situations that for them were inordinately complex.

Impaired Ego Capacity

If the drives are fixated at infantile levels and not sufficiently integrated with memory traces and with the perceptual and executive systems, the ego's capacity to feel will be impared. The feeling of emptiness is a reaction to lack of structure and is intensified by the inability to achieve satisfaction of inner needs because the patient is not particularly aware of his needs due to their incomplete development and he is unable to relate to external objects in order to obtain gratification. The lack of drive differentiation causes the feelings of estrangement, lonely isolation and emptiness. Furthermore, the second patient especially lacked, relatively speaking, the synthesis and skills required to deal with the complexities of the outer world. Without executive techniques that can achieve mastery vis-á-vis objects, a person's drive for autonomy does not develop and the identity sense is defective.

The establishment of homeostasis is dependent on successful mastery and reflects the general ego integration. The balance and harmony of the various ego systems determine whether the self feeling is one of confidence and integration. One can conceptualize identity as a state of self-awareness that is determined by the ego's integration. However, this self-awareness may not be a direct representation of the ego's integration since what one feels about the self may contain defensive elements to compensate for a lack of integration.

What one feels, like any other psychic element, has to be considered as part of an hierarchic continuum, a spectrum ranging from early primary-process id aspects to reality-oriented, conscious, secondary-process ego elements. The self-image contains all levels of the psychic apparatus. The uppermost layers consist of identifying characteristics which become operationally elaborated; for example: "I am————who is—years old, of a particular race and nationality, so many feet tall, etc. I am————by profession who earns his living by———— This enables me to live in a certain fashion and to satisfy a variety of needs." In other words, there is a continuum from identifying characteristics to executive techniques and needs which can be broken down to their basic elements. As the need becomes elaborated from its physiologic substrate, different levels of the psychic apparatus are set in motion to handle this need in preparation for its gratification. Once the higher techniques of mastery come into play, so do the preconscious identifying characteristics. For example: "I am a man, so big and so strong, a citizen who has certain rights, skilled in my work, and adequate to seek the necessary elements from the outer world to gratify what I feel I need." True, he may not be adequate and the self-image may cover up his helplessness and lack of techniques of mastery but the identity sense is determined by what the person believes himself to be. There can be aspects of a defective self-image that have become repressed, but in the cases presented here there was not sufficient structuralization for such a defense.

Only a small segment of the self-representation can be conscious at any one time. *It is the particular conscious element of the self-image that is experienced at the moment that determines the identity sense.* If the drives are strong, they will be experienced as the characteristic feature of the psyche and determine one's identity. A person may think of himself only in terms of eating or being otherwise needful. If one is engaged in problem solving, then the executive factor, the person's particular profession for example, is a predominant identity if one permits himself a self observation. All these elements can become pathologically distorted and the ego's reactive techniques can become predominant elements of one's identity. If, on the other hand, as these two cases illustrated, there is a paucity of such techniques, then one experiences the defects inherent in the identity sense which lead to the subjective states described and in some instances to behavioral aberrations.

One feels alive because one experiences needs, needs that are initially physiologic. They become elaborated; first one feels oneself in an oral fashion; for example, as a hungry mouth and then, with greater structure, there is a wider range of self awareness up to seeing oneself as an aggressive, heterosexual, striving person with a variety of goals that promote self-esteem.

It is conceptually consistent to equate the self-image and the perceptual system's self-observations with the identity sense. What one observes about one's total integration is the essence of the way a person perceives himself. Although integrative mechanisms do not have mental representations, their operations are associated with affects that do, and it is these affects that are felt and observed and related to the ego's integration. Both these patients, as do the character disorders in general, show a faulty structuralization which is reflected in the identity sense.

Summary

I have presented case material from two patients with characterologic defects in order to illustrate disturbances in the identity sense. By demonstrating pathologic distortions of such an important ego function, one is able to construct a conceptually consistent model of the psychic functioning of the patient.

The theoretical understanding that comes from conceptualizing in ego-psychologic terms has predictive utility at the clinical level. The cases that psychiatrists so commonly encounter today often demonstrate serious ego pathology, and consequently one has to sharpen formulations concerning ego operations and ego subsystems such as those dealing with the identity sense.

Chapter 2

Defensive Meaning of a Specific Anxiety Syndrome

Anxiety is a state that the ego finds unbearable. To rid itself of such disturbing tension, the ego musters a variety of techniques and defenses. Freud (1926b) clearly and classically described how the ego handles anxiety and how anxiety acts as a danger signal, leading to a variety of responses, all of which are attempts to reestablish equilibrium and integration. The organism follows the principle of constancy of psychic energy and is motivated when such constancy is threatened to achieve homeostasis once again. Mayer described the constancy principle as early as 1845 and thereby postulated the first law of thermodynamics. He was concerned with physical systems only; Fechner (1873), Freud (1926b) and Cannon (1932) introduced a similar principle in biology.

To go into more detail here about anxiety, homeostasis and defense and symptom formation would be merely to repeat well-established and well-known psychoanalytic principles. I have referred briefly to them because this chapter will describe a distinct anxiety syndrome that cannot be explained in terms of present metapsychological concepts based on these principles. This syndrome, instead of acting as a danger signal that initiates defense formation, whether symptomatic or characterological in expression, is in itself part of an integrating force diffusely incorporated into the ego, and it has a defensive status of its own. Whether this is really an anxiety state, as we have come to understand such states, can be debated and will be discussed later. One is reminded of the paper by Siegman (1954) in which he notes that in the hysterical character certain emotions are utilized by the ego and incorporated in character defense; he described highly charged affective states that served a definite purpose in maintaining defensive equilibrium in some hysterical patients.

The syndrome mentioned here was described by a twenty-six-year-old married woman, who complained of anxiety of a free-floating nature, present from the time of her earliest conscious memories. Her subjective reaction was one of being constantly afraid without any

First published in *Psa. Rev.* 43(1956):373–80. Reprinted by permission.

particular external stimulus. She suffered from all the physiological concomitants, such as palpitation, tremor, increased perspiration, muscular tension and a variety of other somatic symptoms of an adrenergic nature. At the time she entered analysis, she related her disturbance to being left alone and without emotional support. After her husband left for work, she would have to reassure herself that someone was available on whom she could rely if she had to. She did not actually have to have another person with her; knowing that there was someone with whom she could communicate by telephone if she felt the need was enough to make her feel secure. As a consequence she would make elaborate investigations to determine whether a friend or neighbor would be home and accessible. If no one was going to be home on a specific day she would become distraught to the point of panic. The need to call someone never actually arose.

During the course of her therapy a similar reaction, as would be expected, developed toward me. She wanted reassurance that she could call me whenever she wanted and that I would be available to her. I granted this request, but, as in her daily life, she never once made any effort to call me or seek support outside her regular interviews. She slowly became convinced that I would respond and that I could be reached easily, and with this realization she felt less anxious and ceased to be concerned about others' being home and available to her.

The patient's anxiety, however, did not completely disappear, even though the previous stimulus seemed no longer to be effective. At first it was difficult to understand what external factors kept the state of tension operating. Finally the patient confessed that she herself supplied the stimuli and that they were consciously conceived. When she had nothing to worry about, she tried to find something. For instance, while marketing, she would look at a particular person and then start wondering whom the person reminded her of. She picked persons indiscriminately, at random, and not because of any actual resemblance to persons she knew, so that she could not in fact link the strangers to familiar faces. Attempting to do so could keep her in a state of tension for days. She also would wonder if she had met the stranger before and would try to remember where and under what circumstances the meeting took place although she was quite aware of the fact that it never had. In her daily life she used many other devices to stimulate anxiety. In the analysis she would debate whether or not she should verbalize certain associations and would feel very much afraid of my response although she had spoken freely of much more sensitive and embarrassing material without any qualms.

It is not the purpose of this paper to go into complete details concerning this patient but rather to comment on what is pertinent to the study of the anxiety syndrome under discussion. At this point a phenomenological description of discrete symptoms will suffice. What has been described above is not particularly unusual. It has often been found in insecure, guilt-ridden patients who are constantly preoccupied with their dependent needs and in constant fear of being rejected. Such problems existed in this patient too. The unusual factor was that she actively sought out anxiety. Paradoxically, a period free from stress, one of inner calm, was intolerable to her. She felt miserable when she had nothing to worry about. In her own words, she was "afraid not to be afraid." When she had established herself in a therapeutic relationship and knew that in an emotional sense her therapist would always be available to her, she could no longer rationalize to herself that she might be completely alone or abandoned. She therefore developed schemes and techniques that would help her conjure anxiety.

In earlier years similar patterns had been present. Although the external manifestations—i.e., techniques by which she could make herself feel anxious—changed, she always sought tension and inner turmoil. Unlike the obsessive-compulsive patient, she was not preoccupied with, and did not torture herself with, the doubt that she might have committed some hostile destructive act; nor did she attempt atonement for such an act by ritualistic behavior. Generally she was not aware of any external causes for her emotional state. In retrospect she recognized that she had a need to feel anxious, and that in both the past and the present she had considerable control over her feelings. She related many incidents in childhood in which she simply decided that she was no longer going to be afraid and was able to "shut off" her feelings through an act of volition. Similarly she was able to make herself feel tense, and she had the same ability to "turn on" anxiety.

I should like to digress briefly from this case and call attention here to a group of persons who on the surface have similar characteristics although not to the same degree as this patient and not using such elaborate devices in order to maintain tension. Such persons represent a type characterized by apparently unlimited energy that has nevertheless a frenetic quality and never seems to accomplish anything. They are always in a hurry, rushed and overwhelmed by what they have to do, and yet objectively there is nothing unusual about the demands made of them. They seem to be constantly busy, always working at a feverish rate, never able to sit down and relax, but still achieving less than their more indolent colleagues. These persons show a high degree of sensitivity and impressionability and become easily affected even by the most trivial or innocuous issues. Medical students refer to classmates who possess these traits as "spastics" and find them annoying, inasmuch as the anxiety they display is contagious as well as amusing. They always seem to worry about something, usually examinations. Still, they seem to enjoy being distraught. Once the pressure is removed and they do not really have much to do, they become morose and depressed. One intuitively senses that they suffer more under these circumstances than they suffered previously. Ferenczi (1926) described a similar state in his *Sunday Neuroses*. Other authors have written about the defensive meaning of work, but here our concern is with the affective state that accompanies feverish activity.

To seek out anxiety and tension actively is paradoxical, and how can such a paradox be explained? Why should the ego seemingly "enjoy" a state that is intrinsically uncomfortable? As in the masochistic character one can immediately suspect that the state itself must have some meaning for the person, one which protects him from or wards off other impulses that threaten psychic equilibrium. The difference between this patient's ruminations and those of the obsessive-compulsive character has been mentioned. The phobic, too, is constantly preoccupied with anxiety, but the manifestations are different. The phobic patient's symptoms are the result of displacement and externalization to some well-defined, well-circumscribed object or situation (though later in life they may spread and become more generalized). However, a symbolic connection with the original conflict is maintained. In this patient the stimuli were diffuse and inconstant; they covered the complete range of her life activities. None of them seemed to have any special meaning or significance of and by itself. It would seem on initial examination that a certain instance could be explained in terms of specific dynamics. On another occasion, however, the patient might react to the same situation without any symptoms. For example, she would visit a neighbor toward whom she harbored destructive competitive impulses and would feel quite anxious during the visit. Several days later she would visit the same neighbor and would feel only calm and security. As far as could be seen, there were no additional factors to account for the change except the patient's conscious determination before the visit. On one occasion she made up her mind to be anxious and on another not to be, and she always predicted with amazing accuracy.

This remarkable volitional control might make one wonder whether she was not simply a good actress, whether she simply went through the motions of feeling anxious without any real affective experience. In other words, was this a sham anxiety? I thought less of this idea after she had demonstrated the process during the interviews. She reacted much as she did with her neighbors, sometimes feeling anxious and other times not, all by prearrangement with herself. More striking than her subjective reporting of what she felt were the obviously visible autonomic responses such as perspiration, tremor and dilated pupils. Other signs were increased swallowing, gasping for air and a tremulous voice. Because of the analytic nature of the therapeutic relationship, I was not able to make any physiological measurements, such as determining the pulse rate, skin temperature or blood pressure. Though I looked for specific connections with the current of associational material or interpretations that would explain the episodes, nothing convincing was found that had any particular specificity. The lack of specificity was especially striking when the patient exhibitionistically demonstrated her ability to "turn on" and "turn off" anxiety during the same session; i.e., when she "made up her mind" to feel or not to feel anxious, not beforehand, but during the session, and I could observe the stimulus and response at first hand.

To say that specific factors could not be detected is not to stray from a deterministic orientation or to deny the significance of unconscious factors. It was learned that these curious reactions had general meanings to her and were very much in the service of unconscious needs. In order to demonstrate this, additional information on her genetic development must be supplied.

The patient has an identical twin, born ten minutes before she was, and the resemblance between the two sisters is very close even today. The parents' attitudes toward these two very similar children, however, were very dissimilar. Whereas the patient was always in good physical health, her twin had many illnesses during her childhood and early adolescence. She was hospitalized frequently and for long periods of time. Most of the patient's early memories were concerned with her parents' leaving her behind while they went to the hospital to visit her sister. To her it seemed as if the parents' interest was directed solely toward the sister and that she herself was only an afterthought, if she were thought of at all. The patient was not able to express or even allow herself to feel any resentment, since everyone was preoccupied with keeping the sister alive, and any awareness of death wishes or even competitive feelings under such circumstances was so fraught with guilt or fear of complete rejection as to be intolerable. The patient felt pushed into the background even more when relatives and friends became confused by the close resemblance and mistook her for her sister. When she was six, a brother was born, and she felt that her parents' emotional investment in her, previously at a base minimum, then became practically nonexistent. She believed that they had wanted a boy when she and her sister were born and were disappointed in having daughters, but that their interest in the sister was forced upon them because of her ill health.

The patient continued not to express her envious and angry feelings, and she characterized herself as a shy, inhibited, withdrawn and isolated child. Her insecurity was such that she found herself being constantly "afraid," especially when relating to people but also in her loneliness. Her sister was aggressive and outspoken and mingled with people with relative ease. The patient merely tagged along and felt herself to be no more than a reflection, or rather a shadow, of her twin. Only later in life did she have friends and groups of her own. In these earlier years, when not alone or in the care of an indifferent maid or relative, she saw herself as included in a group only out of deference to her twin. She never felt that others accepted her on her own merit and that she really belonged. Her general demeanor was that of an abandoned child, a fantasy she frequently had and one that produced anxiety. Now and then her parents would become aware of the fact that she was frightened of their leaving her and not returning from a visit to the hospital, and she believed that on these occasions they did show some concern, but these were the only instances in which she felt they showed any solicitude.

Although she was left alone most of the time, she felt she never reconciled herself to this state. Yet being alone did not immediately produce the affect of anxiety even though the abandoned child fantasy did. Instead she reported that initially her feeling was one of apathy, as if she were ceasing to exist. At times this sensation was associated with terror, but she distinguished this terror from the anxiety that had been her presenting symptom (see Discussion). Death and ceasing to exist were her main concerns. She found herself constantly preoccupied whether she was an individual in her own right, feeling that she never had an identity of her own apart from her sister. This attitude was reinforced by others, who usually related to the sister and, when they did to the patient, often mistook her for the sister. During early childhood when alone she desperately wanted to be with someone in order to be relieved of the state of apathetic terror, emotional paralysis and "fear of dissolution." (Fear of dissolution are her exact words.) She felt that she was losing knowledge of her identity, but, as this state progressed, being with people did not help. There was only one condition that afforded her relief. If she could feel anxiety, then she was no longer overwhelmed by the catastrophic feelings of being submerged and inundated and of dissolving into nothing. The anxiety could have brought her attention, but she never felt that she needed it. It was enough that she could feel anxious, and as mentioned initially she never really sought anyone while feeling this way. On occasion when she approached panic, someone else's presence would be reassuring, but the patient felt that this was an additional factor superimposed on the reassurance that she already felt in being able to feel something, thereby proving to herself that she existed. Another person relating to her was additional evidence of her existence, and consequently she could then feel less anxious since she did not need such an intense affective experience any longer. However, being able to feel was more effective than an interpersonal contact because she felt that she could not trust people and that sooner or later they would leave her as her parents had.

She revealed the above material, concerning her reactions when alone, only gradually and as the therapeutic process unfolded. Insofar as anxiety dominated her affective tone she did not feel or recall "catastrophic terror." But once she began to relinquish her anxiety, then this state of terror was relived and reexperienced for a short period of time.

The above material stresses the pregenital orientation of this patient and indicates a hopelessly frustrated, dependent child. This theme will be stressed from this point on because it was predominant in the anamnesis and because it occupied a large portion of the therapy. As one would suspect, there were other problems, of a sexual nature, that lay beneath this pregenital orientation and had basic significance in the genesis of her neurosis. Exhibitionistic, melodramatic qualities have been noted as well as certain manipulative tendencies that did not substantiate the helpless, downtrodden, Cinderella-like picture that the patient initially presented. However, for the purpose of this study this phase of her problem does not require elaboration, inasmuch as the meaning of her anxiety is best explained on the basis of more primitive orientations. For the sake of brevity then, the clinical material will be restricted to what has already been presented.

Discussion

Awareness of self and proof of existence were of paramount concern to this patient. Because of the peculiar circumstances of her development she had no clear concept of herself as a person, as an individual in her own right, sharply delineated and apart from her twin. Such low self-regard led to an intolerable, painful state, one of "apathetic terror" and characterized by "fear of dissolution," so that she had to do something to enhance self-awareness. She was able to achieve relief from these basic fears by having an affective experience, one that manifested itself by anxiety. Recognition by others, i.e., seeking attention, played a role in maintaining equilibrium, but it was not of primary importance. An affective experience seemed to be much more significant.

Federn (1952, ch. 11), in contrast to Freud, conceptualizes a psychosis as an impoverishment of ego cathexis. He describes (ch. 16) the state that he calls *Erlebnis* as one of ego feeling, one of self-awareness that has healthy and pleasurable connotations, and he goes on to make distinctions between healthy and pathological narcissism. The effect of anxiety has particular significance in his formulations, and like Freud he postulates that it originates within the ego but that it cathects ego boundaries and maintains identity. With complete ego depletion there occurs a psychic catastrophe, but not one leading to anxiety as we know it. In the same paper (pp. 336–37), he states:

> If there is lack of narcissistic cathexis, the reaction to sudden danger will be apathetic terror and paralysis, but not the very peculiar sensation of anxiety in which the ego feeling, on the contrary, is greatly increased.

From the above one can see that the adaptive significance of anxiety is considered not merely in terms of its potential to lead to defense formation and thereby bring about ego integration, but it is considered also as a positive factor in its own right, one that can lead directly to a better equilibrium by enhancing ego feeling or narcissism.

Similarly, the clinical material presented here requires an elaboration of the concept of anxiety. Here, too, anxiety is seen to be very much needed as a primary force for psychic equilibrium and ego integration. This patient was concerned whether she existed as an individual. One way of gaining the security of autonomy was to be aware of herself by being able to feel, i.e., to have an affective experience. She equated the state of lack of feeling with nonexistence, death or disintegration, the "lack of narcissistic cathexis" that Federn speaks of. To feel something was what she had to achieve, even if it were to some extent unpleasurable, for the something she felt was anxiety. Unpleasant though it was, anxiety gave her considerable reassurance, and it became obvious that she was conjuring the symptom in order to support herself and to maintain equilibrium and self-esteem.

This "fear of dissolution," of ceasing to exist, was, however, only one level of conflict, and although sexual problems are not being stressed in this paper, they did exist and should be briefly mentioned. As her therapy progressed, it was learned that she was also concerned about her self-identity in a more specific sense too, not just a general concern as to whether she existed but as to whether she existed sexually, i.e., as a woman. A comparison or an analogy with castration anxiety can be drawn. At an oedipal level such an anxiety is specifically concerned with the fear of loss of the penis, but when it is observed at earlier levels of libidinal development, the fear becomes more general and is archaically and regressively expressed as a fear of being killed, a threat to life. This patient's symptoms, then, had meaning both at sexual and pregenital levels of organization.

Why she specifically chose anxiety as an affective experience to serve the function of enhancing self-awareness is not entirely clear. Her symptom was overdetermined and was also partially a reaction to unacceptable, guilt-ridden, hostile competitive impulses toward her twin. This aspect of her symptomatology is similar to the reaction that a person experiences when instinctual impulses threaten the ego. The ego reacts with anxiety, and the process can be explained by the signal theory.

However, her anxiety served mainly the purpose of a defense, even in the conventional sense. Recalling her words about being afraid not to be afraid emphasizes how "anxiety" is used as a defense against anxiety. Quotation marks are used because one may question whether that which is described here is really anxiety. Real anxiety exists at deeper levels of the personality, and in this case it is associated with annihilation and doubts concerning her self-identity. What was seen close to the surface was a way of handling this more basic anxiety through affective experience. I feel that the distinction can be made only in a functional and operational fashion because phenomenologically the two types of anxiety are identical.

Gerard (1955) has considered a similar situation in a physiological frame of reference. He feels that the concentration levels of adrenalin or, more generally, sympathins acting on the brain are significant determinants of the level of consciousness. When certain levels were produced experimentally with careful control, he found the subjective response of the person to be anxiety accompanying increased self-awareness.

Summary and Conclusions

Clinical material is presented in order to describe a specific anxiety syndrome.

Anxiety in this case was seen to have a primary purpose for the psychic economy of the personality rather than to be the precursor to defense formation. An affective experience was equated with existence or self-identity, so that to be able to feel had become a positive integrating force.

From a psychodynamic viewpoint an affective state phenomenologically identified as anxiety was seen acting as a defense against a more basic anxiety.

Chapter 3

The Submerged Ego

Maturation and development of the psychic apparatus have become a sphere of central focus and many conclusions have been reached regarding the sequence of such development, the types of structuralization effected, the role of conflict, and the impact of the environment with specific reference to objects. The exploration of the mother-child relationship disclosed the influence of stimulation on primitive ego states and led to numerous theoretical conclusions which are particularly important not only for "normal" development but for the understanding of certain forms of psychopathology commonly seen and often referred to as character disorders.

Geleerd (1956) reaches some retrospective conclusions concerning the early neonatal phases of development. As Freud (1914a) postulated, she also feels that the fantasy of being all-powerful is associated with the infantile stage before the differentiation between ego and nonego. From her clinical material she derives the fact that when the child realizes that neither he nor his mother are omnipotent, he is overcome by a rage of self-destructive proportions. An adult who reacts in this way is fixated at an omnipotent level and is unable to master both inner and outer stimuli.

Boyer (1956) believes that in order to develop beyond the stage of omnipotent organization the child is dependent upon the amount and types of stimuli the mother supplies. A well-functioning mother supplies just the right amount of stimulus and is able to act as a supplementary barrier against traumatic excitations either internal or external. Children whose mothers are unable to provide such protection develop, according to Boyer, ego weaknesses and lack a differentiation between the ego and the id. Bergman and Escalona (1949) also speak about stimulus barriers in describing infants who are hypersensitive to outside stimulation. Referring to Freud's (1926b) concept of the *Reizschutz,* they too conclude that the mother's role is a paramount one: if she cannot reinforce the child's protection against stimuli, he will have a defective ego characterized by premature development in certain areas. There are certain similarities between this concept and the hypertrophied ego described by Gitelson (1958a).

The ministering to a need may not necessarily be gratifying or lead to further development. Here one has to consider the various techniques

First published in *J. Amer. Acad. Child Psychiat.* 3(1964), 430–42. Reprinted by permission.

mothers use in responding to their children's needs. Overfeeding and overprotection do not seem to involve neglect. Under such circumstances, however, the child, as Boyer points out, does not have the opportunity to become separated from the mother and thereby form an individual identity.

Sensory modalities are also involved. The differentiation of the psychic apparatus involves a progressive refinement of sensory modalities and an expansion of the perceptual horizon which in itself is an important element of reality testing. Provence and Ritvo (1961), quoting E. Kris, speak of a "comfort-discomfort index." The child has to feel some kind of tension in order to feel at all. Awareness of needs then is a step that is required for the refinement of needs. In chapter 17 I stress that the awareness of a need in itself can be a pleasurable experience which is not necessarily related to discomfort.

It is difficult to consider the mother's relationship to the child in a stereotyped fashion and to speak of types. However, it is often assumed that there is some homogeneity in pathological reactions that must be paralleled by certain common denominators in the mothering pattern. I would like to explore further the effects on the infantile ego of what seemed to be an excessive amount of stimulation by a mother who could not allow her son to become autonomous. This patient was, from a psychological viewpoint, engulfed by his mother. He felt "submerged" and as a consequence I shall refer to his ego as a "submerged ego." The defenses he employed against such a defect and his reactions to separation I believe are particularly interesting, and may be characteristic of the character disorders.

I would like to make some inferences about a patient's maturational and developmental sequence as reconstructed from the study of the transference neurosis. This is a case where there was serious ego pathology. The type of ego defect and disorganization and the maternal transference can be simultaneously scrutinized.

The patient, a young single man, sought psychotherapy because of general dissatisfaction with professional achievements and the overwhelming distress he experienced when his fiancée jilted him.

He was an only child. He described his father as an insensitive, crass person who had no awareness or interest in emotional problems. His mother, on the other hand, doted on him. He emphasized her forceful, powerful personality, which he found welcome when contrasted with his father's bland, noncommittal, indifferent position. Still, he felt frightened of her. He remembered that as a child he was intimately tied to her. Although the family was wealthy and had several domestics, his care was exclusively in his mother's hands. He was not allowed to attend school until he was ten years old and was not permitted any playmates until then. She took over a tutorial role. When he finally entered a private school, he was academically superior but felt socially inferior, clumsy and gauche.

In adult life he found the simplest social situations difficult. He wanted his surroundings to be quiet, thus trying to create a feeling of calmness and order. Instead, he found everything around him confusing, with a frenetic, inchoate quality. He could not stand loud noises or bright lights and tried to avoid large gatherings although he often found himself in them. He sought male companionship but wanted only one or two close friends at the most. He was afraid of women, once having reached a state of near panic when taken to a brothel. Several months before beginning therapy he met "a beautiful, intellectual girl." He felt she was much above him but believed she would be able to bring him "up to her level." Apparently she tired of his clinging, helpless dependency and terminated the relationship.

In spite of his need for calmness and order, he led a disorderly life. For example, he always looked seedy and unkempt in spite of wearing expensive, fashionable clothes. His apartment was said to be a mess and his performance on the job was reported to be spotty because he was never able to plan and organize. Although he verbalized his wish to keep external stimuli at a minimum, he nevertheless managed to upset everything around him, which in turn confused and overwhelmed him.

His speech had a peculiar incoherent quality. He was hard to follow even though there were none of the grosser aberrations such as neologisms, flight of ideas, or autistic concreteness. At times it was a caricature of free association, although I got the impression that this type of verbalization was not confined to the analytic session. I find it difficult to describe what might be considered characteristic of his attempt to communicate. The confused quality of his speech might have been due to his jumping from one thought to another without verbalizing the connecting links.

Eventually he became easier to understand. For the first two years of treatment he felt little anxiety and his orientation was one of childish dependency and of constantly clinging demands for advice and direction. Then he gradually began to feel anxious. His tension reached paniclike intensity. He felt that I was angry at him and bent upon destroying him. Psychiatry was blamed for all of his difficulties, and he saw me as a devouring, engulfing person from whom he had to distance himself. At the same time he wanted succor and demanded that I take care of him, ascribing omnipotent powers to me. The wish to be taken care of and the fear of annihilation coexisted and were responsible for the destruction he feared. What has just been described is not unusual. Many authors, particularly Lewin (1950) and Balint (1955), have described such phenomena and have discussed them from the viewpoint of ego psychology and object relations.

At this point the patient felt, as he stated, "submerged." He felt as if I were hammering away at him, trying to indoctrinate him with my philosophy. In dreams and associations he felt attacked, saw himself drowning, or had frightening fantasies of indistinct outside forces trying to penetrate, rip him asunder, and then assimilate him as part of themselves. He was now even more sensitive to outside stimuli, again noises and light, but, in addition, much movement or color made him feel as if he would "be caught in a swirl and then be inundated." In spite of what seemed to be a homosexual quality in this material, I was impressed less by its erotic components and more by the fear of dissolution. The fear of loss of identity, under these circumstances, related to global factors of basic existence rather than a focalized identity sense such as a sexual identity.

The patient's behavior reflected his disturbed organization and fears in a striking dramatic fashion, as he constantly asked himself the question "Who am I?" He then began to find his apartment intolerable, rationalizing his discomfort on the basis of his roommate's idiosyncrasies, although he had not complained about him before. He rented another apartment but did not move completely out of the first one. The second one had certain advantages in that it was a hotel apartment similar to one in which his family had lived for a period of about eighteen months when he was three years old. After a week he found out that this building was too noisy. He felt too highly stimulated in these surroundings; so he took a third place, but again left part of his belongings behind and continued to pay rent for the first two apartments. He kept repeating this pattern and finally had a dozen apartments. Each represented a different orientation, and some were similar to places in which he had lived during childhood. However, he found none of them totally adequate and had to keep on seeking. The one common upsetting factor in all of the apartments was that they were all too noisy and not private enough. Still, he felt that by making a composite of all of them, he would, for reasons he could not understand, eliminate all the noise and secure the desired privacy. He would then have an ideal setting.

The patient indicated that in childhood he had felt constantly "bombarded" by his mother. He felt himself to be "flooded" by stimuli, some of which he was able to integrate, as evidenced by his scholastic precocity; others had a disruptive influence. During the analysis his mother still attempted to control and influence the patient. She called me frequently, "bombarding" me in the same way the patient had described, demanding that I do things the way she felt would be best for her son. Finally, I put a stop to her calls and was able to refer her to a colleague (see below). The patient felt that his mother kept him in a state of frenzied excitement and that she was being sadistically manipulative.

Discussion

The clinical material this patient presented, both the transference state and his behavior, showed a constant preoccupation with outside stimuli. His ego became fragmented to a marked degree. Concurrent with this fragmentation was a heightened sensitivity to external stimuli. The perception of his mother as dangerous, threatening, and attacking led to a destructive maternal introject which made it difficult for this patient to synthesize aspects of his environment with perceptual and executive systems and thereby achieve a state of greater structuralization. In so far as early introjects could not be integrated the ego remained in a fragmented state and the identity sense was correspondingly impaired.

Jacobson (1954) emphasizes that the self-representation is the main determinant of the identity sense. The ego's awareness and internal perceptions of its own structure, behavior, and style are factors that comprise the identity sense. Hartmann and Kris (1945) distinguish between self and ego, considering the ego to have functions that are not part of one's subjective awareness. What one is aware of, whether distorted or otherwise, regarding characteristic patterns of perception and reaction that are synthesized into a Gestalt, determines how a person identifies himself. Without such a Gestalt there is the fragmentation described above and a disturbance of identity.

"The character of the ego," according to Freud (1923), "is a precipitate of abandoned objects cathexes." There are, in other words, different levels of identity and different aspects of the self-image. Erikson (1956) emphasizes this point; one can consider the identity sense from different frames of reference, sexual or professional, aesthetic, political, moral, etc.

How one conceives of oneself depends on the synthesis of a variety of subsystems of the ego. The final integration of all the subsystems would be the total general identity of the individual, which would determine a person's basic orientation and attitudes about his role and purpose in life.

Within the subsystems one's orientation would be more specific and focalized. There would also be differences, in some instances, in the degree of organization of one subsystem compared to another. Provence and Ritvo (1961), in discussing the maturational timetable, demonstrate that because of specific vicissitudes there can be an uneven rate of development of different ego functions. Consequently, different aspects of the ego's adjustive elements will be better developed than others and this unevenness affects the identity sense.

Gitelson (1958a) spoke of what he considered to be a hypertrophy of certain ego functions in the character disorders; similar concepts of precocious ego development have been formulated by Bergman and Escalona (1949), Mahler and Elkisch (1953), and others.

This patient demonstrated a precocious development in certain intellectual areas. This is not an unusual finding in children who have been highly stimulated and academically "pushed" by their parents. In such cases one frequently finds outstanding achievement in a certain field such as mathematics and obtuseness or almost complete withdrawal from most other areas which are not valued and may be somehow involved with conflicted object relations.

Intellectualism, in this case, became a modality with which the patient could relate to his mother and at the same time defend himself from what his dreams and transference states indicated he believed to be assaultive stimuli. Bergman and Escalona (1949) think of precocity as a way of reinforcing a defective stimulus barrier which has been damaged by overwhelming stimuli. I feel that the development of precocity as a defense involves other variables than the stimulus barrier and must be viewed in terms of total ego development and adjustment.

When in a state of decompensation, this patient, in addition to being tormented with the questions of who and what he was, was also perturbed and at times panicked by his inability to distinguish what he felt. He said that he was "unaware of his needs." He was not referring to his ambitions or ultimate goals in life, but rather focused upon such elemental desires of whether he felt hunger or thirst, or whether he had to evacuate his bowels or empty his bladder.

He did not feel numb or anesthetized; he was aware of the sensations associated with physiological processes and was able to respond to them by eating or going to the toilet. But he was unable to make clear distinctions. He could, for example, distinguish in a gross way between knowing he had to eat and that he had to defecate. During regressed transference states, the finer sensory elements involved in these needs, such as appetite or pressure, were not experienced, much to the patient's consternation. At other times he was able to make such distinctions, but when he lost this capacity he was very anxious, a situation that I felt was part of a general disorganization. I understand that this lack of sensory discrimination is not an uncommon finding in severely disturbed children. This feeling of dissolution reached its peak when he was unable to distinguish whether he was dead or alive, such doubts being expressed in the form of frightening fantasies.

I am not now concerned whether this patient might be considered psychotic. It might be stated parenthetically that, in spite of severe disturbances, many areas of reality testing were intact and there were no systematized delusions or hallucinations. Whatever the diagnosis, however, the transference reaction was of such a nature that it was possible to make inferences about object relations and ego structuralization and its effects on the formation of the identity sense.

In the transference he felt that I would destroy him and blamed his experience of panicky dissolution on psychiatry. It was at this point that he frequently used the word "submerged" to describe his state. Although he still was able to see me realistically, he was nevertheless obsessed with the thought that I had the power and wish to amalgamate him into myself. He felt helpless and vulnerable, with no will of his own, and at my mercy. I could "submerge" him and he was precariously perched, dependent on my whims. He felt he lost all autonomy and saw himself as a puppet with me up above pulling the strings. To feel submerged referred to having lost all capacity to be aware of what he was feeling and experiencing. He would not react and behave in a fashion determined by his own inner needs but instead had to follow the dictates of an external object. The panic and dissolution were characterized by his not knowing what to do and the feeling that he did not have the equipment to do it even if he knew what his needs were.

He accumulated his many apartments at this time. He was seeking a facet of himself in each apartment. Sometimes an apartment would be associated with some specific childhood period. Others, because of their decor, were representative of the serious professional man or the frivolous playboy.

The mother was now seen by a colleague who reported that she wanted her son to return home. She pleaded with the consultant to give her son back to her and asked him to talk to me on her behalf. When it was pointed out that she was infantilizing her son, she blatantly declared that it did not matter how emotionally crippled he might be as long as she "could have her baby."

In marked contrast to his feelings of weakness and helplessness, the patient believed that he could determine whether his mother would live or die. Because of such omnipotence, he felt responsible for her life and guilty that he might be the cause of her death if he were to separate himself from her. His multiple apartments also meant that he really had no single basic dwelling of his own, one chosen by him. Consequently his only home was with his mother.

A pertinent question is: how do the mother's behavior and needs regarding her child affect his subsequent personality differentiation? The mother could not permit her son to reach sufficient structuralization to enable him to be independent of her. If the patient had sufficient synthesis and a well-established identity sense, the mother could not incorporate him to maintain her stability.

One cannot speculate further about the mother because the information obtained from her is meager and reconstructed only from an anamnesis. However, the meaning of her behavior to the patient is significant. He felt his mother did everything for him, but that even when she became his tutor her role as a teacher was specious. He believed "mother taught me nothing." By this he meant that, although she had given him academic information, she had not supplied him with the techniques necessary to perceive what was going on in the outside world and to get along with people. He considered himself a "babe in the woods." The mother doing "everything" represented an assault which could not be integrated as action units for further structuralization and expand the range of ego functioning.

One noteworthy effect of this lack of differentiation was his peculiar manner of speaking, noted at the beginning of treatment and as it recurred in the regressed state of the maternal transference. There was an obvious difficulty in communication, which also involved a defective understanding of whatever I tried to tell him. Not understanding each other was a phenomenon that replicated the early relationship to his mother. As he was later able to explain when looking back at the transference state and on his childhood, he never felt understood. He could not make his needs known, and he felt a similar frustration toward me. He felt that in part it was his fault; he recognized some aspects of his inner fragmentation and his inability to synthesize needs with the rest of his ego, so his perceptions were vague and disjointed. In the transference he also blamed the therapist for not being sensitive to his demands; he felt I responded only in terms of my own needs rather than being alert to his. This was a clear representation of his infantile evaluation of his mother.

Conclusions

The character disorders, a group of enigmatic conditions, have been explored from the frame of reference of ego psychology. Ego defects and arrested development have been postulated as being the essence of these clinical entities.

Ego structure has been studied in terms of the influence of an early object relationship. The mother's role has been considered as a pivotal developmental determinant. It is generally conceded that the early mothering experience is the most important single relationship in the child's life. For the purpose of this study it has been highlighted and made into a central theme. This does not negate the significant influences of other objects, the father as well as persons met later in life, in the formation of this man's character. The mother's dominance tended to shut out all other potential relationships that might have been significant during the patient's childhood, and undoubtedly the father had been able to make some kind of passive adjustment to the marriage. The mothering pattern was one in which the mother, because of exceptionally strong narcissistic needs, made her son her exclusive possession. He reacted to her ministrations as if he were being engulfed.

This patient's childhood was characterized by a lack of mutuality in the mother-child relationship. Apparently the mother related to the child only in terms of her needs. It seems likely that gratifying her son and helping him progress toward autonomy were not meaningful, satisfying experiences for her. The fact that the patient did not get a response when he wanted one and got one when he did not prevented the synthesis of inner requirements with perceptual and executive systems. When the ego does not experience any need tension, ministrations are felt as assaults.

A further effect of what the child experiences as assaultive is that the drives are not able to be progressively structuralized. A well-integrated ego can experience need tension as pleasurable in so far as it has the confidence that perceptual, synthetic, and executive systems will ultimately attain gratification for such needs. Need tension is disruptive when it cannot be integrated with other ego systems and leads to instinctual satisfaction. In this case the drives remain fragmented and consequently cannot become further differentiated.

A fixated, fragmented ego is a helpless, vulnerable one. The mother in this case, by taking over all executive and even perceptual functions (since she did not acknowledge his needs), reinforced the patient's attitude of helplessness. His difficulties became manifest when he should have achieved a degree of autonomy. These structural defects are reflected in the patient's self-appraisal and are indicated by his lack of identity. Disturbances of inner perception and the fact that the patient did not feel separated from his mother often resulted in panic. He recognized the fluidity of this identity and the precariousness of his organization.

Mothers similar to this patient's have been considered as being overstimulating. Spitz (1951) classifies pathological mothering patterns into psychotoxic ones that involve assaultive overstimulation and depleting ones where direct rejection and neglect are prominent. I do not feel that overstimulation or understimulation are uniform patterns that can lead to a classification of inadequate mothering. I feel that the essence of the harmful effects on the child's ego is that the mother's behavior is disruptive and that she is insensitive to his needs. At times this can be phenomenologically similar to overstimulation when the mother is ministering to a child who is not needful. It can also be similar to understimulation when she cannot perceive and ignores his demands. She is disruptive to the child's spontaneous maturation potential.

The ego defects described in this case, I feel, are frequently found in the character disorders. The importance of early object relationships becomes apparent in the genesis of faulty structuralization which many believe is the essence of the character disorders.

Summary

A mother-child relationship, one considered disruptive and psychically assaultive, is correlated with the ego structure of a patient who is classified as a character disorder. The mother, by responding only to her narcissistic requirements, did not relate to her son's needs. He felt "submerged."

The patient's ego was a fragmented one where drives did not become integrated into perceptual and executive systems. Consequently he felt helpless and vulnerable, *was unable to perceive his needs,* and had a vague, poorly defined identity sense. This type of ego defect may be a characteristic feature of the character disorders.

The concept of overstimulation is discussed. Rather than postulating a distinction between a "toxic" mother and a neglectful one, the disruptive qualities of mothering are emphasized. What is involved is inappropriate "stimulation" rather than too much or too little. The child is unable to achieve gratification from his mother. The developmental path toward autonomy becomes disrupted, so every aspect of the mothering experience is felt as overwhelming and threatening in so far as he cannot integrate it with his needs.

Chapter 4

The Frozen Introject

The role of introjects, since Freud first focused upon it, has become increasingly important, not only as a significant aspect of ego development but because of its relevance to therapeutic considerations. Ego psychology has caused us to focus upon psychic functions and to view the development of the personality, not only in terms of its genetic antecedents but also as a balance between a variety of systems that can be considered from the viewpoint of a hierarchical continuum. The introject is included as an intrinsic aspect of ego structure.

Ferenczi first used the term introject in 1909. Since then there has been considerable debate as to its definition when used as a verb, and how it is to be distinguished from other mechanisms such as incorporation and identification. It has been a subject that was comprehensively considered in the relatively early literature (Fuchs, 1937) as well as in such recent publications as those of Sandler (1962). The role of the introject as a functional mechanism as well as a psychic formation has been stressed and its relationship to other processes, especially identification, has been widely discussed. It is not the purpose of this chapter to pursue these topics further. Here, it is necessary only to give a brief operational definition of the concept of introject and then to proceed with its implications for the study of specific clinical entities. Most psychoanalysts agree that the introject is a psychic formation that results from some interaction with the external world. An object relationship which includes a person and a situation becomes internalized and to some extent unconscious, although, in some instances it may be preponderantly, but I doubt exclusively, preconscious. In any case, what is taken into the psyche becomes part of the memory system and contributes to personality structure. How effective the introject can be in promoting progressive ego differentiation depends upon many factors such as how well it is amalgamated into and synthesized with other ego systems. Heimann (1942) and Loewald (1960) referred to similar mechanisms as internalization, but this concept refers to the loss of the introject's discrete boundaries as it is "dissolved" into the ego.

"The ego is a precipitate of abandoned object-cathexes," Freud (1923) states. Somehow, introjects are instrumental in the formation of the ego not only in terms of establishing a coherent identity, but in initiating a

First published in *Int. J. Psa.* 48(1967), 61–67. Reprinted by permission.

process that leads towards a unified ego organization, one that enables the psyche to deal with both instinctual pressures and the outer world.

The child has to acquire adaptive techniques in order to cope with internal needs and the demands of his environment. Object relationships both gratify needs and help develop techniques of mastery which will lead to further gratifications. As the ego gains structure through maturation and development, it becomes, in a sense, able to retain (register) the gratifying experience of the nurturing situation. At some point, one can refer to the establishment of the good introject, although, as is well known, opinions vary considerably as to when this occurs. However, regardless of the differences of opinion, it is generally felt that this process of retention begins fairly early and determines how well the child adapts.

From the viewpoint of psychopathology and maldevelopment one has to consider the effects of disruptive object relationships. Glover (1930) conceptualizes a stage of primary identification, one which determines the quality of all later identifications and introjects. According to Glover, the primitive mind tends to perceive all states having the same affective tone as being similar, and the objects involved become incorporated as a basic identification. The latter determines the further course of ego development which then has some bearing on the formation of future object relations and may lead in the direction of psychic stability or to faulty structuralization, disturbed object relationships, and the establishment of introjects that will impede the ego from acquiring satisfying, efficient, adaptive techniques.

Disruptive introjects do not lead to ego differentiation. They interfere with the development of specific areas of adaptation. Such lack of development or maldevelopment may prevent the patient from obtaining gratification from persons who may be willing to help him. The patient is not able to utilize or assimilate experiences which another person who does not have the same type of constricting introjects finds indispensable for his emotional development.

Operationally then, the concept of the introject can be sharpened. It can be considered a psychic formation characteristic of relatively early ego states, which is of fundamental importance for psychic structuralization, but which may, when traumatic, also impede the course of further development. Whether introjects are formed by introjection, incorporation or identification is not particularly relevant to the topic that will be explored here. Undoubtedly, all of these mechanisms are involved and may perhaps be characteristic of specific stages of ego development, introjects being acquired over a period of time during the course of development. The fate of the introject and its interaction with perceptual and executive ego systems, however, is relevant and sheds light on specific types of psychopathology.

Patients with character disorders are considered to suffer from ego defects. Consequently, the introject as an elemental aspect of ego structure becomes especially significant for our understanding of such cases.

Before discussing such clinical-theoretical questions, it may be germane to describe briefly the type of case that will be referred to as a character disorder. There is considerable nosologic confusion about the character disorders and here no attempt will be made to distinguish between such entities as borderline cases, schizoid personality, pseudoneurotic schizophrenia, and other labels that place psychopathology somewhere between a psychoneurosis and a psychosis, but not definitely in either category. Every analyst, however, is familiar with a group of patients who have no definitive symptoms, but instead complain of a general inability to get along. They find life to be meaningless and are confused as to the purpose of their existence. Everything is vague, but their dissatisfaction stands out and the world seems too complicated to deal with. Usually there is some disturbance of the identity sense and, in particularly severe cases, the patient may be perplexed as to who and what he is, a state of conflict associated with an inability to perceive his needs and desires. The latter have an amorphous quality and frequently such patients are disturbed, not by what they feel, but by the fact that they are unable to feel anything. They do not feel alive and this can lead to a state of apathetic terror as described by Federn (1952).

Although it is not feasible to construct a homogeneous category from phenomenology alone, one gets the impression that no matter how varied these patients may be, there are, nevertheless, some common denominators. These are persons whose degree of psychopathology is much more severe than that usually attributed to the psychoneurotic. We find them to be in a state of disorganization, and to lack structure, but still possessing some ability to adjust, though unhappily, to the outer world. As in the psychoses, the ego–outer-world conflict in these patients seems to be predominant, but they do not seem to have the same degree of disturbance of reality testing. They seem, however, to have less organization than many psychotics such as the paranoid, who has a highly structured psychotic organization. In other words, these patients have a characterological problem, a faulty, diffusely structured ego that is reflected in all ego functions; but such lack of structure is particularly noticeable in their executive capacities and identity sense, two areas that are intimately related.

There are, of course, many individual variations of faulty ego structure and there are different characterological defences that determine the content of patients' compensatory or maladaptive behaviour. Here, I wish to consider a group of patients whose defences are particularly ineffective; their chief torment is a frantic attempt to establish themselves as separate and autonomous, an attempt that never leads anywhere. Sometimes, one is impressed by the patient's self-defeating behavior, and at other times, one gets the feeling that we are dealing with a helpless, vulnerable babe who does not really know, i.e., has never learned, how to survive, and finds himself in an inordinately complex world.

Elsewhere (chapters 10, 17) I describe patients who complain bitterly about not knowing how to react and behave in various situations that most people would find pedestrian. The ability to perform adequately in a particular role may be markedly impaired. For example, a housewife in her thirties found it impossible to carry on as a mother. She felt she knew nothing about mothering, literally meaning that she did not know how to feed, dress, care for, or play with her child. She could go mechanically through the motions of looking after her child's needs, but she never really understood what her daughter required and she felt she was responding completely without empathy as one would automatically follow instructions from a manual. The analysis revealed that she believed that she had never learned anything from her mother about mothering since her early upbringing was in the care of a series of indifferent maids. The maternal imago was, so to speak, nonfunctional. The patient believed she had never had the opportunity to learn the techniques of mothering as one would by directly experiencing them. Granted that repressive mechanisms were also operating, I was nevertheless impressed by the lack of available experiences the patient had to draw upon in order to cope with the ever-present problems of child rearing.

Whatever conflicts may be involved in threatening the psychodynamic balance, the early introjects have an important bearing on how well the ego is able to handle problems, whether emanating primarily from external reality or instinctual pressures. An introject is functional when it becomes incorporated into an executive system as an adaptive technique. The child learns initially from his parents and he internalizes not only values and limits as in superego formation, but styles and techniques required to solve the problems of routine living. When he forms an introject of the parent he includes many elements of the relationship that involve methods of mastery. Other persons, later in life, add to these initial psychic formations leading to accretions and more sophisticated efficient problem-solving techniques. The factors responsible for an introject being functional and how they become part of the executive system are questions that can be explored further. The study of psychopathology, by pointing out defects and distortions of the developmental process, may shed light on the nature of the process itself. In the short vignette of the "inadequate" mother, I referred to the lack of formation of a suitable introject that had potential for the development of future mothering. The character disorders mentioned above can give us more details as to why the introject is not useful and highlight the relationships between the introject and other ego systems.

From the ego viewpoint this discussion has emphasized executive systems. This does not mean that other systems are not equally involved, but the executive systems can be advantageously studied in patients suffering from characterological defects. As stated, these patients have difficulties in relating to their surroundings and this is reflected in their behavior. Behavior, from the obvious phenomenological viewpoint, is a function of executive systems. Therefore, ego–external-world difficulties are focused upon by these patients and one can begin by assessing the status and development of the ego's executive capacities. The relevance of affects and other phenomena derived from perceptual and synthetic systems can also be considered, but at first the executive system can be viewed as a pivot from which relationships with other ego systems can be studied.

Clinical Material

A young man in his late twenties sought analysis because he felt a vague dissatisfaction with his mode of life. At times he felt awkward and gauche, but he was much more upset by the fact that he was not particularly aware when, in a social situation, he might have committed a *faux pas* or behaved peculiarly. He did not trust his judgment. For instance, during a fairly brisk autumn day he might visit the downtown section of the city in a pair of bermuda shorts. He was not able to decide whether this was bizarre and would only begin to suspect that he was doing something out of the ordinary when others stared at him incredulously or disapprovingly.

During the first interview there was something peculiar about him that was not easy to define. He was dressed in what seemed to be conservative conventional attire and yet looked different. When he walked into the consultation room I noticed his clothes, although there was nothing grossly unusual about them. Later, reflecting on these initial impressions I was able to see seemingly trivial details that contributed to what, in essence, was an incongruous appearance. His coat and trousers did not match, and although his trousers and tie matched, his tie clashed with his coat. He was wearing two-tone shoes, of a subdued color but still not in keeping with the rest of his clothes. His movements suggested a jerkiness such as one would see in the cog-wheel phenomenon of Parkinsonism; but the abnormality of his appearance was very subtle and slight, not definite.

The patient then went on to describe how different he was from his peers. His apartment, apparently, was arranged in such a manner that the conventional division of rooms was ignored. Kitchen furniture might be in the living room, bedroom furniture in the dining room, and easy chairs in the kitchen. In fact, he did not sleep in a bed, just a mattress on the floor.

His unconventional behavior extended to all areas. On Thanksgiving when everyone was eating turkey he had lobster. Obviously, he was motivated by a need to be different, one founded upon a frantic attempt to establish an identity. If he did things in a conventional manner he would not stand out and would become an "amorphous blob, an atom among an infinite number of atoms." To be different was an attempt to define an autonomous boundary, but a fruitless one since he managed to make himself look ridiculous.

In addition to the defensive aspect of his behavior, he stressed the feeling that he was never taught the elements of proper and appropriate conduct. His attitude was the outcome of many factors, including intrapsychic conflict, but it was reflected in a total lack of general accomplishments.

From a productive viewpoint, this patient was "paralyzed." Although quite intelligent he was never able to complete any task he started, and he began many projects. His inability to achieve became particularly noticeable after his mother's death, which occurred shortly after his graduation from high school. He was not depressed, but from that moment on he never finished anything. He had not graduated from college, rationalizing that he would get his master's degree directly. He had been working on his thesis for eight years, never being able to finish it because he had to clean up a desk piled high with papers. If he succeeded in this tidying then he would have to rest from his arduous exertion. During the rest, things would start piling up again.

The patient's father died a month before he was born, and his early years were spent exclusively with his mother. She "protected" him from many experiences, because she had to believe that he was a delicate child and not up to the rougher behavior of his contemporaries. He was able, however, to progress relatively well in school and could complete some projects and hobbies that his mother approved of.

He felt constricted and missed masculine relationships. However, he never expressed his anger, which he felt could reach unmanageable proportions. He was afraid of destroying his mother who, he felt, was also frail. He described her as a timid but haughty person who was afraid of life and people and took refuge in her aristocratic background, considering herself in a state of gracious retirement, one that could be sustained because of her wealth.

That the patient had problems in handling anger was apparent from the first interview. He presented himself as benign and lacking in aggression, but his cloying and saccharin manner and his flamboyant ineptness were offensive. His first and many subsequent dreams were of trapped monsters trying to escape and nearly doing so. They were nightmares and awakened him. After a while, as he felt safer in the analytic setting, he was able to attack me because he felt I was trying to make him conventional, and then the nightmares ceased.

Before developing the course of this patient's therapy further, I will present another vignette of a patient who I believe belongs to the same general category as the above patient and who also emphasizes a similar type of intra-ego defect.

This patient, also in his twenties, was tolerated in his job because he was considered to be very intelligent and of high potential. He was getting only a minimal base salary, his main income being derived from commissions. He had produced practically nothing. But since he also had an independent income he was not distressed.

He found himself uncomfortable because he had no friends and could not remember a single relationship either with a man or woman that had any emotional closeness. He explained his lack of personal contacts as being due to ignorance. His first ten years were almost completely isolated to the confines of his home. His mother did not permit him to go to school, taking over his education herself. He was an only child and had absolutely no playmates. When he eventually went to school his work was brilliant academically, but he felt uncomfortable and inept with his classmates.

His mother died when he was 15, and, like the first patient, he felt no grief whatsoever. However, at this time he involved himself with a beatnik group and drifted aimlessly at school, and later at work, until he sought therapy. He did not finish school and was unable to feel himself in any particular role. He lamented that he never had the opportunity to learn how to behave socially, or to develop skills and techniques that were simply routine habits for others.

The constricted behavior and the emotional paralysis that was characteristic of these patients indicates that more is involved than an intrapsychic conflict. Although these patients do not seem to be psychotic nor to display signs of gross reality distortions, they impressed everyone with the fact that they were very sick, emotionally speaking. It seemed apparent that, regardless of inner conflicts, there was a considerable structural defect.

I would like to focus upon one aspect of their ego pathology, that which refers to the emotional paralysis and the feeling that they "did not know," i.e., had never learned, adaptive techniques. From the affective viewpoint, in making these formulations we shall have also to consider in what context their inner rage belongs.

The lack of manifest expression of anger was striking in both patients. Their predominant psychic state was confusion and there was little other expression of affect. It was particularly striking that they had never experienced depression over their mothers' deaths, this indicating an inability to mourn. They both reported not being able to cry. At the beginning of treatment they were colorless and humorless, and did not seem particularly capable of becoming involved in a therapeutic relationship.

The first patient, however, experienced anger toward me very quickly; but it lasted for only two or three weeks, when he no longer had nightmares or dreams of any kind. The second patient seemed to be completely uninvolved and for a long time (two years) complained of his lack of feeling towards me, comparing himself unfavorably with his friends, who always seemed to be having some affective explosion toward their analysts. But even complaining had a mild, toneless quality to it.

This lack of involvement, in itself, represented a transference attitude. Whether the patients knew how to relate or had to defend themselves from a relationship, their lack of involvement was characteristic of all their object relationships. I interpreted the defensive and transference implications of their distancing, and at the same time pointed out the underlying rage, which was not always well concealed. The first patient then had a dream where he was in an old castle with many rooms. In each room was a body or rather a person, but one who was neither dead or alive. This person (sometimes a man but just as often a woman) was "frozen." To be frozen referred to a state of suspended animation.*
His associations focused on the thought that all these people were use-

*Melanie Klein (1935) briefly describes a manic patient who spoke of internal object representations as being in a state of suspended animation. She did not pursue further the role of the introject in terms of the ego's general adaptation; rather she stressed its defensive function against overwhelming depression.

less (as I was) but not dangerous. If they became "unfrozen," then he would be destroyed, and he now recalled the nightmares he had at the beginning of analysis.

The second patient finally experienced rage toward me following a dream. He dreamed that he could not reach the age of twenty-one. His mother was there but she was unable to help. Even while dreaming he felt he pondered over his mother's presence. She was present but in a unique fashion, neither dead nor alive. The patient then stated that his equipment suffered from "psychosomatic failure" i.e., his table lamp would not light and his car would not start. He then recalled an episode where he brought a classmate home from school and his mother austerely commented that since she had never met his friend she was forced to assume that his judgment about his suitability would have to do. Then she charmed his friend away from him.

Following these dreams, both patients were able to experience considerable anger. The first patient was afraid that I would try to mold him in my image and thereby not permit his autonomous development. The second patient now vociferously complained that I did not help him and all his problems were caused by the analysis. In both cases, there were manifest rebellious behavior and feelings of helplessness and inadequacy. Their "paralysis" continued.

The further course of treatment in both cases is interesting, and in the second case the patient was eventually able to return to school and obtain a professional degree. However, for the purpose of this paper a further description of the therapy is tangential.

Discussion

Fleming and Altschul (1963) have treated similar cases, patients who have lost a parent early in life. Although, in their studies the parent-loss occurred during childhood, their patients also never experienced mourning. Fleming believes that later psychopathology was, in part, caused by the fact that the early parent-loss was never worked through.

To mourn, one has to relive many memories of the relationship with the lost love object. These patients' rage was so intense that they could not cathect further the maternal introject at the time of their mothers' death. Even before they died the maternal introject was not particularly functional in many areas. The patients were not able to "learn" adaptive techniques from their mothers that would have been appropriate to their childhood and later social adjustment. They also found them assaultive and engulfingly destructive. In the absence of the father (in the first patient through death, and in the second because he was passive and ineffectual) as a source of strength, the lack of protection and masculine identification caused them to feel helpless and vulnerable.

Consequently they had to erect specific characterological defences in order to deal with the vicissitudes of the external world, especially their mothers' deaths. The internal percept could not be hypercathected following the loss of the mother; this would lead to a state of disruptive rage and possibly ego dissolution. The patients had to repress the destructive, maternal image by forming a percept that was not a reaction to the mothers' death or a denial of it by keeping her alive. As the first patient's dream indicated, the introject is neither dead nor alive; it is "frozen" in a state of suspended animation. The "freezing" of the introject led to a fixed ego state that maintains a psychic balance just following the mother's death.

The ego then is a paralysed one characterized by complete nonproductivity. If the patient regresses to childhood he brings the engulfing mother who stifles autonomy back to life. If he progresses he has to complete the mourning process; this involves a hypercathexis of the maternal imago and as previously stated he would feel overwhelmed by an uncontrollable destructive rage.

The patient remains frozen. He cannot go backward or forward. The maternal introject causes the suspension of the ego's ability to incorporate adaptive experiences, but in order to preserve self-esteem and to defend himself against the awareness of his helpless inadequacy, the patients had to consider themselves as being in what they called a state of "becoming." They had to go through the motions of accomplishing and believe that they would achieve some future goal but they kept the goal constantly in the future. The first patient as a perpetual student had to have a thesis that he would never finish because by pursuing such a project he would be giving a meaning and purpose to life, i.e., establishing an identity, and at the same time denying his mother's constrictive, paralysing influence. But he had never worked through the destructive aspects of his relationship to his mother and he could not really produce, since his attempts at production depended upon an ego whose energy was expended in supporting a mechanism that was similar to psychotic denial.

Furthermore, since the maternal introject is a core around which other adaptive experiences develop, the fact that it is nonfunctional renders also inoperative techniques of mastery previously acquired. The ego's executive apparatus is thus unable to draw upon the memory systems in order to respond to the requirements of reality.

In the "identity diffusion syndrome" described by Erikson (1959) we note a similar inability to cope with reality. Erickson's patients have much less organization than the two young men described here, and their paralysis is more extensive, including the pedestrian tasks of routine living.

My patients had some degree of organization since the introject was not "lost" or repudiated in the sense that it maintained its structure even though it was not cathected. The remainder of the ego would then not be able to use energy in an effective fashion but it could still appear synthesized and coherent. Consequently these patients were able to go through the motions of adaptation.

To some extent a person's identity depends upon how he functions. If he is, for the most part, nonfunctional this will be reflected in his self-image. The first patient, in particular, tried hard to establish himself as an individual but since these attempts were not based on any concrete achievements he was once again only going through the motions of being a person in his own right. Both patients had many features similar to H. Deutsch's (1942) description of "as if" personalities, but unlike her cases they were not even able to borrow another person's identity. On the contrary, because of the fear of being "swallowed up" they had to construct a nonconforming individuality.

Even before their mother's deaths these patients felt that they had been prevented by them from acquiring the skills that are necessary in order to be effective. The second patient also stressed that his mother did not allow him to seek other experiences which would enable him to be comfortable both at work and socially, and that she did not furnish him with an adequate background so he could learn from others. So again one can stress that because of the relatively ineffective maternal introject the capacity to assimilate other adaptive experiences was impaired. When the initial introject was rendered inoperative after the mother's death the ego's ability to master tasks and to develop further was completely suspended.

The partial recognition of the nonfunctional aspects of the maternal introjects that occurred after their dreams caused the patients to become aware of anger, which was now directed towards me. This transference projection occurred because they were no longer able to keep me "on ice" as they understood the defensive meaning of their emotional isolation. The partially suppressed rage of childhood became manifest in the transference and it was often accompanied by intense fear of being "annihilated" and engulfed by me as I represented the cathected maternal imago.

Summary and Conclusions

Two patients, who are considered as being examples of a particular type of character disorder, are briefly presented in order to focus upon the constricting and paralysing effects of early introjects. In both cases the maternal introject is conceptualized as being defensively "frozen," i.e., neither dead nor alive, following their mothers' death, since a hypercathexis of the lost love object that is characteristic of mourning would be overwhelmingly destructive. The frozen introjects and their paralysing effects on the patients' productivity and acquisition of adaptive techniques are stressed.

From a therapeutic viewpoint these patients are especially interesting since I believe that many of our cases have similar ego mechanisms and are considered untreatable. Frequently these patients give the impression of not being able to form a relationship with the therapist and transference does not seem to occur. However, when one understands their ego structure one learns that their lack of involvement represents a characterological defence to a disruptive nonadaptive object relationship which is reenacted in the analysis and, in itself, is a transference manifestation.

Chapter 5

Compulsory Happiness: Adolescent Despair

The gay, carefree days of adolescence as nostalgically reconstructed by adults is a sharp contrast to the heavy, troubled expressions so frequently observed on the faces of many young men and women. To some extent a depressed outlook, although associated with affective swings, has been considered a typical adolescent mood.

Many authors (Lorand and Schneer, 1962; Blos, 1962; Eissler, 1958) have described features by which they sought to "define" adolescence in terms of psychic processes rather than merely as an entity with chronological boundaries. Although what can be generalized for the group is still a controversial subject, there seems to be agreement about some psychic mechanisms.

For example, since Erikson's (1956) comprehensive description of the identity crisis of adolescence, many therapists are impressed by their patients' preoccupation with both the meaning of life and where they fit. They complain about not knowing who they are and the purpose of their existence. Although severe manifestations of disturbances of the identity sense are an aspect of psychopathology, many adolescents who seemingly adjust well show less intense but similar preoccupations (Grinker, 1963; Offer and Sabshin, 1966). Consequently the identity sense, as a psychic structure, can be singled out as a particularly vulnerable area for this age group.

An invariable manifestation of an imperfectly formed or insecure identity is lack of a subjective sense of freedom or autonomy. The adolescent often feels he has no control over what happens to him. He complains that he is at the mercy of the whims of the adult world and has no security that he can master his feelings.

The above can be viewed as indications of characterological disturbance and when occurring later in life are often signs of severe psychopathology such as occurs in "borderline" cases. In adolescence, however, identity problems and the reaction to what is felt as a lack of autonomy may or may not be indicators of grave emotional disorders. If

First published in *Arch. Gen. Psychiat.* 18(1968), 650–57. Reprinted by permission.

the therapist is oriented to the characterological makeup of the adolescent patient, what may appear to be disparate, clinical phenomena can be understood in terms of underlying homogeneous processes.

Cultural Patterns and Clinical Syndromes

Some aspects of adolescence have frequently been considered an outgrowth of the surrounding culture. Not all cultures have "created" a teenage group sufficiently distinct from both childhood and adulthood. The influence of our society on various psychic structures, however, can be especially highlighted when one examines certain subcultures.

Elsewhere (Giovacchini, 1961) I have described certain behavioral constellations and their defensive meaning in the second-generation immigrant. From the reconstruction of adult analyses, the second-generation immigrant child was seen to be characterized by a need to overidentify with the new culture and repudiate that of his parents. Frequently, during latency there had been a pseudomaturity and a clownish cheerfulness that hostilely caricatured his peers. During adolescence, however, there was much soul searching and an underlying depressive current. In contrast to a somewhat hypomanic latency period they had now become moody and introspective. The question arises as to whether these findings, which are from persons who spontaneously sought treatment, can be generalized to apply to all second-generation immigrants. What was impressive was that, although there were areas of failure, the psychic mechanisms these patients employed are vital for the development of an autonomous identity sense, one that is consonant with the environment. The difficulties encountered in these patients must reflect vicissitudes encountered by all second-generation immigrants and perhaps all adolescents.

These patients especially emphasized identity problems because somewhere in their development they had to "shift" identities. As they became aware of the surrounding world they noted that its values, customs, and mores differed in many respects from those of their parents. Frequently the parents (especially the father) were equated with failure and contemporaries were to some extent idealized. They wanted to be accepted by their peers and to establish an autonomy that would make them distinct and separate from the old culture. They had to shed their national background in order to achieve self-esteem and to construct an ego ideal that valued achievement. Adolescence was a painful struggle for recognition characterized by withdrawal and depression rather than by boisterous gaiety.

Another group of adolescents who come from a markedly different background show a similar depression and identity struggle. Adolescence is often stormy, characterized by restlessness and rebellion, the dominant mood being depressive. I am referring to the children of successful middle-class or upper-class parents. Frequently, these young people live in the suburbs but I do not believe that the locale is a unique factor.

Unlike the parents of second-generation immigrants, these parents are very much a part of the American culture. Many of them are influential and prominent pillars of the community. They are comfortably settled and their dress, manners, etc, are proper and in some instances even imitated. Consequently, from the cultural viewpoint alone, it is difficult to understand why their children should have an identity problem.

Often these adolescents strike a pose that is the complete antithesis of the world the parents value. They do not seek success and reject what our culture considers achievement. They dress sloppily, let their hair grow and wear beards. Heilbrunn (1967) described in detail the cultural subvarieties of this group but regardless of how many different sociocultural factors are involved both this group and the second-generation immigrant have some similar intrapsychic conflicts and psychopathological responses.

Clinical Examples

To illustrate the psychic mechanisms relevant to our understanding of these clinical phenomena, I will present some brief vignettes.

An eighteen-year-old oldest son was referred for psychotherapy because he failed his freshman year in college in spite of high aptitude scores. Though treatment had been urged upon him, it became obvious, even in the first interview, that he was suffering intensively and was eager to establish a therapeutic relationship.

His appearance was unusual. He had long, neatly combed hair and wore a short, disheveled beard on his lower chin. His clothes were informal (jeans and open neck shirt).

His manner of speaking was calm and mature. Occasionally there was some slang phrase typical of adolescence, but I had the impression he was not particularly comfortable with such expressions. What was most striking was his depressed affect, which seemed incongruous with the circumstances of his life.

He described his parents as warm, giving people who judiciously gratified most of his material desires. He did not believe he had been spoiled but he was aware of how easy everything was for him. Both of his parents are outstandingly successful people. His father is a successful and wealthy businessman and his mother, who can trace her ancestry back to colonial days, has gained considerable fame as an artist. In spite of her preoccupation with her work, the patient believed that she was a devoted mother who treated all her children with equal love and care. Although the above description was in part due to the patient's defensive reaction formation, the consistency of his associations later in treatment indicated that there seemed to be considerable accuracy to his report.

I shall not stress the potential of this material for producing intrapsychic conflict. Rather, my specific interest now is to illustrate how the patient's background contributed to the formation or lack of formation of his identity sense. Obviously, many factors are involved, but certain features in this patient's development may be found in many adolescent depressions.

As stated, the patient was eager to begin treatment. He wanted some relief from his inner torment, which at first seemed totally incomprehensible. Along with his agonized outlook, he was preoccupied with "not knowing the purpose of his life." He did not know where he belonged and he had tried forcing himself to pursue a vocation or profession. He had maintained interest only a short time because he could not believe that he had any talent or possibility of success. His depression reached suicidal proportions as his life became a monstrous dilemma. He kept himself isolated and since he lived away from home, he did not let his parents know about the severity of his disturbance.

During treatment he improved; a technical description of the therapeutic process is, however, tangential to the thesis of this paper. The intriguing question was why this patient found it so tormenting and difficult to consolidate his self-representation when, at least at one level, his reactions to his early introjects were positive and seemingly capable of integration with various ego systems. The latter should have resulted in a firm identity sense and yet this situation is not uncommon, as I have gathered from discussions with colleagues and from other cases such as the following.

In contrast to the above case, this patient was an early adolescent, a fourteen-year-old girl, the youngest of three (two older brothers). She wanted treatment because of extreme shyness and severe depression. She had what others described as a marked character change during puberty; whereas she had been fairly active and gregarious during childhood, she changed abruptly as she reached adolescence.

There were sexual conflicts stimulated by the onset of menses, but these were not unusual. Her unresolved oedipus was harder to cope with because of the impetus received from gonadal maturation, but again these are tangential factors. Her description of her family background and the current misery she was experiencing were noteworthy.

She was not as positive as the first patient in the descriptions of her parents, particularly her mother. Still, the parents' concern for her welfare, an only daughter, seemed genuine and warm. She described her mother as a cheerful, happy person who always looked at things from the brighter side. Her father was also a perpetual optimist who was always right both in his judgment and conduct.

She felt, however, that her mother was scatterbrained and impractical. She recited many minor and trivial incidents to illustrate this point. At the same time she also stressed mother's "magic touch." Everything she did, in spite of her disorganized approach, turned out well. She seemed incapable of failing although the patient was unable to understand how anyone as seemingly inefficient as her mother could ever accomplish anything. She reached her goals without apparent effort.

Both parents' relationship to her was giving and indulgent. They made very few demands and the patient accepted responsibilities without being prodded. She knew that her parents would be pleased with academic achievement but they did not push her. On the other hand, they were very much concerned with her being happy. This had become a major issue.

She referred to imposed happiness frequently during later stages in therapy. During the first month of treatment, she described a recent television movie in which a wife berates her husband, who caters to all her material desires, for not making her happy. She screams at him "you don't make me happy. You don't make me happy." This is an isolated statement, standing on its own, outside of any particular context.

This patient illustrated, as did the first case, a paradox. If children consolidate their self-representation by identification with their parents, then these patients are examples of what Erikson (1956) has described as negative identity. Both groups of parents related to the world positively, at least from the viewpoint of surface behavior. The patients' supposedly nontraumatic environment made it difficult to understand why they had to rebel, why they could not incorporate their parents' successful standards and make them their own. To shed light on this paradox, one has to discuss the ego mechanisms of the adolescent process (see Comment). First, I will present more data about the two patients and also about the mother of the first patient.

Both patients were unable to adopt their parents' standards. The young man felt inadequate insofar as he did not believe he could ever equal his father's achievements. His reaction was one of quiet despair since he generalized his comparison with his father and consequently was defeated before he started.

As his therapy progressed, we found that the outwardly optimal relationship with the parents was not so optimal. In subtle ways the parents undermined his early attempts at being autonomous. This was done in such a fashion that the patient was not aware of it. Instead, he could only see helpful parents. For example, he recalled putting together a log cabin set when he was six years old. After having placed several logs in position, he hesitated. Immediately, his father placed the next log in what would have been a logical sequence. However, the patient had not been unsure as to where the next log belonged. He had been thinking of new ways of putting the logs together and his father's seemingly helpful action was actually an intrusion.

The above episode seemed minor, but it became apparent that his life was punctuated with a series of such incidents. Finally, he no longer knew whether any behavior was truly his own or whether it emanated from his parents. He saw himself as a puppet manipulated by strings.

His father, although he verbalized intentions of giving his son complete freedom of vocational choice, had assumed that he would take over the family business as he had done. Consequently, since early childhood he had been groomed for the presidency of the company.

The mother, (see below) without seeming overprotective, had an effect on the patient similar to that of the father. She tried to anticipate his needs and have everything prepared in advance. She had read many books on child psychology and tried to relate to her son in a healthy and warm manner. Since she was currently undergoing psychoanalytic treatment, she believed that she had some sophistication in responding to another person's needs. She was proud of her belief that her son had experienced practically no frustration during his childhood, a marked contrast to his adolescent picture of continual tormenting but outwardly unexplainable frustration. The patient, in turn, cooperated with his parents. He never rebelled because he did not find anything to rebel against. All he saw was kind, helpful people and all the material comforts he could want. Consequently, he felt more miserable as he could not be happy in such ideal surroundings.

As with the second case, his parents "demanded" happiness and paradoxically this was the only thing he could rebel against. He was not consciously aware of any demands in his ostensible permissive setting except the mandate that he be happy.

A colleague has furnished me with material from the mother's treatment. Briefly, he made the following formulation. She was an extremely talented woman who had to use all of her endowments and the acclaim she received to maintain a tenuous and precarious emotional synthesis. Her optimism and optimal adjustment was a thin veneer, a facade to maintain control of an inner disruptive rage and a hold on reality. Viewing the world with rose-colored glasses was a defense against being aware of the ugliness she felt inside herself.

The relationship with her son represented a narcissistic attempt to create an extension of herself that embodied an omnipotent goodness to make up for the emptiness and hatred created by her early introjects. Her self-representation was that of an inadequate, hateful, unlovable person.

The second patient had a similar relationship to her parents. She was not being groomed for anything in particular, but her associations demonstrated that she did not feel she even "owned her thoughts." Her mother constantly interceded whenever she tried to initiate any activity. For example, the patient recalled an excursion she planned with some friends to a local amusement park. This was to be an uncomplicated, pleasant afternoon with lunch at a nearby hamburger stand. Her mother approved of her plans and shared her daughter's enthusiasm. Without knowing how it happened, the patient suddenly found herself completely confused as to what she was going to do. Unobtrusively her mother somehow had managed to change the itinerary and "make it into a big production." The mother's suggestions supposedly made things easier and more pleasant for the patient and her friends. She had volunteered to drive them wherever they wanted to go, but in so doing she was imposing her presence. The afternoon lost its gay, carefree aspect and the patient and her friends felt constrained. The patient was not aware of what had happened and she blamed herself rather than her mother because her trip turned out to be a flop.

Her intense shyness was a reaction to the feeling that she could never do anything correctly. She meant that she had no confidence in her ability to plan a project completely on her own. She was not consciously aware of feeling deficient in this area; she simply felt uneasy. With friends, she never knew where she stood because she did not know just what her role was supposed to be. She brooded over the problem of her identity.

Comment

These patients presented similar clinical pictures. They both were confused and depressed. They suffered from intense feelings of inadequacy and they indicated that their self-representation was poorly constructed with blurred boundaries. Neither patient perceived himself as separate or distinct from parental attitudes and standards.

The description of the parents' preoccupation with being helpful and their attempts to gratify is interesting since many adolescents of affluent families report similar experiences. Adult patients from the same socioeconomic strata and who resemble the mother of the first patient often reveal that their seemingly involved relationship with their children is a characterological defense to maintain some coherence in their self-representation. Consequently, the child feels unsuccessful and miserable rather than using the parental ministrations adaptively.

Freud (1915a) postulates that emotional development requires a degree of frustration. Total gratification supposedly produces no impetus to progress to the next stage of psychosexual development. The parents' attempt to create a nonfrustrating environment does not lead to emotional development. In chapter 17, I discuss my objections to the frustration theory of development other than the impossibility of obtaining total gratification. Here, I wish to emphasize that these adolescents felt that they were being imposed upon rather than helped. They revealed that *even during childhood there is a need to do things for oneself.* Gratification of basic needs is, of course, essential. However, after such satisfaction the child develops other needs which go beyond simply effecting a biological equilibrium. He explores and manipulates objects. To some extent he has to experiment for himself, and to be interrupted even in the guise of being helped, is experienced as frustration. Bettelheim (1964) emphasizes this point when discussing the background of the autistic child. These cases, as did Bettelheim's, demonstrated that from these crude exploratory beginnings develop what is later a firm sense of autonomy, which is a vital aspect of a coherent self-representation.

Adolescents often complain about the unreasonable attitudes of the adult world. Frequently, they reveal that they resent the adult telling them how to live. This goes beyond simply being restricted and having their liberties curtailed. So many of the peculiar and bizarre mores of the adolescent are an attempt to create a culture that they feel is truly their own, one that has not been imposed upon them by the adult world. These patients could not accept their parents' standards of success or even the pursuit of happiness because they reacted to these orientations as if they were foreign bodies and incapable of integration.

To emphasize separateness and autonomy, one has to acquire unique and distinct features. In some instances, this may mean being different. My patients and other adolescents demonstrate that being different from their parents is absolutely essential to the structuring and maintenance of a self-representation. Insofar as the self-representation is not well organized it is not particularly discrete and distinct from the other aspects of the psyche. The adolescent, in order to construct a better differentiated self-image, alloplastically seeks to immerse himself in experiences and ideologies that are different from those of the conventional culture. He is trying to achieve a distinct and unique frame of reference which when internalized will lead to a coherent identity sense, sharply distinguishing his self-representation from other ego systems.

The degree of difference required may, however, be proportional to the severity of psychopathology. It is conceivable that better structured egos can feel their individuality without having to be flamboyantly different or adopting standards that are the antithesis of all contemporary cultural standards.

The differences here included a need not to be happy. This is a paradoxical type of rebellion, since all it can lead to is misery. These patients at one level had to feel unhappy, since being happy meant they were like their parents and not individuals in their own right. Later, during the transference when they had projected parental standards onto me, they experienced panic because of the fear of being just an appendage of mine or of being "swallowed up." Being unhappy was an adaptation by which they could maintain distance between themselves and external objects. A depressive affect had become an indispensable element for character defenses designed to maintain a degree of autonomy and coherence to their self-representation.

The above stresses that *feeling miserable and depressed represents a structured defensive mechanism rather than just being a manifestation of breakdown.* These reactions are purposeful in contrast to being responses to ego disintegration. Still, a reaction or an affect can be adaptive and a product of decompensation depending on the level from which one is viewing the clinical data.

Seeking pain is a manifestation of masochism. Although these patients have some masochistic qualities, what is being described is different. Masochistic behavior protects the ego against a sadistic superego. Such an ego, although pathologically distorted, has a fairly well-defined structure and the conflict is mainly intrapsychic. These adolescents were trying to preserve some unity to ego systems, primarily the self-representation, by protecting themselves from what they considered to be the intrusions of the parental world.

These patients' pain and misery also went beyond adaptive purposes to the point that they eagerly sought therapy and relief. The relative lack of an identity sense in itself leads to a painful emotional state. Viewing oneself as hateful and useless is agonizing. The lower the self-esteem, the more difficult it is to accept oneself, and the more amorphous and poorly structured is the identity sense. This affects the total psychic integration. These patients felt depressed and miserable and unable to find anything within themselves they could value. The defensive purpose of such feelings has been discussed. In spite of their integrative potential, this negative view of the self is also a manifestation of a lack of self-esteem and may be an indication of decompensation.

Many of the mechanisms described above are found in all adolescents and may be considered part of the adolescent process. The need to be different in the context of rebellion may be ubiquitous. With psychopathology, there are both qualitative and quantitative distortions depending upon the degree of disturbance.

For example, once deeper levels of the personality were understood, these patients revealed that they had *not* succeeded in being different than their parents or in constructing unique value systems. *On the contrary, what they felt about themselves was probably very similar to the parental identity.* In the first case, this hypothesis could be confirmed by information gathered from the mother's treatment. In the second case, this formulation is conjecture but the study of adults similar to the patient's parents often reveal a basic underlying insecurity and severe psychopathology.

In the suburbs, one is struck by the cheerful optimism of many of the residents. Their behavior may range from reserved politeness to saccharin fawning. I do not believe that this surface attitude is restricted to suburbia; rather it is probably a characteristic of a certain socioeconomic group that tends to move to the suburbs. In any case, psychiatrists practicing in suburban areas report a preponderance of patients with facades of gentle benevolence who do not acknowledge the seamier and uglier sides of life. Some of my adult patients behave as if they perpetually wear rose-colored glasses. They never say anything derogatory and even when they disagree with a person or position, they always make allowances and became apologists. It is this "rose-colored glasses syndrome" against which my adolescent patients seemed to rebel.

Some adolescents feel uncomfortable with these adults and are sensitive to the artificiality and the insecurity of their supposedly doting parents. During treatment they reveal that their relationship with their parents is only "skin deep" and in some instances they were almost completely ignored, being reared by servants. The decreasing availability of good, warm servants who might compensate for the lack of a significant relationship with the parents may be another factor contributing to current developmental problems in this group.

From another viewpoint, the rebellion my patients manifested during adolescence was not really rebellion. It could be considered rebellion only if viewed from the surface. *They were rebelling against their parents' superficial facade.* At deeper levels, they were very much like their parents.

Each parent has a specific influence upon the child's development. In this paper I am not distinguishing different parental roles; rather, I wish to concentrate upon what might be considered the family "Gestalt" and its general consequences.

Being different from the parents' "rose-colored glasses" attitude meant being grim, depressed, and insecure. The study of many adults indicates that no matter how cheerful they seem to be, basically they feel empty and miserable. The behavior of some adolescent patients reflects the inner emptiness the parents experience. The emptiness and misery that the adults so desperately submerge by a frenetic camaraderie does not escape the adolescent's perception, even though it may be unconscious. He incorporates the basic parental structure into his self-representation. *He identifies with his parents' underlying psychopathology while rebelling against their defensive superstructure.*

With intrapsychic conflict and structural defects, the psyche loses its synthesized unity. Depending upon the severity of psychopathology, the personality will be fragmented. Whereas the hypothetically normal psyche has a harmonious integration of adaptive techniques and ego-syntonic needs, the pathologically distorted personality consists of conflicting needs and opposing defenses. The latter is characterized by a lack of synchrony and different layers of the psyche are split off from and antagonistic to each other. Traversing the spectrum from the normal to the pathological, there is a decreasing unity in the synthesis of the various levels of the personality finally leading to states of schizoid fragmentation.

With less disturbed patients, identifying with deeper levels (more unconscious) of the parents' personality is an important aspect of the healthy adolescent process. Insofar as the parental personality is well integrated the parents' superficial behavior reflects their basic organization rather than being antithetical or fragmented. *Consequently, the adolescent identifies with a synthesized whole which he values as part of himself. Since what he incorporates is relatively lacking in conflict, he does not feel impinged upon and can pursue his individuality and autonomy.*

Defenses that were effective in the preadolescent period were no longer adaptive once these patients reached adolescence. During childhood they were able to incorporate their parents' standards and make what seemed to be good adjustments. Therefore, the question can be raised as to why many adolescents cannot maintain their childhood defenses especially when they are confronted with their parents' seemingly successful adaptation. One answer to this question may be that the adolescent recognizes his parents' failure, although this may be an unconscious awareness. The fact that their drives are much more intense further disturbs his previous defensive equilibrium.

Often some external event or changed life circumstance, such as moving away from home or into a different social milieu, renders previous defensive patterns inoperative. As far as could be ascertained for the patients discussed here, there was no particular precipitating situation to their distress other than that of entering adolescence.

Adolescence is a period of psychic consolidation. It is followed by adulthood where the personality is relatively structured and stable. Emotional development begins during childhood and leads to progressive structuralization at varying rates. During the first year there is a peak of both psychic development and physical maturation. There are apparently developmental spurts during later phases too. Adolescence is a crucial stage when the psyche achieves more stable characteristics. Later, there may be further changes but these are accretions superimposed upon a fairly stable identity sense.

The child's personality, among other factors, is the outcome of transactions with his environment. He tends to incorporate adaptive techniques in the context of a harmonious relationship with his parents. If the parental character, however, is mainly a defensive facade it cannot be successfully incorporated by the child.

A defense has a degree of specificity insofar as it is designed to handle a particular conflictful drive or painful characterological defect. The child may, at first, be able to derive some stability from using techniques that are similar to those of the parents, such as their "rose-colored glasses" attitude or their pursuit of "success." The adolescent's physical maturation and the social mores force him to disengage himself, relatively speaking, from his dependence upon the family. He has to construct adaptive techniques that are consonant with *his* needs beyond simply relating to his milieu. Defenses that maintain the parents' psychic equilibrium are not necessarily appropriate for their children when they reach adolescence and begin constructing an autonomous identity.

Rejecting the parents' defenses was, for these patients, an attempt to form a coherent self-representation. Still they identified with a part of the parent's personality which was characterized by a lack of self-esteem. This resulted in a fragmented and vulnerable psyche since they had inadequate defenses of their own. They could no longer use parental techniques which had now become a further threat to their autonomy. To do so would increase their sense of worthlessness and create a vicious circle.

Some adolescents, in spite of their vociferous rejection of parental standards, adopt their defenses during postadolescence. The initial incorporation, although accompanied by instability and feelings of inadequacy and vulnerability, may, in some instances, gradually lead to a tenuous, though relatively independent, orientation. The latter is, in itself, a defense, but one which may lead to sufficient stability so that in early adulthood it is possible to incorporate parental techniques into their identity sense.

The formation of a differentiated psyche involves more than an identification with the parents during adolescence. Considerable structuralization has occurred during previous stages of development. During adolescence there is an intensification of psychic processes such as identification that were also significant for earlier phases. Psychopathological distortions are highlighted but since the ego is particularly "fluid" and its capacity to incorporate is heightened, the adolescent usually has a good therapeutic potential.

As their readiness to become involved in treatment demonstrated, these patients desperately wanted a dependable relationship with an adult. They missed the stability and reliability of a gratifying mothering experience during childhood. Unlike some schizophrenics, they had not withdrawn. Although they were seeking satisfaction of infantile needs, the reliability of the treatment setting engendered enough security so that they became involved in the therapeutic activity. The incorporation of the nonanxious and nondefensive understanding therapeutic attitude became an important factor in the formation of an autonomous self-representation.

Summary

Some aspects of the adolescent process are studied in the context of psychopathology. The behavior of adolescents demonstrates the need for autonomy in order to construct a coherent well-delineated identity sense.

Two patients are briefly described. Both patients felt miserable and depressed although their backgrounds were characterized by successful, optimistic, seemingly understanding parents. The patients ostensibly rebelled against the parents' "compulsion" that these children be happy.

Actually, these adolescents identified with the parents' core personality. The parents' cheerful demeanor represented a defense against the inner misery they experienced. Their children identified with the latter. Consequently, what seemed to be rebellion was a rebellion only against the surface layer of the psyche, which was fragmented from deeper ego defects of the parents.

The healthier adolescent also incorporates aspects of the parents' psyche to construct an autonomous self-representation. When the parents' psyche is a well-synthesized unit, the adolescent can identify without feeling impinged upon since he is incorporating adaptive techniques rather than defensive fragmentations.

Adolescence is a period where defensive mechanisms utilized in earlier stages become inadequate. As previous techniques fail, there is emotional turmoil but since the capacity to incorporate is also increased, the adolescent is able to identify with the therapist and become engaged in a treatment relationship.

Chapter 6

Fantasy Formation, Ego Defect, and Identity Problems

Viewing the psychic apparatus in terms of a structural hierarchy from a physiological to a psychological-mentational frame enables one to raise the question as to what elements are involved in fantasy production. An inner need is experienced at all levels of the psychic apparatus. As physiological stimuli gain ascendency, drive representations are given shape as they interact with memory traces and reality. Various ego mechanisms are involved, and the cathecting of the appropriate executive apparatus determines how the need is met, that is, actual or fantasy gratification.

The role of fantasy can be considered in terms of its adaptive or disruptive aspects. Freud (1900) emphasized omnipotent wish fulfillment as corresponding to a magical-primitive developmental phase where reality and fantasy are not distinguished. He illustrates how both dreams and fantasies contain id elements striving for gratification, and if reality is too thwarting, the patient withdraws from it, seeking solace in fantasy.

Many patients, especially those suffering from severe psychopathology, are afraid of their fantasies. This is also true of many adolescents who do not permit themselves the freedom of fantasy production. In the consultation room these patients are often cryptic and concrete, unimaginative and incapable of free associating. The underlying id impulses that would become elaborated into a fantasy seem to be too disruptive for their loosely integrated egos, and they have to keep their inner excitement under control. Consequently, these patients are often constricted, repressed persons who keep their feelings at a distance. Fantasy production is inhibited.

In contrast to frightening wish-fulfillment fantasies, one sometimes encounters fantasies that are primarily manifestations of defense. Many grandiose fantasies do not refer exclusively to the instantaneous gratification of all desires; often, they reflect an overcompensatory need for protection against the uncontrollable onslaught of destructive and self-

First published in *Ann. Amer. Soc. for Adolescent Psychiat.* 1 (1971), 329–42. Reprinted by permission.

destructive impulses. In other fantasies one can clearly discern vigilant and repressive qualities against the pressure of unacceptable strivings or parts of the self, whereas still other defensive fantasies are designed to make gratification less dangerous.

I shall present two brief vignettes to illustrate the subtle relationship among characterological pathology, fantasy, and the role of external objects in reestablishing equilibrium when the factors leading to fantasy production threaten psychic stability. These interactions also have relevance to the adolescent process in general.

Clinical Material

A homosexual senior college student was constantly preoccupied with fantasies. He complained of his habit of living almost totally within himself to the point where he had only a minimal awareness of the surrounding world.

In his fantasies he constructed elaborate settings or dialogues in which he would try to master problems that usually took the form of a struggle with another person or situation. Instead of a strong or clever hero, he depicted himself as a bewildered, harassed, vulnerable person (this view of himself was an accurate reflection of his self-representation). He created fantasy situations where he would be in physical danger, ridiculed, or swindled. The activity around him would take place at an accelerated tempo. Objects and people would move at a rapid pace and cause him to feel dismayed and confused. He did not see himself as being able to preserve order or maintain equilibrium. This created further vulnerability and helplessness and made him less capable of coping with the threatening situation or problem that he was facing.

In spite of all these difficulties, he would overpower and outwit his opponent. His success was usually accomplished by his being able to anticipate his opponent's moves by reproducing the course of the latter's thinking and staying a step ahead of the situation.

When he had such fantasies in my office, he would spend lengthy periods of time constructing a situation between the two of us. For example, he would conjecture that I had been about to have intercourse with my previous patient but had to stop my advances because I knew that he was outside waiting for his appointment. I then would want to manipulate him sadistically by doing something unexpected. Perhaps I might act in an insane manner and then he would be faced with the dilemma of determining whether this were genuine or simulated. If I faced him with my psychosis, then he would be completely discombobulated because this would represent a completely unforeseen reversal of roles. He would fantasy "You (the analyst) will think this, then if I say such and such, you will do this, so instead if I say———you will (do something different), but then I would———." After he had anticipated all my possible reactions and responses to his responses, he would then do something definite to counteract my attempt. The latter, after such a buildup, was usually a dull and crass anticlimax, such as simply calling the police. A telephone call would determine whether I were simulating because I would stop acting out if I were faking.

At other times the patient would create a dilemma of such magnitude that he could not find a solution. This occurred more frequently outside the analysis, though I had the opportunity to observe several episodes of such disruption. During one particularly memorable session, he had a sexual fantasy about a young lady he had recently met and who indicated that she was willing to become involved with him. He had never had a sexual relationship with a woman, though now he felt some desire and began anticipating the possibility of having heterosexual intercourse. This anticipation was the dominant theme of the fantasy, and he tried to create a situation in which he would be making love to her. He tried to visualize a room, a bed, and her naked body, but he was unable to form a composite picture. He could only conjure fragmented bits which did not permit any cohesive action. In this abortive fantasy, he continued anticipating the sexual act, but he was unable to form a coherent picture. He stated that he did not have the "equipment," that is, "did not know how" to make love to a woman. Eventually these fragmented images began to whirl around in a "frenzy" and he felt he was losing control over them. He began feeling "bombarded" and "torn apart." His increasing anxiety reached panic-like proportions. When his discomfort reached such a peak that I began to feel it too, I stated that I was in the same room with him. I had learned from previous experiences that the acknowledgment of my presence would have an instantaneously calming effect. He was once again able to compose himself about sex in an abstract sense, not referring to his fantasy again during the session.

Next, I would like to present another adolescent patient who demonstrated somewhat similar phenomena, which in this instance might have some relevance to the adolescent process, that is, ego mechanisms that might be characteristic of adolescence, and then to discuss both patients in terms of character structure and ego processes.

The patient, a nineteen-year-old male student, had always thought of himself as precocious. He was academically ahead of his age group, had achieved adult social graces even before puberty, and had started having sexual relations at the age of fifteen (this was considered premature in his upper-class group). He sought treatment for the same vague, undefined reasons that older patients with characterological problems give. He found life unfulfilling in spite of his social and intellectual endowments. He did not know who and what he was, or the "purpose of his existence." He elicited all those symptoms that are often referred to as an existential crisis. He was moody and unhappy in spite of a seemingly sanguine demeanor, and was often depressed to the point of suicide. He felt his environment was "inordinately complex" and took drugs (marijuana and LSD) in order to withdraw.

Winnicott (1958b) refers to the capacity to be alone and Borowitz (1967a) carries the theme into the sexual sphere when discussing the capacity to masturbate alone. This patient, in a sense, had not acquired the ability to have sexual intercourse "alone" with his girlfriend. He had to have other persons in the same house or apartment but not in the same room. He never had intercourse in anyone else's presence nor had he ever witnessed the sexual act. On the other hand, he had to have a friend or another couple nearby. The latter would also be having intercourse. If he just had male friends nearby, he would fantasy that they were masturbating. He had never had a sexual experience in any other circumstances.

During analysis he became aware of the fact that his mind was "always in the next room" when he was having intercourse. Though he did not completely exclude awareness of his partner, he almost did at the moment of ejaculation. During intercourse he would imagine conversations with his friends (there was nothing characteristic about the content) while they were either having intercourse or masturbating. He would shift his attention sporadically from his partner to these fantasies, but when ejaculating he would be completely immersed in his fantasy.

The patient went out of his way to create excitement, which often resulted in a painful aftermath. He had on several occasions been careless with his drugs and suffered considerable fear that he would be apprehended by the police. On other occasions he would complicate his social life to such an extent that he seemed to have created an intolerable morass. He would even invent competitive games and work himself into frenzied excitement. He could not tolerate calm and peace.

This patient's background was similar to that of the first patient. Both had highly excitable parents. Their mothers were overprotective but also extremely stimulating and seductive. They described scenes in childhood of seeing them naked and bathing with them, and in the first case there is a possibility that he had actually witnessed the primal scene. Both mothers were also extremely ambitious for their sons, and pushed them to academic extremes. With the second patient the mother needed to see him as a "little man" and cast him not only as a narcissistic show piece but also as a confidant. His father was a very successful man but he remained aloof from his family. Both fathers were passively uninvolved with their sons.

Discussion

Fantasy has been referred to as a substitute for action (Freud, 1900). In some persons the content of the fantasy is a pleasurable anticipation of a future satisfaction. These are wish-fulfillment fantasies that contribute to a mood that will enhance ultimate gratification. In some respects this is equivalent to forepleasure and raises the cathexis of the receptive apparatus.

In some patients, particularly those suffering from ego defects, fantasies are not always or primarily pleasurable and usually do not lead to constructive, goal-directed action. The first patient's fantasies, early in the analysis, were elaborations of anticipated gratification, which continued being disruptively anticipated because the ego did not have the resources to turn to external objects to achieve actual gratification.

Fantasy production is an intermediary step between the perceptions of an inner need and the activation of the proper adjustive techniques to gratify that need. In this patient and others suffering from characterological defects, the drives are imperfectly developed (see chapter 11). As physiological needs become elaborated (further structuralized) into a sophisticated desire such as a heterosexual one, the drive becomes mentationally elaborated. Along with the defect in relating to external objects, the first patient's mental elaboration of inner needs was also constricted, and this was reflected in the content of his fantasies. He had difficulty conjuring cohesive pictures, and often everything would become vague and jumbled, the various elements of the fantasy "coming apart" and resulting in chaos.

The occurrence of fantasy, as an intermediate step between the perception of an inner need and the activation of the appropriate technique to gratify the need, raises the question as to whether during the process of gratifying an id impulse, a fantasy inevitably has to be interposed somewhere along the path from sensory stimulation to motor activation. There are many activities that take place more or less automatically (reflexively) where there is no introspection, planning or fantasy that the person can recall. Still, in order to set the executive apparatus into motion so that the person relates to the outer world, higher ego systems, including consciousness, are involved. Some mentational activity takes place, though it may not have the organization of a fantasy.

Some psychoanalysts believe that the concept of unconscious fantasy is useful when considered in a psychodynamic context. Freud (Breuer and Freud, 1895), very early in his writings, describes patients having fantasies that led to ego disruption and then repressing these fantasies as defensive equilibriums were reestablished. The second patient illustrated this phenomenon, and as his defenses relaxed, previously repressed fantasies became conscious. Whether one refers to such repressed psychic elements as fantasies, when they are repressed, is a question of definition. Still, that which is repressed has the potential to be perceived as a fantasy if it can gain access to consciousness.

Arlow (1969a, b)* discusses these questions thoroughly and by constructing a consistent conceptual system has succeeded in demonstrating not only how confusing questions can be resolved but also that many such questions are superfluous.

There are, of course, many differences between these two patients, but I feel that there are some important similarities that are relevent to the process of fantasy production. Both felt assaulted and impinged (Winnicott, 1958b) upon by their early environment. The stimuli they received from their mothers, sexual and otherwise, were poorly integrated within their egos. The sexual overstimulation, in particular, was felt as assaultive and, because of emotional and physical immaturity, could not be smoothly incorporated within the psyche.

These patients described an inner excitement, vague and undefinable, but still related to this hyperstimulation which caused them to feel helpless and vulnerable. They felt unable to master their disruption.

As a reaction to his inner turmoil, the first patient would get himself "in trouble" because of homosexual behavior. Both patients frequently reacted to this turmoil during their analyses, though neither one acted out as intensely as some of Borowitz's (1967b) patients did. Their inability to integrate the mother's hyperstimulation and precociously stimulated sexual feelings with various ego systems and with reality was reflected in their affects and fantasies.

The life of the homosexual patient was practically all fantasy with very little action. He often emphasized how ignorant and hopeless he felt, indicating that he had never acquired the adaptive techniques necessary to cope with the complexities of the external world (see chapter 11). Similarly, he was unable to experience satisfactory gratification in any area, and even though he desired heterosexual relationships, he felt paralyzed and impotent with women.

With analytic progress he began to have fantasies of the wish-fulfill-

---

*Isaacs (1952) and Segal (1967) used the concept of unconscious fantasy in a somewhat different fashion, one that is tangential to the thesis here. See also Beres (1962).

ment variety. Though these fantasies also began by jousting with me, and anticipating my threatening maneuvers, he now saw me attacking him because he was planning to seduce a girl. There was a gradual shift from his defense against me to the more exclusive preoccupation with the details of seduction.

Still, there was a curious reaction to what seemed to be a conversion of a relatively defensive fantasy to one where the elements seemed to become predominantly wish-fulfilling. He became more and more anxious as he moved further in the direction of wish fulfillment.

For example, he could construct a situation in which he met a girl, took her out, and successfully went through a variety of social preliminaries. Once he brought her into the bedroom he began feeling confusion because he literally did not know what to do. Though repressive elements were evident in his associations, he emphasized that he had never learned how to proceed further. At this point what had started out as being somewhat pleasurable now became increasingly painful. Sometimes, as with previous fantasies, his anxiety would reach the point of mild panic. However, his affect would not become so disruptive as it had at the beginning of treatment, and I never found it necessary to intervene.

This patient suffered from two general but interrelated categories of difficulties. First, as the early fantasies demonstrated, he had to defend himself from an inner, disruptive excitement and agitation created by his inability smoothly to incorporate and amalgamate early maternal experiences. These experiences were perceived as threatening and assaultive, and their inner representations (introjects), which remained fragmented and encapsulated, were also threatening and disruptive. His initial fantasies reflected his need to be constantly vigilant and in control; there was considerable rumination and very little action. Second, he believed that he was unable to gratify inner needs (heterosexual) because he did not know how. The second group of fantasies indicated that not only had he found his infantile experiences disruptive but that they also did not form a base that would lead to the acquisition of techniques designed to relate to the outer world.

Because some of the stimuli (particularly sexual) he received from his mother were premature, the patient did not have the biological equipment necessary to respond to them. As an adult, he found himself in analogous (from a psychic viewpoint), though, of course, not identical, circumstances.

During infancy the patient's ego's executive apparatus was not capable of developing techniques that could respond to or master the mother's ministrations. So, in addition to having unintegrated introjects, there was a lack of executive techniques. His later fantasies demonstrated this lack, and in a sense, defined the ego defect. His characterological difficulties were based on a lack of integration and development of the executive apparatus to gratify biologically appropriate needs, in part because the needs were imposed on him when the psychic apparatus was too immature to deal with them. This led to constriction, and he found himself incapable of dealing with the disruptions of the inner world and unable to turn to the outer world for satisfaction.

The second patient's initial fantasies were obviously a defensive technique that helped him achieve orgasm. The fantasies also served as defenses against internal conflicts. The latter has to be understood in terms of his characterological difficulties, problems that I believe are fairly typical of a certain type of character disorder and of many adolescents.

The central psychopathology of this group of patients often involves the self-representation, that is, the identity system. The impact of assaultively perceived overstimulation has marked effects on the self-representation.

The maternal introject in these patients is perceived as dangerous and engulfing. The formation of the self-representation is a complicated process, one that at some stage involves incorporation or identification with external objects. When a precociously stimulating mother imago becomes part (an aspect) of the self-representation, the resulting identity is precarious and insecure.

The second adolescent patient often reported episodes when he felt he was being "eaten up inside" and his sense of existence felt threatened. The accompanying affect was painful panic, and he had all the symptoms that Erikson (1956) described as the identity diffusion syndrome. When capable of coherently describing his sensations, he had the feeling that something inside was pounding and hammering. He felt as if he would explode.

He could obtain relief from such an intolerable state by two maneuvers:

1. He could involve himself with friends and throw himself into frenetic social and sometimes sexual activity. He would give parties, attend meetings, take drug trips with a group; in other words, he did everything possible not to be alone. He indulged in many counterphobic activities in order to externalize inner excitement and then master it. While "high" on drugs, he and his companions would become tremendously excited watching candles burn. Each person would have his own candle. They would sit enraptured, watching them burn down. They reacted during these candle races with the same tension and excitement

someone might experience at a horse race. His deliberate (though unconscious) creation of dilemmas in his daily life had a similar counterphobic defensive meaning. In these instances, however, he was not always successful and his dismay was a reenactment of the turmoil he experienced in childhood.

He might also become passionately involved with a girl and have frequent sexual relations with her. As mentioned, he was creating excitement in order to master and control his inner turmoil, but this behavior had the added meaning of turning to an external object for protection. In the transference this was clearly illustrated insofar as he turned to me as a rescuer from something inside of him that was "swallowing" his individuality. In dreams he was often pursued by engulfing monsters and found himself running toward a protective person. Thus, the external object was, as will be further discussed, an important factor in his fantasies.

2. This patient would sometimes go into a fugue state when his panic reached an intense pitch, and he was unable to reestablish his equilibrium by the activities just described. He would feel emotionally numb. His identity diffusion would occur when he believed that innumerable demands were made of him (school and family), that is, when he felt unfairly imposed on. He felt as if he were in a "fog." He was not particularly uncomfortable, but he saw himself as apart from the rest of the world. In the analysis it became apparent that he was also apart from the rest of himself. He saw everything in terms of extremes, and certain persons were either all good or all bad. This was true of his behavior and various roles. For example, being a student was bad insofar as students are dependent and useless. His involvement with various civil rights movements and smoking marijuana were good. The transference also reflected this split, and my role shifted from being a nonthreatening, secure person who could protect him to a destructive manipulator, clearly projections of two aspects of the parental introject.

He attempted to cope with this turmoil by withdrawal and by drugs. Drugs represented an attempt to deny the existence of an arbitrary, rigid, and sadistic environment. While under the influence of drugs he felt he was in a "protected cage" and "nothing could get to him." He then felt peaceful and everything seemed to have a purpose and place.

The relationship between the identity sense, fantasy formation, and defenses, such as fragmentation and turning toward external objects, has relevance to our understanding of specific characterological pathology.

For this adolescent patient, inner impulses, particularly sexual impulses, were perceived as dangerous. This danger can be understood further from a characterological viewpoint. For example, when his self-representation was altered by a biological need—a sexual stimulus—he would experience tremendous anxiety. Insofar as sexuality and the maternal introject were closely fused, in that much of his maternal imago was constructed in the context of premature sexual stimulation, the maternal introject would be further cathected when he felt sexually excited. This made him feel vulnerable and helpless against the assaultive mother.

He once again faced a situation in which he feared being engulfed. The maternal introject is always instrumental in the formation of the self-representation. When this patient became sexually aroused, the maternal introject, in a sense, became fused with it. Sexual gratification, therefore, threatened to destroy him. This is perhaps an ego-psychological method of saying that he could not master his impulses, but, more precisely, emphasizes the vulnerability of the self-representation owing to the activation of the maternal introject.

He had to defend himself against such a disruptive situation. His defensive techniques against inner excitement and fear of assault generally have been discussed. He used similar techniques when facing specific sexual excitement and fear of assault.

As mentioned, he had to have someone near in addition to his partner while having sexual intercourse. This highlights the function of the external object. The presence of the external object made the self-representation feel less vulnerable.

One's weakness and helplessness is highlighted when alone; a group or a companion may help one to feel stronger and protected. Freud (1921) emphasized the role of the group in the formation of a collective superego. A group or a companion may also be instrumental in the formation of a collective self-representation. Groups assume an identity that transcends the individual's identity.

This patient introjected his companion to form an alliance against the assaultive maternal introject. The dyad helped him control his inner excitement. This does not constitute an actual relationship with an external object; the external object was a narcissistic extension of himself, an accretion so to speak, to the self-representation. The patient had to have someone, but it was the fantasy of a companion being engaged in similar sexual activity that enabled him to reach the climax of his excitement relatively safely.

The production of this fantasy was motivated by the need to get the "mother off his back." He would create a social environment by his fantasy which for the moment gave him the ephemeral security of having mastered the disruptive maternal introject. Though ephemeral, the fantasy created the illusion of strength, one that sustained him through a moment of danger. Once the sexual excitement subsided he could relax, because the maternal introject became relatively less threatening. Borowitz (1967a) presents similar clinical material; his patients had been assaultively and precociously sexually stimulated during childhood. They could not masturbate unless another person were present. The external object was required so that solitary masturbation could occur without being overwhelmingly disruptive.

The ego defects of these adolescent patients involve different systems, but now one can define the problem as resulting from a lack of development of the self-representation because the maternal introject disrupts an autonomous heterosexual orientation.

The sense of identity is the result of the operations of various ego systems (see chapter 9) and is also determined by the dominant psychosexual stage of the current ego state. For example, one feels alive because one experiences needs that are initially physiologic. They then become elaborated. First, one feels oneself in an oral fashion; for example, as a hungry mouth and then, with greater structure, there is a wider range of self-awareness up to seeing oneself as an aggressive, heterosexual, striving person with a variety of goals that promote self-esteem.

It is conceptually consistent to equate the self-image and the perceptual systems' self-observations with the identity sense. Even though one's self-observations may be defensive in nature and be reactions against other painful states of self-awareness, the identity sense is best defined by the way the person perceives himself at the moment.

What one observes about one's total integrations is the essence of how a person perceives himself. Though mechanisms do not have mental representations, their operations are associated with affects that do, and it is these affects that are felt and observed.

The identity sense of both these patients was characterized by a precociously stimulating and assaultive maternal introject. The acquisition of a heterosexual identity was thus inhibited, and the ego can be conceptualized as possessing a faulty integration of the identity sense with memories of satisfying heterosexual experiences. Consequently, the executive system cannot develop techniques for uninhibited and nonconflictual sexual expression. If the self-representation feels threatened by biological sexual arousal because of cathexis of a threatening maternal introject then the required integration between the perceptual and executive systems is traumatic and has to employ various defenses to cope with the situation as was demonstrated by the fantasies of these adolescents.

The adolescent process in the male may very well involve the task of shifting cathexis from the maternal introject to other females. The less the self-representation feels threatened by the maternal introject, the easier it is for the adolescent to incorporate satisfying experiences with girls in his introjects. These experiences then lead to the acquisition of executive techniques which are set in motion when the self-representation's heterosexual identification, not threatened by the maternal introject, becomes cathected through the activation of sexual feelings.

Patients suffering from characterological defects highlight pathological ego processes. Defective functioning and intrasystemic conflict are reflected in fantasies, which as these clinical examples indicate, may have specific defensive functions as well as representing wish fulfillment.

Summary

The production of fantasy is considered in an ego-psychological context. Fantasies serve a variety of functions; in addition to wish fulfillment, the defensive meaning of fantasy is explored. The relationship between various ego systems and the relevance of fantasy as an element to maintain psychic harmony is emphasized.

Patients suffering from characterological defects demonstrate both disruptive and integrative aspects of fantasy. The ego defects of these patients can be generally described as an inability to integrate early disruptive introjects that do not lead to memory traces of satisfying experiences necessary to later activate the executive apparatus. Fantasy often represents anticipated gratification.

The impact of ego defects on the self-representation is specifically discussed. Fantasy production and the relationship to external objects is also explored in terms of their potential in protecting the self-representation from an assaultive maternal introject. The ego processes involved may have general relevance to the developing sexuality of the adolescent.

Chapter 7

Identity Problems

In recent years the study of patients has compelled us to adopt a more ego-psychological orientation (focusing on structural factors) rather than maintain a predominantly psychodynamic orientation. It is apparent that various ego functions and systems are significant. As a source of psychopathology, it is important to understand the structure of the ego as well as clashing and opposing forces. I would like to mention the first case I treated that convinced me of the necessity of expanding our theoretical etiological explanations and concepts regarding treatable psychopathology.

This patient was a married woman in her middle twenties who complained of free-floating anxiety. Previous therapists thought that she had a type of classical anxiety neurosis with innumerable phobias, and they tried to uncover and resolve the oedipal struggle. I discussed this case with two of her former analysts who consistently described her in terms of an hysterical neurotic. What interested me, even at that time, was the fact that these generally calm and experienced analysts appeared to be excited and, to some extent, disturbed. They did not seem to care about the fact that they had lost the patient (because of a "stalemate"); they maintained an intense interest in her welfare, even though both analysts had been solely responsible for the termination of treatment. After I started treatment, these analysts frequently asked me (to an unusual degree) how she was getting along. I felt that they were genuinely concerned and not primarily motivated by therapeutic rivalry; they seemed to me to be confused and frustrated about their approach to this patient.

Agreeing with my colleagues, I believed that she was primarily an hysterical woman with regressive oral defenses. I waited for the usual dependent transference to develop and, putting the erotic components to one side, began to deal interpretatively with her dependency. Instead of resisting or accepting my interpretations, the patient remained friendly and responded to my "insights" as if they were correct but incidental and irrelevant. She was not disparaging but, nevertheless, succeeded in creating a state of anxious confusion in me which, somehow, reminded me of my colleagues' reactions.

Eventually I learned that this patient's anxiety was unique and differ-

First published in *Tactics and Techniques in Psycho-Analytic Treatment,* Vol. I, ed. P. Giovacchini (New York: Jason Aronson, Inc., 1972), pp. 337–50. Reprinted by permission.

ent from that which is usually described. Even though her anxiety had a signal function (to a minor extent), its pervasive omnipresence indicated a more elemental, primitive meaning. The patient informed me that she had constantly suffered from anxiety for as long as she could remember. It was not associated with any particular class of incidents, nor was it ameliorated by any specific conditions. She claimed that she could "create" anxiety (she could consciously produce it) and could also "turn it off," but never completely. During a particularly memorable session she illustrated this affective control, and I could see the spontaneous generation and subsidence of the vasomotor and physiological components of anxiety.

This startling material (I do not believe we would be amazed at such events today) emphasized my lack of psychoanalytic understanding, and I gradually became aware that my professional identity, which, to a large extent, was based upon standard clinical psychodynamic constructs, was being threatened. Insofar as my technical background was inadequate to understand this patient, my role as a therapist was threatened; this accounted for the vague, uneasy confusion I experienced. I must confess that it was only later that I finally understood my identity crisis, and this patient was instrumental in helping me arrive at this understanding.

To summarize her background, this patient had a sister—an identical twin—who, because of frequent physical illnesses, received all of the parents' attention. The patient felt as if she were a Cinderella-like nonentity without an existence of her own. She experienced periods of blankness and described herself as hollow and amorphous (see chapter 2). Since these feelings and attitudes about herself seemed to be fundamental, her psyche constructed what might be called superstructures to defend itself against intolerable emptiness and nonexistence. Her generation of anxiety was related to maintaining organization of the psyche; otherwise, she might have experienced "apathetic terror" or complete psychic collapse.

Thus, anxiety represented feeling, although it was painful. Any kind of feeling at least assured the patient that she was alive, that she was capable of feeling, and that she existed as a separate entity in a real world. As one pinches himself to determine whether he is awake, this patient, by feeling anxious, knew that she belonged to the outer world and was not a shadowy phantom of the inner world. The importance of the self-representation (which is being used here as a synonym for identity sense) becomes increasingly clear when one is confronted with patients like this young woman. As we have learned throughout the years, there are many patients who suffer from similar characterological problems.

Their identity system, as well as other ego subsystems, is always involved.

The concept of identity should be clarified and elaborated because we learn from our patients that psychopathology frequently affects that part of the psyche that has been conceptualized as the self-representation. How the patient views himself, his self-esteem, and his security in various roles are all aspects of his sense of identity. Many analysts, particularly Erikson (1959) and Federn (1952), have written about different facets of identity and have distinguished among the identity system, the sense of identity, and other aspects that are important in development and have pathological vicissitudes. I do not wish to review the literature or deal with the development of the concept of identity. From Freud's (Breuer and Freud, 1895) discussion of identification as both a developmental and defense mechanism that promotes ego stability to Erikson's (1959) graphic description of the identity disorders of adolescence (the identity diffusion syndrome), our focus has become increasingly clinical within a structural context.

I find it theoretically convenient to perceive the ego as containing, among its numerous introjects, a system known as the self-representation, whose function is to define the person's feelings about himself that will become integrated into his identity. Thus, the sense of one's identity can be explained by operational concepts and viewed as a function of the self-representation. Furthermore, insofar as it is a function, it is not static; it fluctuates and changes depending on the general ego state, which always affects every ego system. The self-representation is a complex, multifaceted structure that encompasses many levels that are related to the various stages of psychosexual development. Our hierarchically stratified psychic model shows that earlier stages of development leave their imprint upon later, better integrated stages. Similarly, the structure of any aspect of the ego, such as the self-representation, contains all of its developmental antecedents. The general ego state of progression or regression will be paralleled in the self-representation and the identity sense will be correspondingly affected.

A secure, well-balanced identity sense is one in which the self-representation is harmoniously integrated with the rest of the ego. Integration refers to a situation in which all ego systems can function well and efficiently; it also includes a sense of time continuity as the psyche relates to the external world. With a general ego balance, one can differentiate and integrate concepts of past, present, and future. The self-representation is an ego system that belongs in this time continuum; its ability to utilize its past as well as its anticipated future provides an integration that makes the self-representation especially relevant to the present. Percepts of the external world in the present can be placed in a differentiated context that is arranged in a fashion that preserves the continuity from the past to the future. Therefore, a person's identity will depend upon his present frame of reference and whether it is in context with that frame of reference. His current ego state naturally includes his environment and the interaction of his psyche with it. There is another continuum here—at one end the ego is completely absorbed with the inner world, and at the other end it is completely absorbed with the external world.

Disturbances of an individual's identity equilibrium are often found when there has been a precipitous change of environment. One is reminded of Jacobson's (1959) description of political prisoners and their experiences in a concentration camp. Eissler (1953b) mentioned the phenomenon of depersonalization when he described the reactions of a stranger who had moved to a foreign country. A more common occurrence is when an individual experiences a momentary confusion and a slight degree of identity diffusion just when he begins his vacation or returns to work. In all of these instances, the usual adaptive techniques are not effective in the changed environment, and so the individual has to reorient himself in order to reestablish equilibrium. Adaptive techniques, as part of the ego's executive system, must be included in the concept of identity. The ego's reactions to an id impulse, an affect, or disturbed homeostasis are not sufficient to form a concept of identity, but the techniques used by the ego to establish and maintain homeostasis are what distinguish one person from another, convincing each person of his existence.

The feeling of emptiness against which my patient had to defend herself indicated a lack of structure, and it was intensified by her inability to satisfy her inner needs. Consequently, she always had a low self-esteem and had constantly to seek reassurance that others could relate to her. She required acknowledgment.

The establishment of homeostasis depends upon successful mastery and reflects general ego organization. The balance and harmony among the various ego systems will determine whether the individual feels a sense of confidence and integration or a sense of misery and emptiness. However, his self-awareness may not be a direct representation of his basic ego integration since it may contain many defensive elements to compensate for its lack of integration (as was true with my patient).

What one feels, as with any psychic element, should be viewed as part of a hierarchical continuum ranging from early primary-process id aspects to reality-oriented, conscious, secondary-process elements. The self-image contains, as previously mentioned, all levels of the psychic apparatus. The uppermost layers consist of identifying characteristics that are operationally elaborated, for example: "My name is———and I am———years old, of a particular race and nationality, and I have the following physical characteristics. . . . I am a———by profession, and I earn my living by———. This enables me to live in a certain fashion and to satisfy a variety of needs." Thus, the range extends from identifying characteristics to executive techniques and needs, which can be subdivided into their basic elements. As a need becomes elaborated from its physiologic substrate, different levels of the psychic apparatus are set in motion to handle this need so that it may eventually be gratified. Once the higher techniques of mastery are activated, the preconscious identifying characteristics become more elaborated and sophisticated. For example: "I am a man who has certain rights as a citizen; I am skilled in my work and am sufficiently competent to secure those things that I require to fulfill my responsibilities and to gratify what I feel I need." True, this individual may not be competent and his self-image may hide his helplessness and lack of the techniques of mastery, but what he believes he is will contribute to his identity sense.

The discrepancy between the way the world views a given individual and the way he views himself is often a significant factor in determining the quality and extent of his psychopathology. Those who suffer from severe characterological defects do not have a smooth and harmonious frame of reference that is integrated with the world in general. Consequently, they often have to create their own world; if their world is sufficiently elaborated, it may constitute a delusional system.

In any case, one's self-appraisal only deals with a small portion of his total identity at a given time. This is consistent with the view that only a fraction of the self-representation can be conscious because, according to Freud (1900), the range of consciousness is a narrow one. One's identity sense is determined by the particular conscious element that is experienced at any given moment. If an individual's drives are strong, they will be experienced as the dominant aspect of his identity. Or one may think of himself only in terms of eating—as a hungry mouth and an empty stomach—or as being otherwise needful. If, on the other hand, an individual is engaged in problem solving, then the executive factor—his profession, for example—will probably be the predominant identity.

Once again, the concept of a hierarchical continuum is indispensable. To begin with, one feels alive because he experiences needs that are initially physiological. The experiencing of such needs is reflected in the soma, where formation of the body image begins; at first this image is diffuse, its sensory components consisting of feelings of hungry tension. Then needs become elaborated, from primitive orality to aggressive heterosexual strivings. Experiencing different body parts is paralleled by the progressive structuralization of various drives, and the body image changes from an amorphous, undifferentiated one to one where different appendages and structures are associated with specific feelings. These, in turn, are associated with greater psychic structure, leading to a wider range of self-awareness and a variety of goals that satisfy inner needs and promote self-esteem.

It is conceptually consistent to equate the self-image and the perceptual systems' self-observations with the identity sense. What an individual observes about his total integration is basically the way he perceives himself. Although integrative mechanisms do not have mental representations, their operations are associated with affects that do; it is these affects that are felt and related to the ego's integration. Although conscious awareness of the self is finitely limited and dependent on the activity of the moment, the individual still views himself as a totality at a preconscious level. To summarize briefly, the various images he has of himself are in context with each other—the present, together with the past and future realities. His various self-representations can also be seen as ranging from somatic representations (his body image) to complex, abstract conceptualizations. The integration of all of these levels of self-representation gives the individual a feeling of continuity and relevance.

In psychopathological states these various self-images are not integrated into a harmonious whole. Patients who suffer from characterological problems experience a multiplicity of affective states and symptoms that are explained most economically by assuming some disturbance in the way they view themselves. During treatment, the phenomenon of a disturbed identity has been noted in a variety of behavioral states. Patients who regress because of a disruption of their defenses or an upsurge of conflictual impulses often have difficulty achieving a consistent picture of themselves. The above-mentioned continuity is disturbed.

Adolescence is characterized by doubts and obsessional ruminations about the meaning and purpose of life and is associated with many instinctual upheavals. My patient developed specific techniques to deal with her inner oppression and barrenness. These techniques helped her to maintain equilibrium; to the extent that they were adjustive reactions to a psychopathological orientation, they could be considered defensive techniques. However, unlike the customary defense mechanisms which consist of aberrant, disruptive id impulses and the ego's attempts to achieve repression, these adjustive reactions were not responses to intrapsychic conflicts. They were attempts to keep the ego from regressing to a state of helpless vulnerability where the self-representation would lose its previous organization, and all ego systems would function less efficiently. Reality-testing and the ability to relate to the demands of a given environment (executive ego systems) are markedly impaired when these patients, who have only a precarious identity sense, decompensate.

My patient emphasized how she protected herself against the painful feeling of her loss of identity. Before dealing with her adjustive modalities, I would like to discuss why an amorphous self-representation should be experienced so painfully, sometimes with feelings approaching panic and terror. At first, it might seem self-evident that the loss of individual boundaries is intrinsically disruptive. However, most clinicians can readily recall situations where patients have regressed to very primitive developmental stages—preceding any demarcation of ego boundaries—and have not been anxious or disturbed. In fact, many of these patients have experienced a blissful, calm, Nirvana-like state. Such states are not restricted to the therapeutic setting; those who have taken drugs have frequently described similar states, and they seem to place a high value on such seemingly regressive experiences.

Fusion

Those who do not become anxious or disturbed at the loss of their ego boundaries differ significantly from those who do. Those who remain undisturbed tend to feel a unity with others—persons, causes, or ideals. They experience a symbiotic fusion with something that transcends their own identity; they are uniting themselves with a force that represents omnipotence and invulnerability. Consequently, even though they are sacrificing their own identity, they do not feel helpless because of a loss of control and lack of structure; rather, the symbiotic union gives them stability and security, which, in some instances, may be delusional. This fusion state can also be precarious, as illustrated by a female college student who often took LSD either with a group or with her boyfriend. One evening while she was on a "trip" with her boyfriend, he deserted her for some unexplained reason. Once alone, she psychotically decompensated; a year after this episode she was still in the hospital suffering from a severe catatonic schizophrenia.

Patients who are threatened by the loss of their ego boundaries thus reveal their intense loneliness and feelings of vulnerability. If the regressive process should continue unchecked (get out of control), they may experience a state of psychic collapse, which could take the form of a psychosis, as happened to the young lady mentioned above. In such cases, there is an almost total lack of object relations that could be integrated and used to maintain some contact with the outer world, leading to the development of adaptive techniques for handling both inner and outer turmoil. *The capacity to relate to some external object, even though in a primitive fashion, seems to be crucial in determining whether a regression to an amorphous ego state with its corresponding lack of identity will result in bliss or in terror.*

The capacity to fuse with a person or certain aspects of the environment was one of the defensive techniques frequently used by my patient. I believe this type of fusion happens quite often in the psychoanalytic situation, especially in patients who suffer from characterological problems and identity disorders. Although such patients may regress to very primitive developmental stages, there is no risk of an intractable psychosis if the transference is allowed to evolve naturally and is not hindered by the therapist's intrusion or his desire to manage the patient's life. Eventually the transference regression will reach back to the level of symbiotic fusion, a level that will become, to some extent, stabilized. This ego state will then be utilized as an adaptive defense against disruption, which would manifest itself as an existential crisis. Thus, analysis contains an intrinsic adaptive technique against intractable regression. References to the structuralizing and stabilizing effects of analysis and its intrinsic supportive elements often mean this state of symbiotic stability. To the extent that the analyst is not intrusive, the symbiotic fusion will not recapitulate the destructive assaults of the patient's early development to the same extent. It is this difference between the benign analytic introject and the devouring internalized primitive object relationships that make the regressive fusion bearable and analyzable.

My patient also used fusion to protect herself against psychic dissolution, but to secure her identity she used the mechanism of spontaneously-generating anxiety. Unlike many patients who suffer from characterological defects, she was able to control her affects, although occasionally she lost this control.

As discussed elsewhere (chapter 3), some patients who suffer from a defective self-representation also have poorly developed drives. Consequently, they cannot discriminate among their inner feelings; one such patient could not tell whether he needed to defecate, whether he was hungry, or whether he had sexual feelings. His inability to identify his feelings made him even more confused about who and what he was, and, in this instance, made him more bewildered about what he wanted and needed. His inability to discriminate was also reflected in a vaguely constructed and poorly defined body image.

Perceptual Hyperdevelopment

My young woman patient had well-developed senses and she seemed to have a superior ability to distinguish nuances of feeling. Although she had not had much experience listening to music, she could hear a selection and readily identify the various instruments in the symphony orchestra. She could recognize a work, the conductor, and certain players (for example, the soloist or the first violinist). She became an excellent photographer after very little training, indicating her inherent visual skills; she also had an unusual taste sensitivity as evidenced by the fact that she could tell whether certain sauces had been properly prepared and, more impressively, could identify different wines and their vintage years. Apparently she was also sensitive to smell and had an unusual ability to recognize various perfumes. Her sense of touch was also thought to be very sensitive, and she could easily detect small temperature changes. This patient's unusual sensitivity was quantitative as well as qualitative. Her hearing and sight were much better than average, as determined by testing. Intense stimuli, however, did not disturb her; she probably had a better than average tolerance of loud noises.

At a later time I learned from colleagues about other patients with unusual sensitivities. Although they are not particularly common, they seem to be found among those who have a special variety of characterological disorders with identity problems, Greenacre (1957) described similar patients, but in the context of a study of creativity; although my patient appeared to be creative, my focus here is on structural psychopathology.

The generation of affect in order to maintain a sense of identity indicates another unusual aspect of this patient's perceptual system. An affective experience involves various psychic systems (including the id), but the experiencing of feeling, by definition, is a function of the perceptual system. This patient had an unusual ability to generate, experience, and discriminate among feelings—she had what might be considered a hyperdevelopment of the perceptual system (and her history showed that these qualities had been present since early childhood, indicating a precocious development).

Patients who suffer from characterological problems have a defective development and fixation of various ego systems. However, the ego is not totally affected; some ego systems are more constricted than others. Children who have been intrusively hyperstimulated (see chapter 6; Boyer, 1956) often show premature ego development, especially with respect to the intellect. Of course, they have to have the innate capacity, but intellectualism can be used adaptively as a characterological defense.

Instead of being subjected to the impact of intrusive, nonadaptive stimuli, my patient felt abandoned and isolated. Rather than feeling that her existence was assaultively threatened, she felt as if she did not exist at all; in relation to her sister, no one acknowledged her. This seemed to be an instance of lack of stimulation; an extreme form of this—perceptual isolation—leads to the generation of certain feelings that can become hallucinations. Such feelings often seem to be self-generated.

Still, the distinction between assaultive hyperstimulation and the feeling of abandonment (with a corresponding lack of parental interaction and confirmation) is more a matter of form than of polarized extremes. The intrusive mother is not relating to her child as a separate and distinct person; rather, she is relating to a narcissistic extension of herself and what she does usually has very little relevance to the child's needs. Consequently, the child feels misunderstood and abandoned since he cannot get his parents to respond to his needs. This situation is quite similar to that of my patient whose parents did not really relate at all. This lack of early nurturing care leads to certain ego defects, such as an imperfectly formed and inadequate identity sense, which necessitate special defensive reactions and often involve the perceptual system.

Splitting Mechanisms

A common way to achieve some measure of adjustment with an unstructured self-representation is to use splitting mechanisms. This defence is especially prevalent among adolescents, when they project their repudiated impulses onto segments of the outside world and then reject those segments of the outside world as bad, thus throwing away their potential for future identifications. Regardless of the reality of certain issues, it is the categorical rejection and the extreme concretization of values that betray some adolescents' psychopathological struggles. They also have an obvious identity struggle.

Splitting of the ego here refers to the projection of unacceptable or disruptive aspects of the self-representation into the outer world. Patients who suffer from identity disorders have a very low self-esteem and considerable self-hatred. My patient felt that she had been ignored and abandoned. She believed that she had been rejected because she was bad and hateful, whereas her sister, although delicate and frail, embodied goodness. Therefore, she had both an amorphous sense of nonexistence and a self-representation of a hateful, unlovable person. Her self-representation made her even more tense. She generated affect in order to feel less vulnerable and to feel that she existed. However, the affect did not protect her from the pain of self-hatred which treatened to overwhelm her ego and often led her to contemplate suicide. In fact, she had taken overdoses of barbiturates on two occasions and was considered a definite suicidal risk.

This patient used defensive splitting to protect herself against self-destructive inner hatred. Like many patients who have ego defects, she had a somewhat paranoid outlook and regarded herself in a fragmented fashion. For example, she sometimes blamed her husband for all her difficulties and could not perceive herself in any role other than a most constricted housewife. She would maintain this orientation although she fully understood the importance of the traumatic events in her background. At such times she believed that all of her troubles emanated from outside, and she refused to take any responsibility for her condition. These attitudes, however, were not fixed.

Another patient who did not know if he were "fish or fowl" split his ego in a very graphic fashion with very little paranoia. This young man gradually accumulated about a dozen apartments, each one representing a different facet of his identity. For example, he had one apartment for study, one for relaxation, one for making love, and so forth. No single dwelling could serve more than one function (see chapter 3). This patient's ego-splitting was typical of primitive fixated egos with narcissistic character disorders. His self-representation reflected his ego-splitting and could function only in a fragmented fashion. This patient's identity sense was defective because it had never developed to the level where there was an integrated synthesis of introjects pertaining to his self-representation. The concept of synthesizing seemingly isolated ego elements is, of course, a restatement of Glover's (1930) formulation about the coalescence of ego nuclei.

Whether a defective identity sense will lead to splitting defenses or whether splitting defenses are responsible for a defective identity sense is not a very useful question; these things usually happen simultaneously. In its formative stages the ego is not very well differentiated, and all systems are, to some extent, involved in every aspect of general adaptation. Consequently, when the early environment is traumatic, the imperfectly formed identity sense, together with the rest of the ego, utilizes splitting mechanisms. These, in turn, will determine what direction the self-representation will take in further growth.

Ego defects involving the identity system lead us to raise certain questions about psychoanalytic technique. Many prospective patients are painfully aware of their identity struggle and urgently seek analytic help. I can recall several who had such characterological problems and wanted analysis; they could distinguish to an unusual degree an analytic from a nonanalytic approach. Even though such patients are difficult to treat analytically, it is clear that it would be impossible to treat them with any other method. They understand enough about the analytic process to know that they probably could not gain further structure and integration unless permitted the freedom to regress within the transference framework.

Summary

Clinical experience highlights the need to understand many patients from a theoretical frame of reference that goes beyond an id-oriented psychodynamic model. Clinicians constantly encounter patients who can best be understood as having structural defects within an ego-psychological frame of reference—defects in particular subsystems. By viewing the ego in terms of such subsystems, we can conceptualize much of the material presented by the patient as defects of his self-representation. It is apparent that he has disturbances of his identity sense as well as defenses against the pain caused by such existential problems. Three specific defenses against an amorphous and defective self-representation were discussed: fusion (symbiotic), the generation of affect in the context of a hypersensitive perceptual system, and splitting. These important psychic mechanisms are designed to maintain equilibrium in an environment that might otherwise threaten an ego that feels vulnerable, unloved, and—in extreme states of regression—nonexistent.

Chapter 8

The Blank Self

There are certain characterological types who are believed to be difficult patients because they maintain a protective distance from the analyst. Here, I would like to discuss a particular subgroup in detail— those with the syndrome that Helene Deutsch (1942) designated "as-if." Although this syndrome is reputedly rare, these patients, because of their ego defects, highlight a variety of psychopathological processes; therefore, they may help us understand a larger segment of the patient population and, in turn, improve our therapeutic attitude. I will focus on the significance of early environmental factors and their bearing upon the developmental process and the structuring of various ego systems. Studying the as-if patient one has the opportunity to learn more about such ego subsystems as the self-representation as well as early mother-infant symbiosis and the consequences of both its pathological formation and its resolution as reflected in the treatment setting.

Many discussions of the as-if personality begin with defining the syndrome; Helene Deutsch, herself, distinguished between as-if and pseudo as-if. I do not wish to repeat what has already been said; rather, I shall describe the ego mechanisms and processes underlying a specific phenomenological entity which is an aspect of wider, more heterogeneous behavioral responses. The patients who will be discussed here lack the identity sense and organization that have generally been believed to characterize pseudo as-if patients. Of course, quantitative assessments cannot be precise because the psyche can never be viewed unilaterally; a multiplicity of variables is responsible for psychic functioning and for varying degrees of integration and organization of different levels of the mental apparatus.

Behaviorally, both as-if and pseudo as-if patients lack individuality; like chameleons, they blend in with their surroundings. Supposedly they adopt the characteristics, styles, and in some instances, even the standards and ideals of others. However, such "identifications" are transient and easily exchangeable with others. The pseudo as-if personality is not phenomenologically different from the as-if personality. From the viewpoint of psychic structure, however, the self-representation of the pseudo as-if patients is thought to have a modicum of organization; relatively speaking, the as-if aspects of his personality (the incorporation

First published in *Tactics and Techniques in Psycho-Analytic Treatment*, Vol. I, ed. P. Giovacchini (New York: Jason Aronson, Inc., 1972), pp. 364–80. Reprinted by permission.

of significant external objects) are supposedly defensive superstructures, whereas those of the as-if patient himself are basic.

Ross (1967) pointed out that the as-if reaction can be described in terms of a continuum: at one end is the as-if behavior which is associated with varying degrees of pathology; in the middle are pseudo as-if states; and at the other end are the as-if responses found in fairly well-functioning persons. Greenson (1958) discussed the specific behavioral characteristics that result from the need for object contact (screen hunger), and Gitelson (1958b) stressed the rigid but adaptive ego features that maintain adjustment and prevent psychic dissolution in patients with as-if qualities. Reich (1953) referred to transient as-if reactions as regressive defensive reactions to specific traumatic situations. Various analysts have stressed such behavioral distinctions as the lack of real engagement in object relationships and the paucity of true affect.

Clinical Material

Two clinical vignettes will emphasize the early object relations of an as-if patient from different perspectives. The first patient, a woman, seemed to have the characteristics of an as-if personality as she discussed her behavior and demonstrated it in the transference. The second patient (also a woman) has a son who has been seen by several psychoanalysts, all of whom have been impressed with the as-if qualities of his behavior. Therefore, the first patient will illustrate the impact of the maternal introject upon later personality functioning and the second patient will illustrate specific projections onto the child. Even though there is no relationship between these patients, material obtained from the one complements that obtained from the other. The first patient provides us with a microscopic view of various ego subsystems, permitting inferences to be made about her maternal motivations, whereas the second patient gives us a cross-section of her maternal behavior, permitting inferences to be made about its effects upon the development of her son's as-if character structure. Furthermore, the first patient is also a mother, and the second patient has aspects to her behavior that could be considered as-if.

The first patient's husband called to arrange for her initial appointment. He was extremely concerned about his wife's welfare and, even during our brief telephone conversation, expressed bitterness about the fact that her mother had neglected her. He stressed that his wife was helpless, almost to the point of being unable to function. The patient, a pale woman in her twenties, was brought to the office by her husband; she appeared hesitant and timorous. In spite of her apparent fragility—

almost bordering upon dissolution and panic—she was able to give me a surprising amount of information. As the session progressed she seemed to anticipate what I wanted to know, and so I found it unnecessary to ask questions to satisfy my curiosity. At the time, I was aware of an uneasy feeling within me which I could not explain; there was an uncanny quality to what I was experiencing.

This patient reported that she had always been shy and withdrawn but, paradoxically, had always felt a need to be with people. Whenever she was alone, she would panic for fear that her loneliness would "swallow" her up. She had difficulty "anchoring" herself and knowing who and what she was and what the purpose of her existence was. She had had these attitudes and reactions since early childhood and they dominated her earliest memories. She had had some psychotherapy in college but didn't feel that she had ever been deeply involved in it. This didn't surprise her because she didn't feel that she was capable of involvement. Her husband had insisted on treatment because she had become totally incapable of doing anything (taking care of the house and her daughter, shopping, and the usual routines of everyday life—including personal grooming). This regression occurred precipitously after the husband's job required that they move to Chicago; for the first time in her life, the patient was separated from her mother. During college she had lived in a dormitory, but the school was located in the same city fairly near her parents' home.

Of course, I became extremely interested in the patient's relationship with her mother as she was telling me about herself. Again, without any overt requests from me, she described in detail her relationship with her mother, which was remarkably similar to one described by James (1960). The patient is an only child. Her mother is still an extremely beautiful woman, with an imperious aristocratic demeanor. Her mother had a rather set routine, one that did not include the patient and included her husband only in a superficial, social sense. The patient believes that her mother's only interest in life has been clothes, for which she still spends an enormous amount of money.

The patient was brought up by a succession of indifferent maids; the mother habitually stayed in her bedroom until noon and, consequently, did not speak to either her husband or daughter in the morning. She would have breakfast brought to her in bed and then would take care of her correspondence, which apparently was voluminous and often required a personal secretary. She would spend the afternoon either at fittings or at some rather "high level" social function. Around five o'clock in the afternoon she would return home, presumably for a nap, and then would remain in her room for the rest of the evening. If her parents were entertaining or were invited to some important social function, her mother would appear sparkling and exuberant. Gradually, the patient became aware of how brittle her mother was underneath this facade. For example, she learned that her mother was an alcoholic and that she spent many of her long hours in her boudoir drinking. Once when the patient was nine years old and was sent home from school unexpectedly because she had developed some flu symptoms, she found her mother completely intoxicated, whimpering, and generally disheveled—a startling contrast to her usual proper, impenetrable aplomb.

The patient's father also had very little contact with her since he was away on business trips during the week and usually busy with showy social functions with his wife on the weekend. When the patient was an adolescent it became apparent to her that her father's apparent passivity was actually a contemptuously patronizing attitude toward his wife's alcoholic weakness and vulnerability. He used her as a showpiece and tried to play the role of a protector, but whenever the patient overheard her parent's rare conversations, she was surprised at his cutting and sneering sarcasm; it also had a whining quality. In the vague relationship she had with her father, she felt that he also used her as a show-piece, "a china doll." Her relationship with her husband was similarly patterned, and during his telephone conversation with me, I could sense both a patronizing attitude and a whining quality in his voice.

The patient reported that she never had any ideas of her own—that nothing came from within herself. She saw herself as a "sponge," soaking up the personality and the identity of the person she was with. She could not bear to be alone, for it made her feel that she did not exist. With another person, she felt that she was part of him or that he was part of her. For example, in high school when she was dating a boy who wanted to be a lawyer, she became convinced that law was also her calling. Then he went away to school, and she had an affair with a premedical student; she became persuaded that nothing else mattered but the practice of medicine. When this relationship ended, so, too, did her interest in medicine. Others noticed her tendency to imitate and to incorporate both their ideals and mannerisms. One of her friends suggested that she consider a stage career, but the patient had no interest whatsoever in being an actress.

Interestingly enough, the man she married has no distinct vocational or professional identity. He is an officer in a family-owned business, but it is clear to the patient that he is only going through the motions of having a position. A job was created for him, one that involves considerable busywork, but it has no real significance in the operation of the business, which is completely dominated by his father. All of his earlier pursuits had failed to materialize.

Before discussing the psychic processes that relate to this patient's particular characterological problems, I will introduce the second patient. This woman, in her early forties, also did not seek the initial consultation for herself. Although she made the first appointment, it was because she wanted help for her eight-year-old son. As she described him, he appeared to be shy and withdrawn and could not be left alone. He seemed to be very unhappy although he never complained; consequently, she had not sought professional help before. She changed her mind, however, when her son's teachers strongly suggested psychiatric consultation. They believed that his almost total reading block was due to emotional factors and that some of his mannerisms and gestures might indicate autistism. I referred him to a colleague. Later, the boy's analyst said that he was not autistic but had an as-if personality. The boy reported that he generally incorporated the characteristics of anyone who related to him, and the therapist noted such reactions in the consultation room.

The mother soon revealed she had a number of problems and wanted help for herself as well. She described a lifetime of continual self-sacrifice. She had dedicated herself to others at the expense of her own autonomy and self-esteem. Her parents had lived in genteel poverty; apparently they had lost a large amount of wealth during the Depression. Her mother seemed to be an aristocratic woman who could never quite accept her impoverished condition; the whole family treated her as inadequate and incompetent. Since her mother had never learned to do anything but instruct servants, the patient, the oldest of three children, assumed the responsibility for taking care of the family and the house. The patient's father was an invalid; he had been bedridden with arthritis since the patient's early childhood.

In spite of all her family responsibilities, she managed to finish high school. Immediately afterward she obtained a position as a secretary to the head of a small firm. Her employer was twenty-five years her senior and she admired his distinguished, sophisticated manner. She dedicated herself to her work and in five years she became manager. She worked many evenings and weekends and became indispensable to the business; in effect, she had no life of her own outside of work. She would receive telephone calls at home anytime, and might have to interrupt a holiday or vacation in order to return to the office, but she never complained. As time went by the patient became more and more intimate with her employer. At first, he told her about his personal life, and then there was physical intimacy and she became his mistress.

She did not make any demands on him. However, he felt sufficiently guilty about the relationship and unhappy about his marriage so that he wanted to marry her. His invalid wife, though, would not give him a divorce, and his two sons (one of whom was a year older than the patient) disapproved vehemently of the liaison. This impasse continued for about twelve years, when the wife died. Then he married the patient, and she felt more secure and wanted. However, shortly after the marriage, she recognized that her husband was a totally dependent, helpless hypochrondiac, and that he needed care and attention like a young infant.

Therefore, the patient began to take care of both her husband and the business. She saw herself as a business woman who had no investment in the household. Her life remained pretty much as it had before marriage, except that she went home with her husband and continued the relationship there—a mixed business and nursing one that could not include anyone else. She scarcely mentioned her son at all after she began her own analysis, even though he had been the focus of her first interview. She spoke of her pregnancy and delivery in such a casual, offhand fashion that it was difficult to realize that she was speaking about herself.

The patient described herself as a bland, dull person without any specific individual characteristics. In her eyes her husband seemed to be a strong personality and so she clung to him as a savior. It didn't seem to make any difference that, after the marriage, she had described him as a weak and ineffectual person; she still saw him as an idealized, exalted person. It was clear that she had a well-developed ability to tolerate contradictions. Another example is the fact that during her childhood and adolescence she seemed to have been unaware of her family's poverty-stricken circumstances, even though it was this that led her to assume so many household responsibilities.

The patient often went into what apparently were fugue states; her companions would find her "lost in a fog"—staring in a fixedly blank fashion and unresponsive to them. During analysis she continued to experience such spells, although they were not as frequent as in childhood. Repeated EEG's had always been normal.

Discussion

Freud's first description of the actual neuroses (1898) was of a nosologic entity based primarily upon physiologic tension or depletion states that bypassed "higher" mentational systems. Extending these ideas logically would lead us to believe that if patients with actual neuroses entered a psychoanalytic relationship, there would be no transference relevant to their area of conflict. However, there is considerable controversy over this matter. I mention it here only because both of my patients developed a relationship with me that (on the surface, at any rate) seemed to be devoid of transference projections. I hope to demonstrate that this was not actually the case; rather, these patients developed a unique type of transference that was the specific product of their peculiar characterological difficulties.

It was particularly noteworthy that during our early sessions neither of these patients made any reference to me, either in their dreams or in their associations. As a person to whom they attached some specific emotional significance, I did not seem to exist. They talked freely and gave detailed descriptions of events in their present and past lives, but these "travelogue" narratives (as Freud [1909] called them) were without substance. They told me nothing about their feelings and gave me no clue about the qualitative or quantitative aspects of their object relationships. Similarly, the primary-process factors that are ordinarily associated with primitive affects were so elusive that I could not find an anchor upon which to organize my understanding of the intrapsychic pathology of these patients. I felt that there was nothing I could "grab hold of"— that there was nothing to analyze. I felt a void within myself when I tried to view each patient in terms of unconscious processes and defensive mechanisms, but even more when I attempted formulations in terms of the dominant transference theme.

An elusive transference is not particularly rare, especially when one is treating patients who suffer from severe characterological pathology. Such patients are often afraid of the dissolution of the symbiotic fusion with the analyst, or else they have to maintain a rigid control against intense disruptive regression. One can easily discern the defensive nature of their withdrawal, manifested in rigidity and tension. My patients, however, were perfectly composed and relaxed and (on the surface, at least) did not appear defensive. Although there seemed to be a paucity of analytic material (transference projections), my patients were not boring. I had the distinct impression that I was being confronted with a baffling phenomenon, but one that might eventually be understood in analytic terms.

Gradually both of my patients developed mannerisms that puzzled me, until eventually I realized that they were imitating my gestures, inflections, and favorite expressions. Their behavior was not clearly obvious, and they had no awareness of what they were doing. It seemed that even though they apparently projected nothing onto me, they were especially adept at incorporating parts of me at some level. This did not constitute a solid identification, though, because I learned later on that my patients imitated me only in my presence; once they left the consultation room, they reverted to their usual behavior. When I confronted them with their capacity to imitate many of my mannerisms, neither of them was surprised. However, the subsequent course of events was different for each patient. I believe these differences reflected the unique aspects of their characterological pathology and indicated two distinct types of as-if reactions.

The first patient soon became benignly dependent. She expected me to know what was going on inside of her and to anticipate her needs, as she had anticipated my curiosity during our first interview. She became docile and submissive, and there were many periods of comfortable silence during her analytic sessions. However, unlike patients who project megalomanic expectations upon the analyst, she indicated no melodramatic wish to be omnipotently rescued, nor did she manifest the subsequent inevitable disappointment of such expectations. On the contrary, intrinsic to her dependent expectations was the conviction that they would not be met. Thus, there was a contradiction: she wanted me to anticipate and to respond to her unexpressed needs, yet she knew that I would fail her. *Failure was inevitable in this situation, not because I could not fulfill her omnipotent needs but because I did not really exist;* what she saw was a phantom—a hollow "ectoplasm" that would evaporate if she touched it.

This patient's vision of me was obviously a projection of her self-representation and the principal aspect of her maternal imago. After I pointed out her projection, she brought up material that dealt with her amorphous imago of her mother and her mother's amorphous image of her. She saw herself as a robot with no soul or identity; she alternated between having this view of herself and having a similar view of me, the analyst-mother. The patient's father also contributed to her self-image of nonexistence, but her mother's role was more crucial.

The patient often described ours as a "tape-recorder" relationship. She was completely blank and she projected "blankness" onto me. The only way she could fill the void was to incorporate others into it, but they could not be "held." This was an extremely interesting phase of her analysis because, as her existential anxiety mounted, she was able to obtain some relief by incorporating me. Then she would ignore me again but, as could be seen, this represented a transference fluctuation rather than a lack of transference.

The second patient reacted quite differently after I confronted her with her imitative behavior. This patient idealized me and analysis became her exclusive preoccupation. She transformed me into an omnipotent savior. Unlike the first patient, this one had a certain melodramatic attitude and she fully expected her needs (which she could not verbalize) to be met. She did not see the rest of the world as hostile or persecutory (as happens with patients who use dissociative defenses); it simply did not exist for her. From this patient's point of view, rescuing and being rescued were equivalent. She converted our relationship into an alliance; we would take care of each other. She, of course, knew of my other patients, but through dissociation she believed that I was exclusively attached to her; in a similar fashion, she also had no "life" between analytic sessions. This patient was not delusional. She was fully aware of reality, but these fantasies were vivid and powerful.

A significant aspect of this woman's analysis was the inevitable disappointment of her megalomaniac expectations. Later she experienced states of disruptive rage, which contrasted sharply with her usual tightly controlled self. As with all patients who suffer from ego defects, this patient reacted with anger to two common feelings: frustration, which usually followed her awareness of guiltily denying her anaclitic dependence through self-sacrifice, and a sense of vulnerability, which led her to revile herself (sometimes she even appeared to convulse on the couch), indicating how uncontrollably helpless she felt. Her maternal transference helped us to understand the genesis of her depreciated self-representation. She was terrified at the thought of being completely "swallowed up" by an engulfing, powerful, demanding mother, one whom she believed was intolerant of any individuation. She attributed such qualities to me; I wanted to rob her of all autonomy. During this time she had many nightmares of drowning.

Periods of panic and rage alternated with periods of calm, which were characterized by the fragmentation I noted at the beginning of the analysis. Her ego dissociation (in which everything outside of the analysis ceased to exist) was a defense against her fears of losing her autonomy. During her stabilized defensive states against a threatening fusion, this patient focused upon certain maternal aspects of her self-representation. The patient's need to negate the existence of the outer world was also reflected in her attitude toward her son: she projected her feeling of nonexistence onto him. Her concept of him was one of "blankness"—an important aspect of her self-representation. Her description of blankness resembled Lewin's (1946) dream screen, and I believe it had the same structural and functional meaning.

Blankness was also an important factor in helping this patient maintain a defensive balance. During regressed, disruptive states, she would speak of her son, indicating that she hated him and would like to annihilate and repudiate him. These feelings were, in part, a replication of the murderous rage she had repressed toward her siblings. More pertinent, however, was the projection of her hateful, destructive, vulnerable self. She reported several dreams in which she had given birth to a deformed monster, thereby indicating that her son represented a narcissistic extension of the intolerable parts of her self-representation. Blankness, therefore, served as a defense against this dangerous and guilt-laden projection. Having a nonexistent son protected her from these death wishes; through projection it also relieved her of the oppressive burden of her inner void.

Both patients had specific structural defects and characteristic methods of dealing with them that were reflected in their general behavior as well as in their as-if behavior. Their as-if reactions, including the second patient's behavior during the initial phases of treatment, exemplify neither imitation nor identification. Imitation is believed to be consciously contrived, whereas identification is an unconscious process. These patients, like others who have been called as-if or pseudo as-if, were not conscious of what they were doing or of its significance. Still, they could not form a solid core identity that would endure without the external object. It seems that the as-if patient utilizes an incorporative mechanism that is somewhere between imitation and identification (a point that other analysts have also made).

The capacity of these patients for what might be called a partial or transient identification seems to enable them to sense others' feelings and subtle reactions. During the initial interview with the first patient, I felt that she was particularly sensitive to my feelings and could anticipate what I wanted to know. However (as others have also noted), the sensitivity of these patients seems to be restricted to superficial feelings; when I have experienced deep reactions, including countertransference, these patients show no awareness of them; they seem to have little capacity for true empathy, as might be expected in view of their psychic impoverishment. In fact, my early feelings of bewilderment, I believe, were evoked by their projection of emptiness onto me, a projection that precludes understanding. Patients who suffer from characterological problems have a defective self-representation. Both of my patients considered themselves empty, thin, hollow shells. They always seemed to be trying to fill this void by incorporating significant external objects.

Examining the genesis of this type of identity or lack of identity highlights important aspects of early mothering. Apparently the mother of the first patient was an extremely brittle woman who had little capacity to relate to anyone. She had to preserve whatever libido she possessed in order to maintain a shaky narcissistic balance. Her daughter's early concept of her was vague, remote, and distant. The mother was practically nonexistent, and that which the patient eventually incorporated—the maternal introject—was of a nonexistent (blank) entity. To the extent that the maternal introject contributes to the formation of the self-representation, the patient constructed an identity sense based upon blankness. Another reason for the patient's blank identity sense may have been her mother's projection of blankness onto her. A woman such as her mother cannot relate to her child in any substantial fashion except as a narcissistic extension of herself. Probably the fact that this patient's mother had no definition of her self-representation affected her perception of and relationship with her daughter; she saw her daughter merely as an extension of the amorphous (blank) part of herself.

This description of the patient's mother is, of course, speculative, but it gains plausibility if we recall the sequence of the patient's transference reactions. Of particular interest (and what makes this type of characterological defect unique) is the fact that hatred and self-hatred were *not* prominent in the patient's self-representation or transference projection; feelings of nonexistence and blankness predominated. Usually the mothers of such patients project the hateful parts of their selves onto their children, who then incorporate these parts into their own self-representation. In treatment the hatred manifests itself in deeper transference projections. However, in the case of my patient, her projections indicated that blankness constituted a primary level of her self-image; it was not a superstructure designed to defend her against self-hatred and disruptive rage.

It is important to be aware of such psychic processes for technical reasons. What may appear to be a lack of engagement in some cases is actually a necessary transference projection. A patient will establish a relationship with the analyst in terms of his own character structure (the product of early object relationships); *his adaptation to the analytic setting constitutes transference.* My patient's projection of a blank self-image was, at times, the dominant transference theme. This often made her appear to be dull and uninteresting, too afraid or incapable of analysis, but this projection belied her intense interactions with the analyst below the surface.

My second patient's reactions did not remain dormant very long; she showed hatred and self-hatred and projected them both on the analyst and on her son. This woman differed significantly from the first one in that the blankness she initially projected on me represented a defensive superstructure; it also characterized the way in which she perceived her son. Underneath this blankness, however, was a murderous rage that she later expressed eloquently. She defended herself by feeling blank and empty. Many patients who suffer from characterological disorders have similar problems and reactions. However, my second patient was unique in that she used blankness as a defense against her underlying rage and self-hatred (as well as to demand magical salvation). Her

projection of blankness onto her son was probably important in determining his as-if orientation.

The defensive use of blankness is not particularly rare; Kalina (1969)
has encountered it in adolescents who were struggling to achieve identity. Using blankness as a defense may also indicate that there is some
blankness in the underlying self-representation. I believe that patients
who use blankness as a defense exemplify pseudo as-if personalities and
not true as-if personalities (my patient's son is probably also a pseudo as-
if). However, if there are amorphous elements in the underlying self-
representation, the distinction between my first and second patients (that
is, between as-if and pseudo as-if) becomes blurred, and their differences
are then a matter of degree and not of kind. The capacity to introject and
make solid identifications is generally impaired in both as-if and pseudo
as-if patients. They cannot make clear distinctions between themselves
and the outer world; they tend to fuse with external objects instead of
making selective identifications. Although their superego development
would ordinarily be affected, both of my patients were able to withhold
their aberrant impulses by conforming to the repressive aspects of the
outer world. Their affectlessness resulted from their lack of distinct
structuralization (Zetzel, 1949; Zilboorg, 1933).

In conclusion, as-if and pseudo as-if patients illustrate the interactions
among various ego systems that lead to distinct transference manifestations. In discussing patients with schizoid personalities, Khan (1960a)
suggested that their passivity is the result of specific relationships among
their various ego systems. Although this chapter has not dealt with
libidinal conflicts, it does not mean that there are no such conflicts; it
only means that during earlier phases of treatment they are poorly
developed and not particularly meaningful.

Summary

Patients who display as-if behavior help us to understand a larger
group of patients who suffer from characterological problems. Specific
character defects are the result of unique early object relationships. The
way in which some of these defects manifest themselves in the treatment
relationship may make it appear that there is no therapeutic engagement.
However, such appearances are actually the outcome of an important
transference projection—the projection of the patient's "blank" self-
image.

I believe that the two patients discussed here exemplify as-if and
pseudo as-if personalities, respectively. The essential difference is their
self-representation. The first patient's blankness and emptiness were

primary and resulted from her relationship with her fragile, narcissistic mother who treated the patient as if she did not exist. The second patient felt the same way about herself (that she was a void), and she projected this aspect of herself onto her son, who had as-if symptoms. She exemplifies a pseudo as-if character structure because her blankness represents, in part, a defensive superstructure to protect her against self-hatred and disruptive rage.

The pathological relationships among the various ego systems have important technical implications. The transference projections of these two patients, especially during their initial phases of treatment, involved parts of the self (rather than libidinal feelings) that are typical of this nosologic group.

Chapter 9

The Concrete and Difficult Patient

Questions regarding the applicability of the psychoanalytic method eventually become focused upon two basic issues: (1) What types of case are amenable to analysis (what are the indications for this specialized type of treatment)? and (2) Assuming that the psychoanalytic method can be extended beyond Freud's use (which was limited to the transference neuroses), what modifications of the classical technique are required in order to be able to engage these more difficult patients in a treatment relationship? These questions have been argued from many viewpoints; only the first one will be specifically discussed here, although inferences pertaining to the second one can undoubtedly be drawn.

Freud's main argument against analysis for certain patients was that they could not experience transference. Thus, he distinguished between the transference and the narcissistic neuroses. In recent years other analysts have challenged Freud's belief that there is no transference in the narcissistic neuroses (see Little, 1958; Modell, 1963; Searles, 1963). Psychotic patients, as well as the so-called borderlines, seem to be able to form intense reactions toward the analyst, reactions that are directed at infantile archaic objects (part-objects endowed with considerable primary-process qualities). If transference, as suggested by Anna Freud (1946), consists of an exclusive projection upon the analyst viewed as a whole object (presumably at the oedipal level of psychosexual development), then these intense reactions do not constitute transference. Patients who suffer from severe character pathology often project parts of themselves onto the analyst—a narcissistic transference. Still, it is probably too restrictive to think that transference belongs only to a particular level of psychosexual development, and probably the transference mentioned by Anna Freud is clinically rare. Freud (Breuer and Freud, 1895; Freud, 1900) initially postulated that transference was a projection of the same infantile feelings that characterize primitive object relationships. As ego psychology emphasizes, such relationships are

First published in *Tactics and Techniques in Psycho-Analytic Treatment,* Vol. I, ed. P. Giovacchini (New York: Jason Aronson, Inc., 1972), pp. 351–63. Reprinted by permission.

part-object relationships, and feelings toward such part-objects are often split between one part-object and another.

Regardless of how one defines a patient's irrational reactions toward the therapist, the important question is whether these reactions can be used for therapeutic benefit. Exactly what type of regressive phenomena are we encountering? How can they contribute to our understanding of fundamental pathology as well as determine our treatment approach? It has jokingly been said that psychoanalysts will only treat patients who are not sick. After reviewing the characteristics that analysts usually require of prospective patients (for example, considerable ego strength, relatively little resistance, a minimum of acting out, good motivation, ability to free associate), one has the distinct impression that the only patients who are suitable for psychoanalysis are those who don't need it; "difficult" patients are not believed to be suitable.

"Difficult" patients should be defined in terms of intrapsychic processes, and this can be done by studying the types of transferences they form. At the outset a therapist usually has a quick impression about the patient's potential for treatment. This appraisal is usually based on the patient's ease in becoming engaged in the treatment relationship. At times this ease may be accompanied by considerable anxiety; nevertheless, there is a kind of relaxation that indicates an ability to communicate. The therapist feels secure if he believes the patient can become aware of the irrational nature of his transference projections. "Difficult" patients often give the impression that there will be difficulties in forming or resolving the transference. Frequently they seem to be rigid and inflexible. An analyst may be reluctant to treat a patient because he is afraid that analysis will bring about a dangerous decompensation, perhaps an unmanageable regression.

There are certain patients who appear to be so "tightly held together" that they do not seem to have the freedom to regress; their concreteness might preclude analysis. It is difficult to describe the concrete quality of the mental operations of these patients. Nevertheless it creates an unpleasant and tense atmosphere; regardless of the patient's avowed willingness—sometimes eagerness—to enter into a therapeutic relationship, the therapist has misgivings about the final outcome. One can quickly sense the underlying hostility and the unmanageable dependency of these "concrete" patients.

I am using the term "concrete" to describe a mind that is either unwilling or unable to deal with both inner and outer experiences in psychological terms. In fact, it is difficult for concrete patients to acknowledge inner experiences. These patients can only deal with very simple cause-and-effect relationships, and they do not have the capacity for free-flowing spontaneity that would enable them to capture the emotional nuances of subtle intrapersonal and interpersonal relationships.

Although it is difficult to characterize a "concrete" patient, I have found that my colleagues know precisely what type of patient I am talking about and can quickly supply me with clinical examples of their own. Their exasperation with such patients is evident, and, regardless of their unique countertransference attitudes, it is apparent that they are responding to possible ego defects as well as to a controlling manipulativeness designed to defeat any therapeutic effort in spite of these patients' apparent cooperative attitude.

For example, an unmarried man in his middle thirties sought psychotherapy because of impotence. He didn't seem to have any real understanding of psychotherapy; he was simply following his internist's suggestion that psychiatry might help since all of the clinical tests pointed to the functional nature of his disturbance. Since psychotherapy had been recommended, that was what he was going to "get." He showed his enthusiasm and a willingness to cooperate, as exemplified by the following statement: "Tell me what to do, Doc, and I'll certainly do whatever you say." It seemed ridiculous to talk about spontaneity, and the most we ever achieved was a travesty of free association. At best, this patient went through the motions of analysis. He lay down on the couch and usually waited for me to ask a question to "guide" him. I explained that I didn't want to choose his topic or theme for him; he expressed his gratitude to me for this and then totally ignored it. He would turn and look at me and then say something to the effect that he wanted to choose something I would find useful.

He frequently brought me dreams because he understood that dreams were important. His dreams had some unique and interesting qualities. From his viewpoint they were full of "Freudian symbols." He dreamed of snakes, cigars, chandeliers, holes, and caves; he would often be running up or downstairs. His dreams seemed to be caricatures of those reported in *Interpretation of Dreams* or the *Introductory Lectures on Psychoanalysis*. He also had other dreams that were quite different. These were equally interesting but impossible to work with, *for they were exact replicas of reality*. It was often difficult to ascertain whether he was talking of an actual experience or of a dream. The themes were vivid and organized, the action was sequential and logical, and the id forces seemed to be under complete control of reality-testing.

Some concrete patients seem to be naïve, and of limited intellectual and cultural endowment. Therapists often encounter these characterological types in low fee or free clinics. I do not believe, however, that such patients are a product of any particular socioeconomic group, for my impotent patient came from a socially prominent, wealthy family. He was a business executive and was reputed to be quite talented in his area of specialization. He belonged to the "right" clubs and had been graduated from a sophisticated preparatory school and an ivy league college. His background, therefore, contrasted sharply with his naïve approach to psychotherapy and his inability to relate emotionally.

Analysts sometimes categorize difficult patients by their inability to become "engaged" in the analytic relationship. Some schizoid patients and many adolescents, although they may faithfully keep their appointments, seem to be unable to develop meaningful and deep feelings toward the therapist. They are often reserved and do not spontaneously express themselves. When they do speak, their words tend to be monosyllabic; if the analyst feels frustrated and asks questions in order to "force" them out of their withdrawal and isolation, their answers are cryptic and terse.

Are these clinical situations psychotherapeutically hopeless? In view of the large number of patients who suffer from characterological problems, including the concrete patients described here, I believe that we should muster all of our clinical experience and understanding in order to learn to utilize, as much as possible, whatever inherent therapeutic potential there may be. True, many patients discontinue treatment early in the relationship, but there are some, such as my impotent patient, who, after facing certain fundamental conflicts, lose their need to withdraw and eventually their concreteness.

Perhaps there are important differences among patients who have the same characterological manifestations. Some patients may use concreteness as a defense to protect themselves against intolerable ego states, while others use this type of thinking because of a faulty organization (ego defect). The latter patients have a rigidity to their secondary process, the result of a fairly primitive ego organization that has not developed to any great extent the integrative capacity for abstraction and symbolization, the tolerance of inner disorganization and ambiguity, and the autonomy of self-observation and spontaneity.

These distinctions between a defensive reaction and one due to faulty structure are, of course, the same that are so often encountered in our diagnostic conceptualizations of defensive regression and fixation. However, when patients are viewed from a characterological perspective, differences between regression and fixation have less clinical relevance (see chapter 21). Whenever the ego adopts a certain modality to maintain cohesion and homeostasis, it is still utilizing a characterological stance. This stance may have a defensive function, but not in the traditional sense of a unilateral, unacceptable inner situation (such as an id impulse) and an ego response that is designed to preserve organization by repression. In patients with characterological problems, the ego resorts to a characteristic mode of functioning, determined by its structure and designed to maintain a degree of harmony between the inner psychic world and the environment. In the case of concrete patients, concreteness is both a perceptual response and an executive technique; it is a method used by the psyche to preserve itself. Thus, concreteness can be considered defensive, but it is also typical of a particular type of ego organization. Whether these patients are amenable to therapy, therefore, cannot be answered simply on the basis of a quantitative fixation; other factors must be considered.

It is natural to wonder whether these patients have similar underlying conflicts—conflicts of such magnitude that demand an inflexible noninvolvement in the therapeutic setting. Furthermore, should the analyst try to break through such a needed defensive barrier since he will probably not be successful and could cause irreversible disruption? The analyst almost always thinks about these questions when he considers treating concrete patients; he usually declines treatment if it will involve deeper layers of the personality. It is generally believed that the patients' characterological fragility and withdrawal are insurmountable obstacles.

Before saying anything definitive about therapy it is necessary to understand more about a patient's underlying psychopathology. Since my frame of reference is purposely ego-psychological, other character traits should be considered. When a therapist is able to obtain enough information, he often learns that concrete patients have only a vague idea as to who and what they are and what their purpose in life is. They feel a vague dissatisfaction about not belonging, and they do not see themselves as distinct individuals. As they describe themselves, their identity sense lacks organization. In ego-psychological terms, these patients can be viewed as having defective, poorly developed self-representations. Perhaps all who suffer from severe pathology have disturbances of their self-representation. The differences among patients may be just a matter of degree.

Clinically, not all patients with severe psychopathology have difficulty becoming engaged in a therapeutic, even a psychoanalytic, relationship. *Potential difficulties can be foreseen by determining how much disturbance there is of the identity sense. It is possible that there is a direct relationship between the amount of disturbance of the identity sense and the patient's tendency to isolate himself from the therapist.* The existence of such a relationship is only conjectural, but the subject can be explored further in terms of developmental and characterological factors. I hope to demonstrate that many of these patients can be treated. Rather than simply citing cases that were successfully conducted as empirical proof, I want to formulate concepts based on the therapy of such patients to indicate the feasibility of treatment. Therefore, I will present conclusions drawn from material obtained during the transference regression of such patients (more specific clinical material is abundant elsewhere in this book)—a regression that followed the relaxation of their initial withdrawing defenses.

During relatively deep transference regressions, these patients may have intense antithetical reactions. For example, they may experience blissful calm and have omnipotent feelings of transcendental unity. They may feel that they are harmoniously fused with the analyst and they may no longer recognize the boundaries between themselves and the therapist. They may still say that they have no identity, but, whereas previously such an awareness might have reached the proportions of an existential crisis, now, during the transference regression, they show an almost magical degree of comfort. Instead of feeling amorphous, empty, and chaotic, as they had at times prior to treatment, they see themselves as having a kind of "super-identity" (as reported by one patient)—a transcendental identity based upon the patient-analyst fusion. To stabilize this fusion state, practically every other aspect of their lives loses its previous meaning. Although they go through the motions of relating to people and situations, their meaningful, affective ties are restricted to the analytic situation. Whereas at the beginning of treatment they were maintaining a state of noninvolvement with the therapist, now their relationship with the outer world is largely one of withdrawal. Thus, there is a dramatic and striking change in these patients as treatment progresses.

As with most phenomena that occur during treatment, these changes are not always sudden, nor do they always stand out clearly. These patients showed shifts from one transference state to another; their transference projections and defenses against such projections sometimes underwent rapid alterations. Following periods of tranquil fusion, these patients returned often to their previous aloofness. They might interrupt a long period of silence to say that they were disappointed in the treatment relationship and that they found it meaningless and hopeless. Sometimes they would blame me, although just as often they would blame themselves for being too unworthy or lacking the resources to avail themselves of the potential benefits of analysis. Although they found treatment to be "meaningless," they still kept their appointments and were disappointed and angry if, for some extraneous reason, a session had to be canceled. Then gradually their mood tended to change and once again they would establish a state of fusion. We can establish a sequence from the initial distressing symptom of noninvolvement to a specific transference regression. I believe we can postulate certain psychic processes that will help explain these back-and-forth shifts and enable us to understand that what might initially have been interpreted as the patient's therapeutic inaccessibility is actually analytically meaningful.

Before proceeding with this discussion, I would like to describe another path taken by the transference projection that seems to be almost inevitable when treating these patients. Although clinical events do not occur in an orderly or predictable sequence, the phase I am going to describe usually follows the patient's fusion with the therapist but sometimes precedes it. When the latter occurs, the therapist is more likely to become discouraged. Therefore, it should be understood in the proper context.

The patient may reject everything interpreted by the therapist. He will hold steadfastly to a position of invulnerability—a psychic state that seems to be almost a psychotic exaggeration of his previous reserve and apathy. However, instead of apathy, the analyst observes an intense amount of affect (sometimes anxiety) that may approach panic. Since the patient is actively trying to keep himself separate from the analyst, he may demonstrate a hateful rejection (rather than a passive awareness) of him.

An obvious connection can frequently be observed between the regression characterized by blissful fusion and this phase of hostile rejection. The patient often begins by complaining that the analyst is not meeting his megalomanic expectations. A blissful state cannot survive without some magical reinforcement, which the analyst is unable to provide. The patient's resentment builds up until he finally tries to separate himself entirely from the analyst. The fusion is no longer harmonious, but threatening, and the analyst is perceived as dangerous and engulfing. At this point the patient may have dreams of being inundated or swallowed up and he may complain that the analyst is trying to manipulate or smother him. He fights hard to maintain a distinct boundary between himself and the analyst, one that he needs to sustain a precarious self-representation.

This defense against fusion does not necessarily occur after a period of harmonious symbiosis; it may appear as an extension of the patient's initial nonengagement. This defense seems more apt to come about if the therapist does not actively try to get the patient involved (if he doesn't probe or otherwise try to make the patient respond or talk). In any case, the patient's initial defense seems to gather momentum and to acquire content. The patient will indicate that his noninvolvement is based upon his relationship with the analyst; the analyst is significant to the extent that the patient has to withdraw from him. The patient will specifically defend himself against the analyst, clearly indicating that he means something very special to him, even though it is threatening. Thus, the patient assigns a particular significance to the therapist and this constitutes a transference projection.

Even though the patient's behavior and affect in a state of blissful fusion seem to differ significantly from the state just described, basically they are quite similar. During fusion, of course, the patient shows his admiration for the therapist and finds the relationship vital and life sustaining, yet on closer examination, the therapist can see that his presence is not really acknowledged; the patient is only reacting to an internalized imago of him. The patient has introjected the imago and discusses the relationship between two parts of his own self in the hope of effecting a synthesis. *Since he basically ignores the external object, from a psychodynamic viewpoint, fusion brings about the same results as passive withdrawal or a defense against fusion.*

During periods of contentment and fusion with the analyst, the analyst as a person is simply ignored, whereas during periods of disruptive regressions, the analyst is feared. The differences can be explained in terms of the content of the projections: in the former case, megalomanic expectations are projected and then incorporated (Klein [1946] would call this projective-identification), and the external world is ignored. In the latter case, the hateful, chaotic parts of the self are projected and then pushed away or violently withdrawn from.

Bleger (1967) makes an interesting distinction between symbiotic and autistic mechanisms that operate during narcissistic transference states. In the Kleinian tradition, he elaborates the concept of projective-identification, specifying the position of objects, inside or outside. The symbiotic state is mainly one of projections. The external object becomes a depository of the patient's projections, and then the patient effects a fusion with it. He usually does this in order to defend himself against his own aggression and greed. Autism represents the other side of the coin: the analyst is internalized and then the patient reacts to his imago.

In accord with Bleger's distinctions, the clinical phenomena described in this chapter could be categorized as symbiosis (the blissful state) and autism (the hostile, rejecting state). However, I would like to emphasize the advantage of considering everything manifested by the patient as occurring in his mind. In regressed states the distinctions between external and internal object *representations* are blurred. In both the blissful and the hostile states, the integrity of the self-representation is a central issue. As mentioned earlier, concrete patients have unusually severe disturbances of their identity sense which reflect their general ego organization; consequently, whatever vestige of structure their self-image has must be zealously protected. The transference regressions of these patients help to protect their autonomy, in the one case by defensively withdrawing, and in the other (in a seemingly paradoxical fashion) by introjecting projected, idealized, structured parts of the self and then denying the significance or the dangers inherent in external objects. Both states utilize splitting mechanisms, a general characteristic of schizoid patients.

Whether patients who do not seem to be able to become engaged in therapy are treatable can now be viewed from another perspective. Granted that these patients are difficult to treat, they are not impossible. What may appear to be noninvolvement is really a symptom of their psychopathology; in itself, it represents a type of involvement, that is, a transference manifestation.

Thus, it is apparent that the more amorphous and hateful the self-representation is initially, the more painful and threatening the symbiotic fusion will be. In some instances, the prospective patient will not allow himself to become engaged in analysis because the anticipated symbiotic regression is too threatening due to the intensity of his inner hatred. His precariously constructed identity sense cannot withstand the threat of having his anger turned toward the self as would inevitably occur during a fusion state where distinctions between the inner and outer world are obliterated.

Some analysts believe that it is important to make a distinction between transference and a defense against transference. They do not believe that a defense is a transference; they feel that if it is too intense, it may be a deterrent to analysis. I do not believe that one can make absolute distinctions; patients who suffer from severe psychopathology, especially, develop transference states where the content of the projection and the defense against the disruptive aspects of the projected material are so imbricated that they are virtually inseparable. As in the case of symptoms, there is inherent in the transference projection a relatively primitive defense against the anticipated consequences of that projection.

One could conceptualize a situation in which the patient would muster his resources so that he would not project infantile elements into the analyst. This, of course, would mean that their relationship would be influenced less by primitive factors and more by the better-organized, mature parts of the patient's psyche. The patient would be oriented more at a secondary-process level. Any other type of defense (if the above can be considered a defense and not an adaptation) on the part of the patient against his relationship with the therapist would be more primitive. Certainly, a passive withdrawal reaction clearly demonstrates primary-process factors. Consequently, a patient with this reaction must have already projected infantile elements into the analyst and then defensively retreated. He would not have to withdraw from someone he perceived at a secondary-process level; this person would not be threatening because nothing had been projected into him (there would be no transference).

Perhaps because patients suffering from severe psychopathology have a primitive ego organization (their perceptual and integrative ego systems have not achieved much secondary-process organization and their reality-testing is somewhat defective), they are more apt to perceive the analyst as an archaic object. Others who have a better ego organization can relate to the analyst in a realistic fashion and, in contrast with those who suffer from severe psychopathology, do not develop transference reactions as readily. This view contradicts the usual distinctions between the transference neuroses and the narcissistic neuroses. Stated somewhat differently, the patient with severe psychopathology develops transference reactions more easily than the one who is better integrated.

Since the content of transference projections differs, one can also consider treatability from the perspective of whether a patient can recognize that he is projecting (confusing reality with events that are going on in his mind). Although this is another issue completely, the analyst's ability to perceive and react to behavior in terms of its transference aspects will enable the patient to adopt a similar viewpoint.

Even with the constricted concrete patients described earlier, one is dealing with a transference phenomenon. The defense that characterizes a secondary-process organization is still a reaction to an imago of the analyst. Not intruding into the defense but letting it develop has, in my experience, led to two diametrically opposed reactions. Either the patient will establish an analytic relationship (as happened with my concrete patient) or he will spontaneously terminate. One might ask whether it is feasible to let the patient terminate, especially if he is suffering. If the analyst takes a nonanalytical approach initially, there is no way of knowing whether analysis might have been possible. I believe it is better for the patient to seek help elsewhere if analysis is not, *at the moment,* possible. If the analyst preserves the analytic setting, the patient can always return to it sometime in the future. I can recall three patients who fled from my analytic stance but then came back months or years later. In the interval one had had psychotherapy and the other two had had no further professional contacts. There are many types of noninvolved patients. I believe that the diagnostic types who are called "as-if" or "pseudo as-if" should also be categorized as noninvolved (see chapter 8).

In summary, a group of patients thought to be difficult cases because of their apparent inability to become engaged in a therapeutic relationship is discussed in terms of their ego processes that are relevant to the analytic interaction. These patients are viewed in terms of characterological pathology (particularly their defective self-representation) and in terms of the transference implications of their recalcitrant behavior.

Even though one can generalize about the defective self-representation and say that it is an intrinsic part of the psychopathology of patients who suffer from characterological problems, noninvolved patients are probably more disturbed in this area than those who do not have any difficulty forming a therapeutic relationship. *I believe that the more defective a patient's self-representation is, the more he will be inclined to withdraw from analytic involvement.* There is a logical reason for this; it becomes apparent if one looks closely at the various transference regressions these patients undergo, if they continue in analysis. A patient's initial noninvolvement is, in itself, a manifestation of transference; he withdraws from an imago of the analyst upon which he has projected hateful and destructive parts of the self. After reviewing the distinctions between a transference and a defense against transference, it was concluded that they are not particularly meaningful for the group of "difficult patients."

Part II

DEVELOPMENTAL AND EGO
ASPECTS OF PSYCHOPATHOLOGY

There is, of necessity, considerable overlapping between the sections in which these chapters have been placed. Part I deals primarily with the relation between the identity sense, psychopatholgy and technique in a variety of patients who are commonly seen in psychoanalytic practice. In Part 2, other clinical phenomena are explored and discussed as in Part 1, in an ego-psychological frame of reference.

The close scrutiny of transference regressions highlights the importance of early object relationships and their effects upon psychic development. The traumatic past gains wider significance as the treatment uncovers its psychopathological influence, because patients, in addition to referring to specific relationships with emotionally significant persons, also reveal the significance of the world in general, that is, their private world, which is constructed in a fashion that incorporates early developmental vicissitudes. Within the transference context, the patient recapitulates (not exactly reproduces) early ego states, and the parental role can be surmised from the various introjects which are from time to time projected onto the analyst.

Again, one cannot help but be impressed that the type of psychopathology that confronts us daily can be understood in terms of structural defects. At first this strikes us as disconcerting because if we call to mind analogous situations in organic medicine, our hopes concerning a favorable prognosis are considerably diminished. Indeed, many analysts, including Freud, have taken a pessimistic position, and sociological studies of the ambience surrounding such patients only add to our despair. However, the various movements of regression and progression that punctuate the treatment of patients who are essentially suffering from ego defects cause some analysts to gain respect for psychological resiliency when we see the results of early damage to some degree undone, to a greater degree than is the case with patients suffering from organic congenital defects.

In Part 1, I concentrated on one particular ego subsystem, the self-representation. Owing to infantile experiences that hinder the acquisition of autonomy, patients suffering from characterological problems develop only a minimal or a marginal identity. This is reflected in their behavior, both in the outside world and in analysis, and is a manifestation of a disturbed symbiotic relationship with the mothering source.

The construction and progressive structuralization of ego subsystems can be explained in terms of the acquisition and integration of introjects, a concept which refers to experiences offered by the environment that are potentially helpful (functional) or which may act as impediments to further development (constrictive). The presence or absence of certain functional introjects has a significant bearing upon what types of psychopathology the patient has developed.

In this section, different facets of ego structure and early developmental vicissitudes are examined. The concept of the absence of a particular functional modality, or lacuna, in the ego's executive system is frequently seen as the basis of the problems of many patients. This type of formulation seems almost pedestrian today, but when it was first proposed it met with considerable opposition. I surmise this was due to the influence of training in which the prevailing inclination was to make formulations on the basis of repression and unavailability of various psychic elements rather than their absence.

Still, these formulations proved helpful therapeutically. In what appeared to be a grave clinical situation—and, indeed, many of these patients were severely disturbed—the analytic approach was not only feasible, but, in many instances, indispensable. Finding some explanatory guiding light, in spite of the fact that the explanations were different from those we had been accustomed to expect, helped many of us to maintain an enthusiastic, if confused, perspective toward our patients.

Chapter 10

Maternal Introjection and Ego Defect

Psychoanalytic theory has in recent years focused upon ego operations. This is due not only to the natural continuum that began with an exploration of the id, but also because many of the cases that are being seen by psychoanalysts today require an intensive scrutiny of characterological factors and early object relations. The so-called character disorders, an enigmatic group of patients, have revealed to us many facets of ego structure which in turn have to be expressed in an acceptable and consistent conceptual framework.

Freud was, of course, mindful of the problems that we study today in ego psychology and touched upon many of them in various metapsychological papers which culminated in the formulation of the structural hypothesis (1923). Klein (1932) and Jacobson (1954), although they disagree on many fundamental points, both dealt with the early stages of psychic development. Jacobson's formulations about self and object representations have been significant contributions about ego subsystems and an expansion of Hartmann's (1939) pioneer work on ego psychology. The literature has become quite extensive and need not be reviewed here.

Experience with analytic patients has taught us about the necessity of understanding ego operations, and the subject has been approached from many different viewpoints. The unfolding of the transference neurosis and its special qualities have become the psychoanalyst's most valuable research tool. The clinical data presented in an abbreviated form in this chapter enable us, I believe, to make certain genetic reconstructions that have a bearing on ego development and its psychological distortions. Here I would like to investigate certain aspects of ego structuralization which are associated with the self concept and the mothering function.

The case to be presented has many characteristics that are described by Gitelson (1958a) when he discusses the character disorders. The patient's disturbance and confusion concerning her role as a mother also remind us of Erikson's (1959) concepts about disorders of adolescence and what he called the identity diffusion syndrome.

First published in *J. Amer. Acad. Child Psychiat.* 4 (1965), 279–93. Reprinted by permission.

Case Material

The patient, a woman in her middle thirties who had been married twice, sought analysis because of intense and general feelings of inadequacy as well as an inability to become pregnant. Her gynecologist felt that psychological factors must have a bearing on her sterility since the examinations of her and her husband failed to reveal any organic factors that might account for it.

She reported feeling inferior all of her life; on several occasions in the past she had received psychotherapy. It was at the insistence of her second husband, to whom she had been married only a few months, that she sought analysis and decided to see it through.

She acknowledged that intellectually she was capable and, although she had made only average grades in college, she had done so with a minimum of effort. She did not worry about her appearance and, in fact, was a fairly attractive woman. Her ability to relate to others did not lack charm and she found herself fluent and able to make a good impression at social gatherings.

Although she was both attractive and sociable, she suffered from the subjective sense of being inferior, clumsy, and gauche. She lamented the fact that although of superior intellect she had never accomplished anything constructive. Social relationships, although satisfactory, were transitory and superficial in nature without leading to any deep, warm, satisfying emotional bonds. In this regard she felt she was playing a role, one she had learned by rote memory and did not really feel the part. Giving a dinner party was "sheer torture" because she felt that she would make a fool of herself by revealing her inability to handle what should be a routine task. By this she meant that she was quite literally unable to think of what to serve, how to cook it, how to set the table, and all the other varied details that go along with planning such a social occasion.

She had held half a dozen jobs since leaving college and she believed she was fired from all of them because of incompetence. Though she made good grades in college she did not graduate. There were many reasons for her leaving college when she did but the patient believed that it was representative of her general inability to function in any area.

She did not have a histrionic melodramatic quality and spoke with a good deal of tension, anxiety, and depression. She was extremely bitter about what she considered to be her deficiencies. When faced with a situation that she felt overtaxed her she would react with impotent anger and disorganization. These feelings were sometimes accompanied by derealization and depersonalization. At these times she reported having "no way of knowing who I am or what I am." She would helplessly cling to various friends; she had one in particular whom she considered to be a "bulwark of strength, to tell me what to do and how to do it."

Her father had died when she was six years old and she had only a slight recollection of him. As far as she could ascertain, he was a "nonentity who was completely dominated and submerged" by her "all-powerful mother." (This is a description an aunt gave of him.) Her mother had died in a state hospital five years before the patient began analysis. Her early impressions of her mother were of a very powerful, competent woman, who successfully manipulated the family business and brought the family much wealth. They lived in a big house which the mother handled with the efficiency of a capable overseer of a feudal estate. The patient vividly recalled her mother giving orders to a variety of subordinates, running things with an iron hand, and subjugating all of those around her. According to the patient, mother's strengths served to emphasize everyone else's weakness.

In the course of the analysis, the patient brought up a good deal of material which permitted one to make inferences about the nature of the mothering relationship. Naturally she could not recall the details of her earliest experience, but she remembered mother's inability to handle a four-year-younger sister. Since the family was wealthy, there were many domestics who took over the complete care of the two children. Although the mother was extremely skillful in the hiring of employees to work in the business and to handle her extensive social activities, the patient felt she was obtuse when it came to the selection of nurses and governesses for the children. She vividly recalled the chaos that followed the birth of her younger sister. She considered her mother, for example, to be confused and totally inexperienced in handling the simplest activities of child rearing. She had no idea how to feed the baby, how to select the layette, clothe her, change diapers, or make sleeping arrangements. Furthermore, she was unable to instruct or even to select someone to carry out these functions.

The sister developed severe ulcerative colitis during adolescence and became both physically and emotionally incapacitated. The patient's self-evaluation corresponded to what she described as the sister's actual state.

After four years of analysis the patient became pregnant and gave birth to a girl. I would like to consider this woman's reactions to the pregnancy and her feelings and experiences in the early postnatal period. I wish to emphasize her attitudes about mothering and their relationship to her self-esteem. Her self-representation as a mother naturally included unconscious memories of experiences with her own mother which will be correlated with her reactions to her baby.

During pregnancy she made light of it and did not consider it an accomplishment in spite of having tried to conceive for seven years. She began to depreciate the bearing of children, whereas previously she had lauded it. She further depreciated the role of woman; since the bearing of a child was such an animal process, it was not necessary that the woman possess any other abilities. She felt herself to be intelligent but could not see why it was necessary to have intellectual capabilities simply to breed. At this point she carefully avoided any discussion of what abilities one must have in order to care for a child successfully.

After a fairly easy delivery of a daughter, she became obsessively interested in child-rearing. As I have noted in several other patients who have had similar but less disturbed experiences with their own mothers, she became intensely preoccupied with raising her child properly.

She avidly read all of the recommended books on child development to learn not only the facts of emotional and physical maturation but also the proper psychological handling which would produce a healthy and happy baby. Her preoccupation went far beyond what one would ordinarily expect in a loving mother, and there was a striking lack of affect. She seemed to pursue such information as if she were interested in passing some kind of examination or in producing a model child that would win some contest. It became apparent to both the patient and myself that she had to be a perfect mother to obtain an omnipotent perfectionism that would serve some inner need which had little to do with the welfare of her daughter.

In the analysis she incessantly asked questions about how to handle a variety of rather ordinary situations that arose in reference to her daughter. It gradually became clear that in spite of all her reading and frantic seeking of advice, she showed no more skill or capacity to take care of her child or to relate to her than she remembered her mother having with her sister. I could observe how fatigued and depleted the patient felt, both emotionally and physically. She was exhausted because of the effort and work she put into the taking care of one child, even though her husband was cooperative and they had a full-time maid and a nurse. From the standpoint of work alone it was hard to understand why she was so exhausted.

She then revealed the following ideas: a good mother should not relegate such functions as feeding, clothing, and bathing to a domestic as her own mother had done. These must be her "duties." She also had to be able to relate to the baby which to her meant being sensitive to the child's needs and to be able to play with her.

When faced with these self-assigned functions which she defined as mothering she found herself to be in a state of both panic and confusion. Although she had read considerably about all of these areas, she felt herself to be an extremely poor student who was unable to comprehend what she tried to learn and certainly was not able to apply it. She agreed that it should be simple enough for one of her intellect but in this regard she described herself as an "idiot." For example, her milk supply was such that she was unable to breast-feed the baby. Consequently, she had to prepare a formula. She would have to start preparing one bottle immediately after having fed the child because it would take her that long to get everything ready for the next feeding. At first this was difficult to understand, but once she described how she prepared the bottles it became apparent why it was so time- and energy-consuming. It would take her over an hour to wash a bottle and this whole process can be best summarized by comparing it with certain obsessional rituals, such as a hand-washing compulsion. Then all of the other steps necessary for the preparing of a formula such as the mixing and the heating were handled in the same time-consuming fashion. She used similar methods while dressing and bathing the baby.

Still it was not just the meticulous and the obsessional ritualistic aspects that made taking care of the baby such an arduous task. She often referred to what she considered to be her lack of knowledge, which made it necessary for her to be extra careful. As noted earlier, she felt that she had not been able to learn anything from the books that she had read or from the advice that she had received from friends. She was referring then to a feeling of inexperience and clumsiness in handling tasks with which she had no previous acquaintance, and she felt unable to learn the new skills. One of her most frequent similes was that she was like a student who had never been in or seen an automobile and yet was learning about its operations from a mechanic's manual. She felt that it would be very difficult to learn in such a vacuum and then suddenly to be confronted with an automobile and expected to take care of it as a skilled technician. She felt her task to be equally insurmountable because of the lack of any previous experience. Its difficulties were compounded by a need to be a perfect mother, plus the feeling that she could not learn.

Later she complained she was unable to respond to the child's attempts at communication. It was in this area that her frustration reached its greatest intensity and led to bitter self-recriminations, agitation, and depression. The fact that she was unable to play with her baby, that is to think of any particular games that the child might enjoy, led to the deepest dejection. One day after a friend came in and was able to get her daughter to smile playing peek-a-boo, the patient went into a state of intense rage. She attacked herself for not having been able to think of this game herself, but then revealed that she was not acquainted with it, never having played it or seen anyone else play it with a child. Even cooing or baby talk was something she claimed was entirely foreign to her, but still she was critical of herself because she was not able spontaneously to think of and invent such methods of communication and play for her daughter. She worried whether this would lead to severe developmental defects in her child's character.

Other activities such as weaning from the bottle to a glass, toilet training, and even how to handle the arrival of a sibling did not cause her any particular concern. These functions, which she considered to be "gross" in nature, could be handled mechanistically on the basis of her readings and from the advice she received from friends. But no one could tell her of the innumerable unpredictable situations that arise in the complex relationship between a mother and child. These demanded an intuitive grasp and subtle responses. She summarized her situation by repeating, "I don't know how to do."

In spite of this patient's severe problem, there was never any indication that there were gross disturbances of reality testing. Rather, she emphasized her inability to do things, her helplessness and vulnerability in facing pedestrian tasks. Then she felt completely worthless as if her whole existence and self-esteem depended upon being able to perform in this area, an interesting contrast to her arrogant attitude about the bearing of a child expressed in the prenatal period.

Discussion

The self-image is an important aspect of the ego's structure and disturbances of it have become more frequently observed in recent years. When a person feels dissatisfied with his self-image, he feels inadequate and often helpless and vulnerable. The concept of self-esteem emphasizes the comparison between the self-representation and the ego ideal, as Freud (1914a) pointed out when he spoke of self-regard. He further discussed how the ego ideal, which at that time was synonymous with his broader concept of the superego, determined one's satisfaction with the self. He introduced the concept of ego depletion and demonstrated how it was a causal factor in producing negative self-esteem. All of these are extremely important concepts indispensable to the understanding of the character disorders.

The self-image, to repeat, is a self-observation. It contains an awareness of all the ego's functions, sensory, executive, synthetic, defensive, and otherwise. The operations of ego systems vis-à-vis external reality and the id have definitive characteristics, which Rosen (1961) calls "style" and which give the person his individuality. These qualities in turn are largely determined by one's past experiences, especially those with objects. Satisfactory object relationships cause expansion of adaptive methods of reacting and achieving mastery consonant with reality testing. What is learned therefore is also fundamental for a person's individuality, and identity has been defined by some in terms of the special skills that a person possesses, often referring to a professional or vocational identity.

The concept of identity is a complex one. Many theoretical distinctions concerning the ego and one's self-appraisal have been made and Hartmann (1950) proposed distinguishing between self and ego.

Here I am referring to only one facet of the more complicated rubric of identity sense. I am emphasizing the operational aspects of this patient's self-image, particularly her attitudes about her capacities and abilities to mother. Mothering is also a complex concept, but this chapter will limit itself only to how the patient conceived of her adequacy as a mother.

Some adjustive techniques are learned by everyone early in life and are required for ordinary survival in our culture. The postponement of gratification is not too sophisticated an example of a technique that has to be learned and that involves mastery over and control of one's impulses. With further maturation and development both the needs and the techniques required to gratify these needs undergo a more refined structuralization, one which is considered to belong to the sphere of secondary-process operations. The executive systems develop more efficient and skillful responses because of satisfactory experiences with objects.

Gratifying experiences with objects are incorporated within the memory system and later can become organized into action units by the appropriate executive apparatus. As functional introjects they contribute to the ego's integration and are hierarchically arranged in a continuum from simple adjustive techniques to the complex, subtle problem-solving methods that are required to integrate inner needs with complicated reality tasks. If the ego does not have these techniques at its disposal, this will be reflected in the self-image which may be experienced in many ways, but one common factor is the feeling of unworthiness, inadequacy, and helpless frustration. If the outer world requires a proficiency, to use an analogy, at the calculus level and one has learned only arithmetic, the person will feel weak and helpless. The task of mothering is a complicated one that requires a high order of integration and the executive ego systems have to function at the "calculus" level.

Benedek (1959) has conceptualized parenthood as a developmental phase. She believes that a child revives the parent's developmental conflicts, which lead either to pathological manifestations or to resolution of conflicts whereby the parent may reach a new level of integration. She also emphasized the developmental potentials of an object relationship which lead to structuralization through processes of introjection and identification. This, in turn, leads to confidence which serves as a defense against frustrations and also makes possible other object relationships in addition to the one with the mother, "and it furthers the integration of self-representation within the value system of 'self-esteem.'" This leads to security and a positive identity sense in the child, and later in the parental role.

The patient constantly referred to the fact that she did not know how to do things for her baby and was unable to be spontaneous and to create ways of communicating in the form of games, fondling, baby talk, etc. Her clumsy and time-consuming handling of the baby was characterized by compulsivity and was indicative of guilty preoccupation. Undoubtedly she possessed the motor skills and coordination required for such tasks, but they were now associated with sadistic destructive feelings that necessitated extra vigilance as part of the defense of reaction formation.

This patient had a frantic need for perfection in many areas, especially mothering. I have noted these qualities in several other patients too, and have seen a vicious circle develop. These patients, because they feel so totally inadequate, cannot believe that anything they do or achieve is worth while, at least they cannot utilize any of their accomplishments for the enhancing of self-esteem. As was true with this patient, there was also a minimum of accomplishments, Consequently, in order to feel that anything they did was competent and noteworthy, they set up certain goals to attain. The underlying feeling of infantile helplessness required a perfectionistic behavior of megalomanic, omnipotent proportions to make up for it. The disparity then between the idealized self and the self-representation became enormous, and as they failed in their pursuits of superhuman goals their self-esteem became even lower. Further self-condemnation then led them to strive for even more perfect goals and the whole process repeated itself. In one patient, this process led to a panic state as he saw himself facing the world which was infinitely complex and demanding of one so helpless and base. What he failed to see, of course, was that he himself had set up all of these standards by which he could measure himself so unfavorably.

What has been described is a defensive process, a reaction formation, to handle painful feelings of inadequacy. The defense does not work and merely serves to augment the initial negative self-image.

This patient's ego defect consisted primarily of an inability to perceive her child's needs. Her mother's lack of response and communication compounded by ignorant and disinterested surrogates led to special difficulties when her response to another person, her baby, had to be at its keenest. The rage and frustration, which were reactions to her feeling inadequate, were directed toward her child since it taxed capacities she felt she did not have.

At this point, one can raise the general question whether a person who cannot perform a task is unable to do so because he does not have the basic integration, or whether his inability represents an inhibition due to repression. In the latter instance, one is dealing with symptoms that lead to absence of function, as Freud (1926a) described in a variety of contexts. One might say this patient's inability to mother could be explained as due to a specific conflict situation, perhaps oedipal in nature, leading the patient to repress her knowledge of maternal behavior because of guilt concerning death wishes toward her own mother. The resultant inhibition would thus be a manifestation of such repression. On the other hand, this patient's difficulties can be viewed as an ego defect occurring in a person suffering from a rather severe character disorder whose chief symptomatic manifestation is a pervasive feeling of inadequacy.

Mothering, according to Benedek (1959), represents an advanced state of psychosexual development, and one can postulate that this woman had never reached such a mature libido position. Conceptually one would have to distinguish between fixation and regression. It is possible that this patient, because of an unsatisfactory experience with her mother, never incorporated the functional introjects that would later be required when she assumed the responsibility of motherhood.

The above distinctions are overstatements of what was actually observed in this specific clinical instance. In fairly unstructured egos the defense mechanism of repression still operates, and in well-organized psychoneurotic patients there can still be areas of reduced integration of executive capacities.

Positive self-esteem is a manifestation of a well-integrated ego as well as a factor in its further development. The first rudiments of a positive identity sense contribute to structuralization. Since such a child is not anxious and feels loved and therefore worth while (a positive self-image), the synthetic and integrative systems are not disrupted by conflict and frustration. Other positive influences, i.e., satisfactory object relations, continue to be effective and the ego's integrative capacities reach higher levels of structuralization. In turn, such higher states of organization enhance self-esteem further and the identity sense becomes increasingly acceptable.

In contrast, this patient was obviously very angry with her mother. This was highlighted in the transference neurosis when she became aware of oral-sadistic impulses which, in the relatively undifferentiated state of self from outer world, threatened to devour her. This was experienced as agitation and panic and accompanied by fears of me as I represented the primitive maternal imago. At this point she went into a state of dissolution of practically psychotic proportions. She felt unable to do anything and was obsessively preoccupied with the fear of killing her child. Furthermore, she was both angry and "petrified" with what she felt to be my disgust and wish to get rid of her. With further regression she made me into an elaborate persecutor and the clinical picture was paranoid.

This response to me was in marked contrast to the time when she saw me as a teacher who could supply her with executive techniques to master all problems. That the teacher-student relationship also represented a defense against the above disruptive transference feelings was also true, but for the most part she was attempting to make up for what she considered to be deficiencies in her childhood.

When the patient began to reintegrate she idealized me as the omnipotent good object. Mother could only destroy and be ineffective, a regressed transference state characterized by projective defenses, whereas now the idealized external object could be incorporated and make up for her deficiencies. This state, too, had psychoticlike qualities in so far as it was characterized by megalomanic expectations. The student-teacher relationship, on the other hand, was of a subdued nature and did not point to any specific attachment to the analyst. Anyone, then, could assume such a role if he would make himself available (books, husbands, friends).

Her destructive and self-destructive transference feelings highlighted the hostile cathexis of the early maternal introject. The "poisonous" internal mother did not enhance instinctual gratification and mothering had to become an "encapsulated" experience. The patient was unable to integrate such an introject and thereby attain a higher state of differentiation.

Whenever an object relationship is conflictual, and destructive feelings are predominant, its potential for development becomes minimal and instead of progression may lead to regression. Whatever the psycho-dynamic determinants might be for such a hostile orientation, the earlier such a conflict occurs and the more primitive the stage of psychosexual development, the greater is the likelihood for the occurrence of an ego defect.

Ordinarily the mothering imago throughout the course of psychosexual development undergoes a hierarchical elaboration which in the genital phase becomes the basis for the complex interrelationships of mothering. The primitive maternal introject can be considered as representing the potential which later, because of further gratifying experiences, achieves a degree of structuralization that leads to the expansion of sensory and executive ego systems and causes them to function with efficiency and confidence while relating to the child's needs. In this case the maternal conflict, by not permitting a synthesis and integration of the introject, deprived the patient of a potential which later could lead to satisfying and satisfactory mothering.

These developmental defects have broader implications for the study of the character disorders. The clinical exploration of such cases is of value in furthering our understanding of ego development and the importance of object relationships.

Summary

The smooth functioning of perceptual and executive ego systems is seen to be dependent upon the synthesis of past functional introjects. A positive sense of identity is founded upon the operations of executive systems and the mastery of external situations consonant with the dictates of the ego ideal. In the study of the character disorders one has the opportunity to observe the ego when such a synthesis is not achieved and the self-image is one which is unacceptable to the patient.

This patient, who reported an unsatisfactory mothering experience, found herself unable to function and felt inadequate as a mother. Although the ego was able to function adequately and even more than adequately in many other respects, the patient's inability to function as a mother led to negative self-esteem and self-condemnation.

Early object relationships are essential for the further structuring of the personality. From satisfactory relationships one learns techniques and skills that become useful for the gratification of needs as well as the mastery of external tasks. This patient indicated that her own defective mothering experience did not lead to the formation of the proper introjects which were later essential for her to draw upon in order to take care of her own child. Although repression leads to inhibition of functions and although repressive measures were operating in this patient, it is felt that her difficulties in mothering were due to weakly established mothering introjects. This was seen as constituting an ego lacuna due to the absence of a satisfactory experience from which the ego could further structuralize. Repression implies that the patient has a well-established memory trace of the experience which, because of neurotic conflict, cannot be retained at conscious levels. The distinction postulated here is not an absolute one. What was observed in this patient was a balance between repressive forces and a relative absence of what has been referred to as a functional introject.

Chapter 11

Frustration and Externalization

Various transference reactions occur in patients suffering from characterological defects. Some of these reactions may go unrecognized because of their unfamiliar qualities. The patient's adaptive techniques and defenses often reveal that the apparent lack of transference involvement is in itself a reaction toward the analyst, a response determined by frustrations stimulated by the analytic process.

Here I will discuss two related reactions, frustration and externalization, which occur in all patients but may have unique features in patients suffering from characterological problems. These two reactions belong to different conceptual levels. Externalization represents an ego mechanism that requires theoretical clarification; frustration produces a behavioral response. My clinical data suggest that frustration besides being a reaction to thwarted instinctual impulses is also a result of failure of the patient's adaptive techniques.

Freud (1924a, b) described the psychotic patient's conflict as between the ego and the outer world. Not all patients who suffer chiefly from characterological defects are manifestly psychotic, but all have a more or less distorted perception of the environment. Many of these patients have failed to live in a fashion that corresponds to the demands of the external world as they perceive it. This failure frustrates their adaptive efforts, and the results appear in their analyses. The patient attempts to recreate in the transference an environment that he believes he can cope with. In the transference he is externalizing some aspects of his inner organization as well as projecting affects, impulses, and attitudes. Insofar as he fails in this externalization, he feels frustrated.

Case Report

A middle-aged housewife sought treatment because she felt that everything in her life was wrong. She complained that her husband mistreated her, that her children made unreasonable demands, and that her friends were selfish and inconsiderate. She lacked, however, both the fixity and fervor one often sees in the paranoid patient. It was unclear why the patient wanted therapy when she did rather than previously. It seemed that she was finally unable to tolerate feeling miserable any

First published in *Psa. Q.* 36 (1967), 571–83. Reprinted by permission.

longer; only later did it become apparent that her friends and family were forming attachments elsewhere.

She revealed a traumatic and chaotic childhood. Both parents beat her frequently and demanded that she shoulder the responsibility of raising her siblings since she was the oldest child. Her father was described as an unpredictable alcoholic; the patient "never knew" what to expect from him, a caress or a blow. She believed that her mother was more consistent for varying periods of time, but from the patient's description it seemed that her mother was suffering from periodic agitated depressions. She recalled episodes lasting several months when her mother was warm and loving and very much concerned about her daughter's well-being. Paradoxically, the patient felt uncomfortable and anxious at these times. After such benevolent periods she would find herself in a situation of physical jeopardy when her mother had violent outbursts and continuously attacked her in the midst of agitation and tears.

I rather quickly formed the impression that the patient was not seriously uncomfortable. It was apparent that she wanted me to fight with her but I did not think this was typically sadomasochistic, although at times there was considerable masochism. It seemed that she wanted to preserve the atmosphere of the battlefield rather than experience or inflict pain.

After several months of this behavior, during which I was silent, I pointed out that she had a need to see me as an opponent and that as long as she felt herself fighting with me she could feel some security. I emphasized that it was the battleground that she seemed to find necessary rather than the actual fight. She quickly replied that high-ranking military strategists always fascinated her and she had often seen herself standing over a huge map, planning campaigns, but at the same time she could visualize the enemy playing the same game.

Next day she had lost all her exuberance. She had an air of wistful melancholy which she could not attribute to anything in particular. She then reported her first dream.

> An amorphous person (she could not distinguish whether male or female) came at her with a club, but she was not frightened. She knew that she would not be hit and enjoyed the challenge of being what she later called the "artful dodger."

She spontaneously pictured me as the amorphous attacker, saying this before expressing the feeling that I would want her to talk about the dream. This feeling made her even sadder. She was beginning to believe that I was not at all like the person with the club and this upset her. She now thought of me as a warm, generous person who wanted to understand her.

Primitive pregenital elements now emerged rather than associations expressing the more obvious sexual implications of the dream. Instead of playfully enjoying herself, she presented herself as anxious and desperate. She was begging for a fight, and at the same time she felt that she was "falling apart." She had many dreams of houses crumbling and of drowning, but surprisingly all these catastrophic events occurred in a warm, pleasant setting.

This period of obvious dissolution reached its climax with a short dream.

> She was dressed in tattered rags and walking in a dirty slum. As she continued walking the disordered slum gradually changed into a well-lit and rich neighborhood. She then found herself in front of a mansion, but at this precise moment she disappeared.

This was difficult to describe; she felt panic and thought of herself as a flimsy and empty shadow. After reporting this nightmare, she had an angry outburst at me and emphasized the unmanageable frustration she was experiencing.

I commented that in the dream she would have felt safer and more comfortable in the slum, and that she had made me into a mansion. She agreed and pointed out that she wanted to make me into a slum so that I could be as dirty, horrible, and angry as she was, but it was my stubborn refusal to be anything but kind and understanding that made her feel so miserably frustrated. She then remembered a story she had either seen in a motion picture or heard in a soap opera on the radio during childhood. A kind and beautiful heiress brings a disheveled, deprived ragamuffin into her luxurious home where she has provided a playroom filled with toys. As soon as the heiress is out of sight, the little girl quietly walks to the window and climbs out, getting back to the slums as quickly as possible.

The patient wanted to see me just as she saw herself; she also wanted me to be "at the same level." She had to externalize her feelings, to see the outside world in the same terms as she perceived her inner organization. She felt I was presenting her with an experience she could not integrate with her usual perception of the world; especially did my attitude of desiring to understand her disturb her. This attitude she believed she had never before experienced.

In the course of treatment she gradually began to realize that there was hope of raising herself from the "slum level" to the level she attributed to me. Her view of me was favorable but still primitive in so far as it had megalomanic elements. But the "mansion" was not unattainable; she had after all created it herself. If she could ascribe such qualities to me, it was possible that she could develop them for herself.

The fact that the analytic relationship could survive the regression was also helpful, and she gradually became stronger although, as in any analysis, there were many fluctuations due to emergence of sexual and other conflicting feelings.

Discussion

Paradoxical seeking for a situation that to the observer seems likely to be painful is the essence of masochism. Certain features of the self-defeating behavior of patients with character disorders should be distinguished from masochism. Masochistic behavior requires a degree of coherent ego organization with a fairly well-defined superego and a capacity for experiencing guilt. Patients with character defects have undergone considerable maldevelopment, and their self-defeating behavior is not functionally organized to protect them from the harsh dictates of the superego. Self-defeating behavior that has a defensive purpose must be distinguished from that resulting from a faulty organization or breakdown of the personality.

At the outset this patient's ego had considerable structure. Her provocativeness was well organized and may have contained masochistic elements even though she did not seem to react to interpretations that referred to them. Later her ego lost its organization and her need to construct a painful reality did not result from masochism. It is possible, however, that her psychic disorganization resulted from regression from a masochistic defensive position.

As her ego regressed, she attributed the trauma she experienced to inability to cope with the external world. This is often the complaint of patients suffering from character defects. Their environment is seen as inordinately complex, impossible for them to cope with by the adjustive techniques available to them. Another patient expressed his dilemma by stating that the world was at the level of calculus and he had barely mastered arithmetic. The patient feels helpless and vulnerable, a helpless babe who is cast out into an environment he is totally incapable of handling.

One would expect the reality these patients are describing to be harsh and demanding, and often it is. Some, however, like the woman I have described, react paradoxically. They cannot cope with a warm and nonthreatening environment. They react to a benign situation as if it were beyond their level of comprehension. These patients do not have the adjustive techniques to interact with a reasonable environment. Their formative years were irrational and violent. They internalize this chaos and their inner excitement clashes with their surroundings. When the world becomes benign and generous, the patient withdraws in panic and confusion, just as my patient described herself as doing during a phase of ego dissolution. This was particularly emphasized by her story of the heiress and the slum child.

To feel secure in one's identity one has to know where he stands in his universe. The self-image contains numerous introjects, so one perceives the self in the same way as the external objects that have been introjected. External objects are among the first representations of reality. So one's sense of identity, if it is firm and coherent, corresponds to the environment that contributed to its formation. The early environment of patients with ego defects is different from that experienced by persons with a relatively good psychic organization. The ego of the person with a character disorder is not in resonance with any reality that differs radically from the one he knew in early childhood. The degree of difference determines how well he can master external stimuli and perceive himself as a meaningful person in a knowable, acceptable world.

The ego with primitive fixations or one that has undergone defective development can maintain some coherence in a setting similar to the one from which its introjects were formed. For my patient the analysis represented an infantile situation; being understood or having someone interested in what was going on within her was an entirely foreign experience in which she could not feel at ease.

This woman's requirements from the world are those often seen in persons who have suffered much trauma in childhood. Their egos have been acclimated to a frustrating environment. The person with a character disorder expects and brings about his failure; he adapts himself to life by feeling beaten in an unpredictable, ungiving world. Obviously this situation is different from a masochistic adjustment that is designed to effect a psychodynamic balance; the defensive situation described in this patient is one that is vital for maintaining a total ego coherence instead of dealing with specific conflicting destructive impulses.

This patient's psychopathology can be understood in several ways. Very often she saw herself as a frightened little girl who was given everything but love and intimacy. At other times, her provocative behavior was a defense against her libidinal attachment to the analyst. By regarding the analysis as of little value, she need not become painfully dependent and thus expose her helplessness and vulnerability. She could maintain control by projecting the despised aspects of her self onto the analyst. Her underlying oedipal wishes might destroy her as well as others; to avoid them she forbade herself a warm and receptive relation with external objects, including the analyst. When the analytic situation did not support her defenses, she felt traumatized.

Freud (1920) described the tendency of patients to repeat traumatic situations of the past. He believed that this repetition represented, in part, a need for mastery, but he pointed out that a characteristic of the id, the repetition compulsion, is also involved. Undoubtedly the repetition compulsion is also operative in these patients, who resemble those with traumatic neuroses although the trauma began early in life and was repetitive and cumulative (Khan, 1964).

The analyst is faced with a seemingly paradoxical situation when the patient feels frustrated because the analyst refuses to frustrate him. The analytic setting provides consistency, the constant reliability Winnicott (1955), described and hence is conducive to regression. It causes the patient to hope that infantile needs can be gratified. Because of past experiences this hope cannot be trusted; instead of risking the inevitable disappointment of megalomanic expectations, the patient prefers relating in a setting to which he has learned to adjust. If the analyst does not frustrate him the patient's psychic balance is upset.

To reinstitute ego equilibrium the patient attempts to make the analyst representative of the world that is familiar to him. This defense must be distinguished from projection. Projection was very early described by Freud (1896, 1911b), as the attribution of a disruptive, unacceptable impulse to an external object. In the course of time the concept has been broadened to include not only unacceptable id impulses but also disruptive affects, as well as discrete psychic contents such as introjects (see chapter 3). There is always some interplay between projection and introjection.

Such primitive defenses as projection are often employed in character disorders but what my patient was attempting to achieve in her analysis was more than projection. Although one can describe the inner and outer world only in terms of their content, her reconstruction of reality was not based solely upon unacceptable impulses and affects. These patients are attributing a particular level of integration to reality, a process better described as externalization. The need to be frustrated is not primarily projection of hostile wishes upon a persecutor; rather, it represents a mode of adjustment that makes the interaction between ego and outer world possible. According to Freud (1911b) the patient projects inner impulses that have become disruptive. Externalization provides the patient with a setting that enables him to use adjustive techniques that he has acquired during his early development. Although there is always an element of projection in every externalization (insofar as the construction of reality will invariably involve the attributing of some unacceptable impulses to external objects), there are additional factors.

Externalization can be conceptualized as the "projection" of an ego mechanism whereas the defense mechanism called projection deals with impulses, affects, and self- and object-representations closer to the id. For example, if the chief adjustive modality of the ego is repression, then it seeks a repressive environment. But if the ego makes its adaptation to a world perceived as full of rage and violence, then the mechanism of acting out becomes its chief interaction with the world. The type of acting out displayed by my patient, however, was not flagrant antisocial behavior. Many ego mechanisms can be attributed to the environment; this attribution enables the ego to maintain itself, not in a vacuum but in a familiar even though painful and frustrating world.

Brodey (1965) in a recent article describes externalization as "distancing . . . without separation." According to him, projection also occurs but the manipulation of reality referred to as externalization has the "purpose of verifying the projection." Other aspects of reality are simply not perceived.

Externalization can be defensive in so far as it maintains a tenuous psychic balance. It can also be part of any defense because defenses have to operate in a setting that is to some extent compatible with them. Van der Heide (pers. comm., 1966) stated that in so far as a defense is ego-dystonic the ego changes the environment in order to "justify" the defense. Persons with character disorders do more by their externalization than merely make the environment compatible with their defenses. Their basic identity is involved. The environment has to be constructed so that their total ego organization is maintained.

But externalization is not confined to persons with character defects; it occurs in normal development. In psychoneurosis it helps to maintain defenses, but as the ego develops it helps to establish reality testing. The child's ego not only constructs an imago, it also incorporates the setting characteristic of the object. The mother is a means by which the child becomes adapted to the environment; hence the child not only "registers" a maternal imago but he perceives the mothering process as an adaptive technique. Introjects function by helping the child to establish a relation with the inner and outer worlds and to develop and use subsequent experiences for acquisition of further adaptive techniques (chapter 3).

When my patient tried to make me representative of a specific traumatic environment she was, at the same time, projecting parental imagoes and hated parts of herself onto me. The latter process is, of course, characteristic of transference but with this patient it was an uneasy and conflicting transference because she could not reconcile her projections with the analytic setting. This had, nevertheless, therapeutic advantages, since it did not lead to a transference fixation and made possible the understanding of irrational and infantile expectations.

Anna Freud (1965) discusses externalization as a mechanism that externalizes parts of the self or the inner conflict, or both. She describes how the therapist may become representative of conflicts or of a psychic agency, such as the superego. Clinically this transformation of the environment has to be described in terms of specific content. To speak of conflict and superego is to introduce a categorization that goes beyond clinical observation and description. One can describe the patient's construction of external reality in terms of his perceptions. The psychic mechanisms involved in his conflicts or in a psychic agency, such as the prohibitive or judgmental aspects of the superego, are elaborated into experiences which can be reported as perceptions and feelings. Anna Freud also seems to distinguish externalization from projection but she does not emphasize the differences. Furthermore, she believes that when the patient "externalizes," the therapeutic relationship differs from one in which a transference has been established.

Whether the phenomenon of transference should be restricted to the projection of an object or part object (see chapter 20) or whether it should include the adaptive function and setting of the object is an interesting question. Here I emphasize that some patients suffering from character disorders may find themselves in an analytic situation that is discrepant from their projection of an archaic imago. This can lead to disruptive regression but it can also be potentially useful for analysis.

The analysand's response to the hope stimulated by the consistent analytic situation is of crucial importance. Because these patients present themselves as so needful, the analyst sometimes feels that he must offer some gratification in order to achieve sufficient stability for the analysis to proceed. The patient often misunderstands the analyst's helpful attitude and believes that he is being promised gratification of needs that would have been appropriate to childhood. The analytic situation, by providing a setting that facilitates regression, sometimes causes the patient to believe that such gratification is possible, and if the analyst also seems to offer help, the expectation of primitive satisfactions may be reinforced.

Two of the many possible reactions to this therapeutic interaction must concern us. First, the patient may for the moment relinquish his distrust and his insistence that the environment is frustrating. He acknowledges that gratification is possible, and since the needs he hopes to satisfy are primitive, his expectations will be megalomanic. The transference is characterized by fusion with the analyst; the patient expects to be rescued from his assaultive depriving introjects. In so far as megalomanic expectations are thwarted, this attitude usually leads to bitter disappointment. Second, occasionally this fusion persists and the therapeutic relationship is maintained on the basis of a delusion. Strachey (1934) believes that many so-called supportive relationships continue because the analyst unwittingly fosters such a delusion.

The patient may not accept the analyst's offer of help. Since he has always been suspicious and wary such an offer may lead to a strengthening of distrust. He can then view the analyst as insincere and convert him into a replica of the frustrating environment he once knew. This transformation involves a projection of the bad self as well as externalization.

Either reaction to the analyst's interventions precludes analysis. To some extent, such reactions will occur regardless of what the analyst does. But if he has maintained the analytic setting by avoiding involvement with the patient's infantile needs or defenses he has established a frame of reference in which such responses can be examined. He is an observer and the patient begins to realize that the analyst's primary aim is to understand how his mind works, a unique and new experience for him. This attitude becomes characteristic of the external analytic reality and when internalized (Loewald, 1962) constitutes an ego mechanism. The externalization of this mechanism occurs in an ego that has achieved sufficient structure so that it can maintain itself in nonfrustrating surroundings.

Summary

Patients suffering from characterological defects emphasize certain defensive reactions that are not frequently encountered in the psychoneurotic. Some of these patients have an unusual orientation to the outer world. They *must* fail. They unconsciously attempt to create an environment in which they feel frustrated. This constitutes an adjustment; frustration has become a way of life. In so far as they cannot master a benign environment they construct one that is harsh and ungiving. The patient's attempt to reconstruct such a frustrating environment is highlighted in the transference. The patient feels frustrated because the constant reliability of the analytic situation refuses to frustrate him. This compensatory defense—the creation of a traumatic but familiar setting—is referred to as externalization, which is distinguished from masochism and projection. The techniques of working with such "needy" patients demand further scrutiny.

Chapter 12

Aggression: Adaptive and Disruptive Aspects

Since Freud's *Beyond the Pleasure Principle* (1920), the concept of aggression has become a controversial cornerstone of our metapsychology. The evaluation of a patient's aggressive reactions is clinically useful but when one attempts to make judgments regarding their role in maintaining psychic balance, there is considerable confusion.

Some of the theoretical difficulties have been due to the reluctance of many analysts to accept Freud's last instinct theory, which is based upon the existence of a death instinct. Furthermore, the distinctions between aggression, hostility, violence, and rage are unclear.

I do not wish to reawaken polemics about the death instinct. Rather, I would like to emphasize how I propose to use the above terms so one can proceed with discussion in an orderly fashion. Aggression, hostility, rage, and other terms that have some relationship to activity and violence belong to different conceptual levels. For example, rage can be considered an affect, aggression, an energic modality, hostility and violence are usually discussed phenomenologically, i.e., behaviorally.

Nevertheless, one can postulate important relationships between these various expressions if they are viewed in terms of emotional development, relationships which will also have clinical implications.

These different conceptual frames of reference can be thought of in terms of an hierarchal continuum. The neonate's purposeless and chaotic screaming and kicking represent the primitive primary-process-oriented end of the continuum, and active, aggressive, but nonhostile behavior in the service of adaptation and mastery represents the other mature end of the spectrum. The intermediary stages include such reactions and states from disruptive rage (uncontrollable anger and violence) to reactive and justifiable anger that leads to purposeful action. There are, of course, many gradations, but the main progression is from reactions that are essentially maladaptive in the adult to secondary-process, goal-oriented responses.

This spectrum can also be considered from the viewpoint of the different frames of references mentioned above, and, here again, one can postulate an hierarchal continuum. The neonate's "tantrum" is

First published in *Bull. Phila. Assoc. for Psa.* 19 (1969), 76–86. Reprinted by permission.

obviously overwhelming, a motoric response to some inner state of homeostatic imbalance. What he feels under these circumstances is impossible to ascertain. But, in view of both his developmental and maturational immaturity, it seems likely that he does not have sufficient organization to experience a structured affect. An affect, even hate (see Winnicott, 1947), presupposes a degree of psychic structure that the neonate has not yet achieved. Consequently, his tantrum can be considered a massive, diffuse, motoric manifestation of a state of psychic disruption, one which antedates the feelings of rage and frustration.

With further development, the child gains the capacity to "feel" in a more sophisticated, nonvisceral fashion. From a sensory viewpoint, his experiencing of satisfaction or dissatisfaction is mentationally richer. Affects of pleasure and pain develop, which at these still early stages do not lead to purposeful behavior.

The continuum from neonatal tantrums to goal-directed, aggressive behavior is a description of various characteristics, motor and sensory, of different developmental stages. It should be emphasized that there are many other qualities that characterize these different stages, and that this conceptual scheme does not make any statements about etiological links. Reality-oriented aggression need not be a consequence of neonatal screaming. The development of the psychic apparatus is a complex phenomenon, dependent upon many variables. What we are viewing here are essentially responses that are manifestations of various psychic states. In a sense, they may be considered end products; and, as such, one response does not lead directly to another one. However, each structural level leads to the next "higher" one, and the characteristic qualities of one level can be compared to another one. These comparisons are essential to our clinical and therapeutic concepts of regression and progression and the role of aggression in the context of such dynamic shifts.

Clinical Material

The study of hostility and aggression also has many clinical implications which broaden our understanding of the adaptive and disruptive aspects of psychopathology in the context of developmental factors. To elaborate, I will present a brief vignette of an interesting regressive episode that occurred during the analysis of an apparently very disturbed patient.

The patient, a single man in his early twenties, presented a benign, cheerful exterior. He was soft-spoken, sanguine, and formed friendly relationships easily. However, they seldom lasted, and this transience was one of the reasons that he sought therapy.

During the early phases of the analysis, it soon became apparent that insofar as his friendliness was overdone, his benign demeanor represented a defensive facade. Most of his dreams were concerned with situations of catastrophic violence.

He used such primitive defenses as projection, but in a novel fashion. Unlike the typical paranoid, what he projected was friendly and helpful instead of hostile and persecutory. For example, if he were facing a difficult decision the "voices" would discuss the situation and eventually help him reach an agreeable decision. That patient played a musical instrument. While practicing, he usually heard voices, and it was at these times that they were the most helpful, giving him benign critiques and suggesting methods by which he could improve his technique.

Whether these voices can be considered true hallucinations is debatable. He heard them with the clarity of any external percept. On the other hand, he referred to them casually, without grimness, as if they were not completely separated from himself.

In any case, after interpretation of the adaptive (defensive) nature of his friendliness, the patient changed dramatically. He became frightened and his behavior generally and in my office was infantile. His frustration tolerance diminished, and the most trivial and slightest stimuli caused him to feel intense anger. If I shifted in my chair, he believed that I found him uninteresting and complained of my neglect. At first he whined, but after several weeks he became very angry, and eventually his anger reached the proportions of a tantrum. He would writhe and kick on the couch, scream and cry, clenching and unclenching his fists, beating his head and striking my wall. On one occasion, he rolled off the couch, thrashed around on the floor, and started biting a loose rug until I made him stop.

I had reached the conclusion that his behavior in my office had become so chaotic and, at one level, purposeless (although in terms of the transference, it had intrapsychic determinants), that I had to impose some controls for my peace of mind.

He again changed when I indicated that I could not tolerate the intensity of his tantrums. He continued being very angry, but in a more controlled fashion. In some respects, his anger was even more malicious than previously, but behaviorally was more manageable. He now resembled the traditional paranoid patient.

I was made into the chief persecutor. His benign voices had left him a long time ago, and now he heard the more usual persecutors generally threatening and accusing him of being a homosexual. He believed that I had hired these persecutors to torment him.

His paranoid system became well stabilized, but after considerable vacillation. He would, from time to time, feel less intense about me. Then he sought me as an ally, in some cause against social injustices. He complained, sometimes eloquently and convincingly, against the narrowmindedness and reactionary mediocrity of various institutions.

The above was in inverse proportion to the paranoid transference. Finally, he became less involved at the civil rights level and saw me as his exclusive persecutor. The therapeutic handling of this case is tangential to the thesis of this chapter. Since he had a sufficiently well-estalished therapeutic alliance he was able to develop insights about the paranoid transference. What is important here is the course of the regression as described above and the subsequent reintegration.

Although the course of regression and progression was not a steady one, there was some direction to the general movement. He gradually become affectively less paranoid as he was able to recognize the adaptive qualities of his behavior (to control disruptive rage). His ego "progressed" from a psychotic organization to one where he could view the surrounding world less delusionally. This forward movement was characterized by the same preoccupation with social issues that he had prior to entering his phase of organized, well-adjusted paranoia.

At the beginning he was fervently involved with these issues. My own prejudices and orientation caused me to feel these were laudatory causes and *therefore* realistic, but in spite of my implicit approval, I could recognize that his involvement excluded all other interests in his life. In other words, the defensive aspects of his crusade-like preoccupations were dominant, and he was not a particularly effective participant in the various movements he joined.

Gradually, as he needed the involvement less, he did not feel as "immersed" in these activities and was able to handle himself in a calmer, objective fashion. He found himself less intense and less passive, and became aggressive in many other areas.

Discussion

This patient's regression and subsequent progression can bring into focus many important aspects of the effects of hostile responses upon the psychic economy. From a theoretical viewpoint, I would like to emphasize the following areas:

1. The general effects of hostile acting out upon psychic integration; i.e., whether it is adaptive or disruptive and whether it leads to regression or structuralization.
2. The degree of organization of various hostile impulses and affects and the qualities of the corresponding ego states.

3. The significance of such impulses and affects relevant to developmental phases.

Depending upon its context, a response or a feeling may be either disruptive or adaptive. However, it must be emphasized, adaptation and disruption are in themselves relative concepts. Even during a regressive course, the resultant ego state may be considered a defense against further regression, and in this respect, can be considered adaptive and defensive. However, comparing the ego state with the previous one, it is a product of regression; and insofar as it contains less organization, it is relatively maladaptive and can be thought of as a disruption of a higher organization. When discussing hostile reactions, these distinctions will be kept in mind, but the concept of adaption and disruption will be confined to the general direction of structuralizing processes. If a phenomenon is associated with stabilization or further structure, it will be considered adaptive, and if it leads to regression and psychic imbalance, then it will be conceptualized as maladaptive or disruptive.

Reviewing the hierarchal gamut discussed above, screaming and tantrums do not seem to be associated with later states of higher organization. One cannot comment about the subjective state of the neonate, but if the mother is not able to furnish gratification that will calm him, the child finally reaches a state of utter exhaustion, one which does not seem to have any advantages regarding emotional development. He seems depleted.

When an adult reacts as an infant, one can make more definite statements about his psychic organization. My patient did not seem to gain from the experiencing of intense rage. It was helpless and impotent rage that caused him to feel frightened and vulnerable.

When he started a tantrum early in a session, he was "spent" at the end. He felt often that he would be totally unable to face the world outside my office, and his self-confidence and self-esteem were very low. His reaction had the quality of a negative feedback. Infantile rage, whatever its source, became dominant. This psychic state was one which threatened his adult ego ideal. To behave in such a childish manner caused considerable shame. Furthermore, it recapitulated an infantile ego state (one of relative disorganization) where he lacked the adaptive mechanisms to adjust to the demands of an adult world. Consequently shame and feelings of inadequacy, with accompanying helplessness, caused him to experience further anger.

His anger was not sufficiently organized to lead to outwardly-directed violence, but its self-destructive aspects were obvious, as demonstrated by his behavior in my office. Regression led to further regression. Rage created more intense rage and disorganization as the shame increased and the destructive aspects of the superego became dominant, rendering the previously benign aspects (Schafer, 1960) inoperative. Behavior became regressively disorganized until he was reduced to a state approximating an early neonatal ego state, where ego/non-ego boundaries cease to exist.

Obviously, the above state cannot be endured indefinitely, and the patient had to construct defenses to protect himself from such an intolerable regression. At this point, his anger became better organized and focalized. This was a paranoid adjustment, but nevertheless an adjustment where his ego integrity was partially restored. His paranoid projection, therefore, represented an adaptation, a delusional one, but one which definitely represented a progression from the state described above. He could now cope with the surrounding world, and as he was able eventually to restrict his persecutors to my office, i.e., keeping them focused in the transference; he was able to enjoy some limited successes in his everyday life.

The paranoid adjustment was characterized by vigilance. He constantly scrutinized situations and events in order to assess whether they represented a threat. He looked at everything in terms of its dangerous potential. He was chronically angry and he saw the world mainly in terms of violence. Still, this outlook achieved security since he could put what had been uncontrollable disruptive anger outside of himself and then protect himself from it. Anger had now become a modality, an affect which was instrumental in maintaining ego integrity. As he protected himself from the projected persecutors of the external world by an angry hyperalertness, he achieved a synthesis that prevented him from regressing to the previous state of chaotic disruption.

It is interesting to note how his persecutors, who—as mentioned above—were often projected onto me, changed and became "socialized." The patient's fervent involvement with civil liberty issues was also a defensive stabilization. In a sense, it was an *institutionalized paranoia*. He fused some aspects of his environment with some facets of his self-representation and then reacted to it as if it were outside of himself. The psychic mechanisms used were still typically paranoid but less obviously so since his projections were more in tune with reality.

Insofar as he received approval from his peers for his views, he was gradually able to achieve some success. He was elected an officer in an organization and the members praised his work. His psyche was well-defended, and his defenses were socially acceptable. Consequently, his self-esteem was boosted and he began functioning more effectively. Here we have an example of a positive feedback which had a psychopathological foundation, but which, nevertheless, led to stability and created a setting where therapy could be effective.

In this instance, hostility, dependent upon its context, was both disruptive and adaptive. There was a continuum from primitive disruptive rage reactions to a somewhat reality-attuned anger, which led to aggressive and productive behavior. During regression the patient passed through the various phases of the continuum in the direction of infantile tantrums; and during progression, he reversed his direction, going through similar phases.

Many adolescent patients demonstrate similar mechanisms. Their involvement with social issues, an almost exclusive preoccupation, has a paranoid flavor to it and maintains an otherwise precarious equilibrium. Such involvement is often positive for their psychic economy, not only because of its defensive adaptation, but because it seems to be an activity that precedes the formation of a better integrated adult ego. These patients, by "socializing" their anger, construct a setting that makes further emotional development possible.

Hostility, therefore, can be studied in the context of emotional development. Now, I would like to review the three categories of anger (infantile tantrums, individual paranoid delusions, and institutionalized paranoia) in terms of their corresponding ego states and the developmental scale.

My patient's chaotic rage reactions occurred when he was experiencing the loss of symbiotic fusion in the transference, a transference many therapists would consider psychotic. At these moments he did not distinguish himself from me and often called me by his name, as well as the reverse, referring to himself by my name. His dreams emphasized the dissolution of ego boundaries, depicted by such manifest content as drowning or being engulfed by both inanimate objects and me. These dreams and transference feelings were not in themselves threatening. After he began to believe that I could not fulfill his omnipotent expectations, he developed chaotic tantrums. Direct observations of children sometimes illustrate similar factors, Bettelheim (1964) and Ekstein (1966) give many examples of the emotional upheaval of autistic children, children whose disorder has conceptualized in terms of the symbiotic phase (Mahler, 1952) of development.

The following situation illustrates the genesis of a tantrum within the context of the symbiotic phase: An eleven-month boy toddler was being observed through a one-way mirror as he played, his mother sitting quietly in the background. He crawled on the floor and handled many different toys, some of them being fairly complicated. At times, he was obviously frustrated but he never turned to his mother for help. He totally ignored her, never even looking at her, and ploddingly continued handling the various toys.

The mother unobtrusively left the room as planned. Although her son seemed to have ignored her presence and hardly noticed her departure, he suddenly broke down into a fierce tantrum. He screamed, thrashed, and kicked, and banged his head on the floor. He was inconsolable when a staff member tried to calm him. Finally the mother came back into the room and although the child did not acknowledge her entrance, his tantrum disappeared instantaneously and he continued playing as previously, once again ignoring her presence.

In the history of this boy's illness, and in the observations on the adult patient, primitive rage occurred in the context of a symbiotic developmental phase. The child could maintain a *defiant autonomy* as long as the mother was around. He seemed to be controlling her, but within the symbiotic context, she was vital for his equilibrium. When she left, he ceased functioning. Both the child and my patient demonstrate that the mother or analyst is necessary as an auxiliary or fused ego to maintain ego coherence and functioning. Withdrawal, or the inadequacy of the symbiotic partner to fulfill needs, led to a disintegration which was manifested by purposeless rage.

The paranoid defense can also be viewed in terms of symbiosis. This patient and others have had mothers who use their children as narcissistic extensions of their hated selves. For many reasons (which are not necessarily pertinent here), they are threatened by their children's structuralization beyond the symbiotic fusion; i.e., by their individuation. As a result further structuralization is perceived as dangerous by the child and later, as an adult, the paranoid projection can represent a defense against this danger.

In contrast to the previous rage reactions which seemed to be associated with an inability to maintain "autonomy" within the context of symbiotic fusion, the paranoid response in my patient represented an attempt to keep himself from being "swallowed" by the hovering, engulfing maternal imago. This response represented a movement "away" from symbiosis, an attempt to rid himself of intrusive psychic elements.

In a well-established, therapeutic relationship the paranoid material gradually becomes less grim. The patient not only begins to look at his reactions with curiosity, but even when discussing persecutors, he does so in a calm and sometimes amused fashion. My patient was able to recall the benign voices as he began seeing the unreality of some of his paranoid beliefs. He was then able to attribute some good intentions to his persecutors and was finally able to give them the capacity to behave logically and wisely. These changes occurred shortly before he entered what I have called the phase of institutionalized paranoia.

Studying paranoid projections carefully frequently reveals a benign and partially synthesized core beneath the externalized anger.

In order to preserve themselves from the mother's assaultiveness, some paranoid patients "fragment" and the *healthier* parts of their egos are projected into the outer world. They have to protect better-structured elements of the self from their perception of the maternal imago as vengeful and intolerant of individuation. Whereas the toddler "denied" his symbiotic attachment, these patients have reached another stage where projection is the dominant mechanism.

True, the projections usually contain hostile destructive elements and are experienced as persecutory, but this may represent a superstructure. The maternal introject's destructiveness is superimposed upon better structured ego fragments. The fragmenting process represents an attempt to maintain a degree of autonomy and individuation, as well as a striving for further development. Even though this is a psychotic reaction, it is still an attempt to maintain synthesis. Its direction is forward, a progression with the eventual goal of further structuralization and ego development. This paranoid reaction is designed to prevent a submergence of the self into a symbiotic fusion where all elements of individuation are lost.

By keeping the healthier parts of the ego, to some extent, externalized alongside the maternal introject, he has better control of the latter as it threatens the former. The maternal introject gradually loses its dangerous significance and the projected elements can once again become integrated back into the psyche as structured and nondisruptive.

Thus, the anger and aggression associated with paranoid reactions can be viewed as adaptive and thereby alter our therapeutic focus.

Summary

Angry, violent reactions were conceptualized in terms of an hierarchal continuum, purposeless tantrums representing the primitive end of the spectrum and active, nonhostile, aggressive behavior in the service of mastery, the other. The intermediary positions emphasized paranoid mechanisms leading to persecutory delusions, followed by angry involvement at a more socialized level with various causes. The latter was referred to as an institutionalized paranoia.

The adaptive and disruptive aspects of the above responses were discussed. In this context, the corresponding ego states were described and the clinical reactions of anger and violence were examined, both in terms of structure and their economic position in the developmental continuum.

Chapter 13

Regressed States, Timelessness, and Ego Synthesis

The concept of regression is of fundamental importance to the ego processes underlying psychoanalytic activity. Freud's (1900) description of the three types of regression and of their significance as defensive reactions has led to many insights about the nature of the analytic interaction.

Today, some analysts believe that psychoanalytic treatment is effective in cases suffering from characterological problems. The regressive reactions of these patients can be studied in an ego-psychological context, and their potential as a positive integrative factor, as well as their defensive qualities, can be scrutinized.

Alexander (1956) and Winnicott (1955), among others, have considered regression in terms of its constructive potential in psychoanalytic treatment.

Rather than viewing regression in its total context, e.g., as a developmental vicissitude, or as an aspect of creativity (Kris, 1950b), I wish to emphasize its role in analysis as well as the quality of the regressed ego state from which structuralization occurs during psychoanalytic treatment.

Various ego functions are highlighted during regression insofar as they lose their previous synthesis. The sense of time has been studied by many analysts (e.g., see Eissler, 1952, and Cohn, 1957) since Freud (1915b) postulated the timelessness of the unconscious. The regression of the time function will be discussed as an intrinsic factor in analytic integration.

Some Aspects of Analytic Regression

The analysis of some patients has been considered impossible because their fixation points go back to narcissistic preverbal states. The analytic regression supposedly recapitulates these primitive phases, which preclude verbal understanding. Interpretations are supposedly meaning-

First published in *Psa. Forum* 4 (1972), 294–309. Reprinted by permission.

less to these patients. It has been stressed repeatedly, however, that regression in analysis is not identical with the corresponding fixation point. The ego does not revert totally to primitive patterns, nor does it lose its structure (topographical regression) in a continuous degenerative fashion. Regression is, to some extent, always uneven and selective. Even though the patient's psyche may have qualities characteristic of primitive development, the soma, in general, is still physiologically mature. Usually the patient can still talk, maintain continence, and have sufficient reality testing to perceive, and communicate to the analyst. In severe regressions, as in catatonia, even some of these functions may be lost. However, patients who are able to come to the analyst's office retain some later acquired functions even though significant portions of their egos revert to patterns like that of the neonate.

Regression to phases that presumably correspond to preverbal phases makes manifest certain ego mechanisms that are relevant to emotional development. The study of the antecedents of later adaptational techniques is also significant for our understanding of how the analytic interaction promotes structuralization.

Perception of Time and Regression

The capacity to discriminate past, present, and future represents an ego mechanism that has considerable adaptational significance. The time sense is fundamental to reality testing and is considered one of the higher ego functions. Insofar as the ego is under the sway of the id in regressed states, the time sense undergoes degeneration. Discriminations about the passage of time become harder to make, and the distinctions between past, present, and future are blurred. During analysis the patient sometimes is surprised when the session is over, feeling that it has just begun; in other instances a few minutes seem interminably long. Granted that the fantasied gratification of infantile needs or the pressure of resistance are variables that distort the patient's perception of the length of the session, there is still a faulty time sense due to the relative loss of secondary-process organization. During treatment many patients with characterological disorders recapitulate the timelessness of the unconscious that Freud postulated.

There is a partial loss of reality testing in all analytic patients. This impairment will affect all ego systems and determines the quality of the regressed ego state. "Analytic" time differs from secondary-process time. The perceptual system is involved in the functioning of all ego systems; its perception of time is an important factor that is involved in efficient, reality-oriented, well-synthesized executive responses. During regression, ego systems revert to primitive functioning that includes the distortion of the time sense.

Identity and Structure

Closely connected with the time sense is the identity sense. The definition of identity is an involved and controversial subject. For the purpose of this paper I will consider *identity,* the *identity sense* and the *self-representation* as synonymous terms (*identity* being simply the person's view of himself at any particular moment).

The analytic regression, to some extent, involves the self-representation as it does the time sense and other ego functions. The regressive movement, however, primarily involves ego systems that are the least stable and the most vulnerable to trauma. In cases suffering from characterological problems, the defenses compensating for ego defects are affected profoundly by regression, and the malfunctioning of the underlying ego systems becomes more apparent. Both the self-representation and reality testing are highlighted since these patients have special problems in these areas.

The so-called borderline patient has some difficulty in perceiving himself in a coherent, organized fashion. Instead, he often has doubts about his existence. He does not know where he fits in the general scheme. Sometimes he is unable to perceive his inner needs—feelings of hunger, excretory urges, etc., being diffuse and amorphous. His ego lacks synthesis, and he has not been able to integrate inner and outer percepts with a time continuity into his self-representation.

A self-representation that is poorly structured undergoes interesting changes during the analytic regression. Even though distorted, the formation of the identity sense "in reverse" can be observed, and inferences about the antecedents of the self-representation can be made. The latter are especially important because the construction of the self-representation is intimately involved with ego structuralization in general.

Analytic Regression and the Therapeutic Process

The projection of archaic imagos characteristic of transference occurs in analysis when the ego or parts of the ego have undergone regression. Regression is thus an intrinsic aspect of the development of transference as the therapeutic process is set in motion. Similarly, the primitive functioning of various ego systems can be a factor that is essential to the analytic interaction. Winnicott (1955) believes that the regressed patient who gives up relatively mature adaptive functioning may achieve an ego state that antedates (at least in fantasy) the infantile trauma. Consequently, the ego is better able to assimilate positive integrative experiences. Elsewhere (chapter 20), I have described how the patient regresses to a state prior to the formation of disruptive introjects and thereby makes possible the introjection of the nonanxious understanding analyst, leading to the development of the self-observing function.

Patients with severe psychopathology have had a constantly traumatic environment, as described by Khan (1964) in his concept of "cumulative trauma." They attempt in the transference regression to recreate the frustrating and withholding environment (chapter 11). In addition, these patients also experience themselves in a fashion that seems to antedate the formation of the sense of organized identity.

Case Report

A "borderline" patient in his middle thirties illustrated the regression of the identity sense in a dramatic fashion. He entered treatment because he was generally dissatisfied with his way of life. Despite his high salary, he did not like his job. He believed he should do something creative but was unable to decide what he would like to pursue. He was single, had practically no friends, and led a solitary, lonely existence.

He felt life drifting by and was aware of how time dragged. He felt the days to be interminable and could obtain relief only by withdrawing into sleep. During weekends he might spend practically all of his time in bed; sometimes he found this experience pleasurable, time then speeding by much too swiftly until he would have to face the world again.

He had a vague concept as to who and what he was. He saw no purpose in his empty life but was able to imagine himself as a professional person. He had set up ideals for himself, some of which he believed I would oppose. Even though his identity sense was diffuse, he had been able to erect defenses to preserve some coherence in his self-representation. He used compulsive mechanisms to adhere rigidly to a picture of himself that he valued, e.g., the image of a well-bred, genteel aristocrat. His rebelliousness was designed to preserve an acceptable image of himself. If he could believe that others (e.g., the analyst) would not permit him autonomy, then he could fight for an independent identity. The reconstruction of his past revealed why he needed to feel that external objects were robbing him of the opportunity to construct solid ego boundaries.

In analysis, he rather quickly saw me as a person who wanted to "smother" him and make him into an appendage of myself. This type of projection was short-lived. It was followed by a phase where he no longer fought me and did not see me as trying to incorporate him.

His regression was now manifested by the loss of previous patterns of behavior. His personal habits deteriorated markedly. Previously neat and punctilious, he now dressed shabbily and was unkempt and often unshaven. He became undependable in his daily commitments. He managed to keep his appointments with me, but he was frequently late or sometimes very early.

The patient was aware of increasing disorganization, and at first displayed considerable anxiety. He showed many of the signs of ego disintegration described by Erikson (1959) as the "identity diffusion syndrome." He was afraid of "falling apart," and he indicated that his decompensation was caused by my interpretation of the defenses by which he had sought to maintain a coherent self-image—defenses that manifested themselves as resistance against regression in the transference.

In spite of the patient's discomfort, he did derive some relief from the analytic relationship. After several months, his anxiety gradually subsided and he was able to idealize me as an omnipotent rescuer. He relaxed and felt a "Nirvana" type of equanimity.

His self-image underwent some interesting changes. Frequently, he felt he did not exist and experienced a sense of void or vacuum, which was not always painful. At times he had sensations of floating in empty dark space, which he conjectured were similar to the state before he was born.

There was a significant difference between the patient's reactions to the empty void and what has been described as the identity-diffusion syndrome, a state of ego dissolution. During the latter, he was visibly agitated; now, he felt peaceful infantile satisfaction. Gradually, however, he indicated restlessness and dissatisfaction with this amorphous identity.

During the sessions, the patient's time sense was similar to the dreamer's. He lost all perspective and sometimes felt, when the session was over, that only a few minutes had passed. He described a sensation of "timelessness" which was alternately pleasant and frightening. He experienced anxiety when he became aware of his loss of control and when he could no longer feel secure in the omnipotence he had projected onto the analyst.

Discussion

Though the regressive process is selective, and various ego systems are affected more than others, all such systems are somewhat involved during analysis. The identity and time sense are focused upon because changes in these functions are conspicuous in patients suffering from characterological problems. The psychoneurotic patient also, to a lesser degree, reports attitudes and feelings that indicate there has been a regressive change in his identity and time sense. In him, too, momentary dissociations and transient lapses of subjective time are common.

Can the clinician make inferences about the psychic processes of "forward" development from his observation of the reversion to earlier modes of functioning? Maladaptations and compensatory defenses have led to defects in structure and functional distortions. Consequently, one would not expect that regression would simply parallel relatively non-pathological development in the reverse direction.

The transference neurosis is our most valuable therapeutic tool. In its context, the analyst has the opportunity of learning not only about the regression of ego systems, but also about their subsequent development and structuralization. The latter enables the clinician to learn about the psychic processes underlying psychoanalytic treatment.

Though my patient had a characterological problem and his regression was "deep," I believe the inferences about the therapeutic process in such cases have some general applicability. In the psychoneurotic patient, regression may occasionally reach levels comparable to those seen in more disturbed patients, but there is less disruption than in patients with characterological problems. The psychoneurotic is more resilient in recovering his reality testing and integration rather quickly. However, the effectiveness of analysis in the psychoneuroses is, to a large measure, dependent upon the depth of regression these patients are able to achieve. Despite different facets of analytic resolution in these less fixated patients, there are also similarities to cases such as the patient described in this paper. Characterologic development occurs in all successfully analyzed patients, and the changes in the regressed state that follow therapeutic intervention have certain homogeneous features for both groups of patients.

Kanzer (1967) raised cogent questions concerning regressed states, stressing the difference between a patient's reactions and the ego state of the neonate. There is a marked difference, and what the patient reports has considerable retrospective reconstruction. When a hypnotized subject acts as if he is in utero, he is describing and behaving on the basis of his adult, sophisticated concept of intrauterine existence.

Nevertheless, a patient's changed behavior shows a different kind of organization. In some ways he is less efficient than before the regression and less able to cope with reality, as reflected in his appearance, actions, and words. His disintegration lasts for hours, days, or even longer, in contrast to the momentary disassociation that sometimes occurs in a well-integrated ego. On a comparative basis, he is reacting in a more "primitive" fashion, although, as Kanzer correctly emphasizes, some mature functions are preserved during the regression.

Identity and Time Sense

The changes that occur in the regressed identity sense are of particular interest since they occur whenever there is analytic progress. Both intrapsychic conflict and traumatic experiences affect the self-representation. Any sustained stimulus will have an effect upon the ego and involve all ego systems. Shifts in ego equilibrium will result in some change in the self-image (see chapter 9). Even in psychoneurotic patients, if the analyst directs his attention to material referring to the self-representation, he will note that it undergoes important changes dependent upon the degree of regression or progression.

The self-image develops gradually during infancy until it achieves sufficient consolidation so it can be considered functional. Whether this occurs with the smiling response, "eight-month anxiety," or negation (Spitz, 1957), is conjectural. Any such achievement parallels the development of object relations and the time sense.

My patient started treatment with problems about his self-concept but also with some overcompensatory defenses. When the latter were difficult to maintain because of interpretation, his underlying insecurity about his *existing* became apparent. The final, most regressed state was one where he experienced void and timelessness. This had some similarities to an ego state that is antecedent to the sense of being.

The regression seemed to approximate an early infantile ego where the self-representation was embryonic and amorphous. Again, it must be repeated that this was not an exact reproduction of infancy, because in the regression he "brought back" many later experiences which made his percepts considerably more sophisticated. Nevertheless, the lack of structure eventually became intolerably painful.

This painful state became the impetus for ego integration. Instead of forming pathological defenses he seemed to develop adaptive mechanisms that were realistic and object-directed rather than being compensatory denials. When he felt most anxious, he was particularly impressed because—and commented that—I did not seem anxious. This gave him considerable reassurance. The patient gradually introjected the analyst's nonanxious understanding orientation and developed a self-observing attitude. For example, he began to consider where he stood concerning his world, profession, friends, philosophy, etc., and he was able to crystallize certain goals. At first, he took over, by imitation, some of my personal attitudes which he had been able to detect through various clues that he perceived. Later he was able to select what was most appropriate to his training and background and to reject other aspects of my personality. He acquired the ability to view the future in terms of present and past time. Consequently, the interaction of self-observations, the sequence from imitation to selective identification, and the searching in the outer world for something meaningful, led to an integration characterized by a consolidation of the self-representation, increased self-esteem, and a better-developed time sense.

Is it necessary for patients to experience such painful regressions in order to gain impetus for structuralization? Such ego states are frequent occurrences in the treatment of patients suffering from characterological defects, but a generalization cannot be made for all patients. Furthermore, one does not gain the impression that it is simply the painful features that produce progressive changes. In some situations a painful state may lead to further disruption or to rigid unanalyzable defenses.

Still, the question can be modified as to whether some patients have to undergo an experience where, for a time, they partially recapitulate a timeless state such as that which precedes the formation of the sense of being and its corresponding sense of time and continuity of existence, in order to gain ego structure. Does the resolution of intrapsychic conflict require a regression to "analytic time" so that better secondary process can develop? To some extent, the regression to a void may be an intrinsic aspect of the analytic process, the development of secondary-process time and identity synthesis. In psychoneurotic patients these movements may occur "silently" without great pain. Insofar as there is a superstructure of oedipal conflict and corresponding defenses, these underlying character changes are not apparent but may become so during transient deep regressions. Cases suffering from severe psychopathology, on the other hand, are not so "silent" in revealing basic character structure and regressive or progressive changes in various ego systems.

I believe that the consistent analytic setting in which such an amorphous ego occurs accounts for progression rather than further regression and rigid defenses. Because of the constant reliability of the psychoanalytic situation, disruptive introjects can be projected onto the analyst and the regressed patient is better able to incorporate adaptive experiences and to make use of the analyst's secondary process as he makes interpretations (see Boyer and Giovacchini, 1967).

Interpretation and Verbalization

Interpretation is the means by which the patient gains understanding of inner psychic elements. Whether the patient's lack of self-perception is due to repression or to a lack of integrative and synthetic ego mechanisms, or both, the analyst promotes secondary-process qualities by his interpretations. The patient, in a sense, "borrows" the analyst's secondary process in the course of developing his own secondary-process operations. Both the time sense and the self-representation are involved in this synthesis.

The analytic setting and the analyst's integrative interpretations provide a setting where the borderline patient can synthesize disparate fragmented introjects, unimpeded by the analyst's impingements. This setting fosters the experience of primary-process qualities such as timelessness. However, as the analyst confronts the patient with organized interpretations of his inchoate, incomprehensible inner world, he is introducing order. The patient often reacts to interpretation by converting timelessness into a sense of "becoming," and in so doing begins to develop ego structure from the initial regressed state.

If the analyst maintains the interpretative approach, he is limiting his therapeutic activity to the observational frame of reference. Both he and the patient are *looking* at disorganization rather than *participating* in it. If the analyst abandons the interpretative approach and offers "help" for the patient's helplessness, then he has shifted from the observational frame of reference to another. He has accepted the patient's helplessness as a reality that requires action.

Interpretation also has a replenishing action. Frequently, patients present associations or dreams where the interpretation has acquired a concrete quality and is considered a gift. It may also be conceived of in a negative fashion, as an attacking weapon (Sanford, 1966). When the patient is in a state of regressive decompensation, however, he usually reacts positively to interpretations which in many instances "fill up" the void.

This regressed state represents the void or nothingness from which the patient can develop vital psychic functions. Interpretation leads to structure, but it is also the means by which the patient defends himself against the psychic equivalent of death. The analyst periodically replenishes the patient by bringing him back into the observational frame of reference, saving him from being "swallowed and lost" in his disorganization. Patients with characterological defects reveal these fears in dreams of drowning, and of houses and platforms crumbling beneath them. Some patients convert the analytic relationship into an interminable one, much as the diabetic requires his periodic dose of insulin in order to survive.

A patient described the above situation by comparing himself to an electric bug. This contrivance could explore in many different directions, but it could not travel too far from an electric light socket.

Periodically, it had to plug itself into the socket and recharge itself so it could then go back to its travels. The analysis was represented by the socket and supplied sufficient organization so that the patient could function. This patient found that during an analytic session he and the analyst became observers. Interpretations helped him distance himself from his inner chaos, and he then was able to achieve sufficient structure to master both inner and outer problems. However, unless he was able to return to the analytic session, he would gradually shift from the observational frame of reference and become "immersed" in his intra-psychic turmoil.

To be able to put an inchoate feeling, perhaps of preverbal vintage, into words is a structuralizing experience. What was initially primitive has gained considerable secondary process during the process of verbalization.

Loewenstein (1956) refers to different functional categories of speech, ranging from emotive appeal to communication. Verbalization is instrumental in making a person aware of inner feelings, and is an important aspect of self-observation. Freud (1915b) repeatedly emphasized that the auditory image becomes linked with instinctual content, leading to a psychic state that has considerable structure. Similarly, Loewenstein discusses the different functions of speech as being characteristic of various ego states, communication being the most advanced, and emotive appeal, the most primitive, or regressed, state.

Hayman (1965) also stresses the secondary-process function of speech. Interpretations are usually verbal communications. In addition to the positive aspects of insight, the verbal form of interpretations in itself has structuralizing qualities.

Hayman reminds us that the child can understand words before he can speak. The ability to integrate a verbal communication precedes the development of the capacity to form one's own verbal images.

The question is often raised as to whether the primitively fixated or regressed patient is able to use interpretations. His ego is described as being organized at a preverbal level and not containing the sophisticated integrative mechanisms that make an interpretation understandable. On the other hand, as with the child, the preverbal ego is capable of considerable comprehension. Although it might not be obvious, even the catatonic has retained most of his auditory comprehension.

Development of the capacity to understand and produce words parallels the development of the identity and time sense. The patient retains these auditory images as part of his memory system. Insofar as interpretation refers to some facet of the patient's psychic structure, observations incorporated into the memory system become self-observations.

The organization inherent in these verbal traces gives the patient a concept of how his mind works.

The analyst's exclusive preoccupation is with the patient's psychic functioning. Every interpretation refers to some operational aspect of his personality. The analyst puts into words what was unknown to the patient.

For a variety of reasons, the patient has been unable to achieve such an understanding on his own. Patients suffering from severe psychopathology do not have the synthesizing capacities to form verbal constructs that refer to mental operations. The analyst's interpretation furnishes such a verbal construct. As Loewald (1960) has emphasized, this also constitutes a structuralizing experience for the patient. *Because of the interpretation's verbal form it has greater structure than that which it describes.* As the patient is able to integrate the interpretation and develop insight he is acquiring a view of himself that is more organized than he actually is. However, as his self-perception contains relatively more secondary-process synthesis, that which is being perceived also gains coherence. The act of perception and the percept belong to the same frame of reference. *Consequently, the patient gains structure by perceiving himself in a more integrated fashion.*

Clusters of self-perceptions lead to the formation of identity. As they become organized in the ego they become crystallized into the self-representation. Therefore, the introjection of interpretations is a pertinent aspect of the acquisition of a structured identity.

Insofar as interpretation includes a discussion of the present transference situation in terms of its antecedents and hopeful implications about future reactions, these verbal traces also include a temporal perspective. The present is compared to the past and separated from the future. The intimate relationship between the identity sense and the time sense is highlighted during the analytic regression where past, present, and even future identities are revealed.

Summary

A case of a man suffering from a characterological disorder highlights some aspects of the analytic interaction that are not as obvious in the psychoneuroses.

The therapeutic potential of the regressed ego is an important factor in psychoanalytic treatment. Some patients regress to a state that approximates, but is far from identical with, a preverbal, neonatal ego. This state precedes the formation of the identity and the time sense and is experienced as a void which is not always unpleasant.

The psychoanalytic process is promoted by adaptational techniques to overcome the void. These adaptations lead to a secondary process concept of time and identity synthesis, two structuralizing experiences that parallel one another.

Interpretation is the means by which ego structure is achieved during psychoanalytic treatment. In addition to the integrative effects of insight, the verbal quality of most interpretations also leads to ego structure.

Chapter 14

The Symbiotic Phase

The psychoanalytic viewpoint extends to the so-called deeper and more primitive layers of the personality. Eventually most clinical formulations center on an early and important developmental phase—the symbiotic phase. Here I wish to explore further both the clinical and the theoretical aspects of this early ego state, which seems to be so relevant to understanding psychopathology, emotional development, and treatment.

Since Freud's revolutionary discoveries, early childhood experiences have been recognized as fundamental to our assessment of character structure, defensive and adjustive modalities, and general psychic equilibrium of both child and adult. Since such experiences always include another person, they must be considered in terms of the adaptive or disruptive qualities of object relationships.

Freud (1918) reconstructed the infantile neurosis retrospectively while analyzing adults. Study of the transference neurosis enables one to evaluate how early object relationships have contributed to the current ego organization. Memories of the adult patient about his childhood may be the product of considerable distortion. Some analysts do not think that the exact reconstruction of past realities is particularly important for therapeutic management. But in order to assess the etiological significance of early object relationships on later psychic structure, one has to deal with more than the adult patient's fantasies or memories in which external objects are more or less revised. Still, there is always a reality basis for the archaic transference projections that occur during analysis.

Another research method that has recently achieved popularity is the longitudinal approach. Here one can observe early relationships that do not necessarily lead to psychopathology and are therefore more relevant to the study of normal development. As is true of experiments in general, introducing an observer changes the data, but this factor can be minimized and taken into account. Observing a continuum from the neonatal state to adulthood is valuable, and the data collected have a kind of relevance different from those obtained from studying the transference neurosis.

First published in *Tactics and Techniques in Psychoanalytic Therapy*, Vol. I, ed. P. Giovacchini (New York: Jason Aronson, Inc., 1972), pp. 137–69. Reprinted by permission.

Theoretical Considerations

Data acquire significance only when they can be placed in a conceptual framework. Etiology can be established when process connections can be made among various phenomena and these intermediary links are placed in a consistent theoretical system. Theoretical elaborations frequently lead to predictions about heretofore unnoticed phenomena.

Freud (1900) constructed a comprehensive theoretical system based primarily upon a topographic framework and oriented chiefly around what he later referred to as the id. His metapsychology was biologically oriented, and he postulated a sequence of developmental stages that are determined by increasing maturation. The influence of external objects was recognized but not particularly emphasized except for their traumatic potential.

With the addition of the structural hypothesis to metapsychology (Freud, 1923), the ego was given a more central position in the psychic apparatus. Both reality and psychic systems (the superego and the id) were considered relative to the ego. Introducing the ego viewpoint enabled certain areas, such as object relations, to be more meaningfully integrated into the theoretical edifice.

Ego psychology is a particularly appropriate conceptual frame of reference for studying both efficient adaptation and disruptive psychopathology. This is especially true if the vantage point of observation is the transference neurosis. As the patient regresses to earlier modes of adaptation and projects archaic introjects onto the analyst, both the analyst and the patient have the opportunity to learn how these introjects "precipitates of past object cathexes" (Freud, 1923) are utilized in the service of adaptation and structuralization or how they impede development and cause characterological defects and fixations.

The study of the transference neurosis is essentially a study of different grades of psychopathology, including the psychoneuroses, since psychodynamic conflicts also involve significant persons in the patient's past. However, as implied above, ego psychology, by conceptualizing the influence of early object relations on the operations of ego systems (perceptual, executive, and integrative), focuses upon developmental factors in a microscopic fashion. The latter also has implications for the therapeutic process.

Ego psychology is also a useful framework for a phenomenological approach, which is characteristic of longitudinal anterospective studies. More subtle (unconscious) motivations and "microscopic" ego operations are not discernible when surface behavior is studied. However, such reactions as aggression and techniques of mastery can be viewed in the context of object relations and maturation and development. Behavior, therefore, can be scrutinized in terms of its affective and motoric components; object relationships are the axis around which adaptive techniques become increasingly refined or psychopathologically fixated.

In a psychotherapeutic context Freud discussed adaptation in terms of psychoeconomics, which was based upon a hydrodynamic, drive-energy-discharge hypothesis. Energy resides in the libidinal reservoir (Freud, 1915b) of the unconscious (later referred to as the "id"); as it pushes forward, it creates a tension state that seeks discharge. This is essentially a stimulus-response model where the stimulus originates within the organism, although Freud also acknowledged the influence of the external world upon inner impulses and needs. Nonetheless, the chief emphasis was on how organic tensions become psychologically elaborated and seek reduction of tension.

The concept of psychic energy in the context of a dualistic instinct theory has been fundamental to our understanding of a developmental hierarchy. Both Freud (1923, 1926b) and Hartmann et al. (1949) wrote about the fusion of drives—a process, when proceeding toward integration, called "neutralization." Others (Colby, 1955) have criticized the chemical analogy implicit in the term. Neutralization is the outcome of the fusion of libidinal and aggressive energies and leads to secondary-process-directed activities. If one restricts this process to energic considerations without including ego structure, it is difficult to understand how the fusion of two primary-process-oriented elements can lead to secondary-process operations. Rapaport (1966) and Gill (1963) have discussed the "taming" of affects insofar as primitive energies become bound to "higher" ego structures. But here again energy is considered in terms of a drive-discharge hypothesis with an implied independent status.

A psychology based upon a centrally placed regulatory ego is more internally consistent when energic sources are not restricted to instinctual impulses (Boyer and Giovacchini, 1967; Giovacchini, 1966b). The gratification of an impulse by setting the ego's executive apparatus into motion requires energy. The impulse is the psychic representation of a need that results from an upset of homeostatic equilibrium. The ego's sensory systems perceive changes in the homeostasis if the ego is sufficiently developed, unless repressive forces are operating. Energy is required for repression as well as for perception and the cathexis of adaptive techniques that will gratify the impulse. Energy, however, is not part of the need but is mobilized from an organic-metabolic reservoir in response to homeostatic shifts; energy then makes possible the operation of various ego systems. When either external demands are made or internal needs are stimulated, appropriate psychic systems are cathected (energized) in order to master the problem created by such demands. In some instances this can lead to a feeling of tension, but the mastery of tension-producing needs does not require a discharge concept. Nothing is discharged; no quanta of energy are involved. Rather, various ego systems become functionally active as a response to these needs and reestablish homeostasis. The achieved homeostasis is not necessarily a quiescent state but merely a well-balanced one. After satisfying certain basic needs a person may seek other gratifications; he may create his own needs and pursue more integrated levels of adaptation.*

The course of emotional development can be viewed as a series of adaptations of varying degrees of complexity. The passage from childhood to adulthood, a developmental continuum, can easily be conceptualized as a hierarchical structuralization of the psychic apparatus. All psychic elements, drives, and sensory and adaptational systems undergo progressive structuralization. The neonate's requirements are fundamentally biological and his techniques of mastery and adaptation are minimal. He is totally dependent upon external objects. With maturation and satisfactory nurture (somatic and emotional) and as his range of perceptual sensitivity widens, his needs become more structured. More avenues of satisfaction are open to him; as he learns to introject and assimilate gratifying experiences with external objects, his executive capacities also expand.

From a state of primitive biological helplessness, the psychic apparatus becomes progressively refined. However, the more advanced state of integration is a structural accretion to earlier states of organization. Just as the soma contains numerous types of cells and organs, ranging from primitive embryonic tissue and unstructured connective tissue cells to highly complex systems (such as the brain), the psyche also contains its developmental origins. Freud's (1900) concept that the ego evolves from the id is a prototype for a theory of psychic structure that contains a series of elements representing all stages of development.

Every psychic structure, therefore, can be viewed as a hierarchical continuum that recapitulates the various stages of emotional development. Psychological systems are not rigidly fixed; earlier types of adaptation can become recathected under specific circumstances such as psychopathology, environmental stress, and others that are not necessarily pathological (for example, creativity). This hierarchical ego-psy-

Experiencing a need is not necessarily painful. The psyche may feel stimulated but instead of experiencing disruptive tension it reacts with pleasurable anticipation. Freud's (1905b) remarks on forepleasure are particularly apt.

chological model does not require a hydrodynamic-energic-discharge hypothesis; instead, it emphasizes structure-producing factors. These factors, in turn, focus upon the structure-promoting or psychopathology-producing qualities of object relationships.

Developmental Factors

The newborn is not fully developed neurologically, and, as experiments suggest (Reisen, 1947), there is considerable autonomic instability and an incomplete perceptual sensory organization. From these findings and the neonate's global dependency, it seems plausible to postulate an early stage of development in which the child does not feel that he is a separate unit apart and distinct from the surrounding world.

A study of adults during regression in analysis indicates the existence of an early phase in which the boundaries of the ego are not yet formed and the self and the outer world are not separate and distinct. This phase is supposedly characterized by a megalomanic omnipotence where wishes are magically fulfilled. Insofar as the child feels that he is part of his mother, his needs and their gratification are not separated. From the study of infants and the retrospective reconstructions of adults, this early stage of development is conceptualized as a symbiotic phase.

Benedek (1938, 1949, 1956), who focuses upon the mothering process, and Mahler (1952, 1953), who is primarily interested in childhood psychosis, have discussed symbiosis extensively and presented convincing arguments for its usefulness as a postulate. For the sake of clarity it should be emphasized that the mother's need for the infant is not quite the same as his need for her (chapter 19). If symbiosis refers to an "equality" of needs, this early relationship has some parasitic elements. Still, mothering is a need that has developmental potential for the mother (Benedek, 1959). From the initial symbiosis there is a progressive maturation and development which leads to separateness and object relations (Mahler's separation-individuation phase). Spitz (1965) outlines certain crucial points in time, for example, at two to three months and at eight months of age, when the infant learns responses (smiling response, negation, and anxiety about strangers) that act as "organizers" for developmental spurts. In a similar fashion Erikson (1959) writes of epigenesis where structure leads to further structure.

These descriptions and formulations have explanatory significance for many direct observations of infants, but they are not intended to explain how development occurs and how the psychic apparatus acquires structure and adaptive techniques; these questions require a microscopic scrutiny of the development of object relations.

As stated above, reconstructions made from studying the transference neurosis point to the plausibility of postulating a symbiotic phase. Psychopathology, although distorting, also emphasizes psychic features that might otherwise go unnoticed. Fixation upon the symbiotic phase broadens our understanding of structuralizing processes by highlighting those factors that impede emotional development.

Adult patients who demonstrate difficulties in resolving their infantile symbiosis suffer from serious psychopathology, as do Mahler's child patients. Many are psychotic; some are thought to be borderline or suffering from characterological defects. Others (for example, some psychoneurotics) may not have such severe developmental problems, but in the transference regression are able to recapitulate symbiotic elements.

Clinical Considerations

The following vignettes will illustrate the effects of fixation upon the symbiotic phase.

A middle-aged patient found that he was unable to work. He felt totally paralyzed and incapable of coping with the external world, which he felt had become inordinately complex. He had no perception of himself as having a separate identity and had absolutely no interest in relating to anyone. He felt sorry for his wife because he knew she wanted to be kind and helpful, but he could not respond or even acknowledge her efforts. At first he felt strange, but later he found that he didn't care about anything in the outside world; he was only interested in his relationship with me. This patient had just changed jobs. He left a position that offered financial comfort and status but no hope for further advancement, and accepted one where his horizons were unlimited. Recently he had also married a woman with whom he had been having an affair for two years.

He began suffering from an inability to concentrate, which was sometimes accompanied by anxiety of paniclike intensity. Curiously, he stopped referring to his wife as such and called her his "girlfriend," as he had done before marriage. His associations were prominently oral; he was preoccupied with thoughts of swallowing and eating me or being eaten by me. He was also obsessed with the fear that I would kill him or that he would commit suicide. At first, the patient seemed to be expressing self-destructive guilt because of his vocational success and because of his marriage after so many years of bachelorhood. It was certainly a factor. However, he expressed very clearly that he was afraid of me in a way that went beyond the projection of his superego.

He believed that a job with upward mobility would lead to his separation from me; he equated upward mobility with independence. His previous job, insofar as no advancement was possible, meant a fixated state that posed no threat of change. He explained that having a wife gave him definite status (identity) as a married man, whereas a girlfriend made him feel that he was in an amorphous, ill-defined state. Although he was relatively comfortable in his niche, there were conflicts.

There were many facets to his fears. Thoughts of moving away from me (the symbiotic fusion) led him to be afraid of my anger. He believed that I wanted to maintain the status quo and would kill him if he showed any evidence of "growing away." He was also afraid that he would kill me if we separated. He fantasized that if he literally pulled away, he would tear some vital part out of me that would result in my death. He also wanted to kill me in order to get rid of the hated part of himself that had, to some extent, become projected into me through the symbiotic fusion. On the other hand, because of the fusion he believed that killing me would also constitute suicide.

In summary, all of his symptoms and transference reactions could be understood as the result of the dissolution of the mother-child symbiosis that was being reenacted in the transference regression. He was ambivalent: he wanted to feel autonomous and separated from me, but because such independence was frightening, in many fantasies he questioned whether he could survive without my "omnipotent support." Symbiotic fusion also meant annihilation of his psychic existence as an individual entity, and he experienced this with terror. Consequently, he was faced with the unbearable conflict of wanting an independent identity in the context of magical fusion.

A colleague (Borowitz, 1966) who has had considerable experience with children supplied me with the following material. He has obtained data from both the treatment of children and direct observation of the mother-child interaction that point to conclusions similar to those derived from the study of the transference neurosis in adults. For example, an institutionalized eleven-year-old boy who was autistically withdrawn had to be forcefully taken to his first therapy session. Once inside the consultation room he no longer struggled. He saw a stove in the corner of the room. Without saying a word he walked up to it and lay down in front of it, basking in its warmth but completely ignoring the therapist. Subsequent sessions were similar in that the child said nothing, did not acknowledge the therapist's presence, and continued to curl up in front of the stove. In spite of his apparent indifference, others were impressed when they noticed the boy eagerly running to his sessions, slowing down only as he passed through the consultation room door.

The patient needed to find a situation from which he could withdraw. The therapist respected this need by not intruding; finally, after several months, the patient started talking.

There are many direct observations of the mother-child relationship that have a meaning similar to the one described above. A toddler who could barely walk was playing very actively. His mother was sitting in the same room, one that had an ample supply of toys. He broke several of the toys and could not manage others, but he doggedly continued to play even though he obviously felt frustrated. The mother sat there quietly, but the child never turned to her for either help or comfort. The child displayed a remarkable independence which, in spite of the many frustrating toys, was characterized by determined calm. When the mother finally left the room, the child's reaction was rather surprising. Even though he had seemed to be nonchalant about her presence, he broke down completely when she left. His expression changed to terror and he had a temper tantrum. He looked miserable and began to engage in chaotic and purposeless screaming and kicking. Others entered the room to try to comfort him, but the tantrum only became worse. Nothing could pacify this child until his mother returned. She walked back into the room and he gave no sign that he even saw her; not once did he directly look at her, but his anguish vanished and he returned to his "autonomous" play.

These vignettes are examples of persons suffering from relatively severe psychopathology. Several psychic elements are particularly prominent. The adult patient at the beginning of analysis demonstrated a constricted development of drives. His needs were simple and minimal. To him, eating was a mechanical response to a feeling of hunger—a feeling that had no discriminating features. He had no appetite for any particular type of food. To him there was no distinction between oatmeal and caviar. His sexual drives were also poorly elaborated. He had no fantasies while masturbating; he described it as relieving himself of some ill-defined tension. In fact, he found the urge to defecate and urinate not particularly different from the sexual drive. In general he was not aware of any definitive sensations. He stated that at times he felt a vague uneasiness and then would have to "decide" whether he was hungry, needed to defecate, or was sexually aroused.

Such retarded development of drives is not infrequent. In such cases characterological development is distorted; both the drives and other psychic elements do not structuralize to a level that is characteristic of advanced development. This is illustrated by Spitz's (1957) dramatic and tragic examples.

In normal development the ego boundaries become consolidated after the dissolution of the symbiotic fusion. A fixation at the symbiotic stage also leads to a blurring of ego–non-ego boundaries, which has many manifestations. My patient often did not know what was not part of himself. He frequently demonstrated this during the transference regression, and he also spoke of other situations that could be explained by his inability to distinguish "me from not-me." For example, during his first week of analysis he often pounded the wall with his fist. In this way he would establish where his body (fist) ended and the outside world (wall) began. This patient had difficulty paying his bills, a not too unusual symptom. Paying money meant surrendering part of himself to me. Since his ego boundaries were so tenuous, he was sensitive to many situations that he believed threatened his integrity.

In other cases the blurring of ego boundaries is manifested by a lack of perceptual discrimination. What is, in fact, outside the self is perceived as belonging to the self. Consequently, the external object is only dimly perceived and its distinct qualities are not recognized. This frequently happens with obese and alcoholic patients. Often a markedly overweight patient does not really enjoy food. Bruch (1962) has described such phenomena. These patients rarely allow themselves to feel hungry and seldom have any appetite, a manifestation of a nondifferentiation of drives. But there is an added factor in that these patients do not distinguish between food and non-food; one patient actually did not know when she was eating. For her, eating had become a mechanical, automaton-like procedure; she did not cathect it sufficiently to be aware of what she was doing. Her basic pathology included a fluid ego boundary that encompassed the universe. If, by chance, she managed to perceive something outside of herself, it was only momentary because she was continually incorporating and maintaining a state similar to symbiotic fusion and infantile megalomania. This patient never had an organized meal where she sat down at the table at a prescribed time and ate a particular type of food appropriate to what is conventionally served at that time of day. Her eating habits reflected her general lack of structure; her ego was unable to relate to structured, distinct situations because her diffuse boundaries contained an amorphous, unorganized ego.

The same constellations can be found in many alcoholic patients. They do not enjoy liquor and are often unaware of what or whether they are drinking. One patient said that alcohol was one of her body secretions (see DeLevita, 1965). She could not buy anyone a drink because it would be equivalent to giving away part of herself, thereby establishing a distinction between herself and the surrounding world. When drunk she was very generous and wanted a drinking companion, but she said that at these times she was totally fused with her companion and so, emotion-

ally speaking, she was giving nothing away. Through a vicarious identification, she was merely providing herself with drinks; thus, she was not
forced to distinguish between herself and the outer world, that is, to
disrupt her symbiotic fixation. This patient was not aware of her drinking
(when she said that she never drank, she believed it) because she was
drinking all the time. Alcohol had become so much a part of her that she
did not perceive it as a separate entity, nor did she perceive drinking as a
specific activity.

When an individual cannot distinguish an external object as separate
from the self, there is a further problem in being able to perceive the self.
When early object relations have not led to structuralization beyond the
symbiotic phase, there are identity problems. The patients described
above had difficulty knowing who and what they were and they questioned the purpose of their existence. The obese patient sometimes
found that everything was hazy, including her body image, which
seemed to "blend" with her surroundings. At such a time she "forgot"
her name, profession, and other facts about herself that would identify
her as an individual. Similarly other patients, especially when the transference regression recapitulated the symbiotic fusion, lost their precarious sense of personal identity. There is a relationship between the loss
of identity and fixation upon the symbiotic phase.

Children demonstrate similar phenomena. Dramatic examples of the
malformation of a sense of identity are found in autistic children. Bettelheim (1964) describes a young autistic girl who had no organized identity. Her behavior reflected her preoccupation with boundaries and
borders, a manifestation of the diffuseness of her ego boundaries, which
were the result of an incomplete differentiation from a traumatic symbiosis. Many less dramatic examples are associated with lesser degrees
of psychopathology, demonstrating similar problems and emphasizing
the correlation between diffuseness of the sense of identity and the
degree of symbiotic fixation. Identity is discussed here only from a
phenomenological perspective; to pursue the operational aspects of
identity is beyond the scope of this chapter.

One aspect of identity, however, is related to arrested development
and object relations. A person's executive style is a significant aspect
of his sense of identity (chapter 1). Techniques of mastery and control
of inner impulses are an important aspect of the self-representation, and
vicissitudes in this area are easily observed in children.

At one extreme are the tragic children described by Spitz (1957) who
achieved practically no techniques of mastery or control. Because they
were emotionally impoverished by the complete lack of object relations,
these children never even progressed to the symbiotic level. In other

instances, especially when the symbiotic fusion is traumatic, a peculiar kind of "autonomy" may develop. When the child's psychic integrity (his very existence) has been impinged upon (see Winnicott, 1952), a defensive type of insulation may occur. Winnicott (1949) described the development of a "false self" as a reaction to a traumatic, assaultive environment. This self cannot generally be integrated into the ego and is not synchronous with a cohesive, synthesized ego organization. It is a "false self"—a product of an incomplete differentiation from a constricting and threatening symbiotic fusion.

To relinquish control to others, to relax, and to trust external objects are impossible for these children. In cases of severe psychopathology, the child may shut out the external world completely. The extreme counterpart of this condition in the adult is the catatonic, who, by his withdrawal, maintains megalomanic control. In children, usually under one year of age, there are stereotyped repetitive movements that constitute part of their autistic withdrawal. It is impressive how totally preoccupied body-rockers or head-bangers are with what they are doing and how utterly oblivious they are of their surroundings. It would appear that they are flamboyantly demonstrating that they do not require the environment, that they can maintain themselves without any outside help. Insofar as this is an infantile megalomanic orientation, their methods of control are primitive, rigid, and robotlike in nature. Older children sometimes show similar automatonlike, controlling behavior. If they mature physically (there may be retardation at the somatic level), this behavior becomes elaborated into an obsessional ritual. If there is sufficient involvement with reality so that the adult does not catatonically withdraw, complex obsessional systems may develop.

It is, of course, impossible to know from direct observation what automaton behavior, such as head-banging or body-rocking, means in a child under one year of age. Still, inferences can be drawn from the treatment of adults. For example, an adult patient sought treatment because his obsessional rituals had become so time consuming and constricting that he found it was almost impossible to carry on his routine activities. He reported he was told that, as a child, he had been a body-rocker and head-banger. Although these symptoms in other children may be sporadic, transient, and not necessarily a sign of severe psychopathology, this patient supposedly spent all his waking time from approximately seven to ten months of age either head-banging or body-rocking. After he began to walk at about the age of two, these symptoms vanished.

Several years later he had fantasies in which he constructed a complex city that was run by machines and robots; he was the only human there.

He described the intricate details of how this city maintained itself. Equally complicated were its transactions with the rest of the world. They were handled in a mechanical, precise, mathematical fashion. This city did not directly recognize the existence of the surrounding environment, yet in some ways it operated in the context of something outside itself.

This patient currently seemed to demonstrate a need for omnipotent control and independence of external objects. Still, like the child who was oblivious to his mother's presence until she left the room, this patient seemed to need the framework of his environment to maintain himself. For example, he talked endlessly and without interruption about how crass and intrusive everyone was, never acknowledging that there may have been some redeeming features in the persons or situations he was describing. He spoke calmly and without bitterness and acted as if I were not in the room. If I interrupted him with a comment or interpretation, he would wait politely for me to finish and then continue where he had left off without acknowledging the gap created by my "intrusion." He seemed perfectly content to have me sit there saying nothing. He never asked a question or sought my opinion or advice.

This patient was a striking contrast to other patients who resent the analyst's silence. It is commonplace for patients to complain that the analyst gives them nothing. They feel that they might as well lie on their living room couch and free associate, thereby saving themselves considerable money and time. However, both the analyst and the patient know that this would not work. The resentful patient needs to have someone he can complain about and upon whom he can project his devaluated self-representation.

My patient did not complain, but he demonstrated a need to have someone around from whom he could withdraw and thereby establish his autonomy. He was similar to the young boy who eagerly came to his sessions in order to curl up in front of the stove and have the *opportunity* of ignoring his therapist. This was a primitive, omnipotent autonomy but one that was necessary in order to save him from being crushed, "dissolved," and destroyed by symbiotic fusion. Therefore, this patient needed to have someone around whom he could relegate to oblivion. His action represented mastery but he had to reassure himself continually that he could successfully shut out external objects. Without an external object to serve this purpose, he would lose a vantage point from which he could consolidate an identity, even though it might be a "false self" (Winnicott, 1952).

This patient had a history of head-banging and body-rocking during childhood, and it is possible that other cases of automatonlike behavior have similar histories. These symptoms are autistic and are frequently associated with similar behaviors. Head-banging, body-rocking, and trichotillomania sometimes occur together and can be explained in terms of defensive processes similar to those described for this patient. Spitz (1965) has discussed specific aspects of the mother-child interaction of head-bangers.

Control is needed, not only to separate the patient from the external world but to maintain some order within an otherwise chaotic intrapsychic world. This means that the patient has to control what goes out as well as what comes in. For example, a middle-aged woman who had had trichotillomania for as long as she could consciously remember, as well as a history of body-rocking, head-banging, and enuresis, showed tremendous conflict about relinquishing any part of herself. As in the case of many obese persons (this patient had been quite obese during adolescence), she did not clearly distinguish the boundary between herself and the external world. Eating her hair had many meanings; here it is pertinent to emphasize that she was incorporating something that could be separated from herself. Her action in detaching her hair was part of her need for omnipotent control.

To summarize briefly, various autistic, automaton phenomena that have been viewed as manifestations of developmental vicissitudes are described as examples of reactions to a traumatic symbiotic fixation. The analysis of adults with a history of such behavioral anomalies during childhood sheds light on certain characterological defenses that result from the symbiotic phase. Both the observation of children and the retrospective reconstructions made from the treatment of adults emphasize that difficulties in the symbiotic phase can have the following consequences: (1) drive differentiation is impaired; (2) ego–non-ego boundaries are blurred, leading to a defective sense of identity; and (3) there is an exaggerated need for omnipotent control, leading to the interesting paradox of autonomy within the framework of symbiotic fusion.

Developmental Aspects of Adaptation

The neonate is helplessly dependent and requires a long period of mothering in order to maintain himself as well as to structuralize enough to achieve substantial autonomy. To understand more about the psychic processes required for progressive structuralization, the interaction among developmental phases, maturational sequences, and external objects must be scrutinized microscopically.

From the patients described above, one can make inferences about development in general; these patients can be understood in terms of object relations pertaining to disturbances of the symbiotic phase of development.

Pre-Object Phase

The matter of what precedes the symbiotic phase has been discussed by many psychoanalytic theoreticians. They stress neurophysiological factors because they perceive the neonate as biologically oriented. His sensorimotor apparatus is not sufficiently differentiated so that he can see the external world in a coherent, integrated fashion. Therefore, the neonate cannot distinguish between the inside and the outside; in fact, his psyche is not sufficiently mature so that the concepts "inside" and "outside" have any meaning. Instead, the infant presumably experiences only vague, visceral sensations of comfort or discomfort, which are determined by cyclical biological needs.

The neonate does not have a relationship with an external object since his psyche is not integrated to the point where it can coherently perceive or emotionally incorporate. In a sense the infant's earliest life can be considered prepsychological since mentation has not yet developed. The external object, of course, is important but mainly for sustenance. Bowlby (1951, 1960a, 1960b) believes that the individual qualities of the external object are not important during the early months. He states that the mothering person can be changed during the first 27 weeks of life without disrupting the child's development so long as the nurturing source is competent and nontraumatic. Just how interchangeable the mother is during that period is a debatable question. The ways in which the mother is needed beyond providing basic care require further study. One important function, however, has been established: *During the pre-object phase, the external object (mother) is responsible for preparing a setting in which object relationships can occur.*

There has been considerable controversy about the length of this stage. Some analysts, especially the Kleinian school, ignore this phase and discuss psychodynamic constellations within the infant from the moment he is born. Certain experiments (Reisen, 1947) suggest that perceptual discrimination and learning begin quite early—within a week or two. The timetable of development from a primarily biological orientation to significant mentation is still imperfectly understood. For our purpose it is important to recognize that nothing occurs abruptly; rather, there is a continuum from the biological to the psychological, a gradual progression from one stage to another while elements of a former stage continue to exist with decreasing prominence alongside greater structure.

Symbiotic Phase

As clinical examples illustrate, the symbiotic phase is a developmental one that can be studied in a psychotherapeutic framework. There are incomplete mental representations that can later be activated and observed during the transference regression. At the time when mental representations occur and the external world is perceived coherently enough so that the psyche "wishes" to blend with it, denying its separate existence, this stage can be considered the first phase of *psychological* development.

It is not certain whether one should consider the symbiotic phase an object-relation or pre-object-relation stage. To a large extent this is a semantic question. If the requirement for object relations is to perceive someone else as distinctly separate from oneself, then the symbiotic union with the nurturing object does not constitute an object relationship. However, since the child is "engaged" in a relationship (even though he is fused with someone else), this has been considered a primitive form of an object or part-object relationship. One can argue that the process of fusion requires some concept (even though vague) of something outside the self in order to be able to fuse with it. The previous, so-called biological state, which has no mental representations, is not one of fusion or lack of distinction between ego and non-ego. Fusions and boundaries separating the self from the non-self are psychological constructs; they have not been established during the early neonatal period. In order to be one with the external world, there must be some dim percept of oneself and something apart from the self. The latter can be considered a primordial perception of an object or a primitive form of object relationship.

Maturational factors provide the stimuli for emotional development. In the pre-object phase, there are no mental representations because the neurological apparatus is not sufficiently differentiated to perceive, incorporate, and conceptualize. With the maturation of the perceptual apparatus and the central nervous system generally, the child begins to perceive in a more structured fashion. From another viewpoint the Nirvana (not necessarily blissful but preblissful) state of nondifferentiation is biological; with somatic differentiation it becomes impossible to maintain. Increased biological structure becomes an impetus for corresponding emotional development.

Consequently, the symbiotic phase can be conceptualized as a *transition* phase between a more-or-less biological orientation and one in which external objects are perceived in a somewhat structured fashion and can be used for adaptation. Winnicott's (1953) concept of the transitional object is compatible with this viewpoint since the transitional object is experienced as both outside the self and an omnipotently controlled part of the self. From this control the child can eventually let the object remain in the outside world while retaining its representation within the ego system. The symbiotic fusion is a phase in which an internal object representation begins to form, although it is not consolidated until there has been a partial resolution of the fusion. The child's perception of objects is of part-objects, as Winnicott emphasizes; the transitional object represents the breast.

In a sense, the symbiotic phase can be considered an attempt to maintain a biological orientation or to return to a pre-object level. It is difficult to assign a complex purpose to such early periods of life, but it may not be too teleological to believe that there is some form of inertia inherent in the living organism. As soon as the child's perceptual apparatus becomes structured to the point where he has some awareness of the external world, symbiotic fusion counteracts such a perception and tries to reestablish the earlier state of less differentiation.

On the other hand, fusion with the outside world is, in itself, a form of perceiving and relating that is appropriate to primitive levels of development and represents a *necessary* first stage. By analogy, the more primitive (embryonic and undifferentiated) an organ or organism is, the more global its reactions. Freud (1939) reminds us of Roux's experiment in which he stuck a pin in a group of embryonic cells; this had a profound effect, producing extensive malformation in the mature organism. At a later time, when the organism was more developed, a pinprick would have had only a minimal effect. Similarly, stimulating a neonate produces global effects—the whole body responds, as in the Moro reflex—whereas applying the same stimulus when the infant is older may only cause it to turn its head.

It has been postulated that the first visual perceptions are of shades of light and dark and stillness or motion. Auditory perceptions are believed to be equally undifferentiated in the neonate and to consist of only the recognition of different amplitudes. Certainly he cannot be aware of the subtle nuances and intonations of complex language, although he learns to react to affects quite early.

From a mentational viewpoint it is assumed that the first object relationships and perceptions are also global. It seems reasonable to believe that initially the mother, although a part-object, "fills" the perceptual apparatus whenever she is perceived at all. If one considers her to be introjected, the introject is massive and undifferentiated during the symbiotic phase. To form discrete introjects requires a structured perception and an ego that is able to maintain a well-formed introject. If the perceptual system is part of the ego, it is still operating at a primitive level; the rest of the ego, which is operating on a similar plane, can only maintain an introject that is similarly constructed. In the symbiotic phase, that which is introjected and that which is introjecting are indistinguishable and constitute fusion.

The structuralizing process initiated by innate maturational forces is characterized by responses that move from the general and massive to the coherent and discrete; in psychological terms, these latter responses are conceptualized as secondary process. Consequently, to postulate a symbiotic phase as the beginning state in the development of the psyche is a logical extension of what has been observed in the structural development of the soma. As psychic differentiation proceeds, one would expect object relations to become more circumscribed.

The attempt to achieve consistency within the theoretical framework can be exciting because it calls attention to phenomena that would otherwise not have been discovered. The latter in turn strengthens the validity of the conceptual framework. If our theory has general validity, then the formation of the psychic structure within the context of object relations *must* proceed from a symbiotic global fusion to discrete object relations that are used for adaptation. From this viewpoint teleological considerations recede into the background; whether the child attempts to remain at early levels of development or wants to fuse with the mother's breast is no longer meaningful. Volitional factors are minimal and they arise in inverse proportion to innate maturational factors. The child's development, although profoundly affected by the nature of his introjects, undergoes a sequential pattern in which there is a predetermined method of incorporation based upon structural considerations. What is incorporated, of course, varies with the unique qualities of the environment; each introject, in turn, will affect later ones, but the maturational sequence is not significantly influenced by the environment just before the symbiotic elaboration. Unusual environmental circumstances and intense trauma can upset the innate maturational pattern. Severe development arrests leading to little subsequent development may occur during these early stages and result in emotional malformations. These are, however, extreme exceptions that have been described by Spitz.

Resolution of the Symbiotic Phase

Resolution of the symbiotic phase generally leads to more sophisticated object relations; to the extent that the psyche becomes progressively more differentiated from the external world, the self-representation (for our purposes the sense of identity) becomes consolidated and increasingly distinct from object representations. As stated earlier, biological maturation contributes to this differentiation, but the influence of the external object requires further scrutiny as it becomes increasingly meaningful in the process of individuation.

Insofar as the mother is an adequate provider and does not unduly disrupt her child's homeostatic harmony, the symbiotic phase is relatively comfortable. This does not mean, however, that the child "wishes" to remain in what is becoming a pleasurable state. On the contrary, *the fact that the relationship is satisfying permits maturational forces to unfold without impediment.* The whole psychic apparatus structuralizes; as there is "more" ego, the global relationship (fusion) with an object representation changes and becomes more elaborate. Metaphorically it is as though differentiation were accompanied by a shrinkage of the ego from its previous vast amorphous, diffuse, amoeba-like state. What is perceived undergoes a similar shrinkage so that the external object is eventually "registered" within the ego system as a more discrete entity. It is more sharply delineated and there is more "space" between the object representation (later referred to as an introject) and the boundaries of the ego. In this sense, the ego has "expanded" from a mere involvement with the nurturing source.

Biological maturation and the emerging qualities of the external object are interrelated and should not be artificially isolated. For example, if the mother has been disruptive and assaultive, the infant will find it harder to integrate her into his ego system. In order to perceive trauma as a first step toward mastery and integration, one must have effective structure.

The infant is aware of his basic needs (hunger, thirst, warmth, etc.) and a competent mother provides for them in a nonthreatening fashion. Her smooth, synchronized responses are gratifying because they are appropriate to the child's needs and they are nonintrusive. Simply because a mother feeds, clothes, and holds her child does not mean that she is meeting his needs. To give the child something when he does not need it is felt to be an intrusion, sometimes an assault. Need tension disturbs the homeostatic balance and the nurturing substance reestablishes it. If there is no disturbance in the homeostatic balance, attempts at feeding, for example, will disrupt the child and he will react either defensively or chaotically.

A child cannot use gratuitous offerings. In order to incorporate an adaptive experience smoothly, the experience must be part of the process of reestablishing homeostasis. The ego expands by incorporating the tension-reducing qualities of the mothering interaction. If the relationship leads to a disruption of homeostasis the child will fend it off. Whatever intrudes into his ego is traumatic. Any incorporation that occurs during a disturbed state leads to a similarly disturbing introject.

The period of symbiotic fusion, if satisfactory, is characterized by an ego that has smoothly incorporated the mothering experience. Because it is a fusion the mothering experience and the child's ego are indistinguishable; it is harmonious in the sense that it achieves intrapsychic balance. When the ego becomes more structured and the mothering experience is a more discrete part of the ego, the same harmony and balance are maintained.

Ferenczi (1909) introduced the word "introject"—a very useful concept. Some authors (for example, Sandler, 1956) distinguish between preoedipal incorporations and those that lead to the postoedipal superego. The latter are considered to be introjects. Introjects are formed by the process of introjection, although the terms "incorporation" and "assimilation" are often not distinguished from introjection. As used here, introjects will refer to experiences and objects that have become part of the ego but have a structure of their own that distinguishes them from the rest of the ego. Once they are integrated into ego systems (as adaptive techniques), they lose their introject status and become "assimilated." If the introject is traumatic or disruptive it is not assimilated into the ego.

To return to the progressive developmental sequence from the symbiotic phase: as the diffuse but harmonious mother-ego fusion undergoes differentiation, the internalized mothering experience becomes delineated and develops into what could be considered an introject. Within the ego, boundaries form around the maternal representation. These boundaries mark the beginning of the psychic separation of the child from his mother. As the ego begins to differentiate itself from the maternal introject, the child sees himself as separate and distinct. At this point he becomes aware of his dependency, not in a sophisticated sense, but in terms of needing his mother's presence.

In an immature ego a mental representation has to be reinforced by a relationship with the external object that has been introjected; it has to continue being cathected by repeated gratifying experiences with the mother. Later the ego will be able to retain a mental construct even when the mother is not present. As the maternal introject is increasingly consolidated, the child's behavior becomes organized and goal-directed. His play activity usually includes a problem situation that he has to resolve; often the problem is the actual or anticipated separation from the mother. Freud (1920) illustrated this thesis by describing the behavior of his nephew; he symbolized his mother's departure and return by alternately pulling an object at the end of a string into view and then putting it out of sight, thereby controlling the separation. This child demonstrated both his need for his mother and his need to be autonomous.

The child "learns" the mother's adaptive techniques without having her repeatedly demonstrate them to him. By making her methods his own he achieves further separation and strengthens his ego boundaries. The maternal introject thus becomes part of the child's ego and is no longer a discrete entity like a foreign body. Insofar as the maternal introject promotes psychic harmony rather than disruption, the ego does not have to erect defenses against it. Consequently, the introject loses its boundaries and becomes assimilated.

The object relationship with the mother is functional. That which is introjected is operational. The mother represents nurture and care, and the child's inner representation of her reflects her adaptive significance. As the maternal introject is "absorbed," it helps to structuralize various ego systems, such as the integrative and executive systems. *The executive apparatus expands and acquires further techniques of mastery by incorporating the functional maternal introject. The latter is no longer a distinct entity but has become a modality.*

This discussion has focused solely upon the object relationship with the mother. Although this is a vital relationship during the early months of life, other object relationships are also important for emotional development. The father is a significant contributor to the child's maturation; later on, teachers and others will also be important. Because other object relationships add to the ego's dimensions, the psyche becomes multifaceted. Multiple identifications constitute the elements of a Gestalt, accounting for the richness of personalities. However, the mechanisms by which individuating qualities are acquired resemble those that produced the maternal introject.

In summary, the resolution of the symbiotic phase is, in part, initiated by innate, biological, maturational forces. *If the maternal (part-object) imago and the ego are indistinguishable but harmoniously united, the symbiotic phase is a transitional, developmental stage between a pre-object (basically biological) orientation and one where object relationships are established and self-representation is consolidated.*

Disruptive Introjects

Repetitive gratifying experiences cathect further functionally adaptive introjects, which are then incorporated into the ego. The above are theoretical constructs about relatively nonpathological developmental sequences. Insofar as these are microscopic descriptions, one can ask what type of data would be required in order to make such formulations plausible.

Again, we are confronted with the same methodological considerations discussed in the introduction. Direct observations of children, although helpful, are within a frame of reference that is not particularly appropriate to microscopic formulations about intra-ego processes. Rarely, if ever, is a person analyzed whose early relationships were devoid of trauma.

Still, the study of an adult's psychopathology in the context of the transference neurosis is a relevant approach to this type of conceptualization. Psychopathology is selective. Not all ego systems or object relationships are equally involved; some areas have not been significantly affected or traumatized. One can learn a lot about emotional development in general because the early stages are recapitulated in the transference regression. In spite of the defensive distortions of this regression, many observations can be made. Furthermore, impaired development yields inferences about the customary course of events. The effects of defensive distortions upon ego development relate to our concepts about psychopathology, which have been expanded considerably beyond psychodynamic factors with the inclusion of characterological elements in our formulations. Consequently, the study of cases suffering from severe psychopathology is valuable for our further understanding of clinical phenomena as well as of concepts of intra-ego processes that underlie emotional development.

Insofar as the main emphasis of this chapter is on object relationships and the internalization of the object as an introject, it is not necessary to discuss psychopathology at length. In developmental disorders the influences of the external object will be recognized as traumatic and disruptive rather than cohesive and adaptive, as discussed earlier.

During the biological pre-object phase, the external object is already significant for later psychic development. Even though neurologically the neonate is poorly developed and may not retain potentially conscious memory traces, his mother's positive or negative influence will nevertheless affect his later development. The child's maturational impetus must be augmented and sustained by properly timed nurture. Although the neonate lacks mentation, the mother can set the stage for future psychological elaboration by giving appropriate care.

The symbiotic phase will reflect any improper care received earlier. The child will experience fusion with a traumatizing mother as dangerous. Although infants are not capable of sophisticated fear or subtle perceptions of danger, direct observations indicate that there are situations they find terrifying and noxious. Tantrums characterized by purposeless and chaotic screaming are often seen in children who find their mothers threatening. Mahler (1952) skillfully describes two reactions that characterize disturbances of the symbiotic phase: (1) children who cling to the object in a tenacious state of fusion and will not tolerate separation—symbiotic psychosis, and (2) children who avoid external objects because of a fear of fusion—autistic psychosis.

Some of the clinical examples that were discussed here showed a markedly conflicted attitude about being fused with the external object. The two children had to assure themselves that the external object (mother and therapist) had no significance. One of them could not let his mother leave; in order to maintain "independence," he needed his mother nearby so he could withdraw from her. The adult patient demonstrated the same conflict in the transference. He was afraid of independence in part because he believed he would destroy me if he "tore" himself away from me. He was also afraid of being "dissolved" if he remained in a state of symbiotic fusion.

To reach a state of relative separation is exceedingly difficult. Once there is some dissolution of the symbiosis, the ego has to react defensively or (in some instances) it may undergo a rigid fixation—a state of paralysis where further development is minimal.

If the environment is not in harmony with maturational drives, later structuralization will be distorted. If biological progression does not receive reinforcement from the outside world, the psychic structures will be functionally constricted. Reisen (1947) describes experiments with monkeys who have been blindfolded since birth; he reports that even though their retinas structuralize, their vision is markedly impaired. In the human infant there are many corresponding situations where environmental responses do not stimulate maturational progression.

Introjects become established after the partial dissolution of the symbiotic phase. A traumatic symbiotic phase will lead to the formation of threatening maternal introjects in later developmental stages, and there will be difficulties in "absorbing" such introjects into the general ego structure. The sense of identity will eventually incorporate the mother's hatred as self-hatred, with feelings of worthlessness and inadequacy. The child will feel unlovable and vulnerable; his self-representation will be tenuous because of his lack of self-esteem. Still, the ego attempts to defend itself against the devouring qualities* of the maternal introject. It cannot smoothly incorporate such an introject into integrative and executive systems.

To the extent that the external world is traumatic, its internal representation (disruptive introjects) is also felt to be threatening. The ego, therefore, has two monumental tasks. First, it must protect itself from

Granted that the horrendous, monstrous qualities of the archaic maternal imago as described in the transference regression are the outcome of projecting the child's hatred, symbiosis precedes projection, and hateful self-feeling is the residual of the partial dissolution of the symbiotic fusion.

the maternal introject. This means that it must be powerful enough so that it will no longer feel threatened. It must be able to handle any disruption created by the maternal introjects; this is achieved by a rent in the ego's unity. The ego requires complete control, but it is especially vulnerable because of the split; one part maintains control over the other which contains the disruptive maternal introject. The second task of the ego is to master problems "autonomously." Since the maternal introject is split off and has to be "controlled," the child must deny that the mother has any influence whatsoever—either negative or positive. The child cannot turn to his mother to satisfy his inner needs, and he cannot rely on his own resources because he has acquired only a minimum of adaptive techniques from her.

To augment the defense of dissociation by regression is not entirely satisfactory since the next earlier stage is the symbiotic phase. Regressing to this phase would undo the defensive splitting; the child would again be faced with an intrusive and "swallowing" maternal imago. Because there has been further maturation and development, regression to the symbiotic phase is perceived more intensely. In the transference regression the patient describes this state in terms of fearing annihilation, that is, destruction of himself as a distinct entity. Regression to the symbiotic phase often occurs but, as illustrated during the transference, it is nonadaptive.

The patient or child must maintain a facade of control and autonomy within the framework of a helpless and vulnerable ego. In order to maintain this control the child has to be isolated from the threatening introject which he can achieve by defensive splitting. On the other hand, he must cling to an external object because of the intense helplessness he feels. He requires both nurture and rescue from inner assault by the frightening, disruptive introject. But insofar as his self-representation includes derivatives of the primitive symbiosis, an inner assault also seems to emanate from those hateful aspects of the self that are "precipitates" of the mother-child fusion. The child then turns to the outside world for anaclitic nurture and salvation from a raging, self-destructive self.

Anaclitic clinging is often observed in very disturbed children, but the psychotic transference of patients with characterological defects often emphasizes the need for and the cataclysmic fear of fusion. The need for isolation and control conflicts with the need for nurture and rescuing, as illustrated in all of the clinical examples presented earlier. If one can maintain a relationship with an external object while simultaneously ignoring and withdrawing from it, then one has achieved a tenuous degree of intrapsychic harmony; this is, however, a very precarious balance.

An adolescent patient spoke of the above conflict and its tragic consequences in students taking drugs. He described a young woman who paraded her independence and flaunted conventions by frequently using LSD. As was the custom she took the drug either in a group or in the presence of her boyfriend. The patient said that the various participants ignored each other during a "trip." The last time the young woman tried the drug she was with her boyfriend. For some unexplained reason he left her just when she was experiencing the effects of the drug most intensely. Suddenly she became panicky and incoherent, and was unable to gain control and reestablish normal perception and reality-testing. Eventually she was institutionalized, suffering from a psychosis. Her behavior highlighted her basic helplessness, which was hidden by her facade of control and independence.

In the clinical examples presented earlier there was little ego structure, and the patients needed a specific kind of object relationship for their survival. In contrast, the psychoneurotic patient has considerable autonomy and a variety of useful adaptive techniques.

As a child grows older the world of object relations expands. He comes into contact with more people, and he relates to many facets of different persons. For example, he no longer views his mother as just a source of nurture but as a whole person. Other significant maternal roles increase in importance as the personality expands. Every stage of psychosexual development is characterized by distinct parental functions. The oedipal conflicts that characterize the psychoneuroses, for example, are brought about by a disturbance of object relations in terms of a specific role. The child may find himself in a conflict with the sexual mother whereas earlier he may have had a harmonious relationship with the nurturing mother.

The distinction between suffering from characterological defects and the psychoneuroses is one of degree. Disturbances in object relations do not usually occur abruptly. If a particular facet of an object relation becomes a source of conflict during a later phase of psychosexual development, there was usually some difficulty during an earlier period when the external object was less differentiated. It may not have been a severe disturbance, but, to the extent that there was one, every psychoneurosis will have an underlying characterological problem, minimal though it may be. Since no phase of development can be completely harmonious, everyone has residuals of developmental disturbances. How significant these may be is another question, but the characterological distortion underlying the psychoneuroses is relevant for our therapeutic understanding.

Therapeutic Implications

Infantile disturbances of object relations are reenacted in the transference regression of children and adults. The question has frequently been asked as to whether therapy can undo the effects of severe early trauma and deprivation. Once the personality has been consolidated, can a benign, helpful relationship be as influential as a damaging one was during the early formative months? Most therapists agree that in both children and adults the effects of severe disturbances in early object relations can never be totally eradicated. A defective psychic structure makes it difficult for the ego to profit from potentially constructive experiences.

The psychoanalytic setting stimulates regression, causing the ego to lose some of its cohesiveness. Previous developmental levels are recreated, not as exact replicas of earlier stages, but with enough elements of more mature functioning so that both the therapist and eventually the patient can understand the nature of the early trauma. For example, through the transference projection, the patient revives early traumatic experiences with his mother. He reacts to the analyst as if he were fused with him and reveals megalomaniac expectations or the fear of annihilation. There are, of course, many individual differences, depending upon specific aspects of early object relationships, but, in general, one is impressed by the threatening qualities inherent in the stage of symbiotic fusion in patients suffering from characterological problems.

This transference regression results in greater resiliency than was present in the formed personality before analysis. The rigidity of defective structuralization and the constrictions that prevented further development are not as operative during the transference regression. Consequently, even though object relationships do not have such an intense impact, either disruptive or constructive, upon later developmental stages, the analytic setting creates a situation that not only recapitulates early trauma but has some potential for nondefective development—an opportunity that was not available during infancy.

The resolution of the symbiotic fusion during the course of psychoanalytic treatment can be of considerable benefit. Both children and adults can emerge from such a transference state with an ego that is better structured because it has overcome the forces that previously caused maldevelopment.

During infancy the dissolution of the symbiotic fusion was followed by defensive splitting and denial of the maternal introject. Since this meant the disavowal of significant portions of the psyche, development of the self-representation had to be constricted because parts of the self were "lost" (unavailable for integration into adaptational ego systems).*

There are significant differences between the symbiotic dissolution that occurs in the transference and the one that took place in infancy. These differences can constitute the essence of the therapeutic process in psychoanalytic treatment. The patient projects the traumatic aspects of early object imagos onto the therapist. Instead of reinforcing this projection the analyst can help the patient understand how his mind is working. He does not treat the patient as a helpless, vulnerable baby who needs omnipotent rescuing. Instead, he views his psyche as a phenomenon worth of study. He does not respond to the patient's terror or helplessness, but, with analytic calm and interpretation, he brings his secondary-process organization to the patient's primary-process chaos. *The analyst's availability for projection and his nonparticipation at the level of the transference regression brings some security into the symbiotic fusion. The patient no longer experiences the fusion as threatening because the analyst displays interest (not the feeling of vulnerability due to the patient's destructiveness) and he does not accept the patient's helplessness as a tragic reality that he has to do something about above and beyond analysis.* As the analyst brings meaning into an apparently chaotic state, he is helping the patient achieve organization through self-understanding. By incorporating the analyst during the regression to the symbiotic level, the patient is also internalizing some elements of the analytic attitude.

When the patient achieves separation, or at least partial separation, his ego retains an introject of the interested, analyzing analyst which counteracts the assaultive mother or omnipotent rescuer. The regression to the symbiotic phase during analysis can lead the patient to regain parts of the self that had been split off, and *the catalytic effect of the analytic introject causes them to be synthesized into various adaptive ego systems—not to be dissociated as they were in childhood.* The fusion with the analyst has a corrective potential; although the effects of early trauma can never be completely undone, the patient's ego can still develop sufficiently so that he can respect himself as a person.

Both the children and the adult cases presented earlier demonstrated

A patient described himself as being defective in that he was "missing many parts." At first he described methods of relating to problem situations. He believed that he simply never learned how to handle many situations that were routine for others. During therapy his fantasies indicated that he was worried about lost parts of the self, including both the psyche and soma.

an inability to profit from external objects because of ego distortions following a disruptive symbiotic phase. If the therapy proceeds in the direction of a recapitulation of this early stage, perhaps a purposeful introduction of extra-analytic procedures might blur the distinction between the helpful, nonanalyzing analyst and the omnipotent, rescuing introject. Strachey (1934) believed that active support can help to foster paranoid attitudes where the therapy is perceived as good and the outside world as bad. This may lead to the alleviation of symptoms but not to character improvement. Active support can encourage an ego split, perhaps a more comfortable one; but, in terms of structure-promoting potentials, such a split is similar to the ego dissociation of childhood. Activity designed to help the patient by education or environmental manipulation is often experienced as an intrusion by susceptible, sensitive, vulnerable egos, which characterize patients who are suffering from developmental arrest; this is true of adults and frequently of children (Anthony, 1964).

Summary and Conclusions

1. An ego-psychological model based primarily upon a hierarchy of all psychic elements (drives as well as structure) is particularly apt for the study of pathological and relatively nonpathological development in the context of object relations. This model does not require a hydrodynamic-energic-discharge hypothesis.

2. The study of psychopathology enables one to make inferences about nonpathological development. Here, clinical accounts of children and adults who have disturbed early object relations are presented in an abbreviated form. Data obtained from the direct observation of children as well as from the transference regression can be conceptualized in terms of early object relations.

3. Both types of data can be understood as examples of a disturbance and fixation of the symbiotic phase of development, one in which the child does not yet distinguish between himself and the nurturing source.

4. The symbiotic stage, conceptualized as a psychic fusion between mother and child, is thought to be a transitional period between the early neonatal stage (which is biological and preobject) and the one in which there is a dim awareness of objects as separate from the self. Biological maturational forces serve as the impetus for greater somatic structure and subsequent elaboration of the psyche.

5. The nurturing object can either augment the maturational potential or cause maldevelopment.

6. A disturbed symbiotic phase is followed by fixation. The subse-

quent maternal introject is perceived as dangerous and disappointing. The ego uses primitive defenses, such as denial and dissociation (splitting), to protect itself against the assaultive qualities of the introject.

7. During the transference regression, the symbiotic phase is relived in a modified form. The analyst's interpretive attitude serves as an impetus for resolution of the symbiotic phase, and the subsequent ego states reflect the corrective experience. Whether corrective changes can be achieved if the therapist attempts to provide "support" (other than analytic) by education or environmental manipulation is conjectural. It is believed that, although such support may bring about considerable symptomatic improvement, especially in children, there will be no basic characterological changes. There are limits to what can be accomplished in severely traumatized patients. However, many therapists are hopeful about them; some cases have been reported that were helped considerably.

Part III

SPECIAL TYPES
OF OBJECT RELATIONSHIPS

These sections progress from the general to the specific. Particular aspects of ego functioning, object relationships, are emphasized in the following papers and are studied in terms of their impact on character structure and psychopathology. How the patient relates to other persons defines the dimensions of his personality. In other words, general formulations regarding the patient's psyche have considerable significance for the way a person will relate to external objects. The manner in which such objects are used to sustain emotional equilibrium, either defensively or constructively, will be reflected in the transference relationship during analysis. In some instances a relationship to an external object is clung to and used as a resistance against analysis.

I have focused upon one particular type of object relationship, the marital relationship. My interest in married couples originated when I was a candidate in psychoanalytic training and antedated my interest in the subjects discussed in the two previous sections. However, this volume is not chronologically ordered since, conceptually, a movement from the general to the specific is logically consistent. Our experiences and quandaries are not necessarily ordered in such a sequence and our formulations are usually dependent upon the problem that confronts us.

Before thinking in a more global sense about the patient's psyche and his various characterological modalities, I was struck by a particular segment of the patient's personality that seemed to be frequently stressed in clinical seminars that I attended as a student. If the patient were married, the spouse often received unfavorable consideration by the class. For example, one would often hear the lament that it was unfortunate that the patient should have married such a sick partner. The patient might be described as a fairly well integrated psychoneurotic whereas the marital partner, because of data that the patient presented, would be considered schizophrenic. Sometimes it would be reversed but usually one's attitude toward the patient was positive and toward the spouse, negative.

Apart from the infeasibility of making judgments about another person simply from the report of someone intimately involved with that person, the concept of psychic determinism seemed to recede into the background. Furthermore, my rudimentary clinical experience did not indicate such wide discrepancies in the character structure of married patients, or for that matter, in the psychic makeup of persons involved in any intimate relationship, heterosexual, homosexual, or simply close friends. I was impressed by similarities rather than differences, especially when treating the wives of alcoholics.

When a patient makes significant changes in analysis indicative of the achievement of better integration, striking changes sometimes occur in the marital or otherwise intimate relationship. A delicate balance seems to be disturbed; in the most memorable instances, the partner may assume the very characteristics that caused the patient to seek treatment. With alcoholics, if the drinker happened to be receiving treatment and he stopped drinking, the spouse might begin drinking in the same compulsive fashion as the patient had formerly done.

I found these events to be particularly intriguing and learned that it had been well known as far as alcoholic patients were concerned. More intriguing was the discovery of such equivalence of psychopathology in patients whose behavior was not as flamboyant and whose relationships consisted of many subtle interactions. Analysis, at times, created dramatic situations, which, in some instances, were designed to sabotage analysis and to reestablish the previous equilibrium.

A particular object relationship can be a valuable indicator of the patient's and his partner's general psychic organization. One can move from the particular to the general and then from the general to the particular, a back and forth movement which enriches our understanding of the patient's interactions in the analytic setting.

Chapter 15

Mutual Adaptation in Various Object Relationships

In a well-established object relationship, many factors operate. In this chapter, the mutually adaptive character of certain relationships will be stressed. Mittelmann (1944) studied the psychodynamic features found in intimate ties and demonstrated the complementary qualities of the neuroses of the partners studied. Oberndorf (1939) previously described such complementation in terms of both pregenital and oedipal orientations.

The above studies, as well as those of Hartmann (1946), uncovered psychoanalytic principles that apply not only to the person who was studied microscropically, so to speak, by the psychoanalytic method, but that also extend our understanding to the interaction of two persons; i.e., to various transactional psychological relationships.

The nature of the psychoanalytic patient's intimate ties may have significance for the therapist if he is able to determine something about the persons with whom the ties exist. That is, understanding of the psychic structure or the psychopathology of the patient's wife or husband, close friends, and other intimate associates provide a wider base for study of the patient's psychic state and a wider scan of his emotional horizon. Psychoanalytic understanding, although still chiefly focused on the patient, would be extended into the environment and thereby serve to highlight the vicissitudes the patient has to face in his current adjustments.

The question can be briefly raised whether emotionally meaningful relationships can be considered psychically "symbiotic," a term that is now found fairly frequently in the psychiatric and psychoanalytic literature. De Bary's (1879) original use of the word "symbiosis" to mean simply mutual dependence has been extended to the well-defined concept (as expounded by Benedek (1949) and Mahler (1952) as well as others) of the biologically significant relationship of the mother-child unit. In this relationship, the child's survival and psychological development are at stake, as also are important developmental potentialities of the mother with respect to her motherliness. The relationships to be studied here are of a different order. Although they, too, operate on a

First published in *Int. J. Psa.* 39 (1958), 1–8. Reprinted by permission.

principle of mutual adaptation, such adaptation cannot be considered as positive in terms of potential maturation. It is seen as a defensive manoeuvre and, for the precarious equilibrium that it ensures, the ego has to pay a price.

Environmental Compliance

Psychoanalysis began with the study of hysteria, and Breuer and Freud (1895) understood that a conflict can result in various physical symptoms. According to the concept of conversion, as it was more explicitly stated, the body or a specific organ came to be thought of as placing itself at the disposal of the conflict; i.e., there existed a somatic compliance.

I should like to call attention here to what must be a similar type of compliance in terms not of the body but of the organism's choice of object relations. The soma is not merely a passive recipient of the various tensions, and it is not accidental (even though our understanding of the subject is still incomplete) that a specific organ is picked for cathexis. Similarly, perhaps more obviously, one would expect that a person's choice of another human being to help maintain his ego integrity indicates a type of compliance on the part of the chosen one that might be called an "environmental compliance."* Rather than examine this environmental compliance in its broader sociocultural aspects, I propose to restrict this discussion to the study of specific object relations: the dynamic interrelationship of two persons who have an intimate and, to some extent, lasting emotional tie. This will be investigated from a psychodynamic and psychopathological viewpoint, utilizing insight gained from patients in psychoanalytic treatment.

Environmental compliance should be considered in terms of both participating persons as somatic compliance is considered in terms of two factions. In other words, the person with whom the patient has an emotional involvement must also derive something from the relationship that contributes to his stability, defensive or otherwise.

What is to follow are clinical observations from a number of cases which, I believe, stress the mutually adaptive characteristics of the relationships between the patient and others. In an introductory effort such as this, one can present clinical data which can be supplemented by the observations of other analysts who may discover similar metapsychological principles operating. For the most convincing data are those

---

*I have recently learned that Dr. Heinz Hartmann coined the term "social compliance" in the same context and with similar meaning; cf. Róheim, 1947. Dr. Sidney Margolin (1953) also used the term "environmental compliance."

gathered by the psychoanalytic technique with its particular emphasis on the nuances, shifts, and innumerable complexities of the transference neurosis. The cases to be cited here will, for the most part, deal with such material which must, of necessity, be condensed, since the detailed approach would make this communication untenably long. When considering homosexual object relationships, however, the focus will be on the separation reactions of the partners when, for one reason or another, the relationship had to be disrupted. Focusing on this one aspect does not provide the richness of detail and dynamic conviction that the study of the transference neurosis does, but it is another axis that, when combined with the purely analytic methodology, may give a more comprehensive picture of the transactional process. Finally, when considering social relationships, very little more than a phenomenological description will be given. However, it is hoped that this static, observational approach will be of value when combined with the above.

As can be seen, an attempt will be made to look at the problem both macroscopically and microscopically, proceeding from the more general phenomenological data to those that are extracted from dynamic understanding of the patient's neurosis. As already stated, this approach is an introductory effort, one that would require considerable psychoanalytic exploration before a specific thesis could be formulated. The cases that are to follow show some rather interesting similarities in terms of certain features concerning their object relationships, similarities which may or may not be confirmed or which may be revised and extended by the clinical observations of other analysts.

Clinical Observations

Freud (1921) modified individual psychology in order to apply it to the group, and drew interesting conclusions about the dependence of the members on their leader and on each other. This study was actually a precursor of his formulation of the superego. Piaget (1952) similarly looked into the problem of morality and found that when the conscience was well developed, a close group cohesiveness existed.

Mutual dependence in a social relationship is easy to observe when ordinary moral restraints break down. The fact that delinquent acting-out characters, alcoholics, criminals, and other such groups, flock together illustrates this point.

I observed a twenty-three-year-old university student who repeatedly became involved with friends who seemed to have no sense of personal responsibility. The patient himself was an extremely dependent person, whose general tone was one of marked passivity. As a rebellious gesture towards an aggressive father, he did poorly in his studies (although he was of superior intelligence), squandered his allowance, and had to beg for more money, involving himself with what seemed to be unsavory companions. These consisted of about a dozen men, also students. One day the patient jokingly revealed that every one of them was undergoing psychoanalysis. Even though it seemed astounding, such a situation is not unusual at this particular university, where a large proportion of the student body as well as the faculty has had or is undergoing psychoanalytic treatment. I was able to talk to the analysts of four of his friends and was interested to find that their general psychodynamic formulations were similar to those that I had made for my patient. Such a correspondence in four acquaintances seemed noteworthy. That four analysts, independently of each other and without knowing any of my opinions about my patient, should come to the same conclusions, even though about different persons, seemed most unusual.

All these young men were characterized overtly as passive, experiencing one failure after another. They all kept erratic hours, drank more than they should, and attempted what might be considered sham debauchery. Their relationships with women had been fleeting and each of them felt threatened and withdrew when there seemed to be a possibility of become emotionally involved. Their sexual performances varied from different degrees of impotence to ejaculatio praecox. All in all, the behaviour of each of these twenty-two to thirty-four-year-old patients resembled that of an anxious adolescent. The intensity of their behaviour represented merely a quantitative distinction from ordinary adolescence.

The most noteworthy features of this group were passive dependence and an unusual amount of hostility toward a father who was domineering, blustering, but successful in business. Each patient had developed some personal technique to discharge his angry feelings, and a bond of iconoclasm and rebellion appeared to keep the group together. It seemed as if a collective superego resulted that because of the mutual support of the members was less oppressive than the individual superego operating alone. None of these men had any skill or even good sense relating to financial matters, and they all hated the business world vehemently. My patient dealt with the members both as a group and as an individual, for a time being particularly close to one or two of them and then relating to someone else with equal intensity.

My observations and those of the other four analysts seem to indicate that we were dealing with persons similar in personality structure and main characterological features as well as in overt behavior, types of defences and family backgrounds. Each felt himself compelled to relate either to the group as a whole or to some one member. Although other students envied the cohesiveness of the clique, they sensed that the group maintained itself because the men in it were too frightened to go on without the support of their colleagues; so the sting of envy was soothed by the knowledge that the group was held together by anxiety and insecurity.

The next two cases concern overt homosexuals and demonstrate the operational compatibility of the homosexual object relationship, either in terms of augmenting or reinforcing one partner's defences through identification, or in terms of complementing one defensive system by the other, as in a sadomasochistic relationship. In these instances the relationship was seen as being so intense that when for any of various reasons one of the persons involved decided to disrupt it the remaining partner would react violently. This served to illustrate how intense the homosexual relationship can be and how vital it is for the equilibrium and total integration of the persons involved. The interaction of the total personality can be demonstrated by the intensity and nature of the separation reaction.

The first case was that of a twenty-six-year-old man. He had been involved with a contemporary for several years; although they did not live together, they had frequent homosexual contacts. The general tone of the relationship as well as the nature of the erotic behaviour clearly indicated a sadomasochistic axis. For instance, the patient would supply his lover with many material objects, such as money, gramophone records, articles of clothing, etc., on a loan basis, never getting them back or really expecting to. He willingly inconvenienced himself, allowing himself to be abused and humiliated in order to preserve the erotic union. When his partner's actions or demands were so sadistic that they went beyond the bounds of even the patient's masochism, the partner would coerce him into complying merely by threatening to terminate their sexual practices. These consisted in acting out of various rituals and always put the patient in a helpless, vulnerable position. For instance, the patient would be securely bound with a rope, and then, while he lay helpless, his partner would masturbate him, in so doing making a pretence of castration. At other times he would ask to be beaten with the same rope, but never too hard. The whole experience would end with the patient performing fellatio.

The patient's friend finally sought analysis and, surprisingly enough, responded rather rapidly to the therapeutic process. After a year or so of analysis, he informed the patient in a definite, unmistakable fashion that the affair was ended. The pent-up hatred that underlay his masochistic façade erupted, and the patient attacked his former lover with murderous intent. Fortunately, he was not so strong as his intended victim, and he was subdued, the encounter resulting only in a few minor bruises. Following this experience the patient went into a fairly severe depression, left his job, became careless of his personal appearance, and drank heavily. The pressure of guilt that had been relieved through his suffering was manifesting itself directly, and he was now at the mercy of his superego and his castration anxiety. In actuality his suffering always had been controlled and, as Alexander (1948) has described, constituted a bribing of the superego. But now that the affair was terminated, he really began to suffer and consequently entered psychoanalytic treatment.

The second case was that of a twenty-two-year-old woman who sought consultation not for analysis but because she felt upset about her former girlfriend. The two had known each other since she was 15 and they had engaged in various homosexual practices. It was obvious that the patient's need for the relationship was just as strong as her friend's, but for reasons that came out later in treatment, she had decided to leave her. Her friend rapidly disintegrated into an acute schizophrenic state and had to be hospitalized.

Both these examples illustrate how vital the relationship was for at least one partner. However, further study of the second member clearly indicated that these were not parasitic or one-sided relations. In the first case, a change had actually taken place in the friend because of analysis, which altered his equilibrium so that it was no longer in resonance, as E. Weiss (1950) describes, with that of my patient. Prior to his analysis, his need for such an affair had been particularly strong, and later in analysis, during a stage of extreme resistance and regression, he came back to my patient to reestablish the old pattern. This time, however, he was rejected, and then his behavior became identical with that of my patient when he had felt abandoned.

The second patient tried to seduce another girl and thereby acquire a new partner. Her choice was not prudent, and she failed; she then tried to go back to her former partner, but this was completely out of the question because of the psychosis. When she finally realized that she was stranded, she went into a phase that had psychotic characteristics. Her state was comparable with that of her former lover, and intuitively one felt that the depth of regression was remarkably similar.

Finally, in such clinical observations, one must include those that deal with heterosexual object choices and where there has been more than merely a transient association between the partners. The following cases were in analysis for a considerable length of time.

A twenty-five-year-old male psychologist sought analysis chiefly for scoptophilic-exhibitionistic impulses that from time to time he acted out. He was intensely ashamed of these impulses, feeling that he would be ruined and disgraced if they were found out. His sensitivity was so great that he did not tell me about these perversions until the 25th hour, suppressing them completely when giving his history and emphasizing instead various characterological difficulties, as well as his need for training, as his motivation for seeking analytic treatment. In addition, he had recently married and was completely impotent with his wife; there had been no consummation of the marriage.

To my surprise, I learned that although the patient's wife verbalized impatience towards him in regard to his impotence, her demeanor indicated that she was really quite satisfied with the *status quo*. He described her as attractive, but minimized her physical attributes which he felt were far overshadowed by her scholastic achievements. Her college academic record had been very good, and she received a degree in physical culture, her specialty being classical dancing. All in all, the patient emphasized how well adjusted his wife was in contrast to himself. His description was one of emotional maturity, and from what he was able to tell, it would have been difficult to think of her as being otherwise, except for her complacency regarding the lack of intercourse and, perhaps, her somewhat too perfect academic showing.

At the very outset there seemed to be such a difference in the patient's adjustment in comparison to that of his wife that one could not help wondering how they could ever have formed such an alliance. His wife's "maturity" was a point that he stressed, and because of his obvious need to be related to a "strong character" the objectivity of his description came into question. Several facts immediately created suspicion as to his accuracy. First, her tolerance of the lack of the sexual relationship seemed very strange. Second, her vocation, a dancer, though it would not be significant of anything by and of itself, seemed to take on meaning in relation to his scoptophilic-exhibitionistic tendencies. I wondered what meaning such an exhibitionistic occupation had for her and how well suited it might be to her husband's voyeurism.

Analysis of the patient revealed a very severe character disorder with poor ego integration oftentimes bordering on the psychotic. There was no question that even though he was not psychotic in a phenomenological sense, he could be considered what has frequently been referred to as "schizoid."

During the first year of treatment, he showed a certain demanding tension which was initially masked by calm and rational discussion. Actually he was using words in an affectless, intellectual sense, attempting to set up a friendly relationship. He felt that he could please me by being perceptive and introspective. When he discovered that this type of manoeuvring was ineffective, his dependent cravings burst forth and for a while it seemed that the full intensity of his infantile pregenital strivings dominated the transference relationship. He would cry during the hours because he felt deprived; he would roll and writhe on the couch and at times kneel on the floor. The nature of this dramatic and primitive material became more understandable in the light of his genetic background and his marital choice.

As his analysis progressed, he revealed material that pointed more concisely to the adaptive nature of his marital relationship. His oedipal strivings were such as to create intense fear of castration by his mother. She was a dominating woman who behaved seductively towards him but became threatening when he responded to her sexual provocativeness. She had exhibited herself to him frequently when he was a child, but was severely prohibitive when he showed signs of sexual interest. She actually had threatened castration when she found him masturbating at the age of five. His father was a passive, depreciated person who showed only minimal masculine attributes.

On the basis of the material it became understandable why he had to stress his wife's strength of character; it also could be seen that his appraisal of her integration was not necessarily accurate, but represented his need to find in her what he had experienced with his mother. It was obvious that his mother was also a disturbed person, and it became clear that his wife also was far from well, psychologically speaking. Her difficulties are discussed in greater detail below; at this point I shall take into account only those disturbances that complemented her husband's specific conflicts. She depreciated him in the same way that his mother had depreciated his father. Her manner was decidedly exhibitionistic, and although she never overtly prohibited his sexual advances, it was learned later in the course of his analysis, when he was able to maintain an erection, that sexual intercourse was still impossible because she suffered from vaginismus. The castrative implications of this symptom are obvious.

Although his wife was sexually inhibited, and yet provocative and exhibitionistic, she did tend to gratify his dependent needs. At this level, she was so maternal that her infantilization of him stifled any attempts he might make towards self-sufficiency, autonomy, or potency. He, in turn, treated her with the same infantile consideration and, later in his analysis, after he divorced her, he described their relationship as that of "two babes in the woods."

What was most impressive in this marriage was the way each of the partners got what they unconsciously asked for. The husband needed a woman who was similarly infantile, to protect himself from the threat of castration, but who also seemed mature enough to provide dependent gratification and yet bolster self-esteem. At this point I was struck by the need each of these partners had for the total personality of the other and how their neuroses dovetailed.

The next case is that of a forty-one-year-old woman advertising executive who sought analysis because of increasing dissatisfaction with her marriage. She also suffered from a peptic ulcer that was aggravated by the emotional upheaval created by marital tension. Bleeding of the ulcer led to frequent hospitalizations and caused her internist to fear for her life. Her analysis revealed a severely masochistic character, a woman who had to deny herself any dependent gratification. As a consequence, she was ambitious and had been able to be successful in the business world. This constellation has been described by Alexander et al (1934). However, this patient's demeanor was not that seen in the classic ulcer patient—belligerent self-assertiveness, indicating an over-compensatory denial of oral impulses. On the contrary, she was mild in manner, compliant, with a certain softness that in no way betrayed her business success. From the family history I received from her as well as from her internist, I learned that her husband was a chronic alcoholic, irresponsible, unpredictable, and much her intellectual inferior. He worked as a laborer, making an adequate salary that was, nevertheless, far below his wife's. He hardly ever alluded to the difference in their earning capacity, being quite content to spend all his earnings as well as a good percentage of hers on liquor.

The husband's behavior towards her was sadistic. Though he never acted it out in terms of physical abuse, he managed to cause her considerable distress and mental anguish. For instance, he would embarrass her by arriving drunk at important social functions. She was unable to depend upon him for anything, and was forced to take over the complete management of the household, payment of bills, planning of vacations, and even keeping a record of his job schedule. This marital situation had existed for over seventeen years, and the patient had not been naïve about her husband's character even before their marriage. If it had not been for the severity of her ulcer and the insistence of her internist, it is doubtful whether she ever would have sought therapy.

However, she became involved in therapy rather quickly, developing a basically dependent transference. As would be expected, her initial resistances were designed to keep such needs repressed, taking the form of overcompensatory denial. When the defence was analysed and the patient, as a consequence, felt herself threatened by the strength of her oral sadistic impulses, she began to behave in an extremely provocative fashion, attempting to get me to react as her husband did in order to gratify her masochistic urges. Because of her oral destructive impulses, she harbored unusually intense feelings of guilt which made her feel as if she would be annihilated by an engulfing, incorporative, utterly cruel maternal superego. Masochistic defences were able to placate this terrifying maternal image and to keep dangerous, cannibalistic impulses safely repressed, a condition described by both Abraham (1927) and Rado (1928). This particular characterological defence was genetically determined by her position in the family; she was the second oldest child among three siblings, all brothers, a fact that contributed to her feeling that women have a depreciated, inferior role. Consequently, this successful woman with a humble mask needed an "inferior" in order to feel "superior."

L. Blitzsten (pers. comm.) felt that these dynamics are precursors of a paranoid state should the defensive equilibrium be disturbed. At times during the process of analysis, associations with a paranoid tinge did emerge, but not to a degree indicating dissolution of ego boundaries and loss of contact with reality. Instead, although it took nearly four years before she reached this stage, the patient began expressing and acting out her dependent needs. At the same time her ulcer once again became active and started to bleed. Her acting out was particularly interesting, in as much as she identified herself with her husband and for a while behaved like a typical alcoholic. This was an entirely new pattern of reaction for her, for prior to her therapy she had been only a moderate drinker. The destructive and self-destructive aspects of her response was readily detected, especially in terms of her ulcer and, on an interpersonal level, in the jeopardizing of her responsible status as an executive. She came close to being fired and was nearly placed in a position where she would have to rely on her husband for financial support. Interestingly enough, with the advent of this chaotic upheaval, her husband stopped drinking, took over the running of the household, and held steady employment. His attitude was moralizing but indulgent. In other words, the roles of these two persons were reversed. The transformation was amazing and puzzling to everyone associated with them.

Further analysis pointed out more clearly her need for the kind of relationship she had with her husband. Unconsciously, her instinctual urges (hostile dependent) were similar to his, but because of the unacceptability of such impulses she was not able to act them out in an egosyntonic fashion. His being able to do so acted as a repressing force. This was illustrated in a dream of two springs, where one spring expanded and, in so doing, exerted pressure on the other, causing it to be compressed. As in all defences against unconscious impulses there was incorporated in the defence some gratification of what was being defended against. In this case, vicarious pleasure was gained from the husband's flagrant pursuit of pregenital satisfactions.

Little was discovered about the husband's character structure, since, as might be expected, it was impossible to get him to seek treatment. Still, his response to the patient's almost complete identification with his alloplasticity indicates the delicate balance achieved in this marriage, and how much in tune his needs must have been with hers to effect the juxtaposition of the springs she dreamed of. The reversal of roles, the remarkable Jekyll-Hyde transformation, indicates how involved their total personalities were with each other.

It might be mentioned, parenthetically, that the patient was able, after having for a time gratified her infantile propensities, to reintegrate herself socially. Following this, her need for the marriage was no longer present, at least in a relative sense, so she obtained a divorce. Her husband reacted adversely to her decision, and after final separation was effected it seemed as if he were going to disintegrate into a psychotic state. He managed, however, to find a woman who was willing to assume the role the patient had played and, as far as can be learned, has maintained his usual equilibrium. I was reminded at this point of the same observation regarding total personality involvement in the first case; even though one partner was obviously immature and the patient seemed quite mature, further developments demonstrated that they were really very similar in their psychic integration.

Discussion

What does the patient's object choice tell us about the other person? Laughlin (1954) writes of a pattern of reaction as being the basis for certain unexplained positive feelings and attractions towards another person. He conjectures that an object relationship may be facilitated by similarities in character and personality traits which in some way may explain our interest in and towards other persons.

Hartmann (1946), in summarizing recent studies, indicates how the development of object relationships depends on the participation of both instinctual and ego tendencies. He states that what we call "satisfactory object relations" have not only an id aspect but obviously also an ego aspect. Instead of considering a relationship in terms of a satisfactory-unsatisfactory axis here, I prefer to use the variables of depth of involvement (elaborated below) and constancy of relationship. As stated above, the material presented here denotes the lack of satisfaction, but nevertheless an equilibrium in which the object relationship has a defensive potential.

In all the cases described, the second person had defences complementary to those of the patient. Sometimes such complementation was overtly manifested and easily recognizable; in other instances, it was subtler and less quickly discernible. Perhaps the most dramatic examples were those of sadomasochism. In the analytic situation the polarity of such reactions was seen more clearly; in several instances the passive partner became the active one, and vice versa as a result of the transference relationship.

Less obvious were those cases where the main axis of the relationship was identification with the object. The existence of such identifications was clearly demonstrated by Johnson (1949, 1952) in her cases. After some study it was possible to discover the pleasure the patient received from his partner's acting out. Such vicarious gratification served to strengthen the bond, in spite of the fact that consciously the patient might complain bitterly of the object's behavior and indicate disapproval. Analysis always revealed that these protestations were defensive, and closer scrutiny revealed that these patients unconsciously encouraged the acting out of patterns that they themselves would have liked to act out but, because of superego restraints, could not. An unacceptable instinctual impulse thus was gratified by identification with the person who was able to discharge a similar impulse alloplastically.

In addition to instinctual gratification, psychoeconomic factors play a determining role in the relationship. The husband of the advertising executive, by his impulse-ridden actions, made possible successful repression of the patient's unacceptable impulses. Identification in this case served also to protect the patient's ego, her husband's symptomatology serving as an "expanding spring" (the spring dream) keeping the patient's impulses in a state of "compression" or, in a more familiar term, a state of safe repression.

The defensive meaning of the object's behaviour can be illustrated in another way. Equilibrium can be maintained by utilizing certain symptoms of the object in order to mask or hide the patient's own. For example, a thirty-six-year-old architect complained of social restrictions imposed on him by his wife's phobias, which were of such a nature and severity that they kept him virtually chained to the house. Her difficulties served to maintain his self-esteem and to protect him from the painful recognition of shame-provoking passive needs. Her behavior served as an excellent rationalization to stay at home and not be aggressive or manly, qualities that were frightening to him because of severe castration anxiety. Analysis revealed that he had phobias practically identical with those of his wife—fear of crowds, parties, being too far away from a toilet, etc.—but his wife's symptoms kept him away from anxiety-producing settings so that he never had to experience the phobias or even to admit their existence.

These factors again point to the adaptive nature of an object relationship. These observations indicate the existence of similar or complementary defences in the partners. The persons studied seemed to be similar in their psychic adjustment, showing identical patterns of regression and fixation based on similar or related conflicts. For example, guilt and the lack of homosexual contact caused a female patient to seek therapy after the schizophrenic breakdown of her lover. Then it was discovered that her make-up was essentially schizophrenic, although this was not indicated by superficial observation of her behaviour.

Another example of what seemed to be wide differences, on the surface, of psychic adjustment is that of the psychologist and his wife. I learned from his therapy that he was essentially schizoid in nature, whereas his wife's integration did not seem to be nearly so seriously impaired. Nevertheless, after he had made some rather startling changes, becoming less narcissistic and withdrawn, his wife began to experience overt anxiety. As it continued, she became more and more withdrawn and then developed a full-blown paranoid psychosis that required a long period of hospitalization. Her therapist was able to determine that her regression was precipitated by the demands of her husband's new-found sexual potency, that her ego, which was only loosely held together, simply was not able to cope with the changed reality of the marriage. Moran (1958), who interviewed husbands of patients, found how threatened they were by their wives' improvement or the prospect of such improvement. The possibility of disrupting the adaptive harmony of the marriage may explain the numerous cases of husbands and wives being in analysis at the same time.

The clinical observations cited here seem to indicate that the equilibrium established in an emotionally meaningful object relationship is based on similarities of psychopathology and results in the total involvement of the persons with each other. The clinical material thus indicated the following: (1) similar or complementary defences, which might imply similar underlying conflicts, but not necessarily prove their existence; (2) similar underlying conflicts were found when both partners could be analytically studied; (3) similar underlying conflicts were revealed also when the superficial defences were relinquished and the reversal of the behavioral roles took place during analysis; (4) separation reactions also resulted in reversal of behavioral roles and indicated similar underlying conflicts.

The depth of psychopathology of the two partners seems to be equal when one requires the total personality, or the specific character defences, of the other. Still, one would wonder if there are emotionally meaningful relationships where the above similarities do not exist, and undoubtedly many such examples can be listed. I would like to present one, but also indicate how I believe this patient's object relationships are different from those previously mentioned.

A young and brilliant scientist was unable to explain his lack of success in achieving a stable marriage. He had been married twice before, and now in his third marriage found it impossible to continue. He vacillated in his feelings towards his wife. Even though he wanted a divorce, he did not want to admit defeat again. Nevertheless, he found his wife's behavior intolerable because of her varying and unpredictable moods. At times she would reject him completely and react violently to any affectionate gesture he might make. Just as inexplicably, she would behave in a seductive, warm fashion. The wife's therapist felt strongly that she was suffering from a schizophrenic psychosis and could not face any involvement in an object relationship. On the other hand, her husband was an affable person and outgoing, with many social contacts and close relationships. The impression gained from his analysis was that of a moderately severe character neurosis, with hysterical and obsessive features, but nothing so severe as to suggest any psychotic elements. Nevertheless, his need for his wife seemed to be very strong, as shown by his pursuit of her during courtship and his tenacity toward the marriage, even though it was obviously impossible.

His motivations became clearer when his relationship with his mother was understood. Her main characteristic also was unpredictability. She, too, was openly seductive toward the patient and on several occasions made overt sexual advances. At other times she would be violently anti-sexual and adopt the manner of an incensed Victorian. To overcome his castration anxiety, the patient had to solve the riddle of the mysterious, unpredictable woman. He deliberately associated himself with such disturbed women in order to repeat the experience and master the danger he felt was inherent in his relationship with his mother who later became psychotic and died in a state hospital.

He was preoccupied with problem solving, a motif that had a large share in determining his choice of profession. His need for his wife was not based on characterological similarity; rather she represented a challenge and a problem to him. Such a challenge, by its very nature, could be found only in a seriously disturbed personality. When he did finally leave her, she had very little reaction and did not seem upset in her usual equilibrium. What he really needed was this one trait of unpredictability which he found in this woman and other women of diverse character structures.

This case and others like it indicate that the object relationship is determined chiefly by the patient's conflicts and much less by the partner, as could be seen in the partner's relatively mild reaction when separation eventually occurred. Even as far as the patient is concerned, the involvement did not seem to be one of the total personality. A specific area of conflict seemed to be at work, but it did not include the main characterological features of the psychic structure.

The distinction is analogous to that between a character neurosis and a symptom neurosis. Anna Freud (1949) and her co-workers indicated that there is a marked difference between an object relationship that is need-satisfying and one that includes object constancy, in that the former will exist only as long as the particular need is satisfied. The latter type was seen to have positive integrative aspects in terms of ego development, but Anna Freud, Hartmann (1952), and Kris (1950a) recognized the role of intrapsychic conflict in the formation of object relationships. If the characterological features in their more total and diffuse aspects of the ego are the source of interactions of the partners, then we seem to have a total deep and constant involvement. If, on the other hand, an isolated area of the ego, such as a specific defence or symptom, becomes a pole around which the relationship revolves, then the relationship is less vital for the partners and is more transient, as in the example just cited. Such an object relationship represented a symptomatic manifestation, but only one manifestation among many, whereas the object relationships previously described had become the axis around which transactions with reality were affected and internal equilibrium was maintained, indicating a characterological involvement rather than simply a symptomatic one.

I feel that this subject deserves further study which can be pursued through further clinical observations. I hope that this introductory effort will be supplemented by others and extended to a point where we might have a basis for the metapsychology of object relationships.

Chapter 16

Resistance and External Object Relations

Understanding of the subtleties of emotionally meaningful object relationships has become, in certain cases, an integral part of the psychoanalytic exploration and resolution of resistances. The object relationships alluded to here have been described in chapter 15 and were found to be characterized by a high degree of mutual dependence. The interaction of two emotionally involved persons was found to be a complex phenomenon in which were revealed many basic similarities of character structure, defences, and conflicts. The defences of two individuals were seen to complement each other in many such instances.

In this study I wish to utilize some of the theoretical constructions that were formulated regarding the similarity of character structure in two individuals who have an emotionally meaningful relationship and to apply these constructions to the therapeutic field. In other words, I hope to demonstrate that extended insight about the dynamics of an object relationship can have pragmatic utility in the specific psychoanalytic situation.

Freud (Breuer and Freud, 1895) first described a concept of resistance in one of his earliest papers. His early attempts to get patients to associate freely consisted in placing his index finger on their forehead and asking them to tell whatever came to mind in connexion with the onset of symptoms. The first two or three times he did this the patients stated that nothing occurred. Finally, they admitted that they had had some thoughts even the first time they were asked to speak, but felt these thoughts were inconsequential or trivial, so they did not verbalize them. Freud called this lack of verbalization when something actually did occur to them "resistance." He went on to describe this as a conscious withholding of associational material; whereas defence was described as being unconscious. Later, when formulating the structural hypothesis, Freud (1923) somewhat modified this concept. He now felt that resistance emanated from the ego. It was perceived but not recognized as a resistance or described as such, so it, too, was unconscious. He explained that what institutes and maintains repression is resistance.

With the advent of the structural approach there has been a special concentration on defences, characterological features, and object rela-

First published in *Int. J. Psa.* 42 (1961), 246–54. Reprinted by permission.

tionships. Many of the problems experienced in the therapeutic process have been examined from these particular vantage points, and every analyst is familiar with the phenomena resulting from specific object relationships. In many instances patients have made a degree of progress which is determined by the usual analytic criteria but then stubbornly balk at any further resolution of unconscious conflicts. A therapeutic impasse is reached.

Oftentimes the analyst is able to determine the cause of the patient's lack of response. Here I would like to discuss certain cases where this situation has occurred and the chief determinant in bringing it about has been an object relationship. One might consider this as being an extrinsic resistance or at least a resistance extrinsically stimulated. Such an external factor when acting as a stimulus blocking the progress of analysis is one that is intimately associated with the characterological defences of the patient. In other words, the emotionally meaningful object is somehow able to stimulate or reinforce the patient's resistance and by so doing to create a therapeutic complication of such intensity that it may disrupt the whole psychoanalytic process. It should be stressed that this occurs only in very close object relationships, those that have been described as being mutually adaptive in character, where both partners receive much support from each other.

Disturbances of Equilibrium and Object Relationships

Analysts often learn of anxiety in the husband or wife of a patient who is making progress. After learning of the peculiarities and quirks of behavior in so many of our patients, we often wonder how the spouses manage to tolerate the relationship for so long. Sometimes a marital partner may complain vociferously, but on the other hand he often presents a picture of calm, amazingly stoic.

Frequently enough, as the cases to be described here show, the husband or wife appears to be sincere in encouraging the analysand in working hard to achieve maturity. Although he seems to be genuinely dissatisfied with the status quo, the analyst becomes aware of a difference in his cooperation once some real movement in the analysis occurs that is reflected outwardly in the patient's everyday behavior. At this point one can detect a disturbance of equilibrium of the marriage that is different from the conditions that prevailed at the beginning of therapy. This disturbance somehow seems to have more substance to it, and intuitively one senses a certain ominous tone that in the majority of cases did not previously exist. In other instances, the marital partner reacts with overt anxiety, whose content is determined by his specific emotional constellation but is obviously triggered by changes in the analysand.

Such a shift in the equilibrium of an emotionally meaningful relationship constitutes a threat to the relatively static personality of the individual who is not involved in therapy. How he reacts to this threat depends on his particular psychic structure, so that the manifestations of the response are varied and manifold. Still, I believe that there are some common denominators dynamically if not phenomenologically. I believe, also, that the effects of this reaction on a patient have some potentials common to many patients and that often they produce similar therapeutic complications.

Object relationships can be considered from a variety of viewpoints. Stress has relatively recently (Bowlby, 1958) been laid on the intrinsic instinctual need for the object or the maturational potential of the relationship as described by Benedek (1949, 1959) in the mother-child symbiosis where both participants can benefit. Here the child by receiving from the mother is able to develop and mature, whereas the mother in being successful in her motherliness also achieves higher states of integration. This transaction, however, may also lead to negative results which may be a determinant in the causation of psychopathology in the child and at the same time may augment the mother's already existing problems. The types of relationships to be considered here will be discussed only from the psychopathological viewpoint and not in terms of possible potentials for emotional development.

Oberndorf (1938) and Mittelmann (1944) have described relationships similar to those to be discussed here. They felt that the personalities of the partners were complementary to each other. I wish to stress this point too, when I refer to the mutually adaptive character of the object relationship. Unlike the mother-child symbiosis of Benedek and Mahler (1952), the needs of each partner for the other are equal. In the mother-child relationship this is obviously not so, since the child depends on the mother for his total survival whereas the mother is able to survive without the child, even though, in some instances, the loss of the child may constitute a serious threat to her equilibrium.

A relationship formed between two persons with similar character structures, complementing each other's defences or in some instances reinforcing them, has assumed a vital importance for each of the partners, and equilibrium has been reached not only intrapsychically but also between the two persons. There may, nevertheless, be certain discomforts involved for one partner within the frame of the defensive adjustment; consequently, this person may seek therapy. Discomfort resulting from one's defences is not an uncommon motivating factor leading to the quest for therapy. In the instances to be described there is the additional variable of the partner who also feels uncomfortable because of the patient's discomfort, and therefore encourages the seeking of help. He desires a corrective experience for the patient, but not one that will change the fundamental equilibrium existing between the two of them. What he usually wants is only symptomatic relief without any characterological alteration. The salient difference between this type of object relationship and the mother-child one is that the aim of the partners is to maintain the status quo, whereas the latter, if a mature one, has the development of a child as one of its intrinsic aims.

Clinical Material

An especially striking example of a therapeutic impasse stimulated by an object relationship is the case of a recently married young woman who sought therapy because of various somatic complaints. Her symptoms centered upon the respiratory system and consisted in difficulty in taking a full breath, a feeling of suffocation, and hyperpnoea, all present from childhood on. In addition to this specific somatization there were many characterological features that indicated a basically infantile personality with a strong oral component. Her behaviour and attitudes indicated a person who was naïve and sexually unsophisticated; at least, her appearance gave that impression. Others, especially her husband, described her as a "wide-eyed, cute little girl." In her dealings with men she was forthright and sincere to a point that could have been considered tactless, although there was a certain charm about her manner. Underneath what at times seemed to be a dependent helplessness, there was a haughtiness and a belief that she came from a superior, cultured, aristocratic background (in fact, it was a not unusual middle-class setting). This belief caused her to feel above her intimate associates and, in particular, her husband. She felt that because of inferior breeding he did not know how to treat her with proper respect, delicacy, and consideration, and constantly compared him unfavorably with her parents.

These narcissistic qualities served to bolster an ego that was beset with feelings of inadequacy and one that was dominated by insatiable, oral dependent demands. Her feelings of inadequacy were determined by sexual conflicts that threatened her feminine self-esteem. The character structure seemed to be a basically hysterical one, the physical symptoms representing conversion processes. However, this aspect of her personality, as is so often the case, came to the surface only after a long period of treatment that for the most part was involved with her pregenital oral dependent strivings. The nature and strength of such impulses were so intense that at first I wondered if she were not primarily fixated at such a point of libido development, a point that Marmor (1955) made some time ago about hysteria and one that has recently been referred to again (Rangell, 1959).

Nevertheless, the dream material indicated that no matter what oral fixation was operative, the oedipal problem was nuclear. Her analysis seemed to progress favourably and her improvements were reflected in her behavior. She seemed to be sincerely trying to work through her infantile dependent demands and effected many changes in her daily life which indicated that she was headed for self-sufficiency and a basic resolution of her oedipal problems.

This optimistic appraisal was not confirmed as the analysis continued; subsequent events indicated that the prognosis was not nearly so favourable as it had seemed initially. After about 18 months of what had seemed to be a well-progressing analysis, the patient reverted to her old dependent status. Not only was there an intensification of the physical symptoms that she initially presented, but her haughty, whining behavior returned. In the analysis itself she showed an obtuseness and refractoriness to any and all interpretations. Whereas previously she had been attentive and receptive, insights that at one time seemed to have been operationally useful appeared to have been lost both emotionally and intellectually. Granted that this type of regression and resistance is not unusual in an analysis when deeper layers of conflict are encroached upon, this patient showed a tenacity that seemed peculiar. If it had not been for unmistakable evidence of previous working through of conflicts, I would have felt that she had been completely untouched by the psychoanalytic process. Repetition of interpretations that had previously been effective now left her unmoved, and the tendency to vacillate between oedipal and pregenital material, as is more often the case, did not appear. Instead, she seemed to remain rigidly involved with her pregenital orientations. In the midst of all this she finally began talking more about her husband and revealed information that she had never previously brought up.

She described him as a self-assured, competent person who had always done well both professionally and socially. In spite of her earlier criticisms of his background, she had always seen him as a mature man with considerable strength and with great concern for her welfare. Still, oddly enough, he never raised any questions about her treatment, although he was extremely inquisitive about all other aspects of her life. He had always tended to manage her and to lead her around in a protective fashion. Concerning the analysis, however, it appeared that he was studiously avoiding any discussion of it. In general he seemed to encourage her and to emphasize his eagerness for her to "grow up," but in spite of her regression, which was manifested in behavior as well as within the analytic framework, he did not show the least sign of impatience or discouragement. This was especially odd since the cost of his wife's treatment represented a sizeable financial sacrifice for him. He could be and had often been extremely critical of his wife, but in this area he never evinced any disapproval.

The patient then revealed that he liked certain infantile traits. For instance, he thoroughly enjoyed having her use baby talk on certain occasions. In the past she had done this unconsciously. Since her analysis she found it odious; but she continued because she was afraid of displeasing him. When she had stopped for a period of time, he overtly resented it. He also liked telling her obscene jokes, but he wanted her not to understand so that he could shock and tease her with the explanation. Even though she understood the meaning of the joke as well as he did, she maintained an attitude of naïve bewilderment, since he seemed to enjoy it so much. When she was eating, he often looked at her with a satisfied expression similar to that of a father enjoying a daughter's childish incompetence. When she did actually behave incompetently, his attitude on the surface was benign and patient, but she began to understand that he was really being patronizing and enjoying the situation.

She responded by going out of her way to appear incompetent, sensing his need to have her remain childish. This continued until she began to feel resentment because of the lowered self-esteem resulting from this type of behavior and relationship. Her anger was particularly aroused when she began to consider their sexual practices. Again, he preferred her to be a little girl. He never approached her and showed no response when she tried to be seductive either by direct actions or by wearing provocative nightgowns and perfumes. If she wanted intercourse, she had to get into his bed and cuddle up beside him in what she now considered to be a babyish fashion.

She now believed that her husband unconsciously did not want her to be anything but an infant and that, in spite of his enthusiasm for her analysis, he was well satisfied with the status quo.

The patient, on the other hand, found it difficult to adjust herself to this infantilizing atmosphere. As she reported more material about her husband, the impasse reported gradually gave way and she was once again able to continue with the analysis. This necessitated some changes in her external adjustment which will be discussed later in connection with the husband. Suffice it to say that the husband, because of the disturbed marital equilibrium, became anxious and found himself forced to seek analytic assistance.

This type of impasse has been frequently observed clinically, but in this instance the dynamic interrelationships of these two people can be described in a fairly detailed way since the material of two analyses is available to us. Furthermore, as we shall later see, the changes in the husband were striking and dramatic ones which served to highlight both the mutually adaptive and the resistive meanings of the object relationship.

Another case showed similarly dramatic features. This patient, also a young married woman, sought analysis because of chronic anxiety. For many years she had felt frightened, experiencing a persistent tension that fluctuated in intensity, increasing episodically to a panic state. Her anxiety had practically no ideational content except that she was afraid of being left alone and abandoned. Her symptoms indicated that she was very dependent and beset with infantile fears of being rejected, losing all support and finding herself in a helpless, vulnerable condition. As in the previous case, orality seemed to be the dominant characterological feature. But again the question arose as to how much defensive meaning such infantilism had in terms of protecting her from more disturbing oedipal conflicts. The degree of disturbance manifested was not reflected in the transference situation, nor did she seem to display the type of disorganization that would be typical of a pregenital fixation consistent with such symptoms. She did not make any unusual demands of the analyst and was able to free-associate in a spontaneous, relatively uninhibited fashion. The helplessness she spoke of was more in the nature of a protest and its defensive meaning became apparent.

She too seemed to develop insight with relative ease and was able to utilize what she learned in her analysis by applying it to the problems of everyday living. She gained confidence and a heightened self-esteem, recognizing many potentials and demonstrating them in actual achievement. Her dreams showed even more clearly that she was defending herself against disturbing sexual feelings, which by this time had become part of the transference.

This patient showed features strikingly similar to certain features in the first patient discussed above. A period of apparent progress was followed by one of analytic stagnation, all her symptoms of anxiety and helplessness and the fear of being left stranded returning. Whatever insights she had seemed to gain vanished and further analysis was of no avail. Once again an impasse had been reached.

Because of my previous experience I wondered whether the husband's reaction might have had some bearing on the difficulties encountered. Like the other patient's husband, he initially encouraged his wife. Everything he said indicated that he found her symptoms distressing and aggravating and that he had reached a point where he could no longer tolerate the marriage if things continued as they were. In fact, he had taken the initial step of contacting a physician friend in order to discuss the possibility of analysis for his wife. His attitude was concerned and solicitous, indicating an eagerness not only to relieve his wife's suffering but to do everything possible to put the marriage on a more mature basis. He was even willing to acknowledge that some of the difficulties might have been provoked by his own personal problems. But he felt, in view of his wife's overt distress, that her situation was the most pressing one and demanding of professional attention.

Once she began analysis he frequently inquired as to how she was getting along and made certain that she was keeping her appointments. On several occasions when he felt that she was too disturbed to keep an appointment, he would take time off from work and drive her to the analyst's office. Several times he called me, ostensibly to get reassurance that I would be able to help his wife. His eagerness to see her improve and his concern about her condition was of such a degree of intensity that one might well have become suspicious of his motives.

His attitude gradually changed and was correlated with the subsidence of her symptoms. As these began to improve, he showed less and less interest in what was occurring during the analytic sessions. He still maintained a benign demeanor, although somewhat stoic. Only when her anxiety completely disappeared and her behaviour began showing increasing degrees of competence did he begin to complain. At first he took what might be considered a cautious outlook about her improvement, indicating that he felt it was more apparent than real. Then he began to complain about his wife's behavior, labeling it as selfish. Finally he displayed overt hostility which took the form of depreciating his wife in terms of her weakness (even though she was then behaving in a much more positive fashion than she ever had before) and condemning psychoanalysis as ephemeral and unscientific. He also vociferously complained about the cost of therapy and the many material sacrifices they had to make because of it, a sharp contrast to his former attitude. He had gone along with the analysis for a long time, never raising any objections as long as his wife showed no discernible external changes, but when there was a marked difference in her behavior he began suddenly to voice objections. It became apparent that his complaints and the patient's regression were, at least, temporally correlated.

Discussion

If we consider the mutually adaptive elements in an emotionally meaningful object relationship and note the characterological similarities of the partners involved, the difficulties encountered in these two analyses can be understood in terms of the precarious balance of the marriage, a balance that was disturbed by the progress that the patient made. Anna Freud (1949) has discussed need-satisfying relationships and their influence on further ego development. Hartmann (1946) indicated the important role of the id as a determinant in object choice, whereas others such as Bowlby (1958) have recently postulated an innate instinctual need for object contact. Freud (1911b) demonstrated how an object can represent, sometimes through a process of projection, various aspects of psychic structure.

In chapter 15 I presented clinical material which indicates that a marital partner is not chosen accidentally or haphazardly. On the contrary, any lasting relationship is established because of the many characterological similarities of the partners. Although the wife's symptoms may at one level be disturbing for the husband, he unconsciously needs a woman with that particular psychopathology. Such a relationship has a defensive, protective function and is necessary for ego stability. It was stressed in the previous communication that the psychopathology of the partners involved was similar. The levels of fixations and the basic conflicts were the same in such an object relationship and the defences either reinforced or complemented each other. One cannot generalize that all object relationships are centered upon such a mutually adaptive axis, but the cases that did not seem to have such similarities were those of transient object relationships.

What one partner in this transient group demanded and needed of the other was merely a segment of the personality such as a specific defence or area of behavior which was able to satisfy some circumscribed need. In a sense the partner required only the symptoms (if there were any) of the object, whereas in the relationships discussed here the involvement is a more total characterological one. The reactions of the partner to the analysis were different in these two kinds of object relationships. In these cases of only circumscribed involvement, there was less or no reaction to the partner's improvement and in some instances which resulted in separation there was a minimum of reaction. The cases discussed here were different in this respect.

The partner's attempts to sabotage the therapy became apparent and were voiced as complaints, a phenomenon that Mosse (1954) has frequently observed among the relatives of analytic patients. Usually, one is not able, except by inference, to understand the exact motivations behind the spouse's needs except in the general terms already described. The seeking of analysis by the spouse is not an unusual occurrence, one which is often responsible for saving the marriage.

The motivations of the first patient's husband can now be discussed more specifically. The analytic material indicated that his outer demeanor of self-sufficiency and autonomy covered a basically oral dependent personality. He was very much ashamed of such needs, which threatened his ego ideal, and because of the resultant lowered self-esteem he tended to defend himself by overcompensating. In order to do this successfully, he needed an object to support his defence, and his wife helped in this respect. By feeling superior to her and looking upon her as a baby, he placed himself in the parental role, taking care of someone else who was dependent and thereby denying his own oral impulses. As has often been seen in mutually adaptive relationships, the additional factor of vicarious gratification operated. In these circumstances one can understand why, though on the surface he encouraged his wife's therapy and pushed her to make progress, unconsciously he felt differently about it. When she did begin to make some progress, this was reflected in their relationship. Her progress served to frustrate an instinctual gratification, i.e., his oral dependent impulses, but more important still, threatened his stable defence of reaction formation. He was no longer able to use the object relationship to maintain intrapsychic harmony by protecting him from shame-provoking and, as was learned later, guilt-ridden oral demands.

He would naturally want to reestablish the object relationship on its preanalytic basis, so it is not difficult to understand how he would be forced to respond in some way that would attempt to interfere with his wife's therapy. Although from the beginning of their marriage he tended to infantilize his wife and depreciate any spontaneous attempt she made in the direction of psychic maturity, he intensified his efforts when he began to recognize changes in her.

We can reconstruct the effects of the husband's behavior on her total response, which became manifest in the setting of the transference neurosis. She was not consciously aware of his aversion to her achieving emotional adulthood but sensed it unconsciously. The marital role she assumed was, of course, consistent with her defensive needs. Later, however, she became afraid of displeasing the husband by altering her role, and this fear led to resistance in the analysis. This resistance can be conceptualized as an extrinsic resistance, indicating that it did not result from an intrapsychic conflict alone but was stimulated by the specific object relationship. So the husband's overt resistance to therapeutic progress on the patient's part became a significant factor in motivating the patient to regress. Such a factor, as is well known, can be effective only if it is exercised on a suitable medium, where there is an emotional constellation with capacity for a suitable response. In these cases the husband's reaction reinforced tendencies that were already present but had been partially worked through by analysis. The husband's resistance on the outside can be thought of as intensifying the patient's inner resistance.

The recognition of the husband's role led to startling results in both cases. Nothing was said to either of these women about the speculations the analyst had made concerning the husband's motivations. Instead, the patient's need to please the husband was stressed in the interpretations. Besides protecting them from disturbing sexual conflicts the infantile behavior was discussed in terms of its adaptive features vis-à-vis the husband, and the patients were able to perceive that in many instances they behaved as they did because they were afraid to do otherwise. What was different at this point was the fact that they were able to relate their anxiety to a specific situation that always involved the husband. They were then able to recall incidents where they became aware that at least part of their motivation for behaving childishly was to conform to what they imagined the husband expected of them. The dream material of both patients confirmed the fact that they felt afraid of behaving otherwise because of masculine disapproval. Dream analysis also revealed that these patients believed their fathers wanted to keep them as lovable little girls, not wanting them to grow into sexual women. By assuming this role the patients were able to protect themselves against their oedipal wishes. This drama was being reenacted in the marriage, both patients indicating that they felt they had found mates who were threatened by a mature sexual orientation.

The patients were then able to consider many situations which they had previously accepted as ordinary ones in this new light. They were able to report many details and nuances and subtleties of incidents that had previously escaped them, insofar as they had not seen anything unusual in the specific type of object relationship they had. They had not scrutinized various elements of the marriage too carefully. Now they began to do so. Quite spontaneously both these women began pointing out to their husbands exactly what they were doing in terms of wanting to maintain them in a state of infantilism.

The husbands, at first, tended to make light of their wives' observations. In their usual fashion they treated such reflections in a condescending and patronizing manner. They tried to make it appear as if this were just another example of their spouses' childish incompetence, so they tended to be indulgent. The husbands' denials then became more intense and at times were even frenzied. It became apparent that their equanimity was shattered, and consequently they attempted to depreciate the patients further. The first patient, in particular, was not discouraged since she could not see any reason to be surprised by the fact that he had to be defensive about his behavior. She resolutely continued to convey her beliefs to him and was especially effective when she could demonstrate the truth of what she was saying about him during a current incident. Her confrontations went a little deeper than simply identifying the nature of his attitude towards her. She attempted also to convey to him what his motivations were in terms of his not being able to tolerate a relationship with a sexual woman. At this point it was obvious that the patient was being somewhat intellectual, a defensive device which served her in the analytic experience also. She felt, however, that her observations were accurate and astute and they did have the hoped-for effect on her husband. As time went on his protests became weaker and he even began to behave differently in the areas discussed. He finally recognized, though reluctantly, a need to seek professional consultation.

The night following his first appointment he experienced epigastric pain resembling the symptoms of peptic ulcer. He had had similar symptoms in the distant past and it was suggested that he have a diagnostic gastro-duodenal X-ray examination; he never followed through. The hypothesis that he was reacting to his wife's new-found independence, which resulted in a distrubance of his overcompensatory defences, was interesting in view of his somatic response. Such a con-stellation has been described by Alexander (1934) and his co-workers as a typical situation for peptic ulcer. In this case the material indicated that his dependent difficulties were close to the surface and that oedipal problems were at the core of his conflicts. The first dream indicated a hostile, competitive struggle with his father and an accompanying fear of castration. His defences were overcompensatory ones which helped him to preserve self-esteem in view of his passive needs and resulting feelings of inadequacy. This man's prominent, aggressive behavior was then seen to be overdetermined at both sexual and dependent levels, emphasizing that although the overt picture was different in these marital partners, dynamically there were very striking similarities.

In the second case, essentially similar events took place. The husband could no longer capitalize on his wife's difficulty when she started to maintain constant vigilance over her behavior and her reactions to his attempts to keep her helpless and vulnerable. As with the first patient, she often pointed out to him what she felt was meant either to depreci-ate or to baby her. He did not agree with her or give credence to what she said to the point of seeking consultation. But he did cease his com-plaining and anti-analytic barrages. Otherwise his reaction was one of withdrawal; he reverted to his former behavior and hardly ever men-tioned the treatment.

The patients' reactions were striking, especially when considered in relation to the impasses that had been reached. In both cases nearly all the symptoms disappeared. In the first patient all the somatic difficulties, mainly respiratory, cleared up, and in the second anxiety, the predominant affective state, vanished. The correlation of the improvement following the impasse and the changes in the marital situation was an exact one. The nonsymptomatic states were not permanent, and as in any analysis depended on the general movement within the therapy and the transference relationship. The important fact for our purpose here was that the previous period of stagnation was finally disrupted and the analysis continued once the meaning of the husband's role in relation to the patient was understood. The subsequent course of the analysis was not particularly unusual and need not be dwelt upon further.

The patients' confrontations somehow made it impossible for each husband to continue the sabotage and thereby removed his value to them as a resistance, what could be called an extrinsic resistance. The patients had to refocus on their inner problems when it ceased to be possible to externalize their difficulties in the reality situation.

It is obvious that all these people, patients and spouses, had fairly well-developed ego ideals and high needs for self-esteem. Otherwise these women would have been content to accept the status quo, since it was in the service of their defences. It was not, however, consonant with the ego ideal. Giving up a defence, or the use of a husband for defensive purposes was not necessarily pleasant for them. The first patient, at one stage, regretted what she had done because her "inner" resistance was now threatened and she was in part responsible for this. Although intellectually she understood that from a long-range viewpoint she had acted wisely, for the present she found herself without the support that the marital relationship offered her. She felt as if she had forged ahead and now had to stop and look back with the attitude of "My God, what have I done?" She was frightened, and as is usual, she expressed her tensions somatically; the asymptomatic state was only temporary. But she recognized also that having taken the step she could not give in to her wish to regress, and she was able to continue analysis without any unusual difficulties.

The importance of the object relationship is emphasized in this material. The value and potential of an object relationship in the development and maturation of the psyche can hardly be overstressed. On the other hand, its contribution to psychopathology also requires emphasis. In these instances, one can see the similarities in the basic conflicts, the ego structures and the complementation of defences. This led to a stable psychopathology and to operational stability.

Insofar as the partners' defences are utilized also by the patient's ego and have come to represent an external extension of internal defences, the analytic process becomes a threat to the stability of the marriage and will constitute a problem for both the patient and the partner. The partner's attempts then to reestablish the status quo are understandable since he, too, is losing a defensively meaningful object. In other instances where a patient clings to an object because it is needed for psychic equilibrium and represents some archaic infantile need, the object may not be particularly needful in its own right. In these cases what is being stressed is a mutual need of the partners for each other.

It might be concluded that in order to conduct a successful analysis of a married person the spouse would also have to be analyzed. This is true in many cases, as any analyst knows. It is not necessarily true, however, and such a generalization cannot be made. Many patients make progress in therapy in spite of a spouse's continual sabotage. This factor is dealt with analytically, as is any vicissitude encountered in the patient's daily life. Though it has been postulated that marriage represents a form of stability and indicates a state of emotional equilibrium, marriage is not static. Equilibrium can be maintained even when another variable is introduced in the relationship. The analysis may introduce different adjustments and therefore different needs on the part of the analysand which will lead to a shift in the object relationship, but equilibrium can be reestablished at a different level. In a marital relationship the husband would have to respond to the wife's changes and in turn effect some changes himself. He would have to give up at least some aspect of his defensive needs, those pertaining to the object, and construct his defences in other areas. This can often be done and the defences kept relatively isolated from the marriage. On other occasions, the spouse may actually work through some inner conflicts, thereby being able to keep pace or at least make a degree of progress which makes it possible to continue the marriage in a relatively undisturbed fashion. The analysis of one person has been known to have a maturing effect on his spouse, and such a result can be considered an optimal outcome of an analysis of a married person.

Many cases, however, do not achieve such a favorable resolution. An object relationship can be oriented along many different axes. Although further explorations are required, it seems reasonable to believe that the qualitative differences in an object relationship may in some way be associated with the tenacity of the relationship and how it will react to and withstand analysis. In some instances, the analysand continues to make progress in spite of innumerable obstacles raised by the partner. The partner in turn becomes increasingly disturbed and the relationship eventually becomes intolerable with divorce as the outcome. In my experience, this type of circumstance is most often seen in marriages oriented around a sadomasochistic axis. I recall one particular striking example.

An academician's wife entered therapy because of a depression and revealed that her husband had often inflicted brutal beatings on her, as evidenced by many visible bruises. Like other masochists, she provoked him and received a modicum of enjoyment from this physical abuse, her tolerance for pain being high. With analysis and working through of guilt, however, the acting out of masochistic impulses ceased to be necessary for her emotional equilibrium. Her husband's sadistic urges nevertheless still demanded expression. As with the other husbands discussed in this paper, he did everything possible to upset the progressive course of analysis, but the patient recognized what he was trying to do and his efforts were useless. She suggested therapy to him and he did seek consultation. Though he made this initial effort, he rejected the suggestion that he be analyzed. The marriage became increasingly difficult with the patient no longer tolerating his brutality, a fact that received emphasis when she finally called the police to thwart his intention of doing her physical harm. He then realized that she was absolutely serious about not wanting to continue the relationship on the previous basis; he once again sought professional consultation but, as previously, balked at the suggestion of analysis. Soon after, the patient divorced him. He made a feeble attempt to block the divorce but recognized that the possibility of staying together was remote, so he reconciled himself to the inevitable. From this moment on, he became pleasant and affable and did nothing whatsoever to hamper legal proceedings. When he recognized that it was useless to fight he felt he should be a gentleman about the situation and acted as a man of good taste and breeding. He was able to reconstruct the chain of events in terms of defects in his character and of maturation on his wife's part, but he understood that he did not have sufficient motivation to change at this particular time. Later he married a woman who served the same function as the patient had formerly done.

In all of these clinical instances the object relationship has been considered as a crucial factor involved in the analytic process. The importance of other relevant variables such as the infantile conflicts and the transference neurosis is, of course, no different in these cases than in others.

The object relationship is simply another determinant which may hamper the analysis or in some instances help it in that it serves to accelerate the working through of inner conflicts by emphasizing their effects and reenactment in current situations. The patient's analysis gives us clues about the psychopathology of the object. Not only does such an understanding help us discern the object's motivations, which in themselves would not be of particular importance, but by helping us focus on the dynamic aspects of the object relationship much can be learned about the patient's characteristic responses to reality. In this instance the reality emphasized is a current one, but by understanding the equilibrium effected with emotionally meaningful objects in the present, we are able to reconstruct a good deal about archaic and primitive object relationships.

These are traditionally reconstructed in the transference neurosis and to some extent acted out in this setting. The analyst, however, does not react in the expected fashion to the analysand's infantile demands and needs. The object in the external world does; otherwise the relationship would not have been established in the first place. If the patient feels the frustration of the disappointed transference expectations, then he is apt to strengthen his ties to the defensively meaningful and gratifying object. This has been noted in analyses where both spouses join together in a common and reinforced anger towards analysis, thereby cementing their relationship and for the moment being able to suppress previously recognized negative aspects.

If, on the other hand, the patient is able to resolve at least aspects of the infantile conflicts that determine the transference relationship, then the type of object relationship needed is a more mature one than actually exists. This will lead to the circumstances described in the clinical material and the objects' reactions may be effective in creating a thera-peutic impasse. This particular complication, inherent in the disturbance of a mutually adaptive relationship, has been stressed in this communi-cation. Naturally, the subject can be pursued further from a variety of standpoints, and as our theoretical understanding of object relationships increases, our view of the therapeutic process will also widen.

Chapter 17

Integrative Aspects of Object Relationships

Current interest in ego psychology has caused us to examine closely the operation of intra-ego systems, defective functioning of which is said to underlie character disorders or "borderline" states. Consequently, the operations, development, and maturation of such systems are of increased theoretical and clinical interest.

Studies of the ego have usually included scrutiny of object relations, and the role of the object is pivotal in many concepts. Fairbairn (1954) regards the object as the most important element in the strivings of the drives and believes that the organism seeks not primarily pleasure but rather an object that can afford gratification. Bowlby (1958) believes that there are certain innate needs, species-specific and necessary for survival of the organism. One of the most important needs is clinging and making contact. Bowlby (1958, 1960b) does not believe that the primary goal of the neonate is physiological gratification and does not adhere to the theory of secondary drive, in which the object is seen mainly as a means for securing satisfaction.

Balint (1955) views the subject clinically and characterizes the attitudes toward objects into two fundamental types, object avoidance and object seeking. In chapter 15 I discussed the mutual adaptive qualities of various types of object relationships, emphasizing how the neuroses of two individuals complement one another and concluding that there are striking similarities in the characters of persons involved in long-established mutual object relationships.

Winnicott (1953), in his concept of the transitional object, traced the developmental potential of the object and the child's differentiation of the object as a percept. Freud (1923) wrote of both negative and positive effects of relationship with objects and believed that, although in most cases the object relation contributes to further development, in some instances it leads to ego depletion and "cessation of psychic function." In another paper, Freud (1911a) said that experiences with objects make it possible to lay down memory traces which can be used for thinking and cause the psyche to function more efficiently at both sensory and

First published in *Psa. Q.* 32 (1963), 393–407. Reprinted by permission.

motor levels. He referred particularly to acquisition of reality testing as a result of transactions with the environment.

It is the purpose of this chapter to explore further the psychic structuralization and development effected by experiences with objects. To give the object as central a position as Fairbairn has done may be an artificial separation if the object is considered apart from the experiential situation that promotes ego development. Nevertheless it is true that some patients emphasize the attributes of the object per se and give less attention to the quality of experiences made possible by it.

The character disorders demonstrate how unsatisfactory object relations in early life lead to ego defects which are characterized by specific psychopathology and defenses. These defenses cause the unfolding of the transference neurosis, as it reflects archaic object relations, to have unique and dramatic aspects. By studying the pathological consequences of defective early object relationships, the developmental potential of the object is highlighted.

The transference neurosis, ego development, and defenses of a patient, whose ego defects at times made him appear psychotic, clearly demonstrate the vicissitudes of his object relations. His defenses and the underlying ego defect may be the essence of the character disorders.

The patient, a twenty-six-year-old scientist, was considered by his colleagues to have made brilliant contributions and to have a knack for certain mathematical principles. In spite of his professional achievements, there were long periods during which he was completely unproductive. He sought therapy because he was unsure of his ultimate goals and from time to time had intolerable anxiety with inability to concentrate, confusion, and all the other symptoms that Erikson (1959) categorized as "identity diffusion syndrome." He believed that these symptoms became noticeable during adolescence, but later recalled that he had had them all his life. They became more intense when he was eighteen. He related that even though he could sustain deep friendships with benign, "maternal" women he could not become sexually involved.

His mother was committed to a state hospital when he was three years old and had died there several years before he started analysis. His early life was extremely turbulent and he condemned both parents, although he had no conscious recollection of his childhood relation with his mother except that he recalled with horror his infrequent visits to her, since she was in a regressed, disintegrated state and did not recognize him.

At the age of five, after several foster homes, he lived with a widow who had two sons in high school. He found himself drawn to these boys as ideals. He liked this home and felt that he was treated kindly there, although his feelings about his foster mother were ambivalent. She meant well, he said, but was unable because of ignorance and naïveté to help his anxiety and loneliness.

In hostile, bitter tones he described his father as a man with the intelligence and sophistication to recognize his needs and to give emotional support; he simply had not chosen to do so. Father had "pulled himself up by his bootstraps," emigrated from another country, and worked hard to get an education at night school. Finally he achieved eminence in applied science; the patient admired his accomplishments but felt a certain disdain for the area in which he was successful. During early childhood he had, he said, an "intense and unrealistic admiration" for his father, but this was "catastrophically shattered" when he felt abandoned by being put in a foster home.

He was always able to function in spite of his many difficulties but considered himself "marginal," especially socially. In school he achieved many honors. The teachers found him bizarre but put up with him because of his intelligence and scholastic abilities. He never worked hard at his studies but sincerely admired the field of science in which he later specialized. He read avidly about the great men in his field and was finally able to work under some of them. In spite of these successes and the praises of colleagues, he emphasized his chronic anguish, at times believing he was going insane. He had many nightmares in which he was "falling apart."

The patient told of a series of incidents in which men whom he initially admired as he did his father turned out to have "feet of clay." One reason for seeking therapy was a disappointment in a senior colleague who demanded that the patient collaborate with him on a paper that the patient considered somewhat dishonest in that it distorted data.

Although he had idealized science during his student years, he no longer held it in high esteem. In fact he could now feel deep emotional involvement only in music. He played an instrument, practiced diligently two hours a day, and considered music to be filled with beauty such as science could never hope to approximate. He believed he could never be a great musician but had boundless admiration for those who were.

His therapy began with detailed descriptions of a variety of people. He was extremely bitter about the senior man in his laboratory and frequently behaved in a rebellious, provoking fashion toward him. The senior man occasionally fought back but for the most part showed amused tolerance, ignoring his childish, rebellious antics. Being ignored was, of course, the most painful response he could have received and he became so irritated that he often threatened to quit his job and seek employment elsewhere. His hostile attacks on figures of authority had a somewhat paranoid tinge; he often felt exploited, cheated, robbed of his ideas, and inadequately compensated, financially and academically.

Toward certain men of artistic bent, particularly some musicians, he felt quite otherwise. Several months after analysis began, he happened to see in the street a professional musician whom he regarded as a hero and believed that the man looked at him with a provocative stare. He spoke of him in the same idyllic and rapturous tones that he had used previously about certain pieces of music; he thought him physically attractive and supposed him to possess esoteric skills and genius in playing the same instrument that the patient himself was attempting to master. He thought this kind of talent "transcendental in nature and an ideal worth pursuing," although he was certain that he had begun his musical studies too late in life to achieve such great ability.

As his admiration for this man grew to the point of worshiping him as a god, his bitterness toward his immediate superior in the laboratory reached new heights. This professor, he said, had been working on a problem for many years with compulsive meticulousness, was a master technician but devoid of imagination (a quality so necessary for the artist and scientist), and was unable to produce anything of more than mediocre significance. The problem this man had been working on suddenly captured the patient's fancy and in a day's time, in a frenzy of activity, he solved it. Surprisingly, he was only mildly pleased with what he had done. The next day he solved another problem of equal importance and of fundamental significance, especially as it proved by rigorous mathematics that the conclusions reached by his superior after many years of hard work were erroneous.

Immediately after this creative fervor, he lost all interest in science and intensified his preoccupation with the idealized musician. Several dreams indicated his need for an ideal; they showed the dreamer as "nothing" and the object as omnipotent, grandiose, and godlike. However the same dreams often showed that it was he himself who had such qualities and also that he was afraid he would not be able to control this power which could eventually lead to cosmic destruction.

The patient then began to suppose the musician to be preoccupied with him. At concerts, for instance, he thought he saw the man look at him, whisper to those around him, and then giggle with them. Finally he believed that the musician parked his car in front of his apartment and made critical but helpful comments as the patient was practicing his instrument.

Unlike the classic paranoid, he was not quite convinced that the voices he heard emanated from outside himself or that the evidence he had gathered for this man's presence conclusively indicated that he was acting as a persecutor. He often described himself as having a vivid imagination and as capable of elaborate fantasies. He had heard voices in the past and had known that these were expressions of his own thoughts and feelings. He tended now to believe that what he experienced was part of external reality, but he was not sure. It became apparent that, unlike the typical paranoid, he did not really feel persecuted. The experience was not only enjoyable, for it brought him attention, but also instructive and educational, for the man was giving him free music lessons and was much concerned with his success.

Rarely were there any oppressive, ominous tones in this episode but rather an air of pleasantness and good humor. Perhaps the most disturbing feature was the patient's preoccupation with the musician's welfare, and obviously what he described about the musician's frailness, pallor, emotional imbalance, and loneliness were the very same qualities he had described in himself when he entered treatment.

Finally the patient tired, as he said, of this situation and his good humor became mixed with annoyance. The voices outside his window became more critical. At first the criticism was friendly but later sarcastic and ridiculing. He wished to rid himself of the whole experience and hoped that he could get the musician to enter psychoanalysis, thereby ending all this nonsense. As the episode subsided the patient recognized more and more that there was no musician outside his window and that he had constructed this character because of his need for an ideal figure. He then became aware of frightening, free-floating, destructive impulses. Walking down the street, for example, he would be seized by an urge to commit murder or rape.

The patient then revealed that he had no intention of publishing his scientific discoveries. He wished to avoid discussion, but it soon became apparent that he saw himself able to destroy his superior, at least in a professional sense, if he were to make his work public. He also believed that he would become famous if he did so and he did not welcome the public attention that a famous person receives; it would interfere with his meditative existence and upset his shy nature.

In the transference he showed a childish dependence mingled with the demeanor of an errant, impish little boy. Often, however, he was genuinely distressed and clung to me for reassurance and succor; yet he was fearful of my disapproval, so that he had to turn around and look at me to determine whether he had succeeded in getting me angry.

His feelings about me were consistently friendly and there was much evidence to indicate that he had made me into an omnipotent, idealized figure. For example, he praised me for being able to do almost everything well and especially for an "uncanny genius to know what my hidden feelings are." He carefully avoided hostile, destructive impulses toward me and felt secure in having such a powerful person concerned with his welfare. He was concerned about my welfare, too, reassuring himself that he could not hurt me, being solicitous of my health, and admonishing me to take care of myself. By being friendly he was protected from destructiveness. The patient was able to keep erotic feelings out of his relation to me. His feelings for the musician were, he acknowledged, homosexual. For his superior at work he felt chiefly anger.

He remembered only unsatisfactory early object relations. His mother he recalled only in the hospital, but we may be sure that even at home she had largely failed to supply the nurture and contact that Spitz (1945) and others have found to be so necessary for survival. It became apparent in analysis that his father had been more supportive to him in early life than he had at first thought. His father had been, even before his mother's hospitalization, a fairly stable and accessible object. Yet the patient lamented that his father later failed him; he really had wanted a god, benign and omnipotent, who would take care of him and "allow" him to become great. He assigned this role to me as, in the past, he had idealized outstanding scientists. The musician also had been idealized but was not always benign.

This patient's requirements of the external object were primitive and magical. He somehow hoped to be "restored," since he saw himself as destructive, hateful, and unlovable. He both hoped his discoveries would bring him abundant fame, showing mankind that he was "lovable and not vicious and rotten," and feared that the unbridled power he associated with creative endeavor would destroy him or others such as the senior scientist. To counteract his destructive self-image and the ego disintegration that resulted from "opening the floodgates," he had to find a benign, powerful, idealized object. He sought, not a scientist as he had done when younger, but a musician. In science he was a destructive competitor, and any object found there might share or become subject to his omnipotent destructiveness. Upon his superior he could project his destructiveness.

Musicians, on the contrary, stood for goodness, beauty, love, and warmth. Since he was not interested in a career in music, it offered pleasure without rousing his destructive competitiveness, seeming to provide for him something that brought a sense of well-being, stability, and harmony; it did not abandon and reject him as he felt his parents had.

Identification with the idealized musician (Klein [1958] would have called this process "projective identification") enabled him to have relations with other persons without fear of destroying or being destroyed. His relations with the idealized object nurtured and protected a valued part of himself. This was evidenced by the concern he showed for the object and the way he felt the object related to him. It became clear that all his life he had divided objects into two classes. His father was assigned the role of persecutor, whereas numerous other objects became his mentors. (These latter relationships were eroticized and there were homosexual preoccupations.) This man had an ability to seek objects in the outer world to maintain intrapsychic stability and a sense of identity. A patient may have a realistic relation with objects and at the same time use mechanisms that ignore reality (Giovacchini, 1960); as Kris (1950b, 1955) stated, this quality seems to be important in the creative process.

The hallucinated object was interesting from several viewpoints. Treatment had penetrated his defenses against hostile impulses, and his scientific discoveries augmented his guilt and fear over the omnipotence of his death wishes. He did not want to direct these feelings toward me because he now felt secure and accepted by me, idealizing me and assigning to me, in a controlled way, omnipotent qualities. To base his relation to me on insatiable and contradictory archaic needs meant to risk destroying the analyst or being rejected and abandoned by him. It was safer to construct an object in fantasy and to divide his ambivalent impulses between this and his superior in the laboratory. His infantile longings for the musician could lead only to bitter frustration if directed against the analyst. Thus, the hallucinated object enabled him to remain in treatment.

Nevertheless, this same object was limited in its usefulness, for the ego cannot maintain synthesis and structure wholly by a relation with an object of its own creation. Often the patient spoke of "pulling myself up by my bootstraps," an expression he had also used in reference to his father. He referred often to mirages, remarking that a man may feel better if he imagines an oasis where he can eat and drink, but since his need is not really satisfied he will eventually starve. His idealization of the musician gradually subsided and the phenomena of the voices ceased; at this time he became more aware of angry feelings which often took an obsessional form.

Discussion

This case emphasizes the integrative potential of object relationships by demonstrating the pathological consequences of deficiencies in early contacts with objects. The defenses constructed against such deprivations are typical of the character disorders, a group of enigmatic conditions considered here in line with Gitelson's views (1958a).

The functional aspects of the object largely determine the structure of the ego and the sense of identity. This patient dealt with objects in a primitive way, splitting them into part-objects, one part idealized, the other debased. This he did in treatment when the transference became disturbing. Object splitting was a defense that overcompensated for his ego defect. When treatment enabled him to direct both love and hate to a single object, his ego was better integrated.

When the infant's needs are met, his homeostasis is reestablished; he enters a state of equilibrium marked by absence of tension and a calm, placid demeanor that often leads to sleep. Speculations about the accompanying affective state have to be tentative since there is a tendency to adultomorphize. Presumably he experiences a feeling of satisfaction and comes to recognize the outer world as good. Since this outer world is not yet sharply differentiated from his own self, satisfaction with it is paralleled by satisfaction with the self, and the infant feels worthy, confident, and trusting. We may say that the good object, the mother who is responsible for this happy state of affairs, now becomes internalized and the inner world, like the outer, is viewed as a source of satisfaction; this enables the child to look further in the direction of reality. Jacobson (1954) has emphasized that the neonate does not initially distinguish between self and object, their images not yet being differentiated. Fantasies of being engulfed and engulfing are therefore regularly found together, whereas later, when the ego conforms to secondary-process thought, the two are incompatible.

Satisfaction of needs does not lead to a static state; the drives undergo developmental changes concomitant with changes in the needs of the organism, which do not remain purely physiological. Satisfaction of physiological needs, however, makes it possible to develop other needs that can be considered to lie on a higher plane. For example, one is more inclined—in fact, one is enabled—to seek gratification from aesthetic and creative pursuits when the need for food and other physical comforts is satisfied.

Awareness of needs is not necessarily frustrating. To experience a need with confidence that it will be met is pleasurable. What is painful in some character disorders, as was especially emphasized by this patient, is the fact that the patient is not even aware of the existence of needs or lacks energy to want or pursue anything, to have definite goals the achievement of which will give pleasure and heighten self-esteem. Kurt Lewin (1951) spoke of quasi needs as a replenishment function which must be developed by the organism to maintain homeostatic balance.

Omnipotent expectations of objects may be a central element in the character disorders. A poorly synthesized ego, such as the ego of this patient, may be able to maintain its integrity only while an externalized omnipotent object is available. The paranoid psychotic uses a somewhat different mechanism in that he has internalized all or part of the omnipotent object and his self-image is megalomanic. Like other persons with character disorders, this patient often described himself as "nothing," "empty," "hollow," or "drained out." Perhaps such a patient cannot use an overcompensatory megalomania as a defense and become paranoid. (However, my patient was at times somewhat paranoid.) The need for an external supporting object to whom the patient can impute magical omnipotent qualities is a defense resulting from disturbed early object relations. The subjective sensation of nothingness may be inherent in character disorders; it is possibly an element of the character disorder occurring in all persons.

As the infant grows older, the response to internal and external stimuli is increasingly determined by secondary-process thought. In my patient, however, the functional introjects (especially of the mother) required for more sophisticated responses were lacking, and the stimuli continued to evoke primitive responses. The patient required an object for defensive and developmental needs. His inability to feel caused him to construct an idealized object. Beside counteracting a destructive self-image, he hoped to gain an identity by incorporating the all-powerful object. He was thus attempting to "feel alive" with "pleasurable appetite and lust" rather than feeling "nothing" or "hateful and despicable."

A well-established sense of identity requires an ego with good integrative capacity, including perceptual sensitivities and executive systems that can deal with reality to achieve gratification. The quest for identity puts the object in a central position, whereas satisfaction of biological needs does not necessarily require a personal object since it is the food, warmth, or other physical thing that the infant requires and the object is merely a vehicle that can supply it. Bowlby (1958) does not accept this thesis, but perhaps the distinction between an object and its function has been overstressed. Internalization of the satisfactory object is fundamental for formation of identity. Without such internalization, the executive apparatus in the ego is defective. My patient matured physically, but his physical capacities were not integrated to produce actual ability to perform socially, for this ability must be learned, mainly through transactions with people. He constantly emphasized the fact that he did not know how to do many things, especially how to get along with people; he felt awkward and without social grace. He did not know how to approach a girl sexually. He felt bitter toward his parents and blamed them for never having taught him techniques which he believed to be second nature to others; in fact he remembered no one interested in helping him learn such techniques. During adolescence, when new experiences normally lead to expansion, fusion, and synthesis of past identities and modify them into adult forms, he found "nothing to build upon" from his early development. He then felt especially confused and, although he got over the acute phase of this disturbance, some symptoms lasted until he entered analysis.

He felt the need to incorporate a giving, nurturing object whose skills he might acquire. Loewald (1960) points out that treatment takes place between a person of greater structure and one of lesser structure, and Heimann (1942) parenthetically remarks that an internalized object can become so far assimilated as part of the self that the patient no longer recognizes its external counterpart; this internalization leads to integration. Freud (1923) was first to describe the ego as being a precipitate of past identifications and Menaker (1956) emphasizes the need for an idealized object in certain cases.

The satisfaction of basic biological needs initially occurs before the ego has developed sufficient structure to understand such a sophisticated concept as the personal object. Physiological maturation concurrent with satisfactory experience leads to differentiation and integration of the sensory and motor systems. If the external world does not supply the gratifying experience that leads to learning at a time when the physical apparatus has acquired the ability to master certain skills, a defect occurs which is reflected in the structure of the ego and later in character. Langer (1942) wrote that if opportunity for learning is not presented when the psychic apparatus is ready for it, later attempts to teach particular skills will have little or no success. She quotes the example of learning to talk and postulates a "chattering phase" occurring during the first year. If the child has no opportunity to learn to talk then, efforts to teach him language at later times will be of no avail. An inherent biological potential impels the organism to grow. But the psychic apparatus must incorporate a variety of experiences at the proper times so that it may develop skills consonant and synchronous with the physiological maturation. For these acquisitions the personal object is significant.

Gratifying experiences lead to expansion of the perceptual system, which becomes more sensitive to an increasing variety of subtle stimuli. My patient had always, he said, been able to "hear myself think." Granted that he had hallucinations, was he also possessed of unusually acute perception, a gift that helped maintain the precarious integrity of his ego and caused him to function moderately well in spite of his character disorder?

Studies of gifted individuals often reveal that their special gift has preserved them from mental illness. The ability to hear one's own thoughts might be indicative of disintegration of the ego in an ungifted person.

Mastery of a task requires a variety of skills, and the more adept a person is in attacking a problem the less energy he requires to reach his goal. A well-trained athlete does not tire and can accomplish feats with minimal expenditure of energy whereas the beginner does a good deal of work and gets little done. The well-integrated ego does not exhaust its supplies in gratifying basic needs if it has at its disposal the proper techniques to satisfy them. Such an ego can turn toward the outer world to pursue additional goals and thus further expand its adaptive capacities. Satisfaction in early object relations brings self-esteem, self-confidence, and high capacity in later life.

Summary

A patient with character disorder illustrates the damage sustained by the ego in the absence of satisfactory early object relations. The patient compensated for his lack of an object early in life by splitting of the ego and idealization of an external object to maintain synthesis. The ego defect was experienced as emptiness and unawareness of the nature of his own needs, qualities which may be the essence of the character disorders and which arise from lack of satisfactory introjects for synthesis and expansion of perceptual and executive ego systems. The identity sense was likewise disturbed and the patient had to incorporate an omnipotent object to achieve positive cathexis of his self-image as well as to counteract its hateful destructive aspects.

Chapter 18

Treatment of Marital Disharmonies: The Classical Approach

Marital partners and the subtleties of the relationship between husband and wife have been intriguing subjects since the beginning of civilization. Little wonder then that the basic family unit, beginning with Adam and Eve, should now come under psychoanalytic scrutiny.

The therapeutic approach to any specific problem or situation, if it is to be founded on scientific tradition, must have a theoretical rationale. This statement is true of psychotherapy in general. If the treatment of marital partners warrants consideration as a separate topic, then there must be particular aspects of a more general theory to be focused upon, aspects that will serve to highlight certain areas of the therapeutic process. In looking at the treatment of married partners from a psychoanalytic point of view, we must define it in terms consistent with a theoretical superstructure. Consequently, there is a need to examine both our clinical approach and the concepts underlying it. In a clinical science, as in any other science, there is a need for examination and reexamination, continued evolution, expansion, shifts in point of view, and widening horizons.

Therapeutic ambitions rise and fall; treatment goals are constantly reevaluated. Today there has been a movement away from what is considered the traditional or classical psychoanalytic approach. This shift has been viewed as a modification of the orthodox position, one that is characterized by humanistic interest and the recognition of practical realities. Changes in science are often associated with progress, and the spirit of exploration that goes beyond classical psychoanalysis is considered by many investigators to be a sign of development. Furthermore, the kind and number of cases presenting themselves to the psychiatrist and psychoanalyst have forced them to deviate from the so-called "standard" techniques. These deviations, which Eissler (1953a, p. 1) calls "parameters" (a term that has become almost a classic concept in itself), are widely discussed not only by psychiatrists but also

First published in *The Psychotherapies of Marital Disharmony*, ed. B. Greene (New York: The Free Press, 1965), 39–81.

by social workers, psychologists, and other professionals who deal with the study of man. Other professional workers naturally have their own techniques, but the formulation of the parameter concept by the psychiatrist makes possible a cooperative study of such techniques. Even though the various professions may start from different points, there has been an attempt to formulate concepts with similar superstructures.

Parameters have caught our professional fancy. Still, before we can speak of deviations, we must know from what we deviate. Orthodox classical analysis, although often discussed, has never been thoroughly defined. We speak of the analyst's impassivity, his mirrorlike qualities, his avoidance of any human expression toward a patient, and a variety of other factors that focus upon objectivity and distance. Distance, however, has been viewed by many as coldness, and because of the many emotionally needy persons seeking help, it is believed to be an inappropriate reaction. Nevertheless, these types of description are superficial. The best we can say about them is that they are phenomenological. But we cannot define anything as complicated as a therapeutic approach only in terms of its phenomenology. The "classical psychoanalytic" technique has not received the theoretical attention it deserves.

Freud (1912a, 1914b) emphasized that the interpretation of the transference neurosis was the essence of his approach and that anything else might be detrimental to analysis. It is quite obvious from Freud's writings and those of his biographer Ernest Jones (1953), however, that Freud related to patients in many ways that transcended interpretation. This point does not militate against Freud's dictum, and some of his papers read like primers and directions for psychotherapists, even though he could not practice what he preached. One wonders, though, if the innovator of the psychoanalytic method could not abide by it himself, whether or not it might be even more difficult for his followers. Still, his ideas require scrutiny from a scientific point of view, regardless of their difficulty of application. What followed had many paradoxical features, for some analysts blindly and rigidly adhered to his dicta or thought they did, without particularly understanding the underlying processes, whereas others like Ferenczi and Rank (1924) introduced extensions, or so they thought, that were so sweeping that their roots were no longer recognizable.

The treatment of married partners is especially interesting because, in considering how the classical approach can be utilized, we can at the same time learn more about the underlying ego processes associated with this approach. Any clinical study can be valuable in augmenting our understanding of dynamic interrelationships—in this case, those that occur between patient and therapist. The latter relationship can be pivotal for our theoretical understanding of the therapeutic process. I wish to emphasize that not enough is really known about what has been called a "classical psychoanalytic approach." Here, instead of considering techniques in addition to or as extensions of those already included in analysis, I wish to focus upon a better understanding of these already existing techniques. I also emphasize that I am speaking of the *analysis* of married couples. Another investigator may feel that other approaches are better in particular instances, and it may well be that analysis is not applicable or practical in such instances.

The expense and time-consuming qualities of psychoanalysis are serious limitations. Consequently, anything that may ease the burden on both practitioner and patient is welcome. The characterological problems that are so frequently seen today, according to many psychiatrists, do not lend themselves to a therapy that lacks so-called "supportive" elements. If, however, the therapeutic process were better understood as a process, our conception of what the patient needs and responds to might be expanded. Sometimes it is not possible to substitute another form of therapy, even though the effective form has serious practical limitations. As an analogy, a ruptured appendix must be treated surgically—even if surgeons are scarce or unavailable. Another approach could be disastrous. What I am about to discuss, of course, does not have "life and death" implications in the physical sense, and we know that there are many ways of helping people. I shall address myself exclusively to those aspects that deal with character structure in both a clinical and theoretical framework.

As I have previously remarked, classical psychoanalytic treatment is imperfectly understood from a theoretical point of view. The theoretical understanding that we have has not kept pace with advances in other areas of theory. I shall consider the psychopathology of married partners and its treatment in terms that are consonant with the recent advances in ego psychology.

The insights gained from ego psychology can help us understand the psychic operations involved in the marital relationship. In turn, the deep and intimate ties between two people can contribute considerably to our knowledge about the operations of the ego in general. Marital disharmonies therefore represent a clinical area that can be fruitfully investigated and can, it is to be hoped, contribute to both a theory of therapy and a theory of structure.

Any study of the ego eventually leads us into a study of object relationships. Object relations have been somehow involved in all areas of ego psychology, including development, learning, defenses, and adjustive techniques. Married partners are a particular example of an object relationship. From the point of view of the individual, object relations are of crucial interest in the therapeutic setting. One can easily understand then how significant the patient's relationship with the spouse can be as an indicator of his basic characterological structure and psychopathology.

Here, insofar as our interest is in the therapeutic process, ego developmental factors will be noted but not emphasized; instead, the marriage will be scrutinized in terms of its adaptive potential in the face of individual psychopathology. How each partner adapts to the other's personality and neurosis is in line with our clinical interest. That there is something different or special about the marital relationship, as distinguished from other object relationships, seems clear even at first glance. In a person's development, many objects become significant, each being needed or reacted to in a circumscribed fashion. Initially, the mother represents a global object, but, with development, other persons begin to fill distinctive roles and must have particular functional significance. The spouse, representing a heterosexual object choice, would ideally be associated with ego transactions at the most mature levels of psychosexual organization. We should anticipate that psychopathology would be reflected in a special way in such an object relationship.

There is an old adage that "marriages are made in heaven." Psychoanalysis, because of its strict adherence to psychic determinism, takes issue with this proverb, unless heaven is defined in terms of psychic processes. When a person has developed sufficiently to be able to exercise some autonomy in selecting an object, then there must be reasons, arising from past relationships, that cause him to select a particular person. If the relationship is characterized by strife, is one of disharmony, then the likelihood that he has stumbled upon it accidentally is minimal. It becomes even less likely when that relationship is a conflicted marriage, in spite of the fact that many patients protest that they were not really aware of their spouses' undesirable personality traits, that they had been misled, or that the courtships were too short for them to make accurate assessments. One sometimes senses immediately the need of one partner for the other, although the surface picture may be chaotic, turbulent, and painful to both husband and wife. When such patients are analyzed, certain characterological features become obvious and indicate that, even in situations in which the courtships were short, the patients either manipulated their spouses or themselves into marriage and that the relationships were extremely meaningful for the preservation of their psychic equilibriums.

Psychoanalysis is a therapeutic technique, as well as a conceptual system. The transference neurosis, an entity that Freud (Breuer and

Freud, 1895) mentions in one of his earliest publications, is the analyst's most important tool. Its unfolding enables us to scrutinize microscopically the patient's character structure, as well as to make formulations about psychodynamic conflicts. We learn about the patient's infantile past and his early object relationships as the transference neurosis develops. In psychoanalytic therapy, there is an ego regression that corresponds to, although it is not identical with, infantile ego states. The patient projects onto the analyst archaic imagos of significant past objects. From this vantage point, the analyst scrutinizes the patient's orientation toward objects in a contemporary setting as they represent reflections of attitudes from infantile relationships.

One soon learns that there are many variables that determine the choice of one's spouse. The psychoanalysis of a married person reveals that unconscious determinants are highly significant in determining such a choice. Data from the psychoanalytic frame of reference cause us to emphasize that there is much more than mere contemporary significance in the attraction between two persons and that marital interaction is founded largely on infantile attitudes. I do not intend that this conclusion become the basis of a generalization for all marriages. Obviously not all married persons seek psychotherapy, and those who are seen by psychiatrists have emotional problems that may distinguish their marital relationships from those of people who are not aware of any need for help. The inductive process has its limitations, and what pertains to cases of psychopathology is valuable only in the clinical setting.

Still, the distinction between persons who admit the existence of emotional problems and those who never come to a psychiatrist's attention may not be the same as the distinction between psychopathology and normality. Extratherapeutic experiences have often led us to believe that some persons not in therapy have serious emotional problems, sometimes greater than many patients have. These problems are also apparent in the marital relationship. Although it does not follow logically, many would not disagree with a conjecture that there are elements of the infantile, relatively speaking, in every marriage. I do not necessarily mean that there are elements of the psychopathological in every marriage, nor do I wish to convey the impression that these elements must be considered in value terms, negative or positive. What is crucial here is their adaptive significance.

Many authors have made generalizations about the psychopathology of married partners. Both Oberndorf (1938) and Mittelmann (1944) have commented that the neuroses of husband and wife complement each other and indicate that there is a dovetailing of conflictual and defensive patterns. Oberndorf has described such complementing in terms of both pregenital and oedipal orientations. In chapter 15, I have extended these conclusions and emphasized the mutually adaptive qualities of the marital relationship. I thought of these relationships as being symbiotic in nature, using the term "symbiosis," as DeBary (1879) originally did, to signify mutual dependence. Benedek (1949, 1959) and Mahler (1952) have extended this concept to the biologically significant relationship of the mother-child unit. In this relationship, the child's survival and psychological development are at stake, as are important potentialities of the mother with respect to her motherliness. The concept of symbiosis, as it is used in biology, emphasizes that the need of each organism for the other is equally vital. Naturally such a concept becomes more complex when applied to humans. Symbiosis as it pertains to the mother-child relationship would not correspond exactly to the biological concept in which the child needs the mother for survival. Even though the mother's need for the child may be intense, she has at her disposal a variety of other techniques to maintain herself. One cannot therefore consider these needs as equal.

In the marital relationship, however, I concluded that the partners' needs for each other are equal. If this conclusion is correct, the pattern is symbiotic in the true sense and different and distinct from the symbiosis of the mother-child unit. But the label is not important. What is significant is the psychic process itself and not what one calls it.

The mutually adaptive qualities that are found in marriages are clinically impressive. I have come to the conclusion that the nature and depth of psychopathology are identical for the husband and wife in a long-established marriage. A long-established marriage does not necessarily mean a well-established marriage. Indeed, a marriage may be characterized by strife and turmoil and appear to be on the brink of collapse. Yet in spite of continuing misery, one senses how necessary the marriage is for each partner's psychic survival. The superficial adjustment, in terms of behavior, defenses, and general adaptations, may appear markedly different in each partner, for one may present a picture of relative calm and equanimity, while the other may seem markedly disturbed. The underlying personalities of the husband and wife are similar, however. We find that their basic conflicts, their points of fixation and regression, and their general ego integrations are the same. For example, if the wife presents an obvious picture of fragmented schizophrenia, we can feel relatively confident that the husband, although phenomenologically better defended, has similar underlying disorganization and will, under certain circumstances, become as fragmented as his wife. In fact, very often the wife establishes an equilibrium similar to the one that the husband initially had. He, in turn, may break down in a fashion similar to the wife's previous disorganization.

The data for such conclusions come from several frames of reference. First, we are most impressed by the reactions of one partner when a separation occurs. The importance of the object relationship to the maintenance of psychic equilibrium in both partners is then dramatically highlighted. For example, a man in his middle forties had been married for fifteen years to an utterly helpless, dependent woman. She found the pedestrian tasks of everyday living overwhelming and would frequently withdraw into catatonic-like states, in which she was completely detached from the world around her. She was frightened of everything and found every one and every situation dangerous. There was a paranoid flavor to her thinking, insofar as she believed that people were out to destroy her. She also saw herself as a venomous, destructive person who would be better off dead. In contrast, her husband presented the picture of a very forcible and highly adequate personality. He was successful in his business, very much an extrovert, and related easily and comfortably to people. He did not seem afraid of anything and went through life with a persuasive charm. He consulted a psychiatrist, not because he felt he had any personality problems, but merely to receive advice on how to help and handle his wife. The psychiatrist thought it odd that the husband had permitted such a situation to exist for so long a period of time, but the patient was able to produce a series of rationalizations, all of which made him appear favorably in the light of his forbearance. He wanted advice on how to help and handle his wife, but, when it was suggested that she receive therapy, he balked. Institutionalization was also out of the question, and he rationalized this attitude with moral arguments, insisting that it was his duty to look after her even though it was painful. He insisted that his only desire was to help her and even went so far as to deny all hostile feelings or even mild irritation at the trouble she caused him. In spite of his strict surveillance of all his wife's activities, she managed to run away to some relatives in another part of the country. With their help, she was able to resist both his threats and entreaties to return. She went into treatment in that faraway city. Because of the therapy and because she was away from her oppressive husband, she improved considerably. When the husband learned of this improvement and became convinced that, no matter what he did, she was not going to return, he became acutely disturbed. He presented a picture of total helplessness, had innumerable crying spells, and, like his wife, found every situation threatening and frightening. His air of self-confidence and bravado disappeared, and, in its place, appeared an infantile disorganization, which led eventually to hospitalization because he was unable to carry on routine activities. As in his wife's previous condition, there were also many paranoid elements.

This case shows that, at least phenomenologically, both partners reacted similarly. The marital equilibrium had a protective function for the husband. The later disruption of this equilibrium showed that he had always had the potential for the same kind of disorganization as that of his wife. This case does not prove that their character structures were identical, but, on the other hand, it suggests that they may have been.

We note similar reactions when one partner dies. The survivor frequently marries a person who seems identical with the first spouse. This pattern is particularly impressive in the wives of alcoholics, who, although they may complain about their sorry lots in life and how trapped they are by their irresponsible, acting-out husbands, often marry other alcoholics shortly after the deaths of their first husbands. It is not uncommon to find a woman who has been married to two or three alcoholics.

Another area that suggests a similarity of psychopathology in married partners is the therapeutic setting. The evidence that, when one partner improves in therapy, the other partner soon develops symptoms identical to those the patient initially presented is impressive. Often, the spouse who initially felt that he did not need help is forced to seek therapy for himself if the marriage is to be preserved. In some instances, the marriages were founded on such neurotic bases that, with therapeutic improvement, divorces were inevitable. Such divorces frequently resulted in regression in the untreated partners, which may have been similar to the patients' initial symptomatic pictures. Our earlier clinical vignette also illustrates this point, but there are many instances in which such regression takes place without actual separation. The improvement of one partner upsets the previously established equilibrium, and the defensive compensations that the marriage has held for the other partner are no longer operative.

A very striking example was that of the wife of one patient in analysis, who succeeded, in a relative sense, in overcoming some of her phobias. She was afraid of crowds and social gatherings. Consequently, she was unable to go to parties. She was also afraid of being away from her home, and, because of these symptoms, she was virtually a recluse. Her husband complained bitterly because his business demanded that he entertain and be entertained. He blamed her for his having missed many business opportunities because he was unable to attend various social functions alone. Because of her he felt chained to the house. After his wife had been in analysis for a short time, his wife's therapist suggested that he also receive analysis. The fact that he acquiesced was in itself interesting because he claimed that there was no such need. Still, he seemed glad that such a suggestion had been made. His analysis revealed that he had phobias almost identical with those of his wife, fear of crowds and parties, of being too far away from a toilet, and so forth.

His wife's symptoms served to keep him away from anxiety-producing settings, so that he never had to experience the phobias or even to admit their existence. Her difficulties served to maintain his self-esteem and to protect him from the painful recognition of shame-provoking, passive needs. The wife's phobias became an excellent rationalization for staying at home and not being aggressive or manly, qualities that were frightening to him because of severe castration anxiety. This patient maintained psychic equilibrium by utilizing his wife's symptoms to mask his own. His wife's relative improvement accelerated the recognition of similar conflicts within himself, and for a long period of time during his treatment his phobias became full blown, showing striking similarity to his wife's previous symptomatic picture. In this case, because the husband was in analysis, it was possible to reconstruct his infantile conflicts and to compare his psychodynamic and characterological constellations with those that the wife's analyst had formulated about her. Both analysts were impressed by the similarities of their conclusions.

The analysis of the other partner provides valuable data to support the thesis that there are identical elements in each partner's psychopathology in a marriage. I have often been astonished by the reconstruction that a colleague has given of a husband or a wife of one of my patients, about whose psychopathology he knew nothing, or by the similarity between his conclusion about his patient and my conclusion about mine.

In psychoanalysis, the transference neurosis is the most important investigative tool. In making formulations about object relations, it becomes extremely valuable, for crucial object relationships are reenacted with the analyst and can therefore be studied microscopically in a comtemporary setting.

The infantile basis for the choice of a mate is especially highlighted in the transference setting. As inevitably occurs in any analysis, the patient will at some time or other relate to the analyst as if he were the spouse. The relation becomes apparent in dreams and associations, but what is projected on to the analyst also contains an archaic infantile object imago. The surface form of such an imago may be that of the spouse, but its constituents come from the infantile past. This transference manifestation demonstrates that the meaning of a husband or wife for an analytic patient is, in large measure, derived from past object relations, and the patient reacts to his spouse as if the spouse were a person that had been emotionally meaningful to him as well as conflictual during his childhood. Cases in which patients react to their wives as if to nurturing mothers are commonly encountered by psychiatrists. Or a wife may have for her husband feelings that she originally had for her father or, in some instances, a younger brother or a son.

Clinically I am impressed by the fact that the patient often complains or describes the spouse in terms similar to his own self-description. He is not aware of these similarities, and often a considerable period of time has elapsed between the two descriptions, but it is nevertheless striking how similar they can be. The transference neurosis again becomes indispensable if one is to evaluate such similarities, for one sees a projection of the self-representation onto the analyst.

The transference projections are projections of early introjects. Insofar as what is introjected is first perceived by the ego and then incorporated, the quality of the introject must also have some qualities of the introjecting ego, at least those of the perceptual system. Jacobson (1954) has described in detail the various self- and object representations (acquired introjects) representing different developmental phases. Although all introjects possess some aspects of the self-representation, some do so more completely than others. What is stiking in marital partners when they project elements of the spouse onto the analyst is the fact that what is projected is also a self-representation. One notes, often in dramatic fashion, that the patient's self-representation is the essence of the transference projection. Everything that the patient unconsciously feels about the spouse turns out to be true of himself as well. Consequently, the spouse is viewed as an extension or as a replica of the self. This view would not necessarily prove that the spouse is actually similar in personality to the patient; it merely indicates that the patient's unconscious attitudes toward the spouse are similar to his attitudes to himself, that he needs to perceive the spouse in this fashion. Without the study of the transference neurosis, we should find it difficult to reach such conclusions. I shall therefore present another clinical vignette in order to demonstrate how the transference neurosis reveals that the projection of the archaic imago representing the spouse also contains the self-representation.

The patient, a middle-aged professional man, constantly complained about his wife during his analytic sessions. He thought of her alternately as a weak, vulnerable woman who was unable to carry on the routine activities of homemaking and child-rearing. She drank much too much, and, even though he did not consider her quite an alcoholic, he felt that she was close to becoming one. At other times, he saw her as an explosive, unpredictably aggressive woman who nagged and descended upon him with a fury that made him fear for his life. He filled his analytic sessions with such material, practically to the exclusion of anything that referred directly to himself. He was able to acknowledge that he had some responsibility for this marital chaos and that, in his own passive manner, he contributed to it, but, in spite of this ability to look inward, he continued to complain vociferously. The analyst, however, constantly directed the patient's attention to the defensive meaning of his complaints about his wife and attempted to demonstrate how he had elaborated them into a complex analytic resistance. From time to time, the analyst became aware of subtle similarities between many of the things that he said about his wife and some of his descriptions of himself. As the analyst interpretively elaborated on the possibility that his preoccupation with his wife's inadequacy might be a method of protecting himself against low self-esteem and to cover up his own feelings of inadequacy, he gradually began to relate more directly to the analyst.

At this point, he began having dreams in which the analyst was attacking him or berating him in the same unpredictable fashion that he had ascribed to his wife. In one dream, he was trying to raise himself from the floor but found it difficult because two people were sitting on his back. His associations clearly brought out that these two people were his wife and the analyst. In contrast to his previously mild-mannered, docile attitude toward the analyst, he now became vociferous and argumentative. The contents of his productions were similar to those at the beginning of the analysis, except that now he had considerable affect with them, insofar as he was directing them toward the analyst. He was reliving in the transference neurosis the same defensive attitude that he held toward his spouse, and both the dreams and associations indicated that the wife and the analyst, from an unconscious point of view, were now one.

To view these developments simply as defenses against low self-esteem and feelings of inadequacy would give us an incomplete picture. Obviously, his feelings represented, among other things, projections of infantile attitudes as they related to archaic objects. One can raise the interesting question as to whether or not such must be the case. Might it not be true that he gave a fairly accurate assessment of the wife's behavior and personality and that he was reacting in a realistic indignant fashion to the many burdens and pressures to which she subjected him? Undoubtedly there was considerable accuracy in his appraisal of his wife, and there was some evidence to support his allegations. Still, from the therapeutic point of view, whether or not he was describing reality was irrelevant. No matter what his wife was actually like, his attitude toward her still represented, to a large measure, the projection of infantile attitudes and imagos. This fact became evident as he reenacted the whole drama in the transference neurosis. Certainly, the analyst could not and did not represent in reality the type of person he described, yet he reacted to him with precisely the same feelings that he had reported concerning his wife. In fact, there was considerably more affect toward the analyst since his previous complaints about his wife had been affectively mild and had seemed to have a slight intellectual quality about them. I wish to emphasize, therefore, that, in spite of the reality situation, it is important to note the patient's feelings in terms of his own internal psychic milieu and also to note that there must have been very significant meanings to his complaints other than realistic ones.

The patient also related to the analyst with the same ambivalence he showed toward his wife. In addition to his attacks, there were periods during which he saw the analyst as competent and strong. At times, he described his wife as a person with considerable charm, beauty, and poise, who could be masterful and adept in a variety of social situations. Nevertheless, the predominant emphasis was a negative one.

The transference neurosis revealed the following genetic antecedents: The patient was the younger of a pair of identical twins. His brother was looked upon as the successful one, whereas, for a variety of reasons, the patient was viewed and viewed himself as the "black sheep." What he said about his wife and later about the analyst in the transference neurosis was an almost exact replication of what he reported that others had felt about him during childhood in a role into which, because of guilt and masochistic defenses, he had manipulated himself.

The transference neurosis also revealed that he was projecting various aspects of this self-image onto the analyst. At times, he had to external-ize a hated destructive part of the self and then attack it. This behavior had a defensive meaning in preserving his shaky self-esteem and in preventing his being overwhelmed by loss of control of disruptive feel-ings. On the other hand, he could attempt to repair his damaged self by a Pygmalion type of relationship with his wife. Rescuing her (there were many "rescue" dreams) would be tantamount to restructuring a defec-tive part of the self. During the transference neurosis, when he felt positive, he attributed omnipotent healing qualities to the analyst.

As is common among identical twins, this patient had a serious identity problem. As the concept of identity is a very complex one and tangential to the topic of this chapter, I shall refer to it only in terms of its equivalence to some aspects of the self-image. This patient demon-strated that his wife represented to his unconscious a projection of a hated, destructively cathected self-image or its counterpart (the other side of the ambivalence), a powerful omnipotent self-image. He there-fore saw her as similar to himself. She may not have been, psychically speaking, the "same" as the patient, but we are constantly impressed with how often, when the defense mechanism of projection is used, the object chosen is so appropriate.

This patient felt that, to achieve an identity separate from that of his brother, he must destroy him. This situation was one of extreme danger because killing his brother also represented killing himself, for psychically he could not differentiate himself from his brother. He was then able to gain a modicum of individuation by a split in his self-image, which reflected a split in the fusion of twinship. The separation, which was characterized by the ambivalence between the hated inadequate and the rescuing omnipotent, was then enacted in childhood and determined the core around which his marriage was founded.

Granted that this patient is unusual because of his identical twinship, patients with identity problems are by no means rare. Erikson (1959) believes that this type of problem is practically universal among adolescents, and study of character disorders and borderline states emphasizing ego defects also reveals how deeply disturbed the identity sense can be.

In any case, the transference neurosis highlights the person's need to find himself in the object, although, in a clinical setting, infantile and destructive determinants are stressed.

The psychoanalytic study of married partners, therefore, leads us to several observations. First, we often find similar or complementary defenses, implying that there may be similar underlying conflicts but not necessarily proving their existence. Second, when it is possible to resolve or at least partially resolve these defenses, we are struck by the similarity of the underlying conflicts in the married pair. This similarity is most apparent in the frame of reference provided by the transference neurosis. Third, in some cases, relinquishing defenses causes reversal of behavioral roles. When this reversal occurs in the analytic setting, we once again find identical underlying conflicts in married partners. Finally, the reaction to separation in some instances also results in reversal of behavioral roles, and again we are able to note similar underlying conflicts.

These marriages are characterized by intense involvements of one partner with the other. The marital partner requires the total personality, including the specific character defenses, of the other partner in order to maintain intrapsychic equilibrium. In spite of bitter strife and turmoil, the marriage lasts, and even though it may seem constantly on the brink of divorce, the observer recognizes that divorce is unlikely. To distinguish such a total characterological involvement between the husband and wife, I shall refer to this type of object relationship as a *character object relationship.*

Not all marriages, however, fall into this category of object relationships. There is another group that I shall designate as *symptom object relationships,* which differs from the first group in that the marriage is transitory in nature and does not have the same depth of involvement characteristic of a character object relationship. Frequently such marriages result in divorce, and equilibrium, pathological or otherwise, has never been firmly established. Once again we sense mutual need in such marriages, but it seems less intense than in marriages of the first type. We have the impression that the patient's spouse does not have a specific meaningfulness to him. Analysis reveals that the patient does not require the total personality of the other; he needs only a particular trait or symptom, and the marital involvement seems only a partial one. Other objects with similar traits or symptoms, although differing in many respects, could serve his defensive needs as well, and frequently such a patient has had several marriages in which the spouse had a common denominator, so to speak, and also great differences.

For example, a wife in her late twenties described her husband as a weak, inadequate person. She brought this point up as an incidental finding and was not particularly concerned about him. Nevertheless, she gave an extensive description of his personality and painted a picture of a detached, withdrawn person using schizoid mechanisms and perhaps bordering on schizophrenia. This woman, on the other hand, did not seem so seriously disturbed. She had sought therapy because of a variety of hysterical symptoms, and the analysis finally reached the core of her conflicts, which were basically oedipal. At this stage of analysis, it was learned that she was in intense competition with her mother, who was said to be more beautiful than the patient and covetous of her heterosexual successes. The mother both intimidated the patient and made her feel guilty (at least such was the patient's perception). Consequently, her romances never worked out well; she was defeating herself in order to placate a disapproving maternal superego. She felt unconsciously that, in order to appease her mother, she must have a husband who was passive and inadequate, but the nature of his basic psychopathology was not important. As long as the man she married was not desirable, her mother would not want to destroy her and take him for herself. She managed to find a man who did not rate high on the marital market. At the time of treatment, she was in her fourth marriage, her three previous ones having lasted a year or less each. All her husbands were described as ''weak characters'' who were unattractive physically, lacked charm, and were shallow and intellectually constricted.

Still, there were significant differences among these men. Her first husband had been a gregarious, back-slapping salesman who bluffed and boasted in so obvious and gross a manner that no one failed to recognize his ineptitude. He never achieved status, and his performance was mediocre. The patient considered him crass, dull, and materialistic, lacking in sensitivity, and a bore. In contrast, her second husband had been a high-strung, oversensitive artist who reacted or overreacted to even the most trivial stimuli. His demeanor was usually depressed or angrily rebellious, and he valued aesthetic and intellectual pursuits. He was also a failure, however, lacked talent, and talked more about working than he actually worked. His colleagues thought him a "jerk," and the patient stated that he was physically repugnant, unkempt, and unwashed. The other two husbands also differed from the first two and from each other, but each was inadequate in his own way.

This patient emphasized the circumscribed defensive meaning of the marital relationship. The spouse was not considered as a whole object. She related to only one particular characteristic of the husband, one that she used to defend herself from destructive and self-destructive competitive feelings toward her mother. The need for such relationships was vital, but, unlike patients involved in character object relations, she had greater flexibility and could shift from one object to another. A relationship founded on such a symptomatic basis would be unstable; other attributes of the spouse's personality extraneous to the patient's needs would eventually make the relationship untenable.

Symptom object relations are also found in persons who are not predominantly oedipal in their psychosexual development. For example, a young and brilliant scientist was unable to explain his failure to achieve a satisfying marriage. He had been married twice before, and in his third marriage he found himself distressed because he was going to leave his wife. He vacillated in his feelings toward her, but even when very angry he was reluctant to separate himself from her. Although he wanted a divorce, he did not want to admit defeat again. Nevertheless, he found her behavior intolerable because of her unpredictable and sometimes violently explosive moods. She would, at times, reject him completely and react with great disdain to any affectionate gesture he might make, just as, at other times, inexplicably, she might behave in a seductive, warm fashion. She had had difficulties in other areas too—vocational, academic, and social—and had been in therapy for several years. Her therapist diagnosed her as suffering from a schizophrenic psychosis, one that could not permit her any involvement in an object relationship. On the other hand, her husband was an affable, outgoing person with many warm friendships and social contacts. The impression gained from his analysis was that of a moderately severe character neurosis with obsessive features but nothing so severe as to suggest psychotic elements. Nevertheless, his need for his wife seemed very strong, as had been his pursuit of her during courtship and his tenacity in the marriage, although it was obviously an impossible one.

His motivations became clearer, however, when his relationship with his mother was better understood. Her main characteristic was also unpredictability. She, too, was openly seductive toward the patient and on several occasions made overt sexual advances. At other times, she would be violently antisexual and would adopt the manner of an incensed Victorian. The patient was dismayed and confused and found himself in a position of helpless vulnerability. He felt that his very existence was at stake. In order to overcome his anxiety, he had to solve the riddle of the mysterious, unpredictable woman. He deliberately associated himself with disturbed women in order to repeat the traumatic experiences with his mother and master the danger. The mother later became psychotic and died in a state hospital.

The patient was preoccupied with problem-solving, a motif that had played a large share in determining his choice of profession. His need for his wife was not based on characterological similarity; rather she represented a challenge and a problem to him. Such a challenge, by its very nature, could be found only in a seriously disturbed personality. The descriptions he gave of his first two wives, however, indicated that they were quite different from his third wife. One sounded like a fairly typical hysterical personality with a good deal of acting out, and the other one seemed moderately depressed with self-defeating qualities. Still, when he finally left his third wife, she had very little reaction, and her usual equilibrium did not seem disturbed. What he sought was this one trait of unpredictability, which he found in this woman and in other women of diverse character structures.

In this case and others like it the object relationship is determined chiefly by the patients' conflicts, which are different from those of the partners, as could be seen in this partner's relatively mild reaction when separation eventually occurred. Undoubtedly, the partners had their reasons for marrying the patients, reasons that we cannot ascertain because they have not been studied. Nevertheless, we can conjecture that the particular conflicts that motivated the partners to enter into the relationships were of different orders from those of the patients. In the second case, in which the wife was in therapy, it was learned that she had attached herself to the patient because of a helpless, clinging, dependent need, almost anaclitic in nature, and she, too, would choose any man that seemed to offer these nurturing qualities.

For the patient, the involvement did not seem to be one of the total personality. A specific area of conflict seemed to be the chief determinant of the object relationship, but this area did not include the main characterological features of his psychic structure. This distinction is analogous to that between a character neurosis and a symptom neurosis. Anna Freud (1949) and her co-workers suggested that there is a marked difference between an object relationship that is need-satisfying and one that includes object constancy. The former will exist only as long as the particular need is satisfied, whereas the latter has positive integrative aspects in terms of ego development. Anna Freud, Hartmann (1946), and Kris (1950a) have recognized the role of intrapsychic conflicts in the formation of object relationships. If the patient's characterological features in their more total and diffuse aspects are the sources of interactions between the marital partners, then a total, deep, and constant involvement seems to result. If, on the other hand, an isolated area of the ego—a specific defense or symptom, for example—becomes the pole around which the relationship revolves, then the relationship is less vital for the partner's intrapsychic stability and turns out to be transient, as in our two examples. This type of object relationship is typified by a symptom or rather the manifestation of a symptom. It represents one manifestation among many, however, whereas character object relationships become axes around which transactions with reality are achieved and internal equilibrium maintained, indicating characterological rather than merely symptomatic involvement.

Insofar as married persons relate to each other either in terms of a symptom object relationship or a character object relationship, we can expect complications in their analyses, and because many analytic patients are married we may consider such complications as characteristic of the analytic relationship. In the therapeutic process, these complications manifest themselves as resistances. In chapter 16, I described these resistances as unusual, in that they seem to be initiated by external objects.

Resistances stimulated by external objects occur in the analyses of unmarried patients too. Those occurring in the marital relationship have special characteristics because of the equivalent psychopathologies of the partners. We often note that, although the patient's spouse frequently has encouraged analysis and sometimes even insisted upon it, once the patient begins making progress, his spouse's attitude changes. The analysis brings about the disturbance of a previous marital equilibrium. Then the spouse reacts, at first subtly and later more openly, in a fashion designed to sabotage the analytic relationship.

An especially striking example of a therapeutic impasse brought on by a sabotaging spouse was the case of a recently married young woman who had sought treatment because of a variety of somatic complaints. Her symptoms centered around the respiratory system and consisted in difficulty in taking full breaths, feelings of suffocation, and hyperpnea, all present from childhood but increasingly severe since her marriage. There were also many characterological features indicating a basically infantile personality with a strong oral component. Her appearance was that of a naive and sexually unsophisticated person, one who was described by others and, especially by her husband as a "wide-eyed, cute little girl." Nevertheless, she could be disdainful and haughty, and underneath what seemed a dependent helplessness, she had the attitude of a tyrannical aristocrat. She felt superior to her friends, and, although her husband was a successful professional man, she believed that he was of inferior breeding and did not know how to treat her with the respect, delicacy, and consideration that she deserved.

The defensive nature of this narcissistic orientation became apparent during her treatment, which revealed an ego beset with feelings of inadequacy and dominated by insatiable oral, dependent demands. Her feelings of inadequacy were determined by sexual conflicts that threatened her feminine self-esteem. She was basically hysterical, and the physical symptoms represented conversion processes, but the hysterical aspect of her personality became apparent only after a long period of treatment that was mainly involved with pregenital, oral dependent strivings.

In spite of her narcissistic orientation, this patient's analysis progressed favorably, and she seemed to be sincerely trying to work through her infantile dependent demands. This effort was reflected in marked improvement in her behavior. She seemed able to integrate analytic interpretations and then to utilize insights to effect new adjustments in her daily life. She seemed headed in the direction of self-sufficiency and basic resolution of her oedipal problems.

After about eighteen months of what had seemed to be a well-progressing analysis, the patient reverted to her old dependent status. All her initial physical symptoms returned along with her haughty, whining behavior. She now showed a stubborn naïveté and refractoriness to all interpretations. Granted that this type of regression and resistance is not unusual in an analysis when deep layers of conflict are broached, this patient showed a tenacity that seemed peculiar, especially in the light of her previous receptiveness. If it had not been for unmistakable evidence of previous working through of conflicts, I should have believed her completely untouched by the psychoanalytic process.

Still she was able to bring up new material, which shed light upon the nature of this intense resistance. She began talking in more detail about her husband, whom she described as a successful, secure person. She was aware of her critical attitudes toward him but, nevertheless, she saw him as a mature man with great strength and concern for her welfare. He was enthusiastic about her treatment and had in many ways helped her get started. He handled himself discreetly and never raised any questions about what was going on in her analysis, although he was extremely inquisitive and protective about all other aspects of her life. It seemed that he was studiously avoiding any discussion of her treatment, and, in general, he seemed to encourage her to grow up. In spite of her regression, which was manifested in her general behavior as well as within the analytic framework, he did not show the least sign of impatience or discouragement. This attitude was especially odd because the cost of his wife's treatment represented a sizable financial sacrifice, and he was not a particularly patient man. He could be cruelly critical, but toward the analysis he had never evinced any disapproval.

The patient, however, began to suspect ulterior motives in her husband's attitude and behavior. She discovered that he wanted to keep her infantile. For example, he enjoyed having her use baby talk, something that she had done frequently in the past. Since starting her analysis, she found it odious, but she continued because she was afraid of displeasing him. She was aware of his resentment when she stopped. He also encouraged her sexual naïveté. He liked to tell her obscene jokes, but he wanted her not to understand so that he could shock and tease her with the explanations. Although she understood the meanings of these jokes as well as he did, she assumed an attitude of naïve bewilderment. When she actually behaved incompetently, his attitude seemed benign, but she was able to discern that he was patronizing her.

Consequently, she made special efforts to appear incompetent, sensing his need to have her remain childish. He encouraged her initially to seek analysis because there were various aspects of her symptoms that were annoying to both of them. Nevertheless, he really did not want any basic changes, and his need to consider his wife as helpless and immature represented an overcompensatory defense against his own low self-esteem. This defense became apparent later when he himself sought analysis; his wife's improvement forced him to seek help.

As the patient began to understand her husband's needs, she found it difficult to adjust to such an infantilizing atmosphere. The analytic impasse gradually gave way, and she was once again able to continue with the analysis. The resumption necessitated some changes in her external adjustment, which forced her husband to decide between divorce and analytic assistance for himself. He chose the latter, and a new marital equilibrium was eventually established.

In such cases, the therapist may be led to believe that he is dealing with a difficult and sometimes intractable reality situation. This case involved a resistance for the patient, which was at times sufficiently subtle so that its intrapsychic implications could easily be overlooked.

Although there are, indeed, difficulties in external adjustments, they still offer reflections of each partner's personal neurosis. On the surface, the spouse seems to be responsible for the disruption of the treatment, but he can be effective only if the patient allows him to be. These patients utilize external objects to defend themselves against awareness of their inner problems. True, the other partners attempt to sabotage the treatment, especially if there has been any significant progress, for they feel threatened by any changes in marital equilibrium. Regardless of the many uncomfortable aspects of a marriage, aspects responsible for initiating treatment, any shift in the equilibrium seems threatening to the other person. Nevertheless, the patient also responds to the threatened equilibrium and may in turn become frightened of further progress because it means going on alone without the usual defensive props. Consequently, the patient may encourage the sabotaging aspects of the spouse and may then use this attitude as an analytic resistance.

One cannot therefore focus upon the external situation. This problem is still an intrapsychic one, to which, in many cases, the patient has contributed. On the surface, it seems as if the patient is trying hard to work through inner conflicts and is being attacked by an undermining, sadistic spouse. Such seems to have been the situation in the case of the young woman. Still, as we scrutinize the subtleties of the marital relationship, it also becomes apparent that she had manipulated her husband to react as he did. He felt threatened by her progress and the upset in the marital equilibrium, but so did she. She unconsciously recognized the vulnerability of some of his defenses and attacked him particularly in those areas. She contributed to his feelings of insecurity and stimulated him to intensify his defensive behavior. They were both serving their own needs, but she was able to use his reactions as a protective screen against deeper transference involvements.

Object relations are a facet of ego functions. One has to include them in any study of the therapeutic process. In a marriage, any changes in the marital equilibrium constitute changes in an important object relationship for both husband and wife. These changes affect each partner's psychodynamic balance. Conversely, any shifts in psychic structure are reflected in all object relations, especially the marital one.

Clearly, the development of the transference neurosis gives us an excellent vantage point from which to observe various shifts in object relations. From such observations, we can better evaluate the effects of deviations from the one-to-one aspects of the psychoanalytic relationship. In view of our interest in the therapeutic process, I am raising the question of the significance for the patient of conjoint therapy or collaboration with the spouse. From an analytic point of view, it is important to see how such a parameter either helps or hinders the usual unfolding of the transference neurosis. From a longer-range perspective, we must formulate some hypotheses about whether or not the analytic goal, that is, the resolution of conflict and ego structuralization, can be better achieved if the spouse is somehow brought into the treatment—or whether or not the situation is inordinately complicated by a collaboration that might be reacted to as an interference.

These questions cannot be answered simply by observing symptomatic improvement or remission. Phenomenological criteria are inconclusive and do not add to our knowledge. What may at one time appear to be improvement, behaviorally speaking, may represent an intractable resistance and may really indicate therapeutic failure. Similarly, what may seem a worsening of the patient's condition may actually be a reaction to the relinquishing of a defense and a step toward ultimate resolution. Although we are all interested in the welfare of the patient, there are many ways of helping people that are not part of our professional orientation. To study questions concerning the therapeutic process, we must stay within a consistent conceptual framework, and the phenomena observed, at least in the psychoanalytic setting, must be understood in terms of their transference implications.

To return to the transference neurosis, then, we note that it highlights the significance of contemporary objects in terms of their relevance to infantile objects. A serial hierarchy of object imagos extending from contemporary objects to archaic forerunners is found in any object representation. If this point is kept in mind, we can see that it is meaningless to think in terms of one element's belonging to transference and another's belonging to nontransference. Every object relationship must have some transference element, just as any thought, wish, or impulse has its unconscious determinants. True, the relationship may be founded mainly on conscious contemporary elements, and the unconscious infantile contribution to the relationship may be minimal. In any psychoanalytical study, however, it is the latter factor on which we must concentrate.

The question can now be rephrased. In what ways will a transference neurosis be affected if the analyst has any contact with the marital partner? Although a relationship with the spouse may not seem to have any particular effect on the patient, a microscopic scrutiny of the transference neurosis indicates that something has happened to some aspect of the transference relationship. This point is obvious because the analyst's contact with the spouse is an event, a stimulus, and every stimulus must have some reaction. Of course, the quality of the reaction determines whether such contact is helpful or deleterious.

The clinical example given at the beginning of this chapter suggests that there comes a point in the analysis of a married person when he projects onto the analyst an imago of the spouse. It also suggests that the imago of the spouse is similar to an archaic self-representation. This projection therefore highlights the infantile determinants of the choice of mate, as well as the narcissistic factors involved in such a choice. During this phase of the transference neurosis, the analyst represents the spouse, and the spouse in turn represents an archaic infantile self-image. Insofar as there is a lack of distinction between the patient and the spouse from the point of view of intrapsychic structuralization, there is a fusion between the patient and the spouse. This fusion is reenacted in the analytic setting, and we note during this stage of treatment a similar fusion between the patient and the analyst.

We might justifiably raise the objection here that these conditions are artifacts caused by analysis itself and not necessarily indicators of a basic orientation or even a modality that might exist between husband and wife. What appears in analysis must, however, be present in the patient to begin with. One cannot introduce a mode of reaction into a person for which he did not have the potential in the first place. What we uncover in the analytic relationship are mechanisms that, although not obvious, contribute to the patient's adjustments and determine the character of his object relations. The transference regression highlights archaic qualities that are nevertheless operative even when the patient is not in a regressed state. This point is similar to that about every impulse and acting having its unconscious determinants. The regressed transference neurosis reveals reactions that are the prototypes for later adjustments.

An object relationship that has such primitive elements as fusion embodied within it causes special problems for the resolution of the transference neurosis. As we are dealing here with marital partners specifically; I wish to bring into focus the difficulties that are created when the patient-analyst fusion reflects the patient-spouse fusion. When we are considering the effect a relationship between the therapist and someone known to the patient might have on the therapeutic process, the mechanism of fusion becomes important.

Let us consider the triangle of patient, therapist, and spouse from a conceptual point of view and relate it to various transference elements. To repeat, the patient projects an infantile self-image in the form of the spouse on to the analyst. This projection results in the patient's confusion of the spouse and the therapist. His reality-testing is impaired. If the therapist is having an actual relationship with the spouse, the patient's confusion of the two becomes intensified. He receives support for his distortions by the existence of such a relationship. The extra-analytic relationship with the spouse reinforces the transference projection. The specific nature of the patient's reactions to such a projection would depend upon the content of the inner conflicts. Our task is to determine whether or not such a reinforcement creates obstacles for therapy.

To clarify the nature of the transference, as reinforcement sometimes does, can be helpful. But the main question is whether or not the transference can be resolved. The existence of a transference neurosis is not necessarily helpful to analytic resolution. Transference does and must occur, but it must be an operable transference, one that can be eventually recognized by the patient for what it is. In a large measure, the capacity to distinguish between transference feelings and reality depends upon the patient's integrative abilities and his capacities for reality-testing. The analyst's role, however, is paramount because the patient's reality-testing can be obscured if the analyst has behaved in a fashion that reinforces the transference projection. It is beyond the scope of this discussion to consider the optimal conditions that the analyst might create for transference resolution. Still, if the analyst behaves in a fashion congruent with the patient's fantasies and goes along with the qualities that the patient has projected onto him, then it becomes obvious that the patient will find it difficult to make distinctions between what he has projected and the reality of the analytic situation. It will be more difficult for him to introject an objective, observing, benign, and interested analyst whose chief function is to understand what is going on within him. Such an introject augments self-observing tendencies and, through introspection, leads to the formations of insights that emphasize intrapsychic phenomena. If the analyst, on the other hand, behaves in a fashion that is similar to the role that the patient has ascribed to him in the transference projection, then the formation of an observing introject does not occur. Instead, the patient will react toward the analyst as if he really were an archaic object imago.

If the analyst behaves in a fashion that corresponds to the patient's fantasies, then both the patient's and the analyst's abilities to view the object relationship of the transference neurosis as an intrapsychic phenomenon are impaired. They both respond to what they consider to be reality elements. If the predominant transference results in fusion of the patient, analyst, and spouse and if the analyst has an actual relationship with the spouse, then the boundaries among these three persons become indistinct. The analyst's function is to help the patient be objective about his inner feelings. He attempts to show him that some of these feelings represent archaic reactions and fantasies. This task becomes increasingly difficult if he behaves in a fashion that reinforces the fantasies.

Ego boundaries become blurred, and the patient no longer feels himself a separate and distinct entity. To be fused with the spouse-therapist may give him unconditional security or cause him to feel helpless and vulnerable. The patient's reactions depend upon whether he is projecting an omnipotent wish fulfillment or a destructive rage onto the analyst, these two reactions not being mutually exclusive and usually alternating.

One might object at this point that this type of patient is an example of exceptionally severe psychopathology and that generalizations about therapeutic approaches cannot be made from a particular clinical group. I agree with this position, but many have emphasized the need for more varied approaches because the patients they have encountered have not responded well to traditional techniques. The reason offered for such a lack of response is that these patients are too sick to be treated in terms only of their intrapsychic conflicts and that some degree of environmental manipulation and support is required. It is precisely the type of patient who shows such primitive mechanisms who has been considered from the point of view of "marital therapy," and it is this type of patient who is most likely to develop difficulties in transference resolution if the analyst steps outside the analytic situation.

Furthermore, regressed ego states characterized by fusion occur in cases that do not show serious characterological defects. Such states occur as results of the regression set in motion by the analytic procedure and become manifest in the transference neurosis. Returning to a hierarchical concept of object relations we should expect to find a pre-object fusion state at the primitive end of the spectrum. Insofar as every relationship contains all elements of its development, even the most mature object relations contain some degree of earlier adaptive techniques. The latter may come to the fore in deep transference states and may lead to complications if the analyst has reinforced the fusion with extra-analytic relationships.

The main element of transference resolution consists of the patient's recognition of the archaic nature of his transference feelings. He learns not only of the infantile qualities of his feelings but also that he has projected them on the therapist, thus coming to separate the therapist as therapist from a significantly emotional figure from his own childhood. The resolution of this specific transference state would result in recognition of the projection of an infantile self-representation embodied in the spouse on to the analyst—and the fact that this view of the analyst is a projection.

Boyer (1961b) made a point of not communicating with the relatives of thirteen severe adult schizophrenics, and Weiss (1963) and Anthony (1964) similarly refrained from consulting the relatives of their child patients.

What are the implications, then, of an extra-analytic relationship with or simultaneous treatment of the spouse in terms of the transference neurosis and the regressed ego state of fusion among patient, analyst, and spouse? What are some of the factors that enable the patient to discriminate between what is occurring intrapsychically and what emanates from the external world? In any analytic relationship, the patient, because of regression, reverts to infantile methods of relating to the therapist. Among the techniques utilized is introjection, and the patient introjects the analyst during many phases of the transference neurosis. The nature of the introject is multiply determined and has many facets essential for distinguishing between what is transferred and the object of transferences. The natural tendency of a patient who has fused the self-representation with the spouse-analyst is to confuse internal (introjects) and external reality. Ego boundaries are relatively nonexistent, and there is difficulty in maintaining a separation between self and objects.

Nevertheless, if the analyst has maintained his individuality, so to speak, an individuality that is determined by his adherence to the analytic role, the patient will introject some elements of it. By "analytic role," I do not mean distance or impassivity. Rather, I am describing the analyst's willingness to understand what is going on within the patient, instead of taking sides in his intrapsychic conflicts, and to feel that there is something within the patient worth understanding. This attitude provides a structuring experience for the analysand, one that strengthens his self-esteem. Inherent in the desire to understand is a respect for the patient's autonomy and his developmental potential. The analyst also conveys a nonanxious orientation in his response to the patient's infantile needs and conflicts. All these elements compose the analytic attitude, and to some extent they are introjected.

If the analyst turns to the outer world either to help the spouse, the marriage, or the patient, he introduces another frame of reference, which transcends the technique of intrapsychic exploration. Whereas the purpose of the analyst is to help the patient distinguish inner conflicts from reality and, through the transference resolution, to recognize distortions of reality, the analyst who has a relationship with some facet of the patient's reality dilutes his own function of providing inward-directed attention. The introjection of the analytic attitude (the analytic introject) does not occur or does not occur so definitively, and the transference projection of fusion among self-representation, spouse, and analyst becomes intensified. This process takes place because the analyst is actually behaving in a fashion congruent with the patient's fantasies, assuming a role that involves omnipotence and is reminiscent of the early mother-child fusion or symbiosis. By relating to an area of the patient's reality, the analyst is tacitly (or otherwise) promising the patient that he can alter the external world in ways that will significantly help him, that he can produce changes within the patient that do not require self-understanding, internal readjustments, conscious choice, or autonomy.

Transference resolution becomes difficult under these circumstances, for there is a relatively weak formation (cathexis) of the analytic introject and a fairly intense distorted representation of the analyst determined by the transference projection. The ego is therefore impaired in its self-observing function to the extent that the distinction between the analyst and the transference projection is blurred. The patient is unable to view the analyst as analyst but can see him only in terms of an archaic imago. This state results in a transference fixation, which is a hindrance to further analysis. Instead, the patient continues to react to the analyst in terms of his infantile distortions and expectations.

He is also unable to distinguish between his internal milieu and the analyst. Because the analyst has become "fused" with the spouse and because this fusion is reinforced by the analyst's relationship with the spouse, the perception of such a relationship is reflected within the ego as a fusion of self- and object representations. An external object relationship inevitably reinforces the mental representation of such a relationship even if the initial intrapsychic formation was created by a projection of infantile attitudes. Under these circumstances, various intra-ego systems become less clearly delineated. The ego becomes less structured and amorphous. This result has therapeutic drawbacks, for the ego cannot achieve an optimal distance from the unconscious and is thereby impaired in its ability to discern conflicting motivations and distortions.

These formulations are conceptual descriptions, and reactions and regressions as intense as those I have described are not always the rule. I have emphasized the analytic goal of the resolution of the transference neurosis, which I believe is hampered by introducing an extraneous relationship. The goals of therapy differ, however. I limit myself here to the analytic process, which sometimes continues in the direction of resolution even when vicissitudes are introduced. Still, it is best to be aware of the meanings of parameters in terms consistent with our theoretical understanding.

The study of married couples, insofar as they represent a particular type of object relationship, has many interesting implications for the more general developmental aspects of object relationships. Benedek (1949, 1959) and Mahler (1952) have studied the early stages of development in adults, using reconstructive methods, and in children, and have postulated an early stage of fusion between the mother and child, which they call "symbiosis." Husbands and wives are also bound to each other in symbiotic fashion. But their bond is of a different order from that between mother and child. Pollock (1964) has explored the concept of symbiosis thoroughly, and he has also made the distinction between symbiosis of two adults and of mother and child. He emphasizes the conclusion that the symbiotic process can be viewed at different developmental stages. Married couples differ from the mother-child symbiosis because the needs of one partner for the other are "equal." The mother may have an intense emotional need for the child, and the child is, of course, almost totally dependent upon her. The mother could survive, however, without the child, whereas the converse is not true. The study of psychopathology has revealed that one spouse could not survive psychically if something happened to the marital relationship. At least, he could not maintain an equilibrium unless he found someone similar to the lost partner. These marriages highlight intense mutual dependence. Every marriage, of course, has a degree of mutual dependence inherent in it, one that becomes exaggerated with psychopathology.

Some symbiotic element, therefore, is found in every stable relationship. It is not necessarily the same as that found in early neonatal stages, but it has some resemblance to the initial symbiosis. There are in every object relationship elements of its beginnings, operating even in a contemporary setting. Object relationships reflect their historical development, and, although later derivatives may be the most significant ones, their prototypes still exert some influence.

Early neonatal stages are conceptualized as characterized by a homogeneity between the inner and outer worlds. There is no clearcut distinction between the self and the outer world. If we can speak of an object relationship at all, we should have to speak of a narcissistic one. Later, however, the external object, by promoting ego structure in general, also contributes to a consolidation of the self-representation. From an initial narcissistic stage, a symbiotic fusion between the mother and child develops through gradual differentiation and separation from the external object, an ego that has its own boundaries. This ego, or more precisely, the self-representation still contains introjected elements of the initial symbiotic relationship. With further development, these elements become increasingly structured and then differentiated into qualities that determine later object choices.

The early symbiosis is therefore involved in developmental processes and is a factor in such development. Aspects of this symbiosis as they persist in later object choices are highlighted in the study of the psychopathology of the married patient. Early fusion with the mother, although global, nevertheless represents an embryonic self-image. Separation from the mother leads to a consolidation, an individuation, of the self-image and results in a circumscribed identity. Insofar as the projection of the spouse in the transference neurosis reveals a projection of an early self-representation, we can conclude that the symbiotic elements of an object relationship have persisted with considerable intensity. The patient seeks, at one level, elements of the early symbiotic experience in the marital relationship. He attempts to find an early aspect of the self in the spouse.

If the early symbiosis was characterized by destructive elements and the self-representation was a hated and hateful one, then it would block further development. A hostile cathexis of the self impairs ego differentiation and leads to constriction of adaptive techniques. The developmental spectrum of object relationships is also correspondingly narrowed, and, in cases of psychopathology, especially those with characterological defects, the modality for the choice of objects is determined chiefly by the early symbiosis. Mahler's cases of symbiotic psychoses in children are extreme examples of narrowed object relations determined by symbioses that were felt to be engulfing and destructive.

As a person matures, his capacity to obtain gratification from objects increases. The ego has many adaptive techniques at its disposal, and object relationships have multiple facets enabling the psyche to achieve a wider variety of satisfactions. Both the needs and the techniques of gratification are better developed. One relates to an external object at many different levels. Still, the need to consider an object in terms of one's own self-representation is operative in well developed egos too. The self-representation, however, has many more dimensions than the global fusion in the initial symbiosis. It is a representation that functions in many frames of reference, is well synthesized, and embodies a variety of skills and adjustive techniques. In a well-differentiated ego, the self-representation is close to the ego ideal and is highly valued. Similarly, the object is highly valued in the same way as the self. The initial symbiosis has undergone a series of refinements and progressive development leading to an expansive sense of the self that functions smoothly and often creatively. A person seeks a spouse whom he values in the same way that he values himself. The elements of the earlier symbiosis continue to operate even in so-called "mature" object relationships, but they are expansive rather than constrictive because the symbiosis has undergone considerable organization. The person finds that, in order to value another person, he must know how to value himself, and he must rediscover in the other a valued part of the self.

That the psychopathology of the married person is identical or equivalent to that of the spouse is a conclusion based on observation. It is an empirical generalization, and there are exceptions (symptom object relations, for example). The exceptions, however, consist of object relations on a different axis from that of character object relations. They are characterized by superficial involvement and tend to be transient.

Can such an empirical generalization as the equivalence of married partners' psychopathology be integrated into a consistent theoretical framework? If so, an observation that has been explained in terms of a theoretical process becomes more plausible and gains in predictive value, for it is no longer dependent on mere induction. As a construct, the equivalence of psychopathology and even nonpathological character structures as a characteristic of marriage acquires greater validity and conviction than it has when viewed only as a clinical phenomenon.

The projection of the self-representation is often observed as a central feature of the transference neurosis. The analyst can, at different times, be imbued with qualities characteristic of the patient during periods of his past. Sandler (1962) and the Hampstead group have noted that, in children too, usually those whose conditions have been diagnosed as borderline states, the projection of archaic aspects of the ego may be the chief transference manifestation. In cases of married adults, different levels of the self-image are projected onto the analyst, depending on the predominant psychosexual orientation of the therapeutic moment.

As we have stressed, whenever the self-representation is projected onto the analyst, regardless of the psychosexual level of the ego state, the analyst is also viewed as a spouse. The analyst, by not behaving in a fashion consistent with such a self-representation, enables the patient to correct his distortion and eventually to effect a resolution of the transference neurosis.

Can the spouse also behave in a fashion that is not consistent with the self-representation, while still enabling the patient to maintain this projection? How does the spouse behave if the patient projects an earlier self-representation onto him? Piaget (1951) points out that a mental representation (an internal psychic construct) can be maintained in early stages of development only if there is a corresponding external object to reinforce it. Beres (1960) makes a similar point about ego regression. In a married couple, it becomes difficult to understand how one spouse can maintain a projection of an infantile self-representation unless it receives some validation from the outside world. Even the paranoid psychotic, who uses projection in an extreme fashion, chooses objects that show some degree of appropriateness for the projection.

If the patient is not able to maintain this type of projection, the marital equilibrium is disturbed. The separation reactions and resistances described occur when one partner is no longer able to project because the other partner is no longer willing to allow it. The latter partner has experienced shifts in his intrapsychic equilibrium that are reflected in changes in his adjustive techniques. Consequently, we can raise the question of what type of psychic organization a person must have in order to behave in a fashion that enables another person to project aspects of an infantile self-representation onto him. If a person is able to behave in a manner congruent with another person's infantile self-representation, it seems inevitable that he has an underlying structure consistent with such behavior. To play a role for a long period of time is difficult, if not impossible, unless the role, to some extent, fits.

The patient's requirements of the spouse are so global and involve so many facets of his behavior that for such a role to "fit" would require specific qualities of the most basic and fundamental aspects of the spouse's psychic structure. The patient's projection includes practically all areas of the spouse's life, domestic and sexual as well as vocational and aesthetic. The evidence for this conclusion again comes from observation of the transference neurosis, for when the analyst is considered as a spouse-self-representation, the patient's associations and fantasies delve into all areas of the analyst's life. Whatever conflictual elements are predominant determine what areas the patient will focus upon. Eventually, with psychodynamic shifts, he covers the gamut of the analyst's personal life, indicating that his need to see the spouse as a certain type of person includes the broader aspects of her personality. In contrast, a person whose marriage is founded on the basis of a symptom object relationship shows a more limited involvement in the broader aspects of the analyst's personal life when the transference of the spouse is the essence of the transference neurosis. In other transference states, in which the spouse is only minimally involved, if at all, the patient's fantasies about the analyst may include many areas.

To recapitulate, because the spouse can behave appropriately relative to the patient's projection of an infantile self-representation, it becomes apparent that the spouse's and the patient's self-representations must be similar. We can then conclude that there has to be an equivalence of psychopathology and a similarity of character structure.

In order to understand how similar self-representations indicate equivalence of psychopathology, we must examine the concept of the self-representation further. The patient reveals that he not only projects a subjective appraisal of an earlier self-image, but he also includes both conflictual and defensive aspects in the transference projection. We note the projection of an ego state that contains conscious and unconscious elements, psychodynamic and characterological features. Psychopathology is the outcome of disturbances of an early self-representation. Psychodynamic conflicts and character defects in the adult can be traced back to and are, in large measure, caused by disturbed early object relations, which in turn contribute to the structure of the self-representation. The last then determines how he adjusts and the quality of his future object relations. Adjustive techniques, defensive or otherwise, are the essence of a person's individuality; the nidus of character structure is already formed in the early self-representation. When we think in terms of similar or identical self-representations, it is therefore conceptually consistent to conclude that the personalities of those compared are similar from all points of view, psychodynamic, characterological, and psychopathological.

Summary

To explore the classical psychoanalytic approach as applied to the treatment of marital disharmony, we must understand precisely what is meant by "classical psychoanalysis." Deviations from so-called "classical" techniques are meaningful only if their implications can be discussed within a consistent theoretical framework. The theoretical scaffolding both of psychoanalytic treatment and of parameters requires elaboration and refinement.

The study of object relations, of which marital partnerships are one type, affords us a good opportunity for such a theoretical study. The frame of reference of the transference neurosis, along with the separation reactions of one partner when the marital equilibrium is disturbed, enables us to conclude that a marriage that has endured is characterized by an equivalence of psychopathology of the spouses.

Introduction of parameters causes complications for transference resolution. The projection of the spouse, at a crucial transference stage, involves a projection of an infantile self-representation; this projection is characterized by the psychic mechanism of fusion of the spouse and the analyst. This spouse-analyst fusion is reinforced if the analyst has an actual relationship with the spouse, which makes resolution difficult.

Symbiosis, a term that has been restricted to an early mother-child fusion, exists at later developmental levels too. We can scrutinize the symbiotic process as a serial hierarchy, a continuum that extends from neonatal stages to adult object relations, including marriage. There are symbiotic elements in both nonpathological and pathological relations, and in both instances they determine the quality of the relationship.

Symbiotic fusion is crucial in the early formation of the self-representation, which can be conceptualized in terms of psychodynamic and characterological elements. The partner, as a recipient of the projection of an infantile self-representation, behaves in a fashion that permits the maintenance of such a projection. The partner is able to behave "appropriately" because he has a similar self-representation. To the extent that an infantile self-representation contains the seeds of later psychopathology and determines nondefensive adjustments, similar or identical self-representations indicate similarity of character structure from both pathological and nonpathological points of view.

Chapter 19

Characterological Aspects of Marital Interaction

Adjustive techniques and defensive interaction can be profitably studied from the viewpoint of ego psychology as well as in terms of intrapsychic conflict and instinctual derivatives. Such an orientation is directed toward transactions with the outer world but, of course, the analyst maintains his interest in their intrapsychic components. Thus, object relations represent another frame of reference which is relevant to analytic inquiry and therapeutic understanding.

Marriage is a special type of object relationship which can be understood from several viewpoints. One immediately perceived function of object relations is their adjustive potential, which in many instances can become defensive in view of intrapsychic conflict or characterological defect.

Benedek (1949) and Mahler (1952), among others, have designated certain stages of the mother-infant interaction as being symbiotic in character with considerable mutual dependency. Although the child's dependence upon the mother is total, the mother can turn elsewhere. However, as Benedek (1952) has emphasized, the mother's relationship with the child may be a "total" one during early neonatal stages and represents a developmental phase for her as well as for the baby.

Symbiosis also refers to a developmental phase that leads to the structuring of object relationships and the formation of an integrated, coherent identity, distinct from the outer world. Such developmental levels determine the qualities and nature of object relationships appropriate to the particular psychosexual stage. (See chapter 18; Pollock, 1964.)

The symbiotic aspects of the marital object relationship have been described in chapters 15, 16 and 18. Here, I wish to elaborate the thesis that marital partners have constructed a symbiotic object relationship which stresses equal needs of one spouse for the other. This equality of needs, however, has unique manifestations that reflect the total personality integration.

Total emotional involvement—the need of marital partners for each other—often involves massive projections that are vital for psychic

First published in Psa. Forum 2 (1967), 7–13. Reprinted by permission.

survival. The following vignette illustrates the role of projection (akin to that described by Melanie Klein [1946] as projective identification) in maintaining psychic balance in the marital setting. This type of marital interaction also teaches us about the intimate and unique characterological involvement often encountered in marriage.

Clinical Illustration

The patient, a housewife in her middle thirties, was urged by her husband to seek therapy. She presented herself as completely helpless, unable to carry on the pedestrian functions of everyday living. She could not take care of the house, raise her children or even perform routine shopping chores. She described a state of perpetual anxiety bordering on panic. (Though married eleven years, the situation she was now presenting was no different from that at the beginning of her marriage.)

Her husband had to assume complete control and responsibility for the household in addition to conducting a successful business. He seemed to be an extremely patient person who was kind, tender and concerned about the welfare of his family. He telephoned for the initial appointment and voiced his concern and willingness to spare no efforts or money to help his wife.

There were no obvious precipitating circumstances that accounted for her seeking treatment at this time. The patient had made some attempts at self-improvement by registering for a technical course that would have enabled her to be self-sufficient. In view of her extreme helplessness, it was difficult to understand her having taken such initiative. The patient revealed that throughout the years she had made attempts to obtain help, either by receiving further education in a vocational setup or by seeking therapy. What was astonishing was the husband's reaction to these endeavors. Although he did nothing overtly to stop her, he subtly depreciated whatever she attempted and the patient felt absolutely no support from him. On the contrary, she saw him as obstructing whatever progressive steps she was trying to pursue.

The patient's ego organization was an extremely unstable one and she experienced many episodes of depersonalization. Frequently, she had ideas of reference and there was a paranoid quality to her associations. She had no overt delusions but in view of her intense helplessness, inadequacy, and the looseness or fragmentation of her associations, I believed this patient was bordering on psychosis.

In marked contrast the husband presented a picture of a gregarious, affable, flexible, mature person with genuine concern for his wife's welfare. His sabotaging her attempts at self-improvement was inconsistent with the picture he presented when making arrangements for her treatment. However, the situation changed as therapy progressed.

The patient related well to the analytic situation and rather quickly formed an anaclitic type of dependent transference. She idealized me and made me into a person of omnipotent goodness who could somehow counteract the badness she felt was inside her. She saw me as a rescuer with whom she could fuse so that together we could exercise a cosmic control over both our inner feelings and the universe.

In spite of her seeming helplessness it became apparent that this patient could effectively manipulate others who responded to her intense anxiety in a sadistic fashion which enhanced their self-esteem. In the treatment her helplessness was designed to destroy me by first aggrandizing me. But in spite of her precarious equilibrium the patient was able to withstand the frustration accompanying her recognition that I was not trying to rescue her.

After about one year of therapy she showed marked symptomatic improvement. Her anxiety disappeared and she gained some self-confidence. Her previous endeavors at self-improvement materialized and she learned a vocational skill that enabled her to obtain a relatively lucrative position.

As her improvement became manifest with lessening of anxiety, her husband became increasingly dissatisfied. He had been cooperative when the patient was helpless and anxious, but now he took every opportunity to make disparaging remarks about analysts, myself in particular. He seemed to be doing everything possible to destroy the analytic relationship. The patient steadfastly refused to terminate; finally the husband stopped paying for her analysis. However, the patient had some money from an inheritance, and her job was paying sufficiently so that she could continue the treatment.

Her husband now became violent. He had fits of rage in which he attacked his wife and children. The patient remained resolute, and when he lost control, she called the police. At this point he began to realize he could not force her to stop treatment. The only avenue that remained open to him was to threaten divorce, and he was amazed when she seemed relieved at his suggestion.

The husband became increasingly upset, calling on the telephone and threatening me. He was incoherent and showed unmistakable signs of paranoid ideation. When he became convinced that I would not discuss his wife's situation with him he threatened to leave her and finally did. He went to a hotel in the downtown section of the city, became intensely frightened and signed himself in the psychiatric ward of a local hospital. He was diagnosed as suffering from paranoid schizophrenia. He remained in the hospital several months, finally reintegrated and later obtained a divorce. While in the process of getting the divorce he started going out with a patient whom he had met in the hospital, and shortly after the decree was granted he married her. It was interesting to note that his second wife was described as being quite similar to my patient, a helpless, vulnerable, panicky person.

Marital Object Relationships

Initially, there seemed to be a wide divergence in characterological stability, but subsequent events indicated the basic personality organization of these marital partners to be similar. The patient seemed to need the husband for her psychic survival, but, as the course of therapy indicated, the husband was just as dependent upon her. When the patient improved, the husband regressed to a position that was at least phenomenologically similar to the one the patient presented when she first started treatment.

Similar cases (chapter 15) demonstrated that the underlying conflicts, levels of psychosexual development and characterological structure in such marital partners are remarkably similar. Each marital partner requires the total personality, including the specific character defenses, of the other partner in order to maintain intrapsychic equilibrium, and regardless of intense strife and turmoil, the marriage lasts. This type of object relationship, where the involvement is such a total one, has been referred to as a *character object relationship*.

Not all marriages, however, establish an equilibrium on this basis. There is another group of relationships that I shall call *symptom object relationships,* which differ from the marriages described above in that the marital bond is transitory and superficial, the marriages frequently result in divorce, and the need of one spouse for the other is less intense than that described for character object relationships. The partners do not require the total personality of one another; each must have only a particular trait or symptom to serve the other's defensive needs. Frequently such a patient has had several marriages in which each spouse had a common denominator, so to speak, but in other respects differed markedly.

For example, a young married woman in her late twenties stated that her husband was a weak, inadequate person. Even as she was criticizing him it was apparent she was not particularly concerned about his drawbacks and that her involvement with him was only superficial. She was able, however, to paint a picture of him as a detached, withdrawn schizoid person. The patient, in contrast, seemed outgoing, reality-oriented and in no way so seriously disturbed. She sought analysis because of a variety of hysterical symptoms, and the treatment finally reached the core of her oedipal conflicts. She revealed that she was intensely competitive with her more beautiful mother and covetous of her heterosexual successes. The mother intimidated the patient and made her feel guilty. Consequently, her love affairs never worked out well; she was defeating herself in order to assuage a disapproving, maternal superego. To appease her mother she felt she must have a passive, inadequate husband, but the nature of the husband's psychopathology was not important. So long as the man she married was not desirable, her mother would not want to destroy her and take him for herself. She managed to find men who did not rate high on the marriage market. At the time of treatment she was in her fourth marriage, each previous marriage having lasted a year or less. All of her husbands were described as "weak characters" who were physically unattractive, lacking in charm and intellectually shallow and constricted.

These men were not alike although the patient felt that they were all inadequate and undesirable. Her first husband was a gregarious back-slapping salesman who covered his ineptness with bluffing and boasting. No one failed to recognize his mediocrity. The patient considered him crass, materialistic and an insensitive bore. Her second husband, markedly different, was described as a highstrung, oversensitive artist. His mood was usually depressed or rebellious, and he valued esthetic and intellectual pursuits. But he, too, was a failure and lacked talent, talking more about his work than actually working. The patient felt he was physically repugnant, unkempt and unwashed. The other two husbands also differed from the first two and from each other, but she described each as uniquely inadequate.

The analysis revealed the circumscribed defensive meaning of the marital relationship. The spouse was not considered as a whole object. The patient related only to one particular characteristic of the husband, one which she used to defend herself from destructive and self-destructive competitive feelings toward her mother. The need for such relationships was vital, but unlike persons involved in character object relations she had greater flexibility and shifted from one object to another. Relationships founded on such a symptomatic basis were unstable; other attributes of the spouse's personality extraneous to the patient's needs would eventually make the relationship untenable. This woman could not relate to hypomanic, depressive, or schizoid qualities.

In symptom object relationships the spouse represents the personification of a defensive need. There may be similarities in the manifest expression of some defenses and differences in the underlying personality organization. Character object relationships, in contrast, involve a projection of the self-representation onto the spouse, which then makes the establishment of intrapsychic and marital equilibrium possible.

Developmental Aspects of Symbiosis

The marital object relationship has been discussed here primarily as a defensive stabilization in psychopathological situations. Whatever the level of psychosexual development, the spouse is fundamental to the maintenance of that level, so that a homeostatic balance can be maintained. The function of the marital object relationship can be generalized to include marriages that have only a minimum of psychopathology. Object relationships are not only important determinants of emotional development, but once optimal development has been achieved they continue to be vital for the maintenance of ego integration.

From the viewpoint that the initial fusion with the mother leads to an integrated ego with a coherent identity, the symbiotic element can be considered in terms of its positive differentiating potential rather than in terms of its defensive psychopathological implications.

The neonate's dependence upon the mother is total. If the mother relates to her child as a whole object during the stage of symbiotic fusion (a situation analogous to a character object relationship), the child may develop a well-differentiated autonomous ego. The well-developed ego possesses a coherent self-representation that views itself as a whole object and also responds to external objects as whole objects in the same fashion the mother related to the child during early developmental stages.

The neonate's symbiotic fusion has been conceptualized as being a total immersion of a rudimentary self with the nurturing source. In psychoanalytic treatment the patient may "fuse" with the analyst, especially in cases where the patient suffers from characterological defects. When he is able to reconstruct personal boundaries, his ego has undergone an expansion; parts of the ego that have been repressed and unavailable are now regained. Such a symbiotic fusion with the analyst, once it is "dissolved," can result in therapeutic benefits.

With emotional growth, more sophisticated and relatively autonomous adjustments develop; but, as with any psychic element, its precursors are in some way still operational, although usually in a modified form that is consonant with the "advanced" psychic level. Consequently, the early symbiotic adjustment is still operating in current object relationships, and, as the clinical material indicates, this is especially so in marriage.

In order to maintain a particular level of psychic structuralization certain basic requirements have to be met. The ego cannot exist in a vacuum. Perceptual stimulation and a continuous interaction with an integrative environment are important factors for the stabilization of a developmental position. The marital relationship is especially suited for the maintenance of ego integration.

Equivalence of psychopathology indicates a similarity of character structures. The extent to which the recipient of the projection "fits" the role assigned to him determines the stability of the object relationship. Stable marriages emphasize the durability of such a projection. The spouse has been conceptualized as being the recipient of the projection of the self-representation. The introjection of the spouse-self-representation image is instrumental in reinforcing the general ego coherence and the identity sense in particular. Freud (1923), in describing sublimation, spoke of libido becoming desexualized as it was withdrawn from objects and "passed through" the ego. It is returned to external objects in a neutralized (desexualized) form. In the marital relationship an analogous, but not identical, situation occurs insofar as a "passage" of a psychic element through an external object representation and then a return to the initial structure leads, not necessarily to an increase in structure, but to preservation of a functioning ego.

Unlike Freud's concept of the process of sublimation, an aspect of the self is projected on to the spouse. How much of the self-representation is projected will depend upon the level of object-relatedness the ego has achieved. Primitive ego organizations are characterized by splitting and relating to the external object as if it were a part object. In these cases simply ridding oneself of a hateful and vulnerable aspect of the self-representation by projecting it upon a part object representation constitutes a precarious adjustment. Here the "passage" is outward and there is very little introjection of integrative mechanisms that external objects might offer. On the contrary, because of the projection of the hateful self-representation, and since the object is viewed only as a part object, the ego is not able to turn to the object for the acquisition of adaptive techniques. In a sense it is unable to learn and has to rely upon its own meager resources.

Persons with more advanced states of psychosexual and characterological development view the object as a whole object, and their introjective-projective process is continuous. The self-representation is projected in toto onto the spouse and then is introjected back into the ego, often with a positive integrative outcome. The analogy with Freud's concept of sublimation becomes clearer if we reverse our directions. Whereas Freud stated that the passage of libido through the subject's ego has an integrative effect, in the marital relationship in projection of the self-representation onto the spouse is equivalent to the synthesizing aspects of converting object-libido into ego-libido. Finding someone with whom one can feel in complete harmony is an experience that both enhances and maintains self-esteem. Complete harmony is, of course, a fictional ideal state but there are relative degrees of such an integrated equilibrium. If one values oneself, then one is able to find similar values in another person. In marriage, one can be constantly rediscovering valued parts in the spouse which correspond to similar positive attitudes about the self. This leads to a further integration of the self-representation and it achieves a functional and gratifying equilibrium.

Introjection is a continuous process which reaffirms the self, but projection is also continuous. This introjective-projective mechanism, a replenishing action, leads to flexibility that includes many ego modalities. The initial symbiotic method of relating remains as a core which has undergone modification throughout the course of development. There have been innumerable accretions, the incorporation of subsequent experiences which have occurred in progressively structured settings.

Summary and Conclusions

Ego psychology enables us to focus upon object relationships such as the marital relationship, and in this chapter I have discussed marriage from several viewpoints: (1) In terms of character structure, the partners in lasting, but not necessarily healthy, marriages are found to be similar at all levels of psychic organization. They may have similar or complementary defenses, equivalent underlying conflicts and the same level of psychosexual development. This type of relationship is referred to as a character object relationship. In contrast, transient marriages are not so firmly anchored and the involvement of the partners is only partial. One partner needs only a particular attribute of the other. These interactions are called symptom object relationships. (2) Symbiosis, a concept borrowed from biology, can be applied to the marital interaction. In the character object relationship, the total involvement of the spouses can be thought of as a symbiotic adjustment. (3) The self-representation requires contact with the external world in order to maintain itself. Introjective-projective mechanisms operating relative to the spouse are continuous processes that reaffirm the identity sense.

Part IV

CLINICAL AND TECHNICAL ISSUES

All clinical psychoanalytic investigations finally lead to technical issues. Basically, the clinician reads papers and attends meetings in order to gain some knowledge which helps him treat patients. He may have other related interests such as applied psychoanalysis or abstruse theory, but when his therapeutic orientation is in the foreground, he wants to learn something that will further his understanding and give him insight into how to deal with his first patient the next morning.

I have heard many clinical papers criticized because the data did not justify the conclusions and the material presented could be interpreted in another fashion. Even when I agree with the discussant, I have the conviction that such critiques are irrelevant. If the author has made a point which I find useful and could apply to my patients, then the validity of his conclusion is established. Any lengthy, well-stated hypothesis that is extensively documented on the basis of considerable data and can be facilely integrated within an already existing clinical edifice, but which cannot be brought to bear upon clinical interactions is, from the viewpoint of clinical theory, not particularly useful or applicable. Thus, validity is a relative concept, depending, within the practitioner's frame of reference, upon pragmatic utility.

Many analysts have separated two types of theory (often with further subdivisions): clinical theory and metapsychology. Here, I do not wish to get involved with methodological issues; I merely wish to emphasize that the abstractness of a theoretical construct is not a significant factor.

261

If it can be included in a series of concepts representing different levels of abstractions, then no matter how far removed from clinical observations such a construction may be it is potentially testable and useful if it can be ultimately traced back to the patient's material.

The observations made in the following articles are concerned with technical issues. I refer to Freud's pessimism about treatment and his dictums about the untreatability of patients such as those discussed here. Without belaboring the issue, these patients were treated by what I consider to be classical psychoanalytic technique without the introduction of parameters. That one will encounter difficulties in the treatment of such patients is not surprising, but in my opinion that does not justify abandoning the psychoanalytic approach. Very few cases, of any type, proceed without difficulties, complications or impasses.

Understanding as much as possible about the nature of such difficulties, and the countertransference situations and problems they provoke, gives us deeper insight into the psychoanalytic process.

Chapter 20

Transference, Incorporation and Synthesis

Formulations about psychoanalytic treatment have evolved mainly from the study of the development of the transference neurosis. In this chapter, I shall study regression and other changes in the ego state that occur in analysis and shall focus upon a clinical group that has often been referred to as borderline states and character disorders. In cases with characterological problems, there is an opportunity to view ego processes and transference more clearly than in cases where ego defects are not prominent. However, I will also consider the psychoneuroses, emphasizing features that are common to all patients who can participate in a psychoanalytic relationship.

As noted in a recent panel discussion (Waelder et al., 1958) of the International Psycho-analytical Association, a comprehensive definition of the character disorders is a difficult and controversial task. In this paper I am referring to a clinical group that is familiar to all analysts because of the special and characteristic difficulties they present in analysis. I use the term character disorder to refer to patients who have reality testing sufficient to distinguish them from a psychotic and yet who find it difficult to relate to objects in an affectively significant fashion. These patients, instead of suffering from circumscribed symptoms, find the task of ordinary living and relating to others difficult and frustrating. Many variables have been considered in order to make such a nosological distinction meaningful. Modell (1963), for example, feels that these patients form an object relation in the transference that is similar to Winnicott's (1953) concept of the transitional object. The conclusions of the recent panel concerning arrested ego development and ego defects are also pertinent both to the understanding of this clinical group and to the thesis of this paper.

Some analysts believe that patients with ego defects present special difficulties in developing a transference neurosis. They make a distinction between transference neurosis and transference reactions. Such distinctions become useful only if one can understand the ego processes underlying these phenomena.

An investigation of the historical development of the concept of

First published in *Int. J. Psa.* 46 (1965), 287–96. Reprinted by permission.

transference clarifies many questions. In the *Studies on Hysteria* (Breuer and Freud, 1895) and the Dora case (Freud, 1905a) transference is discussed in a therapeutic setting, while in Freud's papers on technique (1912a,b, 1914b) the emphasis is mainly on clinical theory. We are, however, frequently imprecise in our use of the terms "transference reaction" and "transference neurosis" and I shall here define my use of them.

Transference reaction refers to a person's reactions to an object as they are determined by infantile unconscious factors. Viewing the object in terms of archaic imagos and a primary-process orientation leads to irrational attitudes and distortions. This is the essence of any transference phenomenon, but transference reactions are responses not limited to the analyst. They may occur toward any meaningful object and be well rationalized and justified. The transference neurosis has features which distinguish it from transference reactions and which are important in determining its therapeutic value. The transference neurosis has been defined as a condition in which the patient projects certain infantile feelings exclusively on to the analyst. Anna Freud (1946) believes that if infantile feelings continue to be projected on to persons other than the analyst, one is not dealing with a transference neurosis. She states,

> But, in spite of these manifold and variegated transferred reactions of the child, the author has not, so far, met a single case of a child patient where the original neurosis was given up during the treatment and replaced by a new neurotic formation in which the original objects had disappeared and the analyst taken their place in the patient's emotional life. It is only a structure of this kind which deserves the name of transference neurosis.

Many analysts have doubted whether an "exclusive" projection on to the analyst can ever occur. They reason that insofar as the patient is living in a world of objects, the patient cannot "exclude" them completely from distortions based on the projection of infantile imagos. From a metapsychological viewpoint, the "exclusive" nature is questionable in that the archaic objects that are projected are not integrated as well-synthesized whole objects. The archaic objects are at best, owing to the unstructured state of the infantile ego at the time of their development, part-objects, and can be projected only as such. In this regard, the patient's part-object projections may give the analyst a specific role and significance while some other role may be ascribed to another person. The fragmentation and splitting of objects is a characteristic feature of primitive infantile ego states. The roles assigned to the analyst as a part-object are frequently evanescent and interchangeable. Sometimes, for example, the analyst is rather suddenly changed from a "good object" to a "bad object" and the original savior becomes the persecutor.

Conflicting and ambivalent attitudes toward archaic objects and the later elaborations and revisions of the object are determinants of the transference projection. There are different levels of transference neurosis and dynamic shifts occur differing from the stereotyped repetition of what has been described as a transference reaction. Here the transference neurosis will be considered as a focal object relationship which for the moment may supersede all other object relations.

The most important therapeutic aspect of the transference neurosis is not whether it occurs, but whether it can be resolved. One that can be resolved is a therapeutically workable transference or an operable transference. I would like to emphasize the necessity of considering not only the presence of a transference neurosis, but also the mechanisms necessary for its resolution.

The technical difficulties that occur in the therapy of patients with character disorders are related to defects found in various ego systems. Gitelson (1958a) has emphasized the ego distortions found in this group and has considered such defects as typical of this clinical entity. The ego distortions associated with arrested development affect all ego systems. An important aspect of the ego defect and one that will be critical in determining the course of analysis is the disturbance in relations to objects. These patients have a limited capacity to view an object from a realistic secondary-process orientation. They have an impaired ability for object discrimination; they tend to see objects in a primitive fashion and look at the world in terms of a distorted infantile organization. Although particular objects may serve specific roles, defensive or otherwise, their perceptual system operates with relatively larger amounts of primary process energy than that of the psychoneurotic. Therefore, distinctions between present and past are not precise and the boundary between reality and what is projected is blurred.

Technical problems occur more or less in all cases. To some extent, all patients have characterological problems and insofar as there is an ego defect, the patient will have special difficulties in the resolution of the transference neurosis. Searles (1963) believes that a psychotic transference is characterized by different levels of symbiotic fusion with the analyst and he discusses the various aspects and manifestations of this fusion as it occurs with schizophrenic patients. He points out, however, that psychoneurotic patients have many elements in the transference neurosis that are similar to the psychotic transference. According to

Searles, even with the psychotic patient it is difficult to make absolute distinctions from the neurotic; there are elements of a "transference psychosis" in all patients.

The psychoneurotic patient is able to make better discriminations than is the patient which character problems and consequently is able to appraise external objects, including the analyst, with more of a secondary-process orientation. This greater ability is of value in making the transference neurosis an operable one.

The Need for Omnipotence and Disruptive Regression

In this section, I would like to discuss certain demands some patients may make upon the analyst; the management of them may lead to disruptive complications. The specific psychopathology of these patients frequently leads them to assign to the analyst a role which may lead to an inoperable transference.

The patient is frequently initially suspicious. He has found it difficult to obtain security and gratification from objects or to relate at a level of object constancy. Since he may have little capacity for self-object differentiation, all objects can become a source of danger, insofar as hateful introjects and external objects become fused. Early in analysis, the analyst is often invested with omnipotence, this representing an attempt to counteract the destructive internal objects which have caused the patient to feel helpless and vulnerable and to consider himself a hateful, unworthy person. The analysis is cast in the role of a savior who, in some magical fashion, will be able to give the patient "power" and "love" and thereby make him into an invulnerable, omnipotent person.

An inevitable consequence of such expectations is that the patient is eventually disappointed, insofar as megalomanic expectations cannot be fulfilled. When this disappointment occurs, the patient experiences rage and further regression may occur leading to disorganization and sometimes panic. The feelings may be of such intensity that the patient withdraws from treatment. If the patient remains in treatment, this regression may finally reach a stage that corresponds to, although it is not identical with, the ego state that preceded the formation of systematized defences. At this point characteristic ego defects are revealed and deficiencies in basic capacities become apparent. At such times, the analyst is often confronted by a patient experiencing intense waves of anxiety and accompanied by a fear of dissolution and the loss of control of destructive and self-destructive impulses. The transference neurosis at this point may be characterized by a projection of hostile introjects as a consequence of frustration. If there has been no reinforcement from the analyst this projection may not become overwhelming and the image of the interested and benign analyst may develop and coexist with the transference object projection (see below).

During the course of his life, the patient has met other benign and interested people who have tried to help him. The significant difference between the analyst and other helpful external objects is that the analyst does not take sides in the patient's intrapsychic conflicts; he does not deal with them as only part of a current reality. The analyst considers both sides of the conflict, the patient's genetic background and current reality representations, in his interpretations. He examines the ambivalence and explores the adaptive and defensive reactions to the conflict.

Projection of omnipotence on to the analyst is inevitable in many of these cases and, as stated earlier, is indicative of the projection of an archaic megalomanic imago. This attitude concerning the analyst must be analysed and, as with any element of the transference, such an analysis can be effective only if the patient is able to make a distinction between the analytic reality and his distortion of it. The patient's need to keep the analyst omnipotent will cause him to seize upon whatever opportunities the analyst may unwittingly supply to maintain the idealized external object and to deny it as his own construction. The loss of the omnipotence makes the patient feel a prey to his destructiveness. Under any circumstances, it is difficult to work through an attitude which the patient considers vital for his psychic survival.

The regression that occurs in the analysis of cases with ego defects leads to an ego state which corresponds to earlier phases of psychosexual development than the regressions that occur in the analyses of the psychoneuroses. In both types of cases, however, the ego fixation that is the basis of psychopathology is not directly reproduced in the therapeutic regression. Although there are greater segments of the ego in psychoneurotics which continue to function within the analytic situation at adaptational levels characteristic of later stages of development, in the cases with character disorders there are also still many functionally adaptive areas, as evidenced by the fact that the patient is able to carry on with his daily life even if it is only a marginal adjustment.

This cycle of megalomanic ambivalent expectation and disappointment need not occur as a sudden crisis, although it frequently does. It can lead to an intensely painful state of awareness. Often the patient avoids the full development of such a state by withdrawing from treatment, or by attempting to manipulate the therapist into establishing a relationship which is nonanalytic. To a large measure, the possibility for continuing the analysis will depend upon the analyst's purposeful avoidance of reinforcing the patient's omnipotent expectations of him.

In the development of any transference neurosis, defences are reinstituted to protect the subject against emergent forbidden or disruptive impulses and intolerable regression. The defences characteristically utilized by patients with ego defects are restitutional and primitive, and it is not uncommon for these patients to experience transient episodes that are phenomenologically similar to a psychosis. At these times, the analyst has been made into a destructive external persecutor, a projection of the patient's uncontrollable megalomanic destructiveness. The need to protect himself from the analyst or to protect the analyst from himself is a transference state based on hatred and hating infantile introjects and is characterized by a blurring of boundaries between the self and the outer world. In spite of the gravity of the condition and the considerable reality distortion associated with paranoid defences, a recovery to a less disrupted, more manageable state often occurs rather quickly.

I do not wish to give the impression that all cases of character disorders in therapy react in a rigid stereotyped sequence. The above description should be considered as a theme with many variations. Frequently, the reaction to the projected omnipotence is a fear of dissolution, a fear of being "swallowed up" by the analyst.

The depth of the transference regression is also variable. The analyst's interpretive activity is a factor that will control its disruptive aspects and in some instances its duration. From a functional viewpoint, the regression can sometimes be confined to the analytic session and the patient may continue his usual modes of adjustment to the outside world.

I wish to emphasize that a transference neurosis occurs in the analyses of patients with ego defects, but it embodies specific vicissitudes which require further understanding. Specifically, the frustration of the need for omnipotent gratification leads to a transference regression, which can lead to a therapeutically workable transference neurosis if the analyst's attitude and behavior do not reinforce the patient's megalomanic expectations, and if the analyst's integrative interpretations have continuously kept pace with the shifts in the patient's reactions.

Adaptive Potential of Regressed Ego States

An ego dominated by primary process has numerous characteristics which are not found in a more highly integrated ego. In many ways, the primitive ego is more labile and has a lower threshold of reaction to traumatic experience. Similarly, because of its lability, and in specific favourable circumstances, it may be affected by positive experiences that can increase its adaptive range.

The acquisition of adaptive techniques which lead to higher states of integration involves the process of incorporation. The ego develops by acquiring introjects that lead to more efficient functioning. Such introjects may have several modes of action. On the one hand, the introjects may act defensively, reducing the disruptive potential of intrapsychic conflict or ego defect and permitting the ego to achieve a more stable homeostasis; as a consequence areas of functional autonomy may develop. On the other hand, the ego may utilize an introjected positive experience not only in regard to its defensive potential; it may benefit from the experience directly, by having "assimilated" an adaptive technique, a point that is clinically illustrated in chapter 17. The ego's "armentarium" is expanded and its functional range is increased. Under these circumstances, the ego has better integration (greater structure) than previously.

In the regressed transference state, the ego has undergone a loss of a previous integration, a disruption, that may be experienced as painful. It is less efficient and less able to deal with both inner and outer stimuli. If the disruption is not too intense, however, the ego may not display the same rigidity and inflexibility of the better defended state. During regression, although some adaptive capacities of the ego are impaired, with the loss of certain defensive modes of operation (in contrast to introjects that reduce disruption), the ego gains the potential for structuralization. The functions of later-acquired adaptive and defensive structures, some of which are responsible for stereotyped and rigid responses, are often lost during such a regression, but because of such a loss the ego may acquire other adaptive techniques that are more efficient and flexible.

The reaction to regression is dependent upon many factors and need not always be disruptive or painful. Kris (1950b) thoroughly explored the potential benefits of the regressed state in artistic creativity. In the analytic situation, the analyst's integrative interpretations reduce the anxiety that is produced by the loss of defensive stabilization, leading to a trusting, dependable relationship which makes the regression not only tolerable, but useful (see below).

Regressive Sequence and Transference Resolution

As discussed above, the regressed state may lead to flexible adaptive techniques. However, the degree of regression is variable and there are differences in the therapeutic potential of different regressed states.

I have often noticed, in a broad sense, two types of regression which occur sequentially and differ in their functional capacities. One ego is more primitive than the other and is characterized by relatively less organization, a greater degree of fragmentation, and an inability to relate to objects, including the analyst. Such a fragmented ego is impaired in its ability to incorporate and form stable introjects. The patient's lack of organization does not enable him to form object representations that are coherent and oriented along a secondary-process organization, and as a consequence there is no operable transference with this narcissistic organization.

Nevertheless, the ego may move forward from this position to a state, although primitive, in which it has the capacity to form introjects. Because it has undergone the dissolution described above, the ego now has a capacity to incorporate new objects, a capacity that it did not previously have because of hostile destructive introjects leading to constrictions (see below). By regressing to such a level of disorganization, the ego has also lost its capacity to maintain destructive introjects when it "progresses" to a slightly advanced position. It has gained from the loss of such introjects insofar as it has the capacity to incorporate experiences which can expand its adaptive potential.

In summary, the degree of disruption accompanying the transference regression is variable. The degree to which the regression is "controlled" depends upon the integrative effects of the analytic relationship. In the development of an operable transference, we usually find a particular sequence of ego states. The regressed state is followed by one of greater organization in which the patient has sufficient ego structure to relate to the analyst. Insofar as the ego, although still regressed, is better synthesized, aspects of the analytic relationship can be internalized by the patient and then utilized to examine transference projections.

I believe that a twofold sequence leads to the development of a transference neurosis, particularly in cases with ego defects. First, there is a state of relative disorganization in which the patient cannot maintain old introjects without fragmenting them. Second, this stage of disorganization must be followed by another ego state in which there is sufficient organization to permit the *formation of new introjects*. The patient has usually undergone one and often more states of disruptive regression before he is able to have an analytic "orientation." Psychoneurotics (or neurotics in whom there are only minimal ego defects) do not, as a rule, experience the transference regression in a violent, explosive form. This would indicate that their egos can gain from the analytic situation without having to revert to such disorganized infantile states. The regression of these cases is one in which there is still considerable organization and secondary process, but as always, there are exceptions.

"Supportive" Aspects of the Analytic Attitude

Analysts have constantly been preoccupied with the nature of the broader helpful factors of the analytic situation. The essence of their ideas is that the patient, by internalizing certain aspects of the analysis, achieves a synthesis that enables him to take a relatively objective viewpoint of his inner problems. In this regard, the analyst's feelings towards the patient have been emphasized as being instrumental.

Spitz (1956a, quoted by Gitelson, 1962), writes of the "diatrophic attitude" which he defines as the analyst's healing intention to maintain and support the patient. Nacht (1962) believes that the analyst must have a feeling of "love" for the patient. In all that has been written on the subject, the importance of the analyst's wish to help the patient is one idea which is constantly expressed.

Silber (1962) has described certain therapeutic situations in which the patient, overburdened with anxiety, attempts to displace this anxiety on to the therapist. He believes that if the therapist is able to master the conflicts presented to him by the patient, the patient can learn a technique of active mastery rather than remain in a state of helpless passivity. Silber seems to indicate that the patient learns an adaptive technique from the therapist. This implies that the analyst is able to introject the patient's conflicts and then, presumably because of a better organization, is able to solve them. For the analyst to react to the patient's problems in this manner, however, implies that the analyst has an ego whose structural characteristics make it compatible with the patient's conflicts. I do not believe that this is the nature of analytic "help."

The analytic situation has intrinsic qualities that lead to regression and then to a better integration. The patient brings his inner torment, tension and anxiety to the analyst who is not overwhelmed or destroyed as the patient sometimes wishes and fears, but instead is keenly interested in a nonanxious fashion. Gitelson (1962) has stressed this nonanxious interest, believing that the patient derives his "support" from the qualities of the analytic relationship in which there is a change of narcissistic libido to an object libido, a sequence that, in itself, has stabilizing effects.

The patient reacts to his inner conflicts and archaic destructive introjects as if they were reality. The analyst would be stepping outside the therapeutic role if he were able to react to such problems as if they were capable of producing similar anxiety or other effects within him, for this would serve to reinforce and fixate the patient's attitude that his problems are "real" rather than fantasy. As Loewald (1960) has stated, the analyst, because of the differential between the analyst's and the analysand's ego structures, is able to help the patient to structuralize his needs. The analytic situation, characterized by an interested, but non-anxious attitude concerning the patient's problems, communicates that the therapist has not only a greater integration, but one that is different from the patient's, insofar as the analyst's ego would not be anxious or over-whelmed by similar problems. The patient becomes aware of this differential and gains security.

The analytic attitude gives "support" because eventually the patient recognizes that his problems do not consist of external realistic threats. The analyst's willingness to analyse without imposing his own standards eventually reassures the patient that there is something within him to analyse and he becomes aware that there are irrational elements within his personality that do not have to be reacted to, mastered, or defended against, but simply have to be understood, an understanding that leads to integration and ego expansion. Only then can the analysand understand the anachronistic nature of his fears.

Psychic Development and Disruptive Introjects

To understand the intra-ego processes associated with the achievement of a higher state of integration, one has to explore further the analytically stimulated regression.

Certain features in the psychoneuroses are more easily discernible in cases with characterological problems. Ego defects reflect maldevelopment consequent on traumatic nonintegrable early experiences. Conflict leads to fixation and its impact as a trauma depends on the child's predominant psychosexual orientation; prior ego organization determines whether an ego defect will occur or whether there will be the selective repression that leads to neurosis. These two reactions are not mutually exclusive nor are these distinctions absolute. Many significant external objects are considered dangerous and destructive and their object representation instead of being synthesized into the ego (at a preconscious level) has to be repressed. Object representations repressed in the form of destructive introjects not only have no value in expanding the ego's adaptive techniques, but the presence of these repressed elements interferes with maturational and developmental processes. The hostile introjects interfere with the "normal" course of development in that the ego does not acquire the synthesized smoothly functioning techniques necessary to be able to relate in a mutually satisfactory and beneficial fashion to other objects. Chronic frustration and its various consequences are, therefore, repeatedly experienced.

These destructive introjects later contribute to the formation of pathological self- and object representations. Insofar as the child experienced an assaultive and rejecting external world before there was self-object differentiation, adult levels of ego functioning will reflect disturbances in structure instead of the id-ego conflicts of psychoneurotics.

In analysis, when the ego has reached a certain level of regression, the transference neurosis reveals the disruptive effects of the destructive introjects. The archaic primitive ego that is revived in the transference is characterized by a reduced self-object differentiation. As the analyst interprets the various defences against the awareness of this primitive undifferentiated state, the patient experiences the pain of psychic dissolution (a state of helpless vulnerability) and is overwhelmed by anxiety and rage. His natural tendency is to use the defence mechanism of projection and to feel assaulted and engulfed by the analyst. Interpretations keep the patient's feelings focused upon the analyst and prevent the patient from generalizing the projection, thus keeping the problem within the analysis. If the analyst is successful, or at least partially successful, the patient loses some of his ability to project and the resultant state may be similar to the one that preceded the need to project. The patient feels confused and disorganized and suffers from a pervasive sense of inadequacy; he clings to the analyst and demands succor from him. His identity sense is disturbed, he has doubts concerning who and what he is, and he often complains that his behavior is disorganized and that he is not able to perform tasks that were pedestrian.

As previously stated, the depth and manifestations of the regression vary. What is uniform is that there is a loss of organization when compared with the previous state of defensive adjustment. One observes a greater vulnerability and need in the patient that may or may not be reflected in his general behavior.

As discussed earlier, the patient seeks protection by turning to an omnipotently constructed analyst. He now uses an even more primitive psychic mechanism than projection, fusion. However, since the analyst has constantly been interpreting the projected anger, this fusion is less destructively cathected than when the patient felt frustrated mainly because he was disappointed in his demand for omnipotence, and is characterized chiefly by attitudes of helpless dependency. Insight and understanding are, nevertheless, observed to follow awareness by the patient of his fusion with the analyst. Parts of the ego that had been repressed because of the formation of destructive introjects are now regained. Fragmented ego elements become synthesized and what was previously a fusion becomes an incorporation of the analyst. These processes represent an ego expansion, one that usually occurs as a result of a series of regressions and repetitive integrations.

Regressed States and the Analytic Introject

In the regressed condition described above, the patient's self- and object representations are in a fluid nonintegrated state, a state described by Jacobson (1954) as being characteristic of the neonatal period. This state developmentally antedates the one in which the patient projects his destructiveness. In the latter state, one founded on hate and fear (affects with a certain degree of structure), there is an organization and an ability to perceive objects. The difference between these two states cannot simply be summarized on the basis of one being primitive and the other less primitive. The organization of the projecting ego is still pathological, characterized by rigidity and the inability to assimilate integrating experiences from the outer world. In contrast, the further regression, which I shall refer to as an anaclitic state, is not rigid, but fluid. This fluidity is of vital importance. It is at this point that the presence of the analyst becomes important for the patient's development. To recall, the frustration caused by the analyst's failure to gratify the patient's need to be omnipotently rescued as well as the fear of being engulfed by the analyst contributes to projection of destructiveness on to the analyst.* Regression to an anaclitic state resulted from the internalization of rage, which is brought about by relating all the patient's feelings to the transference. In the anaclitic state, insofar as this is a stage preceding the establishment of introjects, there is a potentiality for establishing new object representations.

In therapy there is no clearcut reversion to a particular psychic state. The two regressed stages outlined here are not finite and distinct. The ego vacillates back and forth and shows elements of both, but with greater emphasis on either anaclitic or projective elements.

The painful and disruptive qualities of regression vary and are dependent upon the kind of analytic situation that has been established. The patient regresses in that he gives up some of his defensive and constricting ego operations, but if this occurs in the context of the analyst's integrative activity, the patient does not feel overwhelming anxiety. The internalized rage may be confined in its expression to the analytic hour or to other more circumscribed situations and be less disruptive than prior to the transference regression, when it was generalized.

The process of incorporating the analyst with his nonanxious attitude and willingness to understand are part of the developmental aspects of

---

*My impression is that the paranoid psychotic has succeeded in stabilizing a generalization of his projection which in a therapeutic setting would represent a transference resistance and a defence against regressing to the anaclitic state. It would also result in not being aware of the analyst as analyst.

the "adaptive synthesis" that Gitelson stresses. Although this is not immediately evident, the patient finds the analyst's nonanxious presence a source of strength. To feel his world crumbling and yet to have a person around who is not afraid as he is, but interested in learning and understanding, gives the patient considerable reassurance. Because the analyst does not accept or respond to the patient's infantile disorganization as a real catastrophe, the patient becomes able to look at himself as a psychic phenomenon rather than as a human tragedy. *Interpretive activity becomes a concrete and implicit demonstration of the analyst's confidence in the patient's developmental capacity.* Introspection is fostered as a result of the incorporation of the anaclitic relationship.

The multiple "transference reactions" that are part of the patient's daily life become recognized as products of infantile responses during the course of analysis. The analyst by confrontation and interpretation reveals the unconscious factors in the patient's behavior. He thus introduces a new frame of reference causing unconscious determinants to become associated with himself, and the various transference reactions when viewed as id responses tend to converge around the analyst.

The patient now has two views of the analyst. One such view, that of the "analytic introject," makes possible a workable transference neurosis by augmenting the ego-autonomous self-observing functions. When such functions are available, the ego responds differently to destructive introjects (or the introjection of imagos projected on to the analyst); it tends to deal with them with some degree of objectivity and not feel overwhelmed by them. Such operations are the essence of, and precondition for, the resolution of the transference neurosis.

The nature of the analytic attitude is difficult to express in concrete terms. Because it is mainly an attitude, a description of it in terms of content is at best vague and ambiguous. I believe one of its main elements is the analyst's response to the patient's anxiety. The analyst, not overwhelmed by the analysand's anxiety, responds in a different frame of reference; he is interested in understanding the patient and helping the patient understand himself. Because of emotional involvement, previous relationships could at most have given him only a limited understanding. To be understood, i.e., in terms of inner needs, tension, and anxiety, is a prerequisite to normal development. Patients with character defects experienced minimal, if any, understanding of their needs during childhood. The understanding the analyst offers is an entirely new experience, one that is the essence of the support intrinsic to analysis. The patient's capacity to acquire the analyst's attitude towards himself makes it possible to resolve the transference neurosis.

The experience the analyst offers has its prototype in normal development. The analyst supplies, through integrative interpretations, what the adequate mother supplies in correctly perceiving and responding to her child's needs. Need satisfaction may be considered in terms of a hierarchical continuum. At first the infant seems to be concerned only with the product that is needed and later with the object that supplies the product. The child achieves his greatest confidence and feels accepted when he has the security of feeling that his mother is aware of his needs and is capable of responding appropriately to them. At this point, he feels his mother understands his inner requirements, even at times when he does not understand them himself. With further development and ability to form abstractions, the security associated with such concrete infantile gratifications as being fed become generalized into self-esteeming feelings of worthiness, confidence, understanding and being understood.

Now alongside the destructive introjects and the patient's angry attitude towards the analyst is the analytic introject. With this development, the ego has the capacity to distinguish between two perceptions of the analyst as well as two different aspects of the self-representation. The patient becomes increasingly able to distinguish the analyst as analyst from the analyst as persecutor or rescuer, and concomitantly more able to recognize certain irrational forces within himself.

The qualities of the analytic introject will vary with the ego state. The imago of the understanding analyst may be incompatible with a primitively fixated ego, especially during the early phases of treatment. As the analyst interprets the patient's unconscious defensive attitudes, however, he demonstrates his ability to understand and pull together what to the patient was disparate, frightening and unknown. This integrative activity, analogous to the mother's understanding of the child's needs, leads to ego structuralization.

I believe that the analyst's integrative activity is the essence of the structural gradient that Loewald (1960) describes. In order to introject the analyst, the patient's ego has to have sufficient structure to perceive the analyst as being able to understand his needs. The analyst in his analytic role has "greater" structure than the patient.

The megalomanic wish for the analyst to be omnipotent represents a regression from the imago of the analyst who understands the patient's needs. The primitive imago instead of representing integrative understanding is now imbued with magical qualities that understand everything and enable it omnipotently to satisfy all needs (and even creates the needs). If the analyst attempts to gratify unconscious needs or to reinforce defences, a technique often referred to as support, he is responding to the patient's irrational demands and contributing to the maintenance of the infantile organization and equilibrium, one that contains a preponderance of primary-process elements, whereas the therapeutically desired development and synthesis always heads in the direction of the secondary process. The incorporation of an interaction that is based on primary-process operations cannot become a basis for ego development.

Many authors believe that there is an innate developmental drive. Under proper circumstances, the ego expands its adaptive capacities and reaches high degrees of synthesis and structure. Winnicott (1958) writes of the "good enough environment" which augments and gives form and substance to the psyche's propensity toward differentiation. The analyst becomes the chief representative of the structure-promoting environment.

Noninterference and acceptance are an essential aspect of the analytic attitude. In the regressed state, everything is tentative and the identity sense is poorly consolidated. Potential maturational forces have been and continue to be disrupted by nongratifying and threatening external and internal objects. The analyst responds differently to the innate development potential of the psyche by not doing anything to suppress it.

As an analogy we can consider the learning process. The ultimate learning achievement is to perform the task alone, autonomously to master the problem. The teacher supplies the student with certain information which he integrates and thereby expands his adaptive capacities and skills. Similarly, the introjected analytic attitude becomes the basis for transference resolution and ego structuralization. As with information imparted by a teacher, it has to become integrated and part of the patient's ego; the incorporation must become an aspect of the ego's synthetic functioning. A good teacher provides a setting in which a student may attempt his own spontaneous solution rather than demonstrating how something should be done. Any attempt on the analyst's part to impose his own standards or to play a role, even though consonant with certain of the patient's conscious or unconscious needs, will not be smoothly incorporated. It will be disruptive to the ego's drive towards autonomy. The analyst, emphasizing understanding by interpretation, is implicitly encouraging the patient's autonomous potential. The patient's developmental drive toward autonomy emerges as interpretation increases the patient's ability for self-observation.

The analysand expects to be responded to in terms of content of conflict, but the analyst scrutinizes his conflicts and interprets their adaptive interrelationships. The patient, by adopting a similar attitude, begins nonanxiously to observe himself, a process that promotes autonomous integration. *This leads to a synthesis of previously fragmented elements and to the formation of Gestalts, adaptive techniques and structure formation.*

What inhibited or blocked the ego's progress was, alongside other factors, an environment that interfered with its developmental potential. The destructive parental relationship is an example of a pathological vicissitude that may lead to psychic chaos and which is experienced as helplessness and vulnerability. Under these circumstances the child cannot become autonomous. A child's experiences with his parents, optimally, are smoothly incorporated and synthesized by the ego and contribute to mastery of the drives and enhancement of the ego's autonomous potential. If the relationship interferes with this autonomous potential, the ego institutes defenses against an experience which is felt as traumatic and assaultive. These defenses prevent the establishment of introjects that can be utilized for ego functioning and adaptation; instead, this traumatic aspect of the parental relationship remains fragmented from the rest of the ego.

The projective aspects of the introjective-projective features of the transference neurosis facilitate the directing of affect to an external object. The analyst becomes cathected and as a consequence there has to be a relative withdrawal of cathexis from introjects, including destructive archaic ones. Turning to the outer world has a structuring effect insofar as what was attached to the primitive and disruptive within the self becomes attached to an external object which is eventually recognized as having structured qualities that are in the service of understanding and promoting autonomy.

To summarize, the formulations concerning regressed ego states and transference resolution refer to stages which correspond to primitive, unintegrated, preverbal phases of the infant. A regressed ego in an adult is not the same as an infantile ego insofar as many of the functions of the adult ego are retained. However, the impact of object relations as an integrative factor is highlighted in the transference regression, and incorporation of the analyst corresponds to the acquiring and synthesis of introjects in the infant. The reaction to the introject is multi-determined and all stages of development contribute to it. These reactions are dramatically relived in the transference and a variety of factors pertaining to ego development, synthesis, and the analyst's role are emphasized.

Chapter 21

The Influence of Interpretation Upon Schizophrenic Patients

The treatment of schizophrenia is a popular topic that has been as varied as theories concerning its etiology. It has ranged from a strictly interpretative approach to total environmental manipulation and support. Eissler (1951), Little (1966), Sanford (1966) and others believe that some modification of a strictly interpretative approach is required for the treatment of patients who have been severely emotionally traumatized during early childhood. The amount of literature on this topic is immense and will not be reviewed here (see Boyer and Giovacchini, 1967).

The relevance of interpretation as it affects the schizophrenic process has been an important aspect of the study of the treatment of such cases, and the structure of the interpretation can be scrutinized further. Many authors* have directed their attention to what might be called the *operational composition* of an interpretation. However, the qualities of interpretations that are specifically directed to certain types of ego defects have not been emphasized. Instead, many papers concentrate on the disruptive effects of interpretation, or argue that interpretation, at best, is meaningless unless a stabilizing relationship has been first established (Eissler, 1953b).

The study of the elements of particular types of interpretation as they affect specific ego systems is relevant to the understanding of the psychoanalytic process in general. There are undoubtedly differences between the therapeutic interaction of patients suffering from "classical" psychoneuroses and that of schizophrenic patients. When reactions to interpretations are viewed microscopically, i.e. in terms of changes within the ego, many of the differences may be only of manifest expression rather than due to fundamental structural factors.

Various Perspectives Regarding Interpretative Activity

Before one can discuss the therapeutic effect of interpretative activity, interpretation has to be more explicitly defined. Generally, any inter-

First published in *Int. J. Psa.* 50 (1969), 179–86. Reprinted by permission.

*Freud's technical papers, of course, focus upon this topic. More recently Bibring (1937), Greenson (1965), Kris (1951), Searles (1961b), to mention just a few, have made relevant contributions.

pretation represents a communication between analyst and patient. It is an important aspect of an object relationship. *An interpretation is not simply a disembodied stream of words.*

As is true of any communication, it contains two fundamental elements: content and affect. The latter encompasses many different levels of the analyst's psyche. Primarily, such affect conveys an attitude—a calm, analytic, observational attitude. The patient may receive insight from other sources, but the analytic relationship is unique in that the analyst is primarily devoted to fostering self-observation whereas other helpful persons have motivations based upon their personal needs that are not concerned with sharing an observational platform. The analyst forms an object relationship with the patient which will lead to both participants understanding how the patient's mind works. The professional elements of the analyst's psyche make such a relationship possible. The affective component of the interpretation creates an atmosphere that is oriented·around such self-understanding.

The object-relationship qualities of an interpretation are the outcome of the transference projection. It has been found useful (Boyer and Giovacchini, 1967) to assume that every association the patient produces has a transference aspect. Granted, some of the patient's material may contain only a minimum of transference projection, but it is that factor that the analyst responds to. The analyst may wait until transference elements develop or become relatively obvious. The therapeutic efficacy of interpreting content that is only minimally or perhaps not at all involved in a transference projection is debatable and especially so in cases suffering from severe psychopathology.

Interpretation can be considered in terms of more specific qualities than the above. Often one hears about a distinction between superficial and deep interpretations. The former may refer to simply a rephrasing of what the patient says. It may be a restatement of the obvious in a coherent fashion. However, as clear as the material may be, the patient may not have been able to synthesize it and therefore is unaware of its meaning. Bibring (1937) referred to this type of interaction as confrontation rather than interpretation. Still, something is being conveyed to the patient that he was not previously aware of, although the hidden material may have been at preconscious levels rather than deeply repressed. In the treatment of cases suffering from characterological defects, such as schizophrenics, the distinction between superficial and deep is more apparent than real (see next section).

Interpretations can also be viewed in terms of their deterministic elements. To some extent what the analyst reveals to the patient has explanatory qualities because it refers to etiological connections; the patient's productions are placed in a perspective that highlights causal relationships. The very fact that the analyst is trying to understand how the patient's mind works implicitly assumes that there is some rationale to what the patient feels or does, that his emotional situation is not hopelessly chaotic but can be understood in terms of fundamental causes. By being able to explain primary-process-oriented material and behavior in terms of etiology the analysis is effecting a secondary-process synthesis which can be a structuralizing experience.

Some interpretations are more explicit than others in pointing out etiological connections. They focus upon stimulus and response, as did Freud's (1900) original model of the psychic apparatus. Freud discovered that certain attitudes and symptoms were caused by underlying wishes and his interpretations often took the form of explaining the patient's behavior, pathological and otherwise, in terms of id impulses.

Freud also referred to stimuli in the external world as being responsible for some psychic productions. His concept of the day residue made the initial stimulus an extrapsychic one, but still he did not ignore the influence of intrapsychic factors. He conceived of all responses as multiply determined and the day residue, a seemingly irrelevant event, becomes fused with an id element and acts as a stimulus to that element. The same concept of the day residue can be applied not only to dream formation, but also to behavior in general and the analytic setting in particular. An interpretation may make a causal connection by referring to the day residue which may be the stimulus for the flow of the patient's associations or for some otherwise unexplainable behavior. These interpretations link events in the outer world with intrapsychic phenomena. The establishment of outer world–inner world stimulus–response is the essence of this type of interpretation, one which can be distinguished from other types. These *linking interpretations* are especially important in the treatment of schizophrenic patients who suffer from considerable fragmentation and who do not make sharp distinctions between reality and intrapsychic phenomena.

To summarize briefly, interpretation is a communication between analyst and patient. It need not be verbal, but the consideration of other modes of communication is an irrelevant extension of our topic. Interpretations during analytic treatment are made in the context of the transference regression and refer to psychic elements that were not previously available to the patient. As discussed here, there are different types and aspects of interpretation but its ultimate purpose is to help the patient understand how his mind works.

Patients, especially those suffering from severe characterological problems, sometimes treat the interpretation as though it were a concrete offering, designed to gratify or frustrate rather than to communicate understanding. The patient reacts to the symbolic connotations of the analyst's interpretative activity. Some therapists believe that, because particular patients react positively to the symbolic connotation, the understanding gained from interpretative activity is not particularly meaningful for therapeutic progression.

Schizophrenic patients utilize projective defences to a greater extent than do psychoneurotics. Consequently they are more apt to distort any interaction between themselves and the therapist. Interpretations are often imbued with qualities that are initially within the patient and part of his primary-process orientation. Both the integrative and disruptive features of such distortion by projection, as well as how it can be used in the interest of treatment, have to be scrutinized further. The question of whether interpretative content is therapeutically useful in severely disturbed patients is complex and cannot be categorically answered; it requires further study.

Psychopathology and Integrative Interpretations

There are various formulations regarding the schizophrenic process, even when one remains in the psychoanalytic frame of reference. Still, the concept of ego systems operating with a preponderance of primary process is generally accepted.

The schizophrenic patient has "defects" (Gitelson, 1958a) in perceptual, integrative and synthetic ego systems. The executive systems may or may not be significantly involved since one can recall schizophrenics who are very successful, though possibly delusional, in adapting to the external world, and others who are totally incapacitated and incapable of doing anything. Insofar as one's identity sense is determined by how one functions and perceives (chapter 9), one would expect schizophrenics to suffer from an imperfectly formed and conflicted self-concept. Often the disturbance of the identity sense is obvious, but it may be obscured, in some instances, by a well-systematized delusional system. A delusional self-concept may give sufficient stability for a fairly comfortable adaptation, at least one that is not plagued by the disruptive tensions of existential crises.

From a particular viewpoint some schizophrenics can be considered as suffering from extreme failure to adapt to the surrounding world. Freud (1924a, b) referred to the conflict as being between the ego and the outer world in contrast to the psychoneurotic where the conflict is between the ego and the id. Regardless of how the schizophrenic constructs his world, he still lacks the adjustive techniques to deal with reality. This lack of adjustment is reflected in the analytic situation.

Two paranoid patients who had been hospitalized in the past complained about not being able to get along in life. They literally meant they did not "know" the ordinary social conventions that enable people to relate to each other. These patients believed that they had never been "taught" common social techniques such as salutation, conversation or how to dress for specific occasions.

Regardless of the defensive meaning of such attitudes, these patients revealed that they never had experiences that would have led to the acquisition of adjustive techniques or were unable to gain from such experiences.

A middle-aged woman was particularly impressive in that she revealed that she was lacking (at least relatively) the memory trace, i.e. the introjects. of the mothering experience. Consequently, she was unable to deal with her child spontaneously. Her mothering behavior was stiff and hesitant as if she had learned it by rote from a manual. This was actually the case (chapter 10).

The relative absence of structuralizing memory traces and subsequent defects in adjustive techniques is an intrinsic aspect of the psychopathology of patients suffering from character disorders and schizophrenia. Therefore the relevance of interpretation for these patients has to be considered in the context of defects in various ego systems. Interpretative activity has to be scrutinized to determine whether there are certain conditions under which particular facets of the interpretation have a structuralizing effect. Since these patients are suffering, in a sense, from a lack of or defect of structure, the question of how self-understanding can lead to the acquisition of previously nonexisting adaptive techniques has to be discussed. Not only is this question related to that of the effects of insight, but it focuses upon the further question of what other facets of interpretative communication are important for the therapeutic interaction with very disturbed patients.

Structuralizing Effects of Interpretations

The essence of psychoanalytic technique is interpretation within the context of transference. Interpretation of the transference projection has emotional impact and can lead to therapeutic benefit. Freud (1912a) explained that the transference enabled the patient to relive his conflicts in the present thus providing the stage for their resolution.

In more disturbed patients, the transference has even greater significance in that it represents more of an adaptation and its successful working through leads to more than just the resolution of conflict.

The psychotic patient often seeks treatment because he is unable to maintain a balance between the intrapsychic, the somewhat delusional world he has created, and his external environment. The paranoid patient, for example, wants to be treated not because he is paranoid, but because, for some reason, *he is no longer able to be paranoid.* In other words, something has interfered with his adaptive use of projective defences. The psychoanalytic setting provides him with the opportunity to project. The analyst can be assigned a variety of roles from omnipotent rescuer to hateful persecutor. This is an adaptation, a defensive, perhaps a psychotic one, but one that reestablishes some equilibrium. The transference phenomenon may at first promote fragmentation. Insofar as one reason for the patient being disturbed is that he cannot keep positive (megalomanic rescuing) and hateful introjects separated he can now do so by splitting his internal objects into good and bad, and projecting on to the analyst. Viewing the analyst as an omnipotent persecutor or rescuer, and perhaps assigning a complementary role to other persons in the patient's life, promotes a paranoid organization which can replace chaotic fragmentation. The analytic setting, however, by providing the *opportunity* for projection makes the outside involvement less intense and disturbing. There are, of course, many variations of the sequence and types of projection. One can ask what is the role of interpretation at this early stage of treatment. During early phases of treatment many analysts agree that there should be very little if any interpretation. Usually the therapist waits until the patient's associations crystallize into a dominant theme and at the same time this theme becomes interwoven with feelings toward the analyst.

Still, one should not be too specific because there are many variations in the patient's reactions in the beginning of treatment. Some patients, and this is more likely with schizoid or schizophrenic patients, develop transference very quickly, often during the first interview or even before the patient has his first appointment. They may have to be handled interpretatively in order to permit the analysis to continue (see Segal, 1967).

In many instances the patient can project on to the analyst and continue doing so in an adaptive manner without the analyst having made an *overt* interpretation. The analyst has, however, conveyed something very important to him without having been verbally explicit. He has done so by revealing an attitude.

The patient brings a psychopathological frame of reference into the consulting room and, since to him his world is all-pervasive, he tries to mould the analytic setting so that it will fit into his private world. The analyst, however, maintains his own frame of reference and does not merge with that of the patient. The above is achieved by the analyst's general approach and manner. First, he does not intrude by "entering" the patient's material. More explicitly, the analyst does not become incorporated into the patient's defenses; for example, a patient who uses withdrawal as a main defence may be provoking the analyst to probe in order to justify and thereby reinforce his defence. In some instances, the analyst may have to withhold his curiosity if it interferes with the patient's spontaneity. His initial attitude is directed toward understanding the adaptive significance of whatever the patient presents. He does not treat the patient's productions as a manifestation of a human tragedy but rather as phenomena worthy of study. One cannot prescribe precisely how this is done; it depends upon the analyst's style. Without necessarily verbalizing anything, the analyst immediately directs himself to understanding how the patient is relating to and often trying to manipulate him. In other words, from the start he examines the transference–countertransference axis.

This is an analytic frame of reference and is the essence of the psychoanalytic approach. Insofar as observation of a present relationship is the analyst's exclusive preoccupation, he is encouraging observational activity (which heightens self-observation and cognition) and, since the purpose of this activity is to understand and to explain how the patient's mind works, it is an *interpretative* orientation. Therefore, although the analyst may not initially verbalize interpretations, he is, nevertheless, conveying an interpretative framework. By so doing, he is maintaining a coherent setting that seeks to explain the incoherence within the patient. The patient eventually joins him on the observational platform and shares his interpretative attitude.

The analyst seeks to understand whatever the patient says or does in terms of what it means regarding himself. He tends to interpret the patient's productions as aspects of the unfolding transference. Adopting such an interpretative attitude implicitly tells the patient that the analyst is available for his projections. The analyst's attitude is both nonjudgmental and unharried. His continued interest in interpreting transference phenomena as they are occurring demonstrates to the patient that what is occurring is of mutual interest and is valued.

In many instances, the hopeful outcome of such an interpretative attitude is that the patient develops a similar interest and orientation. Pressman (1969) has referred to this development as the acquisition of "incognition." Others (Greenson, 1965; Zetzel, 1960) have referred to the "working and therapeutic alliance." In chapter 20, I made a similar formulation by referring to the analytic introject, stressing, as others have, that the incorporation of the analytic viewpoint augments the self-observing function. I would only add now that the self-observing function includes the observation of the self as it is relating to the analyst.

The interpretative attitude focuses upon the reciprocal aspect of this transference relationship.

The manifest qualities of this early therapeutic interaction are often characterized by the analyst being overtly inactive. He may say little or nothing. Some patients are very comfortable with such silence. I have often noted especially with patients suffering from severe psychopathology that they actually seem relieved. Invariably later in treatment frightened, vulnerable schizoid or schizophrenic patients emphasize the security they felt because of the analyst's nonintrusiveness. Since the analyst was not impelled to probe or comment, the patient felt that he was being receptive, uncritical and not threatening. This has an integrative and supportive effect.

In other instances, the regression stimulated by the analytic setting may become chaotic. The fact that the analyst is available for the projection of disruptive impulses minimizes anxiety and disorganization, but he sometimes has to induce integration by making an interpretation. He usually points out what is going on between the patient and himself. This limits the chaos to a specific setting and situation which, in itself, is reassuring. For example, during the first interview, a schizophrenic patient experienced mounting anxiety which bordered on panic. At the same time he increasingly withdrew from me, first by talking in clipped sentences, then silence, and finally, as his agitation increased, by restlessly moving about the room and ambivalently approaching the door. I intervened by pointing out that I would respect his *decision* to stay or leave. I commented further that he felt that if he revealed himself to me, he would destroy me. His withdrawal, therefore, was designed to protect me. This interpretation was made not just because of his behavior, but also from certain other clues he had given me about his depreciated, hateful, destructive self-image. In any case, my interpretation reassured him that we would not confuse his feelings with reality consequences. The fact that I could convey to him my understanding of what was occurring within his mind reassured him that I was reacting with interest rather than being threatened or frightened. This halted the disintegrative process and the patient was able to calm down sufficiently to continue his treatment.

The above refers to general effects of the interpretative attitude and interpretation. One can consider this topic more specifically in regard to the treatment of patients suffering from severe psychopathology. For example, interpretations have been formulated as being either superficial or deep (see previous section). Does this particular aspect of an interpretation have relevance to the treatment of schizophrenia?

Freud's (1924a, b) formulation that the schizophrenic's conflict was between the ego and the outer world emphasizes the pathological distortion of the ego apparatuses and minimizes the role of intrapsychic conflict. It is often impossible to delineate depth and surface in some patients. Primary process seems to be everywhere, so to speak, and, insofar as there is only a minimum of secondary-process activity, the personality cannot be viewed as a hierarchically differentiated psychic structure. Consequently, the acquisition of insight through interpretation does not follow the sequence from the rational to the irrational. The question can next be raised as to whether the analyst interprets whatever the patient presents, regardless of how primitive. Some reports of case histories indicate that this has been done, the main focus of the interpretation being upon id impulses.

Schizophrenic behavior is often dominated by primitive impulses and wishes without much reality-adaptive superstructure. Still, to relate strictly to such a wish leads frequently to adverse reactions, sometimes at the moment but more often later in treatment. Focusing upon irrational wishes can be experienced as an assault on a sensitive, vulnerable ego. The patient may feel attacked and criticized, even if no such censure was intended.

The same may result if we put into words supposedly more superficial reactions, associations that have relatively more secondary-process organization. The interpretation has to achieve more than making the patient aware of content which he may not have consciously known. Simple confrontation does not lead to any particular synthesis in my experience. Altogether, I do not believe that interpretations can be considered in terms of superficial or deep with schizophrenic patients.

The more primitive the ego organization, the more apt it is to use a primitive defence such as splitting and fragmentation. Consequently, regardless of whether the material is deep or superficial, unconscious or conscious, the patient is often unaware of the causes or source of his reactions. He has a tendency to believe that "things" are happening to him and that he is not responsible for what is happening; he does not recognize that his feelings have an intrapsychic origin. *One function of interpretative activity is to put matters on an intrapsychic basis.*

Unlike the treatment of the psychoneurotic patient, the further question as to whether one is interpreting a defence or underlying conflictful impulses is not an especially significant one when discussing schizophrenics. As long as an interpretation leads to clarifying the origin of the patient's feelings, the level of content (an obscure distinction, at best) is not of crucial importance. The choice of the content to which the analyst responds is determined first by its potential for stressing the intrapsychic sources of the patient's disorder. Second, as the analyst interprets the dominant transference theme, he concentrates on the adaptive value of the patient's attitudes, for example, as they protect him or the analyst. Even anxiety and frustration (usually of magical wishes) can be viewed in terms of potential adaptiveness. The patient has been able to have expectations and feel hope that gratification is forthcoming. The analyst's failure, from the patient's viewpoint, can advantageously be used to help the patient know about the nature of his needs. Often this approach makes the patient's anxiety nondisruptive and manageable.

Stressing intrapsychic sources and adaptive value implicitly informs the patient that the analyst is not reacting directly to the transference projections. He deals with them with the same analytic curiosity and objectivity he would have toward a dream or fantasy. This also tells the patient that the analyst's attitude is not judgmental and that he does not feel threatened by some of the more destructive elements of the patient's projections. Consequently, this creates an atmosphere that emphasizes the analyst's availability for further projection.

Not getting directly involved in the patient's psychopathological frame of reference clarifies the unilateral nature of the patient's feelings. When the analyst responds to content by actively trying to help or support or by a frontal correction of distortion, the clinical picture becomes confused. The analytic frame of reference is no longer distinct and schizophrenic patients, especially, feel that they are either being offered omnipotent rescuing or the other side of the coin (ambivalence), being intruded upon or assaulted. In either case, such responses do not lead to understanding; instead, they reinforce the patient's feeling that the external world is responsible for his personal tragedy. Such a viewpoint does not permit the patient to acknowledge his participation in and responsibility for what is occurring. In a sense, it also robs him of some autonomy insofar as his chief focus is on the way in which he is a helpless, vulnerable victim of a cruel, withholding and assaultive reality.

Granted, there are some patients who are incapable of accepting any other approach except involvement at the content level. *Not clinical diagnosis, but the patient's ability to allow the analyst not to intrude may be a criteria of analysability.* The acting-out "psychopathic personality," for example, is not usually diagnosed as psychotic, but he cannot be analysed if he forces the therapist to become involved in the management of his life.

Another important factor responsible for the integrative qualities of an interpretation is that it makes etiological connections (see previous section). This is an especially crucial function for patients suffering from severe psychopathology since their deterministic discriminations are markedly impaired and distorted. These patients can behave both in analysis and in their daily lives in a totally irrational fashion. Their actions often seem purposeless and one cannot find an obvious cause for them. The interpretation attempts to clarify the stimulus for their psychotic behavior.

During the analytic session, it is often possible to discover etiological factors. Within the transference framework, the patient may be involved in endless primary-process ruminations and resulting behavior. Frequently, such behavior is precipitated by particular events in the external world. The patient is unaware that anything significant has happened. These occurrences are not important or apparently traumatic, such as a major loss or reversal. The patient's associations unwittingly reveal this trigger which acts in a fashion identical to that of a day residue in the formation of a dream.

For example, a young mother felt utter dejection and depersonalization for several hours prior to her appointment. This was puzzling to both of us because she had throughout the course of her treatment improved considerably and this was manifested by increased feelings of competence and self-esteem. Now she experienced intense feelings of inadequacy and helplessness and during the session she became more and more disorganized. Her associations became chaotic to the point that they assumed the qualities of a word salad.

Her regression even involved her motor behavior in that she thrashed around the couch and her movements were jerky and uncoordinated. As she started crying, she reached into her purse for a handkerchief. Her movements were so clumsy that she spilled all its contents on to the floor. She got up to retrieve them but tripped and fell. As she sprawled on the floor, the contents of her purse were further scattered. She then had considerable difficulty in gathering them together and nearly panicked when she was unable to find her car keys, although they were prominently visible.

Knowing what difficulties this patient had in learning to drive and what a sensitive area the automobile was for her, I told her that I wondered whether this reaction of chaotic helplessness that she was displaying to me might have been associated with some incident during the day while driving. She could not recall anything unusual, but while reviewing the events of the day, she once again became composed, collected her possessions including the car key and returned to the couch. She sank into it comfortably as if it were a haven and gathered her recollections concerning herself and driving that day. She had been scheduled to pick up her daughter and a playmate and drive each child home. She was aware of some trepidation since the roads were somewhat slippery and she was not too secure with her driving skill, having learned to drive recently, an accomplishment she credited to analysis. Going downstairs from her apartment, she met a neighbor, the mother of one of her daughter's playmates. As the neighbor's car was in front of the building and the patient was parked farther away, the neighbor volunteered to drive. The patient felt both relieved and ashamed.

Her associations next revealed the intensity of her destructiveness toward all the children, her sadistic murderous wishes. She also felt that I would despise her and be destroyed by the poison within her. To sum up briefly, her feelings following the ride with the neighbor, and her behavior in my office, highlighted both the intense guilt and panic that followed the "triggering" of her murderous impulses. The neighbor's offer was unconsciously construed as not only an offer of rescue, but also as confirmation of the reason for the need to be rescued, i.e. her destructiveness. This, in turn, emphasized the need to be rescued from the hateful self. She then feared revealing her destructiveness and shame to me. Consequently *her disorganization also had purpose;* she was trying to reassure me that she was weak and helpless and could harm no one but herself.

There were, of course, many other details to this complex situation. Still, pointing out the connection between a seemingly trivial incident in her daily life and its role in causing irrational, puzzling behavior became a synthesizing revelation. This interpretation emphasized etiology and can be considered a *linking interpretation* in that it linked events in the external world to behavior within the transference context. Linking interpretations are especially significant for schizophrenics and patients suffering from characterological defects. By pointing out in what frame of reference the causal factor belongs and how such a stimulus has disrupted the patient's inner world, the analyst places the patient's behavior within the context of reality. If the environment has to some extent contributed to the patient's disturbance then he can be reassured that his reactions are understandable in terms of secondary process rather than coming from some mysterious and mystical, unknown, uncontrollable force. The all-pervasive intrapsychic turmoil is placed alongside events in the environment. This delineates the inner from the outer world, which parallels the formation of ego boundaries. These linking interpretations, by revealing the sources of the patient's behavior, reestablish reality contact. *They prevent interminable primary-process fantasy activity, split off from the patient's total ego and daily life.*

Summary

Before one can discuss the role of interpretation in the treatment of schizophrenics or other very emotionally disturbed patients, the structure of the interpretation has to be studied.

General aspects of interpretation are briefly discussed. Their communicative object relationship qualities as well as their symbolic meaning are stressed.

The level of the psyche toward which the interpretation is directed is considered in terms of "depth" or "surface" qualities as well as to whether it refers to a defensive superstructure or an underlying conflict. These aspects of an interpretation are not particularly relevant for the treatment of schizophrenia.

Next, the interpretation is considered in terms of establishing etiological connections. Schizophrenic patients with impaired capacity to understand the internal and external determinants of their behavior can gain considerable synthesis by being made aware of causes for their irrational attitudes and behavior. A special type of etiological interpretation is described. It is called a linking interpretation because it establishes a sequence between some occurrence in the external world, similar to the day residue of the dream, and behavior that can be viewed within the context of transference during an analytic session. These interpretations are described further regarding their leading to the strengthening of reality testing in schizophrenic patients.

Chapter 22

Modern Psychoanalysis and Modern Psychoanalysts: A Review

Psychoanalysis was born out of clinical necessity. Its value in organizing the clinician's understanding about hithero confusing patients has been inestimable, and even many antianalytic practitioners who are inclined to question its therapeutic efficacy or practicability admit that it is the only rational clinical theoretical system that goes beyond descriptive phenomenology. Though details regarding the content of psychoanalytic theory can be and have been argued, its place as an explanatory system has remained relatively unshaken.

Within the psychoanalytic movement there has been considerable enthusiasm concerning Freud's formulations, and his technical therapeutic principles have in the main been accepted without hesitation or question. Although Freud, especially in his later writings, was not particularly optimistic about applicability and results of his method, some of his followers considered themselves "classical" analysts, restricted their treatment to the so-called transference neuroses, and rejected any later modifications or technical revisions as nonanalytic.

Modern analysts have become considerably more flexible. Still, there is what might be called a persisting subtrend that has some interesting paradoxical features. Many analysts are extremely interested in applied psychoanalysis and have extended its principles and investigatory techniques to art, literature, biography, anthropology, and more recently, to sociology, history, and politics. Moreover, this "widening scope" of psychoanalysis began very early in its development. At the same time, however, its clinical applicability was rigidly restricted, and attempts to extend its therapeutic range have been, until recently, sparse. Thus, on the one hand, even though psychoanalysis began as a clinical science, many of its practitioners remained fixed to a particular viewpoint about its indications, a viewpoint that in some instances became a dictum; on the other hand, they exercised little restraint in plunging into other fields of knowledge where at best they

First published in *Psychiat. Soc. Sci. Rev.* 4 (1970) as a two-part review article, discussing H. Spotnittz, *Modern Psychoanalysis of the Schizophrenic Patient* (New York: Grune & Stratton, 1969, and R. Greenson, *The Technique and Practice of Psychoanalysis* (New York: Int. Univ. Press, 1969). Reprinted by permission.

would be scholarly amateurs. As professionals they were reactionary; as amateurs they made bold speculative formulations—not an uncommon sequence.

This paradox becomes accentuated when we look at other academic endeavors. Mathematics, for example, has an almost universal applicability; yet many pure mathematicians covet their position and do not venture outside their own realm. Indeed, they look upon such excursions with disdain.

Perhaps I am exaggerating for the sake of emphasis, but it seems that the situation among analysts is the reverse of the above. Many analysts, although this is much less true today, resent implications that perhaps concepts and techniques of psychoanalytic therapy might be improved, whereas they will applaud the study of some long dead genius formulated in terms of a detailed id analysis.

Freud formulated the principles of psychoanalytic treatment, and being a cultured, scholarly man, he pursued and encouraged applied psychoanalysis. His influence has been and is enormous. Notwithstanding his acknowledged genius, one can still ask why he has had such an impact generally and, specifically, why his word about treatment has so often been the last one and why many analysts have preferred to do their exploring only in the safer area of applied psychoanalysis.

The question of Freud's influence is an interesting one from several viewpoints. Other men who have made comparable monumental contributions have not attracted such fervent adherents. It is questionable to make comparisons with other cultural epochs such as those of Galileo and Newton, or perhaps even Darwin. Einstein, however, worked and lived contemporaneously with Freud. Einstein's impact has also been global, but physicists, especially quantum theorists, have had no hesitation in extending, challenging, and modifying his ideas.

The subject matter may account for some of these differences. Einstein dealt with abstractions, at the time, far removed from personal considerations, whereas Freud's universe is man himself. But this is merely an obvious difference, not an explanation. This question of influence is inordinately complex, and its answer would undoubtedly involve sociocultural factors as well as the unique elements of Freud's personality.

Another possible factor may be the extent of Freud's contributions. Perhaps not enough time has elapsed for us to integrate Freud's insights and then to progress beyond them. Time may be of greater importance for progress in psychoanalysis than for other fields, since the insights psychoanalysis offers are aimed at the very core of psychic turmoil, and because of their revealing qualities they are more difficult to assimilate. Nevertheless, there have been many extensions and modifications of fundamental psychoanalytic concepts since Freud; "fixation" has been confined primarily to technical treatment issues.

Dr. Spotnitz[1] is a representative of a movement that wishes to remedy the above situation. He begins by examining the indications for a fairly orthodox psychoanalytic approach to the treatment of schizophrenic patients. He carefully traces the history of past efforts in this direction and reviews Freud's developing ideas about the limits of psychoanalytic treatment. He proposes that treatment can be beneficial without deviating from the analytic spectrum. He discusses special techniques required for this group of patients but distinguishes them from parameters.

I found this first part of the book heartening both from a personal viewpoint and for what I believe it means for our field generally. Although I have received considerable support from private conversations and closed seminars with colleagues, I recall how bitterly attacked I was on two occasions when I presented to *psychoanalytic audiences* papers espousing the thesis that psychoanalysis was even more valuable than Freud believed. At present I find the psychoanalytic community much more congenial. These matters can be talked about relatively freely, and the fact that books such as *Modern Psychoanalysis of the Schizophrenic Patient* are published and talked about reflects a much more relaxed scientific attitude. Colleagues are letting their hair down and are saying things they wouldn't have dared to say a decade ago. As Dr. Lindon pointed out in an editorial of the recent *Psychoanalytic Forum,* the current psychoanalytic atmosphere is exciting because we are examing established concepts with a fresh perspective and with less acrimony. Analysts are talking to each other about these issues, and two recent meetings of the American Psychoanalytic Association held workshops on the psychoanalytic treatment of schizophrenia.

If the development of transference is the essence of psychoanalytic treatment, then the question of whether schizophrenic patients can develop transference is crucial. Dr. Spotnitz asserts that they can; I and many others have repeatedly made such observations. Dr. Spotnitz goes further and distinguishes between narcissistic and object-related transferences and describes the development of the latter from the former in his patients. This, too, has been observed by other analysts.

Whether something occurs and whether something can or cannot be done is an empirical question. The occurrence of transference (which in some instances is therapeutically useful) represents data and is not an arguable point. Nonetheless, I have repeatedly heard analysts say that

[1]Spotnitz, H. *Modern Psychoanalysis of the Schizophrenic Patient.* New York: Grune and Stratton, 1969.

transference does not occur in schizophrenic patients. When asked upon what they based their opinion, they quoted Freud. This always struck me as amazing, a situation that as far as I know has no precedence in modern science, *i.e.*, that evidence for a decisive and far-reaching conclusion consists simply of the pronouncement of a master. This is an ecclesiastical rather than a scientific approach. More recently, however, I have heard more searching objections, such as the admission that narcissistic and psychotic transference occur but that they are not therapeutically amenable.

In any case, the question of resistance to technical innovations belongs in a larger context, one that necessitates briefly viewing the effects of the training and background of the modern psychoanalyst before one can discuss modern psychoanalysis itself.

Training institutes concentrate predominantly on Freud's writings. This is only natural. Psychoanalysis is still a young science, and Freud's principles are so fundamental and broad that they represent the basic foundation of psychoanalysis no matter what superstructures are erected.

Such teaching (sometimes flexible and at other times dogmatic and intolerant of questions) has produced two extreme reactions. Although the majority of modern analysts fall somewhere within these extremes, one can define two antithetical types. One group is characterized by rigid "classicism." Any mention of concepts that are not included in or cannot be logically derived from Freud's writings is rejected, sometimes vehemently. On occasion this attitude has even included a rejection of present-day ego psychology. The other end of the spectrum consists of dissident analysts who finally renounce analysis. They usually see themselves as liberal and flexible, and as having been emancipated from Freud's tyrannical specter. Their iconoclasm may lead to a total abandonment of psychoanalysis, or they may continue to identify themselves as analysts but hold viewpoints and practice in a manner far removed from the usual psychoanalytic orientation. This group consider themselves scientists and see present-day organized psychoanalysis as a cult rather than a science. While I was a resident, a member of this group, one who still retained his membership in the local and national psychoanalytic societies, advised me to seek formal analytic training because (1) the G.I. Bill of Rights would pay for it and (2) when in the future I might attack psychoanalysis at public meetings, my opponents could not discredit my arguments because I was not an analyst.

Some analysts have attacked the training system, mainly because, they assert, it is dogmatic, rigid, and infantilizing. I do not wish to discuss this involved topic except to point out the bearing of such an attitude on the reactions described above. Without formulating precisely how Freud's influence or the present training system (which is not static) have had their effects, we can note that psychoanalytic training has somehow led to characterological orientations that go beyond the clinical and theoretical aspects of the subject matter. It is difficult to ascertain whether the training experience has necessitated such responses as adaptive reactions of a basic character structure that must feel threatened by such an experience, or whether such responses are part of a general defensive orientation that has simply become more manifest with age and security. Of course, these factors are not mutually exclusive.

Furthermore, I have noted even in the "contented" psychoanalyst certain character traits that relate to the topic of clinical-therapeutic inertia. One particular prominent and famous psychoanalyst, who has done outstanding work in the treatment of psychotic disorders, seemed somewhat disturbed about a very difficult patient because of what he believed was the inordinate length of his treatment. The analyst really felt guilty, this particular facet of his superego being a result of his training and reinforced by his colleagues who held similar views. I questioned him as to why one should be "shocked" at the lengthy treatment of a difficult patient, a patient who owed his life to the treatment and who continued to receive benefits from the therapeutic interaction. The length of treatment could be justified both conceptually and practically, but these factors, which my colleague was more than capable of formulating, had remained obscure to him. Sharing my similar experiences was reassuring.

There are many instances in which an emotional orientation of the analyst—for example, idealized identification or the incorporation of Freudian principles in the superego—dominates scientific objectivity. Dr. Spotnitz attempts to place psychoanalysis more firmly in the scientific frame.

Many people, including some psychoanalysts, are quick to point out that psychoanalysis is not a science. I believe this viewpoint is naive, even though it has been discussed by academicians who purportedly are experts in determining what is or is not science. Moreover, the question itself of whether or not psychoanalysis is a science is meaningless and erroneously constructed. After all, science is a method, a unique way of looking at things. What is being observed is not restricted to any particular area. The term *science* implies a systematic collection of data based on a formulated hypothesis (or only minimally guided by previous concepts when one is seeking hypotheses); the formulation of concepts from this data; and the inclusion of data-derived concepts into a larger, consistent, more abstract theoretical system. Certainly, Freud conducted his inquiries along these lines, and although there are many other details that one can discuss about the requirements of scientific method, a careful scrutiny of the origins of psychoanalysis will demonstrate that there is nothing particularly unique or unusual about its conceptual development.

Returning to the question of training: Is there anything about the subject matter of psychoanalysis, aside from its deeply personal references, that particularly influences the intensely emotional reactions of some analysts at the expense of scientific judgment and inquiry, reactions which Dr. Spotnitz believes have led to an inhibition of clinical progress? In the United States (where ideas about what is treatable are much more rigid than in England) the analytic candidate is practically always a physician—his background, therefore, medical. Medical training can be roughly divided into two mutually supporting areas, the basic sciences and the clinical. The basic sciences are the foundation and constitute the underlying rationale of clinical techniques (both diagnostic and therapeutic). At times (often during the formative years of the field) discoveries in the basic sciences have been made quite apart from any clinical experience and only later have led to diagnostic understanding and treatment. The practicing physician need not be an expert in the basic sciences; in some instances, he does not have to know very much about the underlying pathological processes in order to make a proper diagnosis and to institute correct treatment. He feels secure that such knowledge is available to him when he needs it and knows that the foundations of the field of clinical practice rest securely in the hands of capable scientists. The aspiring psychoanalyst begins training with such a background.

He then enters a new field which has many similarities to clinical medicine, e.g., the study of diagnosis, indications and contraindications, prognosis, and so forth. In many institutes, diagnostic history-taking is recommended, and possible complications are reviewed. Freud maintained such a diagnostic orientation at the beginning, but initially for psychoanalysis there were no underlying basic sciences—sciences that would have made such diagnostic and predictive procedures logical extensions of well-worked-out psychic processes. That is, the psychoanalytic method did not emerge from an already established general psychology. In medicine, on the other hand, the basic sciences lead to the refinement of clinical procedures useful in the diagnosis and treatment of a specific disease, and these in turn lead to the establishment of further general fundamental principles. But psychoanalysis did not have such positive feedbacks during its origins. It had to create its own basic science, a task that fell almost exclusively to Freud. Thus, the student of psychoanalysis, as a physician, relies on Freud's metapsychology as he might have relied on the physiologist or pharmacologist. Since Freudian principles are the only basic science, in psychoanalysis the student tends to cling to them rigidly and to idealize their creator. Students and analysts who proclaim their lack of interest in theory rationalize their position by asserting that their exclusive interest is clinical, allowing themselves no questioning of the Freudian theoretical edifice.

The medical clinician does accept changes, of course, but for the most part these changes come from the work of the basic scientist. Although there is some blurring of boundaries, boundaries still exist that separate the practicing clinician and the concept-builder engaged in research. In psychoanalysis we have a preponderence of clinically oriented physicians who respect the above boundaries—and very few have a "basic science" orientation. Freud was an exception—that rare combination of scientist and practitioner. When psychoanalysis became more closely allied to medicine (a development that Freud did not encourage), this division, I believe, became accentuated. The development of boundaries was subtle and covert and manifested by loyalty to Freud, but it lacked the benign critical questioning of concepts which is the essence of the scientific orientation.

I do not wish to attribute the attitudes discussed solely to the medical background of most American psychoanalysts. That would be not only erroneous but a churlish repetition of what has been frequently stated, often to justify a prejudicial viewpoint. I simply wish to relate the analytic candidate's intensely clinical background to a clinical field which had to create its own basic sciences, and to point out that this background is a significant variable (among many others) in helping us understand why traditionally the analyst has consciously or unconsciously avoided delving into or questioning analytic principles regarding the therapeutic process and its applicability.

For reasons that are both tangential to this topic as well as inordinately complex, there has been a gradual change. More and more analysts, at first privately and now often publicly, have been willing to question old dictums based upon some of Freud's early theories. Thus, we are entering the era that Dr. Spotnitz calls modern psychoanalysis.

Patients, being therapeutically and even diagnostically confusing, have "forced" us to reexamine old concepts and dictums. In additon, however, each modification that is offered must be seen in proper perspective. Too often, when there is a pressing need, there is a tendency to embrace eagerly any change that has the appearance of an innovation. The need for change does not necessarily justify a particular change.

And in this connection I would like to make some remarks about Dr. Spotnitz's *Modern Psychoanalysis.*

I can only applaud Dr. Spotnitz's effort. But after the first flush of enthusiasm passed I found myself a little let down. I do not make Dr. Spotnitz responsible for this feeling; I am aware that we (and I believe Dr. Spotnitz himself can be included here) ask for too much and hope to find quick and sustaining answers after struggling and groping in puzzling psychopathological labyrinths. Still, it behooves all of us to stop occasionally and reflect; even though we may learn that we have not progressed a fraction as far as we had thought. A sobering appraisal does not destroy our curiosity, enthusiasm, and efforts.

Many of Dr. Spotnitz's ideas about the handling of patients demonstrate his experience and wisdom, but I doubt that we can think of these ideas as modern psychoanalysis. They are techniques, some of them humanely self-evident, that do not involve either different conceptual foundations or suggest new ways of looking at patients. And some of Dr. Spotnitz's techniques are new *in that he does not withold them from a disturbed group of patients.*

However, when he discusses concepts per se, such as defining schizophrenia or the qualities of narcissistic versus object-directed transference, Dr. Spotnitz retains Freud's hydrodynamic energic principles. The resultant picture is constricted, and one does not get a broad cross-sectional view of the psyche with emphasis on structure and process. Instead, many of his conclusions have tautological elements.

The fact that books such as this are being written represents a tremendous advance, perhaps even a new era, in psychoanalysis. New eras, however, necessitate a considerable extension (not destruction) of the underlying conceptual frame. As yet we do not have enough extensions, but we have some. For example, our concentration on characterological adaptations causes an increased focus on the ego and helps us construct an ego psychology that alters our clinical observational focus, i.e., somewhat less emphasis is now placed on ubiquitous id factors. In turn, our understanding of the adaptive aspects and intrapsychic sources of behavior can lead to a more tolerant view of which patients are treatable. Interestingly enough, this increased understanding intensifies our own looking inwards and leads us to make fewer judgments about reality and to be less inclined to be therapeutically rejecting.

Dr. Spotnitz tells us how he handles schizophrenic patients. Can his recommendations be universally applied? I believe some can, but many cannot. The latter are idiosyncratic; every therapist has his idiosyncratic *modus operandi,* which determines how he conducts therapy and what he can treat. But these techniques are not the outcome of theoretical extensions; they are usually conditions that we set in order to remain comfortable and to create a setting where therapy is possible. It is to be hoped that such techniques (1) do not intrude too much on the patient's autonomy and (2) do not represent participation with the patient's defenses so that the transference distortion becomes impossible to analyze.

Schizophrenic patients have defects in reality testing, and their degree of autonomy is minimal. They find it especially difficult to distinguish between what emanates from within them and what is caused by the outside world. The therapist's intrusion makes such distinctions more difficult and further submerges autonomy.

In even a cursory discussion of technique, the concept of the therapist's intrusion should be accented. The patient brings his psychopathological frame of reference into the consultation room. (This discussion, as is Dr. Spotnitz' book, is limited to outpatients.) He attempts to manipulate the analyst into responding to him within that same framework. For example, if a patient's main characterological defense is schizoid withdrawal, he often provokes the therapist into doing "something" to prevent withdrawal. This may take the form of asking questions (history taking), persuasion, suggestion, giving advice, or other manipulative procedures designed to maintain the patient's contact with reality. The patient, on the other hand, often withdraws further (even though this may not seem to occur immediately). It takes at least two people to play tug-of-war. The patient requires the analyst's intrusion to maintain his defensive stance; he cannot withdraw in a vacuum.

This tug-of-war enables the patient to blame the environment. Blame implies that one's behavior is caused by factors outside the self. Thus, the patient feels that he is not withdrawing defensively because of an inner problem; rather, outside circumstances justify his behavior. He is, therefore, relieved of responsibility for his actions and can successfully continue projecting.

However, denying responsibility for his actions also means that he is vulnerable. He is at the mercy of his environment and has no autonomy. This helpless attitude, although it may become defensively stabilized or dependently fixated, makes further development and ego structuralization difficult.

Keeping the analytic observational frame of reference separate from the psychopathological orientation of the patient makes it more difficult for the patient to deny the intrapsychic sources of his difficulties. He experiences the opportunity of learning about the adaptive aspects of his behavior (see above). His recognition that he is withdrawing because of something within himself rather than being forced to withdraw by an intrusive outer world leads him to at least a glimmer of autonomy.

There are some patients who demand intrusion, however. Their inner wishes are experienced as too destructive and cannot be acknowledged. These patients may make a successful psychopathological adjustment. In an ordinary psychoanalytic practice one does not see such patients. The analyst does not see the successful paranoid patient; rather, *he sees patients who are no longer able to be paranoid.* The patients we see have been unable to keep their defenses in context with their environment; they have been unable to acquire reinforcement from the outside world to maintain them adaptively.

The patient seeks treatment because of this rent in his defensive stability and attempts to use the therapist to achieve pathological stabilization. I believe that here we have a criterion of treatability, one that does not involve diagnostic categories. Using the concept of intrusion we have been discussing, I believe that insofar as a patient refuses to let the analyst *not intrude,* he becomes less and less analyzable. One can recall schizophrenics who would not relate at all unless the therapist intruded. Perhaps the regressed catatonic is an extreme example; by being mute and immobile he "forces" the environment to become involved with him in a nonanalytic fashion. Such patients suspend all autonomy and leave all decisions (except the decision to forsake making decisions) to the outside world.

I believe that insofar as there is some manifestation of autonomy by the patient within the therapeutic setting, he is treatable. It may not even have to be manifest at first, but if the combination of therapist and analytic setting can cause a patient to feel, even minimally, that he can make decisions, analysis is possible. The analytic setting is designed to facilitate the patient's understanding that, at least there, he has some freedom to choose.

Patients suffering from severe psychopathology utilize the analytic interaction in a unique fashion. It becomes a vital part of their lives. The psychoneurotic patient does not become so deeply involved, nor does analysis become the mainstay of his existence as so often happens with the more severely disturbed patient.

The segment of time that the patient, especially the severely disturbed patient, spends in the analyst's office contrasts with time spent elsewhere. Sometimes one notes that a patient isolates his psychosis to the office, behaving rationally elsewhere. By not participating in the patient's defensive struggles, the analyst often becomes almost the sole recipient of his transference projections. Some patients "carry" the analyst with them in their daily lives, talk to him constantly, and thus maintain integration, but their behavior in the office is stormy. One also notes an opposite pattern, i.e., fairly rational behavior in the office and somewhat chaotic behavior elsewhere. In both instances the integrative aspects of the analytic interaction is highlighted.

The above discussion simply focuses on intrinsic aspects of the analytic process, principles that are taken for granted by many practitioners. Still, I believe that it is germane to remind ourselves of fundamentals and make them explicit. By so doing one can understand their relevance to the treatment of all patients. But our understanding of the schizophrenic patient from a characterological (ego-psychological) viewpoint, rather than either a phenomenologic-diagnostic perspective or even Freud's psychodynamic concepts (based upon a hydrodynamic energic model), demonstrates how applicable and indispensable such principles are to the treatment of this group of patients. Especially today, such fundamental principles are sometimes neglected in favor of more social, environmentally manipulative approaches, and this is true not only for the very sick patient but for others that are regarded as being suitable for analysis.

Does the combination of a broader conceptual framework regarding severe psychopathology with concentration on fundamental technical principles lead to the acquisition of new treatment techniques which in turn may cause us to appreciate subtle aspects of psychic processes that add further to our theoretical understanding? Are we entering a phase in which positive feedback between the basic sciences and the clinical is occurring in psychoanalysis? I believe we are, even though, as in any movement, there are resistances and digressions—such as a greater interest in group and community aspects and in applied psychoanalysis. (Digression is not meant pejoratively; such pursuits may be ultimately useful in their own frame of reference.)

Modifications of technique can occur within a psychoanalytic context and need not be parameters as Dr. Spotnitz states. I was first impressed by the need for reevaluation when a middle-aged woman who was referred to me as a "classic" phobic developed an intense paranoid transference after three years of treatment. She then sought consultation from a colleague, and in the space of one interview she *recapitulated* the whole transference movement of three years—i.e., at first being friendly, dependent, and eager for his advice; then gradually becoming suspicious and distrustful; and finally feeling delusionally persecuted. This hour seemed to be a replica in miniature of the sequence of her reactions during the course of treatment. The consultant did not probe nor was he previously aware of the patient's difficulties.

Since then, I have encountered patients who during the initial interview anticipate the future course of the therapeutic interaction. In these instances I find it useful to call attention to their characteristic defensive techniques and to the types of feelings they are developing toward me. For example, a young quasi-mute schizophrenic kept trying to provoke me into asking questions and drawing him out. After I interpreted his withdrawal as a manipulative technique both to frustrate me and to defend himself against revealing himself, he became visibly agitated and showed considerable ambivalence as to whether he should pursue treatment. He finally relaxed when I told him that his indecision was based upon a need to reveal himself and get close to me and his fear of doing so. The greatest part of his treatment focused on his defensive withdrawal owing to extreme ambivalence about symbiotic fusion, the need for omnipotent merging and the terror of annihilation. This is, of course, a capsule summary; but it describes the similarities between the panoramic movement of the first interview and the subsequent therapeutic course.

The replication at the beginning of analytic contact of what might be the future therapeutic progression may be necessary in order to involve some patients in analysis. In reviewing case histories of schizophrenic and borderline patients, I found some patients who would not continue with the interview if the therapist did not initiate some activity or indicate some direction. In other instances the opposite situation prevailed, i.e., the patient did not want the analyst to interfere with his spontaneous stream of associations. It is, of course, impossible to determine how therapy would have progressed if one had used another approach, but it seems likely that patients with whom it was felt necessary to engage in a panoramic prevision of "things to come" would not otherwise have been able to form a therapeutic alliance. How those who preferred no therapist-interference would have reacted is difficult to predict; however, their associations—and in some instances past therapeutic contacts—indicate that they would not have remained in treatment if the analyst had tried to guide them.

There are no exact criteria for determining how to distinguish patients who want intervention and guidance from those who do not. In general, the patient with whom one has to anticipate the future course of treatment by interpreting some general aspects of his anxiety and orientation towards the therapist is taciturn; sometimes he is visibly frightened and withdrawn. He seems to be less integrated, or at least does not have as much defensive stabilization, as do those who do not want guidance.

In reviewing data about both groups of patients, I noted an interesting sidelight: "Panoramic" first dreams were reported only by the group that did *not* want the therapist to be active. The panoramic first dream, described by Freud, occurs at the beginning of analysis; it outlines the structure of the neurosis in a sweeping fashion and depicts the sequence of the unfolding of the transference neurosis or psychosis. The seemingly better integrated group (5 patients) all had such panoramic dreams; three had them on the eve of the first interview. None of the other (more withdrawn) group ever reported such dreams.

Fragmentation of the ego was, however, made manifest in the dreams of patients who did not have panoramic dreams. Frequently, especially during early phases of treatment, specific defensive patterns were reflected in their dreams. In the dreams, however, these defensive patterns were not connected with other aspects of psychic functioning, such as other defenses or underlying conflicts. For example, the patient whose initial defense was withdrawal dreamed about hiding in holes and caves. These dreams seemed to be fragmented from the general associative stream, and although quite revealing, they did not give the comprehensive view presented in panoramic dreams.

These patients seemed to need a synthesizing experience, one that leads to ego integration and unity. Although being fragmented represents a primitive defensive adjustment, considerable anxiety may be stimulated if the patient feels there is going to be further uncontrolled fragmentation. The analysis may be perceived as a force that will disrupt a precarious equilibrium. An initial interview that outlines the course of the unfolding of the transference may give the patient considerable reassurance. Having someone who perceives him as a totality is a stabilizing experience.

Perhaps the techniques just described are specific for certain types of character structure. The reason that books such as Dr. Spotnitz's often leave us more or less dissatisfied, I believe, is that an impasse is created by increased clinical understanding that fails to generate any immediate concrete implications for therapeutic technique—an impasse that may be inherent in the subject matter and may be a recapitulation of our early training. Most of us recall how we wanted to learn how one "does" therapy. All of our psychodynamic understanding did not spell out precisely how one treated a patient; no one seemed able to tell us what to say to a patient during specific circumstances. What made matters worse was that when an instructor did venture this type of information, we were seldom able to use it. Today, when we speak of treating schizophrenia within an ego-psychological frame of reference, we may be facing a situation similar to trying to use our beginning didactic understanding to develop a personal therapeutic style.

It may be that techniques of treatment in the concrete sense discussed above simply cannot be taught and, as a consequence, resistances against innovations develop. Besides personal analysis and supervision, which usually involves broader treatment principles, the important factors are time and experience. Time is necessary to assimilate gradually the knowledge of psychic processes into our perceptual and integrative systems and to relate them to our observations in the consultation room. In other words, there may be no direct transcription from the basic science aspect of psychoanalysis to the direct treatment of the patient— unlike some other fields of medicine. Instead, one incorporates theoretical knowledge and clinical experience and consolidates his professional self-image. The treatment of patients previously considered inaccessible to psychoanalysis broadens one's respect for both the patient's psyche and the psychoanalytic method. The modern psychoanalyst gains in the sense that his belief in the patient's potential autonomy and developmental capacity increases his faith and security in his analytic identity.

Books dealing with the technique of psychoanalysis have greater significance today than ever before. The current professional atmosphere, in which so many lament the psychoanalytic method as disappointing, is not particularly felicitous to efforts such as those of Dr. Ralph Greenson.

Dr. Greenson has written a book[2] which, for the most part, pulls together the cogent historical and technical elements underlying the clinical application of psychoanalysis. Lucidly and in simple understandable language he describes the practical and conceptual evolution of the therapeutic process. This is, understandably, a development of Freud's concepts, with the greatest emphasis placed on the analysis of resistance through transference interpretations. In a second volume he will deal with complications of treatment and presumably focus upon special technical problems.

Discussions of this book with residents (a few who have read it) and psychoanalytic candidates brought to light responses that I could not have predicted. They all liked the book for its organization, scholarship, and the meticulous care that must have gone into it; but, as new as it is, there was a vague feeling that much of the discussion of technical factors underlying treatment procedures was anachronistic. This was especially surprising because there was little disagreement over the specific ways Dr. Greenson handles his patients (the book is replete with candid and frank examples of actual interviews). All in all, they felt that this book is a valuable contribution to the growing literature on psychoanalytic treatment but that, in a general sense, something undefinable is lacking.

[2]Greenson, R. *The Technique and Practice of Psychoanalysis*. New York: International Universities Press, 1969.

I purposely mention students of psychoanalysis because colleagues have had different reactions. They, in contrast, are more prone to argue with specific treatment maneuvers but much more ready to accept Dr. Greenson's theoretical constructs, many of which are regarded as self-evident.

These differences subtly indicate, in my opinion, another variety of the generation gap. The student cannot criticize the therapeutic behavior of a venerable and proven psychoanalyst such as Dr. Greenson, whereas a colleague, being confident of his own skills, can challenge Dr. Greenson's techniques or indicate how his own therapeutic style differs. However, the student is not committed to any theoretical position, and on many occasions he has found the traditional formulations inadequate to his needs.

For example, Dr. Greenson's development (both historically and technically) of the concept of resistance as something to be "overcome" creates an atmosphere, a moral tone, that is antithetical to analysis. Considering the personality in terms of layers and strata of opposing forces that should be dealt with from the surface downward is a useful and orderly approach when dealing with patients. Analysis of resistance, nevertheless, is not the same as overcoming resistance, and what may seem to be only a trivial distinction can in fact be what distinguishes analysis from an exhortative struggle to make the patient give up something in the interest of analysis. The latter is really a managerial intrusion, which hinders the acquisition of insight and does not foster autonomy.

Freud made rules about patients making decisions, free association (the fundamental rule), the rule of abstinence, and so forth. Such rules were designed, as Dr. Greenson points out and agrees, to curb acting out so that the patient recalls rather than translates his feelings into behavior. No matter how well motivated the therapist may be, I have found that such a stance is to some degree always felt as an intrusion by the patient. True, there are always some intrusions—paying fees, use of the couch, even coming to the analyst's office. But the "rules of abstinence" (including abstaining from keeping secrets from the analyst) represent an added increment which is related to the patient's symptomatic adjustments, whereas the requirements just mentioned are usually related to the needs of the analyst and are not, as a rule, a significant aspect of the patient's adjustive modalities. By "forbidding" behavior, no matter how analytically rational it may seem to be, one is trying to do away with something that in itself demands analytic scrutiny. I have found British analysts sympathetic to this viewpoint, and they react approvingly to the recommendation that the word *resistance* be deleted from our technical vocabulary because of the aura of opprobrium the term has accumulated throughout the years—even though Freud may have attached a more benign significance to it.

Students usually find it difficult to impose such restrictions, or when they do not they grossly caricature an analytic stance. When supervising residents, especially beginning residents, I have often heard them admit they feel foolish and presumptuously authoritative telling another person, sometimes of comparable education and often older, how to live his life. The resident's practice of forcing himself to do something which he finds uncomfortable, or caricaturing without integration, cannot be therapeutically successful.

Another relevant factor besides lack of experience has to do with the changing patient population. Our culture differs in many respects from Freud's. The question of sociocultural differences is both beyond the scope of this essay and the competence of this reviewer. Still, some differences are outstandingly obvious. Freedom, as vague as the concept may be, is cherished to a degree unknown in Freud's mid-Victorian milieu. Dependence on the family, even to the extreme of obliterating a unique individuality, was part of the social structure of nineteenth-century and pre-World-War-I society. Today the emphasis is on autonomy and "liberation" from the values of the Establishment. Many adolescents even insist on the "right" to make their own mistakes rather than unconditionally accept the values of their elders. The rule of abstinence—or telling a patient what is best for him, even analytically best—is fundamentally at variance with the ideals of the younger generation, and even older patients have developed values that are somewhat similar in principle.

Dr. Greenson's traditional approach would preclude consideration of such social factors. His approach would also preclude the treatment of a wider group of patients, such as those suffering from characterological disorders and schizophrenia. Since Dr. Greenson believes that some psychic states are "good" for analysis and others "bad," it is natural that he does not focus upon the latter, traditionally untreatable, disorders, although he does consider the contraindications or modifications that are required in their treatment. Both he and Freud also justify their conclusions on theoretical grounds, but even Dr. Greenson's own extensions of clinical theory (which are impressive) are not given sufficient weight or integrated with the clinical problems that all analysts are currently facing. Perhaps he will do so in the second volume. But if he does, he will have to alter a basic orientation about the limits of psychoanalytic treatability.

Optimal conditions for analysis, according to Dr. Greenson, occur once there is a good "working alliance." This concept is somewhat similar to Dr. Zetzel's "therapeutic alliance," although she points out that her concept does not emphasize activity and purposeful work, as does Dr. Greenson's. In any case, Dr. Greenson believes that the feelings which a patient develops toward his analyst motivate the patient to look at and work on his problems. An alliance based on confidence and trust in the therapist is formed, and there is only a minimum of transference involved in the patient's reactions. Technically, negative transference should not develop until a working alliance is firmly established, and such an alliance is an indispensable condition for analysis.

It is important, I believe, to review this concept of alliance in some detail because it is germane to the important and elusive theme of the analytic process. Such terms as "working alliance" and "therapeutic alliance" are commonly used by psychoanalysts, and often one makes the assumption that something significant and modern is being said about how psychoanalysis occurs.

Words often clarify, and the concept of an alliance between a patient and his analyst has an inherent appeal. But does the unique and clever combination of either adjective with the noun introduce any concept that goes beyond already established concepts? Is such a combination part of the modern psychoanalytic theme, i.e., having technical implications about both how and what to treat—for example, including advice to tone down the development of negative transference initially and the warning that such alliances do not develop or are less apt to develop in cases Freud described as narcissistic neuroses?

Both Sterba (1934) and Strachey (1934) developed concepts in terms of ego functions and introjects that referred to the analytic process. Over forty years ago Sterba wrote of the ego's self-observing function and said that without such a function, analysis is not possible. Strachey emphasized that gradual changes occur in the introjects after a "mutative" interpretation has been made, which in turn makes the assimilation of further insight easier. This constitutes a positive feedback, whereas psychopathology is characterized by a vicious circle created by a cycle of projections and introjections. The interpretation, by focusing on the distortion created by the transference projection, interrupts the process of reintrojecting ever increasing amounts of privitive disruptive and constrictive elements. Both authors explore the therapeutic process in a detailed fashion, especially in terms of ego subsystems.

Strachey's formulations would not, of necessity, cause clinicians to reject patients suffering from characterological defects for analysis. It is also conceivable that negative transference could be utilized at the very beginning of treatment.

Still, I believe that Dr. Greenson has made an important point in his discussion of alliance. If a patient's initial reactions to the therapist are hatred alone, even if the patient has the capacity to recognize this as an irrational response, it is not likely that he will remain in treatment. *There has to be some other ingredient present, obviously something positive, but it can coexist with an intensely negative transference which in turn can be worked with analytically.*

Many writers, both in the early and recent literature, have written about this positive factor. The majority find it hard to give a precise description, but they agree that this positive element has something to do with the analyst's attitude as it creates a setting where the patient does not feel overwhelmed by anxiety. The analyst communicates security and calm as well as exclusive devotion to the understanding of the patient's psychic processes, thereby fostering a setting where both regression and insight can occur. Gitelson (1962) wrote about the analyst feeling less anxious and depressed than the patient; Spitz (1956b) referred to the diatrophic attitude; and now Greenson sees such positive factors as part of the working alliance.

All descriptions of what the analyst does to engage a patient in treatment remain vague. This may be due to the fact that there are many variables involved and that there are different, but equally effective, analytic styles consonant with the analyst's personality. On the other hand, if one attempts explanations in terms of ego concepts, as did Sterba (1934) and Strachey (1934), there may be some common denominators conceptually which may have diverse manifestations at the behavioral level.

Dr. Greenson states that a patient is "in analysis" only after the establishment of a working alliance with his therapist. However, I believe that the patient is in analysis from the first moment he walks into the office. Actually, the concept of being in analysis is, in my opinion, anti-analytic. If the therapist views a patient analytically from the beginning and does not impart to him that he has to "achieve" some particular point of view to be in analysis, then the atmosphere is relaxed and the patient has more of an opportunity to become interested in what is going on inside of himself. I believe that the metapsychological foundation of this type of interaction can best be approached by focusing on those exchanges between therapist and patient that we consider to be the essence of psychoanalytic treatment.

Interpretation of the transference is considered the chief mode of communication in the analytic setting. What aspects of the transference are interpreted, and when, has been debated. Whether the content of the interpretation is particularly important is not a settled issue. Still, there are many analysts who retain the "classical" position, and even though they permit themselves some other forms of communication, they believe that only the transference interpretation is analytically relevant.

I believe there is considerable truth in the "classical position," as does Dr. Greenson. However, from time to time I have found myself saying something to a patient that did not seem to be a transference interpretation, and yet I had the conviction that I was analytically "correct," and the patient's subsequent behavior seemed to bear out that conviction.

Dr. D. W. Winnicott illustrates this point splendidly (Giovacchini, 1972). A patient of his became excited after accomplishing something which previously, because of inner constrictions, was beyond his capabilities. He then chided his analyst by asking him why he was not as excited as himself. Dr. Winnicott replied that he was not as excited but then again he did not despair as much either. Later, he added that he was, indeed, excited but not elated (presumably he was referring to the patient's hypomania).

On the surface, this interchange does not have the appearance of a transference interpretation. Dr. Winnicott is responding to content and seemingly not exploring the patient's motivations for wanting him to be excited nor their transference implications. Still, I and some colleagues with whom I discussed this clinical interchange had the firm conviction that Dr. Winnicott responded to his patient in a "correct analytic" fashion. In fact, some colleagues who did not know my purpose in presenting this material to them never even considered whether this interchange had anything unusual about it. The patient's subsequent behavior in the consultation room also indicated that the flow of the analysis had in no way been disturbed; in fact, it seemed to have been enhanced.

Dr. Winnicott is, in fact, telling his patient that he is capable of reacting and having feelings about what the patient does in his daily life; on the other hand, he delineates the limits of his reactions. He does not become as excited or as desperate as the patient. He only becomes excited, not elated or hypomanic. In essence, Dr. Winnicott's reactions retain considerable secondary process and do not become enmeshed with the patient's psychopathological extensions of his feelings. In effect, Dr. Winnicott explains that he sees himself reacting as a reasonable human being, who has empathic feelings toward his patient and who can share in the pleasure that the patient's progress and further ego integration produces. The analyst is, in a subtle fashion, defining the realistic limits of the patient's reactions and indicating the quality and extent of his counterreactions. In essence, he is defining the *analytic setting*.

I have learned that patients suffering from characterological problems (a group that Dr. Greenson does not consider particularly suitable for analysis) require during various stages of their analyses frequent definitions of the analytic setting. The content of definition varies, depending upon the dominant material and affect, but the definition always aims at clarifying the same elements. It focuses on the analyst's function and stresses that he will react to the patient's feelings as intrapsychic phenomena that are interesting and worthy of understanding. The analyst is not reacting to the content per se; rather, his frame of reference is primarily an observational one in which he does not feel elated or despairing or, in other instances, seduced or threatened by what he observes. He is devoted to understanding both the intrapsychic sources and the adaptive significance of the patient's productions. In other words, he is maintaining an *analytic* attitude, and by defining the *analytic setting* he is conveying this position to the patient.

This type of activity is often a useful "intervention" when the patient feels threatened by uncontrollable regression. It is understandable that the analyst sometimes believes it is necessary to make the analysis less painful, since otherwise it may become so disruptive that it is no longer possible to continue. Many authors have explained how they handle such situations. If one carefully examines what they do, e.g., Eissler "talking metapsychology" to the patient, one finds they are describing a particular definition of the analytic setting. Dr. Winnicott makes this point explicit when he speaks of the constant reliability of the analytic hour and remarks that the analytic setting also defines the limits of regression.

I believe that defining the analytic setting is also useful when the patient is not particularly disturbed. This procedure is not limited to patients suffering from disruptive psychopathology or to moments of decompensation. There are specific indications for such a technical maneuver regardless of the category of patient or phase of treatment. It seems that the definition of the analytic setting has created a situation which facilitates analysis. The transference aspects of the patient's feelings become clearer, and he often finds himself capable of understanding their significance. This may occur even when the patient's reactions are silence or "resistive" in nature.

As developed thus far, in addition to the transference interpretation the defining of the analytic setting is *another* technical factor necessary for analysis. This would indicate that we are dealing with two closely related *but nevertheless distinct* factors. Defining, and by so doing creating an analytic setting, could be considered supportive. Because of the reassurance he receives, the patient is better able to investigate the transference further. Moreover, defining the setting could be considered as leading to the formation of a working alliance.

I believe such distinctions are artificial and to a large measure metapsychologically inconsistent. I hope to demonstrate that *the definition of the analytic setting is, in itself, a variety of transference interpretation.* If this is true, the distinction between this kind of support and analysis no longer exists. Separating the working alliance from the activity of analysis would also no longer be necessary. I do not mean to imply that Dr. Greenson insists on maintaining sharp distinctions; on the contrary, he points out just the opposite. I am merely stressing this point and wish to carry it further.

Emphasizing that the analyst will not react in the same way as the patient indicates that either the analyst or the patient is reacting idiosyncratically. Analysis always assumes that in certain respects the analyst is more integrated than the patient. The patient accepts this assumption; otherwise he would not seek analysis. Dr. Winnicott indicated that he would not let his feelings develop beyond a certain level. The increment of the patient's feelings that went beyond this level was unique to the patient and an outcome of his psychopathology. The fact that the patient expected the analyst to feel similarly to himself represents a *transference expectation:* He assumed that his analyst would have the same responses as himself. Isn't this a particular form of transference projection? The patient is projecting his feelings onto the analyst. This constitutes a projection of infantile responses, and even though the patient continues to attribute such feelings to himself, too, that portion which is projected constitutes transference. By keeping the observational frame of reference separate from the patient's (see Part I), the analyst indicates that his reactions are different, and he emphasizes that some elements of the analysand's reactions are due to transference expectations. Thus, a step is taken in making a transference interpretation, emphasizing to the patient that a significant portion of his feelings result from transference. Dr. Winnicott, in essence, is *correcting the transference distortion* by his response, and by so doing, emphasizing that the patient's reactions are idiosyncratic, or at least different from his. The "difference" becomes a subject for further investigation. The interaction that Dr. Winnicott initiated is not simply a direct statement to the patient that the analyst is not really his father or mother, etc. (a type of confrontation that I have seldom found effective), but is instead an active demonstration of transference distinctions in the current affective setting. The definition of the setting leads to the recognition of transference. It not only distinguishes in what frame of reference the material has to be scrutinized, it also tells something about what is being projected.

Every analyst recognizes the unique features of the analytic frame of reference; what has not been sufficiently emphasized is that *the setting itself helps the patient to consolidate his ego boundaries and to see himself as a separate discrete individual.* The analyst, by affirming this setting, communicates that he is different than the patient. This also means that there are three combinations of people in the consultation room: (1) the patient-analyst combination, a transference fusion, (2) the analyst as analyst, and (3) the patient as a *person.* Thus, explicit references to the analytic setting refer to transference and are specifically directed toward an acknowledgment of the symbiotic fusion. They are designed to resolve this fusion, which refers to content and represents a reliving in the current transference setting of an early developmental phase. Although the definition of the analytic setting seems on the surface to be different than the usual interpretative activity between analyst and patient, when viewed in terms of clinical theory it has, one finds, all the ingredients of a transference interpretation.

The value of analytic activity that has the aim of resolving the symbiotic fusion is apparent in cases suffering from severe psychopathology, such as borderline patients and schizophrenics. However, even with patients whose egos are relatively integrated, explicit statements about the analytic setting help create a favorable atmosphere. Perhaps such patients have fewer developmental defects and not *as much* fixation upon the symbiotic phase. *Still, every transference projection, insofar as the patient retains within him some portion of what he projects onto the analyst, represents a fusion; and to the extent that it does, it is a replication of the symbiotic stage.* The difference between the so-called healthier and the more disturbed patient is one of degree. Insofar as there is a capacity for transference projections there is also an element of symbiotic fixation underlying this capacity. True, the better-integrated patient develops transference displacements upon objects that are considered to be more whole objects than partial objects, and the patient perhaps uses displacement mechanisms in addition to projection. Still, to some extent, elements of projections and fusions become apparent during the analytic regression. Such elements are often displayed in a less stormy or disruptive fashion than may occur with more disturbed patients, but they nevertheless have to be resolved if analysis is to be effective in creating a developmental progression as a consequence of the achievement of higher states of ego integration. Even analyses of so-called classical patients are directed toward characterological factors as well as at resolution of the oedipal complex.

Precisely how does one define the analytic setting? As previously stated, such definitions are varied and occur in diverse analytic circumstances. In many instances it is far from apparent (even to the analyst) that he is engaged in such activity. Perhaps a few brief descriptions will illustrate at least the flavor of what is meant by defining the analytic setting. I will begin by once again using Dr. Winnicott's clinical material on the same case. Dr. Winnicott had interpreted to his patient that *"satisfaction annihilates the object for him. He had obtained some satisfaction last week and now I, as the object, had become annihilated."* This is, from any viewpoint, a transference interpretation. Later, Dr. Winnicott says, *"I made an interpretation concerning the continuation of my interest during the period of which I seemed to be annihilated."* I was fascinated by the way Dr. Winnicott phrased his sentence, "I made an interpretation," because what he says refers to his interest and does not explicitly say anything about the patient. Unlike his comment about satisfaction and annihilation, this is not an obvious transference interpretation. Still, I believe he was eminently correct, and again the subsequent material flowed smoothly. In my opinion, he is indicating his interest in being a transference object. This also emphasizes that he does not feel threatened by the patient's wishes to annihilate him; rather, Dr. Winnicott implicitly states that he is available for transference projections, an important attribute of the analytic setting. The fact that he is interested means that there is a phenomenon to be interested in, i.e., the patient's feelings, and the specific use of the analyst in regard to these feelings communicates to the patient that he has separateness in a transference context. This is a variety of transference interpretation, and, in this instance, the patient continued to unfold the transference and began to understand how he used frustration (a symptom) to protect the object from being annihilated.

Now I will present briefly another example from my own practice. During the course of free association, a patient confronted himself with a situation that he could not understand. He remained silent for several minutes and then by his expression and exclamation indicated that he had had a sudden insight and now understood what had previously puzzled him. Quite spontaneously he stated that he was not going to tell me about what he knew, and he seemed very pleased. Equally spontaneously I said that all that was important was that he knew; it was not necessary that I know. Both the patient and I had very strong feelings about the correctness of this statement. It had a tremendous impact upon him and facilitated meaningful reversible regression. Clearly the patient saw that I was not envious of his autonomy. The analytic setting produced an environment where he could withdraw from an object who he could feel wanted to rob him of his individuality and yet at the same time who respected his need to withdraw. At this point, the patient could permit himself further regression and fusion because the analytic setting, by affirming his "right" to withhold (i.e., a transference defense), made it unnecessary for him to continue defending himself so rigidly. I would not be destroyed by his withholding, permitting him to continue using me as a transference figure, and thus leading him to implicit recognition that he was defending himself from an engulfing imago he had projected onto me. Defining the analytic setting as a place where he could keep secrets from me was a pithy way of interpreting a transference defense.

These types of "setting interpretations" lead eventually to the formation of what I have previously described as a solid *analytic introject*. The patient incorporates the setting which leads to the analytic attitude becoming a characterological modality. I believe Dr. Greenson has something similar in mind when he speaks of the working alliance. My formulations do not necessitate a distinction between relatively healthy parts of the ego or feelings that are relatively free of transference and countertransference. The analytic introject is a specific introject which, like all introjects, undergoes constant revision and, hopefully, gradually gains more secondary process qualities. The transference interpretation is an integral factor in the formation of such an introject, but the concept of transference is now extended to include the definition of setting. Finally, such concepts logically lead to a further extension regarding the range of applicability of the psychoanalytic method.

Chapter 23

The Need to Be Helped

Clinicians are constantly faced with the seemingly increasing number of patients who do not fit current diagnostic categories. These patients, instead of presenting definitive symptoms, confront the psychiatrist with vague, ill-defined complaints. The latter usually consist of distressing general questions such as who and what they are, and what the purpose of their life is, i.e., where they fit into the general scheme of things. Some authors have referred to such reactions as existential crises, and Erikson (1956) has described an acute variety of this type of disturbance as the "identity diffusion syndrome" which occurs in some adolescents.

I shall not attempt any further diagnostic categorization. This would be a difficult task that has been discussed by many authors. Suffice to mention here that Knight (1953) very early called attention to this group and coined the term "borderline syndrome." Since then there has been much discussion as to where these patients belong within the continuum from neurosis to psychosis, but as Grinker et al. (1968) aptly point out, a phenomenological approach to diagnosis has severe limitations.

Recently the study of character structure in terms of ego adaptation has proven a fruitful approach to the understanding of this large clinical group (Boyer and Giovacchini, 1967). Both developmental factors and current maladaptations can be focused upon.

Here I would like to consider a particularly distressing feature frequently encountered in such patients. This characteristic is distressing not only to the patient but to the therapist as well when it is brought into the treatment situation.

Often these patients relate to the world in an urgent, harassed manner. They display tension which is seemingly unrelated to any specific object or situation. It is general and pervasive.

During treatment they very quickly direct these feelings toward the therapist in the form of a request for help. However, it is a very abrasive request. The patient displays a clinging demandingness. There is an insistent urgency about his pleading, one which seems to compound itself, and which, from the very beginning, appears fruitless. Nongratification seems to be an intrinsic aspect of this interaction.

Oftentimes the therapeutic setting becomes utterly confused. The therapist finds himself acutely uncomfortable and is unable to determine

First published in *Arch. Gen. Psychiat.* 22 (1970), 245–51. Reprinted by permission.

why. Residents whom I have supervised have frankly confessed their helplessness to deal with such situations, and blamed themselves for their lack of experience and sophistication. I have, however, heard colleagues in more frank moments describe identical reactions and I have often found myself in the same dilemma.

This is an especially interesting situation since the psychiatrist's orientation and background (medical) should not cause him to feel that he is in an alien territory when someone asks for help, even a life-saving type of help. In other clinical instances many psychiatrists function especially well as "rescuers," but not with this type of patient.

Another interesting sidelight has been that when I refer to "this type of patient" practically everyone knows to whom I am referring. To describe a needful person should not evoke any specific recognition, but when one describes the emergency-taut atmosphere these patients create, there is usually an immediate recollection of a case that fits this description.

I believe that the intensity of the psychiatrist's reaction, which is quickly recalled during such clinical discussion, is an extremely important factor. Without considering idiosyncratic elements that contribute to our reactions, there are some common denominators that can lead to insights about this group.

In a previous publication (Giovacchini, 1966a) I described the needfulness of patients suffering from characterological problems in terms of an hierarchal continuum. A person's requirements were viewed as ranging from the total care required by the neonate to a psychic organization that has control over its needs and is able to exercise a maximum amount of autonomy in obtaining gratification. At the primitive end of the spectrum, one finds a psychic organization which is poorly structured and mental processes that are primitive and devoid of abstraction. Communication is primarily at a physiological level. One intuitively responds to an infant. With these adult patients one feels distressed when there is no communication. The psychiatrist cannot respond to what he cannot understand. The patient in turn is unable to articulate what he wants because it is *incapable of being articulated.* All he knows is that he wants help but he does not really know what he means. The concept of being helped is not sufficiently structured so that it can be placed in an interpersonal context. At the level of the psychiatrist-patient interaction, there is nothing one can respond to. Neither the patient nor the therapist comprehends the true nature of what is being sought.

In order to be more specific in outlining this frequently encountered clinical picture, I will present two vignettes which I believe are typical of this group.

Report of Cases

The patient, a middle-aged businessman, came to see me after he had been in treatment with three other psychiatrists. He had almost continuous therapy for the last twenty-five years, having begun when he was an adolescent.

He was especially distressed about his last therapist because they became very angry at each other; the patient believed that his therapist's anger was irrational and they reached the point of mutual insults. His psychiatrist supposedly called him schizoid and paranoid in a pejorative manner. The patient responded by calling him vain, controlling, and manipulative. Still, when he was told he would not be given any further appointments, he was furious and felt betrayed.

This reaction about discontinuing treatment, on the surface, seemed strange later in his treatment with me, because he spent most of his time talking about the worthlessness of treatment and lamenting all the years he had wasted and all the money he had thrown away. He not only blamed me for ineffectiveness but also made me responsible for the total amount of time he had been involved in therapy and for the failure of his previous psychiatrists.

During the end of the first session the patient had already begun to protest that he wasn't getting sufficient help from me. I wasn't telling him enough about himself, and later whatever I interpreted didn't do anything for him. He continued feeling miserable and frustrated and I was in no way alleviating his turmoil.

As a rule he never presented anything definite or concrete. His business was moderately thriving; there were no particular domestic problems. He simply felt that he was unable to enjoy life and demanded that I do something about this.

Unlike some other complaining patients he did not depreciate me in a manifestly hostile way. He had very little self-esteem and saw himself as an unworthy, inferior person but he did not project this negative self-appraisal onto me. Even though I was not of any use to him I was still held in high esteem. It was simply that I could not or would not help him; treatment was of value to others but its benefits were unavailable to him. This caused him to think of himself in an even more negative fashion since this made him into a hateful exception.

Frustration was a dominant theme and he made it the central issue in our relationship. As mentioned above I found myself also frustrated because it seemed that whatever I did was wrong. The treatment in such cases requires another level of understanding that is not inherent in the above data. Before discussing the characterological features of this patient that are relevant to technical factors, I want to present another vignette that illustrates similar psychic elements and highlights further this clinical dilemma.

A young housewife in her late twenties began treatment in a similar but much stormier fashion than the first patient. She came an hour and a half early for her first appointment. When I saw her in the waiting room she looked calm and composed but when she recognized that I was a psychiatrist, her face became tense and anxious. However, when we had ascertained that she had "mistaken" the time and would have to wait in order to see me, she regained her former composure.

She entered my consulting room in a highly melodramatic fashion. Even though there were many histrionic qualities to her behavior, her anguish seemed genuine and she was suffering intensely.

At first this took the form of physical complaints which were an odd mixture of somatic pain and the physiological accompaniments of anxiety. She first focused upon the gastrointestinal system, suffering from very severe stomach cramps and "butterfly" sensations. Then she spoke of "splitting headaches" ranging from migraine to tension headaches. She had visual and equilibratory disturbances as well.

She was also disturbed from a motoric viewpoint. She stumbled when she came into the office. Later she dropped her purse. During the interviews she frequently lost her car keys or misplaced her gloves.

As is so often the case, she turned to me for help. The physical discomfort caused her much pain but she would become just as upset when she misplaced a needed object. She then would revile herself but expected me to do something to relieve her anguish. Matters reached an extreme when by turning a wrong valve she somehow managed to flood her basement. She called me on the telephone and told me about the situation but this time she didn't even know what to ask of me.

She constantly demanded succor which frequently took the form "tell me what to do." However, her requests simply went beyond asking how to conduct herself in a problem situation; a problem that was never defined, but also involved being told how to "feel." She was asking to be supplied a sensory response but as usual the stimulus was not explicitly stated.

The patient created a picture of utter consternation, confusion, and helplessness. She managed to make everyone involved with her feel the same way. Her family, her husband especially, tried to avoid her because she would rouse him to the point of utter exasperation. They didn't know what to do to make her comfortable. On the other hand the husband had severe emotional problems of his own that caused him to put up with such a situation. The reason for seeking treatment at the time she did was associated with certain changes that occurred in the marital equilibrium as a result of his psychotherapy.

The backgrounds of both these patients have some striking similarities. Both seemed unable to obtain gratification, relatively speaking, during childhood.

The first patient had a completely unpredictable mother who was committed to a state hospital when he was eight years old. He visited her at regular intervals until he was thirteen, when she died. He reported many childhood incidents that were characteristic of his relationship with her. The patient felt overwhelmed by her and never knew whether she would be affectionate or cruel. She often attacked him physically, on occasion even when he was in bed asleep. One particular memory kept recurring. They lived in a rural area and had a cat for whom his mother showed considerable affection. She would hold the pet on her lap and fondle him for hours. One day the cat was in the back yard. Without any apparent reason she got a shotgun and killed him. The patient still recalled how she had "cut him in half."

He felt this was an exaggerated model of her behavior toward him. He never knew what to expect. She could be unusually affectionate, even doting. However, the patient felt that she had an uncanny ability to sense when he was not receptive, and then to impose her affection. These moments occurred when he was deeply involved and interested in some other activity. Similarly she tried to feed him when he wasn't hungry. She bundled him in clothes when it wasn't particularly cold. *She ministered to needs he did not have.*

On the other hand, when he was hungry, cold, or otherwise uncomfortable, she ignored him. If he appealed to her, she might withdraw further or bitterly attack him. He reported how helpless he felt but in spite of all the cruelty he was also depressed by his mother's helplessness.

The latter was especially manifest and poignant in her reaction to certain incidents that indicated that the patient wanted to master a problem, a resolution that would signify a developmental advance. For example, the patient suffered from enuresis. The mother took him to several pediatricians and he had a complete medical workup. Many types of regimes and several mechanical devices were tried, but to no avail. Finally, when the patient was sixteen years old, he asked her what she would do if he stopped wetting the bed. She looked at him with a glazed, pale expression and tremulously answered, "I don't know."

From that point on the patient saw himself as a person who did not know. He didn't know what he should do. He also didn't know what he wanted. He simply felt unfulfilled and exasperated.

The second patient also had a very traumatic background both physically and emotionally. The first three months of life were precarious. She was marasmic because she was not able to retain food. She vomited after every feeding and screamed and kicked with colic. The mother, a timid, frightened, naive woman, was said to have blamed herself for her daughter's inability to obtain nutrition. This self-blame, however, prevented her from consulting a physician.

Finally, when she was described as dying of starvation, relatives (the father was a depressed nonparticipant) insisted that the mother seek medical help. The mother's remorse and ambivalence made her immobile; one afternoon an aunt practically kidnapped the patient and took her to the hospital. The physician diagnosed a pyloric obstruction and the patient underwent surgery. She gradually improved postoperatively, especially while in the hospital. At home she continued improving but at a rate which the surgeon felt was too slow. Although the patient no longer suffered from gastrointestinal pathology, she continued having some symptoms. She vomited often but not with the same regularity or intensity as previously. She also continued having colic. It is difficult to say whether it ever stopped because she still had stomach cramps when she first sought treatment.

Her relationship with her mother in contrast to the first patient was predictable. However, here was another situation where the patient felt she was incapable of being gratified. During treatment she drew a parallel between her stomach not being able to "receive" food and her psyche not being able to make experiences with the outer world "helpful." Consequently, she constantly felt "empty," weak, and vulnerable.

She described her mother similarly, i.e., as weak and vulnerable. Furthermore she thought of her mother and herself as hollow shells with thin, egglike covering that could crack any time.

Apparently her mother had sufficient guilt that she tried to take care of her daughter. The child in turn was especially difficult to care for, which only added to the mother's sense of inadequacy and guilt. The latter caused her to be even more inadequate in her mothering, creating a vicious circle.

When the patient reached puberty she became overtly aware of the fact that her mother was an alcoholic. The mother became increasingly helpless and finally the care of the house was completely taken over by a practical nurse. The mother died of a stroke when the patient reached twenty years of age.

Comment

In the discussion of any specific clinical material, one can focus upon many issues, and the same data may allow a variety of interpretations that are not mutually exclusive. For example, some investigators might concentrate upon seemingly masochistic elements of these patients' behavior. The self-destructive aspects of their reactions was related to the repetition of unsatisfied primitive needs but this topic is not germane to the thesis that I wish to explore in this chapter.

Here I want to emphasize the dilemma described above regarding the patients' insistent plea for help. What does help mean to these patients and why do the patients' pleas have such a desperate and agonizing quality?

Both of these patients indicated that in early childhood they experienced defective mothering. Patients suffering from characterological problems have had difficulties during the course of emotional development, which in some way involved the mother-infant relationship. There are developmental fixations in this group of patients which involve early developmental phases and specific constrictions of various ego functions.

Because of these fixations the patients have special problems in relating to the external world. Their problems reflect their early object relationships.

The first patient emphasized his mother's erratic behavior. This caused considerable confusion because no matter what he communicated to her, he did not know (could not predict) her response. This led to the further inability to express himself and make his needs known in a coherent and organized fashion. As he continued experiencing frustration and inconsistency, he began knowing less about what he needed, i.e., the nature of his instinctual requirements.

This patient demonstrated, as do many other adult patients and children suffering from severe psychopathology, a reduced capacity for distinguishing inner stimuli. He often felt tension but usually did not know just what sort of inner needs were responsible for his discomfort. At times he was literally unable to distinguish various bodily requirements; he could not, for example, distinguish hunger from other physiological needs, such as the need to urinate or defecate. Matters became hopelessly complicated when his visceral sensations began achieving sexual qualities.

When one's needs are imperfectly perceived and the external world's responses are either assaultive or nongratifying impingements, the patient finds himself in a situation where he believes he is *incapable of being gratified*.

Because his needs are imperfectly structured, and have undergone, relatively speaking, a limited emotional development, they are, as mentioned above, incapable of being articulated in a sophisticated adult setting. The outer world in turn is therefore incapable of giving satisfaction.

The mother initially could not, because of her psychopathology, respond appropriately to her infant's primitive needs. Because of this neonatal impasse, the patient never received satisfaction adequate to give him the assurance that gratification would be forthcoming. He did not form memory traces of satisfying experiences, nor could he structure a current situation so that it would represent a potential gratification.

Why did he then pursue gratification so avidly? To shed light on this question, the second patient furnishes some valuable data.

During her neonatal period she literally could not be gratified. Food did not nurture and the external world was incapable of gratifying her needs. Her mother, similar to the mother of the first patient, was incapable of responding to her daughter's requirements. This mother had both physical and emotional reasons that impeded the establishment of a nurturing mothering-relationship.

Lack of gratification and inability to make one's needs known cause a child to feel helpless, vulnerable, and unloved. This problem may have been especially intense in the second patient, since no one was capable of responding to her inner tension.

In adult life she showed her helplessness and vulnerability directly, and in the course of events brought these feelings into the therapeutic relationship. Such an orientation, however, was pervasive, and as far as could be ascertained, was typical of all of her relationships. As with the first patient, her helplessness was not only displayed but she insisted that something be done about it.

Before discussing why both these patients fruitlessly demanded "help," I want to mention a very famous case that has not been studied from the cross-sectional viewpoint of psychotherapy, but has been carefully followed longitudinally over a period of many years. I am referring to Engel's (Engel and Reichsman, 1956; Engel, 1968) patient Monica who was also unable during her neonatal years to obtain adequate nourishment because of an esophagal stricture.

Engel has carefully documented (motion pictures and tape recordings) Monica's development from the time she was marasmic, at five months, to the present, when she is an attractive and active adolescent.

Briefly, Monica's early reactions to strangers were characterized by hypotonic withdrawal. She would turn her head away when a stranger walked into the room. In the film it seemed as if she were trying to deny the stranger's existence.

Monica's reactions to separation were equally interesting. She had been able to become dependent upon some of the staff throughout the months and years following her surgery. When they left her she did not show the usual separation anxiety or protest reaction. Her reactions to the care-taking object appeared apathetic. In my opinion it seemed as if she were depleted, and then she would turn to feed her doll, clearly a compensatory activity and an attempt to master her hopelessness.

The interpretation of her separation behavior has to be speculative, since it is impossible to ascertain exactly what Monica was actually feeling. However, her later behavior graphically pointed to certain uniform patterns.

I wish to call attention to one pattern which I believe is especially pertinent here.

Monica was able to manipulate people into waiting upon her. Her high school teacher spent a disproportionate amount of time doing things for her. In the moving pictures it was interesting to note how she would agilely move her body so a staff member would help her off with her coat. She was particularly intriguing when she smoothly and unobtrusively handed her smock to the staff member whose only possible response was to help her put it on. This was done so subtly that it did not seem as if anyone were aware that she was being dependent and taken care of. However, a large percentage of her behavior consisted of a subtle request for help, and obtaining it. Even in her conversations (Engel has taped recorded interviews) Monica did not initiate anything; she was not autonomous and usually managed to get the other person to structure the situation.

The above was particularly interesting since it is reminiscent of many therapeutic sessions with the patients being described here as well as many adolescents. Monica (and patients) simply would not respond to the implicit or explicit request that she talk about whatever she might choose. She refused to make an autonomous choice and forced the interviewer to structure the relationship, similar to patients who cannot free associate and clingingly demand that the therapist take over complete management.

Since Monica's inner tension could only be imperfectly soothed, strangers became disruptive. Ordinarily the infant cries when a stranger appears and becomes upset and protests when the gratifying object leaves. The infant feels threatened by a stranger and abandoned when the nurturing source leaves her perceptual range. Insofar as Monica did not have or had a relative lack of internalized adaptive experiences, she was unable to feel that something valuable was being threatened or lost. She withdrew, it seemed, in order not to experience further failures. She did not cry when abandoned, because feeling abandoned meant she must have known *what it was like to feel accepted (nurtured)*.

Monica's biological helplessness must have caused considerable awakening of her mother's vulnerability and helplessness (there was considerable evidence to indicate that her mother had significant emotional problems) as was the situation with the second case, the young housewife. Later with maturation and the establishment of good object relationships in the hospital, Monica was able to achieve some gratification (otherwise she would have died) and, I believe, to develop a capacity to raise certain questions, unconsciously. Insofar as her needs have been impossible to meet, she must have wondered whether her needs were impossible. Her ego defect may have been founded upon the fact that early in life neither she nor the external world had the executive techniques to gratify her.

Consequently, she must constantly strive to prove there are persons in the outer world who can help her. Because of her neonatal frustration, Monica is relatively unable to internalize adaptive experiences. She has difficulty in forming stable mental representations. Therefore, she must constantly reassure herself that others can take care of her; that she can survive and is lovable.

What was especially interesting was that neither the person she related to nor the audience watching and listening to the data felt resentful. One had the impression that those involved with Monica enjoyed the relationship. The high school teacher, for example, was fond of her.

This reaction is in sharp contrast to that towards the group of patients I am discussing. I believe a significant difference is that Monica was able to be gratified in her current life. This apparently led the teacher to feel increased self-esteem rather than to feel constantly imposed upon by her. It seemed that she unconsciously, or maybe consciously, understood that Monica presented a challenge, a problem, and being able to give her what she wanted represented mastery. It reassured Monica that she could be helped and caused the helper to feel that she could get through to her. I believe that, although Monica could only imperfectly incorporate an adaptive experience, she had in the course of her early hospitalization, postsurgically, succeeded in experiencing satisfaction which led to her later successes.

The group of patients I am referring to apparently did not experience very much in the way of satisfaction during their crucial formative years. Monica's hospitalization was life-saving from more than one viewpoint. She developed some ability to "extract" help from her environment. My patients never had corresponding experiences during childhood, and therefore created further frustration both for themselves and for those to whom they appealed as adults.

These patients thus can be understood as seeking reassurance that they can be nurtured. This reassurance is also intended to prove to themselves that they are capable of being loved, that they have something inside of themselves that is worthwhile. In a fundamental sense they are trying to prove that they exist.

As noted in the beginning of this paper, these patients suffered from identity problems; a self-representation that has no confidence in the ability of the external world to gratify is precariously constructed.

Many patients with characterological problems need to structure their relationships with the external world in terms that are consonant with their needs and defenses (chapter 11). The particular patients referred to here had to construct an identity based upon the unproved premise that they could be "helped."

Recognizing why these patients are so desperate has been of some help in dealing with them by helping us recognize why we cannot deal with them at the manifest level of their demands. If the self-image of intrinsic and preordained frustration can be dealt with therapeutically rather than reacted to with counter-frustration (which is also to some extent a projection of the patient's frustration) or by a reactive attempt to show him that he can be helped, there is hope of further integration. The discussion of the therapeutic process can only follow from such formulations but it is beyond the scope of this essay.

Summary

In discussing patients with characterological problems, attention is called to a group of patients who are insistently demanding and make clinging pleas for help. These demands only intensify their frustration, since what they seek cannot be comprehended or even articulated.

The therapist feels threatened by the urgent atmosphere the patient creates. He also feels frustrated because whatever he does is wrong and he finds himself in the uncomfortable position of facing a therapeutic problem he cannot master.

The developmental antecedents and the character defect of these patients is discussed in the context of two clinical examples and some speculation stimulated by data presented by Engel about his famous patient Monica.

Understanding the adaptive significance of the patient's characterological defenses lessens the therapist's frustrations and makes it somewhat easier for him to deal with this group therapeutically.

Chapter 24

Technical Difficulties in Treating Some Characterological Disorders: Countertransference Problems

All psychoanalysts and analytically oriented psychotherapists are aware that their feelings toward patients vary. Granted, a certain amount of positive feeling is required to conduct any treatment; still some patients are liked better than others. In this discussion I wish to put aside idiosyncratic factors operating in the therapist, since I hope to demonstrate that there are certain qualities of some patients' character structure that cause most therapists to react in a fairly homogeneous fashion. If these qualities are sufficiently intense, many therapists would conclude that such patients might not be psychoanalytically treatable.

The therapists' reactions cannot be completely reduced to liking or disliking the patient. More often, one is confronted with the vague feeling of discomfort when treating a particular patient. Discussions with colleagues have made it abundantly clear that there are varying degrees of comfort with patients; one looks forward to sessions with some patients and experiences a certain degree of aversion to other sessions. If the daily schedule consists only of the former group, the analyst looks forward to the day and can refer to it as an easy and tireless one, whereas after a day with the latter group he often feels exhausted in the evening.

Focusing upon the homogeneous aspects of countertransference reactions reveals that most therapists and analysts find some character traits especially tedious. From a clinical viewpoint this usually means that the patients with these traits are more difficult to treat than others. Thus, making explicit some of these interactions should be of value for both technical understanding and therapeutic technique. Many adolescent patients, who have been considered as suffering from characterological psychopathology, fall in the category of patients presenting problems

First published in *Int. J. Psa. Psychoth.* 1 (1972), 112–27. Reprinted by permission.

that may be beyond our therapeutic tolerance, if one is concentrating upon an insight-producing, one-to-one relationship.

Many reasons have been given for the therapeutic impasse created by this group. Some clinicians believe that the character structure and identity sense is too fluid and transitional for the establishment of an analytic relationship. Others add that there is not sufficient libido free for the formation of a stable transference relationship, because there is too much involvement with the outer world in terms of maintaining contact and adapting to it, or psychic energy is completely bound up in narcissistic self-preoccupation. These latter involvements often result in a concrete, nonpsychologically minded patient whose approach to therapy is mechanistic, shallow, and noncommunicative. These are monosyllabic, unspontaneous patients who, if they are able to report anything, emphasize their feeling of blankness.

The adolescent's instability, frequently results in acting out. Acting out, which has been considered characteristic of this period of life and type of psychopathology, is particularly disruptive and has sometimes been regarded as incompatible with psychoanalytic treatment.

The subject of acting out, a theme that will not be developed here, requires considerable examination, since even what constitutes acting-out behavior is debatable. Furthermore, various analysts evaluate acting out differently; actions that one therapist regards as destructive to treatment are considered adaptive behavior, valuable for analysis, by another. Nevertheless, some patients behave in a fashion that causes discomfort for most therapists and analysts. Still, the reasons for the therapists' disturbances, unlike their reactions to gross behavior, are far from obvious. Again, I wish to emphasize that I am referring to familiar clinical situations and not to idiosyncratic countertransference reactions. I am, however, referring to countertransference reactions, which, of course, consist of individual personal elements, but such factors are common to the character structure of many analysts and produce fairly similar responses.

Countertransference reactions are as varied as are personalities of individual therapists. Still, one can raise the question as to whether patients suffering from specific types of characterological pathology are most apt to evoke particular types of discomfort in the majority of therapists. I believe there is such a tendency and I will try to illustrate it by some clinical vignettes.

Clinical Material

A particularly striking example of a provocative patient is a college student who succeeded in alienating every student health psychiatrist who saw him, as well as one psychiatrist in private practice. The therapist who finally treated him, a colleague, also felt a vague, irrational reaction toward him. It was decided to look in greater detail into the patient's ability to provoke because everyone who had been involved in therapy with him knew something subtle was going on. I asked my colleague to tape-record an interview, and then I had several colleagues and residents listen to portions of the tape. Interestingly enough, they all felt irritated by the patient.

I then recalled other patients who evoked similar reactions; all of them could be classified as borderlines with severe problems centering upon individuation. The problem is especially puzzling, since the reactions were not related to acting out; these patients were not being nasty or necessarily unpleasant. Furthermore, in view of the patients' obvious helplessness and vulnerability, why should reactions not have been moderately tempered and helpful, rather than critical and irritable? I do not mean to indicate that therapists and analysts are not, in general, inclined toward a sympathetic fondness for patients; otherwise, they could not survive in their profession. I am only referring to periods during treatment that deserve to be understood further, because they act as hindrances until such understanding is achieved.

Acting out refers to transposing intrapsychically derived problems into behavior that serves to keep the person totally immersed in the outer world and allows him to distance himself from the inner world of his psyche. Although the provocative patients I am referring to did not act out in this sense, they accomplished the same goals. But instead of using motor behavior, they confined what I will call their acting out to words. This may seem paradoxical, but let me explain what I mean. When closely examined, their associations revealed their exclusive preoccupation with reality and did not take into account any significant etiological contributions arising from within the self.

The tape-recorded interview by my colleague clearly revealed how the patient constantly blamed forces outside himself for his problems, assuming no responsibility whatsoever for his contribution. Something traumatic occurred during childhood, and, according to the patient, everything had to be understood in these terms. He insisted on such an approach. The possibility that early trauma had been internalized and that now he was creating his own difficulties by self-defeating and provocative behavior never occurred to him; instead the idea was strongly resisted. Even when the therapist became the representative of this traumatic external world, the patient had no capacity whatsoever even to consider that this orientation came about through his own projections. The patient also talked constantly about astrology in an exalted fashion. This, too, led to peculiarly irritable responses in all the listeners.

Similarly, one of my patients constantly talked about the superiority of certain schools of psychotherapy, which were different from the one I find useful. I understood that these schools represented different orientations and tried not to be judgmental, but I was unable to maintain a calm, benign acceptance. I found myself becoming irritated and, at times, could not stop myself from debating with him. Finally, when I was able to appreciate that the patient, among other things, was keeping the analysis from penetrating into his psyche, I became more comfortable. I tried harder and found it easier not to respond to content. Instead, from time to time I made comments referring to transference projections and their intrapsychic sources. Nevertheless, during one particular session the patient was furious because he believed that during the previous session I had made harmful comments—comments that were based upon my needs rather than his best interest.

This memorable session brought several important elements to light. Since I was aware that some kind of countertransference elements had been disturbing our relationship, it seemed wise to give credence to his complaint rather than simply assume that it was based completely upon irrational feelings which he had projected. Still, I was not aware of having been either threatened or angry. I decided it would be best to investigate the situation, in order to learn what had been going on within each of us.

During this interview the patient concluded that my hostility was based upon competitive feelings. It must, to some extent, always hurt an older man to see a younger man achieving in areas, which might eventually threaten him. He related this to both intellectual and sexual areas. I was willing to regard this as a plausible explanation, but somehow it did not strike me as being the case. On the contrary, my thoughts turned to a father taking pride in his son's achievements. But wishing to remain receptive, I conceded to myself that something akin to competitive feelings may have been going on at unconscious levels.

As the patient reviewed the previous session's production, he referred to material, which in its distortion unmistakably indicated transference projections. He had read considerably about the principles of psychology and psychotherapy, and, as he was discussing the virtues of a particular school, he referred to a psychiatrist whom I allegedly disliked. It was also clear from previous material that the patient viewed the psychiatrist in the same way he saw his emasculated, depreciated father. Since I had never even known the name of this man, it was unlikely that I could have had any feelings whatsoever toward him. I pointed this out to the patient and added that he probably was projecting some of his own attitudes onto me. He was silent for almost a minute and then, completely ignoring my comment, continued discussing the same school of psychology that had occupied him before my attempt to put matters on an intrapsychic and transference basis. During the next session I realized that I had felt irritated after this event and, from then on, tended to deal imprudently with the content of his associations.

One can easily ask whether I am focusing upon an idiosyncratic countertransference problem which has little relevance to the technical difficulties in the therapy of most borderline patients. After all, this is simply the description of a patient who tends to externalize his difficulties, a not-too-uncommon situation with those who tend to be somewhat paranoid. Why should either of the two patients discussed here present special difficulties? There may be therapists who, because of special endowments (both nonpathological and pathological), are immune to these patients' provocativeness. But, in general, therapists' feelings about difficult patients have something to do with psychic mechanisms similar to those provoked by these patients.

Let us return to the examples. In the first case it became quite apparent, in a specific sense, that the therapist was reacting to some special aspects of the content of the patient's projections. It is not unusual for a paranoid patient to attribute his difficulties to the external world and then to deny personal responsibility for his dilemma. However, this patient seized upon a segment of reality—science—and considered astrology, which the therapist regarded as a special type of omnipotent myth, an exact science. In spite of the fact that he understood such an exaltation of astrology to be the result of the patient's need for a defense against feelings of helpless vulnerability, the therapist, nevertheless, felt threatened. If the patient's delusional needs had been more directly expressed, illogically and flamboyantly, it probably would not have created any problem. The fact that the patient was displaying a problem of delusional proportions was obscured by a seemingly rational superstructure, and it was this rationality that disturbed the therapist. He found himself arguing with the patient, using logic, rather than considering the patient's intrapsychic motivations. With obvious craziness, the therapist would have been comfortable.

Again, one might ask why an experienced therapist should find such a situation vexing. Paranoid patients try to cloak their delusional projections in as much secondary process as possible. They select situations, persons, or causes that seem to justify their position and, in many instances, are eminently rational on the surface. Although the external world is reacted to in a seemingly logical fashion and their beliefs seem to be even sensitive and thoughtful, they nevertheless contain a delusional core, which has to be dealt with in the psychotherapeutic relationship.

This adolescent patient and many others like him, however, have a propensity to clothe their primary-process projections in secondary-process garments that represent areas the therapist *values*. Making astrology a science was the method this patient used. The therapist, who valued science, perceived how the patient distorted and made use of specious arguments. Since the therapist's value system and ego ideals included scientific integrity as a very important element, the patient's arguments, which were considered denigrations and falsifications of the scientific position, ran counter to his ego ideal, and he reacted. Undoubtedly, it would have been better for the therapist to continue focusing upon the delusional core, but this became especially difficult because the patient, by subtle means, upset the therapist's personal equilibrium. When the therapist became aware of what he was reacting to, the treatment lost its horrendous qualities.

In the second case my patient created a similar situation. When he extolled the virtues of the other schools of psychology, he devalued my particular orientation. In retrospect (and even at the time) I could see that he was projecting helpless, depreciated aspects of himself onto me and then adopting an attitude of condescending superiority. This set of circumstances was the outcome of transference, an inevitable and necessary therapeutic consequence, and should not have led to complications. Still, the content he used to depreciate represented an attack on something that mattered to me. He was impugning not only my modus operandi but an important aspect of my identity. Furthermore, when I attempted to put matters back on an intrapsychic basis by pointing out an obvious projection, *he totally ignored me* and continued with a seemingly logical discourse on systems of psychotherapy.

The patient, it will be remembered, believed that I was jealous and competitive. After reviewing the material, I came to the conclusion that something more fundamental and primitive was the basis for my countertransference difficulties. Competition may have been a factor, but, if such a feeling is traced back to its infantile roots, one becomes aware of anxiety regarding survival.

When I attempted to operate in an intrapsychic, a psychoanalytic, frame of reference, the patient treated me as if I did not exist. Not only did he resist my efforts to explore the operations of his mind, but he displayed the ultimate depreciation by politely pausing to let me make my comment and then proceeding, as if he had heard nothing—as if there were nothing to hear. The logical nature of his productions only served to accentuate my existential problem.

With this recognition the treatment situation became more relaxed, at least for me. It also became apparent that my countertransference response corresponded exactly to the patient's fundamental psychopathology—a failure to see himself in terms of a coherent existence, the achievement of a firm and structured identity. In a sense, his treatment of me as a nonentity represented a transference projection of his amorphous self-image.

Although phenomenologically different, this patient brings to mind a group of patients, previously referred to, who are particularly irksome because of their literal approach and concreteness. Often they are silent and their communications are frequently confined to muttering or practically inaudible, monosyllabic replies to questions. This behavior, often referred to as typically adolescent, is cited as another reason why this age group is difficult to treat. My experience, which is probably not typical, does not support the equation of such behavior with adolescents; on the contrary, I have seen such behavior more commonly in adults. In any case, it occurs often enough in adults suffering from characterological problems. These patients often stimulate countertransference reactions, which lead to disturbances and therapeutic disruptions similar to those discussed here. However, the frustration evoked by such patients can be examined in greater detail.

Patients whose thinking is mainly concrete and nonpsychological— that is, devoid of feeling, imagination, and ability to scrutinize emotional nuances—are, of necessity, burdensome to a therapist, who operates in an entirely different frame of reference. These patients are also unable to free associate and incapable of producing fantasies. Even their dreams are usually realistic replicas of their surrounding world, containing none of the bizarre, but often instructive, elements of the dream's primary-process productions. They seem to operate strictly on the basis of the secondary process.

Still, their organization is quite primitive and cannot be principally described in terms of either primary- or secondary-process, energic considerations. Their organization is rather an extremely rigid ego structure, but, if I may be permitted a metaphor, a brittle one that would succumb to stress by crumbling and complete collapse. The ego maintains a shaky organization, not being able to sustain any mobility or flexibility. Momentarily relaxing its rigid organization constitutes an overwhelming threat because there is practically no elasticity. Consequently, the freedom or turbulence of the unconscious, the possible lack of boundaries of fantasy, have to be forcefully avoided.

Thus, rational organization is a superstructure that defends these patients from psychic dissolution. The chaotic is kept in a state of strict repression. The chaotic need not be described only in terms of instinctual impulses. Their basic psychic structure is weakly organized and inadequate to meet the requirements of both inner needs and external mastery. Ego subsystems are poorly systemized, and in states of decompensation the patient's basic inadequacy reveals itself by helplessness, vulnerability, lack of self-esteem, and the feeling of inchoate terror. These patients, when they are able to function marginally and avoid psychotic collapse, are frequently classified as borderline.

These patients and others with similar, but less severe, ego disturbances are able to create special technical difficulties and to provoke specific countertransference reactions. Projection, a relatively primitive psychic mechanism, is a predominant defensive modality for patients suffering from characterological defects. One commonly observes the projection of parts of the self rather than discrete impulses in this group. Often the self-representation is the chief element projected onto the analyst.

The patients in this group, which includes many adolescents, lack a well-defined self-image; they suffer from identity problems. They basically view themselves as worthless, unlovable persons, although they may cover this assessment with provocative arrogance. Their fundamental identity is unformed and is essentially an amorphous, hollow shell, consisting mainly of the feeling of nonexistence. It is this vacuum that they project onto the therapist.

Many authors have emphasized how some patients project hated aspects of the self into the analyst, and this, as negative transference, is manifested by a hostile, demeaning attitude. The experienced clinician does not find this situation intolerable, even though it can be exasperating at times. I am referring to something different; the therapist definitely feels threatened and, unless he acquires understanding of the therapeutic interaction, the effects upon the stability of the analytic or psychotherapeutic setting can be disastrous. Often such understanding is difficult to acquire. These patients produce upheavals similar to those that occurred with my patient. They are especially adept at creating what might be called an existential crisis in the therapist.

When the analyst, as a recipient of the patient's destructive projections, is attacked or demeaned, he still maintains a firm sense of identity. Indeed, an attack is an affirmation of one's existence. There has to be a person to attack or to project into. On the other hand, when the patient projects his blank, amorphous self into the therapist, he transforms the therapist into a similar, blank, nonexistent self. If the analyst is not aware of this particular transference situation, he reacts to the projection with anxiety. He has to defend himself from painful affects and this may take the form of professional rationalizations, which condemn the patient as untreatable because he is too rigid and resistant. The patient's capacity to provoke existential anxiety in the analyst becomes the main

determining factor of treatability. Thus, it is the analyst's inner disturbance that brings him to classify certain groups of patients as difficult.
Since adolescence is a stage of life in which the self-image is particularly
undeveloped, one is apt to encounter such patients in this age group.

Discussion

The discussion of countertransference, as it has been provoked by the
patient's material, has interpretative significance and leads to the acquisition of insight. The therapist has to be careful, however, to distinguish
between what is provided by the patient and what emanates from his
own inner, irrational attitudes. Of course, all reactions have an intrapsychic source, but here one is dealing with a quantitative question. These
patients make many therapists feel uncomfortable in their professional
identity. They possess a provocative attitude, which is a manifestation of
their basic psychopathology.

The patient gains security when the therapist admits that there is
validity to his assertion that something has gone awry. If the therapist
denies the possibility of his having given in to something disturbing
within himself, and sees the problem solely as a transference projection,
the patient feels hostilely demeaned. Often, this is the actual situation.
The therapist uses analysis as a defense against an accusation of having
acted in an improper fashion. On the other hand, to admit that it is
possible that the patient may be correct and to investigate further what
might have occurred shows respect for the patient's integrity as a
sensitive observer, who is concerned about his self-esteem. Furthermore, it also demonstrates that the therapist is not ashamed of the
irrational within himself, making the patient more accepting of his own
inner primitive forces. A calm acceptance of the possibility of a countertransference reaction and a willingness to investigate further represents
an active demonstration of the therapeutic process and a convincing
example of the faith one has in psychoanalysis. The patient once again
sees how much the therapist values the observational frame of reference,
to the point that he is quite willing to apply it to himself. Such an
approach is also reassuring in the transference context. The patient is
neither destroyed by, nor need defend himself against, the component of
his reactions caused by his transference projections. Eventually, the
patient begins to realize that what is going on inside him is not really
dangerous. In essence, I am emphasizing that the best therapeutic
approach to any patient, but especially to the borderline patient, is
honesty. Difficulties in treatment more often than not are caused by
countertransference difficulties. Once a therapist is able to identify these

difficulties as they occur within himself, the honest revelation of them to the patient frequently breaks an impasse. If one is honest enough to admit that he might be having a countertransference problem, the discovery of the problem is usually not too difficult.

It should be emphasized that *honesty* here is not meant in a moral sense. Often one hears about the importance of honesty between patient and doctor, and it sometimes sounds like preaching. One is simply told to be honest, which sounds noble, without any further qualifications or explanation. Rather than being peremptory, I wish to stress that honesty is a pragmatic approach which makes sense in terms of the therapeutic process and its transference-countertransference aspects. Honesty is a powerful therapeutic tool for the above reasons and not a general virtue. It simply happens to work.

Nor should one think of honesty in a promiscuous sense. One has to be selective and use it for therapeutic purposes. It is possible to be too honest and burden the patient with extraneous details. This usually takes the form of revealing our personal neuroses—a burden the patient does not need and which, sooner or later, he experiences as an intrusion. It is usually sufficient for the therapist to admit his irrationality and to treat it as a valuable discovery; it then becomes profitable for the patient to consider how he has contributed to the irrationality. Thus, the therapist opens the door to the analysis of projections, the essential therapeutic task.

Fundamentally, this type of transference-countertransference interplay is the outcome of an important segment of the patient's infantile past. When examined closely, these events can be traced back to early childhood constellations and, from a genetic viewpoint, they supply us with valuable information. Furthermore, these reenactments are always accompanied with considerable affect, by both the patient and the analyst, and they usually lead to meaningful insights which enrich both.

Freud (1912a) has taught us that lifting infantile amnesia through the resolution of the transference neurosis is the essence of psychoanalytic treatment. He discussed these therapeutic maneuvers mainly in the context of hysterical neuroses. Others (Khan, 1960a; Klein, 1948; Winnicott, 1963; Kernberg, 1969; Boyer and Giovacchini, 1967) considered such therapeutic reactions in a wider clinical context, including patients with characterological psychopathology and the psychoses.

One does not often encounter dramatic moments in therapy, in which repressed memories of traumatic events from childhood emerge (Lindon, 1967). *Still, I believe that the type of transference-countertransference reactions just described, if correctly handled, becomes an event that is equivalent to lifting infantile amnesia.* When my patient treated me as a nonentity, he was, in fact, repeating a series of events that characterized his relationship to his father. I will give a brief description of the family structure, to indicate its relevance to the above thesis. The patient's mother was a forceful, resourceful person who valued intellectual achievements. The father, on the other hand, was a poorly educated, immigrant tradesman who provided well for the family, but otherwise was excluded from any consideration. The mother taught the patient to regard his father as a nonentity and to seek his identificatory models elsewhere. She constantly confronted her son with the virtues of her idealized brother and encouraged him to follow in his uncle's footsteps. Thus, the patient, in order to mold a self-image, had to pursue his mother's idealization, which included the denial of his father's existence. This task was especially difficult because he had no actual object contact with his uncle; the uncle was really a fantasy which never received any confirmation from reality, and the patient sometimes received information about his uncle which contradicted his mother's descriptions. Nevertheless, the exclusion of his father was vitally important, in order to construct an ideal self-representation. What he was trying to exclude, nevertheless, became the basis of his identity (chapter 4), and he sought treatment because of the low self-esteem associated with a self-image that was, in fact, modeled after his father.

His reactions toward me can now be seen as reenactments of this early situation with his father. What he produced in treatment was not the recall of a repressed infantile memory; instead, he acted out within the transference context feelings belonging to an early developmental stage and, for the moment, I reacted within this frame of reference and felt uncomfortable. Briefly, an infantile memory, for therapeutic purposes, is equivalent to the emergence of behavior characteristic of early development. The latter dominates, and both the analyst and the patient experience affects associated with primitive developmental levels.

A colleague told me of a similar situation with one of his patients. For some time he was aware of feeling uncomfortable with a middle-aged woman patient. He found himself burdened in her presence and looked forward to her appointments with reluctance and uneasiness. Finally, the patient accused him of wanting to kill her. On reflection, the analyst had to agree, at first only to himself, that she was probably correct. As he considered his feelings further, he was convinced that this was precisely what he felt about her and he wondered why, because up until this period in her treatment he had found her interviews stimulating and informative. Finally he admitted to the patient that he agreed with her and wondered how she had managed to manipulate him into wanting to murder her. The patient's indignation immediately disappeared, and both therapist and patient soon learned that this was an exact replica of a relationship with her parents during early childhood. Of course, the analyst now felt quite differently about her, as he learned more and more about the context of his countertransference reactions.

Searles (1961a) makes an important point relevant to the above observations. He states that, in order to treat certain schizophrenic patients, the patient has to become the most important person in the therapist's life. He is referring to his wish to help the patient. I believe that the wish to rescue the patient, who has become so tremendously important to the therapist, is frequently equivalent to the other side of the coin, the wish to kill him. Whereas the latter is a reenactment of the actual infantile reality, the former is often the patient's compensatory wish fulfillment against such a painful reality, which is then projected into the therapist. In either case, the patient and analyst are completely immersed in a relationship similar to the traumatic infantile environment and, unless the therapist can understand its context, the analysis or psychotherapy may become an unrewarding, disruptive struggle or a doomed attempt to achieve magical salvation.

Patients, of course, project all types of feelings onto the therapist. Nevertheless, there are certain feelings which cause the analyst to be particularly sensitive, as has been discussed above. These transference situations, then, are different because the analyst responds, and his response is capable of contributing to therapeutic progress. The impact of the patient's projection is greater precisely because it is felt by the analyst and because the analyst, for the moment, is completely immersed in the content of the patient's early developmental phase. Since such an immersion is disturbing and introduces a therapeutic obstacle, the analyst is *forced* to gain insight and *share* it with the patient (Winnicott, 1947). In other words, he has to emerge from the patient's frame of reference and, once again, return to an analytic, observational context. Perhaps it would be better for the analyst to remain in an analytic frame of reference and not to have countertransference reactions. This is difficult to evaluate. However, the fact remains that such countertransference reactions occur fairly frequently, especially when treating patients suffering from characterological psychopathology. Consequently, it is gratifying to discover that what began as an obstacle and a therapeutic complication can be utilized for analytic and therapeutic benefits. The understanding of technical complications thus enriches from many viewpoints and the analyst or psychotherapist and his patient, in terms of ego integration, both gain.

Concluding Comments

Certain types of patients who are found to present special difficulties in treatment have been discussed here. Adolescents and some patients suffering from characterological disorders often present themselves in a cryptic, concrete fashion. They tend to be mechanistic and unable to free associate; they cannot express feelings and emotional nuances, and the psychological modality seems to be absent. These constrictions are viewed in terms of the self-representation and the need for a concrete organization to maintain minimal integration.

Technical complications and countertransference reactions have been discussed in terms of the analyst's and psychotherapist's ego ideal. Furthermore, specific transference projections seem to evoke reactions within the therapist that can be disruptive to the treatment.

Nevertheless, these potentially disruptive reactions can lead to valuable insight. They are often replications of early developmental phases and infant-parent constellations. Once understood, their significance is equivalent to the lifting of infantile amnesia.

Chapter 25

The Treatment of Characterological Disorders

Opinions about the types of cases that can be psychoanalytically treated are constantly changing and the number is being enlarged. It is interesting to note that many analysts have presented clinical material that, if diagnostic categorizations were attempted, could be included under the rubric of character disorders, borderline syndromes, and even psychoses. These are all experienced psychoanalysts and some of them were raised in the classic tradition among the original pioneers of psychoanalysis. The fact that the clinical material presented for the discussion of psychoanalytic treatment comes from what we could broadly refer to as sick patients, regardless of diagnostic category, obviously indicates that many analysts believe that these cases need not be abandoned to other treatment modalities.

Since the clinical material I am going to discuss is familiar to most clinicians, perhaps diagnostic considerations are superfluous. Still, for the sake of clarity and precision, although custom may be the more precise term, I will briefly outline some nosologic distinctions.

I have in mind a group of patients who have what we might call character disorders. In contrast to the usual psychoneurotic patient, they do not present distinct symptoms; rather, they complain of general and vague dissatisfactions relating to who and what they are, where they fit in today's world, the purpose of their life, and the meaning of life in general. These are, of course, existential questions and they relate to the patients' identity. These patients may have symptoms, too—anxiety, depression, and paranoid preoccupations—but their primary concern is with difficulties in adapting to the world. Their maladjustment goes beyond social issues because they suffer substantially and feel truly miserable.

The question frequently arises as to how one distinguishes such patients from those diagnosed as borderline or psychotic. Once one understands the character structure and the underlying psychodynamics of this group, the problem is more difficult rather than easier. This is not particularly unusual since there are often differences that manifest themselves on the surface but fade away as epiphenomena when looked at

First published in *Tactics and Techniques in Psychoanalytic Therapy,* Vol. I, ed. P. Giovacchini (New York: Jason Aronson, Inc., 1972), pp. 236–53. Reprinted by permission.

more deeply (microscopically). Still, from a behavioral viewpoint, patients who suffer from characterological problems maintain an operational relationship to reality and, even though it may be constrictive, make an adaptation. They do not often become psychotic in the sense of suffering from florid delusions and hallucinations for protracted periods of time.

I am being purposely tentative because what I am calling character disorders can, at times, develop qualities that are phenomenologically indistinguishable from a psychosis. This happens most often during the course of therapy, but, as a rule, such episodes are transitory, and these patients seem to have considerable resiliency when compared with more traditional psychotic patients. It is equally difficult to distinguish the borderline patient. Unlike the character disorders, one usually thinks of this patient as one who can decompensate to a psychotic state rather readily. His ego state is never far from a schizoid disorganization and his adjustment is believed to be precarious. To repeat, these variations are imprecise and, in my opinion, not particularly useful except for statistical and classificatory purposes. When one wishes to study the therapeutic interaction—the main interest of the clinician—such diagnostic distinctions are of limited value.

Here, I would like to consider once more the question of specific therapeutic approaches that constitute variations of the psychoanalytic method but are not deviations or parameters. Some patients do not want the therapist to interject himself into their associations. They feel his interpretations or comments are intrusions. In some instances these patients are willing to answer questions about their histories or provide other factual information in the interest of clarity, but they become disturbed when the therapist makes a statement about what is going on inside their minds. Other patients who may be more difficult to treat behave in a completely different fashion, demanding that the therapist lead and manage them. Most patients can be placed somewhere between these two extremes, requiring specific therapeutic tactics. I shall illustrate several types of psychopathology and various treatment maneuvers.

The Patient and the Nonintrusive Therapist

An example of a patient who resents any type of interpretative activity was a thirty-five-year-old businessman who believed that he was a chronic failure and felt markedly depressed and generally worthless. He reviled himself for his emotional lability and what he thought were totally unjustified bouts of anger. During the initial interviews he presented, without being asked, a well-organized, complete history. If I asked a question he would gladly answer it in relevant detail. Otherwise, I had the distinct impression that he would resent any comment that I might make about him. He could gratify my curiosity and give me information; however, he seemed to be irritated by even my most casual impressions.

I do not usually make interpretative comments early in the therapeutic relationship, although there are exceptions. This patient signaled to me in many subtle ways not to make any comments. At times I felt tantalized since he brought material that was so easily understood, yet he did not seem to see its significance. I very much wanted to say something, but I rarely gave in to this feeling; when I did, he would frown and otherwise indicate his annoyance. During the initial interviews he ignored my comments, sometimes with forbearance.

As he continued treatment on the couch, he sometimes credited me with having taught him something important about his relationship with some significant figure in his past (for example, his mother); he thought that this type of insight indicated progress and demonstrated my analytic skill. These were essentially nontransference interpretations but, rather curiously, I had not made them. These interpretations were the products of the patient's ruminations that he attributed to me and then praised me for having made.

His reactions were quite different, however, when I made my first *transference* interpretation. I pointed out that he needed to maintain a certain distance between the two of us, which he accomplished by drawing a curtain of intellectualism between us. My comment was not intended as criticism nor did he take it as such. As a matter of fact, I was intrigued by both the form and the content of his associations, and I was just as interested in the specific details of his defense as I was in the underlying anxiety that made him keep us psychically apart. His responses were especially interesting. At first, he was confused. Even though my statement consisted of a simple declarative sentence, he claimed he did not understand what I had said. He asked me to repeat it several times and, since I felt that his response was puzzling and full of anguish, I did. As he painfully and slowly grasped the meaning of my interpretation, he became increasingly sad.

Although the subsequent material more than abundantly indicated that the patient was, indeed, maintaining distance through intellectual control, he felt that he had been completely misunderstood. He resented the idea that I would have anything to say about his feelings and motivations; he felt that no one could know anything about them except himself. He believed that what I said could only be a projection of myself and not a true understanding of him. This, oddly enough, was the way he felt about every transference interpretation I made. Although this patient's reactions struck me as being particularly bizarre, I have since noted other cases who behave in a similar fashion, and sometimes in an even more circumspect fashion. For example, another patient, a professional man, told me during our very first session that he wanted me to remain silent. He did not want me to "intrude" into his thoughts; the time was his alone and I was not to introduce parts of my psyche into it.

Inevitably, the question arises as to how to handle such cases psychoanalytically when the chief therapeutic tool avowedly is the transference interpretation. Must our technique be modified when a patient apparently resents or "forbids" such interpretations? Several factors should be clarified. Although it may not be apparent, these two patients (as well as others I have subsequently seen) had a highly idealized attitude toward me. In some instances this idealization developed quickly during the beginning interviews. In others, they had already formed an idealized concept of me before the first interview. The first patient was referred to me by a former patient, one who praised me "to the heavens," apparently because of an unresolved positive transference. The second patient had read some of my writings and found himself very much drawn to them. Both patients had formed rather exalted pictures long before they actually saw me.

These patients seemed to present a paradox. On the one hand, the therapist is idealized but then whatever he wishes to impart is summarily rejected. In any discussions of therapeutic handling, one must first understand the psychopathology. In these cases, there is a specific type of relationship that has transference significance. Understanding the nature of this relationship should reveal a lot about these patients' specific characterological difficulties, and these insights might indicate the most reasonable therapeutic course.

To understand more, let us return to the clinical material. I found it prudent to take a wait-and-see attitude, and both the patients and I felt more comfortable after I decided to remain silent. The subsequent material emphasizes several themes. First, both patients indicated that I was intruding parts of myself into them. They perceived this as an assault and an attempt to rob them of their precarious autonomy; consequently, they had to keep me "at arms' length." Next, there was an antithetical factor in that they felt very close to me. They were referring to a symbiotic fusion where the boundaries between us did not exist. They saw the relationship as consisting of total unity between patient and therapist.

If I made an observation about our relationship, it indicated that a relationship between *two* people existed. If I commented about situations that were outside of the transference—that did not involve the two of us—it was not threatening. However, any transference interpretations upset the symbiotic unity that seemed to be so vital. Furthermore, the atmosphere of magical omnipotence seemed to be disturbed by a transference interpretation. To remain a deity one must stay concealed; gods do not reveal themselves if they are to preserve their omnipotence. If I said anything I ran the risk of being wrong and of exposing my frality. My remarks about situations outside the transference did not particularly matter because they could be made within the context of symbiotic unity and so their validity did not matter. Within the transference, however, my interpretations were intrinsically wrong.

When a patient laments that I do not understand him, from his viewpoint, he is correct. By intruding, I do not understand his need for symbiotic unity; therefore, his idealized view of me is shaken.

In a witty moment, Dr. Winnicott said that he makes interpretations for two reasons: one is to let the patient know that he is still alive and the other is to show the patient that he can be wrong. Perhaps in this pithy statement, Dr. Winnicott was summarizing the above points. To let the patient know he is alive points to the fact that the analyst exists, separate and apart from the patient, and the second reason indicates that he is not divinely infallible. These formulations remind me of an unusual situation that I hesitate to call clinical and yet may illustrate to an extreme degree the type of interactions described.

A colleague referred the husband of one of his patients to me for psychoanalysis. The wife gave her husband my name and he promised to call me. About two years later my colleague complimented me on the progress this man had made in his treatment. His patient would, from time to time, report about her husband's behavior which, at least descriptively, seemed to be much better integrated than before; certain phobic symptoms had disappeared. At times she would describe what happened during one of her husband's sessions, and the general movement seemed to be a gradual resolution of an idealized transference. In this case, there could be no question of my intrusion simply because the "patient" never called me and so I never even saw him! I was astonished at my colleague's remarks about a *proxy analysis* and an even more remarkable *proxy transference*.

I do not believe that these patients who cannot tolerate transference interpretations require a specific approach or basic alteration of the psychotherapeutic relationship. Once the analyst becomes aware of the transference and adaptive significance of the patients' reactions, they need not hinder analysis. Even though the aim of analysis is to achieve further ego integration by acquiring insight, these patients can reach self-understanding in a setting where they do not feel intruded upon. Gradually, the analyst can augment the patient's self-observations, and eventually the patient will begin to view the analyst's interpretation as an extension of his own.

To reach such a state of mutual cooperation requires considerable patience and respect for the patient's autonomy. It can be an especially difficult analytic relationship because the analyst has to "suspend" his analytic operations and seemingly relegate his professional identity to the background. Once he recognizes, however, that his so-called lack of activity is, in itself, an active demonstration of his analytic forbearance—which may eventually help to clarify the patient's symbiotic needs—the analyst can relax and allow the analysis to continue unhampered by any intrusion of his own needs.

Other Characterological Types

In contrast to the inactivity demanded by the patients just described, there is another group that requires the analyst's intervention, those that can be described as being in need of a panoramic prevision of the therapeutic course. Briefly, they need a unifying, cohesive experience during their first interview; without it, they seem to be unable to become engaged in treatment. The experience usually consists of interpretations of what will later be expanded into the main transference themes. Here I would like to discuss the manifestations of psychopathology that may help to determine our initial therapeutic approach.

Some patients do not want any intrusion; this is quite clear because of their reactions to our comments. Other patients may not resent interpretations and yet do not require an analytic demonstration "in miniature." Both types of patients will indicate, sometimes subtly and sometimes quite openly, that they want the analyst to participate in their psychopathological frames of reference; otherwise they will feel anxious.

A patient often seeks therapy not because he really wants to change; rather, he hopes to have his defenses reinforced in order to feel more comfortable with his psychopathologically determined adaptations. He does not want to give up his symptoms; he merely wants them to work better. However, when the therapist creates an analytic observational framework—a platform from which to view the psychic turmoil going on within the patient—instead of supporting the patient's defenses by educative or managerial activities, there is inevitably some tension. If the tension is very intense, analytic treatment may not be possible. The patient will indicate if he can tolerate the analyst's refusal to take sides with one or another aspect of his intrapsychic conflicts.

I believe that the occurrence of panoramic first dreams is a positive indication for analysis without intervention; it signifies a unity and cohesion of the personality. These patients may suffer from severe psychopathology, and there may be defective and primitive functioning (even considerable asynchrony among various ego systems), but there is a relative degree of integration reflected in their behavior and manner of relating. In retrospect, it seems that this group of patients tends to view both situations and feelings in a holistic fashion; they do not deal with certain matters in an isolated way. Even when they are markedly obsessional, they can still place their preoccupations in a larger context. This capacity is not necessarily a sign of psychic health because the larger context may be delusionally constructed.

For example, a young scientist was quite dissatisfied with the way he was being treated at work, especially by his immediate superior. He believed that this man was jealous of his creativity and was doing everything possible to hinder his advancement. There was an obvious paranoid element in this patient's feelings, and it resulted in a florid, paranoid psychosis later on. Although he spent considerable time marshaling evidence to support his view that he was being persecuted by the senior scientist, he did not restrict his associations mainly to this area. He was able to think about his work in relation to the other areas of his life. He hoped to achieve fame from his scientific discoveries, as well as money, prestige, and admiration; then he hoped he would be successful and popular with girls.

His paranoia was not confined to his mentor; he had a rather paranoid attitude about everything but his attitudes were not exclusively paranoid. Although he tended to be generally suspicious and mistrustful, he could also be friendly and cheerful. Sometimes he used his suspiciousness productively: since he did not trust the motives or reliability of a colleague's reported data, he might repeat the colleague's experiment. He often obtained different results, which then permitted him to carry the formulations further. In retrospect this patient seemed to be able to coordinate the different facets of his life. Perhaps his chief adjustive (characterological) modality was paranoid, but it had many themes and variations. It even had a certain flexibility because it varied according to the situation and was determined by many factors.

This patient's early dreams were panoramic in the sense that they depicted the structure of his personality in a sweeping fashion and were predictive of the course of the transference. His first dream, which took place the night before his initial appointment, was long and involved. He was taking an ocean voyage with a very skillful and highly respected captain. However, somewhere during the voyage the patient found himself in the midst of a storm; he described the ship's precarious balance and indicated that it was in serious danger of sinking. The captain then became the villain because the danger being faced was his responsibility. The captain was not basically irresponsible or careless, but he knew he could save himself and did not particularly care about the patient's welfare. For the rest of the dream, the patient worked with the captain (the period of animosity having passed) and together they weathered the storm.

The dream was not quite this coherent. Some of its meaning was obvious from the patient's associations, and in presenting it here I undoubtedly used some of my secondary process. Nevertheless, there was a remarkable coherence between this dream and most of his others. *I did not feel it was necessary to do anything in particular except allow the transference to develop.* As the dream predicted, after an initial idealization, the patient became quite paranoid about me and had to be hospitalized briefly. However, he reintegrated and the analysis continued without any unusual complications.

Other patients may require a different initial approach. For example, one patient—an attractive, single woman in her thirties—was referred to me as a "classic" hysteric with phobic symptoms. She vividly described these symptoms; the main one was agoraphobia and there were numerous lesser phobias. She was afraid of riding in trains, automobiles, airplanes, or other form of public transportation. These fears, however, were overshadowed by her fear of open spaces, which was equated with leaving home. As a consequence, she was virtually confined at home and continued to live with her parents.

In view of her crippling symptoms, it seemed remarkable that she had managed to come to my office. She, herself, complained about the great effort and then said that she could control her anxiety somewhat if her father were with her; he had driven her to the interview. This was the first time she had sought therapy although her symptoms first appeared after she graduated from high school. Because of her anxiety she did not go to college. The only change in her life that seemed to be associated with entering treatment was her father's illness. He had just recovered from a coronary, and it was fairly obvious that the patient was very much afraid of losing him.

The patient, although soft-spoken and demure, seemed to create an air of tension and urgency. At first, she appeared to be able to speak freely and to impart considerable information; her attitude was pleasantly cooperative. Nevertheless, I felt a vague sense of uneasiness and soon recognized that I knew very little about her. The patient went into considerable detail about her numerous phobias and gave an exact description of her house; however, she imparted no feeling about her relationship with her parents, siblings, and other significant persons. In fact, her descriptions of other people, which she never gave spontaneously, were mechanistic and wooden; although initially I believed I was learning something about her interpersonal relationships, later I realized that this was not so.

It seemed that her life consisted of only her phobias and being at home. She did not discuss the vocational, social, or sexual areas of life; I saw that she seemed to be isolated in these respects, but I was reluctant to make any inquiries. I may have been afraid of offending her or of upsetting a delicate balance, although she presented a picture of sophisticated poise. She seemed to have a delicate, porcelain veneer that appeared as if it could easily crack.

Although her symptoms were supposedly characteristic of a high-grade, hysterical neurosis, I came to believe that I was dealing with a fragmented person. I also saw her as a "difficult" patient. This feeling came to me toward the end of the interview. The patient finally reached a point where she had told me all she could and had nothing more to say. I would have preferred to let her continue talking or to remain silent if she chose. However, after she indicated that she had nothing more to say, I had the distinct impression that if I remained silent I would lose her as a patient.

She looked at me with both an imperious expectancy and a pleading helplessness. Her narcissism was manifested by her straight, regal posture. She was immaculately groomed, with not one hair out of place. Still, the picture she presented was incongruous. When she turned her head, her profile impressed me, perhaps because of a hypnagogic distortion of mine, as that of a six-month-old infant. I thought I saw two distinctly separate ego states, indicating a serious fragmentation. She also convinced me that I would have to "do something" if I were sincerely interested in treating her.

This patient never had what could be considered a panoramic dream; they all dealt with circumscribed themes and had very little, if any, action in them. In the first dream she reported, she simply sat in her living room with a strange man; there was no movement or conversation. Later she had dreams in which she was imprisoned in a cave behind an iron grill. Further on in her treatment she dreamed of storms and holocausts, but she was always standing off at a considerable distance.

Technical Considerations

The phobic patient impressed upon me the need to do something definite, therapeutically speaking. It is sometimes difficult to ascertain why one feels such a need and what exactly is signaled by the patient, but the feeling is unmistakable. With some patients it is possible to sit back, relax, and adopt a wait-and-see attitude, but with others this cannot be done. These two types of patients cannot be distinguished by the severity of their psychopathology. It is clear that the first patient described had many obvious psychotic features, whereas the second one presented an almost classical picture of an hysterical neurosis with phobic symptoms.

From an ego-psychological viewpoint, there were distinct differences between these two patients in the degree and kind of psychic organization. In spite of the predominant primary-process thinking in the first patient, his ego was fundamentally unified. On the other hand, the second patient was markedly fragmented. Her ego used the defense mechanism of splitting to keep various facets of her life separate from each other. The outside world was no longer part of her experience since she confined herself to her parental home, where her father, in particular represented a lifeline.

As treatment later indicated she had split off parts of herself—unacceptable, destructive fragments—and then phobically isolated herself from them. The paranoid scientist also projected parts of himself but he did not separate himself completely from them. He interacted with others actively, which required the maintenance of inner unity. The so-called hysterical patient withdrew from and, to some extent, even denied the outside world, which she equated with the unacceptable within her. Thus, she lived a highly constricted life with only part of her total ego. She sought treatment because the equilibrium of even that part was being threatened by her father's illness and possible death, and if she split off a painful part, this time she would have nothing left, so to speak, for herself.

One is reminded of a situation in organic medicine where a patient may not be able to function efficiently because he is missing a part of himself, perhaps a limb; the problem for that patient is rehabilitation. My phobic patient was missing parts of herself but, unlike a missing limb, they were potentially recoverable.

My patient wanted treatment so that she could continue to live with her constrictions. As her first dream indicated, she wanted to have me simply replace her father without establishing a relationship; the dream was set in her living room, and she and the stranger did not communicate.

These constructions are all retrospective; actually I understood very little during the first crucial interview except: (1) I could not wait for understanding to come, and (2) I was dealing with an ego with many split-off components.

In contrast to the first dream (which was reported at a later session), she felt uneasy with and did not seem to tolerate silence. I definitely felt she wanted me to talk *to her,* which is quite different from communicating with one another. I could feel an immense dependency when she expressed needs that were so primitive (and belonged to preverbal developmental stages) that they could not be articulated. Still she wanted something verbal from me; in this instance words would have concrete, magical powers. Her fragmentation seemed obvious in spite of the fact that such structural characteristics were part of a neurosis that is supposed to represent the highest order of psychosexual integration. Many psychoanalysts have noted the close proximity of a surface hysterical picture and an underlying, often malignant, schizophrenia.

As mentioned above, I did not know how to meet her expectations for silent, magical support. I wondered if such a part-ego could tolerate both a regression inherently stimulated by the psychoanalytic setting and an analyst who would not actively try to provide such elemental support. I knew that this patient would attribute (in fact she had already done so) omnipotent qualities to me, but how would she respond if I maintained an analytic stance and did not try to respond within her frame of reference?

From my theoretical understanding, although minimal, I surmised how a fragmented ego might respond to the psychoanalytic approach. This patient seemed to be able to generate considerable and disruptive anxiety if her needs for magical subsistence were not met. I soon realized that if I could give her what she wanted, she would probably have a fixation, perhaps a delusional one. However, the idea of giving her what she wanted was simply an academic conjecture for me because I would not have known where to begin if I had decided to respond to her at the level she herself presented.

I felt that it was not feasible just not to respond at all except with analytic expectancy. A fragmented ego, per se, does not exclude an analytic approach, but the analytic patient has to learn to see the outside world and his reactions in terms of what is going on within himself. In other words, there has to be some cohesion among the parts of the self and a recognition of the external world toward which he is responding.

My phobic patient did not seem to be able to discriminate between different parts of herself and the qualitative and quantitative aspects of her environment. She did not understand how situations are related to one another and how one event determines another; it could be said that she had little concept of dynamic interrelationships.

Psychoanalysis as a procedure seemed to be incomprehensible to her. I now believe that this fairly common phenomenon among patients suffering from characterological problems is the product of the patients' fragmented view; they have no appreciation of deterministically related interactions. Psychoanalytic treatment requires an observational frame of reference where connections between parts of the self and feelings and behavior toward external objects are made. The analytic process has, in a sense, a unity of its own. My patient and many others have no feelings about analysis because they have none of the unity that is inherent in the analytic process. However, it is precisely this type of patient who needs the unity that analysis offers. Although they can only fragment (and this may prevent them from tolerating an analytic approach), they are in dire need of a unifying experience.

I became aware of an impasse in my thinking and had a strong desire to try analysis even though it might be beyond the patient's capacities. I also realized that I wanted to impress her with my wisdom in knowing what was best for her—in this case, analysis. Without being completely aware of what I was doing, I asked the patient why she put herself entirely in my care on such short acquaintance. The patient was not at all astonished to have me speculate about her trust in me; she simply wondered why I felt her trust was naïve and why I questioned her at all. To her it was perfectly natural to see me as a father substitute and she was incapable of questioning her own motivations or the defensive and adaptive functions of such an interaction.

After she replied, there was a period of silence. This time the silence did not seem to bother her. On the other hand, I felt a need to collect my thoughts, and as I struggled with them, I became uncomfortable. Later that day, I recognized that the patient was displaying total dependence upon me and was making me responsible for her life; I felt uneasy because of the magnitude of that responsibility.

During later sessions I also felt inhibited about making interpretative comments if I had something to say. My reluctance to look for intrapsychic sources of behavior and attitudes became quite intense. I finally concluded that I was responding to her fragmentation and that if I continued doing so, analysis, at least with me, would not be possible. Consequently, I told her that she had an inhibiting effect upon me, which

I believed she purposely, although unconsciously, created in order to keep me under control. At the same time I implied that she had to render me powerless because she was afraid I would attack her.

Again, she did not seem to be upset by my observations but was able to relax and speak freely. For the next ten minutes, she was warm and friendly and made many positive statements about me and my office. I had the distinct impression that she was in a state of starry-eyed idealization. I found this oppressive rather than narcissistically enhancing. Although I felt controlled by her idealization, I decided to wait and see what would happen.

The patient began to have periods of silence, and it became obvious that she was visibly struggling with certain feelings or thoughts. I said that maybe she had feelings about me that were difficult to express. I also indicated that I would respect her decision if she chose not to express them. Her affect changed immediately and she became increasingly angry. She confessed that she felt I had suddenly become unsympathetic and was not the least bit interested in either helping or understanding her. She believed that I actively disliked her and would do her harm if I could. Just then I felt much more relaxed and believed that analytic contact had finally been made, if the patient did not, in the meantime, walk out on me. I felt impelled to make an interpretation that would "pull together," that is, unify her fragmented behavior. Therefore, I told her that her reactions were understandable in view of her intense need to see me as a godlike protector, a need that would be disappointed as she became more aware of my limitations. To some extent, she perceived my ineptness as dangerous.

At this time the patient relaxed and seemed pleased; we had reached the end of the session and there was no doubt about further interviews. We both assumed that therapy had begun. In fact, I felt that she was a long-standing patient and that all we needed to do was to set up a schedule. I emphasize this point because initially she had asked many questions and raised objections about treatment hours and how to get to and from my office. She said nothing more about such difficulties and was quite flexible about fitting into my schedule.

The next session seemed to be a continuation of the material she had presented before she became angry; her associations repeatedly referred to her need to both idealize and control me. Although no treatment proceeds with predictable regularity, this woman's treatment went through various phases. For a long time she was extremely dependent and attributed omnipotent powers to me. There was often marked evidence of a symbiotic fusion. After this she displayed increasing anger which finally reached paranoid proportions. She became delusional about me and developed somatic delusions. She believed that a small freckle on her left forearm was a cancerous mole and sought verification from me and other physicians. Her paranoia increased tremendously and she bitterly reviled me. Strangely enough, however, these attacks were usually confined to my office. She talked of quitting treatment but never too seriously. She went only so far as to demand a consultation. In spite of my lack of understanding and competence she asked me to make the referral.

At first, the patient idealized the consultant but, during the course of the consultation, she developed a paranoid distrust. She finally considered him an ally of mine and, therefore, worthless. The consultant's description of their one-hour interview was an exact replica of the three years she had been in treatment with me. (He had had no previous information about my patient.) It was also remarkably similar to what I had experienced with her during our initial interview.

Although she was angry, she was impressed when I spoke of the similarity of her reactions toward me and the consultant and the similar movement in the two first interviews. Recalling our first interview made it easier for her to see that there was a preordained quality to her reactions. From this point on, there was nothing unusual in her treatment. She experienced regressive fluctuations but was consistently able to recognize them, often with considerable affect, as transference manifestations.

General Comments

Patients who suffer from characterological problems bring into focus both diagnostic factors and technical considerations. My phobic patient illustrates the fact that symptoms alone do not provide an adequate understanding of the more subtle aspects of psychopathology. It is preferable to rely on the patient's reactions toward the therapist as they occur in the here-and-now of the consultation room. My patient presented an interesting sequence of reactions during our first interview that were identical with the later unfolding of the transference. The young scientist, however, reacted in a more conventional fashion. Each patient's reactions and the resultant technical approaches were attributed to certain structural qualities of their egos. Holistic unity and ego fragmentation lead to different therapeutic events.

It can be asked whether all patients with fragmented egos will react in the same fashion as the woman described here; one can also examine the criteria for treatability. I can recall other patients whose egos were probably fragmented who reacted differently from this woman. In fact, it has been reported that these patients cannot tolerate an analytic relationship and that they require a modified therapeutic technique in order to derive any support from the relationship.

Patients' reactions are determined by many factors. My phobic patient might have responded quite differently if I had actively probed or tried to be reassuring. *Her reactions seemed to be a response to my nonintrusive approach. Maintaining an analytic attitude (which simply means relating the patient's attitudes and behavior to his feelings toward the analyst and patient's attitudes and behavior to his feelings toward the analyst and analytic setting) seems to be the instrumental factor that produces a sequence of reactions that indicate the development of the transference. I have repeatedly noted such reactions whenever I was able to respond as I did with the patient discussed here.*

The criteria for treatability cannot be dealt with on an absolute basis. The qualities that make a patient treatable or nontreatable do not reside wholly within the patient. Rather, it is important to look at the reactions and counterreactions; the relationship itself between the patient and therapist may determine whether the patient is treatable. This perspective emphasizes the interpersonal factor. A patient may be nontreatable by one therapist but treatable by another. The responsibility for success or failure, from this viewpoint, resides in their interaction. This does not mean that technical issues and the structure of the patient's personality are not important. Nor does it mean that therapeutic failure is always due to some idiosyncratic countertransference element. Because of specific defenses or ego defects certain patients cannot respond to any approach that is designed to foster self-observation and introspection.

On the other hand, many patients who seem to be analytically inaccessible may respond very well to analysis. Therapists, of course, may abandon the analytic approach for a variety of reasons. *Some patients (and I believe those with fragmented egos can be included in this category) are especially skillful in stimulating the therapist's ambivalence about analysis.*

If a patient's ego is fragmented, the therapist tends to be protective toward him. The therapist senses his helplessness and his relative lack of adaptive techniques to cope with the exigencies of the external world. The patient may create further frustration by not being able to articulate his needs; if he can, the therapist may still not understand what he is seeking, and his wish to be protective and helpful while not knowing how, creates an impasse that is of greater urgency than conducting analysis. The therapist may be impressed with the patient's needfulness and, for some reason, believe that it is inconsistent with an analytic approach. Consequently, there is a tendency to want to offer the patient a constructive experience but not an analytic one; it may be experienced intensely as an urge to "do something," which dominates the entire treatment setting.

The primitive fixations of these fragmented patients involve preverbal ego states. The urge to "do something" for them cannot lead to constructive gratification in the sense that it will produce higher states of psychic integration. At best, the patient may achieve a defensive stabilization which may be reflected in greater comfort. However, this is usually a precarious and temporary adjustment.

I have found that once I become aware of my inability to respond to needs that neither the patient nor I understand, the easiest path to follow is that of analysis. I find it is an effective way out of a dilemma since the analytic viewpoint does not require me to become involved at the level of content. Instead, I can view the patient's overt and covert demands in terms of intrapsychic forces and their relationship to the defective functioning of various ego systems. The patient's material is not seen as a problem per se but his productions are viewed in a broader perspective. Using analysis the therapist is not faced with an impossible request; rather, he tries to understand what is happening in terms of psychic determinism. Engaging once again in a familiar frame of reference makes the analyst more comfortable, and his comfort is transmitted to the patients. This, in itself, may be instrumental in making the patient analytically accessible.

Chapter 26

The Analytic Setting and the Treatment of Psychoses

As we move further into the matter of applying the psychoanalytic method, we must face the question of what type of case is analytically treatable and what modifications of technique are required because a patient cannot fulfill a "condition" that is believed to be necessary in order for him to be analyzed. Extending psychoanalysis to the treatment of schizophrenic patients has been a rather controversial matter. It is often felt that such patients can be treated psychotherapeutically but not psychoanalytically. The psychoanalytic clinician is obliged to decide which patients he will treat; the patients we encounter frequently do not fit the standard categories that we were led to believe were psychoanalytically treatable.

Freud (1915a) said that schizoid patients had narcissistic neuroses and therefore could not form a transference. I will not discuss the matter of whether a transference occurs since many analysts (besides myself) believe that it does and that it can be managed therapeutically (Boyer, 1961a; Boyer and Giovacchini, 1967; Little, 1966; Searles, 1961b; Modell, 1963). Rather, I will focus on two topics: (1) the relevance of the analytic process to specific aspects of the psychopathology of the schizophrenic or other severely disturbed patient, and (2) whether there are special technical features and modifications required for the treatment of certain psychotic patients. I am not speaking of modifications that represent a departure from analysis, but of techniques that are particularly relevant to characterological or schizophrenic pathology and constitute, in themselves, particular facets of the analytic process. As I hope to demonstrate, such maneuvers represent a stronger adherence to psychoanalytic technique and not a temporary abandonment. Both topics require us to consider whether and how contact is established with such patients, thereby making therapeutic engagement possible.

Besides the lack of transference, what special problems are presented by severely disturbed patients so that they are believed to be analytically inaccessible? Perhaps the most important and uniformly agreed upon problem is a high degree of reality distortion. These patients are thought

First published in *Tactics and Techniques in Psychoanalytic Therapy,* Vol. I, ed. P. Giovacchini (New York: Jason Aronson, Inc., 1972), pp. 222–35. Reprinted by permission.

to be so withdrawn and narcissistically fixated that the therapist and therapeutic situation has little meaning to them (Freud, 1924a, 1924b).

The lack of contact with reality also creates difficulties in the transference resolution. Some analysts who feel that psychoanalysis is not possible with such patients admit that there is a transference but, because of its psychotic delusional nature, believe that it cannot be resolved.

Undoubtedly, there are many patients who are so out of contact that it would be ludicrous to attempt a standard analytic approach with them. Let us consider, however, just what are the special characteristics of their withdrawal and whether it would be possible in cases that were not rigidly fixated to create an atmosphere where such obstacles could be overcome. Could some patients benefit from an analytic relationship if it were "offered" to them? Or must we make the a priori assumption that other methods and parameters have to be employed?

The Analytic Setting

Psychoanalytic treatment needs to be understood in terms of the psychic processes that take place in the context of interlocking frames of reference. There are, of course, two persons present, the patient and the analyst. The patient's orientation embodies the whole gamut of his developmental experiences and their psychopathological elaborations. The analyst, on the other hand, tries to maintain as much as possible an orientation based primarily upon his professional experience. Although all levels of his personality are to some extent involved, he still has a way of looking at things that differs fundamentally from the patient's experience. The therapist's ability to keep his frame of reference from becoming enmeshed and confused with the patient's will determine whether psychotherapy is possible.

For the purpose of this chapter patients can be divided into two groups—those who come for treatment more or less on their own and those who are forcefully brought for professional help (usually in a hospital). My experience has been almost exclusively with the former group. The differences between these two groups may perhaps determine their treatability. In the few instances in which I saw involuntary patients, I noted that some could become involved in an analytic relationship when I offered an analytic setting from the beginning. Often it became apparent that the patient had manipulated others to "force" him to do what he actually wanted because he was unable to do so himself. Patients are often unable to make spontaneous choices because of the constrictive qualities of their psychopathology.

Something happens to the patient's usual adjustment. His defensive balance becomes upset. His frame of reference, so to speak, loses some of its earlier integration. The paranoid, for example, constructs a world of persecutors. He lives in that world, perhaps not too comfortably, but he makes an adaptation. He becomes a patient because he is no longer able to hold his private world together. *The analyst seldom sees paranoids in his office; rather, he sees patients who are no longer able to be paranoid.* The patient wants to repair the "rent" in his defensive adaptation; he wants treatment to reestablish his usual equilibrium. Generally speaking, he wants the therapist to enter his private world and supply what has been lost in his decompensation. He comes to treatment with a particular frame of reference and tries to put the therapist into it. The analyst's frame of reference has to be congruent with his. The patient, hoping to establish a relationship that will correspond to his level of psychopathology, attempts to blend the two frames of reference. These maneuvers vary in form, depending upon the specific psychopathology. Some patients want an omnipotent savior who will help both to maintain and to vanquish persecutors. Others are unable to continue projecting in their daily life and need a therapist to make up for the lack of external objects that can be used for defensive purposes.

Winnicott (1949) writes of how the mother may "impinge" upon her child because she is more concerned about her own narcissistic needs than with him. She reacts when the child is not needful and neglects him when he is. In his treatment of such children, Bettelheim (1964) carefully avoids repeating what the mother did.

What should be emphasized is that the patient wants the therapist to intrude. Intrusion may take many forms. It is analogous to Winnicott's "impingement" and consists of any behavior on the part of the therapist that is designed to gratify instinctual needs or to support or undo a defense. The patient uses various defenses to get the therapist to intrude, *including withdrawal.* This may at first seem paradoxical because if intrusion is as traumatic as the mother's early assaults, why should the patient seek to repeat a painful situation? Before decompensating, the patient was able to adjust in some way to a traumatic reality, and he finds that it is even more painful to have this adjustment disturbed (chapter 11).

For example, a young, hospitalized schizophrenic man said almost nothing spontaneously and when he spoke his words were practically inaudible. The patient was being interviewed by me so that his case could be discussed in a class for psychiatric residents. His presenting illness was characterized by severe withdrawal, even though he had always been a shy person. I could either respond or not respond to the patient's withdrawal. Responding meant asking questions (for example, trying to take a history) in a fashion that would not let the patient get too far away. This is sometimes referred to as getting the patient engaged or helping him maintain his hold on reality. As his later behavior indicated, he was extremely ambivalent about effecting a symbiotic fusion with me. He wanted to get emotionally close but feared being swallowed up and thereby annihilated. Still, he wanted the megalomanic support he felt such a fusion would give him. As with all defenses, withdrawal protected him from merging with an external object but it also represented a wish to do so and a fantasy of having done so.

By responding to the patient's withdrawal, I would be intruding into his world, providing the patient with someone to withdraw from; thus, he could justify his defense. He could not withdraw from a vacuum. *A defense has to be in context with a segment of the environment; it requires some support from the outside world for the ego to be able to maintain it adaptively.*

In this case I tried not to intrude, but to some extent I had to. This may be a criterion of treatability. To the extent that a patient will not let the analyst *not intrude* he becomes decreasingly analyzable; there are schizophrenics who will not relate at all unless the therapist intrudes. Perhaps the regressed catatonic is an extreme example; by being mute and immobile he "forces" those around him to deal with him in a nonanalytic fashion.

To repeat, the patient tries to reestablish his former equilibrium by incorporating the analyst into his defensive system. This results in a situation where the patient cannot separate the analyst, as analyst, and the analyst as an archaic object; he cannot distinguish between the therapeutic relationship and his general environment. Paralleling this is a blurring of ego boundaries to the extent that the patient cannot distinguish between behavior initiated within himself and his own reactions to external stimuli.

Because of the schizophrenic's primary-process orientation, the therapist's intrusion is experienced as similar to his mother's "impingements" during early childhood. Longitudinal studies (Spitz, 1965) demonstrate that this type of maternal behavior makes it difficult for the child to construct a coherent self-representation. The mother's motives are usually destructive, and she does not recognize the child as a separate entity; rather, she sees him as a hated, narcissistic extension of herself that she has to rescue from her destructiveness. The psychodynamics of the mother-child relationship vary, but it has been repeatedly demonstrated that the mother's impinging behavior brings about a defective character structure. Thus the child's identity sense is imperfectly formed and his autonomous potential is submerged (chapter 3).

Schizophrenic patients have especially severe characterological problems and their autonomy is minimal. They do not see themselves as separate and distinct. Because of their extensive use of such primitive defenses as splitting, denial, and projection, they find it especially difficult to decide what feelings emanate from within and what behavior is motivated by the external world. The therapist's intrusion makes this distinction even more difficult.

The young schizophrenic man tried to provoke intrusion by withdrawing; there were long periods of silence, vagueness, and inaudibility. At times he was so incoherent that his speech was like a "word salad." Instead of responding to him by asking him to speak louder or questioning him for the sake of clarity, I eventually interpreted what I believed were the motives underlying his behavior: to withdraw from me by both hiding from and confusing me. Of course, there were also many exhibitionistic elements, but these were not essential for understanding the general movement within our interaction. The patient then blamed his inanimate surroundings for his behavior. Since our interview was videotaped, he had much reinforcement from the environment: camera, lights, and the knowledge that eventually he would be seen by an audience. Still, it was obvious that he was trying to avoid expressing feelings about me; he emphasized what was *around me* and then became inaudible and talked about the past.

It became apparent that the patient did not want to acknowledge that he had any specific feelings about me at that time that originated within himself. Therefore, I asked him what he believed *I* felt about him, and he spoke relatively freely. I assume he felt free to speak because he was being asked about someone else's feelings. In any case, he indicated that I must hate him and find him an unworthy person. Then it became my task to show him that these feelings were the outcome of projections— that these were attitudes he had about himself but attributed to me. In other words, I was attempting to keep our frames of reference separate by attributing his feelings, defensive or otherwise, to intrapsychic sources.

When he asked me what I wanted from him, I said that I was there to listen to what he *chose* to tell me—that I would respect his decision either to reveal himself or to withdraw, if that was what he needed to do. Following this interchange, his previously detached and seemingly apathetic demeanor changed dramatically. He complained of stomach cramps, yawned, and showed considerable anxiety. I said nothing. Then he got up and agitatedly walked around the room. He asked about leaving and headed for the door. Again I did nothing to stop him, hoping to indicate that it was for him to decide whether to stay or leave. As a result, he was unable to make a decision; he reached for the doorknob and then walked back into the room, and then repeated this maneuver several times. Finally I pointed out that part of him was eager to reveal himself but that he also perceived this as dangerous. (I believed I was referring to his ambivalence about symbiotic fusion.) I also said that this was a problem that originated within himself and that it might be amenable to psychoanalysis. He visibly relaxed.

My aim was to keep the patient's feelings in the consultation room. If I had taken a family history, for example, he would have been able to escape into the past and the world outside. He could have avoided his current reactions which, because of their immediacy, were able to be examined. I wanted to indicate that his responses were intrapsychic in origin and, to some extent, had adaptive value. If I had asked this patient to free associate, I believe he would have interpreted it as another imposition he could resist. To order someone to be spontaneous (the fundamental rule) is in itself a contradiction. On the other hand, to let the patient "choose" what he will or will *not* say leads to an intrapsychic focus. Since I did not participate (intrude) in the patient's frame of reference, he found it increasingly difficult to blame the environment, that is, attribute his behavior to factors outside himself.

A schizophrenic patient does not feel as though he defensively withdraws because of an inner problem; he uses outside circumstances to justify his behavior. In this way the patient is relieved of responsibility for his actions, and so he can successfully continue to project. To deny responsibility for his actions also means, however, that he is vulnerable. He avoids acknowledging his psychopathology by blaming others. On the negative side, this deception and relationship with the outer world submerges his potential autonomy. This submergence may result in a defensive stabilization but it also makes further development and ego structuralization difficult.

When I spoke of autonomy, the young schizophrenic man's equilibrium was upset. By stressing that it was up to him to decide whether our interview would take place and whether he would speak, I indicated that I was doing my best not to submerge his potential autonomy. Afterward the patient began to experience a glimmer of autonomy through an awareness that he was withdrawing because of something within himself rather than because the outside world was forcing him to do so. He paced back and forth when withdrawal was no longer an effective defense. He began to acknowledge that he had wishes of his own (for symbiotic fusion) that might destroy him; however, these were his *own* wishes and they were manifestations of a core autonomy.

I believe that to the extent that there is some manifestation of autonomy, a patient is treatable. This autonomy may be hidden at first, but if the therapist and the analytic setting can lead the patient to feel, even minimally, that he can make decisions, analysis is possible. The analytic setting is designed to enable the patient to understand that there, at least, he has some freedom to choose.

Interaction Between the Analytic Session and the External World

Stepping outside the analytic situation by becoming part of the patient's life may lead to stability, but such therapeutic maneuvers by themselves are likely to produce fixations. The patient's primary-process orientation will be reinforced and there will be no movement in the direction of structuralization. Strachey (1934) referred to this psychotherapeutic situation as a mutual delusion of patient and analyst, although in some instances it may endure and be adaptive.

What is lacking in this blending of the frames of reference is the opportunity for the patient to achieve states of regression within the context of the analytic structure. The segment of time the patient spends in the analyst's office differs significantly from the time he spends elsewhere. Sometimes a patient isolates his psychosis to the office, while he behaves fairly rationally in his everyday activities. This occurs because the analyst has not participated in the patient's defensive struggles and can thus become the recipient of his transference projections. On the other hand, especially during the early phases of treatment, some patients behave sanely in the office and delusionally outside. Both of these examples illustrate the structuralizing qualities of a stable, reliable analytic environment (Winnicott, 1955). The consistency of the session and the fact that it has a beginning and an end help structure the experience so that it is unique and separate from the rest of life. When the patient's insanity is restricted to the analyst's office, there is considerable reassurance in the fact that at a specified time his regression will, to some extent, end.

A middle-aged schizophrenic woman spent most of her time during the hour crying, whining, and asking for nurture (sometimes literally). She emphasized how miserably helpless she felt and how totally paralyzed and incapable she was. Before treatment I had learned from the referring colleague that she lived a completely chaotic life. After six months of analysis this same colleague reported to me that this woman's behavior had changed to an extraordinary degree. Although she was still rather disorganized, she could conduct her life in a reasonably orderly fashion. Gradually she began to report episodes in which she had been able to master situations that previously would have been insurmountable. Then she revealed that she spent most of her time "talking to me." Whenever she had a problem or began to experience anxious tension, she fantasied that she was talking to me as a *patient talks to an analyst.* This was always a calming and organizing experience. Apparently this patient had succeeded in taking the structuralizing element of the analytic session (even though her behavior was quite regressed during the hour) into her daily life and using it adaptively.

Technical Considerations

Regardless of the specific interaction between patient and analyst, the question still arises whether one should modify the analytic approach when treating psychotic or severely disturbed patients. Instead of discussing purposeful deviations from analysis, I will deal with modifications thought to be within the context of analysis. These are technical considerations that are part of the analytic approach; opening gambits and maneuvers, of course, vary according to the patient's psychopathology and the analyst's style. Do patients who suffer from severe psychopathology have to be approached differently from those whose ego is better synthesized?

One modification was impressed upon me some years ago when a colleague saw one of my patients in consultation. This female patient in her thirties had developed such an intense paranoid reaction toward me that it could not be used for therapeutic purposes. Initially she had been referred as a "classic" phobic. Her beginning sessions were characterized by both dependency and idealization. She responded to interpretations as if they were correct, but, as I learned later on, she was not particularly attentive to their content. Instead, she felt she was gaining omnipotent goodness by absorbing within herself the magic she attributed to these interpretations. During this period of analysis we seemed to have a good rapport. In spite of our apparently good relationship, she was unable to gain any insight that might lead to higher levels of integration.

As her primary-process-oriented demands were invariably frustrated, her friendly demeanor gradually changed. She stopped glorifying our relationship and idealizing me; she became aware of a mounting anger. Her rage was handled by projective mechanisms. At first she felt mildly paranoid about me, but later it increased to the point where she felt the only thing wrong in her life was my persecution of her. These feelings could have been utilized but the patient did not want to continue treatment. Leaving treatment could constitute an adjustment, but in order to justify herself she sought consultation with a colleague. Her reactions to the consultant were extremely interesting. She started the session by being extremely dependent and positive, but as the hour passed she gradually became suspicious and paranoid. In the span of one session she reenacted our entire three-year therapeutic interaction.

Regarding my patient, the consultant's report indicated a panoramic miniature recapitulation of what had occurred in treatment. The patient's transference seemed to cover the same ground in one session as it had in three years of treatment. This reenactment occurred spontaneously since the consultant did not probe nor was he aware of the details of the patient's difficulties in treatment.

The young schizophrenic interviewed on videotape caused me to wonder whether I had altered my interviewing technique. Of course, the encounter was different from one that would take place in a private office because it was to be displayed for classroom purposes and there was no intention of initiating an ongoing relationship. In trying to overcome my own anxiety (which subsided surprisingly quickly), I was not particularly aware of how I was conducting the session. However, the patient tried to use the unique aspects of the setting for defensive purposes, and soon it became apparent that the source of his anxiety was somewhere else.

When I looked at the videotape later on, I concluded that I had been somewhat more active (intrusive) at the beginning of the interview than I would have been in my own office. To some extent I attributed this to my anxiety and my eagerness to impress the psychiatric residents favorably. Silence might not have been detrimental to analytic treatment but it would have been very dull for the class. I wondered if some other approach (regardless of the setting) would have encouraged the patient to speak more freely, and I wondered if ordinarily I would have made so many interpretations in a first session.

There were certain similarities between the videotaped interview and the consultant's report on my patient. The interview seemed to anticipate the probable course of treatment if it had been undertaken. The patient began by withdrawing and defending himself against acknowledging that he was attempting to withdraw from the interviewer. Later, after a few interpretations and questions, he acted out his ambivalence about symbiotic fusion. Because this acting out threatened to disrupt the interview, I offered a final interpretation about his ambivalence.

For some patients to enter analysis, they may need a replication at the outset of possible future therapeutic progression. In reviewing case histories of schizophrenic and borderline patients it is clear that some would not continue with the interview if the therapist did not initiate some activity or indicate some direction. Other patients, however, do not want the analyst to interfere with their spontaneous streams of association. Among the former group I have tried to modify my approach in the same fashion I did in the videotaped interview. Of course, it is impossible to know how therapy would have progressed with some other approach, but it seems likely that the patients who appeared to need a panoramic prevision of "things to come" could not otherwise have formed a therapeutic alliance. It is also difficult to predict how the other group would have reacted, but their associations and some of their past therapeutic contacts indicate that they probably would not have remained in treatment if the analyst had tried to guide them.

It is not easy to distinguish one group from the other. Generally, however, the patient with whom one has to anticipate the future course of treatment is taciturn and sometimes visibly frightened and withdrawn. He seems to be less integrated or to have less defensive stabilization than those in the other group.

In reviewing the data about both groups of patients, it was interesting to note that a "panoramic" first dream was only reported by those patients who did not want the therapist to be active. (A panoramic first dream is one that often occurs at the beginning of analysis, outlining in a sweeping fashion the structure of the neurosis and depicting the sequence of the unfolding of the transference neurosis or psychosis [Freud, 1900]). Five patients in the seemingly better integrated group had such panoramic dreams, three of them on the eve of the first interview; none in the other group ever reported such a dream.

Fragmentation of the ego was, however, clear in the dreams of those patients who did not have panoramic dreams. Frequently, especially during the early phases of treatment, their dreams reflected specific defensive patterns. However, in the dream these patterns were not connected with other aspects of psychic functioning, such as other defenses or underlying conflicts. For example, the dreams of a patient whose initial defense was withdrawal (not too unlike the young schizophrenic man) consisted of hiding in holes and caves. His dreams seemed to be fragmented from the general associative stream; although they were quite revealing, they were not comprehensive, panoramic dreams.

Patients who want the therapist to take an active part seem to need a synthesizing experience. Although fragmentation represents a primitive defensive adjustment, there may be considerable anxiety if the patient feels there will be more uncontrolled fragmentation. He may perceive analysis as a force that will disrupt his precarious equilibrium. If an initial interview can, in a sense, outline the course of the unfolding of the transference, the patient may receive considerable reassurance. Just to have someone around who perceives him as a totality is a stabilizing experience. Even though the patient's self-understanding is distorted and fragmented, he is, at some primitive level, aware of his psychic organization. He can only perceive certain aspects of himself at a particular moment and cannot integrate them with the rest of his personality. By actively demonstrating the unfolding therapeutic drama, the analyst can show the patient that there is a fundamental unity to his psyche. He needs to know that the analytic setting will provide a structure. Although analysis may stimulate regression and further fragmentation, it will take place in the context of an observational frame of reference that is designed to promote synthesis and secondary-process organization. The panoramic interview will reassure the patient that the analyst is, to some extent, aware of the total picture and that there is more to the patient's psychic organization than the fragmented element he perceives at the moment.

Those patients who would react to the panoramic interview as an intrusion are also fragmented and use fragmentation as a defense, but at times they are able to view themselves as a synthesized whole. The fact that they have panoramic first dreams may indicate this capacity, but they are not *always* able to effect synthesis by viewing themselves as a whole or mastering problems with the external world. They hope to regain this diminished or failing capacity in analysis. The analyst does not need to supply specific integrative experiences directly, but the analytic setting may provide a context in which the patient can pursue cohesive individuation without hindrance.

Summary

The analytic setting is discussed in terms of emphasizing whatever autonomy the patient possesses. Once the patient recognizes that there are two frames of reference—his psychopathologically distorted one and the analyst's nonintrusive, observational one—he can acknowledge that he is to some extent responsible for his nonadaptive or defensively adaptive behavior.

Some patients need an initial analytic experience where the course of the analysis is demonstrated, so to speak, in miniature. This type of interaction may be essential for severely fragmented patients whose capacity for synthesis is minimal, whereas for other patients who can function in a better integrated fashion such an approach might be considered an intrusion.

Chapter 27

Interpretation and Definition of the Analytic Setting

Interpretations aimed at overcoming resistance are believed to be the essence of psychoanalytic technique. The setting in which insights are communicated to the patient is one where regression and transference projections predominate. Within this framework, interactions between the patient and analyst can be scrutinized in detail. Working with patients who suffer from severe psychopathology makes such an examination mandatory, and certain technical concepts we take for granted in work with better integrated patients may be seen in a different perspective.

For example, the *goal* of undoing resistances, one that most analysts accept unquestionably, may not be as feasible as Freud had initially thought. The concept of resistance as something to be "overcome" creates an atmosphere, a moral tone, that is antithetical to the analysis of many patients, especially those suffering from severe psychopathology. True, looking at the personality in terms of layers and strata of opposing forces that should be dealt with from the surface downward is a useful and orderly approach. Analysis of resistance, however, is not the same as overcoming resistance, and what may seem to be only a trivial distinction can, in fact, be that which distinguishes analysis from an exhortative struggle to make the patient give up something in the interest of analysis. The latter is really a managerial intrusion, which does not help the patient acquire insight nor foster autonomy.

Freud made rules about such things as patient decision-making, free association (the fundamental rule), and abstinence. Such rules were believed to be necessary in order to make the patient recall events rather than translate his feelings into behavior that would dissipate tension which might otherwise be amenable for analysis. No matter how well motivated the therapist may be, I have found that such rules are, to some degree, always felt as an intrusion by the patient; they signify to him a need to dominate his life and suppress whatever residual autonomy he might have. True, there are always a few intrusions—paying the fee, using the couch, even coming to the analyst's office—but the rules of

First published in *Tactics and Techniques in Psychoanalytic Therapy*, Vol. I, ed. P. Giovacchini (New York: Jason Aronson, 1972), pp. 291–306. Reprinted by permission.

abstinence (including the withholding of secrets from the analyst) constitute an added burden on the patient's symptomatic adjustment; the few intrusions mentioned are usually related to the needs of the analyst and are not, as a rule, a significant aspect of the patient's adjustive modalities. By "forbidding" certain behavior, no matter how analytically rational it may seem to be, the analyst is trying to do away with something that, in itself, demands analytic scrutiny. I have found that a number of British analysts sympathize with this viewpoint, and some of them even approve of the recommendation that we delete the word "resistance" from our technical vocabulary because of the opprobrium that is now attached to it, even though Freud used the word in a more benign sense and did not view resistance in moral tones.

Restrictions, in general, are difficult to impose. Even though patients want to cooperate and seem to comply with the doctor's instructions, they still behave, by and large, as their inner needs dictate. More often than not, both the analyst and the patient deceive themselves when they believe that they have agreed upon the conditions necessary to establish an "analytic contract." The very word "contract" seems inappropriate to me when an analyst is discussing a relationship that is designed to achieve states of higher ego integration in the patient and to release his autonomous potential.

Student therapists usually find it difficult to impose any kind of restrictions upon their patients, or, if they do, they grossly caricature an analytic stance. The student therapist's behavior is mechanistic and robotlike, and soon it is readily apparent to the patient that he is following some prescribed technique. When supervising residents, especially beginners, I have often heard them admit that they feel foolish and presumptuous in authoritatively telling another person, sometimes of comparable education and often older, how to live his life. The resident's practice of forcing himself to do something that he finds uncomfortable, or of caricaturing without integration, cannot be therapeutically successful.

Since many analysts adhere to a rigid diagnostic distinction of what is treatable and what is not (and consequently consider some psychic states as "good" for analysis and others "bad"), they obviously do not accept patients with a traditionally untreatable disorder. Some analysts, however, will modify their treatment in view of their belief that the more standard analytical approach is contraindicated. This usually means that they do more than merely interpret transference projections; for example, they may give advice, try to educate the patient, and set up conditions for his conduct at the beginning of treatment.

Other analysts (for example, Greenson, 1967) believe that the optimal conditions for analysis will come about once there is a good "working alliance." This expression is somewhat similar to Zetzel's (1956) "therapeutic alliance," although she points out that hers does not emphasize activity and purposeful work as much as Greenson's. In any case, Greenson believes that the positive feelings that a patient develops toward his analyst motivate him to look at and work on his problems. He feels that an alliance based on confidence and trust in the therapist is preferable to one where the patient tacitly follows the analyst's edicts.

In a working alliance there is only a minimum of transference in the patient's reactions, that is, the bulk of the alliance is based upon rational, realistic factors and not upon primitive, unconscious, infantile feelings. Technically, a negative transference should not develop until a working alliance has been firmly established, and such an alliance is an indispensable condition for analysis.

Concepts such as working alliance and therapeutic alliance are enjoying widespread acceptance today. Because psychoanalysts are commonly using these terms, one may assume that they are saying something significant about how psychoanalysis occurs. Words evoke images, and the concept of an alliance between a patient and his analyst has an inherent appeal. To me, this concept is much more attractive than that of contract. But does the combination of this particular adjective and noun actually introduce a new idea? Is such a combination part of the modern analytic theme, that is, does it have technical implications about how and what to treat? For example, does it implicitly advise the psychoanalyst to tone down the initial development of negative transference and warn that such alliances do not (or are less apt to) develop in cases described by Freud as narcissistic neuroses?

Both Sterba (1934) and Strachey (1934) developed concepts about ego functions and introjects in the analytic process. Sterba wrote of the ego's self-observing function and said that such a function was a prerequisite for analysis. Strachey emphasized that gradual changes occur in the introjects after a "mutative" interpretation has been made; these changes, in turn, facilitate the assimilation of further insight, and thus there is a positive feedback. Psychopathology, on the other hand, is characterized by a vicious circle—a cycle of projections and introjections. Since interpretation focuses on the distortion created by the transference projection, it interrupts the process of re-introjecting an ever increasing number of primitive, disruptive, and, of course, constrictive elements. Both authors explore the therapeutic process in a detailed fashion, especially in terms of ego subsystems.

Strachey's formulations would not, of necessity, lead clinicians to reject patients who suffer from characterological defects for analysis. It is also conceivable that negative transference could be utilized at the very beginning of treatment. Still, the idea that the patient must have some positive feelings toward the therapist in order to be able to start treatment is valid. The analytic setting has to engender some feeling of comfort and trust, and the analyst's relaxed attitude can help to bring this about. If the patient felt nothing but hatred for the analyst at the outset, and even if he could recognize that this was an irrational response, it is not likely that he would remain in treatment. Something else has to be present—something positive—which can coexist with an intensely negative transference so that is can be analyzed.

Many therapists, past and present, have written about this positive factor. The majority cannot describe it precisely, but they agree that this element affects the analyst's ability to create an appropriate setting—one in which the patient will not feel overwhelmed by anxiety. The analyst can communicate security and calmness as well as his effort to understand the patient's psychic processes; his aim is to foster a setting in which both regression and insight can occur. Gitelson (1962) said that the analyst feels less anxious and depressed than the patient, and Spitz (1956b) spoke of the diatrophic attitude; such factors must be recognized as part of the working alliance.

All descriptions of what the analyst does to engage a patient in treatment remain vague. This may be due to the fact that there are many variables and that each analyst has a different, but perhaps equally effective, style. On the other hand, if one tries to explain the analytic process in terms of ego concepts (as did Sterba and Strachey), there may be some common conceptual denominators that have diverse manifestations at the behavioral level.

I have often heard analysts speak of patients being "in analysis." This presumably occurs either after a trial period or after certain resistances have been overcome. What happens prior to being in analysis is considered undesirable and antianalytic and something that should be dispensed with as quickly as possible. I believe, however, that a patient is in analysis from the first moment he enters the office. Actually, the concept of being in analysis is, in my opinion, antianalytic. If the therapist views the patient analytically from the beginning and does not convey to him the idea that he has to "achieve" a particular point of view in order to be in analysis, the atmosphere is likely to be relaxed and the patient has more of an opportunity to become interested in what is going on inside himself. I also believe that the theoretical foundation of this type of interaction can be elaborated by focusing on those exchanges between the therapist and patient that are the essence of psychoanalytic treatment.

Although interpretation of the transference is believed to be the chief mode of communication in analysis, there is disagreement about what aspects of the transference should be interpreted, and when. It is not even clear whether the content of the interpretation is particularly important. Many analysts who adhere to the classical position may permit themselves other forms of communication, but they believe that only the transference interpretation is analytically relevant.

I believe there is considerable merit in the classical position and have usually found that my difficulties in treating patients occurred when I abandoned the interpretative approach. However, from time to time, I have found myself saying something to a patient that did not seem to be a transference interpretation, and yet I had the conviction that I was analytically "correct" and the patient's subsequent behavior seemed to bear out that conviction.

Dr. D. W. Winnicott illustrates this point splendidly (Giovacchini, 1972). One of his patients became inspired after accomplishing something that previously, because of inner constrictions, had been beyond his capabilities. He then chided his analyst by asking him why he was not equally excited. Dr. Winnicott replied that although he was not *as* excited, he had not despaired as much either. Later, he added that he was, indeed, excited but not elated; presumably he was referring to the patient's hypomania (see also chapter 22).

On the surface, this interchange does not seem to be a transference interpretation. Dr. Winnicott is responding to the content and apparently not exploring the patient's motivations for wanting him to be excited nor their transference implications. Still, I (and others with whom I discussed this interchange) had the firm conviction that Dr. Winnicott responded to his patient in a "correct" analytic fashion. In fact, some of my colleagues (who did not know my purpose in presenting the material to them) never even suggested that there was anything unusual about this interchange. The patient's subsequent behavior in the consultation room also indicated that the flow of the analysis had not been disturbed at all; in fact, it seemed to have been enhanced.

In the interchange Dr. Winnicott was telling his patient that he was capable of reacting and having feelings about what the patient did in his daily life; on the other hand, he spelled out the limits of his reactions— indicating the boundaries and stressing his control. He did not become either as excited or as desperate as the patient; he was only moderately excited, not elated or hypomanic. In essence, Dr. Winnicott's reactions retained considerable secondary process and were not enmeshed with the patient's psychopathological extension of his feelings. In effect, Dr. Winnicott explained that he saw himself reacting as a reasonable human being who has empathic feelings toward his patient and who is pleased by his patient's progress and further ego integration. In this way, Dr. Winnicott was, in a subtle fashion, also defining the realistic limits of his patient's reactions and indicating the quality and extent of his own counterreactions. He was, in fact, defining the *analytic setting*.

I have learned that patients suffering from characterological problems (a group that Freud felt was unsuitable for analysis) require definitions of the analytic setting at various stages of their analyses. The content of the definition varies, depending upon the dominant material and affect, but the definition always tries to clarify the same element. The analyst emphasizes his function, indicating that he reacts to the patient's feelings as intrapsychic phenomena that are interesting and worthy of under-standing. He specifies that he is not reacting to the content per se; rather, his frame of reference is primarily an observational one in which he does not feel elated or despairing or, in other instances, seduced or threatened by what he observes. His purpose is to understand both the intrapsychic sources and the depth and significance of the patient's productions. This is equivalent to maintaining an *analytic* attitude; by defining the *analytic setting* he is conveying this attitude to the patient.

Defining the setting if often a useful "intervention" when the patient feels threatened by uncontrollable regression. It is understandable that the analyst will do what he can to make the analysis less painful, for if it should become too disruptive, it could no longer continue. Many thera-pists have explained how they handle such situations; they frequently write about clinical situations similar to the one presented here by Dr. Winnicott. As mentioned earlier, the content of the interaction will vary but the communication received by the patient will indicate how much protective stability there is in the analytic setting. Dr. Winnicott makes this point explicit when he speaks of the reliability of the analytic hour and says that the analytic setting also defines the limits of regression.

I believe it is also useful to define the analytic setting when the patient is not particularly disturbed. (This procedure need not be limited to patients suffering from disruptive psychopathology or to moments of decompensation.) There are specific indications for this technical maneuver regardless of the category of patient or phase of treatment. Defining the analytic setting often facilitates analysis, even if the patient responds with silence or "resistance." The transference aspects of the patient's feelings can become clearer, and he may find himself capable of understanding their significance. Since defining the analytic setting is another technical factor (in addition to transference interpretation) that seems to be necessary for analyses, it appears that we are dealing with two closely related but nevertheless *distinct* factors. Defining (and thereby creating) an analytic setting could be considered supportive. Because the patient receives reassurance, he is better able to investigate the transference further. Moreover, defining the setting could lead to the formation of a working alliance.

Here is another example of how the analyst's attitude and orientation help create a setting that may be conducive to analysis. When the analyst conveys to the patient what he expects the "ambience" to be, he is explicitly indicating that he will behave in a specific fashion; no matter how much the patient may wish to introduce another level of interaction, he will not succeed. The analyst will confine himself to psychological realities, thereby enabling the patient to see his productions in terms of their intrapsychic origins. The supportive and reassuring aspects of the definition help to make integration of the transference interpretations possible.

Furthermore, distinctions between support, definition of the analytic setting, and interpretation, I believe, are to a large extent metapsychologically inconsistent. I hope to demonstrate that *the definition of the analytic setting is itself a variety of transference interpretation.* If this is true, there is no distinction between this kind of support and analysis, and it would no longer be necessary to separate the working alliance from the activity of analysis.

If an analyst says that he will not respond in the same way as the patient, either the analyst or the patient is reacting idiosyncratically. Analysis always assumes that in certain respects the analyst is more integrated than the patient. The patient accepts this assumption; otherwise he would not seek analysis with that particular analyst. Dr. Winnicott said that he would not let his feelings develop beyond a certain point. The fact that his patient's feelings went beyond that point was unique to that patient and an outcome of his psychopathology. His expectation that Dr. Winnicott would feel as he did represented a *transference expectation.* In this case the patient projected his feelings and expectations onto the analyst. This constituted a projection of infantile responses; even though the patient continued to attribute such feelings to himself as well, the portion that he projected was transference. By keeping his observational frame of reference separate from the patient's, an analyst thereby indicates that his reactions are different and that some of the analysand's reactions are due to transference expectations. When an analyst tells a patient that many of his feelings are the result of transference, he is taking a step in making a transference interpretation. Dr. Winnicott, in replying to his patient, was correcting the transference distortion, thus emphasizing that the patient's reactions were idiosyncratic, or at least different from his own. This "difference" can become a subject for further investigation. Dr. Winnicott was not simply telling his patient that he was not his father or mother (a type of confrontation that I have seldom found effective), but was actively demonstrating transference distinctions in the current affective setting. Defining the setting leads to recognition of transference. It distinguishes the frame of reference in which material is to be scrutinized and also tells something about what is being projected.

Thus, the patient finds himself—together with all of his archaic introjects and infantile orientations—in an environment that does not "blend" with these distorting and psychopathological elements. Defenses, in order to be integrated into the psyche and to be adaptive, have to be supported by the environment. There must be a congruence between the intrapsychic structure and the external world so that defensive interactions can maintain their adaptive qualities. To some extent congruence always fails and the degree of failure will determine whether the patient seeks treatment. Still, the patient attempts to create a setting where his projections need not be viewed as projections. Insofar as the analyst specifies what the frame of reference will be, he is introducing an element of order and is creating an environment in which the patient's reactions and attitudes will be highlighted—clarifying which reactions and sources emanate from within and which from without.

In such a setting, time distinctions become blurred. The past is the present; the patient can more vividly perceive his experiences if they are not confused with external realities. Analytically speaking, the only reality is the here-and-now of the consultation room. The patient cannot remove himself from his feelings by retreating into the past. It is not significant if the patient views the analyst as his father; what is important is the content of the projection itself in terms of its adaptive or maladaptive qualities.

Every analyst recognizes the unique features of the analytic frame of reference; what has not been sufficiently emphasized is that the setting itself *helps the patient to consolidate his ego boundaries and to see himself as a separate, discrete individual.* The analyst, by affirming this setting, communicates that he is different than the patient. Thus, there are three combinations of people in the consultation room: (1) the patient-analyst combination, a transference fusion; (2) the analyst as analyst; and (3) the patient as a person. An explicit reference to the analytic setting indicates transference, specifically an acknowledgment of the symbiotic fusion. Defining the analytic setting is intended to resolve the fusion; it represents a reliving in the present of an early developmental phase. Although defining the analytic setting seems, on the surface, to be different from the usual interpretative activity, when viewed in terms of clinical theory, it has all the ingredients of a transference interpretation.

The value of analytical activity whose aim is to resolve the symbiotic fusion is apparent in patients who are suffering from severe psychopathology, such as borderline cases and schizophrenia. However, even with patients whose egos are relatively integrated, explicit statements about the analytic setting help to create a favorable environment. Although such patients probably have fewer developmental defects and less fixation upon the symbiotic state, *every transference, insofar as the patient retains within him some portion of what he projects onto the analyst, represents a fusion; and to the extent that it does, it is a replication of the symbiotic phase.* The difference between the so-called healthier and the more disturbed patient is one of degree. Insofar as the patient has a capacity for transference projection, he also has an element of symbiotic fixation. True, the better-integrated patient develops transference displacements on objects that are thought to be more whole than part-objects and he may use displacement mechanisms in addition to projection. To some extent elements of projection and fusion become apparent during the analytic regression. In a healthier patient such elements are often displayed in a less stormy or disruptive fashion than may occur with more disturbed patients; nevertheless, they have to be resolved in order for analysis to be effective in creating a developmental progression as higher states of ego integration are achieved. Even analyses of so-called classical patients are directed at characterological factors as well as at resolution of the oedipal complex.

Certain characterological modalities, such as fusion, are believed to be specific for primitive ego states. Nevertheless, even among patients with relatively well-integrated egos, one finds evidence of fusion during the transference regression. This should not be surprising because if one accepts the existence of a symbiotic fusion as a beginning developmental phase, one should expect its persistence in the context of more integrated superstructures. During regression it can become activated once again. Consequently, when the patient's expectations of the analyst are similar to his own, he is, at some level, demonstrating a fusion mechanism. Depending upon the principal ego orientation, there may be other psychic mechanisms as well. However, viewing any psychic interaction in terms of a hierarchical continuum enables us to detect the more primitive elements of this continuum as they become energized, or at least partially energized.

Definition of the analytic setting refers (sometimes indirectly) to the patient's attempted fusion with the analyst or to his defense against such a fusion, as, for example, when he wants to keep secrets. Precisely how does one define the analytic setting? As mentioned earlier, such definitions vary and can occur in many different analytic circumstances. Perhaps a few brief examples can indicate at least minimally what is meant by defining the analytic setting. In many instances, it is far from apparent (even to the analyst) that he is engaged in such activity. Dr. Winnicott, in the clinical material referred to, interpreted to his patient that "satisfaction annihilates the object for him. He had obtained some satisfaction last week and now I, as the object, had become annihilated." This is, from any viewpoint, a transference interpretation. Later, Dr. Winnicott said, "I made an *interpretation* concerning the continuation of my interest during the period in which I seemed to be annihilated" (italics added). I was fascinated by Dr. Winnicott's comment—"I made an interpretation"—because it refers to his interest and does not say anything explicit about the patient. Unlike his reference to satisfaction and annihilation, this comment was not an obvious transference interpretation. Still, I believe he was quite correct in his assertion that he had made an interpretation, and the subsequent material flowed smoothly. In my opinion, Dr. Winnicott was showing his interest in being a transference object. His comment also emphasized that he did not feel threatened by the patient's wish to annihilate him; rather, he implicitly stated that he was available for transference projection—an important attribute of the analytic setting. The fact that he was interested meant that there was a phenomenon that interested him—the patient's feelings—and the specific use of himself in regard to these feelings communicated to the patient that there were two separate persons in the transference context. This is a type of transference interpretation; in this instance, the patient continued to unfold the transference and began to understand how he had used frustration (a symptom) to protect the object—in this case, the analyst—from being annihilated.

Another example comes from my own practice. During the course of free association, a patient confronted himself with a situation that he could not understand. He remained silent for several minutes and then, by his expression and exclamation, indicated that he had had a sudden insight and now understood what had previously puzzled him. Quite spontaneously he stated that he was not going to tell me what he had discovered, and he seemed very pleased. Equally spontaneously I said that all that mattered was that he knew; it was not necessary for me to know. Both the patient and I felt very strongly that my statement was correct; it had a tremendous impact on him and facilitated meaningful, reversible regression. Clearly, the patient understood that I was not envious of his autonomy. The analytic setting produced an environment where he could withdraw from an object who, he believed, wanted to engulf him yet also respected his need to withdraw. The setting enabled the patient to feel that the analyst (or analytic situation) might rob him of his individuality and that he was free to react to that feeling. On the other hand, he realized that I would do nothing to reinforce those feelings. The patient could permit himself further regression and fusion because the analytic setting, by affirming his "right" to withhold (a transference defense) made it unnecessary for him to continue defending himself so rigidly. Since I would not be destroyed by his withholding, he could continue to use me as a transference figure and eventually reach the implicit recognition that he was defending himself from an engulfing imago that he had projected onto me. Defining the analytic setting as a place where he could keep secrets from me was a way of interpreting a transference defense.

These interpretations of the setting eventually lead to the formation of what I have described as a solid *analytic introject*. The patient incorporates the setting, thus enabling the analytical attitude to become a characterological modality. The therapeutic (or working) alliance is similar in many ways to the concept of the analytic introject, but my formulation does not require a distinction to be made between the generally healthy parts of the ego or feelings that are relatively free of transference. The analytic introject is a specific introject that undergoes constant revision and, hopefully, gradually gains more secondary-process qualities.

During the initial stages of introject-formation, the introject may react as if it were a foreign body. Gradually, however, the introject becomes integrated until it is finally incorporated (amalgamated) as an aspect of the ego's executive system. The development of the analytic introject is basically the same as the development of any introject. However, insofar as it is formed in the context of an analytic relationship, it has certain unique qualities, particularly self-observing and autonomous elements. The transference interpretation is an integral factor in the formation of such an introject, but the concept of transference now includes the definition of the setting. Such concepts lead logically to a further extension of the range of applicability of the psychoanalytic method.

Part V

PSYCHOSOMATIC CONSIDERATIONS

As mentioned in the preface, psychosomatic medicine can present a transition from clinical medicine to psychiatry and then to psychoanalysis. The following papers are grouped in this final section and would ostensibly represent a chronological reversal. Nevertheless, I believe there is some logic in this seemingly incompatible arrangement.

Perhaps one can think in terms of a full circle. To recapitulate, there is a natural flow from the study of bodily processes to a focus upon a combination of somatic and mental variables and finally to an exclusive concentration upon psychic operations. The last lies within the domain of psychoanalysis, especially when one directs oneself toward psychopathology. One can now proceed further and extend the domain of the psyche to include some control and domination of somatic spheres. Increased knowledge about mental processes, structure of the psychic apparatus and developmental factors contribute to an enriched understanding of the subtle interplay between psychic and somatic forces. Rather than focusing upon the traditionally historical approach, which asserts that the mind can be understood best by an organic approach, that is, by the study of its somatic constituents, here I am emphasizing an opposite viewpoint. Knowledge of psychic operations and developmental vicissitudes will teach us considerably about somatic processes and somatic dysfunctions and, as the last paper in this series emphasizes, this applies to diagnostic considerations as well. However, I must assert that this is a point of view, a useful one indeed, but not mutually exclusive of an approach that is initially somatic.

These papers are parallel to all the other papers in this volume. One can think in terms of a microcosm. In the previous sections there is a general movement from an id-oriented approach to psychopathology to an approach that is predominantly but not exclusively focused upon the ego. In a more circumscribed sense here, there has been a movement away from psychodynamic aspects of somatic problems to one which concentrates upon psychic structure and maldevelopment. The latter may not have the melodramatic and inherent appeal of specificity theory but it seems to be a better conceptual basis for understanding the somatic phenomena patients present to us. Perhaps, we are dealing with features common to all scientific fields. First, one's enthusiasm is stimulated by bold and ingenious speculations and formulations. This phase is then followed by sober testing—in psychoanalysis this means treating patients—and is finally followed by ostensibly less dramatic but more serviceable concepts.

Chapter 28

Some Affective Meanings of Dizziness

Vertigo is a common symptom of neurosis. Fenichel (1945) stated that vasomotor disturbances, frequent among the manifestations of affects, are channels for emergency discharge whenever direct motor activity is blocked. He further stated: "Often sensations of equilibrium . . . become . . . representatives of infantile sexuality in general. Many persons who have no conscious memory of having masturbated as children do remember various games and fantasies involving the [position] of their bodies in space, . . . changes in the size of their bodies, . . . ideas [that] their beds [are] being turned around, or of still more vague sensations [that] something is rotating." Federn (1928) traced anxiety about disequilibrium to repression of more archaic pleasures. Freud (1905b) was the first to discover a relationship between infantile sexuality and the erotization of equilibrium.

Others have discussed vertigo primarily in terms of its pregenital aspects. The dizziness of Bacon's patient (1948, p. 134), for example, was related to a conflict between oral receptive needs and his compensatory striving for independence. This forty-year-old man would become dizzy after some such receptive pleasure as reading, "dizziness apparently being an expression of his infantile desire to return to the dependent state of the infant who cannot maintain its balance without the help of others." Ferenczi (1924, pp. 239–42) ascribed the dizziness of a patient to his unwillingness to give up the gratification of feeling passively loved by the analyst. French (1929) noted this symptom in a patient who wished to be carried about in his mother's arms, and it represented a dependency conflict.

There is great vagueness about what "dizziness" means unless a patient is asked in detail about his symptoms. Neurologists define vertigo as a consciousness of disordered orientation of the body in space (Brain, 1940). The patient experiences a sense of rotation of his body or of his surroundings. In the latter, the external world may seem to move, usually in a rotatory fashion though sometimes other forms of movement such as oscillation are described. He may have a sensation of falling, or the sensation of movements may be referred to a body part, such as his

First published in *Psa. Q.* 27 (1958), 217–25. Reprinted by permission.

head; his lower limbs may seem to be poorly coordinated. Vasomotor disturbances including pallor, perspiration, tachycardia, hypertension, nausea, vomiting, and diarrhea are common.

Dizziness usually appears either as a transient state or an incidental finding. Among three patients in psychoanalysis, the first gave a history of vertigo during adolescence; in the second case it was present only as a transference symptom; in the third, it had been diagnosed as Ménière's disease.

The first patient was a twenty-four-year-old single woman for whom life had "little meaning," but who was not clinically depressed. She was attractive, had lovers, but became attached to none of them. She led an active social life, had a variety of intellectual and other interests, and was financially independent. Still, she gave the impression of having an intense inner conflict which almost completely depleted her energy.

She was the only child of an erratic, alcoholic father and a sympathetic but ineffectual mother. Her father could be very charming and understanding and showed considerable solicitude when he was sober or when he felt guilty about his behavior. His actions bordered on seductiveness. In the middle of the night he would come into her bedroom and sit on her bed just looking at her. If she acknowledged being awake, he would engage her in light banter. Her reaction to this peculiar nocturnal habit was a mixture of fascination and repulsion, the latter especially when she detected the odor of alcohol on his breath.

Her memories of family life were dominated by recollections of parental quarrels during which her father not infrequently became physically abusive. Her mother repeatedly threatened to leave him, but the patient soon learned that these were meaningless gestures. Whenever the patient became angry about her father's behavior, he would then turn against the child and beat her, the mother making a feeble attempt at what was at best a token interference. Unlike her mother, the daughter fought back and tried to avoid getting hurt. There were times when the father would chase her around the house or try to break down the door of the bathroom in which she had locked herself. She would either wait for him to fall asleep or spend the night at a friend's house. The patient learned to expect no protection or effective support from her mother.

Coincidentally with the menarche in her fourteenth year, she developed an interest in theatrics, and discovered that her absorption in acting protected her from feeling as distressed as she had been. She was told she had talent for acting, with a realism and sensitivity that were unusual for an amateur. To her it now seemed that her real feelings were expressed on the stage and all other feelings she experienced were synthetic. She was aware of some purpose in this arrangement. On the stage she could anticipate what would happen and allow herself to react; the unpredictable threatened to overwhelm her. It was during these initial experiences on the stage that she first became dizzy. The following is a typical situation.

At seventeen, during a party, she persisted in exploring a young man's wallet despite his agitated protestations. That she discovered what she was seeking is attested by her seeming belated recognition that she found and displayed a condom, whereupon she felt dizzy. Other episodes of dizziness, not so well recalled, were inferentially associated with a similar state of "surprise." In each, it was clear that unconsciously she was expressing an exhibitionistic or voyeuristic impulse that her ego could not suddenly assimilate. Whenever she suddenly had a precipitous surge of sexual feeling, when her usual defenses were not mobilized, she did not know which way to turn and experienced the sensation of dizziness. When she approximated gratification of her genital sexual needs, her fear of being suddenly overwhelmed disappeared.

A second patient's dizziness occurred only in the transference. She was a thirty-year-old unmarried high school teacher in treatment because, although she had numerous women friends, men seldom paid any attention to her. She had a natural bent for many sports and although she was proud of her skill, she had come to realize that it served to keep away men who did not like being beaten by a woman.

An only child, she had been reared strictly by possessive parents. Her father she described as a martinet and a petty tyrant about the most trivial matters. She was, however, able to fight with him and often won the argument, at which point he would walk away in disgust. The mother was stingy, suspicious, and taught the patient that all men were stupid and not to be trusted. She often told her daughter in detail the suffering she had endured from intercourse on her wedding night.

At twenty-three the patient had considered marrying a man who seemed eminently suitable, but both parents were so bitterly opposed that she broke the engagement. Her intense hostility and consequent feelings of guilt kept her helplessly bound to her parents. She seemed to be perpetually seething with rage, some of which she discharged in competitive sports, mercilessly beating her opponents, male or female. The patient gradually became aware of her pugnacious attitudes. She found it easy to express her rage at her father, but it became apparent that her anger toward her mother was far more intense. She reconstructed from memories that her mother had inculcated the belief that to be a woman was a painful degradation.

Finally, after a bitter struggle with her parents and her conscience, the patient moved into an apartment of her own. At this point she had homosexual dreams which revealed that her masculine identification served as a defense against destructive heterosexual feelings. Her concept of the sex act was one in which she would be killed.

One day she reported the following dream: "I was in a party dress. It was a beautiful day. A man in a gray suit came to me and we walked together. All of a sudden the sky became dark with black clouds. I was frightened." She awakened feeling that she had had a nightmare.

The evening before she had been at a dance and for the first time seemed not to frighten men away. In fact, a rather attractive man had been with her most of the evening. During one of the dances he led her to a dark corner and suddenly pushed his erect penis against her. Although initially she had felt that the dream was innocuous, she had repressed the experience with the man at the dance, and she recalled it with considerable resistance as an association. She then remembered that I frequently wore gray suits. As soon as she became aware of the connection between me and the man in her dream, she was overcome by a feeling of dizziness; she felt that the room was spinning and the couch turning. These sensations lasted for approximately thirty seconds, and she then composed herself.

The patient continued her associations but made no further comment about the dream. When I questioned her about what she had said regarding my wearing gray suits, she was unable to recall that she had said so. I then quoted what she had said and went on to add that I was the man in the dream. At this point she was again overcome by the sensation of vertigo, this time more intense and lasting perhaps twice as long. After recovering, she had repressed the whole dream.

That the erotic transference was only slightly disguised gave the dream its nightmare quality. Subsequently, each time her associations or the interpretations led her to an awareness of her sexual transference, she reacted with dizziness. Her ego was unprepared to cope with the forbidden wishes of her oedipal conflict. Her ego for the most part was able to keep potentially dangerous sexual impulses repressed. It was during the transference neurosis, when oedipal feelings were intensified and breaking through the bonds of repression, that she first experienced vertigo. The wish to have a child by her father then became apparent, and the process of childbirth, or the possibility of her having children, was considered unconsciously as so dangerously destructive to her that at first it led her to the verge of panic. Later in the treatment all such reactions disappeared.

The third case, a forty-year-old woman, had an intensification of phobic symptoms that she had had in a milder form as long as she could remember. They included fear of the dark, of going out on the street alone, of shopping, of going to the dentist, and a general insecurity in her object relationships. It proved that she was presently more anxious and depressed because her husband had recently begun having friendly relations with his first wife.

Born in Russia, the first of two children, she had experienced innumerable hardships in childhood. She recalled pogroms during which her parents took elaborate precautions that the family might survive. When she was nine years old the family emigrated, and the enterprising father established himself successfully in business. She felt that she was his favorite child, and idealized him. He was unpredictably kind and gentle, or erupting in fits of anger. More disturbing to her was his impulsive seductiveness which would occur when she least expected it. While he was being unpleasant to everyone in the house, he would suddenly seize the patient, draw her close to him, and sometimes kiss her fully on the lips. These vagaries kept her in a state of vigilant tension. She dared not be caught unawares. At adolescence she had become so keenly sensitive and alert that it would be impossible to face her with an unfamilar or an unanticipated experience.

Later she was employed with success as a secretary. She felt sufficiently secure in a routine with a friendly middle-aged employer—the father of a family—whom she admired so much that for ten years she devoted herself almost exclusively to her work. She was at this time a virgin thirty years old. One evening, when she had worked late, her employer proposed marriage to her. She had to grip the table for fear that she would lose her balance and fall to the floor. She felt that the room was whirling around furiously, and she was nauseated. Thereafter these sensations recurred periodically, often lasting as long as several hours and accompanied by tinnitus. Medical consultations established a diagnosis of Ménière's disease, though she was considered somewhat young for this syndrome. Tests indicated a slight loss of hearing. Treatment for an allergy was instituted, and she improved. She gave her employer no definite answer to his proposal, and he did not press her, presumably because he was not divorced.

A month later he had intercourse with her. The patient believed she was taken completely by surprise. Consciously she was not displeased by this event. Soon following, however, she had a sudden severe attack of "Ménière's disease," and her various phobias became defined. During the two years that her sexual relation with this man continued, she came to note a relationship between some of her attacks and sexual intimacy.

Ultimately married to her employer and mother of a child, she continued to be haunted by feelings of guilt. Symptoms of vertigo and phobia continued although not to the degree of disabling intensity. She was aware, she said, of a certain "strange sensation of surprise" whenever her husband made sexual advances, which she defined as guilt and a vague sense of uneasiness. Still employed in her husband's business, she tended to consider her relationship with him as it had originally been. It transpired that whenever he made love, she was repetitively "shocked and surprised." This eventually irritated her husband and he began to see his first wife again. The patient felt that she was now being punished for her illicit relationship with him. She was frightened and depressed.

Discussion

The similarities among these patients are an intense need—engendered by early experiences—to suppress and repress responses to hypercathectic stimuli. They tried to control their feelings; they attempted to avoid situations where there might be undue stimulation. Their childhoods were highly emotionally charged with experiences with their fathers. They strove consciously to avoid any life experiences which would recreate these past traumata. Because intense affects were so painful, they had developed attitudes of preparedness to meet any situation without being overwhelmed. Consequently they lived in a state of extreme caution, anticipating any contingency. Their repetitive compulsion was to plan their lives so carefully and categorically that their object relationships would not catch them unawares; otherwise a delicate balance would be upset. These features are closely related in each instance: strict self-control by constant vigilance; powerful repression.

These three patients were, of course, sexually inhibited. This was not so obvious in the first patient. But in her case she was frigid and sexual relationships were meaningless. All three patients developed symptoms when they became aware of genital sexuality, either in reality or in the analytic transference.

There were also similarities of instinctual patterns. Each of these patients had repetitively seductive experiences with their fathers and were prematurely sexually stimulated. They were both fascinated and repelled and, according to the well-known reaction in such instances, they believed sexual relationships to be brutal, violent, destructive experiences for a woman. The symptom of dizziness occurred when there was a consciously unexpected stimulation of sexual feelings.

Greenacre (1947, 1950) discusses sexual traumata and precocious sexual stimulation in the first two years and in the prepuberty period. In each instance she notes particular somatic reactions such as visual disturbances and headaches, as well as specific character defenses such as "masochistic justification for a defense against sexuality."

However, what seems to have been specific for the evocation of vertigo in these instances is not simply a sexual conflict, but the way the ego may react momentarily when it is overwhelmed by a precipitous surge of previously well-repressed impulses which in these cases happened to be sexual. This occurs in an ego that has been rigidly disciplined to anticipate such stimuli. Why the repression that had previously functioned so well should have become weakened is determined by individual case study.

Summary

The symptom of dizziness in three women is found to have similar ontogenetic influences and closely allied precipitating factors. Characterologically, these patients had many similarities. These women had been precociously sexually stimulated and their constantly vigilant egos tried to be prepared for any situation that might lead to sexual excitement. The three patients developed sensations of dizziness in response to unexpected sexual stimulation. The symptom, in each instance, was correlated with a disturbance of psychological equilibrium.

Chapter 29

The Ego and the Psychosomatic State

Many investigators, Alexander (Alexander, French et al., 1948) and his coworkers, Margolin (1953), Grinker (1953), Deutsch (1953) and numerous others, found that a psychotherapeutic relationship revealed meaningful data that could be organized into a theoretical framework and thereby add to an understanding of psychosomatic reactions.

Elsewhere (Giovacchini, 1956), I discussed the fruitfulness of investigating patients who were found to have two or more coexisting syndromes, each of which could be considered from a psychosomatic viewpoint. Here I will report two cases, both of them in psychoanalytic treatment. Although there were no coexisting organ neuroses these cases were especially interesting in that during treatment they recovered from one somatic symptom and then developed another which had never previously existed. This phenomenon is well known but will be explored further in terms of the transference neurosis, with special focus on the ego's operations. I shall attempt to correlate levels of ego integration and psychoeconomic shifts with the somatic syndrome. Naturally, in summarizing the psychoanalytic data I have had to extract from a voluminous mass of material.

Clinical Material

Case 1. A thirty-seven-year-old, married woman, mother of two children, sought therapy because of free-floating anxiety and a variety of obsessive ruminations. These symptoms dated back to adolescence but had become progressively worse during the last several months since she had begun to suspect her husband of infidelity.

Her obsessional ruminations consisted of feelings of wanting to knife her children, two girls, ages twelve and fifteen. In earlier years, similar feelings were directed toward her mother and her only sibling, a nine-year-younger sister.

The history establishes that the earlier disturbance began when she felt that her father's attention was being shifted from her to the sister. She had been her father's favorite up to that time but he then started

First published in *Psychosom. Med.* 21 (1959), 218–27. Reprinted by permission.

giving his attention exclusively to the sister. The patient found herself turning to the mother but considered her a poor substitute, as she was a nagging, complaining woman with a "martyr-like demeanor." The patient became withdrawn, shy and submissive, felt herself to be a frightened, insecure, and inadequate person who was no longer aware of her anger, but noted the onset of destructive thoughts.

Concurrently with these symptoms, the patient developed headaches which were later diagnosed as migraine. She suffered from episodes of pounding, "explosive" left hemicranial pain, gradually increasing in intensity over a period of one and a half to two days, reaching a peak and lasting for another day, and leaving her in a state of prostration and utter exhaustion. These symptoms were ushered in by visual scotoma and were accompanied by nausea. They had occurred once or twice a month for twenty-five years. Otherwise the referring internist found no evidence of illness, and reported a blood pressure of 124/82.

Therapeutic Course and Somatic Changes

The initial material concerned a seemingly endless preoccupation with feelings of inadequacy and guilt over the content of her obsessional ruminations. Her behavior in the analysis was like her mother's, nagging and complaining. She never showed anger directly, but always presented herself as much abused (especially because of her husband's indifference and caustic behavior) and as one who was constantly taken advantage of by her demanding family. Nevertheless, she categorically denied ever experiencing anger. On the contrary, she saw herself as a docile, submissive person who could not understand why others, particularly her husband, ever felt anger towards her, since hostility was something she hardly ever felt in her adult life. She could recall early angry feelings towards her sister, which she believed she had outgrown.

The dream material, however, revealed manifest content such as war, death, and destruction, atomic bomb explosions, and other cataclysmic elements and clearly pointed out the underlying instinctual state. When she had a dream involving only a minimum of secondary elaboration, one usually stimulated by a fairly active interpretation of defenses against hostile impulses, she would awaken with a migraine headache. Up to this point in the treatment, she had not yet been able to feel angry.

After about eight months of therapy, repressed anger entered consciousness and she had great difficulty in controlling its expression. The migraine, although constantly present for twenty-five years, disappeared and has not returned (four years have now elapsed). Nevertheless, the patient was neither thankful nor pleased by this symptomatic relief, for she had found the ensuing emotional state even more intolerable than the previous excruciating pain. From time to time she would find herself struggling with every ounce of energy she possessed against expressing what she considered dangerous quantities of anger. She believed herself actually capable of murder and that if she lost control she would "blow up" or "fall apart."

The transference neurosis made it possible to understand the instinctual frustrations responsible for her previously repressed anger. As she indicated the relevance of her past to the current situation, significant genetic material emerged. Her mother was described as a withholding, ungiving woman who manipulated others by "parasitically devouring." Consequently, the patient had to seek security elsewhere, from the father. The father was able to supply such needs even though he, too, was described as a selfish person. He sought object relationships insofar as he required an audience; and as a child, the patient loved him. Toward her mother, however, she felt an all-consuming rage at finding herself abandoned. The father was her "savior." When he turned his attention to the newborn sister, at a time when the patient felt especially insecure because of the emotional upheaval of puberty, she felt betrayed and once again as if she were going "to fall apart."

During treatment the patient had other reactions of both a psychic and somatic nature along with the emergence of destructive impulses. At first she feared such impulses would destroy her; and in the transference showed the characteristics of a helpless, panicky infant. She was plagued by anxiety and would state, "Please help, please help me. I beg you to help me. I am eating myself up." In this infantile state she was unable to carry on simple functions such as cooking, shopping, driving the car, etc. She felt isolated, desolate, lonely and abandoned. Physical examination at this time revealed a hypertension of 200/110.

The patient had always been plagued with the thought of dying and concerned about her physical status. Consequently, she had frequent checkups with her family physician who ascertained that her blood pressure rose from a normal level to a hypertensive one in a period of three months. This period coincided with the above-described transference state.

After about six months of this turmoil she felt able to handle the expression of her feelings. She thought herself competent and, although still aware of the immense quantities of anger, no longer feared that she would "let loose." Her attitude was that now her life could be serene.

Her internist, however, reported increased hypertension which averaged 260/140 in spite of medication. Ophthalmological examinations revealed a beginning hypertensive retinopathy.

I will not present the rest of the course of her analysis except to point

TABLE 1.   Summary of Clinical Data and Shifts in Ego States

Somatic Symptom	Ego State
A. Migraine	Well defended. Obsessive-compulsive character structure, anger being deeply repressed
B. Migraine disappears, hypertension first discovered	Breakdown of defenses. Ego is "flooded" with anger that is consciously suppressed
C. Hypertension with retinal changes	Confident of ability to control murderous impulses. Similar to A, but greater defensive stability. No anxiety
D. Hypertension disappears	Further breakdown of defenses. Regression to panicky, infantile, orally incorporative state. Anger openly expressed instead of suppressed as in B

out the shifts observed in ego states and to indicate the correlation between her hypertension and integration when her anger became manifest. On occasion, the patient would again fear loss of control and her ego state would become a primitive regressed one with open expression of rage. Somatically, to everyone's surprise, she would be much improved, with normal blood pressure, and disappearance of retinal changes. She presented herself in the treatment as a frightened, timid, self-demeaning person with an attitude of supplication. The patient found her general adjustment worse, but such coincided with the disappearance of hypertension. During the analysis, three cycles were observed, each consisting of two phases, regression accompanied by normal blood pressure, and repression of hostile impulses accompanied by hypertension. The first episode of hypertension occurred when she was suppressing anger, a condition described by Saul (1939).

Once the ego's integrity was restored, and her hostile conflicts were reconstructed from the genetic material and worked through in the current setting, she maintained normal blood pressure; whereas previously when she seemed to have control of destructive impulses, she was merely denying her anxiety and repressing the angry affect.

The above correlations are consistent with the conclusion of those who regard a somatic symptom as a defense against psychosis. Schwartz and Semrad (1951) have reported similar phenomena and many other investigators have reported psychoses resulting from or occurring at the time of the disappearance of such diseases as ulcerative colitis and neurodermatitis. I feel, however, that such cause and effect formulations are oversimplifications and ignore other relevant variables. Schur (1955) has considered the psychosomatic symptom as one of the somatic ego qualities* accompanying the particular emotional state with which it is associated. He further formulated that the primary process has its somatic counterparts.

Just what particular functional role the somatic symptom plays in the operations of the ego will be considered later after the following additional clinical material is presented.

Case 2. The next case, a thirty-three-year old scientist, complained of episodic left hemicranial headaches (diagnosed as migraine) that had been present since the age of thirteen. From a somatic viewpoint he was otherwise well.

In addition to the migraine, there was a variety of characterological features which caused him concern. He felt that his social life was narrow because he tended to isolate himself and to withdraw. His general demeanor was passive, as he stated, affecting not only social areas but particularly sexual and professional areas. He was unable to maintain a relationship with a woman for any protracted time. When he found the girl or himself becoming emotionally involved, he would behave in such a fashion that she would become angry at his lack of spontaneity or initiative, and finally give up. At work his colleagues and superiors were greatly impressed by his talents but dismayed by the fact that he never carried any research project through to its conclusion.

A brief summary of his past history indicated that he was an only child of emotionally disturbed parents. His mother was described as dominating, overwhelming, and unpredictable, subjected to fits of anger directed both at the patient and his father. He recalled many episodes during his childhood when she would be possessed by a "maniacal rage" and would descend on him, frequently beating him viciously for some minor misdemeanor. At other times he might get into serious mischief and receive only kindness and indulgence. Before he was thirteen the mother had been committed to a mental hospital three times. The father, on the other hand, was a mild, meek, permissive individual who was obsequious to the mother and never paid much attention to the patient. He

---

*Alexander (1950) does not feel, for instance, that the psychosomatic condition is a resolution or a somatic defense against an instinctual conflict (i.e., a pregenital conversion) but instead believes that the psychosomatic condition reflects visceral tensions that accompany psychic conflicts which cannot be expressed or discharged through higher mentational or integrative centers.

was ineffectual in his menial work. His interests were definitely constricted; he had no particular ambitions or hobbies and drank sufficiently to be considered a mild alcoholic. Neither parent suffered from any somatic affliction until old age. The mother had died of an arteriosclerotic condition in a mental hospital shortly prior to the patient's therapy. The father was senile and in a nursing home. The patient resented the fact that he was forced to take over the financial responsibility for his care. In general, his attitude toward his father was an extremely angry one, more so consciously than toward the mother; although he felt angry towards women in general and considered himself a confirmed bachelor and misogynist.

He left home when he finished high school. His life had been drab and gloomy, but he did receive some distinction because of superior intellectual abilities, and received scholarships through college. He was then hired in the department in which he specialized and where he remained up to the time of his treatment. While there he kept to himself, occupying his time almost exclusively with his work, but also indulging in the hobby of amateur radio.

Therapeutic Course and Somatic Changes

The somatic changes in this case were even more striking than those observed in the previous one. Here, too, the migraine soon disappeared. After three months of treatment, he had no further attacks, five years having now elapsed. The initial phase of analysis consisted of outpouring of anger toward his father, mother, self, and the world in general, for having treated him so unfairly. He cursed the fates for having given him such parents. He then reviled others, including the analyst, because they expected him to do things socially and professionally that he felt were beyond his constitutional capacity. He hated women simply "because they exist." He also hated his biological makeup for causing him to have disturbing sexual feelings that demanded gratification, but about which he felt helpless because of his hermitlike orientation.

His ventilation of anger did not cause him to feel any more secure, nor did he consider it to be helpful that he now had this opportunity to express these feelings. His migraine disappeared, although he was unwilling to connect this with the following events in the treatment.

In condemning the world around him he revealed that he was aggressively asserting himself. The material indicated that he was very insecure, thought of himself as professionally inept and generally inadequate, although all the evidence pointed to the contrary. He was afraid of people, saw himself as having many unmet needs, and often complained of not knowing why he existed—or what he was. He freely verbalized his vulnerability and the helpless rage associated with it, but then would quickly cover up such feelings with the self-assertive anger that was so much on the surface.

I interpreted his anger to him as a defense against the fear of finding himself completely helpless and abandoned. I felt that the dream material indicated a feminine identification with a psychotically angry mother in order to protect himself from the fear of being destroyed by her—an example of identification with the aggressor as classically described by Anna Freud (1938). However, I will not present the data that led to these conclusions since they are not relevant to the thesis to be expounded.

Confronting him with his defensiveness did not diminish the outpouring of rage but only served to make it more concrete. He now began to complain specifically that he never received sufficient care, attention and love, and as one might expect, verbally attacked me because I was not helping him, preferred other patients to him, and did not give him enough time, etc. His anger was now much more obviously a reaction to frustrated dependent needs *and it was specifically at this time that the migraine disappeared.*

Shortly after the cessation of migraine headaches the patient developed symptoms of bronchial asthma. Bacon (1956) has described the hostile, attacking qualities that she noted in some asthmatic patients. In this case there had been no previous history of asthma.

His asthmatic attacks occurred daily and the consulting internist found it difficult to control them. Similarly, his emotional state and behavior showed a marked lack of control, and his usual logical and coherent thought process now showed signs of disorganization. He felt he could influence others with his thoughts as well as destroy them by simply wishing to do so. He also felt that others were attacking and persecuting him. His behavior had a hypomanic quality in contrast to his usual reserved, inhibited and withdrawn demeanor. At this time his attitude continued to be cold, and he frequently said that he could not trust me.

In spite of his anger and what appeared to be a beginning schizophrenic process, the patient gradually began to experience deeper and warmer feelings toward me. This transference state unfolded gradually, the anger slowly subsiding as I constantly interpreted frustration of his dependent needs. He indicated his dependence on me and although at this point he was unable to verbalize any positive feelings, it became obvious that he was fond of me and his verbal attacks became less and less frequent. The manifestations of ego disintegration also ceased. Instead, he appeared a somewhat proper, dependent person who put himself completely at my disposal. He hung on every word I said and gave the appearance of a person who would naïvely follow any direction given to him.

The asthma, too, gradually subsided, appearing less and less frequently, each attack being milder than the previous one until it disappeared altogether. This transference shift occurred over a period of approximately a year. Skin tests showed numerous sensitivities and when repeated three years afterwards (even though the asthma did not return) continued to show the same sensitivities, a phenomenon that has been recorded by numerous other investigators.

His emotional state became one of calm and relative comfort, but he developed epigastric distress and other digestive difficulties, symptoms which again were entirely new. Fluoroscopy and x-ray revealed the presence of a duodenal ulcer. The patient's placidity nevertheless continued and, in contrast to his earlier behavior, he did not complain or lament the cruel fate that reduced him to such a state.

It may be stated, parenthetically, that the patient also recovered from the ulcer. However, the ensuing emotional state was no longer a calm one but fraught with anxiety. At this time he had to face fundamental conflicts that would be interesting to discuss but somewhat tangential to the purpose of this paper.

In this case, then, we note the existence of three conditions that have been considered from the psychosomatic viewpoint. The migraine headaches, present for many years, disappeared very quickly during the initial phase of the analysis, when he was expressing anger but maintaining a state of stability and balance. Even before coming into treatment, this man had achieved an equilibrium in which he was able to function, though in a constricted fashion. A correlation, then, can be made between the existence of migraine and an ego state of relative stability.

During the asthma, on the other hand, the ego seemed to be in a state of dissolution. Phenomenologically, the patient behaved as though he were undergoing a general libidinal withdrawal, as one observes in an early schizophrenic process. The greater the disintegration the more frequent and intense were the asthmatic attacks. The instinctual meaning of bronchial spasm has been interpreted by French (1939) and other investigators as a suppressed cry of the infant desperately calling for the rejecting mother. In this case, too, the patient regressed to a state analogous to the desperately clinging child, who fears complete abandonment and starvation. Asthma, as a somatic accompaniment of disintegration, occurred when psychic equilibrium was disturbed by insatiable oral demands and rage. There was associational material that emphasized the lack of control of a poorly integrated ego, in contrast to the cases described by French. The patient often described an asthmatic attack in colorful language such as, "the feeling of suffocation seizes me. I believe that I am being cast away. My body feels as if it is going to fall apart, as if something inside of me, supplied from the outside, were removed, and my whole foundation crumbles. Nothing is going towards me. I can no longer breathe. Everything is taken away from me. Nothing is given to me. I can no longer breathe, I can no longer survive." This is an excellent description of asphyxia as well as of an ego experiencing the threat of disintegration because it feels abandoned, depleted, and unable to maintain contact with the external world.

With the disappearance of the asthma, there was a return to integration and balance. The ulcer became manifest when once again the ego had achieved balance, perhaps a comfort and placidity previously unknown to the patient.

Discussion

Aside from the question of causality, a temporal correlation certainly can be made between the state of ego synthesis and the occurrence or remission of the somatic processes.

That somatic states have some process connection with the ego is inherent in the concept of the ego, defined as including both somatic and psychic systems. These hierarchically arranged systems are integrated into the conceptual framework, ego.

I would like to consider two general kinds of interrelationships between a syndrome and psychic equilibrium that theoretically could account for these clinical data. One type of relationship is that in which the syndrome along with other factors can be considered as contributing to ego integration. In this sense, the condition could be considered as part of the ego's integrative system. In an emotionally impoverished person who has had a minimum of satisfying object relationships, somatic preoccupation or hypochondriasis can serve as a binding force holding the ego together. The emotional energy bound up in the symptom itself contributes to maintaining ego synthesis, even though the symptom represents a somatic dysfunction.

A second type of relationship between the somatic condition and the ego state is one where the organic symptoms are interpreted as dysfunctions associated with a regressive disorganization.

These two views are not mutually exclusive if we consider various levels of ego adaptation. Hartmann (1939), in his many contributions to ego psychology, has postulated conflict-free spheres of the ego that contribute to homeostasis in a nondefensive fashion. This indicates that

TABLE 2. Summary of Psychoeconomic Shifts

	Somatic State	Ego State	Dynamic Relationships
A.	Migraine present	Affective state of anger but a relatively stable ego	Anger represents an overcompensatory defense against a more basic cataclysmic hostility that is associated with a fear of ego disintegration and passive vulnerability.
B.	Migraine disappers. Onset of asthma	Helplessness and rage associated with ego disintegration	Underlying repressed factors in A are now being experienced and acted out in the transference neurosis. Unable to permit himself gratification from the therapy.
C.	Asthma disappears. First onset of peptic ulcer	Calm and placid. Orientation, a dependent and integrated one	Dependent transference. Previously frustrated oral demands are being, to some extent, gratified.

there is a hierarchy of levels involved in the handling of drive discharge. Rather than dealing with the specific drives and the conflicts attendant to them, as Alexander does in his specificity theory (Alexander, French et al., 1948), I would like to examine this hierarchy further in terms of what might on one hand be considered more primitive methods of handling psychic energy, and on the other hand more advanced methods that are the result of maturation and development. Landauer (1938) and Fenichel (1941) believe that massive affect discharge recedes with maturation.

If, because of its genetic development, the ego is unable to handle a particular drive through its higher integrative centers (secondary-process operations) the drive energy must be dealt with in a diffuse fashion by more primitive ego systems. The somatic system, or somatic ego, constitutes such a primitive system. Engel (1954) saw the loss of an object relationship as leading to a regression and to a more primitive mode of ego functioning that included the psychosomatic disorder. I wish to emphasize, too, that in a psychosomatic disorder the ego functions at a primitive level, more in terms of primary-process operations, and that the distinction between ego integration or disintegration becomes a relative one. If the somatic organization of the ego is compared with more refined, integrative, reality-attuned mechanisms, then on a comparative basis the somatic ego can be seen as less integrated. However, in view of the fact that it does maintain some kind of organization it also has integrative features. The psychosomatic symptom, of course, always represents dysfunction of an organ system, a system that has lost some of its previous organization.

Next, I would like to consider some variables which have relevance to the somatic state in my patients. Others may find different constellations and consequently different clinical pictures. Mirsky (1953) in speaking of multicausality demonstrated the existence of what might be considered a constitutional determinant. He also felt that such a factor became related with others and that the interrelationships between a group of variables determined whether a particular somatic syndrome would develop. Similarly, here, I believe that the interrelationships of several factors have to be considered.

The amount of gratification or frustration the patient experienced in the transference neurosis is a variable that can be specifically observed in this data. It is generally indicative of what the patient experiences in significant object relationships. The effectiveness of his ego defenses is another related variable, both of these reflecting the patient's general adjustment and transactions with reality. These variables are also important factors concerned with inner organization, i.e., homeostasis. They, therefore, have to be considered in terms of ego integration. The ego's integration would, in turn, indicate whether the organism is functioning and handling psychic energy at mature or primitive levels, i.e., in a reality-adaptive fashion or in terms of visceral patterns. It must be emphasized that no single variable can be considered alone and correlated with the somatic state. One cannot formulate a single dynamic pattern; rather a complex relationship between a variety of factors has to be investigated, if correlations are to be made.

I shall now consider my data in terms of these particular variables. The first patient had been able to keep anger repressed through the use of obsessive-compulsive defenses. Because of repression the anger affected the higher, reality-oriented ego systems only minimally, and this pent-up state was associated with migraine. One can see that if the ego defenses become inadequate as happened in this case, the previously pent-up anger can gain access to motility and discharge, threatening a disruption of higher integrative faculties leading to behavioral disorganization. When this occurred the migraine disappeared and hypertension was first discovered.

Reestablishment of defenses was accompanied by continued hypertension, yet conscious behavior showed good integration and a remarkable lack of anxiety. I would surmise that the intensity of repressed anger might have been less than in the previously well-defended state since the patient was receiving some instinctual gratifications through the transference neurosis. Why there was a shift from one somatic symptom to another is not explainable by these data and must involve other variables, perhaps physiological ones.

The second case further demonstrates the importance of the variable concerned with gratifications received from the outer world as observed in the transference neurosis. I believe Engel stresses the same variable when he focuses on object relationships. When this patient had headaches his defenses were to a large measure repressing anger. When decompensation occurred and defenses broke down, the somatic symptoms of asthma were first noted. Unlike the first case, who was also disorganized but able to demand and receive much dependent gratification from the analysis, this man had to withdraw from the therapist, feeling abandoned. He still erected barriers against the outer world and suffered an overwhelming frustration that disturbed the equilibrium of both deeper and surface levels. I do not mean to indicate that in other cases (as in the first case) all levels are not affected simultaneously. Relatively speaking, this case, through lack of external gratifications, suffered from greater frustration, that caused disturbance at all ego levels, whereas in the previous case the deeper levels obtained relief when defenses were relaxed. However, it must be remembered that even in the first case, during the beginning phases and first episode of behavioral disorganization, there was some hypertension.

When the patient developed an ulcer, his ego defenses kept anger repressed but were qualitatively different in that he did not erect barriers against certain dependent gratifications from the outer world. His level of instinctual tension was, for him, low.

One can see that in different circumstances varied psychological and somatic syndromes may be associated with differences in the defensive status, external gratifications and levels of ego integration. The maturational factors of ego development, its somatic and physiological components and their ability or inability to bind tension, all have to be understood further. Mahler (1952), from a psychoanalytic viewpoint, conceptualizes the development course of libido from a splanchnic-visceral position through a progressive cathexis outward onto the periphery of the body and finally to a perceptual conscious system. Here, too, a hierarchy of ego systems has been stressed, and the place of a particular somatic organization in the hierarchy, along with other variables, contributes to the final somatic outcome.

Summary and Conclusions

From observations of the transference neuroses of two patients, data have been obtained from two frames of reference, one dealing with psychic integration and the other with somatic dysfunction. As a consequence it has been possible to make a temporal correlation between the state of ego integration and the appearance or remission of a somatic symptom.

Migraine, hypertension, and peptic ulcer were seen to be associated with a well-defended state of psychic equilibrium, whereas asthma occurred when the ego seemed to have lost its unity and organization.

Rather than viewing the specific drives and the conflicts attendant to them, or the symptoms in terms of their defensive or tension discharge potentials, psychoeconomic shifts were correlated with ego integration. Since different ego states can be associated with somatic symptoms there must be a complex relationship between a variety of factors rather than any single dynamic pattern.

In this chapter, the object relationship of the transference neurosis and the stability of the ego defenses were considered as variables, relevant to the state of integration that determined the level (primitive or mature) at which the ego would function. From this material it is evident that tension was, at times, handled by primitive ego systems when other parts of the ego were defensively adjusted to reality.

The single affect consistently present was that of anger. However, since this study does not purport to investigate specific drives, it must be stressed that anger is not being considered on an instinctual basis. Angry tension is considered a sign of a disturbed homeostasis reflected in both psychic and visceral systems. Its origin certainly includes the frustrations and vicissitudes of early development.

Disequilibrium was reflected in the particular ego system handling the anger, in terms of behavioral aberrations and level of control, or in a somatic dysfunction. I believe the data are consistent with the thesis that frustration from failure of higher ego systems to achieve instinctual gratification in relation to objects, led to the development of libidinal and aggressive tensions that disrupted the integration of the lower, visceral, ego systems and contributed to the somatic syndrome. It is apparent that many factors rather than any single specific one, could contribute to this result.

Chapter 30

Somatic Symptoms and the Transference Neurosis

The transference neurosis, a crucial and characteristic aspect of psychoanalytic therapy, is also its most valuable research tool. Research in the field of psychosomatic medicine has taken many forms, but it is now obvious, as many have pointed out, that a psycho-analytic relationship provides a meaningful frame of reference for the understanding of somatic as well as of other processes.

Schur (1955) came to a variety of conclusions concerning somatization, which he was able to fit into the theory of metapsychology. He was able to detect certain characteristics which he considered significant for the patient who might develop a "psychosomatic disorder." In the cases he studied, dermatoses, he found a prevalence of narcissistic and pregenital elements associated with widespread impairment of ego function. His patient's object relationships were tenuous and characterized by extreme ambivalence. He thought these cases could be called "borderline states" and discussed somatization in terms of ego functions. He described a parallel between a prevalence of primary process thinking, the failure of neutralization, and the resomatization of reactions. He referred to an undifferentiated "psychsomatic" phase of development, a concept similar to Hartmann's (1939) undifferentiated stage of id-ego development.

I would like to extend some of these concepts outlined by Schur without necessarily dealing with those of neutralization or undifferentiated id-ego mass. However, an attempt to understand a somatic process that has been studied from a psychological frame of reference and in terms of its relationships to a variety of defences and other ego functions will also be made here. Regressive phenomena that so frequently seem to accompany the various diseases that have been studied from a psychosomatic viewpoint have been referred to by many authors, and their significance discussed from a variety of viewpoints. Greenacre (1945) and Bergmann and Escalona (1949) speak of a predisposition to anxiety and to regressive types of anxiety as contributing determinants to the choice of the reacting organ system. Margolin (1953) refers to a physiological regression, whereas Grinker (1953) thinks in terms of the

First published in *Int. J. Psa.* 44 (1963), 143–50. Reprinted by permission.

overloading of different ego systems leading to a disturbance in synthesis. Menninger (1954) also focuses on disruption of homeostatic regulatory ego functions under stress resulting in disturbed somatic responses.

These theoretical formulations can be reconstructed in the clinical setting. I would like to expand upon certain aspects of ego adaptation that are related to homeostasis and include somatic systems. In chapter 29 I was impressed by some patients who had two or three somatic disorders that have been psychosomatically considered. I reached certain conclusions about the significance of the disease process from a psychoeconomic viewpoint. Here I would like to discuss one of these cases further with special emphasis on the transference neurosis, since it served to highlight the significance of the organic illnesses. The changes in the physical condition could be directly correlated with changes in the transference neurosis. The various ego states accompanying each illness have been described in chapter 29. I feel that a more detailed study of the transference aspects of one patient will enable us to make some formulations regarding ego development with special reference to regulatory factors. This may add to our understanding of the relevance of object relationships, defences, and other integrating features to homeostasis and somatic disturbances.

The patient, a thirty-seven-year-old married woman, sought analysis because of free-floating anxiety and a variety of obsessional ruminations which included thoughts of knifing her children, aged twelve and fifteen. In earlier years, similar feelings had been directed towards her mother and her only sibling, a nine-years-younger sister.

Her recognition of a need for analysis was precipitated when she could no longer deny her husband's infidelity or the fact that her daughter was becoming a woman, as evidenced by the daughter's popularity with boys and her father.

The patient had been her father's favourite for the first nine years of her life. With the sister's birth, however, he started giving his attention exclusively to the new baby and turned away completely from the patient. She then found herself clinging to the mother, but considered her a poor substitute, as she was a nagging, complaining woman with a "martyr-like demeanor." The patient then became withdrawn, shy, and submissive, and felt herself to be a frigtened, insecure, and inadequate person.

Analysis revealed similarities between the current situation and that of childhood. Her husband travelled a good deal because of his business, was never particularly attentive to her, and was sexually passive and withdrawn. He was fairly discreet in concealing his numerous affairs from her but, as is usually the case, furnished her with some clues if she chose to pursue them. He began behaving seductively towards their daughter when she began to acquire secondary sexual characteristics. At this point, the patient's earlier competitive feelings with her sister were reawakened and the repressed rage associated with the helpless feeling of being abandoned and rejected became more intense. She was able to handle angry feelings with a variety of obsessive-compulsive defences, and at the time of beginning treatment was unable to recall or admit any conscious feelings of anger. Even though her thoughts were unmistakably destructive, they were "only thoughts," completely devoid of any affect.

Since the age of fifteen, her late onset of puberty, she had experienced typical migraine headaches which consisted of episodes of pounding, "explosive," left, hemicranial pain, gradually increasing in intensity over a period of one and a half to two days, reaching a peak and lasting for another day, and leaving her in a state of prostration and utter exhaustion. In a typical fashion, these symptoms were ushered in by visual scotoma and were accompanied by nausea and sometimes vomiting. The fact that her daughter had now reached the age at which she developed these symtpoms was striking. The patient spontaneously remarked that the daughter did not develop migraine and betrayed resentment over the fact that she "had to suffer" and her daughter could enjoy the frivolities of adolescence.

The development of the transference was especially interesting since various phases were accompanied by specific somatic changes. Her early associations contained a seemingly endless preoccupation with feelings of inadequacy and guilt over the content of her obsessional ruminations. Her behavior in the analysis was like her mother's nagging and complaining. In spite of this highly-charged material, she never showed anger directly, but always presented herself as much abused (especially because of her husband's indifferent and caustic behavior) and as one who was constantly taken advantage of by her demanding family. She categorically denied ever experiencing anger. On the contrary, she saw herself as a docile, submissive person who could not understand why others, particularly her husband, ever felt anger towards her.

The dream material, however, revealed manifest content such as war, death and destruction, atomic bomb explosions and other cataclysmic events, clearly pointing out the underlying instinctual state. When she had a dream involving only a minimum of secondary elaboration, one usually stimulated by a fairly active interpretation of defences against hostile impulses, she would awaken with a migraine headache. Up to this time, she had not yet been able to feel angry. Toward the end of the first year of analysis, the patient began to experience difficulty in maintaining her usual controls and in being able to feel herself the master of her emotions. She gradually became aware of angry feelings toward me, but did her best to suppress them. Whenever I made an interpretation of her death wishes as directed towards me, she became extremely anxious. As is so often the case, her associations would produce material that indicated a recognition of similar feelings toward her husband and oldest daughter. It became apparent that she was struggling desperately against expressing what she considered to be dangerous quantities of rage. She believed that she was capable of murder and that if she lost control, she would "blow up" or "fall apart."

The dreams were nightmares, and the underlying state was one of panic. As Schur (1958) has described, there is a complementary series of anxiety responses whose understanding is indispensable to formulations about the somatization process. This patient's rage represented an affective response to a panicky fear of dissolution which was associated with intense frustrations at various levels of psychosexual development.

She complained that I was not sufficiently interested in her because I was unable to recognize the intensity of her need to be taken care of. She became jealous of other patients and showed the usual manifestations of pregenitally oriented feelings of rejection and sibling rivalry. The transference neurosis made it possible to make genetic reconstructions. Her mother was recalled as a withholding, ungiving woman who manipulated others by "parasitically devouring." She used the defence of isolation to deal with such a denying and controlling mother. She also sought protection and security from the father and cast him in the role of a "savior," requiring an omnipotent object to fulfil this role, and the father, because of narcissistic needs of his own, was glad to play the part. When he turned his attention to the newborn sister, she felt betrayed and once again as if she were going to "fall apart."

The transference neurosis reflected all these disturbances, and she relived these frustrations in a very dramatic fashion. Anger was being consciously experienced, but expressed very cautiously and in limited amounts. She became helpless and displayed the traits of a panicky infant. She would cry out, "Please help me, please help me. I beg you to help me. I'm eating myself up." The signs of ego disintegration were general, and she was unable to carry on simple tasks such as cooking, shopping, driving the car, etc. She felt isolated, desolate, lonely, and abandoned. Even though she seemed to be asking for help directly, the material was by no means object-directed. Her movements on the couch, verbalizations, and emotional outbursts were of a random variety and never specifically focused toward the analyst. Even when she was pleading with the words, "Please help me," she did not seem to be talking to anyone in particular. I frequently questioned her about this point and she often acted as if she did not hear me or as though she was hardly aware of the fact that I was present.

From a somatic viewpoint, she reported the striking feature that the migraine had disappeared. After having been continually present for over twenty years, it cleared up completely and has not returned (five years have now elapsed). This patient, as one might expect, had always been plagued with the thought of dying and was very much concerned with her physical state. Consequently, she had frequent check-ups with her family physician, who ascertained that her blood-pressure rose from a normal level to a hypertensive one, 180/100, in a period of three months. This period coincided with the above-described transference state, and at least a temporal correlation can be made.

One might characterize the patient's reactions in the analysis as being dissociated ones. She reported several dreams which reflected her disturbed equilibrium and her longings and needs for nurturing. The manifest content consisted of houses crumbling around her, falling off boats and drowning, and falling through empty space. There were certain erotic components present, but what is most relevant to the present thesis is the fact that when the analyst was represented, he was usually in the background and at a very great distance from the patient. As previously stated, this was reflected in her behavior also, and she often spoke of the analyst as being in another world or another frame of reference, one that she could not get to or even comprehend. This orientation, or rather lack of orientation, was reflected in all other object relations as well.

Although the dream material represented the object relationship of the transference in terms of distance or lack of relatedness, her behavior and associations pointed out the complex aggregate of functions that belong to objects by stressing her needs and her inability to achieve gratification. The subtle contribution of the object to structure formation which is accompanied by efficient secondary-process integrative techniques for drive satisfaction was also emphasized by its absence. Previous disappointments and the specific aspects of her relationship to the mother made the patient fearful of being engulfed by and helplessly vulnerable to the infantile imago of the devouring mother and resulted in a general withdrawal.

Slowly, the ego once again achieved synthesis and integration. After about six months of the turmoil described, she once again felt able to handle the expression of feelings, believing herself competent and, although still aware of immense quantities of anger, no longer feared that she would "let loose." Although she was able to have superficial object relationships, none of these contained any real feeling or warmth. They were patterned exclusively along intellectual lines.

Again, the evidence for this conclusion came from the study of the transference neurosis, or rather the defence against the transference. When the analyst was not conceived as a person or responded to with affect, she was able to be pleasant and to communicate on a sophisticated and intellectual level. In dreams the analyst was represented as being somewhere off in the distance or hidden behind a cloud. Previously, when she showed an intense degree of disintegration, and had similar dreams, she seemed to want to reach out toward me in a clinging, helpless fashion, but could not permit herself to do so. Now she did not seem to have a need for an object except to demonstrate the success of an omnipotent, controlling orientation.

This defensive state was characterized by obsessive compulsive techniques similar to the personality organization noted when she entered analysis. Both sexual and pregenital elements were responsible for such an orientation and were further elaborated, indirectly of course, in terms of her relationship to her mother.

If she could control and magically manipulate objects she could feel safe. Her underlying state was precarious, one that could easily be flooded by uncontrolled anxiety. When able to achieve equilibrium she used anal defences which served to protect her both from a denying and devouring mother and later from a disappointing father and now from the analyst. Oedipal as well as oral frustrations were involved and had to be denied by an isolation from objects as well as repression of affect.

Physiologically her condition became worse. Her internist reported increased hypertension, usually 220/120, and sometimes higher in spite of medication. Ophthalmological examinations revealed the beginning of a hypertensive retinopathy.

As in any analysis, there was a back and forth movement from one particular organization to another, dependent on many variables, not the least being the frustrations and gratifications of the transference neurosis. She returned to this well-developed obsessive compulsive state at least four separate times, and exhibited some transient obsessional defences on other occasions also. The internist, toward whom she related in a less intensive, though parallel, fashion than she did towards the analyst, always found severe hypertension at such times. Reiser (personal communication) has raised the question whether her increased blood-pressure may have represented a "transference reaction to the internist." Undoubtedly her relationship there, too, was founded upon the projection of infantile imagos, but during the states of helplessness which alternated with the obsessive compulsive state he found her blood-pressure to be lower and even normal, so that a consistent correlation could be made in terms of what he found when he took the blood-pressure and the ego state.

To summarize, these striking temporal correlations could be made: (1) when her behavior was disorganized and without the ability to relate to the analyst, she suffered from hypertension; (2) when her behavior was organized but her relationship to the analyst was a distant intellectual one, she had an even more severe hypertension; and (3), when she was able to experience feelings, even though disruptive ones, toward the analyst, her blood-pressure returned to normal.

From a phenomenological viewpoint, the last regressed state was very similar to the first state of regression when the hypertension was discovered. The differences, however, are significant for understanding the relationship between the psychological state and the clinical somatic state.

First, the recognition of the existence of anger and a need for a target which became part of the transference relationship also enabled the patient to recognize the existence of objects in an affective fashion. In the first state of ego regression and panic, she felt herself at a great distance from others, finding herself unable to relate to them except in a tangential way. In the well-defended obsessive-compulsive state, she related to objects mainly in an intellectual way. Now she recognized them as being instrumental to her rage, which meant that she was able to detect their frustrating (but also gratifying) potential.

As the analyst became a more significant figure in her life, she was able to experience dependent, affectionate longings as well as anger. All analysts have at one time or another experienced the rather remarkable and dramatic changes that occur when the patient who is withdrawn or who rigidly holds himself back from forming a relationship is finally able to tolerate affect toward the analyst. Distrust and negative feelings regularly accompany libidinal expression under these circumstances, since the affects are derived from infantile imagos. One has the opportunity to observe a variety of primitive mechanisms in this state, and in contrast to the previously constricted, withdrawn, apparently objectless state, correlations between the somatic and the rapidly shifting emotional reactions are more readily discerned.

Discussion

The observations of behavioral integration and breakdown in this patient become meaningful if considered in terms of the capacity for object relations during various ego states. The archaic and infantile object relationships are the axis around which the transference neurosis revolves. The existence of a somatic dysfunction could then be correlated with the variables of the developmental position of the ego and the intensity of affect in object relationships as well as their quality in terms of psychosexual development.

The superficial adjustment of the patient was not a true indicator of her total psychic and somatic integration. In the rigidly defended state she was unable to participate in affective experiences and her way of relating to the outside world was cold, sterile, and intellectual. The transference neurosis was characterized by a lack of object involvement. Her somatic symptoms were intense in spite of a good surface adjustment. During helpless, desperate states where she was making demands of megalomanic, omnipotent proportions, her operational energies were primary process in nature and were also accompanied by somatic dysfunctions. The physical illness disappeared concurrently with her ability to relate to the therapist and recognize him in a more structured fashion. True, she was still helpless and desperate, but the transference state was markedly different. Somatic signs were absent, even though on the surface there seemed to be some phenomenological similarities to the periods of helplessness that were accompanied by hypertension.

I feel that the manifestations of the transference neurosis of this case indicate relevant correlations between object relations and the appearance of the somatic symptom. The following hypothesis emerges if we generalize from these observations: an ego state that is sufficiently structured to be able to maintain cathexis of a meaningful object relationship, although this may not be phenomenologically apparent, is not found in conjunction with certain signs and symptoms that have been considered from a psychosomatic viewpoint. This relates once again to the thesis that somatization is more consistently correlated with a primary-process- than a secondary-process-oriented ego.

We presume that the earliest perceptions of the neonate are bodily sensations without ideational components. The responses observed are massive and global in nature, involving motor discharges as well as vasomotor and other autonomic phenomena.

Many have suggested that the first representation of the outside world is the breast (or other source of nourishment) experienced as a part-object. Later a variety of part-objects become integrated into a whole object. The latter is not just a sum of the various part objects but constitutes a new gestalt, one that transcends the somatic nature of the part-object, and begins to involve elements of a more structured nature, including the psychological or mental.

The sensory registrants of the neonate are impressed on the diffusely and primitively organized ego where the qualities of mentation and consciousness are still embryonic. As external experiences impinge on the maturing organism, higher perceptual centres are established which lead to the development and differentiation of all the sensory modalities as well as to consciousness. Herrick (1956) describes many experiments demonstrating that the development of sensory functions, such as the visual, depends on transactions with the outer world. Without appropriate external stimuli, neurophysiological maturation is defective and the perceptual function fails to develop. The corresponding development of the executive apparatus is even more obviously dependent upon gratifying object relationships and the incorporation of satisfactory experiences.

What has been postulated for sensory impressions is a hierarchy (isolated sensations and part objects, to gestalts and whole objects), and the executive systems can be considered in a similar fashion. From a developmental viewpoint, we can conceive of a continuum from the involuntary nervous system whose responses are unlearned to primitive, reflexive levels of the voluntary nervous system, and finally, to deliberate reality-attuned, planned alloplastic behavior.

When the ego adjustments undergo regression, we usually note the return to a primitive state, at least relatively speaking, which involves all ego systems, sensory, motor, and integrative. With the advent of primitive needs, we often note a lack of integration and in extreme cases a state of disintegration which may be accompanied by panic. The ego attempts to reestablish a balance which is oriented more along the lines of the primary process than previously and includes more autoplastic and vegetative responses. In terms of a continuum we note a regression from secondary-process-structured needs and responses, which include object relationships, to both affective and somatic dysfunctions.

Jacobson (1954) gave a detailed description of the primitive phases of development and the shift of energies in regression as they underwent a process of "defusion." Freud (1923) had discussed this point in terms of his structural hypothesis and libido theory, emphasizing that the ego is flooded with destructive, aggressive forces as it regresses. The preponderance of destructive energies over libidinal occurs in an unstructured state where the organization and synthesis of the ego is disrupted. Freud (1920) feels that in states of greater organization, such as a multicellular in contrast to a unicellular one, there is a neutralization of the death instinct and the diversion of destructive impulses towards the outer world.

Without becoming involved in questions of instinct theory, we can emphasize that in regression there is a loss of functional unity and the various ego systems, both sensory and executive, operate in an asynchronous fashion.

In regressed states, higher-order gratifications from object relationships are not attained, a circumstance that adds to frustration and rage. In turn, the behavior becomes less efficient; e.g., purposeless kicking and the screaming of a tantrum are less efficient than suckling, the autonomic responses being integrated in the latter and not in the former. The unintegrated visceral systems that accompany the tension, rage, and frustration are likely to lead to the formation of somatic symptoms. In the decompensated, regressed state, the unity and synthesis that is characteristic of the secondary process breaks down and the types of responses and gratifications become characteristic of a more primitive developmental level and less effective.

The techniques that the ego has at its disposal in dealing with its needs have been acquired through a variety of gratifying and structuralizing experiences which have become introjected. These functional introjects include the objects that have made gratification and mastery possible. In the regressed, relatively objectless state such integrating experiences are not available and the disruption of various ego systems may be associated with visceral symptomatology as previously described. The object is being considered from an operational viewpoint and need not be separated from its functional significance in terms of gratification of drive needs and structuralization and synthesis.

The case, I believe, highlights some of these mechanisms, although it should be emphasized that the psycho-analytic material does not give us any evidence to determine why a particular organ system has been involved; e.g., the disappearance of the migraine and appearance of hypertension cannot be explained by the psychoanalytic data. We can focus upon the particular ego mechanisms operating at the time of the somatic dysfunction. Interesting comparisons between particular traumas and organ neuroses can be made, although we should be cautious in drawing any conclusions regarding causal connections between these two sets of data.

This case material reveals the intimate involvement between somatic dysfunctions and states of psychic equilibrium. In view of the varied ego states observed in the transference neurosis, it will be difficult to make any one-to-one correlation here between the state of psychic integration and the somatic symptoms. The varied phenomena of reality-adjusted behavior and what at other times seem to be states of ego disintegration do not consistently correlate with the presence or absence of a somatic syndrome. Consequently, it would be difficult to view the somatic symptoms as part of a specific ego defence or instinctual tension as Schwartz and Semrad (1951) and Saul (1939) have done. Alexander (1950) has frequently written about the lack of symbolic significance of the symptoms of an organ neurosis, and here, too, I am considering the physical phenomena as being manifestations of physiological pathology, not having achieved any mentational representation.

During regressed phases, when hypertension was present, the drive needs were not organized in a secondary-process fashion and did not have psychological characteristics such as imagery, thought, or some element of conceptualization and abstraction. The ego operations were somatically and viscerally oriented.

The study of regression leads one to a formulation of a hierarchy of needs and of responses which gratify these needs. The object relationship is a factor in the maturation and development of drives and ego structure as well as a result of such structuralization. With the acquisition of efficient responses the drive needs also become more sophisticated, enabling the ego to relate at more highly organized reality levels which again include objects. In regression there is an ego disruption which affects object relations also, which in turn may lead to a further disruption and regression of ego functions.

What can be correlated with the somatic syndrome in this case is the presence or absence of an object from whom gratification is sought, as was observed in the transference neurosis. This patient demonstrates that as long as she hoped or expected to have her needs met in an object-directed and more or less reality-attuned fashion, she was free of somatic ailments. When she withdrew from objects or regressed to such primitive modes as viewing objects only in terms of magical omnipotent qualities, her somatic symptoms reached their greatest intensity.

The frustrated id impulses included both pregenital and oedipal elements. Both the wish to possess the analyst exclusively during the father transference and the need to receive dependent care and nurturing were apparent when she was able to relate in an object-directed fashion. Still, she had often to retreat from this position because she felt it was inevitable that she would be disappointed, as occurred with her father when he turned to the younger sister.

Her anal defences served to protect her from such a disappointment as well as to erect a protective barrier from what she later revealed was the fear of a maternal assault. During her obsessive-compulsive adjustment, she was able to conceptualize an object but not to seek gratification from it. She withdrew from an affective relationship and maintained omnipotent control by using the defence of isolation. If she relaxed this control, as she had done earlier in the analysis, she would be faced with the catastrophe of feeling engulfed by an all-powerful, destructive mother imago. These mechanisms were clearly indicated during the regressed state that was accompanied by hypertension.

When the patient's behavior was disorganized and indicated a state of ego disintegration, her capacity for object relations was inadequate for a variety of reasons. When she withdrew in a helpless, panicky fashion, although it was so obvious that she needed a sustaining relationship, it became apparent that the perceptual, synthethic, and executive ego mechanisms responsible for transactions with an external object had become inoperative as they were flooded with rage. Her behavior and associations seemed to indicate that she had erected a wall between herself and the analyst and then she would "beat her head against the wall" to find a measure of sustenance. Without the object to save her, she felt she would be devoured by her rage, but then she felt she would also devour the object.

The later stage of regression in treatment was not accompanied by hypertension and showed different mechanisms of relating to objects. Her capacity to seek from an object was different. Now she could reach out and cling in an anaclitic fashion. The object was able to counteract her destructive rage as her father had been able to do in childhood. This transference reaction was a synthesizing force. Furthermore, she was able to externalize her hostility and direct it towards the analyst, and this process also had an equilibratory effect. This type of object relationship was a primitive one, but still she was able to utilize it in the interest of maintaining an equilibrium, even if it was an infantile one and manifested by behavioral disorganization.

One other aspect of the patient's reactions will be commented upon. It was noted that a good deal of this woman's struggle concerned the repression of angry impulses. In this instance, her anger is considered as representing a sign of the disrupted ego which was reflected in both psychic and visceral systems. Its origin certainly would include the frustrations and vicissitudes of her early psychosexual development and included reactions to penis envy, oral frustration, etc. The effects of the anger on the psyche cannot be separated from the frustration of the drive needs that caused it. So once again the patient's position vis-à-vis objects remains an important axis.

Summary

This clinical study uses the frame of reference of the transference neurosis in order to determine what role object relations have for the satisfaction of drive needs and the total psychic integration of a patient who suffered from two somatic syndromes, migraine and hypertension.

Drive needs and object relations are conceptualized along a continuum, a hierarchy whose spectrum extends from primitive, omnipotent, megalomanic, primary-process modes of operation to judgmental, reality-tested, sensory and motor phenomena that are organized in a second-ary-process fashion. The somatically oriented drive needs in a primitively fixated or deeply regressed ego do not have a mental representation, since the qualities of mentation and consciousness relative to such basic needs are still embryonic. At the other end of the spectrum, the drive is experienced as a conscious impulse that can potentially be gratified in an object-directed fashion.

The study of the transference neurosis of this patient revealed the following striking correlations. When she was able to relate in a nonautistic way towards the analyst, which, of course, reflected her general status of object-relatedness, she did not suffer from somatic illness. When she was unable to relate affectively to an object which was also reflected in the transference neuroses and which was indicative of a regressed, primary-process-oriented ego state, she suffered from somatic signs.

Here the organ dysfunction is considered as an indicator of a disturbed psychic equilibrium. Any physical illness is the outcome of some disturbance of homeostasis and in turn contributes further to disequilibrium. When the ego was able to handle its needs at a reality-oriented object-directed level, then the function of the lower visceral systems was not disturbed. From a phenomenological viewpoint, the correlation between the surface adjustment and somatic illness was not consistently maintained; there were times when the patient seemed well adjusted and the hypertension had reached dangerous levels, and times when she seemed to be in a state of almost complete dissolution and would be practically free of cardiovascular signs. The subtleties of the transference neurosis, however, revealed aspects of her psychic integration which did correlate consistently with the somatic states.

Chapter 31

Ego Equilibrium and Cancer of the Breast

The relationship between personality structure and the occurrence of invasive disease has been studied from many different viewpoints. Profile descriptions, psychodynamic constellations, and the use of specific defenses—all have been studied. In some instances such studies have implied, perhaps, even an etiological connection between certain intrapsychic forces and the appearance of cancer.

With the advent of ego psychology, many additional hypotheses have been postulated. For example, the correlation between separation experiences and the onset of cancer have been investigated vigorously for the past two decades. Investigators such as Greene et al. (1956), LeShan (1960) Renneker et al. (1963), Schmale (1958), and Muslin and Pieper (1962), to mention but a few, have attempted to gain further insight into a relationship between a significant psychological event and the onset of cancer. Other authors such as Giovacchini (see chapters 29, 30) and Schur (1955) have studied psychosomatic problems from an ego-psychological viewpoint exclusively. Giovacchini, for example, discusses somatic symptoms as one aspect of a disorganized, regressed ego that is unable to turn to external objects for gratification of basic needs. Schur postulates that somatization is an aspect of the primary process and characteristic of a regressed or primitively fixated ego.

In this study, we propose to make use of the concept of the ego as a central pivot around which our formulations will revolve. Our simplest model, the stimulus–response prototype, illustrates that exposure to psychological events will produce effects felt at all levels of somatic and psychic integration. An invasive disease process that threatens a person's homeostatic balance must not only disrupt the physiological equilibrium but must also be traumatic to the psychological aspects of the ego organization. This would result in a disruption of psychic equilibrium that would have mental representation and affective components. Our purpose is to explore the effect of carcinoma of the breast on the ego and attempt to detect its manifestations before the patient is aware of having the disease. A neoplastic disorganization is occurring for some

In collaboration with Hyman Muslin, M.D. First publsihed in *Psychosom. Med.* 27 (1965), 524–32. Reprinted by permission.

time before "the lump" is produced and detected. In many subtle ways
the invasive process must upset a previously functional equilibrium.
From a psychological viewpoint it is plausible to assume that mentational systems are also involved, although the greater part of such
reactions are unconscious. However, there is a heuristic advantage in
proceeding with the assumption that, despite the fact that such impingements are unconscious, they are detectable.

A condensation of material from the analysis of a patient who developed carcinoma of the breast during treatment is presented below.
Although this illness introduced complications, there was opportunity
under such circumstances to assess the effects of physical illness on
psychic systems. With the patient under scrutiny observations could be
made that are not available to the investigator later on. With the passage
of time not only are there considerable distortions as defensive superstructures are erected, but the reliving of infantile traumas in the current
transference setting is, naturally, not directly observable. One cannot
predict when such a situation will arise, but when it does it can be
considered as being a "natural experiment." Undoubtedly "natural
experiments" where a particular illness occurs during treatment are not
too unusual, and although the therapist may not be particularly interested from a research viewpoint, his data would still be valuable to the
investigator. As long as one can reconstruct the data they will be of value
in forming or validating hypotheses. This is true even if the therapist had
not been particularly oriented to making observations and connections
between physical illness and various psychic states. In fact, there may
be an advantage in the lack of research interest on the part of the
therapist, since he will be less prone to distort the collection of data with
previous biases or research ambitions.

A hypothesis is strengthened by the amount of relevant data that
support it. The study of a single case has obvious limitations; one must
be cautious about generalizing from such data. Still, patients developing
malignancies during the course of psychoanalytic treatment are not
easily found, and if one has the opportunity to study such a case in
"depth," he can observe a sufficient number of events that can be
correlated with a variety of variables that may support a particular
hypothesis.

In the future we will present data from 100 patients undergoing
surgery for breast tumors who were studied preoperatively. Dream
material was collected and, in some instances, similarities were noted
between two statistically significant groups of patients and the material
that will be presented below.

Case Report

The patient, a married woman in her early forties, went through a regressive period that had many puzzling features. After two years of therapy, she reverted to a psychic state characterized by an anxiety of paniclike proportions and showed all the signs of ego dissolution.

When this patient first sought therapy she had symptoms that were similar in quality. At that time she was unable to carry on with her daily routine. She could not do her housework, drive a car, shop, or take care of her three children. She had had similar decompensations after the birth of the first two children, girls, but the birth of the third child, a boy, upset her to the point where she felt she could not survive without treatment.

Since the therapist had observed the patient's decompensation when she first sought treatment, he was able to compare it with this later regressive episode. Behaviorally, she was much more disturbed during the latter episode. Whereas previously she found herself unable to carry on routine responsibilities, she now felt herself to be completely immobilized and could not even perform the most pedestrian tasks such as brushing her hair, bathing, or even remembering; she felt herself incapable of enough organization to take her meals at prescribed times. This disorganization was reflected in her disheveled appearance; when she first started therapy, in spite of her anxiety, she was always neat and presentable.

She had all the symptoms that Erikson (1956) has described as being characteristic of the "identity-diffusion syndrome." She was preoccupied as to who and what she was and whether there was a purpose to her life. Previously she was concerned about not being able to function, but she knew what her functions were. At that time she was dismayed that she could not fulfill her role, but now she was no longer aware of her role.

As in the beginning of treatment, she felt intense anxiety. In addition she was visibly angry, mainly at herself, but there were also frequent outbursts against the therapist. This was in contrast to her initial state in which her feelings seemed to be predominantly anxiety and a clinging, anaclitic helplessness. During this later episode she also felt considerable guilt and viewed herself as a hateful, contemptible person unworthy of anyone's concern.

The dream material was particularly interesting. The dreams at the beginning of therapy and those noted during the later regression were remarkably similar, at least, in manifest content. For example, while experiencing feelings of helplessness and vulnerability she would often dream of drowning and being inundated. Water was prominent in her early dreams. Dreams of falling were also frequent during the beginning phases of treatment, and her associations usually revealed a fear of losing her identity, of being swallowed by a threatening, unknown outside force. She was also terrified of losing control and being over-whelmed and destroyed by her inner rage.

Although her dreams during this latter period were similar in manifest content they additionally showed some subtle differences. The theme of losing control and being inundated was the same and was a dominant thread in her associations. However, the dreams seemed to be some-what more structured than previously. Instead of the patient being amalgamated into a powerful, indistinct force or being dissolved in such a universal medium as water, she dreamed of houses and rooms and was able to describe many details of her surroundings. As with other patients with an ego defect, she would then feel her surroundings crumbling about her, the floor collapsing, and then falling. In her earlier dreams she was falling from no particular place, whereas now she was falling from a setting that she could describe in considerable detail. She felt just as frightened, even more so, but the dream picture differed in that it was better "put together," instead of vague, indistinct, and amorphous as her early dreams had been.

The patient's history revealed that her previous episodes of decom-pensation were similar to the one that caused her to seek therapy. They were postpartum reactions, characterized by helplessness, clinging dependency, and anxiety, but not by self-recrimination, guilt, or anger. She related these reactions to her relationship with her mother and siblings.

Her mother was described as a self-centered person who was beautiful and could be manipulatively charming. She managed, according to the patient, in such a fashion that the "world revolved around her." Conse-quently her husband and daughters seldom mattered. The patient felt as if she "didn't count" and felt powerless and inadequate in general but especially so when comparing herself with her austere and narcissistic mother. In addition, she was the middle child, having a sister three years older and a brother four years younger than herself. The patient felt that the sister was also treated as a nonentity, but she was extremely bitter about her brother who was an exception because the mother idolized him.

Her ambivalence toward motherhood was intensified during her preg-nancies. She could identify with her unborn child and gratify narcissistic and dependent needs in an ego-syntonic fashion. To "lose" the child by giving birth involved a repetition of what she felt to be an abandonment by her own mother.

The associations also revealed that by giving birth to a child she had lost a valuable part of herself, rendering her inadequate and vulnerable. The birth of a son was particularly traumatic for many complex reasons; her destructive impulses toward her brother contributed to the more disruptive regression following her son's birth. Retrospectively she fantasied that she gave birth to a monster, having expelled a hateful part of the self, but she emphasized her "inadequacy for having had such badness" inside of her rather than her anger as she did during her regressed episode two years later. The mothering experience, therefore, had no developmental potential, as Benedek (1959) discusses, but instead intensified conflicts and fixations and upset the ego equilibrium.

A noteworthy feature of the regression during therapy was the absence of any obvious precipitating factors. She was not pregnant, nor could the time of the regression be correlated with any anniversary reactions, e.g., her birth or those of her siblings and children. As far as could be ascertained the onset of the regression did not seem to be related either directly or symbolically to any significant event or trauma of her past. There were no interruptions in the therapy as had sometimes occurred because of meetings or vacations.

Initially the patient presented to the therapist, as she did to everyone, a picture of helpless vulnerability. She was demanding and clinging and in an agitated fashion indicated a need to be rescued. The analyst was cast in the role of an omnipotent savior from whom she could expect sustenance and nurture. The therapist, however, constantly confronted her with her magical expectations to be saved from what she considered to be a hateful, destroying self. This is not an unusual transference situation in patients with character disorders, although as the transference unfolded, many hysterical elements became apparent too.

The fact that the therapist was able to understand that she felt so depreciated but did not react by attempting to reassure or "rescue" her had a stabilizing effect. The patient next related to the analyst as though he were a benign, ideal parent. She rather quickly adjusted herself to the comfortable role of being a little girl receiving a dependent affection from a nonthreatening devoted parent. Although there were many infantile qualities to her behavior, her improvement was impressive, and she was able to handle routine activities effectively. She continued to idealize the therapeutic relationship, but it did not have the awe-inspiring, magical and desperate quality that she had previously projected onto the analyst.

As the patient was able to project the rejecting maternal imago onto the therapist, she was able to integrate interpretations that emphasized her narcissistic frustration and her disappointment in her father, who did nothing either to supply what she felt the mother failed to give her or to further the development of feminine self-esteem. Her feeling of inadequacy became more specific and began to refer chiefly to the sexual area. She became aware of sexual competitiveness toward her mother and found herself struggling with the conflict of being overwhelmed by her mother's beauty and what she felt to be her superiority as a woman.

What seemed to be progress and analytic integration ended abruptly with the regressive period described above. The transference projection reverted back to wanting the therapist to be an omnipotent savior. She associated to evil and poison within her* and expected the analyst to counteract this destructive hatred with his powerful "goodness." However, in contrast to her earlier transference feelings, there was a greater feeling of hopelessness, a realization that the analyst either did not have any power or that she was so hateful that no one would want to help her. She felt that all objects, including the analyst, were slipping away from her. This created panic and made her feel formless. She found it increasingly difficult to preserve an identity, and she found it impossible to reach out and get some gratification and protection from the therapist. The resulting feeling was one of panicky isolation and dissolution.

There had been, of course, a movement back and forth between defensive dependency and sexual competitiveness throughout the course of treatment. Her responses to interpretations usually led to ego integration, although during more defensive periods she would regress. Still the regression described was of entirely different proportions from anything that she had previously experienced. It was cataclysmic and totally disruptive, and she withdrew from the therapist, being seemingly analytically inaccessible, no longer responding to or even acknowledging interpretations—a lack of response that had never occurred in the past.

The regression lasted for four months without relief. Shortly before she once again established psychic equilibrium the patient discovered a small lump in her left breast. A biopsy revealed a Grade I, slow-growing adenocarcinoma, and a radical mastectomy was performed within ten days of diagnosis. There was no evidence of metastases. Her behavior was striking because she completely recovered from her panic and went through this trying period with equanimity. She neither minimized the danger of her illness and surgery nor became desperately anxious. Her reaction seemed mature and calm, and not defensive.

*One might be tempted symbolically to associate feelings of being poisoned and possessing inner evil and destructive forces with an insidious neoplastic process. However, this type of reaction is a complex and structured psychological one and, therefore, difficult to equate with physiological disruption at the cellular level.

After a relatively brief convalescence, she resumed psychotherapy and continued in the same manner as before her disruptive regression. There were no further episodes as severe as the one described, although there were the usual defensive regressions. At no time did she show signs of ego disintegration.

Her dreams also reflected this change. From this point on, there were no longer dreams of elements falling apart or content indicating loss of control. All of her dreams were in some way object-directed and referred to the transference.

The treatment continued for approximately two more years, and there were no further organic complications. Her emotional integration continued, and at the time of termination the patient was quite satisfied with her progress. Six more years have elapsed (eight since surgery) and there have been no recurrences of the breast cancer.

Discussion

Causal connections between psychic states and physical illness cannot be made when the patient is studied only from the viewpoint of the transference neurosis in the therapeutic setting. Still the sequence this patient demonstrated is extremely interesting, and one cannot dismiss the occurrence of her physical illness and the changes in psychic states as having no relevance to each other.

What is most striking in the patient's reactions was the occurrence of the regressive episode and the absence of apparent precipitating factors. Inability to find a precipitating factor in either the external world or because of some subtle transference shift does not mean that one does not exist; it may merely indicate that the therapist was unable to discover it. However, the discovery of a nodule by the patient and the subsequent psychic integration is too striking to be considered coincidental.

This patient's ego showed considerable vulnerability, and the tendency toward regression seemed to be a marked one. Therefore, her reaction to the knowledge of having a potentially fatal illness is paradoxical. Everybody reacts to illness, and being made aware of a dangerous disease, apart from the direct effects of the disease which may be minimal at early stages, is understandably upsetting. When it is not, we usually assume that some masochistic need of the patient is being satisfied or that he is being otherwise defensive.

Although there were undoubtedly defensive elements in this patient's reaction to her illness, they did not seem to be a prominent theme. Ordinarily such behavior, when defensive, is not particularly efficient,

and its constricting effects are easily detectable. The impression gained
here was that there was structure as well as defensiveness and that, in
many ways, she had mastered the trauma of being confronted with a
dangerous disease, especially when the disease could be dealt with at
conscious, well-organized psychic levels.

If her equanimity represented mastery, then one has to examine her
disruptive behavior. It could be viewed as a stage that the patient moved
away from—i.e., from an intolerable ego state to a reestablishment of
equilibrium. Her panic might have been a reaction to her illness—a
response that occurred before the patient was consciously aware that
anything was wrong. *We are postulating, therefore, that at some level
the patient was aware that something threatening was occurring inside
of her and that the disrupted ego state was a reaction to the beginning
carcinoma.*

The question has been raised as to whether it is possible that the
patient detected the lump before the regression occurred and then
defensively denied its existence. Insofar as this would result in the
shutting out of an external percept the denial would have to be massive.
This hypothesis raises many interesting questions concerning such matters as the nature of the relationship between such a massive defense and
the occurrence of psychic decompensation, and the factors which finally
caused her to acknowledge the existence of the nodule. However, there
is evidence that the lump was not detectable for at least one month after
the regression began. At that time she had a routine gynecological check-
up and her breasts were found to be free of nodules. Three months later
when the patient finally discovered it, it appeared to be no larger than
twice the size of a pea, although it was found to be at least 2 cm. in
diameter when it was excised.

One can consider as an alternative hypothesis that the emotional state
is in some way implicated in the genesis of the neoplasm. If one wishes
to skirt etiological connections, the question still remains as to whether
the psychic disorganization might have accelerated the cellular dedifferentiation that is characteristic of malignancies. These hypotheses are
difficult to evaluate in a clinical study such as this one, since the
psychoanalytic method does not enable the investigator to make process
connections between psychic equilibrium and somatic dysfunction. Furthermore, one would then have to find an explanation for the ego
decompensation either in the transference setting or some traumatic
(direct or symbolic) event. However, these possibilities cannot be
excluded, nor are they necessarily exclusive of what we have postulated
because it is not implausible that the somatic pathology affects psychic
systems and that, in turn, the latter contribute to the somatic disequilib-

rium. Collection of similar cases as well as cases that have family histories of many malignancies (this patient could not recall a case of cancer in her family) will help us to focus upon a particular hypothesis. Silverman (1959) reported the analysis of a woman who had somatic preoccupations affecting many organ systems which were related to rage and feelings of hateful self-depreciation. During treatment she also developed a carcinoma of the breast that Silverman feels may in some way have been related to inner aggression, but he is also cautious about making direct etiological connections. Sanford (1957) described a patient in whom carcinoma of the lung developed during treatment. There were changes in the emotional state (hypomanic) that had never previously been observed, a reaction she believed to be due to the developing cancer.

If we review the dream material with our hypothesis in mind, the manifest content of collapsing floors, tumbling walls, and caving-in ceilings becomes understandable. Such dreams indicate a disruption of an ego integration, a dissolution of a previous unity of organization. A disease process, neoplastic or otherwise, always disrupts organization at some anatomical and functional level. Thus, it is reasonable to assume that such disorganization is also reflected in the psyche. That the patient will be consciously aware of an invasive process before it is possible to make a medical diagnosis is not likely; but that the disruptive effect will, in some way, be reacted to might often be the case.

The dreams that this patient had during the regressed period were "representational." Freud (1900), in describing Silberer's experience, writes of similar types of dreams, and more recently Seitz (1963) also described a patient's dreams that depicted ego mechanisms. Every dream, to some extent, is representational—i.e., the structure of the psychic apparatus is represented in a pictorial form. Of course, dreams also depict process and function and one cannot, and need not, separate structure from function. However, these dreams differ from the "ordinary" wish-fulfilling dream in that the manifest content emphasizes structural elements rather than unconscious impulses even though they are still present. These dreams occur usually when there are gross changes in the ego state.

A careful scrutiny of dream elements could be especially valuable in the study of patients developing somatic pathology. In addition to reflecting changes in the ego state, some dreams might contain elements that refer to the tumor itself, again before it is medically detectable. It is possible that an invasive process is somehow represented in the manifest content. In this patient, the therapist, not being alert to the possibility, is unable to recall if there were such dreams.

Dreams of invasive processes constitute valuable data for the support of our hypothesis. Consequently, one can search for such evidence in other cases where there have been sudden and, on the surface, unexplainable changes in the ego state. In the large number of cases we have collected this type of dream has been frequently noted. For example, patients who have proven malignancies of the breast have had dreams of rats or crabs burrowing through the skin or eating their way through the body. When these dreams occur before the patient is aware of being ill, they are particularly significant for the study of the effects of somatic pathology on psychic systems. This topic, however, should be pursued in a separate study.

Alterations of physiology are inevitable with organic disease. In the beginning phases of a disease process the manifestations may be subtle and undetectable. However, is it not possible that impingements on the ego state may occur long before it is possible to perform a diagnostic test? One would expect such changes to reflect a loss of organization. The patient's flexibility and integration determine the ego's degree of reaction and its recuperative powers. It may reestablish equilibrium very quickly by constructing defense, and/or through other integrative mechanisms achieve mastery. Still, at some point during the course of developing illness one would expect to find a period of relative loss of ego organization.

This disintegration could be so short-lived, the defensive reintegration so immediate, that it might be hardly noticeable. If the patient is receiving therapy one has a better opportunity to observe even short-lived shifts. When they are detected it might possibly behoove us to consider the possibility of the development of an organic disease process.

Can one generalize from the experiences of this patient? The introduction of the ego concept, one that includes somatic systems, makes it unnecessary to postulate a dichotomy between psyche and soma and highlights the interplay between somatic processes and psychic reactions. Granted then that any change in one's physiological status also represents an alteration of an ego state, is it not possible that such changes may not be apparent until the somatic process develops to the point where it is so obvious or at least sufficiently manifest that it can be diagnosed? If this is so, then the assessment of the ego state is still useful and has significance in the terms of our therapeutic handling. But it would not be too meaningful in effecting an early diagnosis or in alerting one to the possibility of an organic disease.

Another problem relates to the specificity of the disease itself. Would some diseases disturb the ego equilibrium more profoundly or earlier than others? One may conjecture that the more somatically damaging the disease the greater will be its effects on psychic systems too. A proliferating disease, characterized by cellular dedifferentiation and chaotic, invasive growth destroying anatomical and metabolic organizations, would have widespread consequences long before one becomes consciously aware of them.

Referring to the ego's recuperative powers brings to mind similar qualities in the soma. Many diseases although destructive are limited in their effects because the body sets in motion a variety of defensive maneuvers that prevent spread of the pathological process. Consequently there may be only a minimal disturbance of the physiological equilibrium and still less disturbance of the integration of the ego state. However, any changes in the soma are also reflected in the ego state— even defenses. One would expect that bodily defenses in some way have psychic representations and operate in maintaining emotional homeostasis.

Diseases of the central nervous system, especially multiple sclerosis, are often accompanied with denial of its existence or its later crippling effects. Seemingly the patient continues with his usual adjustment and anticipates no curtailment of activities, even though his relatives and friends are painfully aware of the obvious limitations. The intensity and compulsive quality of the patient's denial are also obvious, and what may on the surface appear to be an establishment of equilibrium turns out to be a desperate and frantic attempt to hold on to an illusion of health in the face of a disease that threatens to undermine the patient's previous defensive organization. Oftentimes the denial succeeds in helping the patient maintain adjustment, but it may have to reach delusional proportions in order to continue doing so.

A neoplastic process, a breakdown of a previous somatic organization, is not well defended against. Carcinoma of the breast, although insidious in onset, is characterized by a gradual, destructive growth. The body is unable to halt it and defend itself against the spread. A somatic defensive equilibrium is not established.

In this patient, the ego underwent changes that emphasized (1) traumatic aspects—it felt threatened and reacted with panic; and (2) a disruption of synthetic and integrative ego systems; the picture was one of decompensation. There were no obvious external traumas. The carcinoma might have been an internal trauma that the ego was reacting to and, for the time being, unable to master. Perhaps because the trauma was not yet at conscious or preconscious levels the ego was unable to deal with it—i.e., unable to harness its higher mentational centers for the purpose of synthesis and integration.

The symbolic meaning of such an illness as carcinoma of the breast in respect to the patient's feminine self-esteem has purposely not been discussed. That it had meaning that involved fantasy systems is certainly true, but there was no evidence from our frame of reference that indicated that the disease process in any way was responsible for the symbolic content of the associational material. Rather, the patient made what seemed to the therapist to be a retrospective construction about her disease in terms of its sexual connotations only after she was consciously aware of its existence.

Part VI

EGO ADAPTATIONS
AND CREATIVITY

This section did not appear in the first edition. It was added because it concentrates upon psychic structure and aspects of ego functioning that stress the adaptive elements of the mind. As psychoanalysts we attempt to understand what our patients present to us in terms of its adaptive potential.

The character changes that analytic treatment achieves can be viewed in terms of increasing autonomy. Creative accomplishment is the outcome of maximum autonomy and represents a high order adaptation. Through the creative product the world is changed and the creator acquires a new adaptation, expanding the range of ego functioning as the scope of the executive system widens.

The study of the creative process leads to explorations of the better-structured elements of the psyche. However, it is also relevant to our interest in primitive mental states because the creative act involves all levels of psychic structure, from the primitive to the most advanced.

The chapters in this section illustrate the interaction of the creative process and psychopathology. The creative act is the outcome of a subtle blending of primary and secondary process. When this balance becomes upset, the psyche has to resort to psychopathological adaptations. The clinical picture frequently seems to be a psychotic reaction. Undoubtedly, the erroneous equation of genius and insanity is based upon such observations.

On the surface, disturbed creative patients may appear to be psychotic, but the resemblance to a psychosis is mainly phenomenological. They may quickly return to reality and are not rigid or bound to psychotic adaptations. Neither their megalomania nor their paranoid projections are particularly threatening; they do not provoke disruptive counter-transference responses. These patients seem benign.

The harmonious interplay of advanced levels of integration, exceptional talent, and primitive mental states is the background of creativity. This process is completely independent of psychopathology. However, the presence of psychopathology in a creative person is an informative opportunity that can teach us about the formation of psychic structure, primitive mental processes, and the functioning of higher integrative systems.

Chapter 32

On Scientific Creativity

The creative process is a topic that attracts any person engaged in the study of human emotions and has become a subject of widespread interest and manifold research approaches. Within the psychoanalytic frame of reference, more than one approach is possible. Although Freud (1937) felt that the so-called "higher ego functions" would not lend themselves easily to psychoanalytic scrutiny, many analysts have written about creativity, usually focusing on the artist. The problem has been approached most frequently in terms of content of conflict, and analytic material and pathobiographies have often been used to shed light on the instinctual factors involved in the personalities of creative persons. A thorough review of the psychoanalytic literature on creativity is beyond the scope of this communication; however, a few brief statements will be made.

The sublimatory aspects of creativity were first pointed out by Freud (1916/17). Stekel (1920), Rank (1932), Sachs (1942), as well as many others, elaborated on the theme of the creator becoming free of mental conflicts by expressing them in creative work. More recently, Kanzer (1955) pointed out that the research scientist gratifies voyeuristic demands by satisfying conscious curiosity through discoveries.

Although Lee (1940) disagrees with formulations that consider the creative process a result of the desexualization of sexual instincts, he also focuses on instinctual factors. In addition to considering the creative product a derivative of id impulses seeking sublimatory expression, he believes that creativity is part of a healing process following a depression.

Others, mainly Klein (1929) and Sharpe (1930), have expressed similar views, though they do not regard the creative process as simply a derivative of unconscious factors. They have written that significant emotional figures who were destroyed in fantasy are unconsciously restored by the creative process. Sharpe stressed that the ego obtains relief from anxiety caused by the incorporated parental image when it is externalized into an art form. The difference between art and science consists in the fact that the artist externalizes the introjected images by doing and the scientist by knowing. It is not the conflicts themselves, but the methods of handling

First published in *Journal of the American Psychoanalytic Association* 8:407–426. Reprinted with permission.

conflict, that determine the differences between artists and scientists (Sharpe, 1935).

In a most intriguing article, Beres (1957) compares the creative process in general with what he considers to be creative in the psychoanalytic relationship. Beres feels that communication plays an essential role in both and that recreating childhood fantasies and communicating them to the self and to the analyst constitute a form of creativity. The mechanisms involved are externalization, projection, and communication.

Although such formulations explain the role of creative activity in the personality, they do not tell us much about the creative process itself. These hypotheses deal with id content and describe conflicts that are found in noncreative persons, too. Certainly, the conflict must be associated with another factor to produce creativity.

To state the problem simply, and perhaps redundantly, the creative scientist must have some very special talent. I would like to examine some aspects of this talent, fully realizing that not too much can be said regarding its origin and development. Its sources may be manifold and include hereditary and constitutional factors. I shall assume that creative abilities are facilitated by or even characterized by particular modes of ego operation and examine them in that light. It is postulated that the ego has special faculties and particular ways of reacting both to the internal and external milieu that make possible the expression of the creative urge. It was at this point that Freud felt that the method of free association would not be too fruitful in examining such ego factors.

More recently, however, there has been an increased emphasis on ego psychology. The works of Hartmann, Kris, and Loewenstein have to be taken into consideration in any study that deals with these higher ego functions. Their hypotheses and formulations give us a theoretical structure that can be used in guiding observation and in the collection of clinical data. Hartmann (1952) has described a nonconflictual sphere of the ego. Discussing the autonomous factors of ego development, he indicates that such factors remain in the conflict-free sphere. Even though they may retain their relationship with the drives, they do not necessarily become involved in conflict. Kris (1955) points out in this connection that these autonomous factors lead to creativity; however, when they become invested with conflict, they lose their autonomy, their organizing and integrating capacities, and their creative potential. Rosen (1955) studied the intrasystemic relationships of the ego of a mathematical genius who had very distinct methods of handling psychic energies and object relationships, methods that Rosen felt were the *sine qua non* of his productivity. In another case (1953) he stressed the importance of object relations and a certain ego reaction which he saw as being associated with "illumination." It is this approach of ego psychology that I would like to expand upon.

Focusing on the ego does not by any means ignore the richness of unconscious material, fantasies, dream productions, or special conflict. Anna Freud (1951), speaking of the instinctual ego, and Hartmann (1952), emphasizing the mutual dependence between the ego and the id, describe the ego not only in terms of perceptive, integrative, and executive functions but as an admixture of primary and secondary process. A well-functioning ego maintains a balance between the rational and the irrational, not excluding the latter, but dealing with it in a specific way. The modus operandi of the reality-testing function must be explored further in the creative individual in order to determine whether there are any unique qualitative or quantitative factors operating. Such a study can best be conducted when there is a disturbance of the function, which serves to highlight it and make possible intensive scrutiny that would not have been possible without psychopathology.

Case Material

The material I have gathered comes from the analyses of eight men who were either physical or biological scientists and whose ages ranged from the mid-thirties to the mid-forties. In spite of the diversities present in such a group, it was truly remarkable how many similar patterns existed. I shall emphasize what I consider to be the features common to these scientists.

They were all creative. I shall not attempt an exact definition of creativity except to mention that what these patients considered to be creative had the approbation of academic colleagues. The scientist is able to refine a crude idea or a disturbing question into a hypothesis that can be tested and formulated into something new. In studying the psychic operations responsible for this sequence, we will investigate the creative process.

At one time or another during treatment, most of these men had symptoms that were akin to psychoses phenomenologically or at least indicative of severe regression and decompensation. During these periods their thinking showed definite paranoid elements. They felt suspicious of those about them. For example, several believed that colleagues were attempting to undermine their reputation or the value of their work. Their thinking processes were accelerated and usually there was a rapid flight of ideas that made sleep impossible. Some of these men even had feelings of depersonalization and unreality and experienced phenomena that were akin to hallucinations and delusions. I am purposely vague with regard to the latter, for although they did hear voices or were preoccupied with extremely bizarre fantasies that to some extent replaced reality, even in their most disturbed moments, none of these men actually accepted these productions as real. Even though they might have heard voices, they did not really believe that they emanated from a source outside of themselves. They saw such phenomena as products of their own disturbed self. These experiences were frightening to them and often led to panic, however.

Four of these scientists sought therapy because of symptoms such as those just described. Their colleagues had become extremely concerned and usually had made the arrangements for therapy. These particular men were highly esteemed by their scientific confreres and their work had won them international recognition. The other men, although considered bright and promising, had not yet achieved anything that they felt was up to their ultimate capacities. This latter group sought analysis because of various characterological difficulties but did not present the dramatic, bizarre symptoms of the more established group. However, several reported similar episodes in their histories and two developed such symptoms in the course of therapy. Each had gone through a period during which he was more or less incapacitated emotionally and professionally, and his ability to create was interrupted.

During childhood, these men had fulfilled self-esteeming needs by being academically outstanding under the wing of some enthusiastic teacher. Very early in their lives, science had held a fascination that included elements of fear. This anxiety was proportional to the abstractness of the subject matter. If the material had some direct contact with reality, they felt at ease; but while studying theory that dealt only with symbols necessary for an isolated theoretical organization, they would feel frightened. None of the men were mathematicians, although most were quite proficient in mathematics, which they usually regarded merely as a tool to aid in solving problems that dealt with the world of visible experience. Some of these men liked to dabble in mathematics, which held a particularly dangerous fascination for them, and they had to make conscious efforts not to get too involved in it. One patient told me how he would sit down and start studying some known mathematical system such as non-Euclidean geometry. He would separate the particular system from its applications to the physical world and begin considering it in its own right. He would then derive various modifications that were logically connected but new. At this point he felt his ideas were beginning to stray beyond the boundaries of logic and would become completely wild. Then panic would ensue and he would have to terminate the whole exercise, which had begun simply as an intellectual process but had become "sheer fantasy."

The creative talents of these men lay in their abilities to produce experimental models, and they tended to be mildly disdainful of the theoretician, whom they considered more a philosopher than a scientist. They felt that their role was to observe reality, manipulate it, and isolate some facet of it to add to a common fund of knowledge. Their reality had to be tangible rather than symbolic, theoretical, and without direct correspondence to the external world.

One patient told of the following reactions to an experiment that he devised during treatment. He worked hard and used considerable skill in setting up apparatus to get data on certain natural phenomena. Most of the experimental work was concerned with recording measurements. The next step was to organize numerical results so that they would have quantitative significance. The patient was adept both at obtaining the required measurements and at manipulating them mathematically. However, one evening he became dissatisfied with what was a relatively mechanical operation. He started studying his tables and correlating the figures. He realized that his equations were beginning to indicate the inadequacy of the current theoretical system. Although the motivation for the experiment was just such a recognition and the patient was on the brink of fulfilling the purpose behind his work, he began to feel disturbed. As his calculations led him into hitherto unknown and unsuspected constructions and changed some previously held concepts, he noted gradually increasing anxiety and a variety of somatic sensations involving muscular tension. He recognized these feelings as similar to those that initially had brought him to therapy and was afraid that if he continued in this fascinating but dangerous preoccupation, he would precipitate a psychosis. His work held him spellbound and fascinated, yet created such panic that he felt it prudent to stop and put it into the hands of a theoretician. This he did, although others could not understand why he did not pursue the matter further on his own.

It was obvious that certain id impulses threatened to overwhelm the ego integration during a creative phase. Still, these men were attracted to the primitive, and all of them had more than passing interest in mystical religious systems and tended to treat with respect even naïve ideas, theories, and superstitions about natural phenomena. They were interested, usually without disdain, in naïve ideas about nature, for example, that weather could be predicted by an aching corn. One said that these notions were "down to earth," devoid of sophistication, and uncontaminated by "intellectual gymnastics." Even though they were erroneous in content, they maintained a direct contact between man and nature. As long as these men could feel themselves in close touch with nature, they felt secure. They enjoyed such activities as walks in the woods, hunting, and fishing;

one man found that sitting under a tree and looking at the fields and sky produced inner contentment and harmony.

I will mention two other striking similarities in these men's conscious attitudes; one concerns their feelings about science fiction, and the other, attitudes about gadgets. Their feelings about these two subjects are related to what has just been described. They all were critical of current science fiction, most frequently because of the impression that the world created by the authors was a cold, sterile one, devoid of any correspondence to human feeling and emotions. They felt that the complex technological and mechanical societal systems of modern science fiction failed to take into account the subtle interactions of people. On the other hand, the Jules Verne variety appealed to most of them because it considered altered reality in terms of its effects on the individual's psychology and interactions with the milieu.

They tended to regard gadgets as unwelcome barriers against direct contact with nature and noticed that gadgets could come to have meaning in their own right rather than for their function. One of these patients told of a colleague who failed to recognize meaningful data in his experiments because he had so many unnecessary gadgets attached to the apparatus. The results finally obtained were misinterpreted as being an artifact created by the gadget and, consequently, certain fundamental relationships were ignored. Later, when the experiment was repeated with the simplest apparatus, the desired measurements were easily obtained and their meaning seen clearly in terms of fundamental natural laws.

From this material, one can see that these men are describing two contradictory tendencies. On the one hand, they indicate how intolerable intense effects are because they threaten to lead to ego disruption, as evidenced by the psychoticlike symptoms some experienced. In order to protect themselves, they have to deal with the world of concrete reality and not stray too far afield in abstractions that do not require a reality model. Yet they are fascinated by the primitive both around and within themselves. They value feelings highly and, during stable phases, have been considered quite warm, emotional, and loving, the antithesis of the stereotype of the cold, calculating, and austere scientist. These men prevented themselves from feeling too intensely and yet could tolerate a modicum of affect and delight in its content. One patient said, "I cannot allow myself to feel too intensely. Such unbounded feelings are too frightening. They are like children watching fireworks or a circus and being exhilarated. I cannot allow myself such exhilaration."

Returning to the subject of productive and creative work, several interesting patterns were noted. These men considered lack of productivity a symptom. During the treatment they equated their work capacity with their general state of integration and used it to measure therapeutic progress. When defenses became more stabilized, they were once again able to create. When, for a variety of reasons, defenses were disrupted, they were unable to work.

The defenses that served these men in their daily life and the resistances that they displayed in treatment were characteristic of the obsessive-compulsive character neurosis. With increasing stability, the tendency to intellectualize also increased. They tended toward ritualism and found it difficult to be flexible or to deviate from a set course of action. They liked order but were basically disorderly. Reaction formation was a prominent defense, but, as with most obsessive-compulsives, the underlying instinct was apparent in their behavior, too. When they were operating at the obsessive-compulsive level, they were able to work; but when these particular defenses no longer protected them, panic ensued and productivity was completely inhibited.

Still, the facts were not simply that, as long as they had the protection of their defenses, they were able to function. If they became too enmeshed in ritualistic systems, strong reaction formations, or intellectualizing, they found they could not create. Constriction made imaginative activity impossible. Under these circumstances, they could work and carry on routine and sometimes difficult but dull tasks that did not produce new or stimulating ideas. During these periods, they thought only in concrete terms and their interpretations of reality were masterpieces of detail and observation but literal and dull. Curiously enough, some then became interested in gadgets and quite materialistic in other ways. In these instances, reality-testing functions were highly developed and received priority over anything else. Strong defensive measures were operating in order to keep expression of id impulses in a state of repression.

Because of the obsessive-compulsive orientation, one wonders about the significance of the mechanism of isolation. The relevance of isolation to creativity is a very complex topic that has been discussed in a panel (1959) and deserves further consideration. However, this will not be attempted in the present communication.

Correlation of obsessive-compulsive character structure with creativity has been reported by Stein (1953) and Roe (1953) in their statistical observations. Sharpe (1935) remarks, "The anal fixation seems more marked in the scientist than in the artist, the urgent need to control and make right what has been done and what is being done, rather than to make good by doing, which is the artists' course." Although the need to know and the need to control are features that operate in all scientific endeavors and are seen also in the obsessive-compulsive character, such a similarity does not necessarily indicate that a similar mechanism operates in the creative endeavor and the neurotic state.

The histories of my eight patients were strikingly similar. I shall highlight the common features. All eight men reported extremely domineering mothers who ruled the household by their aggressiveness. They were demanding and pushed their children to achieve status that would gratify their narcissistic needs. They all had a tremendous investment in the patient and hung onto the relationship with the son tenaciously, using both direct and indirect means. The latter usually took the form of seductive manipulation. These mothers also tended to be somewhat inconsistent, in that they could be extremely gentle and forgiving of some childish but perhaps serious transgression and inexorably cruel or punitive for some minor misdemeanor. Two of the mothers were definitely psychotic and died in state hospitals.

All these patients considered themselves to have been their mothers' favorite child. Three were only children. Two never had married and had had no heterosexual contact whatsoever. Others had married somewhat overbearing, maternal women who tended to infantilize them and reactivate the state of helpless dependency experienced in childhood. One patient had married several times in an attempt to overcome his castration anxiety, which centered mainly around the fear of the vagina. All his wives had severe emotional disturbances, one being overtly psychotic. His need was to master the fear associated with unpredictable women, whom he found dangerous like his mother. This need to master also contributed to his persistence with research problems.

The patients' fathers, on the other hand, were described as mild, submissive, passive men whose role in the family was a subordinate and, in some cases, an inferior and depreciated one. All the patients manifested considerable hostility toward them; they felt cheated because the fathers had not protected them from the overwhelming, threatening mother. Their model for masculine identification was an insecure one and some of them had long recognized this. Even though they handled this deficit in a variety of defensive fashions, confusion as to what constitutes masculine identity was present in all of these men.

Fear of being overwhelmed by hostile, destructive impulses that were predominantly anal and oral sadistic in nature emerged during analysis. The strength of the instincts and the particular methods of handling them, both defensive and nondefensive, are relevant to these patients' creative ability. However, the equation of psychopathology with creativity is a unidimensional correlation that ignores other important variables. In some instances, it may explain the why of creativity but not the how. To attempt an operational approach requires the scrutiny of other ego processes and the transactions between various intraego systems.

These patients sometimes presented a state with paranoid features of varying intensity; at other times, they showed a rigid, obsessive-compulsive adjustment. The former state was notable for a breakdown of the usual defensive patterns. This led to an instinctual flooding of the ego, which then became oriented in terms of the primary process. The obsessive-compulsive state was characterized by rigid defenses and secondary-process modes of operation. In one state, reality was distorted; in the other, reality testing was a strong and efficient ego function. I want to stress that I do not regard creativity as necessarily part of a continuum between a compulsive and a psychoticlike state. Even though these patients demonstrated such a continuum, one should not conclude that the creative state must occur during transition between two specific poles of psychopathology. Rather, I wish to focus on and attempt to clarify the process associated with creativity, which may or may not be related to any particular pathological state.

Hartmann's constructions (1956) emphasize the point that certain ego nuclei are unhampered by conflict and work at maximum efficiency in terms of the secondary process. Such efficiency leads to an unusually keen evaluation of reality and a sensitivity to the external world. Not only are the reality-testing functions enhanced, but the appraisal of reality leads to a larger span and depth of perception than would have been possible if the perceptual system of the ego were constricted by conflict. As has been indicated here, an ego that is defended by rigid reality orientation is incapable of the kind of communication with the environment which leads to creative work. Stein (1953), quoting Frenkel-Brunswick, states, "The creative individual may be characterized as a system intention, sensitive to the gaps in his experience and capable of maintaining this state of affairs."

Even though my patients illustrated fully the importance of maintaining a hold on reality by obsessive-compulsive mechanisms, it is also apparent that something else must exist in addition to this kind of communication with reality. Much of the material presented indicated a fascination with the instinctual and the primitive. True, this fascination at times led to threatening instinctual upsurges that could produce psychoticlike pictures, but patients' creative potential was at its maximum when they were able to achieve a balance between secondary and primary process.

Discussion

These patients' unconscious furnished the content for their probing explorations of reality. At the ego level, one can say that the unconscious furnished the raw material, which was then subjected to secondary-process operations. The established order of the universe had to be imposed upon the chaotic disorder of the unconscious. The universe, which behaves according to laws and is characterized by logic, coherency, and simplicity of design, corresponds to secondary-process ego operations.

The significance of disordered ideas or impulses is described by Kris (1952) who divides the creative process into two phases, the phase of inspiration and the phase of elaboration. He also indicated (as these patients demonstrate) that alternations between inspirational and elaborational phases may be rapid. The following discussion corresponds to this biphasic division although, during the actual creative period, it was difficult to distinguish between inspiration and elaboration since they seemed to be operating simultaneously. In creating, these patients had to discover a new reality, one that extended beyond the borders of the established and accepted order. Unlike the rigid adherence to reality they maintained during the obsessive-compulsive phase, they were able to perceive and tolerate ambiguities and lack of closures (Frenkel-Brunswick, cited in Stein, 1953). The gaps were threatening but also pleasurable and made it possible for them to explore further and make accretions when they were able to effect closures.

During creative phases, they were aware of chaos and disorder and it became a scientific task to extract order from it. What started perhaps impulsively and always disturbingly from id sources had to be subjugated to what the patients themselves referred to as conscious forces. They were aware of two different types of operations, operations that are easily recognizable as primary and secondary process. The metapsychological aspects of the struggle consisted of refining crude, unconscious forces and divesting them of primary-process factors by use of secondary-process operations.

The impetus and the mobility of the instinctual is imposed upon the static rigidities of reality. The perceptual system is then confronted with an expanded reality that transcends the old, familiar boundaries in that it first appears incongruous with well-established systems. For my patients, this phase (the inspirational phase of Kris) was characterized by a pleasurable erotic and aggressive upsurge, alertness, and increased vividness of sensory experiences. In addition to the heightened instinctual awareness, the integrative ego systems were functioning at peak efficiency. Consequently, the chaotic id impulses that emerged were subjected to organization (the phase of elaboration), and the expanded reality was synchronized with established reality systems by such an organization. This could result in an accretion to, or modification of, the accepted reality.

Freud (1911a) traced the genesis of thought from the id impulse to the cathexis of memory traces and, finally, to the perceptual system, which functioned judgmentally to effect synthesis between the drive needs and their motoric expression and discharge in an acceptable reality. Hyper-cathected thought (as in the obsessional neurosis) was seen by Freud (1909) to represent a regressive action, naturally without the same discharge value as motoric expression. Freud alluded to the subtleties of the interactions of ego systems as early as 1900, when he postulated a mobile cathectic energy of the *Pcs.* which was responsible for the process of becoming conscious. One can see, then, that Freud was definitely thinking in terms of a hierarchy of ego systems, each being able to bind id impulses and each requiring a residual cathexis in order to be functional. In my patients, the id drive led to a cathexis of the higher integrative and perceptual systems. The cathexis of the memory trace and its later fusion and synthesis with reality, which occur in the normal thought process, may not occur when the thought leads to a creative product. During creativity, the id drive bypasses memory traces and cathects the perceptual system directly, leading to its expansion. At the same time, the integrative functions also are being cathected and can deal with the id impulse, which to some extent has been decathected, and effect its fusion with reality. This leads to an expansion of reality, represented by the creative product. Since memory traces are not involved (or at least are less involved), the expanded reality may be not only an extension of something previously learned but actually something new. Briefly, one can state that the higher ego systems obtain their energy from the id in order to deal with the id and refine the emerging impulses into secondary-process modes.

Why the ego in one instance is able to bind id forces and to lead to the creative product, and in another instance forms rigid, constricting defenses or is flooded and becomes disintegrated, is a topic that requires detailed individual case study. The traumatic stimuli that led to decompensation in these patients were of the usual variety and need not be stressed. Three of the cases succeeded in resolving many basic problems, terminated their analyses, and were able to continue creating uninterruptedly without phasic variations. This outcome is at variance with conclusions of investigators such as Lee (1947) that creative work occurs at specific times, corresponding to certain phasic variations in a cyclical depression.

The question has been raised whether the creative process involves a "regression in the service of the ego," i.e., a controlled regression, as Kris (1950a) defined the term. According to this concept, the ego's regulation of regression under certain conditions is considered. The organizing function of the ego is seen as temporarily decathected. The ego is then in the service of id drives, functioning according to the primary process, with mobile, unbound energies. Kris stated, "the integrative functions of the ego include voluntary and temporary withdrawal of cathexis from one area or another in order to regain improved control" (p. 522). In terms of the instinctual orientation of the ego, the concept of controlled regression certainly applies to my patients. However, if the concept of regression requires a temporary suspension of organizing functions, then it would not seem to apply here. The data did not seem to indicate such a suspension while these patients were creating. As a matter of fact, there seemed to be a simultaneous increase in the cathexis of the organizing, integrative, and perceptual systems, with the increased energies being supplied by the id. Some of the evidence for this conclusion came from the fact that the upsurge of the instinctual was perceived with pleasure and zest rather than with anxiety or panic. Kris (1936) noted that, during the process of creative activity, there is freedom from guilt and shame about fantasies that become conscious. This seems to be due to withdrawal of cathexis from the ego ideal and from the more primitive functions of the superego. My patients had a heightened perception of external reality and functioned with more vigor in all areas, vocational, social, and sexual. Reality-testing was not suspended. It was not the rigidly constructed, photographic reality-testing of the obsessive compulsive, however. It retained an instinctual flavor in terms of freedom.

Even though these patients' egos used primitive mechanisms, such as fantasy and picturelike symbolic elements, they still continued to function at highly integrative, reality-testing, and adaptational levels simultaneously. Kris emphasized that the ego's countercathexis against the id is temporarily suspended during inspirational phases and that this represents regression. These patients clearly demonstrated the same process. Kris went on to say that, during the "elaborational" phase, countercathexis may be restored, with increased cathexis of other ego functions such as reality-testing and "communication with the public." My patients' productions did not indicate that there was a reinforcement of countercathexis; instead, they pointed to a reorganization of the instinctual that did not involve repression. For, in any ordinary reinstatement of psychic balance through repression, an ego constriction results from the use of countercathexis. The creative process has been observed to be different in that there is not an ego constriction but what I have described as an expansion of the ego. I have postulated that, during the creative process, energy formerly used to maintain repressive countercathexis becomes available for ego expansion.

Hartmann (1955) described a neutralization of energy in the transformation of an instinctual mode of operation to a noninstinctual one. In my data, it seems clear that energy bound to id content became unbound and then was used in secondary-process operations. This might possibly be thought of as neutralization if one stresses that there did not seem to be any change in energy itself but only in the system cathected. Earlier, Hartmann, Kris, and Loewenstein (1949) indicated that neutralization occurs by binding, which takes place according to a hierarchy ranging from the instinctual to the higher, organizing ego functions.

Referring back to the previously mentioned continuum, it is not known under what circumstances id energy leads to heightened organization, reality expansions, and filling in of closure, and when it leads to panic and disorganization. This may be related to specific conflicts and to constitutional and developmental influences that have not yet been identified. Greenacre (1957) stated that creativity is a special capacity that becomes significant when it is a part of a certain constellation of special abilities and drives. She, too, indicates that creative persons have great sensory sensitivity as well as an unusual capacity for awareness of relations between various stimuli, "a greater sense of actual or potential organization, perhaps a greater sense of gestalt." The data presented here could be interpreted as substantiating these views, for they demonstrate special capacities and potentials of the integrative and perceptual systems to become hypercathected during periods of creative accomplishment. Greenacre (1956) indicated that creative persons describe the experience of awe in childhood with special intensity, pointing to a particularly sensitive perception of external objects. In her view, such children glorify the parents and the identification with a powerful, Godlike father. Their capacity for heightened sensitivity can lead to vibrant, ecstatic bodily feelings. She commented that contact with an actual individual may not be required for an identification with such an idealized image, however. My patients tended to make accretions to such an image from contacts with fatherly teachers, in part to compensate for the disappointment in their actual fathers.

These patients spoke frequently of their bitter resentment of their fathers. Even though, in some cases, the father was successful, more often than not he was considered a nonentity and his work was viewed as unglamorous or lacking in integrity. The oedipal phase was characterized by fear of the overwhelming, castrating mother and an inability to achieve masculine self-esteem through identification. Frequently, one noted overcompensatory factors, in that these patients tended to be forward and aggressive heterosexually, and characteristically sought depreciated women for their casual sexual satisfaction. Early masturbatory fantasies also involved the image of themselves as a "man's man" who picked up prostitutes or became involved with *femmes fatale*.

Other fantasies of a more intellectual nature involved the admiration of elderly men, revered teachers or famous scientists who were particularly fascinating to them and who recognized the patients' potential and made them protégés. Although these men were clearly father substitutes, the patients believed they had no resemblance whatsoever to their real fathers. Greenacre conjectured that creativity is a "gift from the gods." These men created their own father image, which was not modeled after their experience with their parent. They therefore created their own gods, but these were the gods of science. In autobiographies of scientists, one frequently encounters a reference to science that has mystical, religious overtones (e.g., "the hallowed halls of science," "the temple of learning and truth," "the giants and gods of science").

Their masculine identification was self-created. One can say that the introjected father image involved more than identification; its creation transcended the developmental and maturational potentials of patients' biological environment.

Ghiselin (1952) noted similar features in many creative persons, but since he was a literary artist he did not record his observations in metapsychological terms. Still, much of what he writes is strikingly similar to what was learned from these patients. For example, he states,

> even to the creator himself, the earliest effort may seem to involve a commerce with disorder. The first need, therefore, is to transcend the old order. New light comes always from outside our world as we commonly conceive that world. This is the reason why, in order to invent, one must deal with the indeterminant within himself or, more precisely, with certain ill-defined impulses which seem to be the very texture of the ungoverned fullness which John Livingston Loews calls "the surging chaos of the unexpressed" [p. 14].

He further indicates that creative production by a process of purely conscious calculation seems never to occur. Nearly every introspective researcher has indicated that both unconscious factors and conscious calculation were important in creative work. For, as Chekhov states, "to deny that artistic creation involves problems and purposes would be to admit that artists create without premeditation, without design, under a spell. Therefore, if an artist boasted to me of having written a story without a previously settled design but by inspiration, I shall call him a lunatic." The details of this "settled design" require much more intensive scrutiny.

Summary

The case material of eight scientists who have been universally recognized as talented and creative was presented and discussed. An attempt was made to investigate the creative process in terms of the ego operations that may facilitate the creative potential. An approach that focuses on specific id factors or neurotic dynamisms and conflict situations does not add to our knowledge of the sources of creativity. These eight patients all showed varying degrees of decompensation, which made it possible to study the various levels of the personality. When their defenses were reestablished, the character structure seemed to be that of an obsessive-compulsive. Decompensation occurred when the ego was unable to subject id impulses to binding by higher ego systems. In the decompensated state, the ego was overwhelmed by primary-process operations, and patients were unable to work. However, when compulsive defenses were working well, secondary-process operations predominated, and patients were logical and coherent but crass, materialistic, and unable to think imaginatively or produce creatively.

The creative operations of the ego were seen to consist of a balance of primary and secondary process. A creative ego has the ability to bind the chaotic impulses emerging from the unconscious, fuse them with external reality, and refine and integrate the product. When this was achieved, a new segment was added to reality. During creative periods, the higher ego systems received energy from the emerging drives, which led to hyper-cathexis and greater functional capacity in dealing with the very same drives and in subjecting them to the laws of the secondary process. Finally, the role of the memory trace in thought processes and creativity was discussed.

Chapter 33

The Ego Ideal of
A Creative Scientist

Recent emphasis on ego psychology has been paralleled by an intensified interest in the creative process. Many authors have studied the adaptive role of various ego mechanisms in creativity.

Conceptualization of the ego as an apparatus with diversified functions in subsystems is one of Freud's contributions. The history of ego psychology need not be explored here; I will only note two articles that are particularly pertinent in introducing the line of inquiry to be pursued. Freud (1911a) discussed the interaction of id impulses, ego mechanisms, and memory traces in normal thinking. Hartmann (1956), in a similar and comprehensive fashion, expanded this theoretical approach, making the ego a pivotal concept in a theoretical framework. He attempted, in his formulation of autonomous ego functions, to explain phenomena outside the realm of psychopathology. There has been considerable debate as to whether creativity is such a phenomenon.

In the last chapter, I attempted to demonstrate by clinical observations that psychopathological processes hindered and sometimes completely inhibited creative activity. Lee (1940), Klein (1948), and others have considered creative activity a healing factor in overcoming a depressive episode. Kris (1950a, 1952) studied the various ego mechanisms in somewhat more detail and concluded that the ego undergoes a controlled regression during creative activity. Eissler (personal communication) believes that there is an expansion of the ego which has to be differentiated from regression and, in his pathobiographical study of Goethe (1958a), concludes that conflict has to become encapsulated so it cannot interfere with other ego functions responsible for artistic innovation.

No attempt is made here to define creativity, since the definition itself is controversial and cannot be settled on a purely descriptive basis. Rather, the ego process accompanying creativity is considered the essence of creative phenomena. The special environments, developmental potentials, and particular sensitivities of both creative artists and scientists have been discussed by many authors, particularly Greenacre (1957). These studies have also helped us in our understanding of psychic structure. The study of the creative process, one of the higher ego functions, may contribute to the formulation of a comprehensive ego psychology. The circular situ-

First published in *Psychoanalytic Quarterly* 34:79–101. Reprinted with permission.

ation of conceptualizing within a fluid and impermanent theoretical system from a series of clinical observations may have paradoxical elements but is not unusual in an empirical science. It should not make too much difference whether one is using ego psychology to study creativity or vice versa, as long as our observations are extracted from psychoanalytic material.

Here I wish to discuss theoretical principles derived from the observations of scientists in psychoanalysis (also see Chapter 32). I will scrutinize energic shifts between primary and secondary processes and the increased efficiency of various integrative and synthetic ego mechanisms in the creative process. Instead of exploring psychoeconomic factors and specific energy distributions, the role of memory traces and their organization as introjects will be stressed, with specific reference to the formation of the ego ideal. The nature of the ego ideal, the specific introjects, and the ego's constriction or expansion when faced with conflict distinguish one person from another. Although the creative person tends to handle conflicts in a characteristic manner, defensive techniques common to the noncreative person are also used.

The infantile experiences to be described are not to be considered determinants for creativity. One cannot reach conclusions about the source of a scientist's talents from a clinical study. The men I have studied were precocious, and constitutional factors must have been significant. Certainly they were not creative because they had particular psychic conflicts.

This study stresses that the techniques used to master problems may be effective in creative activity. Similar ego processes may operate during psychic development and in scientific creativity. The concepts discussed are derived from observations of the transference reactions of a patient who received universal acclaim for his discoveries. Genetic material is considered when it is relevant to the primary data. In the interest of discretion, the following presentation is purposely vague about data that is of minor importance to the thesis.

Case Material

Mr. Y., an unmarried man in his thirties, sought treatment because of episodically recurring depressions during which he could not do creative work. Although many people sought his company, he did not believe that they were really interested in him but felt that they gravitated toward him because of the fame he had achieved as a scientist. He was particularly vexed because he was not able to form any deep, lasting, or "inspiring" friendships.

His relationships with women were transitory; he indulged in occasional sexual relationships but felt no emotional bond with any of his partners. He was unable to effect any particularly close tie with men and his friendships were characterized by shallowness. He had idealistic notions concerning a deep bond with both a man and a woman and desperately wanted someone that he could look up to and respect.

The only area in which he did not feel disappointed was science. He spoke of science in anthropomorphic terms and worshiped the ideals of truth and discovery. It was sometimes difficult to distinguish whether he was talking about a deity or concepts from his particular field of work. He emphasized the strength of science, its immortality, omnipotence, and trustworthiness.

Mr. Y. described his mother as a dominant, ambitious woman who idolized him, her only child. The patient enjoyed this attention and the fact that he was in the spotlight, but was also made uncomfortable by being shown off. He was sensitive to the fact that he felt "exhibited" and, as a consequence, grew to distrust her. An aspect of this conflict was his recognition that his mother was inconsistent. She tended to revere and praise him but could also act very cruelly. He was never able to predict her outbursts of anger. For example, serious transgressions were overlooked or forgiven quickly, while on other occasions he was treated harshly for only minor offenses. He developed the belief that women were paradoxical and unfathomable creatures.

He also described his mother as charming, talented, and able to use tact, which sometimes bordered on manipulativeness. She displayed an outward demeanor of selfless submissiveness to men and had a superficial feminine attitude, indicating docile and gentle qualities. The patient felt that this was deceptive, however. He remembered that after he had come home late from a date during his adolescence, his mother went into an intense rage and spanked him brutally. He could never forget the anxiety as well as the shame and humiliation of this assault.

His father ostensibly had a position of supreme authority. He was dominant, vocal, and seemingly made all the important decisions in the household. He demanded and commanded respect and was considered sagacious, cosmopolitan, and intellectual, a veritable fountain of wisdom whose authority and strength would protect the family against any calamity. This idealistic picture received more than just reenforcement from the mother; in fact, she clearly helped create this portrait.

Mr. Y. reported a rude awakening during latency in his estimation of the father. As his social world expanded beyond the confines of home, he was able to compare his father with those of his friends. Perhaps he "had never noticed before," but now he compared his father's competence and social poise with that of other men, and recalled instances, such as parties, social events, scout meetings, or other community affairs, where his father had been shy and withdrawn and had behaved in an inept and ineffectual manner. He stressed the fact that his negative reevaluation had occurred precipitously, almost overnight, and that his disappointment had known no bounds. He was extremely melodramatic when he revealed this material.

This reaction, which is frequently seen in adolescents, occurred when Mr. Y. was seven years old. In retrospect, he believed he had decided then that his mother was really the ruler of the household. All of her ambitions were directed toward him and she tended to exploit his intellectual abilities. She had supreme confidence in his talents, and the patient became accustomed to thinking of himself as potentially creative.

This close relationship also had erotic components. She would often undress before him and not only bathe in his presence but sometimes take her bath with him. The relationship with his mother became the pivot around which all activity revolved and his father was pushed into the background. He was treated as a "miniature adult" and was given the prestige, authority, and status that "should have belonged to Father." The mother treated him as a confidant, discussed matters of adult importance by the hour with him, and respected his comments and decisions. Mr. Y. revealed how frightened he was of this "honor," although, at the time, he believed he was pleased.

During latency, he became a hero worshiper. Eighteen months after having experienced the disappointment, he sought and found an understanding and sympathetic male teacher whom he greatly admired. From his description it became apparent that the reverence and adoration he had felt for the father had shifted to the teacher. The teacher reciprocated, in that he was enthusiastic about the patient's scientific potential. Since he was always so far ahead of his classmates and displayed a sophistication considerably beyond his years, Mr. Y. constantly found himself in the position of a protégé with an enthusiastic mentor. He had a series of such teachers, many of whom spent much time tutoring him. During high school, he continued to receive praise and more definite encouragement to pursue science. He recalls being engaged even then in innumerable discussions that were passionately devoted to scientific ideals. Although he maintained some contact with his contemporaries, these relationships meant less to him.

Even in elementary school, the teachers treated him as if he were an adult. He felt that his teachers opened up a new vista, showed him a horizon with unending possibilities, and pointed out a world that he never suspected existed. Through them, he achieved an "intensive learning experience that reached sublime and blissful levels." His propensity for hero worship reached even greater heights when his mentors introduced their own personal heroes through conversations and literature. These were the great geniuses of science, the builders of the foundations of the particular field the patient later pursued. First Mr. Y. revered them; then he arduously and eagerly assimilated the pioneers' work, which led increasingly to an attitude of self-reliance. This form of idealism continued in his adult life. The original teachers were left behind, but Mr. Y. succeeded in forming a relationship with the scientist his first teacher revered. It was shortly after this man's death that he sought analysis.

The transference neurosis revealed in meaningful detail the sequence of object relationships in the genetic background of this patient. He began his analysis with complete trust and confidence. As observed in other scientists, Mr. Y. had a feeling of reverence for psychoanalysis and considered Freud one of the greatest geniuses of all time, ranking him at the same level or even above some of the great scientists in his own field. Consequently, he thought of the analyst as a god who could accomplish almost any miracle and attributed qualities of flawless perfection and infinite wisdom to the analyst.

The patient's unconscious wish was to incorporate the omnipotence he had assigned to the analyst, not only to gratify all of his infantile longings but to become a superman in his own right. His idealization took on grandiose and magical qualities. For example, his dreams always portrayed the analyst as a person of supreme strength who would nurture him and rescue him from some mysterious and destructive force. The alliance of patient and analyst would make Mr. Y. invulnerable and superior.

After about six months, the inevitable disappointment occurred and the patient was so bitter and depressed that he nearly terminated the analysis. At this point, he felt that the analyst was unable to do anything for him, and described him in exactly the same terms he had previously used in speaking of his father, i.e., dull, materialistic, passive, ineffectual, crass, and stupid. Interpretation, which he had previously valued so highly, now became meaningless. He was depressed and withdrew from all object relationships. His interest in science diminished and he was unable to produce anything. He vehemently denied that he had ever learned anything from the analysis and told of a dream in which a man who was a composite of the analyst and his father gave him something to eat that he found distasteful. He did not feel the substance was particularly harmful but believed that it would not do him any good or have any nutritional value. He then defecated the substance and felt relieved because of the bowel movement. His associations dwelt on the conviction that his father was unable to teach him anything useful and that he had to extrude what had been incorporated from him and of him after he discovered his weakness. This dream is very much like that discussed by Abraham (1927) in his classic paper on the dynamics of depression. Abraham told of his hair turning gray after the death of his father, which he interpreted as indicating his introjection of the lost love object; he overcame his depression when he was able to expel this introject anally in his dream life. Shortly after Mr. Y.'s dream, his depression lifted and was followed by a period of enthusiastic creative activity.

After this, the patient felt he was able to see the analyst in a new light. He commented that he now realized that what he wanted from life did not really exist and that the ideal qualities that he had believed the analyst possessed (similar to those his father had prior to the "catastrophic disappointment") were not to be found without some special effort. He could not passively wait for some such person to appear. On the contrary, he felt that he had to construct such a person himself.

As he elaborated on this, he indicated that it was not simply that he had to create such a person in fantasy. He did mean that but, more important, felt that he also had to turn toward the outer world to find a person to whom he could give the ideal qualities his father lacked and which I also could not supply. He was preoccupied with the task of creating an ideal person and of including this ideal in an object relationship.

He gradually began feeling positive toward me and his behavior vacillated between the position of a student and a teacher. At times, he cast me in the role of being able to learn a good deal from him and patiently preached standards of conduct, integrity, and scientific idealism. He wanted me to learn what it meant to be curious and to pursue knowledge assiduously for its own sake. On the other hand, he felt that I had a good deal of technical information and was a master in logic, well-grounded in the philosophy of science, and thereby could supply him with the power to master the mysteries of the universe. This latter attitude was similar to his earlier deification of the analyst, but he now felt that these qualities were not inherent in me but that he had been able to help me develop into an omnipotent person. He definitely felt responsible for my omnipotence and the material clearly revealed that he believed that he had succeeded in creating a "superman."

Often, his descriptions of transference feelings indicated that he was not speaking of a person. His "creation" became so esoteric that it gradually lost most of its human qualities. His descriptions of me became so abstract that my person was no longer required. In other words, he was speaking of his ideal, science, but his conviction was that he had created it. As he incorporated elements of this ideal within his personality and grew more confident, he did not feel he acquired his abilities from me. Rather, he believed that he had created his own ideal in the outside world, in this case by making a superman out of me, and then introjecting it. At this time, the patient was reaching a peak in his creative abilities and was so ecstatic that, once again, he saw no need to continue analysis.

Fortunately, some inroads had been made into the defensive meaning of such an idealization and into his need to believe that no one gave anything to him. He now spoke of his fear of his mother and brought it up contiguously with his precipitous disappointment and consequent irreverent attitude toward the father. His reconstruction was that she subtly exerted a marked influence on his attitudes and loyalties. She was the one who had set the father up as a god and he, being somewhat a martinet, had enjoyed the role. She had propagandized for the father to her son; as a result, his reverence had been founded more on her influence than on actual experiences in his relationship with his father. His mother was equally adept at tearing him down and had subtly undermined his confidence in his father for a long time. His confidence and esteem in his father gradually eroded under the influence of her insidious destructiveness, but the final collapse seemed to be traumatic and sudden. At this point in the analysis, Mr. Y. became preoccupied with unpredictable women. He felt that he had to turn toward the outer world and find a protector against his mother's engulfing destructiveness. The need for an idealized father was particularly strong, in that he represented an escape and a protection from mother. He had to be alert against a surprise attack.

During the latter phases of analysis, when he had insight into the conflicts just described, his ego ideal had considerably less magical, omnipotent qualities, as its protective function was less evident. He still felt that he had created his own ideal and had had few actual life experiences after which to model himself, but he acknowledged that his mentors as well as his father in some way contributed to the content of this ideal.

Discussion

The unique quality in this case was the timing and manner of the patient's attempt to master conflicting parental ties. He actively sought the idealized teacher, remote from the original parental object, during latency rather than at puberty or adolescence, when this more frequently occurs. Many children go from disappointment to disappointment in an attempt to recapture the lost object and, in some instances, may even find it in an abstraction or cause.

His mother was reported as being extremely involved with him in early infancy. Similar to the description of Loewald (1960), it is possible that her narcissism provided her with sufficient empathy for his needs so that he gained the strength to seek new objects. The first disappointment may have occurred when her narcissistic investment blocked his maturation but had already contributed enough to his ego strength* to facilitate his turning to the father rather than remaining fixated.

Mr. Y. was able to withstand the maternal onslaught because his father helped him in more ways than he was willing to acknowledge. After age seven, however, with the broadening of his social world, his father no longer afforded the needed protection from his frightening fantasy of being engulfed by his mother. Seeking a remote idealized object was an attempt to make up for this lack.

The patient prided himself in believing that he had a forceful personality and no difficulty in answering the questions of who he was and where he fitted in the fundamental scheme. Undoubtedly, his self-appraisal was narcissistically tinged, but a good deal of his self-satisfaction was without smugness, as his life was a sharp contrast to his father's passive orientation and mechanistic, materialistic outlook. He had a need to stress that his early introjected version of the father was for the most part repudiated and replaced by something else. The ideal qualities that had been previously attributed to his father not only ceased to belong to him but also ceased to be ideal.

In this connection, the autobiography of the physicist Michael Pupin (1925) is revealing. Pupin gave lengthy and admiring descriptions of his mother's strength of character, her confidence, and her interest in him, without which he felt he never could have reached the pinnacle of academic achievement that he finally obtained. His father is infrequently mentioned and one does not get a clear-cut impression of him as a personality.

Pupin described his highly personal attitude toward science. That he had a need for a father is quite evident, but apparently he was disappointed in reality and had to seek an idealized father elsewhere. Science, which he endowed with spiritual and religious overtones, served this purpose. He stated that "every American college and university could raise an invisible capital consecrated to the eternal truth and fill it with the icons of the great saints of science." He felt that the "saints of science" imparted their knowledge (secrets) to their "sons," the young, eager, and

---

*Phyllis Greenacre (personal communication) stated that the mother "contributed to the development of the autonomous ego inherent in gifted children, in that she permitted and encouraged his activities."

sincere students of science. Finding people of his own age inadequate as teachers, he sought older men and then revered them as if they were gods. He also implied that his attitudes were acquired without the help of a father in real life, but certainly the mother's role is not neglected. He felt that she inspired him to pursue what he considered to be the pathway to immortality.

The creative product is an expansion of reality, a new accretion to the outer world that is constructed and given form by the scientist. In a study of the ego processes accompanying creative activity, I have observed that this expansion occurs when the scientist is able to effect an expansion of the ego, reflected in heightened inner and outer perceptual awareness and unusually effective executive responses. The executive, integrative, and synthetic ego systems operate with greater efficiency and economy. They seem to have at their disposal energy that was not dissipated in counter-cathexis. The ego is free of conflict and, as Kris (1952) has emphasized, secondary process extends to include primary-process instinctual elements.

In describing reality-attuned behavior, Freud (1911a) pointed out that the id impulse cathects an appropriate memory trace that associatively corresponds to its content. These memory traces, which are found in the preconscious system, represent intrapsychic registrations of past experiences, situations, or relationships that have been meaningful to the developing psyche. When a need is stimulated, the ego executive system must function in accord with reality in order to supply the elements required to satisfy that need. Needs seek immediate gratification, but survival necessitates that executive systems be integrated with inner and outer reality. Freud pointed out that the process of thinking includes delayed action and testing potential action in graduated doses. In order to achieve this, the well-integrated ego draws upon a series of memory residues that have been gratifying and pleasurable or frustrating and painful. Integrated in these memories are the objects that have made possible the pleasure or pain.

Freud (1923) said that a thought whose formation is stimulated by an inner need reached preconscious existence "through becoming connected with the word-presentations corresponding to it." The verbal image constitutes the content of the preconscious memory system. Rapaport (1956) extends this concept somewhat in that he believes that an idea, initially an instinctual representation, becomes conscious by being hyper-cathected and may or may not include a "relationship to the verbal trace." However, when an idea is elevated to the position of a thought, it retains its relationship to reality, which, according to Rapaport, occurs "through experientially meaningful connections of ideas." The latter are part of "an experiential connection system of progressively more differentiated and discrete ideas" and the memory system. Freud (1900) wrote that when the id impulse does not go through the secondary-process refinement of thought, hallucinatory wish-fulfillment may result. In this instance, the memory trace of the archaic object affording gratification is revived, and the aim of the psychic apparatus is merely to reexperience that perception, which is connected with the gratification of the need. The object is viewed in a primitive fashion rather than as part of a gratifying, reality-attuned experience. According to Freud (1915a), ideas are cathexes of memory traces, whereas in a hallucination "the cathexis passes over the memory system to perceptual consciousness" (1923). In this connection, Piaget (1951) wrote that a thought requires no outside object to produce it (similar to Beres' concept of a mental representation) because it occurs from a combination of memory traces. Beres (1957) considered this combination of memory traces a determinant of imagination and part of the process of creativity. It should be stressed that, in the case of thought oriented to reality, the id impulses seek gratification through techniques acquired through past satisfactions and made part of the memory system. A hallucination does not work this way.

For Mr. Y., the object was a most important memory trace that could become integrated in behavior governed by the secondary process. During regressed states, his magical attitudes about objects were highlighted, but these attitudes became more sophisticated and refined when his integrative capacities were functioning once again. Earlier, he felt that he could "command" the appearance of the archaic object for the satisfaction of infantile wishes or for protection. His fantasy was that, like a magician, he could conjure up the object. The belief "I see it, therefore it must exist" and the subsequent "because I can bring it into view I am responsible for its existence" coexisted with intense scopophilic needs and might have been related to his vivid external perceptions.

By observing the transference neurosis, I could detect the megalomanic aspects of the "peek-a-boo" creation of the object alongside Mr. Y.'s abstract scientific credo, passionate idealization, and creative fervor, all of which had become synthesized into an ego ideal.

The belief that he created the object stemmed from such primitive mechanisms of control. Later, when secondary-process integrative mechanisms were also effective and he could turn to the outer world, an expansion of the ego resulted in psychotic defenses and constriction of the ego. Greenacre (1957) has called the ability to find substitute objects a "talent" and has included it in the concept of "collective alternates." According to her, the gifted patient turns to a variety of objects in the outside world to fulfill needs and seek protection in areas where the patient has been disappointed by the parents. I think that Mr. Y. and other creative scientists demonstrate this phenomenon, which is accompanied by a high and abstract ego ideal.

The formation of the ego ideal is not being considered here as a causal factor of Mr. Y.'s creative abilities; nor is the reverse being implied, i.e., that his innate creative potential would inevitably lead to the formation of such an ego ideal. That creative ability and the ego ideal are in some way imbricated is obvious, but the connection cannot be understood without further exploration of genetic factors.

One of the first determinants of Mr. Y.'s early idealization of his father was the anxiety he felt in relation to his mother. The image of the idealized father protected him from this anxiety. Since it was characteristic of him to use the mechanism of seeking a new external object even as a child, as evidenced by his finding enthusiastic mentors, it is not surprising that his father image underwent changes, including partial decathexis, when his expectations of the idealized father were disappointed. The decathexis of the initial image enabled him to use the energy to cathect the ego systems active in seeking and creating new objects.

The decathexis of the father image was reenacted in the transference neurosis, but in this case it did not lead to what Eissler (1960) described as the canceling out of a psychic element. Rather, the change in the image or in the elements superimposed on it lessened its power to deal with inner impulses and master external situations. The position the idealized father previously held as the central core of the ego ideal was no longer an active one; instead, he had been relegated to the negative realm, and any remaining elements of the earlier identification led to a negative self-esteem and a sense of shame. Many of Mr. Y.'s derogatory self-descriptions were almost identical to his descriptions of his father. As a defense, he sought out objects that he felt conformed to the standard he had constructed. He then had to establish an object relationship in order to reenforce the "self-constructed" qualities he wished to achieve. He did what is done by every patient as the transference neurosis unfolds—he attributed certain qualities to an external object.

Heimann (1942) has commented on a similar process in sublimation and internalization. The ego normally "assimilates" the qualities of the internalized parent if it succeeds in replacing the fantasied objects of early oral and anal sadism with more benign objects. The patient experiences such revision of objects as "creating [or recreating, according to present views] his parents rather than swallowing them."

The introjected archaic object that is later transferred is not identical to any person. A continuous revision of internalized objects occurs in the service of both the pleasure and reality principles. Nevertheless, certain elements of infantile and archaic mental representatives, which vary according to the analytic situation, are transferred. In Mr. Y., the early father ideal was replaced by the ideal of science, which had to be "objectivized," as the patient called it. After this occurred, he responded to the analyst in the same way as he did to his esteemed mentors. Later, in deeper transference states, the early idealized father image became prominent.

The influence of the idealized preoedipal father became apparent in spite of the fact that the patient denied its significance. This early image contributed to the later ego ideal, and certain positive attributes seen in the father were projected onto others and reintrojected. Later, the elements of the introject formed part of a larger context—scientific idealism and ideals that Mr. Y. had attributed to teachers were introjected. Then this image was elaborated by many details, which became further and further removed from human attributes and took on an abstract quality. It is particularly significant that the megalomanic fantasy of creating a needed object which was originally utilized for defensive purposes, was refined and applied to realistic, creative tasks.

The megalomanic fantasy of creating the object had a strong visual cathexis associated with it—its "peek-a-boo" quality. Greenacre (1956, 1958) describes a strong sensory awareness and an unusual vividness of sensory impressions in such patients. Mr. Y. demonstrated a similar vividness and had many fantasies with intense scopophilic elements. He was very curious, which was somehow related to seeing. The visual modality was preeminent in all his fantasies and he sought objects primarily by seeing. His thinking was also dominated by visual elements. Obviously, he was involved with primal-scene elements, but these need not be elaborated.

The integration of a primitive id impulse with scopophilic elements into such a sophisticated mental representation as an abstraction necessitates a reality-oriented refinement of the impulse. The elevation of a psychosexually induced need to an abstract idea is similar to the formation of the scientific ego ideal from the need for a supportive father figure.

In his autobiography, Pupin commented that his most meaningful learning experiences came from his mentors, who introduced him to the works of some "great ones." My patient, like many scientists, felt that the elements of his most meaningful and lasting experiences were transcendental. He could not explain in any logical, coherent fashion what he actually experienced while learning but felt that his most potent knowledge was assimilated in some magical way. This included experiences of awe (cf. Greenacre, 1956) vaguely related to his highly esteemed hero teachers. Others have described this more graphically as learning "through the process of osmosis" or, as one patient said, "by fusion with an outside powerful inspirational force that comes from another reality." My patient's descriptions of his teachers were so esoteric that they did not seem human or concrete at all but, in themselves, represented a kind of abstraction. This was the direct antithesis of what he felt about his father, but it is interesting that he could feel so powerfully about object relationships and elevate them to superhuman levels.

In this connection, Greenacre (1958, p. 11) states, "the developing gifted child, even in very untoward circumstances, will sometimes be able to find a temporary personal adult substitute or even to extract from a cosmic conception some useful personalized god conception on which to project his necessary idealized father and himself to enable him to develop further." Greenacre also felt that one of the parents, usually the father, had to "qualify for the mantle of greatness." Although my patient denied any such qualities in his father, it was quite apparent that his father's role was significant.

In this analysis, Mr. Y.'s idealizations enabled him to avoid experiencing hostile feelings toward the revered object while directing them toward the debased one. The self-image and the ego ideal became fused and the debased images were decathected during zestful creative activity. Klein (1948) spoke of this decathexis of a debased image as a restoration of it in the ego ideal. The restorative quality of creativity has been referred to by many authors, Lee (1940, 1947) in particular.

Mr. Y. insisted on the important distinction between creating something new and simulating creativity through the elimination of an interfering element. Removing crabgrass was not the same thing as creating an original landscaping arrangement. To exorcize devils within oneself or destroy their projected counterparts in the outside world is a process of constriction, in contrast to the expansion of the ego in the creation of an "addition" to reality. Since Mr. Y.'s father had become an object of disappointment, the patient had to find moral and aesthetic values in the external world. Being unable to depend on father as a model produced a "gap." He had to fill it by seeking other models, for he could not accept the paternal image, either as he saw it at the time or as he had previously seen it in its positive version. This he felt was a laudable pursuit, in that it represented independence. Independence and initiative also had defensive qualities, of course, in that they represented a reaction-formation against passive longings. He did not believe that he had been "discovered" by his teachers. Instead, he emphasized that he had found the teachers and attracted them to himself by being an active and brilliant student.

Ordinarily, there is a continuum from the father, to a culturally accepted hero, to values and ideals. The progressive abstraction of Mr. Y.'s ego ideal led to a similar abstraction of the discovered outside objects required to sustain it. The primary identification with archaic and primitive features furnished later objects with primary-process qualities, giving them their transcendental, superhuman, magical, awe-inspiring characteristics. Abstraction, on the other hand, is a secondary-process function, the antithesis of the concreteness of the id. *The combined action of the primary process associated with this early father introject and the progressive abstraction of the later object into a scientific idea or concept led to an ego ideal that valued creative discovery.*

In the formation of the ego ideal there is a synthesis of a variety of perceptual experiences that later determine the roles and strivings of the person. Rosen (1958, 1960) speaks of a progression from early stages of image formation to later stages of concept formation that require the synthesis of projective mental contents along with an introjection of external objects. He considers such processes in terms of their relevance to imagination and discusses how such operations are pertinent to abstraction.

Thoughts, like any psychic element, must be viewed in terms of a developmental continuum. The psychic model has been conceptualized as consisting of a variety of systems, including the physiological as well as the psychological. Freud's earliest model basically was one of stimulus and response. An outside stimulus was conceived as passing from lower systems to higher ones; at the highest levels, it was experienced as a thought. An impulse passes upward through a variety of stages, from a vague visceral sensation, to an animistic affective perception, to an autonomous idea separated from personalized factors.

Similarly, in the development of the ego ideal, the synthesis and introjection of percepts of external objects take place gradually in a serial, hierarchical fashion, each object being perceived in a progressively more sophisticated manner that is consonant with the particular phase of psychosexual development. In many instances, the progression (from primitively perceived part objects to the complex and sensitive evaluations of individual persons) is beset with a variety of vicissitudes. Its course is not necessarily smooth and, as with Mr. Y., there can be severe disappointments. The child may go from disappointment in objects and finally turn to an abstraction or a cause.

As I discussed in Chapter 32, there is a wide range of energy, a broad spectrum of extremes of primary and secondary processes, operating during creative activity. The ability to vacillate between primary and secondary processes has been noted by many authors as a particular feature of the creative person, one that involves all ego systems, including the superego and ego ideal. At the secondary-process end of the spectrum, the psyche can form concepts and deal with abstractions. One notes that, for Mr. Y., the early father introject determined the direction of the later abstractions. Finally, abstraction proceeded to a point where a person was no longer required (Piaget, 1951); instead, elements that extended beyond the perceivable, concrete reality were sought. Bronowski (1958), Poincaré (1952), and other introspective scientists have noted that a theory or an abstraction always extends beyond the observable data and that extension constitutes the creative product. The creative activity, the mastery implicit in such activity, becomes the axis around which the ego ideal maintains itself.

The activity described here—turning toward the outer world to seek objects in order to construct an ego ideal, with progressive abstraction of the object—constituted a talent that was relevant to Mr. Y.'s creative ability. Nevertheless, it must again be emphasized that the developmental vicissitudes that he experienced are in no way responsible for his special abilities. The origin and source of his talent cannot be discussed here, since there are no data from the frame of reference that I have introduced that would be relevant. The sources of creativity are still as much a mystery as ever, and all one can attempt to do is to explore further certain developmental factors in a person known to be creative.

Summary

Pertinent object relationships of a creative scientist undergoing psychoanalysis are given in order to understand the development of his ego ideal. The transference neurosis highlighted some of the introjective-projective mechanisms used to form a composite father-science image of lofty proportions transcending any concrete experience.

The patient remembered an early attachment to his father, whom he viewed as forceful, confident, and tyrannical. At the beginning of latency, he suddenly saw his father as an ineffectual, passive martinet. His previous image of him was destroyed and the reaction was extreme disappointment. His seductive, dominant, manipulative, and unpredictable mother significantly affected his assessment of the father. In order to master the conflict in his relationship to his mother, the patient sought a strong, consistent father image with spiritual, esoteric qualities, one that was best embodied in the canons of science. This led to a progressive abstraction of the personified aspects of the ego ideal, as his ability to abstract was a well-developed talent.

The techniques employed in the formation of the ego ideal were particularly relevant for later creative activity. The acquisition of such techniques is not discussed, since the psychoanalytic data do not contribute answers to the question. It is possible that specific developmental vicissitudes, by producing a need for such integrative methods, served to stimulate their use and led to their development, though other life circumstances could have had a similar influence. The same circumstances in other patients can produce an entirely different clinical picture that shows no significant creative ability.

Chapter 34

Dreams and the Creative Process

The creative process has been studied from many different viewpoints. The psychoanalyst has found that, in the study of the creative scientist's or artist's biography, fantasies and dreams are of considerable value in learning about inner motivations and intrapsychic conflicts. In this chapter I will describe two dreams of a patient who received high acclaim for his scientific discoveries, dreams that occurred while the patient was engaged in intense creative activity. In fact, the second dream occurred at the time he made a scientific contribution that established his reputation as a renowned scientist. The interplay of psychic conflict, as reflected in the transference regression, and creative activity has many fascinating facets that are highlighted as we examine manifest dream content.

Patients with character disorders where the basic psychopathology is an ego defect sometimes reflect regressions and ego dissolution in their dreams by such elements as crumbling houses, the floor collapsing underneath them, or the ceiling falling down. These manifest elements, overdetermined as they are, frequently represent the ego and its loss of synthesis. Consequently, I have referred to such dreams as representational, the dream image being at one level a pictorial self-observation. Freud (1900) concerned himself with how various psychic elements and processes are represented in dreams. Sandler and Rosenblatt (1962) use the term "representational world" to describe aggregates of introjects. I use the term in a similar sense, since psychic structure is determined by introjects that become amalgamated into the ego, a process that Loewald (1962) refers to as internalization. All ego systems depend upon introjected adaptive experiences for their development; the synthetic functioning of these systems determines the characteristic structure of any particular ego (see discussion).

All dreams are to some extent representational and it is not possible to separate wish-fulfilling dynamic forces and structure. However, one can emphasize structure; in the character disorders and in creative activity, such an emphasis is useful for the exploration of intra-ego processes.

The study of dreams occurring during creative activity calls attention

First published in *British Journal of Medical Psychology* 8:105–115. Reprinted with permission.

to positive aspects of ego functioning. The character disorders have been mentioned because they represent the other side of the coin. Perhaps there is a continuum with the character disorders at one end and the creative ego at the other. However, this does not mean these are mutually exclusive conditions. It is well known that a person with a severe ego defect can also be highly creative. Nevertheless, some analysts believe that the ego defect is not relevant to creative ability and, although a defect and such ability may coexist, one does not contribute to the other. In fact, if there is a relationship, it is an inverse one, as Eissler (1958a) has postulated in his study of Goethe.

Freud (1900) mentions Silberer, who assigned himself a mental task and then drifted into sleep. In one dream, Silberer translated the self-assigned task into a concrete action, as the sleeping ego was unable to deal with higher abstractions. The reversion to primitive modes of representation may accentuate defective integration obscured by later defensive super-structures or, on the positive side, it may emphasize expansive ego operations that occur during creative activity. This expansion consists of a widening and extension of perceptual and integrative systems, which leads to an increased range of functioning.

There are many examples in the general literature of dreams and fantasies of creative scientists and artists. Perhaps two of the best known are Poincairé's fantasy (1952) and Kekulé's dream (described by Freud, 1900). Poincairé, while on a walk, visualized brilliantly colored balls and hooks being arranged in a variety of ways, at a hectic pace. When he "recovered" from his fantasy or reverie he was able to formulate certain mathematical elements known as Fuchsian functions. This was an important mathematical discovery. Kekulé, it will be recalled, was struggling with the problem of the benzene formula, one that defied the leading chemists of his time. After having unsuccessfully pursued this problem, he had a dream of a snake who curled around itself and put its tail in its mouth. On awakening, Kekulé was able to retain the image of the curled-up snake; he realized he had resolved his dilemma by postulating that carbon atoms arrange themselves in a ring.

In these and other examples, one has to raise the question as to whether any creative activity occurred during the dream. Does the dream have any problem-solving qualities? Freud felt divided on this point. In Chapter One of *The Interpretation of Dreams* (1900), he implies that the process of dream function has creative qualities. For example, he states:

Reports of numerous cases . . . seem to put it beyond dispute that dreams can carry on the intellectual work of daytime and bring it to conclusions which had not been reached during the day, and that they can resolve doubts and problems and be the source of new inspiration for poets and musical composers [pp. 64–65].

Yet he feels that the dream does not in itself lead to a creative product. During the day the dreamer may be intellectually preoccupied, and this preoccupation is reflected in the dream. Intellectual activity does not occur while dreaming, but the dream in some way expresses intellectual activity that had already been going on. Freud reached the following conclusion:

> the dream work carries out no other function than the translation of dream thoughts . . . and that the question whether the mind operates in dreams with all its intellectual faculties or with only a part of them is wrongly framed and disregards the facts [p. 445].

Later, when one is awake, the primitive representation of intellectual activity can bring to consciousness a solution which was latent, presumably already close to consciousness. Freud does not pursue the topic further. The psychic mechanisms involved in what phenomenologically appears to be a "flash" of insight or an immediate, momentous discovery have, as far as I know, never been conceptualized in the frame of reference of ego psychology. These questions will be discussed after the presentation of some dreams that occurred during a creative phase.

Case Material

Mr. Y., an unmarried man in his late thirties, had won worldwide renown for his scientific accomplishments. He was both pleased with, and frightened by, his creative abilities. He described a gradually increasing anxiety that could reach paniclike proportions when he was involved in work that was going to lead to a discovery. His creative abilities were episodic and he described himself as dull, sterile, and unproductive when he was not doing some exciting research. Although he was frightened at the time of creating, he also felt exhilarated and found life zestful and exciting. It was the fear that such feelings would become too intense and get out of control that caused him to feel anxious and seek therapy.

The background of this patient is discussed in Chapter 33; I have discussed similar patients in Chapter 32 and elsewhere (Giovacchini, 1959). Briefly, he felt his father was passive and weak, dominated by and beholden to the patient's mother. Up to the age of seven he idolized him, encouraged by his mother. When he started going to school and moving out of the confines of his home, he felt he was able to measure his father against other men and his idol was "dethroned." He described this reaction as one of "catastrophic disappointment."

The mother doted on her only child. She cultivated and stimulated intellectualism and then took tremendous pride in showing him off to her friends. He was pleased with the attention he received but also resented it. He was somewhat aware of the fact that he was being manipulated and felt his mother to be unpredictable and dangerous. He felt uneasy about the tremendous responsibility and adult position she forced upon him, although he did his best to handle it. As a result he was precocious, not only intellectually but in his general behavior too. He acted like a "miniature adult."

Mr. Y. became involved with and idolized his teachers, who made him into a protégé. This was an acceptable way of defending himself against his mother, and also represented a substitute for the disappointing father, who was not able to protect him against what he felt to be mother's onslaught.

In the analysis he began by idolizing me, became bitterly disappointed, and then tried to "teach" me how to be a person he could idolize and feel protected by, but he was unable to feel secure. The transference regression was characterized by a fear of "falling apart," "losing" himself, and being engulfed, but it never reached paniclike proportions. He felt disappointed and unprotected and was very disturbed, but his reality-testing remained fairly intact. He was also afraid of his impulses but felt omnipotent and therefore able to gratify instinctual demands, oedipal and otherwise. He felt "surges of power" and believed that he could possess his mother, annihilate his father, and even control the world. To be so powerful was awesome and frightening and he was concerned about being overwhelmed and destroyed by his impulses. My role was to protect him from such powerful feelings. He clung to me helplessly, but his anger often reached paranoid proportions because of his disappointment.

The genetic antecedents of both his omnipotence and anxiety became apparent as he focused upon his relationship to his mother. She treated him as being all-powerful, making him feel that he was the most important person in her life. This was accompanied by precocity and superficial confidence. However, insofar as the relationship he had with his mother was inappropriate for his immature ego, he sensed that it was dangerous.

During creative phases, he reexperienced the conflict between narcissistic gratification and the fear of becoming all-powerful and losing control. The fear of loss of control was, of course, the fear of an overwhelming destructiveness, which became associated with the omnipotent aspects of his creativeness. While creating, he felt he was "unlocking the floodgates" and would have to stop himself from pursuing his research problem further.

The problems he worked on always had some bearing on someone else's work. He would supercede other investigators' discoveries. In fantasy, he felt that by destroying another scientist's work he had also destroyed the scientist.

His dreams reflected the fear of being overwhelmed by his impulses and the resultant anxiety and fear of ego dissolution. For example, in the midst of working on a problem, he had the following dream:

> I was sitting at my desk trying to figure out how to achieve a more elegant solution to some equations that Professor X felt he had solved. Things became pretty exciting as I began to find an answer that was more precise than his. Professor X appeared momentarily and although, as you know, I detest him he looked pale and wan and I felt sympathy for him. I wanted to take care of him for I felt now I could do anything and transcend petty, trivial rivalries. The room then got all mixed up and I got scared. Things started whirling around, the walls began caving in, and I could feel the floor start giving way under me. I woke up and had to pull myself together.

When fully awake, the patient regretted that he could not recall the "elegant" solution he had dreamed about. He felt that he had actually solved a problem, but the problem in the dream was a different one than the one he was working on, even though his recall of the dream problem was imperfect.

His disappointment was tremendous because he had been pursuing his research in a frenzied fashion. All of his thoughts were concentrated on seeking a solution, one that he hoped would bring him recognition, yet he was afraid of succeeding. His preoccupation with his research was all-pervasive and, when associating to the dream, he discussed his scientific dilemma in considerable detail.

Professor X had worked in a similar scientific area and had painstakingly and laboriously arrived at and published some conclusions. Mr. Y.'s work was beginning to reveal that these conclusions were partially erroneous, and he frequently verbalized his concern that he was destroying Professor X, at least in a scientific sense.

He was particularly concerned because he was very angry at Professor X, who had been his teacher and who had an international reputation. At first, the patient believed it was an honor to be his student and expected to become a "colossus" in his field because of what he would learn from his mentor. Instead, he was bitterly disappointed. He saw Professor X's successes as being due to a dull, plodding, and unspectacular pursuit of a problem. He lacked brilliance and dramatic appeal.

The patient felt he had surpassed him even before he received his graduate degree. Some colleagues agreed with him. He also felt that Professor X was resentful and that he made things unpleasant for him. For this reason, Mr. Y. moved to another institution, where he was given complete academic freedom.

The theme of angry disappointment in a man who was set up to make him omnipotent recurred frequently. Mr. Y. then feared he would not be able to control his anger and felt both frightened and guilty.

The transference neurosis was the scene of the reenactment of his early disappointment in his father for not protecting him against his mother's narcissistic demands. He had been feeling similarly resentful of me, insofar as analysis had not fulfilled his earlier expectations and he had not been able to sustain his initial enthusiasm. Still, he was ambivalent and was concerned as to whether he had hurt me or whether I would become angry with him. He frequently turned around to look at me to reassure himself and, at the time of the dream, often remarked about how wan and pale I looked and urged me to take care of myself.

His creative activity was associated with several factors. He had tremendous conflict in creating because, on the one hand, it was an omnipotent experience and, on the other, he was exposed to the impact of anger. To be creative meant the destruction of his mentor, but, at the same time, especially in such a transference regression where ego/nonego boundaries are blurred, it also meant that he would be destroyed. In this instance, it became clear that his concern with my health was reflected in the dream; he felt he would destroy me by being creative. As the "elegance" and purity of the creative product became contaminated with destructiveness, his ego was faced with a "flooding" of disintegrative impulses. The patient stated that the crumbling structures in the manifest content reflected his crumbling self (see discussion).

The need to cast me in the role of the omnipotent protector gradually lessened as it was constantly interpreted. Consequently, the angry disappointment that occurred because of the inevitable frustration of such a need was considerably diminished. At this point, the mother transference came to the fore, but since it is tangential to the study of psychic processes reflected in dreams during creative activity, I will describe it only briefly. He was afraid of being assaulted and engulfed by her. He felt threatened, fearing that she would rob him of any autonomy and identity by making him a narcissistic appendage. He accused me of manipulating and exploiting him, the purpose of the analysis being to fit him into a mold and divest him of any semblance of individuality. He also felt engulfed by oedipal feelings that threatened to inundate him; possibly because during childhood they may have been unusually intense, since he saw himself as being put in the precocious role of being a "miniature adult." This role was disruptive in that he must have found it difficult to handle the sexual excitement that was prematurely stimulated.

As Mr. Y. was able to understand the archaic nature of his object representations, his confidence about maintaining control increased and he became much more comfortable when facing instinctual impulses. This had an effect on creative activity.

Previously, he could create only episodically and, as has been described, found such episodes to be situations of extreme tension that left him "drained." He did not know when an idea or a project would occur to him. He could not predict the occurrence of what Kris (1952) has described as inspiration, and equated the lack of predictability with lack of control, helplessness, and vulnerability.

He reported that he was no longer at "the mercy of ideas." He found that he could involve himself in creative activity at will and did not have to wait for inspiration. Furthermore, the exhilarating effects of work were not nearly as disturbing and had less of a tendency to get out of hand. He still experienced a state of omnipotence but was able to emphasize the enjoyable and exciting aspects of it rather than the fear of destroying and being destroyed. In other areas, he found himself "very much alive." All activities were experienced with zest, whereas previously he had been isolated and withdrawn.

As Greenacre (1956) has described, he seemed to experience heightened responses to external stimuli. Everything seemed much more vivid than usual during creative periods. Rather than being totally immersed in his work, he continued to be actively involved with the external world. He enjoyed food, drink, and an active sexual life as he continued working.

His mood was expansive and accompanied by mild euphoria. Still, his contact with reality was not disturbed and one was able to observe a mixture of excitement and sound, logical thinking. He noticed many subtleties in his interactions with persons with whom he was emotionally involved, and made many keen observations that he ordinarily would not notice.

After finishing a research problem, he would relax for a while and not pursue intellectual activities. Previously, he had been depressed between creative periods. Some (Lee, 1940) have considered the creative experience a healing factor in overcoming a depressive episode. In any case, after some analysis, this patient was no longer depressed but did not have the same zest for living that he experienced when creative.

He was still productive but now was dealing with routine, somewhat mechanistic, tasks. He would watch television for long periods of time or become inordinately interested in gadgets (Giovacchini, 1959), pursuits that he found reprehensible when creating. He never reported any dreams at such times.

In contrast, he reported many dreams during creative periods. These dreams were characterized by intense activity; often he would be aware of bright colors and lights but, in spite of the turbulent activity he dreamed of, he felt pleasure. Frequently, he was able to recall only the pleasure and the sensation of considerable activity but would not be able to attach any of these feelings to a specific content.

There were dreams, however, where he had a vivid recall of the manifest content. During a particularly inspired period, he solved a problem that had perplexed him for a long time, a solution that he prized. On the eve of the day that he solved this problem, he had the following dream:

> I was in this modern, ranch-style house similar to the one I've been thinking of buying. This place was pleasantly furnished; tasteful but nothing out of the ordinary. The room was of average size, not large but not small either and reasonably comfortable. I remember particularly looking out the window and the garden and the surroundings looked pleasant but nothing spectacular. Everything seemed to be cast in grays; varying shades hinted at color but there was still a dullness to the whole picture. Perhaps everything was just a little bit drab. I was fairly calm and maybe even a little contented at first. But as I kept looking around, I sensed tension and began to get increasingly restless. I felt peculiarly dissatisfied, as if I wanted to do something but not knowing exactly what. All of a sudden everything started whirling around. I mean literally. There were bright lights and everything, the furniture, the house, myself, even the garden, looked as if it had been caught in a tornado. As I think of it now, it's funny that I wasn't the least bit afraid. Instead, I found it fun like I find riding a roller coaster. I felt like a child watching fireworks and getting exhilarated but I knew things would calm down and not get out of hand. It finally stopped and now the scene had an almost spiritual quality to it. It was the same room but it was larger and more elegant. It had lost none of its previous simplicity. The furniture seemed to be better balanced, more functionally arranged, and there were several new pieces that I hadn't seen before. Everything seemed bright. Now there was no dullness and drabness. Looking outside the window gave me a totally different feeling, as if an incredible change had occurred in the whole world. The outside was also brighter. Here again the garden had other shrubberies and bushes that I had not noticed before. The colors were deeper and vibrant.

The report of this dream was a verbatim one. As one can see, the patient had a dramatic sense and was able to express himself in a vivid and, at times, poetic fashion. Concerning this dream and others that were similar in manifest content, he immediately associated it to creative activity.

His first associations to the dream were in terms of the various degrees of organization that characterized different aspects of the dream. The way the room expanded—that is, the extension of its initial state as well as the rate of change—was closely connected to the problem he had been arduously pursuing. I cannot go into more detail here concerning these associations; suffice it to say that any person whose daytime preoccupations were as intense as this patient's would naturally reflect them in his dream life. How the highly focalized day residue interacts with the unconscious is the main element of analytic interest and highlights aspects of the creative process as well as the intrapsychic balance of the particular transference situation.

In this dream, Mr. Y. once again felt that the room was representative of his mental state and that the expansion, vibrancy, and "elegance" were the result of creative activity. There was a minimum of contamination by destructive feelings and he felt that his newly established room—an expansion from the previous state—represented the creative product.

As with any dream, there were many different levels of meaning to this dream. The dream thoughts were concerned with his "whirlwind" relationship with his mother, which he now felt he had under control but which had overwhelmed him in the first dream. There were sexual and pregenital elements that threatened to engulf him. His ability to create depended on how much control he had of primary-process instinctual elements, whether he could master them and subject them to secondary-process forces.

Discussion

These dreams can be considered from many viewpoints. Instead of emphasizing psychodynamic factors and dealing with the conflictual dream thoughts, this discussion will focus on psychic structure. Dreams can be used to study the relationships between various ego systems, which is also useful for the study of the creative process.

As Seitz (1963) has pointed out, a dream can reflect a psychic state. He believes that some dreams can include in their manifest content some elements that represent specific ego structures. He illustrated this thesis by presenting dreams that he interpreted as containing instinctual regulatory systems, represented by transformers and rheostats. In contrast, the dreams presented here do not represent specific psychic structures.

Silberer (in Freud, 1900) illustrated how psychic processes can be transformed into pictorial form. He did not speak of structure in an isolated fashion, but, following Freud, demonstrated how the dream work handled a particular mental task that the dreamer had assigned himself. He would fall asleep while thinking about a problem. The resultant dream picture was often a metaphorical expression of that problem. He did not dream of a direct representation of a psychic structure but, rather, of the thinking process itself.

Structure and wish-fulfillment psychodynamic forces cannot be separated. The psychic apparatus has been conceptualized as consisting of various units that are characterized by their functions. Freud (1923) formulated the structural hypothesis in operational terms, so too finite a separation between structure and impulse is artificial and conceptually inconsistent.

The manifest elements of houses, rooms, and furniture were often found in my patient's dreams. These elements realistically represent a dwelling, a place where one lives or is housed. They have been found to be symbolic of the mother but, in any case, are symbolic of an object or a part object that was instrumental in caring for the dreamer. They refer to a situation where the person felt supported and maintained regardless of the conflict that might be associated with such sustenance and nurture. The infantile ego can relate to objects only as part objects and in a concrete fashion. Still, these part objects become the building blocks of the child's psyche. The dream occurs in a sleeping ego that has reverted to primitive modes of functioning and utilizes infantile methods of representation. This ego's perception of the self would contain infantile elements that, because of their part object and concrete qualities, are particularly suitable for pictorial expression. The representation of the regressed sleeping ego would consist of the early introjects of the nurturing source.

Freud (1900) discusses the symbol of the house as being especially apt to represent the organism as a whole; different sections of rooms refer to specific bodily parts. The soma, however, is included in the concept of the ego, and during regressed states the ego reverts to its primitive core, which contains somatic elements. Consequently, it is not surprising that a house in a dream often designates an ego state.

Silberer believed that "functional phenomena" (the translation of abstract thought process into concrete images) occurred during a transition state between sleep and wakefulness. The dreams I have described here also occurred during a transitional state—in the first, the ego was entering a condition of narcissistic regression; in the second, it was emerging into an organization that was less narcissistic and more structured and object-directed. In other, noncreative patients, similar dreams of collapsing elements may reflect a chronically tenuous ego organization that is precariously balanced and where the range of either regression or progression is narrow.

The admixture of primary and secondary process has been referred to by many authors as characteristic of the creative process. The dreams of my patient Mr. Y. illustrate this thesis and reveal other subtle relationships between various psychic structures. Both dreams begin with a state of calm. At the onset there is an equilibrium and the activity of the dream is coherent and organized. In one instance, the patient is carrying on a routine activity—sitting at a desk and working on a problem; in the second dream, he is peacefully contemplating his surroundings in a fashion that seems to be reality-directed. His thoughts in both dreams, as he recalls them, have some secondary-process characteristics.

Whenever a patient reports a dream that is well organized and realistically constructed, one can raise the question as to how much secondary elaboration occurred in reporting it. Insofar as the patient has to take various images and put them in a verbal form and then communicate them to a therapist, the dream must undergo significant revision. The process of making it communicable must add considerably to the manifest content.

This reality-oriented revision occurs, more or less, with all dreams. It has to be taken into account but does not prevent us from detecting the balance between primary- and secondary-process elements. Many dreams are bizarre and incoherent in spite of the secondary revision they have been subjected to while being communicated. Consequently, one can look at a dream and compare one part of it with another and reach conclusions about relative degrees of primary and secondary process. Similarly, the dream can be scrutinized in terms of its general organization, enabling one to observe shifts and changes in equilibrium which reflect the ego's integration and synthesis, as French (1954) has done. This does not mean that we have any other method of dream analysis that is as valid as the study of the dream in the context of the transference neurosis. The manifest content has many interesting features, but one cannot isolate the study of the dream to its manifest aspects alone. The patient's free associations and their transference implications enable us to make formulations about the meaning of the dream. The scrutiny of Mr. Y.'s dreams emphasizes that his free associations are valuable in reaching conclusions about psychic structure and ego processes, as well as id impulses and psychodynamic conflict.

In this patient's dreams one sees two different states. The reality-oriented state contrasts sharply with the second state, where the previous equilibrium is shattered and the patient experiences a chaotic disruption. This "whirlwind" activity can be identified as being primary process in quality since it is characterized by lack of organization, violent forces, and an absence of coherent, goal-directed activity. The whole experience is primarily an affective one, which reveals further that it is closer to primary-process operations than to secondary-process ones. An affect is a complex reaction but, from one viewpoint, represents an ego reaction that contains less reality elements than an abstract thought. The activity in the dreams was at a particular point devoid of any degree of abstraction and totally affective.

To create, the patient had to be able to orient himself along the lines of the primary process. Instinctual content contained many elements that were perceived as threatening and disruptive as they reached ego levels and approached consciousness. His destructive impulses led to chaos and contaminated, so to speak, his creative efforts. Rage threatened to overwhelm him and, insofar as such a feeling became the dominant aspect of the primary process, he was unable to create. In the first dream, one can see clearly the disruptive aspects of primary-process operations. In waking life, all creative activity stopped and the patient felt immobile and paralyzed. He had to take drastic action while asleep, as evidenced by waking up, to protect himself from inner feelings; similarly, when awake, he had to use strong repressive measures to protect himself from uncontrollable feelings. Consequently, the ego had to expend considerable energy in countercathexis and the perceptual system had to focus on reality exclusively, as in waking up. It had to maintain a rigid hold on the external world to maintain the countercathexis against primary-process elements. The ego's orientation would be strictly secondary process but would be crass, dull, inflexible, and characterized by obsessional ritual and routine and vast expenditures of energy on trivia and gadgets. Imagination would be constricted, since fantasy and free-floating connections between external and internal percepts require a primary-process mobility as well as the logical secondary-process refinements.

The second dream had many similar elements to the first but a different outcome. As in the first dream, a period of relative calm is followed by chaotic activity. The same formulation applies here, in that there is movement from a fairly well-organized secondary-process orientation to a "tornado"-like activity that contains many primary-process elements. The chief difference between this dream and the first one, as revealed by Mr. Y.'s associations, is that he did not feel overwhelmed by the second dream. He again experienced intense waves of effect but he never felt afraid that he would lose control. He did not have to awaken, and the last part of the dream was associated to the creative product.

Initially, the room was described as well balanced and comfortable but lacking in color, being drab and dull. At one level, he was describing an ego state, insofar as he was well organized and his ego was operating in a reality-oriented secondary-process fashion. Among other things, the quantity and arrangement of the furniture referred to his inner arrangement, in that he felt he was "well put together" but lacking in imagination and verve. His view of the outside world was also one of orderly arrangement but there was nothing picturesque or exciting in what he saw. He indicated that the scene outside the picture window was the way that he looked at the world when he was not rapt in creative fervor. His ego status prior to the disruption brought about by creative involvement showed considerable synthesis and his perceptual system was well organized but not particularly sensitive or able to make interesting connections between various percepts. Everything was in its proper place and comfortable but there was an obsessional rigidity with a minimum of primary-process flexibility and mobility.

After the whirlwind, exhilarating activity that has been postulated as being a primary-process activity, one containing erotic elements, there was a further organization that differed in quality from the previous one. The room was bigger, which Mr. Y. felt represented an inner expansion, one accomplished by relatively nonconflictual creative endeavor. He associated the additional furniture and the more efficient, functional rearrangement of all the furniture to the creative product. He had, in fact, discovered a new method that could be used to solve various problems. This method was simple in principle and much easier to use than previous approaches, which were clumsy, laborious, and led only to approximations, whereas the results from his new method would be precise and would detect subtle functions.

The scene outside the window reflected his increased sensitivity, as it referred to his perception of the outside world. As with the room, he noted a "larger" scene with vibrant colors and a better balance. He produced associations indicating that this extension of the outside world, in that it was an accretion to his previous reality, might also be the pictorial representation of the creative product (in the same way that Kekulé's coiled snake might have represented the benzene ring). One could not, however, be definite about this point.

As with many other talented persons, he did not have an intense emotional investment in his discoveries. Once he had solved the problem, he felt detached from it. However, unlike the reports of some creative persons (Ghiselin, 1952), he did not feel any aversion to what he created. He felt he could separate himself from the product and look at it objectively. Criticism or praise did not disturb him and he could join with others in appraising his work. The creative product per se was not associated to his expansiveness; rather, the process of creative discovery was the important factor.

The question can be raised as to whether these dreams contain evidence that the patient was creative. It is apparent that they indicate a loss of structure, a regressed episode, that may be characteristic of a patient suffering from severe psychopathology. Assuming one accepts the thesis of "representational" dreams, were these dreams evidence of a crumbling ego structure such as one might see in a psychosis or a response to a creative endeavor resulting in the pictorial depiction of a creative product?

One must keep in mind that every dream element is an expression of some aspect of the psyche and that representations of the external world are held only as a vehicle for the dream work. Freud (1900) emphasized that dreams are totally egoistic. Are external objects, including the creative product, depicted in the dream directly or are some dream elements metaphorical or symbolic expressions of such objects? Dream elements, whatever their counterpart in the external world, always refer to the subjective world; the creative product does not enter into the dream as such, but the ego processes (as Silberer's "functional phenomena") associated with the thinking activity of the moment become concretely expressed. If a metaphor is involved, it refers to inner processes. When my patient believed the rearrangement of the furniture, the additional furniture, and the expansion of the room were a metaphorical expression of his discovery, he was, in essence, describing connections and psychic rearrangements accompanying an ego expansion. From this viewpoint, the question of whether Kekulé's snake was the benzene formula is not particularly meaningful; rather, a particular thinking mechanism was the essence of the dream picture. With both Kekulé's and Mr. Y.'s dreams, the specific form of the dream elements was determined by id factors as well as current ego processes.

While Mr. Y. was creating, there was a wider range of functioning of all ego systems—sensory, executive, and integrative—but this could occur only if he were able to function partially along a primary-process axis. The ego was functioning with primary and secondary process simultaneously. The flexibility of the primary process expanded the functional range of ego systems that are instrumental in maintaining intrapsychic balance in terms of both internal and external objects. Instinctual elements led to more efficient, reality-oriented secondary-process operations.

The concept of controlled regression (Kris, 1950b) might be applicable to these formulations. However, if repression (even though transitory) is a necessary mechanism in such a process, then what has been observed is a somewhat different phenomenon. Mr. Y.'s second dream and other similar ones were noteworthy for the absence of symbols or actions that point to an inhibition representative of the ego's repressive struggle. If repression was operating while the patient was creating, it was not reflected in the dream.

Naturally, the above formulations do not by any means account for the innumerable complex and subtle facets of creativity; nor does the study of a few dreams enable us to construct comprehensive hypotheses about the origin and psychic operations of scientific talent. These dreams, however, are a source of useful data when considered in the context of the transference neurosis. Shifts and changes in the dream picture reflect corresponding shifts in the psychic apparatus and are of considerable value in confirming or helping us to modify various hypotheses that are primarily concerned with different levels of ego operations.

Summary

Rather than studying creative activity in terms of its immediate psychodynamic content, this chapter concentrates on the ego's operations during creative episodes and, by focusing on ego structure, attempts to scrutinize the relationships between various ego systems.

The study of dream material is a valuable supplement to other methods of clinical investigation, such as those focusing on the transference neuroses, but even dreams have to be considered in the context of transference in order to be meaningful.

Two dreams were discussed; one occurred when the patient had considerable conflict that interfered with and sometimes completely stymied his creative endeavors. The other dream occurred when many of the conflicts attendant to creativity had been partially resolved and the patient was able to create in a relatively effortless fashion.

There were both outstanding similarities and marked differences in these dreams. The settings of these dreams consisted of a room and various pieces of furniture, which referred to the patient's psychic apparatus (primarily the ego). As the dreams progressed, marked activity occurred which was associated to creating and was a picture of primary-process forces. In the first dream, such forces became disruptive but, in the second dream, they led to an expansion and rearrangement of the dream setting.

These changes effected in the second dream represented in pictorial form the ego's increased synthesis and heightened sensitivity to both external and internal stimuli, which were associated with the process of creative discovery.

Chapter 35

Characterological Factors and the Creative Personality

Studies of the creative process and the creative character continue to intrigue workers in different disciplines. I have noticed that psychoanalysts in particular grow enthusiastic when the topic is mentioned. Insofar as psychoanalysts tend to be interested in artistic, cultural, and humanistic affairs, it is not surprising that they should find the study of the creative experience valuable and interesting. The intensity of their interest is in itself a phenomenon worthy of study. Perhaps an investigation of our own reactions will add to our understanding of creativity in general.

Participants in seminars, workshops, and discussions on creativity often describe various factors associated with creative experiences of their own. Their candor in revealing themselves during a creative moment is sometimes remarkable. In fact, one often gets the impression that some authors have made formulations on the basis of self-observation rather than from data gathered from patients.

The revelations reported, however, seldom reveal anything shameful or embarrassing, so the candor does not involve an agonizing self-appraisal and the possibly critical judgment of one's colleagues. On the other hand, there is always some exposure of intimate feelings and orientations that one would ordinarily feel reticent to make public. In these instances, it is apparent that the speaker takes great pride in having had a creative experience. He or she is flattered to find some personal endowments and character traits identified as suggesting creative potential. Such judgments afford the speaker considerable narcissistic gratification.

The pride in and gratification from a creative accomplishment, usually completely apart from either materialistic gain or elevation of status, indicate that the character structure of the creative person has self-esteeming qualities. Structure and function need not be separated. Consequently, it can be stated that psychic functioning associated with creative accomplishment also elevates self-esteem. Although there is often

First published in *Journal of the American Psychoanalytic Association* 19:524–542. Reprinted with permission.

considerable gratification associated with the creative product, observations of patients and of colleagues discussing their creative experiences clearly indicate that their greatest joy was experienced *while creating*, not when contemplating the finished work. In fact, interest in the creative product wanes rather quickly, whereas the memory of the creative experience itself can be suddenly rekindled, and some of the feeling previously associated with it can be reexperienced as enthusiasm for the discussion and investigation of creativity.

To broaden our conceptual understanding of how working creatively can lead to a sense of exhilaration and a heightening of self-esteem, I shall examine various ego subsystems that are particularly affected by creative activity. This is not an investigation of the creative process, nor do I propose to define creativity. In Chapter 32, I stated that the only definition of creativity possible at that time was an operational one, that creativity could only be defined by the ego processes associated with it. I also recognized that there is a degree of circularity to this type of definition, but this situation is not unusual in science, especially when the problem involved is a relatively new one, i.e., the investigation of creativity in an ego-psychological context. Creative activity, regardless of how it is defined, is experienced as creative by the person engaged in it. Whether the product will later be accepted as truly innovative is not decisive because the impact of the experience has definite consequences, and it is these consequences I wish to investigate here.

One might raise the objection that, if one cannot be certain that the psyche is involved in creating, conclusions about the reactions of various ego subsystems cannot be unequivocally attributed to the creative process; they may be the outcome of some other psychic activity not necessarily related to creativity. I question the validity of this oversimplified objection, for what we are examining here is an ego state that is without doubt consumed by problem-solving activity, and there are definite reactions associated with the belief that the problem has been solved. The person believes that he or she has done something creative, and it is a combination of this belief and the activity leading to it that is responsible for the changes in the person's psychic state. It is this kind of activity that seems to raise self-esteem so tremendously, and the context (ego structure) in which it occurs may have some homogeneous qualities. The relationships between various ego systems may have specific features that are related to productive thinking. And the latter, in some instances, undoubtedly includes creative thinking.

The clinical data presented here pertain to eight scientists and were gathered during their analyses. Some of these scientists had received the highest approbation from their colleagues; all were unquestionably creative. I am for the most part referring to a scientific mode of thinking rather than an artistic one, although in terms of ego functioning I do not believe there are major differences.

My patients and my discussions with colleagues do not give me the impression that there is much homogeneity in terms of basic psychopathology among creative scientists. My patients demonstrated a broad spectrum of psychopathology ranging from primitive existential conflicts with overtly psychotic manifestations to behavior indicative of fairly well-integrated egos with oedipal-based conflicts. At the level of basic id conflicts, it is difficult to think in terms of *a* creative type. There are no ubiquitous conflicts. I have emphasized that creativity and psychopathology are completely independent variables; one is creative in spite of psychopathology rather than because of it. On the other hand, there may be some homogeneity in various character traits that do not necessarily stand in a causal relationship to creative activity but are associated with it.

Roe (1953) and Stein (1953) noted a variety of similarities in their studies of scientists, many of which were brought into focus by responses to psychological tests. In a sense, they were able to create profiles. Here, too, one can think in terms of a profile but not one dealing with either behavior or attitudes; I am referring to ego systems that are reflected in character traits. However, even though there may be both functional and structural similarities in various parts of the ego, these do permit a wide range of manifestations involving all types of perceptions and responses. Consequently, the "creative profile" is not phenomenologically obvious.

When one discusses ego systems, distinctions between pathological and nonpathological functioning become blurred. There is considerable variation in the way a particular ego system may react and still be harmoniously integrated with the general psychic equilibrium. The ego of a creative person may exhibit varying degrees of reality-testing without necessarily being either psychopathological or regressive (see Giovacchini, 1969). The creative person seems to have resiliency and a wider spectrum of reactions. At times, because of the almost elastic quality of such a person's reactions, one may be led to believe that the person is strange and bizarre and that this is the outcome of infantile psychopathological fixations. The creative person, as is true of any person, may exhibit behavior based upon psychopathology, but behavior associated with creative activity, although at one level it may appear pathological, is often based upon a wider range of functioning rather than upon neurotic or psychotic constrictions.

Perceptual System

For example, a patient frequently had auditory hallucinations, especially when involved in intense problem-solving activity. He heard male voices that made helpful and constructive suggestions about what he was doing.

He was not frightened or even concerned about this phenomenon. He welcomed their appearance, and even though what he heard was vivid and distinctly "outside" of himself, he was able to recognize it as an extension of his conscious thinking processes. His auditory perceptual sphere had a wider range of functioning, insofar as it could perceive his thoughts in addition to sounds from the outer world. It could perceive his thoughts with the same clarity and volume as an external percept. He could literally hear himself think. When not creating and in the throes of regression, however, he could have hallucinations of the usual paranoid variety, reacting to them as would any paranoid patient.

Another scientist patient experienced eidetic imagery. He could conjure up pictures of equations, geometrical figures, diagrams, and formulas—whatever was appropriate to the problem he was struggling with—with photographic clarity. He first had an eidetic image in college. He was taking a chemistry examination with considerable trepidation because he had done no formal studying and believed he was poorly prepared. The examination consisted of only one long, complicated problem. It happened that this problem was an illustrative example in the textbook used for the course. The student, although he believed he had not paid much attention to this problem, suddenly saw the page of the book containing the problem flash in front of him as if it were on a screen. He saw it with the same sharpness of detail as if it were a slide, including the page number and other irrelevant details. He felt almost as if he were cheating when he "copied" the answer from the "slide." He subsequently had many similar experiences, although with the passage of time the images tended to become dimmer, more like what one sees "in the mind's eye." As with the patient who had auditory hallucinations, this seemed to be an example of a benign, productive hallucination. These are hallucinations, however, only in a descriptive sense and have none of the other qualities associated with a hallucinatory experience. The second patient could, in a sense, see himself think by projecting essential components required for his problem and then effecting the combinations necessary in order to obtain a solution. In the first experience, it would seem that he had already solved the problem at levels below conscious awareness and then simply sharpened secondary-process synthesis by projection. His later experiences included a more active manipulation of what he "saw," as if he were working at a blackboard.

One can view these phenomena as the outcome of an increased range of functioning of ego systems—in the first example, the auditory-perceptual system, and in the second, the visual-perceptual system. The increased capacity of perceptual systems to expand may be an inherent talent that develops further as it is exercised. It may also be a talent that operates during a certain period of life, i.e., when the character structure is still fluid. Later, once there is increased ability and security, it may not be so necessary. If the constitutional factor is significant here, then these characteristics of the perceptual system will not help us understand what ego qualities are involved in persons who value creativity. It must be emphasized that these systems function in this expanded manner only under the pressure of problem-solving activity. In the first example, in particular, the patient's colleagues considered him brilliant and his problem-solving ability extraordinary.

Perceptual and integrative ego systems must function in a distinctly unique fashion when involved in problem-solving activities. Here, the operations of auditory and visual modalities have been described only in general terms. They seem to be best conceptualized as expansions or extensions of ordinary perceptual activity, a quantitative distinction. One can also surmise that such functions can be formulated more specifically.

Many scientists as well as many patients have repeatedly indicated that they can look at almost anything and find it interesting. In addition to perceiving with greater depth, so to speak, they are able to traverse their memory system swiftly and find some experience or constellation that can be synthesized with the new percept, and, by so doing, add dimensions that lead to novel and interesting viewpoints. In some instances, this may lead to a creative product; in others, the psyche experiences a special pleasure from a seemingly insignificant or trivial situation.

Two of my creative patients, for example, often "indulged" themselves by looking at television programs such as crass Westerns and insipid mysteries, which, as they recognized, had no artistic value. They also read trashy novels and sporadically immersed themselves in sexy books or pornographic movies. At the same time, they read books with literary value and went to concerts, plays, and good movies. They derived considerable pleasure from the crass and smutty as well as the cultural and artistic. In fact, they believed that the two levels of entertainment were mutually enhancing. They also stated that their need for pornography, for example, enabled them to be creative. These patients gained gratification from areas some would find dull or disgusting. Their sensory responses seemed unusually intense, as well as varied, and they described themselves as particularly sensuous. Although some of their responses were in part the outcome of intrapsychic conflict, they were also the result, particularly later in analysis, of freedom from the restrictions of a standard morality. Their behavior, however, was not in any way unconventional.

Perhaps these are examples of perceptual ego systems operating with more autonomy than usual. Thus, these patients could focus their sensory scan upon a large variety of external percepts and memory traces. This ability might be lacking in those who do not value creativity, partly because they have less autonomy or have incorporated less meaningful experiences in their memory system.

The creative patients I have just described emphasized that their interest in trivia had a "replenishing" effect which, after a time, led to serious creative work. They were, in essence, describing a continuous cathexis of sensory systems, a pleasurable experience, without much in the way of the integrative and executive activities associated with work, which were also experienced as pleasurable. The interest in trivia represented a rest period, but at the same time they were keeping themselves "primed." Once they again became creatively involved, they would not have to "start all over"; the perceptual system had been constantly active and now they merely had to bring it more in conjunction with other ego functions.

The readiness of the psychic apparatus for creativity has been striking in all of my creative patients. This does not necessarily mean that creating occurred in a sequential pattern. These patients would very quickly abandon "replenishing" periods for productive work and then just as quickly return to them. These patients showed considerable mobility, often making the switches described several times a day.

Other patients who value creativity but who are not particularly creative often demonstrate similar mechanisms. For example, some frequently find themselves reacting to situations in what they have called a perverse manner. Like the scientists, they are not perturbed or ashamed of their responses but, rather, amused. They may find something sexual or funny in an experience another person might classify as embarrassing. Such patients also have fantasies of how they should act in certain situations, and sometimes, although rarely, they behave as their fantasy dictates. These responses are usually idiosyncratic but often very clever and ingenious.

As a group, patients who value creativity engage in many hobbies and have a wide range of interests. In some instances, their activities seem to be at variance with each other, as was the case with a highly competent, intellectually oriented professional man who had an avid interest in racing his motorcycle. I have the impression from my practice and from casual discussions with colleagues that the majority of patients seeking psychoanalysis belong to the category of those who value creative accomplishments, and their sensory responses approximate the ones just described.

The Ego Ideal

Creative people and colleagues idealize creativity, persons, and causes (see Greenacre, 1956, 1957). They can passionately worship a hero, usually a venerable personage in their field. This occurs with greater fervor during their physical, emotional, and academic development, but even later they tend to romanticize their work and, in many instances, the accomplishments of colleagues. There seems to be a transition from an almost magical devotion to one of the "giants" in their field, sometimes a teacher or mentor, to a more realistic, sober fondness for a senior scientist or the ideas of colleagues (see Pupin, 1925).

This respect for ideas is an important aspect of the ego ideal. I have found that, in spite of rivalries and jealousies, those with reputations for being truly creative generally are benignly inclined toward and enthusiastically involved with the ideas of others. Freud is a good example. He had an immense tolerance for and even tended to idealize the ideas of others such as Fliess (Bonaparte et al., 1954), and Ferenczi and Rank (1924), even when they were dissident to his. He did his best, on the basis of his need to idealize, to accept their ideas; it was only after considerable struggle that he finally abandoned the effort (Jones, 1953). Later, as is true following any disappointment in someone who has been idealized, there were bitter feelings.

The development of the ego ideal of the creative scientist is discussed in Chapter 33. Here I simply wish to emphasize that a person who places high value on creative work also has a well-developed ego ideal. Creative accomplishment, in turn, seems to make the ego ideal attainable, which by definition is a self-esteeming experience and an important factor in determining why so many persons, such as colleagues, are interested in the subject of creativity.

There are also megalomanic elements to creative activity (creating something from nothing) that enhance narcissism and that are also significant to the intense appeal being creative has. Many people, however, have no interest whatsoever in being creative; in fact, in some instances it is doubtful whether they really understand what creativity means. Consequently, one must conclude that there are special characteristics in the character structure of both the creative person and the person who values creativity but may not be creative.

A "high" ego ideal is the outcome of emotional development, rather than a constitutional endowment. The relationship between the ego ideal, the self-representation, and the developmental antecedents of the ego ideal are especially germane to the question regarding specific characteristics associated with creativity. The discussion of the self-representation of creative scientists is therefore relevant. I use the terms "identity sense" and "self-representation" synonymously. The concepts of identity and ego ideal I use in much the same fashion as do Erikson (1956), Jacobson (1964), and Sandler and Joffe (1963).

Self-Representation and Fusion States

Regardless of the nature of the psychopathology that caused the scientists I have described to seek treatment, their self-concepts were outstandingly distinct while creating. The more intense their creative fervor was, the clearer the boundaries of their identity were. Unlike patients suffering from characterological disorders, they very definitely knew who and what they were and what their purpose and function in life were. Their feelings were zestful and, although they seemed to be totally absorbed in their work, they related well in other areas, too. They did not restrict their identity to just one modality, i.e., that of the creator; they could also function well socially and, in some instances, sexually.

The professional aspect of the self-representation was particularly noteworthy, in that it blended harmoniously with the ego ideal. They felt themselves to be invulnerable and capable of achieving anything they desired, scientifically speaking. They not only admired the "giants" of their field, but they felt themselves to be among them. They spoke of themselves and their heroes with almost religious overtones (see Pupin, 1925). This was a peculiar type of megalomania because, in spite of their grandiosity, they did not seem arrogant or even particularly unrealistic. There was a relaxed quality about them and, paradoxically, their mood was almost humble.

Again, I wish to emphasize that the clinical sample of eight patients was far from a homogeneous group. During noncreative periods or periods of decompensation, they exhibited a wide variety of reactions which covered a broad characterological and psychopathological spectrum and was reflected in their self-representation. During creative periods, however, this fusion of the self-representation with the ego ideal was manifest in all of them. Colleagues have reported many similar instances.

To achieve a self-representation that basks in the security of having achieved its ego ideal by creating sheds light upon the question of why so many of us find creativity such a fascinating subject. Here is an exquisite combination of achieving both one's standards and megalomanic invulnerability and, in spite of the fusion involved, maintaining the integrity of the self-representation. This was amply demonstrated by my patients.

Several questions, however, come to mind. One has already been alluded to, but it requires further amplification. How does this exalted state differ from any state of fusion between the self and a magically endowed idealized person, a situation fairly common in patients suffering from severe psychopathology? In the latter fusion state, patients do not see the self as separate and distinct. They have lost whatever boundary their self-representation had and are now involved in a blissful, nirvanalike state in which they, as individuals, have ceased to exist. They are in a state of transcendental unity; magical omnipotent qualities dominate the picture; autonomous and secondary-process elements recede into the background. Grandiosity, delusional orientation, and lack of reality-testing are conspicuous. There are also marked differences in behavior. Instead of the calm, relaxed, almost humble mood characteristic of the creating scientist, the omnipotent fusion state is often characterized by tenseness and urgency. Even when the subject speaks in blissful tones, the atmosphere is taut. The severely disturbed patient does not really relate to the analyst; instead, there is symbiotic fusion with an omnipotently endowed imago of the analyst. External object relationships are sparse; the patient's involvement with the external world is minimal.

To be creative involves special talents, but the effect of creative activity described among the scientist patients may be the outcome of particular qualities of the self-representation that may be present in noncreative or relatively noncreative persons as well. If there are such specific features involved in the formation of the identity sense of many besides the true innovator, this may constitute another reason why creativity has such a wide appeal.

To pursue the topic of the structure of the self-representation further, I wish to refer once again to clinical observations of the group of eight scientists, and to consider their self-representations in a broader context. As has been emphasized, these patients had a very firm identity sense during creative periods, and even during noncreative periods there did not seem to be an unusually intense disturbance of the self-representation. During both creative and noncreative periods, however, they sometimes referred to themselves as if the previously distinct elements of the self-representation had disappeared. Like patients suffering from characterological defects, they sometimes described themselves as "amorphous, hollow, and empty." They literally spoke of losing their identity, and three patients reported difficulties remembering where they were, what they were supposed to do, and even their names. In spite of the bizarreness of what they were reporting, none of them spoke in ominous or anguished tones, as is so often the case when noncreative patients make similar observations about themselves. My patients did not seem concerned, and I later detected that some actually took pride in being able to "reduce" themselves to a primitive, amorphous condition. During noncreative periods, some patients showed concern and mild anxiety about the state of emptiness. One sometimes regressed and developed the delusional identity of Christ the Savior. This patient, however, had considerably more resiliency than the ordinary psychotic patient, and he would rather quickly return to an amorphous ego state, experiencing only minimal anxiety.

During creative periods there was no anxiety whatsoever, and the zest ordinarily associated with creativity persisted along with the feeling of emptiness. As all of these patients became more and more immersed in the scientific problem they were attempting to solve, the euphoria and sense of emptiness reached peaks that "swallowed" them up (see Chapter 32, this volume). Reminiscent of patients in a transference state of symbiotic fusion, they saw themselves merging with their work. They experienced this as a psychic dissolution with loss of ego boundaries. This state would then be followed by psychic synthesis, i.e., a firm conviction of their identity status, at which point the problem also would have undergone consolidation and synthesis. The sequence from a structureless state to a highly structured one was subjectively exhilarating. Others have described processes such as controlled regression (Kris, 1950b) and stages of inspiration and elaboration (Kris, 1952) as typical of the creative psyche. For the sake of exposition, I have also described a sequence, but, at times, the fluid self-representation and the well-structured one seem to occur simultaneously. Furthermore, I am specifically emphasizing the role of a unique characterological feature, the identity sense, in contradistinction to the ego in general. Whether regression, even controlled regression, is a useful concept for understanding the creative process has been thoroughly and ably discussed elsewhere (Bush, 1969).

Because the focus here is on characterological factors associated with creative activity, it is again useful to compare similar factors in patients who are not particularly creative in order to highlight differences that may be essential, and perhaps determine how creative activity is distinguished from pathological processes.

The megalomanic fusion that occurs in noncreative patients suffering from severe psychopathology is often accompanied by tenseness very unlike the comfortable and calm state mentioned above, especially since this defense cannot be maintained indefinitely. Delusional omnipotence cannot be sustained unless it receives reinforcement. Thus, these patients experience considerable anxiety, even panic. They suffer the pain of psychic dissolution, which is the outcome of an amorphous, empty self-representation. The latter is threatening and emphasizes patients' vulnerability, helplessness, and misery.

In contrast, creative patients did not defend themselves from feelings of emptiness while creating. The "empty" state was not painful, and they often associated it to wiping the slate clean, constructing a *tabula rasa* that could incorporate stimulating and exciting ideas. At this point, they were extremely receptive to the ideas of others and even seemed to be gullible and naïve. They often appeared passive and highly suggestible. However, they were not accepting for long, and what seemed to be passivity was, in fact, an *active acceptance* of any innovation which was then subjected to critical scrutiny and evaluation. The latter activities may take place at preconscious levels and need not be manifest.

The self-representation is not really a vacuum. It has an increased capacity for incorporation, but, unlike the "as-if" character, it is not categorically accepting, and it exercises considerable selectivity in what it chooses to incorporate. At most, one can say that the self-representation is characterized by *pseudoemptiness,* a factor which is perhaps responsible for the creative scientist's high tolerance for ambiguity and ability to suspend final judgments. Nevertheless, it has definite boundaries and structure and will incorporate what can be potentially integrated into its preexisting framework.

Furthermore, such a receptive self-representation is reflected in all ego systems. When the ego is considered in terms of "taking in," however, one is once again primarily faced with the operations of the perceptual system. The creative person demonstrates both an increased range of functioning of perceptual modalities and the effects of a receptive self-representation. The former refers principally to internal perceptions, such as auditory or visual thinking, whereas the latter refers both to the incorporation of the ideas of others and to the inner registration of external stimuli that would be unnoticed by the ordinary (noncreative) observer. The combination of these two activities leads to states of integration which finally become elaborated into a creative product.

Thus, the relationship between a particular type of self-representation and the perceptual system is highlighted. The interaction of these two systems may also reflect the interplay of constitutional and developmental factors, but the specific nature (psychic processes) of this interaction requires elaboration if one is to understand further characterological factors associated with the creative process. During the creative moments when the above interaction occurred, my patients indicated that the predominant ego modality was fusion. These scientists had a tendency to fuse "everything." External percepts that were distinct and separate would be combined. Disparate thoughts would be superimposed upon each other. There was a general confluence, and their thinking seemed superficially bizarre.

Distinctions between creative activity and irrational, bizarre behavior were difficult to make, because creative persons are in no manner exempt from psychopathology. The scientists I have been referring to were patients, and all of them sought treatment because they were suffering. They also uniformly complained about having lost the ability to create, a loss of a very important self-esteeming function. Their egos could, in moments of extreme decompensation, regress to states of emptiness and amorphousness of the self-representation similar to those described for patients suffering from characterological defects. They used megalomanic symbiotic fusion states as a protection from psychic dissolution in the same way many noncreative patients do.

Still, these creative scientists had considerable resiliency no matter how deeply they might have regressed. Their character structure demonstrated a fundamental solidarity and flexibility, and the creative experience was one which led to ego expansion and the achievement of progressively structured ego states.

The relatively noncreative analytic patients who value art and new ideas often show similar psychic configurations. They are, in general, open-minded and have a similar tolerance for ambiguity. During regressed states, they do not seem particularly threatened or fixated and seem to have a fair degree of resiliency. These features are indicative of a type of self-representation similar to that described for the scientist patients, although the ordinary patients lack, relatively speaking, the security regarding the integrity of the self-representation seen in the creative group.

The content of the ego ideal of these noncreative patients who value creativity is almost the same as that of the creative scientist. What seems to be lacking is the ability to project it onto the outer world, i.e., to find venerable and enthusiastic mentors, and to introject them as part of themselves. They also seem to lack the ability to idealize their area of endeavor. Their interest is directed toward the unattainable, although, when internal conflicts are minimal, they succeed in being reasonably well adjusted to their vocation and can enjoy the fruits and accomplishments of others in the field they value. As a rule, this group is intelligent and well educated and, when not hampered by intrapsychic conflict, shows considerable aptitude in problem solving.

The creator discovers new solutions. Noncreators who value creativity often do well in solving known although difficult problems. The distinction is between effecting and creating solutions. Noncreators rely upon what they have learned, and their skills are reflected in their ability to utilize instructive past experiences.

One particularly talented patient graphically emphasized his need for external experiences in order to maintain his high productive level. The psychopathological extension of this dependency upon external objects was reflected in his fear of loneliness, which highlighted his inability to feel autonomous and self-reliant. He learned easily and could effectively utilize what he learned but, unlike the creator, was not able to "teach himself."

One scientist exemplified the antithesis of such complete reliance upon the environment when he spoke of creating his "own reality" in his research. He explained that the questions he had to answer were hitherto unknown questions; consequently, the answers could not be worked out according to any established system. In terms of ego functions, his position might be described as follows: whereas other people turn to the outer world when they need help, the outer world had nothing to offer him. He therefore had to find the answer within himself. But because none of the introjects acquired from past experience were relevant to his new question, he had no relevant memory traces to aid him in the solution of his problem. He therefore had to select diverse elements from various object representations and synthesize these into a Gestalt, thus producing a new, self-created introject. The patient then would have a tool to solve his problem, a tool that he himself constructed. While it was derived from past experiences, no single experience would have been adequate to the task. The externalization of this introject as it relates to the novel question constitutes the creative product, one which the patient considered the creation of a new reality. Now he and others could incorporate this "reality" and use the corresponding introject as an adaptive technique. Noncreative persons can learn from the creative product and incorporate it in their memory system, but they cannot form introjects without incorporating discrete experiences from the external world.

From a structural viewpoint, the noncreative person who values creativity has much in common with the creator. The functional range and the interactions among various ego systems, such as the perceptual system, the self-representation, and the ego ideal, may be the areas that determine a person's creative capacity.

Finally, one can never be absolute regarding creative accomplishments. There are gradations; the limits of operations of ego systems are not intrinsically fixed or predetermined. There are also other variables that extend beyond intraego relationships, such as specific developmental experiences and the nature of the environment in general. All of these areas require considerable study. Such pursuits should be fruitful and should augment findings from the ego approach, which is the focus of this chapter.

Summary

Creative activity is valued by many, and those fortunate enough to have creative talent invariably derive considerable esteem from the process of creating. The ego systems referring to the identity sense (the self-representation) and the ego ideal seem to be particularly instrumental in determining how one reacts to creative activity *per se* and how much one values the act and subject of creativity.

The perceptual system of the creative scientist, in some instances, has a broader range of functioning than that of other people. Examples pertaining to the auditory and visual perceptual system are given. In one instance, a scientist had what phenomenologically appeared to be auditory hallucinations, but the "voices" were benign and helped him solve the problem he was struggling with. In similar fashion, another scientist had the ability to conjure up clear visual pictures, eidetic images, which were also helpful.

Whereas there seem to be some similarities between the psychic structure and behavior of creative persons and those of disturbed, noncreative patients, the similarities seem to be mainly phenomenological, and there are important fundamental differences. Although the creative scientist may regress to states characterized by unstructured, helpless, and vulnerable self-representations, he or she has greater resiliency than the ordinary disturbed patient. The scientist's self-representation fuses with the ego ideal, but not in a defensive fashion. It effects a fusion to achieve higher states of integration rather than from a need to be magically rescued from immersion in self-hatred and chaotic dissolution.

The self-representation of those who value creative activity may, at times, appear to be unstructured, a state designated here as pseudo-emptiness. The identity sense has a different kind of structure, a fluid and incorporating one with considerable capacity to tolerate ambiguity.

Finally, although one cannot at this time do more than speculate, it seems likely that the group that ranks creativity high in its value system, even though it may not itself be particularly creative, has characterological features similar to those described for the creator.

Chapter 36

Creativity, Adolescence, and Inevitable Failure

The essence of the creative process is the production of something that did not heretofore exist. It may be the discovery of a realm, a new frame of reference, a better explanatory hypothesis, or a novel combination of already known factors or concepts. Our current reality is expanded by the creative product.

We can make a comparison from the psychic viewpoint. What had been previously unstructured, inasmuch as it had no access to conscious or cognitive processes, becomes sufficiently structured so that it can be perceived and used. Certainly the creator furthers his or her own emotional development and attains higher levels of ego integration as a result of creative activity. I believe that much of the appeal creativity has for many of us is based upon its potential for self-growth as the spectrum of primary to secondary process is lengthened (see Chapter 35, this volume).

There are many perspectives by which we may explore this topic. I have investigated the relationship of the creative process to insanity (I do not believe there is any process connection between the two) and the special role of the ego ideal in the psyches of especially gifted scientists (see Chapters 32 and 33, this volume).

Here I will investigate the way in which the adolescent process of character development becomes intertwined with creative activity. I emphasize that I am not equating growing up emotionally with a creative act; we would all be geniuses if that were the case. The obvious flaw here is that we would be confusing the product with the process. I believe the word "creative" has been much misused and applied to a variety of areas and products that, at best, could be called clever and skillful but not truly creative.

During adolescence there are many internal rearrangements that have to be differentiated from creativity. Adolescence itself may supply a setting that is favorable or unfavorable to such activity. Defensive adaptations to psychopathological disequilibrium, although they may appear to involve areas that are thought of as representing creative endeavors such as artistic pursuits, are not creative. This is a repetition of the negation that genius is equivalent to madness. Furthermore, simply because a

First published in *Adolescent Psychiatry* 9:35–60. Reprinted with permission.

person paints, writes, or dabbles in the laboratory does not mean that he or she is engaged in the creative process. Creativity, by definition, is something special.

This does not mean that such accomplishments cannot have a beneficial and restorative effect on a vulnerable psyche, a vulnerability that is common among adolescents. Furthermore, the adolescent may be particularly receptive to accepting new ideas and working them over into a useful and novel coherence. Adolescents' open character—their psychic structure is still relatively unconsolidated—is a factor determining their capacity to incorporate elements within the psyche that the more structured personality could not integrate.

There are other features to the adolescent personality that facilitate innovative strivings. For example, adolescents are typically idealistic. I cannot say whether it is true for artists, although I strongly suspect it is, but all of the highly gifted scientists I have had the opportunity to analyze were passionately idealistic (Chapter 33, this volume). Within the adolescent's psyche, the intensity of the ego ideal may be another favorable element that can be used for the promotion of creative activity.

Characterological features that are considered more or less typical of adolescence are involved in the creative process. I believe there are developmental tasks that propel a person toward the goal of being creative but which, in most instances, fail to achieve this aim. In some respects, failure is inevitable. Truly innovative persons can convert what most often is experienced as inevitable failure into a higher level of psychic structure, shifting goals as they change their idealized objects.

Case Material

I will first present a scientist whom I analyzed as an adult, after he had already made his mark in the world. I will focus, however, upon what I learned about his adolescence. This patient's creativity had reached fruition before entering analysis, but his psychopathology interfered with his being able to continue to perform at such high levels.

When I first saw the patient, a man in his late thirties, he described his childhood and adolescence as being fairly happy. He was the second of three children and his two sisters adored him. His father was a successful businessman who reputedly had his share of charisma. The mother, said to be a beautiful woman, apparently doted on the patient and immensely enjoyed his precociousness.

The patient was gifted and a fast learner. His father, who was somewhat scholarly, started giving his son private lessons when the patient was only two years old. He could multiply and divide by the age of three. At four, he knew Euclidian geometry and was able to construct his own theorems. He was also taught geography and history by his father, but by the time he started school he had already outstripped his father in all of these subjects, pursuing them on his own. He feared his stern, volatile father.

He was popular with his peers and had an outstanding number of playmates. He was also very active physically and preferred sports that stressed individual skills, such as boxing and wrestling, to team sports such as baseball. He played hard. He graduated from elementary school at age nine. He did not threaten anyone even though he usually was the teacher's favorite. The bigger boys did not resent him because, in the physical area, he was no competition. Instead, they used him to help them; he did their homework for them. Since he could do it without any effort, he gladly complied. The girls and female teachers thought he was "cute" and tended to mother him, which he remembered fondly. He told me, with a nostalgic, wistful look, how he remembered the older girls hugging him and how he loved the smell of their perfume. Apparently his female teachers were also in the habit of hugging him, something he still thought about fondly.

Outside the classroom he played with boys his size and age and he was comfortable there too. They admired his intellect but, since they had no competitive strivings in that area, they were content to just give him a nickname such as "the genius" and let it go at that. With his peers, he was accepted as a teacher rather than a follower and enjoyed this position.

The patient recalled being afraid of his father in early childhood. At first, he had viewed him as a strong, stern character who could easily lose his temper, but he had a tender, loving side as well. Perhaps what disturbed the patient most was his father's emotional lability. By the time he was five, so he reported, he had become aware that his mother hardly ever talked about her husband and acted as if he did not exist. When the patient moved beyond the confines of his home and came in contact with other adults in school, he was able to make comparisons. He also noted that on the rare occasions his mother or older sister spoke about his father, they were subtly deprecating.

During the oedipal phase and early postoedipal period, he had many omnipotent fantasies, which continued well into adolescence, although by then they were cast in erotic tones. During childhood he would build enormous space ships in his mind and travel to and discover distant planets. He would also encounter all types of obstacles which he always successfully overcame. He would fight monsters and giants.

As is often the case with creative persons, he had many "lucid" dreams (dreams in which the dreamer is aware that he or she is dreaming). These are pleasant dreams, in that one can do all kinds of things, satisfy diverse needs, take unusual risks, etc., and since it is only a dream no one can get hurt. One involved being able to fly and possessing prodigious strength, as evidenced by his ability to lift steamships and buildings.

As he began to idealize a teacher who had become intensely involved with him, the patient began to deidealize his father. He began to see his father's shortcomings; that, underneath some superficial bluster, he was passive and submissive to his wife and older daughter. He also reported that now he felt his father could not have helped being jealous of him. Still, in spite of his superior position, one part of the patient was still afraid of the father.

He emphasized his conflicting viewpoints. On the one hand, he was clearly the victor in the oedipal triangle. On the other, he had an internalized image of his father as a powerful, strong, wise man. When the patient measured himself alongside his father, he felt inferior, a feeling he had seldom experienced.

He became passionately involved in science. Even in his prepuberty years he had a reverential awe for what he was learning and the teachers who taught him. As he advanced in school he always managed to have at least one teacher whom he idealized and who, in turn, would admire and encourage his talents. One instructor of whom the patient was especially fond spoke with almost religious fervor about a very famous scientific genius with whom he dreamed of studying. The instructor was not good enough to achieve his coveted position, but my patient got his Ph.D. under this scientist and became almost equally famous. Afterwards, he continued idealizing, although the objects of his idealization became increasingly more abstract. He idealized his work and the principles and goals of science, which he saw as the objective search for truth.

Compared to his childhood, my patient's adolescence was relatively unhappy. In high school and, later, at the university, he continued to attract people because of his academic brilliance and personal charm. However, he was aware of a developmental lag. By the time he passed through puberty, his colleagues seemed to be well established in their sexual identity and social relationships. He was no longer satisfied being cast in the role of the young ladies' "darling." Instead, he wanted a girlfriend and a sexual partner, but he could not believe that any girl would relate to him at that level. He now suffered from feelings of inadequacy and felt defeated in an area in which he felt he did not have the endowments required for success. He thought that other young men were better looking, stronger, and more appealing.

As might be expected, he was extremely sensitive and was easily wounded by any rebuff, actual or imagined. He tried to overcome his sense of inferiority by directly confronting what he feared. During his first year at the university, he mustered his courage and started asking girls for dates. His record of success did not please him, but he managed to go out occasionally and petted fairly heavily. He also joined a fraternity, carousing a good deal with his fraternity brothers. In summary, there was some heterosexual activity, but most of his time was spent in "bull sessions" and drinking beer. He was also aware that he was covering up for his basic sense of insecurity. In the sexual area he felt very much a failure.

Academically, he continued in his usual brilliant fashion. There was no problem too difficult for him and soon he had a reputation for being able to do anything. In this regard there was an aura of omnipotence about him. He actually believed he could create at will.

His capacity for visual imagery was developed to the point that he could conjure pictures of pages he had read when he needed information on those pages. He did not exactly have a photographic memory, but he could produce eidetic images. He could also visualize a solution and then reproduce it and, in his mind, have a rather effortless resolution of an extremely complicated, difficult problem. After adolescence, his eidetic experiences disappeared, although he was still able to have powerfully vivid visual experiences.

Again, the responses of his fellow students were surprising, as were the patient's responses to his own talents. His peers apparently identified with his grandiosity, as evidenced by their enthusiasm and pride when they talked about his "miraculous" feats of intellect. They were proud to know him personally since he was gradually becoming a legend. Equally remarkable was that he was in no way arrogant or prepossessing, in spite of a megalomania which seemed to say, "if I can see it, that is, if I can conjure it in my mind, then it exists."

He endeared himself to his colleagues by being interested in their interests. There was nothing that he found dull. Though deeply immersed in science, he also found his other subjects—the humanities, history, art, and music—fascinating. He was a good listener as well as an eloquent speaker. Still, everything was not well. In the sexual area he remained very insecure, became increasingly shy around girls, and stopped dating altogether when he started graduate school. He became sufficiently depressed and concerned to contact a psychiatrist but stopped seeing him after several months because he did not feel any better about himself. Nevertheless, he continued to do extremely well in his work, and it was this success that sustained him.

Creative persons operate within broad spectrums, a fact this patient illustrated in various ways. He demonstrated many of the qualities that have been considered characteristic of the creative process. He was grandiose but not arrogant, inquisitive and curious but not intrusive, and although he valued what he did to the degree of idealization, he could also appreciate the involvement and enthusiasm of others for areas in which he had little interest, such as economics and business. Roe (1953) and Stein (1953) outlined traits and qualities commonly found in the true innovator. The sense of failure, however, was not on their lists.

The clinician could rather easily focus upon elements of this patient's past history and make speculative formulations that would explain his adolescent sense of sexual inadequacy. Freud (1905b) emphasized how conflicts, including guilt as well as castration anxiety, are reawakened after the latency period and during the early prepubertal period. Blos (1962) also refers to the reawakening of old conflicts during adolescence. Do feelings of inadequacy, during what many authors have considered the vulnerable period of adolescence, necessarily constitute psychopathology? Is this sense of inevitable failure perhaps part of the process of facing adult aspirations, such as sexual satisfaction, with the psychic equipment of childhood?

My patient, having sought treatment as an adult for very disturbing symptoms, indicated that his conflicts were more than just the manifestations of the insecurities inherent in a developmental phase. We can ask if his situation is a matter of degree in which ordinary occurrences become intensified to psychopathological proportions.

In the same context, we have to examine how his creative talents were related to his dilemma. Were they simply artifacts that ran parallel to his intrapsychic conflicts, thereby leading to what seemed to be enigmatic contradictions to his characterological orientation? Certainly, his good feelings about his scientific proclivities and his bad feelings about his heterosexual capacities and their social extensions did not cancel each other out; this was not a neutralizing interaction (Hartmann, 1955). Furthermore, the bad feelings did not "spoil" the good ones (Klein, 1929). Again, the creative factor may be implicated, in that such an ego is able to keep separate these two aspects of the psyche with what we can identify as a special strength, a special ego capacity of the creative character structure.

From another perspective, we can consider whether creative talents or the infantile environment in which they developed lead to vulnerabilities that become manifest during adolescence and adulthood. I believe that focusing upon these issues will provide us with further insights about both the creative and the adolescent process and their psychopathological vicissitudes.

Another patient, an adolescent, was known to be gifted but failed to perform up to his enormous potential. He was so obviously disturbed during adolescence—in contrast to the first patient—that he and his family sought intensive treatment while he was a freshman in college.

When I first saw him, he had all the symptoms that Erikson (1959) described as constituting the "identity diffusion syndrome." Several months after he started college, his personal habits broke down completely. He stopped bathing, shaving, brushing his teeth, and functioning socially. He just sat in his dormitory room doing nothing. Finally, his classmates took him to see the student-health psychiatrist, who at first diagnosed him as an acute schizophrenic. However, after his parents came to visit, the patient became less apathetic and did not have the signs and symptoms of a psychosis. He gave the appearance of a frightened, confused young man who had very little self-confidence and an amorphously constructed identity sense. The parents questioned whether analysis might be feasible, and, since the patient also seemed to show some interest in intensive treatment, he was referred to me.

The patient is an only child of a wealthy, socially prominent family. Both parents are talented, successful persons. From an early age, the patient showed considerable proclivity for mathematics and various branches of science—physics, chemistry, and biology. He was also interested in astronomy but dealt with it as a fascinating hobby. His parents were proud of him and doted on him. They bought him powerful telescopes and, during adolescence, big motorcycles and expensive sports cars. The patient enjoyed them, but he never felt truly happy. Something was missing in that he could not experience a solid sense of gratification and fulfillment.

The father did not expect his son to succeed him in the empire he had created. He prided himself about his liberal attitudes and his respect of autonomy. I learned later that both he and his wife had been analyzed. In view of his son's interest in biology, he had hoped that he would seek a career in medicine. Ostensibly, however, he did not push him, but he did once joke when his son was only two years old that he would give him complete freedom of career choice—he could go to any medical school he chose.

My patient quickly revealed how much he revered his parents and how he basically hated himself. The latter was based principally on his failure to live up to the expectations his parents had of him. He felt even worse because he had nothing to rebel against. These were expectations he felt they had of him, but he could not justifiably accuse anyone of having imposed anything upon him.

During treatment, it slowly became apparent that he experienced the infantile environment as oppressive to his autonomy. As an adolescent he had become aware of painful feelings that he described as disruptive agitation. When he was taken to the student health clinic, he was deeply disturbed. He had withdrawn completely from the external world because he believed he could not hold himself together. He described feeling as if he would "explode," and there was nothing he could find that would calm him. The underlying sense of futility, misery, and hopelessness was most impressive. He reviled himself mercilessly for his lack of accomplishment in view of the tremendous advantages and opportunities he had had all his life. He stressed his failure.

At the same time, he was not without some grandiosity. His narcissism was not totally depleted, as it might have seemed at first. In the back of his mind, he was convinced that he had the capacity to make momentous discoveries. During his treatment he often seemed megalomanic. He boasted about his brilliance, his photographic memory, and how he could conduct experiments that would prove the validity or invalidity of various controversial hypotheses. However, when he entered the area of mental development and health, he was naïve, sophomoric, and for the most part incomprehensible, so it was difficult for me to determine whether he was being delusional about these capacities. I had no inclination to challenge him but even if I had, the other dismal picture he painted of himself would have forced me to remain silent.

To reinforce the assumption that I am discussing creativity when I present material about my adolescent patient, I merely need to add that some ten years later he made various discoveries that revolutionized some aspects of the industry in which he worked.

Discussion

Mental Mechanisms and Ego Developmental Processes

Both patients demonstrated a curious clinical phenomenon—contradictory ego states existing almost simultaneously. The first patient displayed the coexistence of grandiosity and a sense of failure. The second patient could feel megalomanic at the end of a session dominated by bitter self-recriminations. This young man, because of the quantitative exaggeration of psychopathology, made clearer the processes and character traits illustrating certain parallelisms between elements of the creative process, adolescent character consolidation, and ego development. For example, a mechanism essential to creativity might decompensate into a pathological defense or become involved in a disintegrative, regressive current, causing it to lose adaptive and creative capacities.

I am referring specifically to dissociation, the splitting mechanisms that have been so frequently implicated in borderline psychopathology (Kernberg 1975). This mental mechanism, however, can be taken out of the context of psychopathology and viewed in terms of its adaptive capacities, inasmuch as it permits the ego to continue functioning at very high levels and to reach innovative states of integration which lead to creative products or consolidations. Both patients used dissociation extensively, but the first patient was able to maintain self-esteem and to function efficiently and creatively.

Is dissociation a defense for these patients as it is for noncreative patients? Does it allow them to maintain psychic equilibrium? Ordinarily, we think of defenses as reestablishing a balance, a compensation to counteract the decompensatory effects of psychopathology. At best, this can be considered a psychopathological equilibrium because the psyche expends a tremendous amount of energy to maintain a precarious balance; we would not expect there to be enough remaining for creative activity.

This was not true for the first patient. He was very productive becuse he was able to maintain the split between those parts of his personality that bordered on the grandiose and megalomanic and those that caused him to feel inadequate and a failure. In later adulthood, he temporarily lost his capacity to effect such a dissociation and was unable to continue with his creative work. The second patient could not function because he could not use dissociation well enough. He had some grandiose moments, but they were not highly cathected, as was his sense of inevitable failure.

Eissler (1958a) tells of a similar situation with Goethe, who apparently had an "encapsulated" psychosis. Goethe usually was able to keep the creative and psychotic parts of his psyche separate. When he was unable to do so, his psychotic parts dominated and rendered him unable to function. However, it was part of his genius that he could reinstate splitting mechanisms.

Does the concept of splitting, as I use it here, correspond exactly to the dissociation we find in severe psychopathology? Inasmuch as we formulate dissociation as a mechanism in which connections within the ego are dissolved, then I believe something similar happened with my patients. This is an intraego process and involves similar levels in the psychic hierarchy; whatever splitting occurs involves the same ego subsystems. For example, in my patients we witness dissociation of the self-representation rather than of executive skills.

Norbert Wiener, the father of cybernetics, exemplifies various types of dissociation. It is reported that he was so poorly coordinated that it was necessary for his secretary to write on the blackboard for him. Yet, when Wiener was doing research in a hospital in Mexico City he was a favorite among the interns. He would become involved in their two most popular pastimes, wrestling and chess. I naturally surmised that he must have been a chess master but an ineffectual, unskilled, and awkward wrestler. I was completely wrong; he was the best wrestler and the worst chess player of the group.

Regarding memory, Wiener was well known for his almost total recall for practically everything he had ever read. Still, there is an apocryphal anecdote told at the Massachusetts Institute of Technology, where Wiener held his academic appointment. Around noon he encountered a colleague and the two stopped to chat for a few minutes. Before departing, Wiener asked his friend in which direction he had been heading. After being told, he replied, "Then I haven't had lunch."

The dissociations discussed here are structurally similar to splitting mechanisms in general, but I believe there are fundamental differences. As adults, both my patients had little, if any, dynamic interplay between the split-off parts of their egos. There was very little connection or continuity between the grandiose, competent self-representation and the inadequate, failing part of themselves. To maintain this separation, the first patient did not require large expenditures of psychic energy. His grandiosity and success did not constitute a compensatory defense against what he perceived as weakness and vulnerability. These were two states of mind that coexisted without intruding into each other. This isolation of structural configurations permitted him to make innovative discoveries.

Psychopathology cannot be conceptualized on an absolute basis; it is always a matter of degree. Nevertheless, when discussing creativity, it is valuable to make as many distinctions as possible. Being able to effect a dissociation was a necessary psychic activity so that my patient could be creative. According to Eissler (1958a), this was also true of Goethe. Can we then state that dissociation is a defense required for creative functioning? I cannot generalize, of course, but it is necessary for some. I would question, however, whether dissociation would be part of a defensive system if its outcome were the preservation of creativity. Here, we can distinguish an adaptation which maintains the highest level of functioning possible and a defense that protects against a psychotic breakdown.

We can question whether dissociation is fundamentally involved and intrinsically related to creativity. Both my patients emphasized how they were able to make use of splitting mechanisms since childhood. As I have stated, the patients and I concluded that their ability to not have various parts of their minds intrude into the other was a talent, a strength associated with creative capacity. Greenacre (1956) stressed that there are ego strengths, unusual disciminatory sensitivities, that are found in creative persons, but they cannot be considered etiological factors. Still, we can ask whether there are unique and special childhood environmental configurations that are particularly conducive for the development of creative ability, as Greenacre (1957) explored, or for the development of dissociative psychic mechanisms.

Environmental Factors and Psychopathology

Both patients had mothers who were unusually devoted to them. They were breast-fed well into the first year. The first patient actually had two mothers, in that his oldest sister also doted upon him. Jones (1953) tells us about the devotion between Freud and his mother.

As their precocious talents flourished, they were increasingly idealized, inasmuch as others joined the admiring throng. It would seem that they were able to incorporate life experiences, that is, to integrate them into their memory systems, since they were so gratifying. With the increased self-esteem that was produced, they proceeded to further accomplishments. Such positive feedback and harmony between the inner and outer world would seem to preclude the need for dissociative mental mechanisms.

This is where their fathers enter the picture. The first patient emphasized his disillusionment with his father once he was able to see that underneath the facade of competence and self-confidence his father was insecure and not successful. The second patient's father, by contrast, was successful. Still, as his son grew older, he became unhappy with the materialistic attitudes that surrounded him. He wondered about his father's ethics and integrity and became less and less pleased with the gifts that his father lavished on him.

When I first saw my adolescent patient, he was in a state of identity diffusion. In addition to having lost his sense of identity, he was in a painful quandary about his value system. He did not know what he aspired toward and what he could respect. On the one hand, he regretted the crass materialism of his father's world, but at the same time he was perceptive enough to know how pleasant and comfortable the state of lack of want could be. He enjoyed his sports cars, for example, but he felt he should not.

As treatment progressed, he relived his conflict in the transference. He reviled himself for having no integrity and for being rich and privileged. This was not the ideal image he wanted for himself. He would then attack me because of the way I lived, my high fees, and other qualities that he attributed to the materialistic, greedy Establishment. These angry attitudes are not unusual during adolescence, but what distinguished my patient was his ready propensity to internalize his feelings against himself.

It became clear that he was projecting and reintrojecting his father imago.

He had been able to keep his idealization of his mentors and science dissociated from the image of the father who, during latency years, had fallen from grace. This accounted for both his self-aggrandizement and self-depreciation. The latter was the outcome of his introjected father; as he was hating himself, he was also attacking his father.

When he first started treatment, the first patient was phenomenologically psychotic. He was an angel in God's entourage and at war with the devil and his cohorts. The split between good and evil had reached paranoid proportions, but his psychosis, if that is what it was, was colorful and even entertaining rather than grim and painful. For example, he patterned his "delusions" around the plot of Anatole France's fascinating novel, *The Revolt of the Angels*, where the forces of evil and the forces of good were not only juxtaposed but reversed. The protagonist's guardian angel rejected God and wanted him replaced by the devil.

He began treatment by challenging me to analyze him and for a long time would not lie down on the couch. He was suspicious of me, and accused me of working for the Mafia and wanting to destroy his brain. He soon saw me as the devil but he also saw himself as behaving devilishly. At times he was the guardian angel and at other times he was the protagonist, somewhat of an amoral libertine who preaches virtue to an angel who does not believe in God. He reenacted this interplay with me, and some of his sessions were amusing, something I seldom feel with psychotic patients. He often told me of a particular conversation between the guardian angel and the protagonist, Maurice. The angel is arguing with Maurice and trying to enlist his aid in order to raise funds so that he can organize a cadre of angels and dethrone God and replace him with the devil. As the angel argues more and more heatedly, Maurice, in an astonished voice, exclaims that it seems that the angel does not believe in God. The angel replies that of course he believes in God, his very existence depends upon that belief, but he protests that his is not a just God.

As long as he mixed his delusions with the plot of the novel, my patient was animated and comfortable, although he was totally paralyzed as far as work was concerned. However, as he gradually internalized the feelings attached to them, he began experiencing the same coexistence of grandiosity and self-debasement and confusion my adolescent patient experienced. He projected and reintrojected the hated parts in the transference and later, idealized me. Both patients carried their idealizations from my person to psychoanalysis in general.

The adolescent patient's psychopathology intensified to the point where he could not function during his teenage years, and he was not able to achieve his creative potential until late in young adulthood. It is doubtful that he would have been able to reach the heights he did without treatment. In some respects, the other patient had a difficult adolescence but still functioned continuously at a very high level until he had his "psychotic" decompensation.

Perhaps the relationship of these patients to their fathers might have been a variable that determined whether psychopathology or creativity would gain the upper hand. The adolescent patient deidealized his father, but his father remained powerful and competent. The disillusionment concerned only one facet of his character, that involving moral integrity. This father remained strong, whereas the other patient's father was totally discredited. The latter patient later developed symptoms that have been associated with severe psychopathology, but he could cling to his grandiosity and be sustained by it because the depreciated father did not threaten his megalomania. By contrast, the adolescent's father's strength interfered with his son's capacity to generate enough self-esteem to function and he was not able to maintain an effective dissociation between the valued and devalued parts (the paternal introject) of the psyche.

Omnipotence and Creativity

The truly creative product, whether it is material or an idea, constitutes something that has never previously existed. Even if its component parts are known, their combination is novel. In a sense, the creator can be thought of as producing something from nothing. Of course, the fundamental law of conservation of matter and energy does not permit a something-from-nothing sequence, but in the mind of the creator this seems to be the case. Thus, the sense of omnipotence and creativity are intrinsically related to each other.

Once the scientist patient had achieved considerable integration during treatment, he would calmly relate how he could "will" himself to have an idea. He would describe his mind as being "empty." He would then "command" himself to think of something brilliant and there, as if by magic, it would appear. We both knew it was not that simple, effortless, or magical; that his training, experience, and knowledge were operating at levels below perceptual awareness.

As I emphasized in Chapter 33, creative patients do not seem at all arrogant when they talk about their feelings of omnipotence. The scientist patient was not offensive to me or others. He was casual and, although proud of his talents, not prepossessing or deprecating of others, who generally did not approach his level of performance. On the contrary, he respected the efforts others made and was even naïvely accepting of ideas that, on closer inspection, often proved to be pedantic and sophomoric.

There was an idealistic quality to his feeling of omnipotence. Rather than idealizing a person, an institution, or a cause, my patient idealized his own creative potential, which he considered to be a "gift from God." He had the same attitude that some very talented tenors have about their "golden" voices (e.g., Caruso and Pavarotti have referred to their voices as something God gave them to keep). This is an interesting combination of megalomania and modesty. The implication is that the possessors of these talents do not deserve any special credit; they were privileged in that they were given these gifts by a deity for the good of humankind. They have obligations in view of this sacred trust.

Kris (1952) stressed that, in addition to the construction of something new, the creative act involves communication. The creator has to have an audience. Whether or not the creator is understood is not the point. While creating, he or she is synthesizing and integrating in such a fashion that the creation will be potentially understandable. My scientist patient and other scientists I have treated sought analysis because, among other reasons, they possessed a gift they could not use. They meant that they felt they could not maintain contact with the external world, which heightened their sense of painful alienation.

Inevitable Failure

According to some authors (Blos, 1962) adolescence is a stage of life in which some developmental tasks that could not be dealt with in childhood are confronted once again. Arnstein (1979) questions whether crisis is a necessary factor in the quest for identity. Sharfstein (1978) emphasizes that creative activity enhances the progression on the path toward autonomy.

Freud (1905b) stated that children experience failure as their sexual instincts develop, which creates a breach in infantile omnipotence. This will carry over as a sense of failure in early adolescence.

According to Freud (1914a), early developmental stages from auto-erotism to the secondary narcissism of beginning object relationships are characterized by a sense of omnipotence if the infantile environment has been optimally gratifying. Though there are inevitable frustrations throughout the course of development because instantaneous gratification is not possible (or, according to Freud, even desirable), on the whole, children know that their needs can be met and that they are capable of being gratified.

In any case, when the young child faces strong oedipal urges, there is no possibility of gratification. For the child, gratification would mean victory over the giant adult of the same sex. It would also mean that the child has the somatic equipment to achieve heterosexual satisfaction which, of course, is not the case. The little boy cannot successfully pursue the goal of sexually possessing his mother. At this oedipal level, failure is inevitable. Thus, the sexual instincts become associated with failure. It might also be said that there is an asynchrony between instinctual development and the acquisition of the appropriate somatic apparatus for sexual fulfillment, which could be incorporated in the ego's executive apparatus. From this viewpoint, instinctual precocity is part of normal emotional development.

The line between normal and pathological development is often difficult to discern. This is an especially hard distinction to make when we study the adolescent phenomenon. Many children develop feelings of vulnerability and inadequacy during the oedipal phase, and these feelings are reawakened with the biologically stimulated sexual urges of the postpubertal period. They are then felt in a pervasive fashion as a sense of inevitable failure in the anticipation of a heterosexual relationship. Establishing a sexual relationship becomes a perplexing problem.

There has been considerable cultural support for the maintenance of the sexual mystique. According to the traditional masculine viewpoint, women can never be understood by men; they are attractive but unfathomable creatures. They represent a problem that can never be solved and man will always remain inadequate in the face of its enormity.

These attitudes fit better with a mid-Victorian milieu or any society in which sexuality is to a large measure repressed. In view of the current liberal attitudes about sex, this orientation would not be expected to be prevalent. Nevertheless, it is not an unusual one among a fair number of adolescents and some adults. It is not restricted to patients seeking treatment, although I have seen it in all the creative men I have analyzed.

I have discussed a scientist (Chapters 32, 33, and 35, this volume) who avidly pursued different women and who had married several times because he wanted to make their behavior predictable. Otherwise, he felt inferior and a failure. He had to master a problem and this compulsion to seek solutions carried over onto his creative work.

He illustrated an interesting conclusion first reached by Zeigarnik (1927). A completed task does not keep a person's interest. Once the problem is solved, there is little further investment in it. For the creator, it loses its cathexis, or at least, its major force since there is still pride in the accomplishment. However, the act of accomplishing is much more important than what is accomplished. Zeigarnik discovered experimentally that an unfinished task, that is, an unsolved problem, retains its cathexis. If abandoned, it still vividly remains in the person's mind. Even after years have passed, an incompleted action is easily remembered in contrast to completed tasks. My patients constantly had unfinished tasks even after they gained security in the sexual area.

Creativity, Precocity, and Psychic Structure

Regardless of psychological factors, in the final breakdown, creativity is a quality found in persons with special gifts. There must be an inherent constitutional factor of which we know practically nothing. However, there are attributes of innate talent that can be understood in terms of both emotional and psychic developmental factors. I have already presented clinical material emphasizing such elements, but now I wish to derive some generalizations from data obtained from the treatment of patients.

The creative persons I have treated, read about, or known showed their proclivities early in childhood. They were destined for greatness. I know there are exceptions but, in general, creative scientists usually were precocious and attracted attention while very young.

Psychoanalysts have discovered that precocity may be the outcome of psychopathology, a defensive response to a traumatic assaultive infantile enviornment (Bergman and Escalona, 1949; Boyer, 1956). The patients I have reported found that their precocity helped them maintain psychic equilibrium; whether it was primarily a defensive adaptation is difficult to determine. In view of their later creative accomplishment, it is not surprising that their talents flourished early. Their precocity led to success.

The precociousness of the sexual instinct Freud (1905b) wrote about and that of the creative person permit some interesting comparisons. Freud was referring to instinctual precocity, whereas in creative persons I am emphasizing an early unfolding, a premature appearance of talents. The ego's integrative functions and executive apparatus develop and structuralize to a degree that is further advanced that what is usual for that particular age period. In contrast to what Freud was describing, precocity here refers to overdevelopment of certain aspects of psychic structure relative to instinctual organization, the reverse of his formulation in which the sexual instinct is developmentally ahead of the rest of the psyche. To repeat, these are two antithetical situations, two types of precocity: in one, psychic structure outstrips instinct; in the other, instinct outstrips psychic structure.

The first type of precociousness is associated with creativity whereas the second type, according to Freud, is innate to infantile development. In the former, precociousness can become the vehicle for a successful, creative adaptation; the latter is always doomed to failure. My patients, especially the scientists, demonstrated this peculiar combination of success and failure. Is such a combination necessary to activate the creative process?

We do not know what psychological variables are involved in creativity. The psychic processes of adolescence, however, often seem to be related to creative activity. For example, as an adolescent, the scientist had the capacity for eidetic imagery and a photographic memory, but these abilities diminished as an adult. He did not totally lose them but they had reached their peak during his college years.

During adolescence, there is considerable rearrangement of various psychic agencies, which finally leads to character consolidation. With puberty, there is a biological heightening of sexual impulses. Unlike children, adolescents have the somatic equipment to seek sexual gratification, but they do not yet have the psychic structure and orientation to have a satisfactory experience. During adolescence, they recapitulate the oedipal failure of childhood.

The creative person can convert failure into success. The heightened excitation induced by the hormonal accretions of puberty produces a generally higher energy level that is not restricted to sexual urges. There is an all-pervasive zest for life in the well-adjusted adolescent. For the creative or potentially creative adolescent, this energy is harnessed to serve the talent that precociously appeared in childhood. In other words, a connection is established between precocious psychic structure and instinctual activity. Thus, sensual urges that were associated with inevitable failure during childhood begin to be linked with successful activities during adolescence.

I do not mean that creativity is the outcome of sublimated sexual energy. I am purposely leaving the concept of psychic energy vague because I do not wish to engage in irrelevant controversy in the context of this discussion. Rather, I am stressing that to gratify needs and to function generally requires energy. This energy is used in many ways, both sexual and nonsexual. The task of adolescence is to acquire psychic structure so that a variety of needs, including sexual, can be gratified and to use the upsurge of energy that occurs with maturation in a harmonious and efficient fashion.

Instinctual forces are associated with primitive psychic levels. During the course of emotional development, a structural progression establishes a hierarchy. The psyche can be thought of as a spectrum ranging from the primitive, relatively unstructured, and instinctual to the well-integrated, differentiated structures that function at secondary-process levels. These two ends of the spectrum are joined together by intermediary levels, forming a continuum. This continuum, or bridge, is poorly established in the precocious psyche of childhood and during adolescence.

During the creative act, primitive parts of the psyche governed principally by the primary process come in apposition to structured secondary-process levels. There is no bridge between the two. The continuum is temporarily relinquished. As stated, psychic structures that developed precociously become connected with instinctual elements without a modulatory bridge between the two. This lack of a bridge is characterized by what appears to be the coexistence of contradictory elements, as if the psyche were split or dissociated. The creative act culminates in a synthesis and a reestablishment of a connecting bridge and continuum.

The lack of a continuum between various levels of the psyche, as it occurs with the precocious child and during adolescence, may produce a creative person and or it may lead to psychopathology. There are many factors that determine the final outcome, as my patients demonstrated.

Summary and Conclusions

The lack of rigidity in the adolescent's character structure could provide a fertile setting for the realization of creative potential. Fluidity of character structure, however, could also be an element in the production of psychopathology. The combination of creative ability and emotional illness seems to be fairly common.

Still, comparisons and combinations do not mean that there are causal connections between what is being studied. Similarities may be only at the surface level. For example, during the creative act, the creator may seem to be using primitive psychic mechanisms such as dissociation. The creator may also appear to be indulging in magical thinking, as evidenced by megalomania. However, on closer scrutiny, it becomes apparent that the creator is in control of the primitive aspects of self, as he or she is simultaneously operating at higher levels of integration. The creator has a tremendous amount of energy, which causes him or her to perceive and feel more intensely than usual.

I presented two patients. The first demonstrated psychopathology in coexistence with creative capacities. His adolescence was characterized by an ego dissociation. One part of his psyche preserved his capacities for innovation, was experienced as pleasurable, and was associated with success, grandiosity, and high levels of self-esteem. The other part of his psyche contained the remnants of his childhood oedipal humiliation, which he carried with him as a sense of failure and inadequacy. As long as he could maintain this dissociation, he functioned well. He sought treatment when, as an adult, he could not maintain this split and developed symptoms that were phenomenologically psychotic but from a prognostic viewpoint not nearly so serious. The second patient decompensated into an identity diffusion syndrome during adolescence and did not realize his creative potential until after his treatment was terminated.

Various parts of the creator's psyche are hypertrophied, such as the perceptual apparatus and the ego ideal. Hypertrophied is not the most apt term because it implies constriction, which is not at all the situation in creativity. I mean that these structures and functions are better developed than usual and that they become apparent earlier during the course of development. This can also be considered precocity.

I discussed two types of precocity: one characterizes the creative person and the other is an instinctual precocity that Freud (1905b) postulated as typical of the sexual instinct. The former refers to ego functions and structures, such as the integrative system and the ego ideal, which are advanced for the child's age, whereas the latter consists of oedipal sexual urges that are also premature in the sense that the ego does not have the apparatus to ensure their gratification. Thus, there is, on the one hand, a precocity of structure which heightens self-esteem and, on the other hand, a precocity of instinct which leads to feelings of inadequacy. Both my patients demonstrated the effects of these processes in the dissociation they experienced to a fairly intense degree during adolescence.

During the creative act, the modulating bridge that forms a continuum between the primitive and the integrated structures parts of the personality is temporarily inoperative. During adolescence, such a bridge is in the process of being established. Talented and secure adolescents can take advantage of their relatively unstructured ego and use it for creative activity. This may be a reason why so many innovators, particularly mathematicians and physicists, have flourished during their youth.

Creative adults retain the capacity to reproduce an ego state in which connecting bridges and continuums are abolished. They are reproducing and reliving an adolescent ego state, a vibrancy and youthful zest that are the essence of the creative process.

References

Abraham, K. 1927. Notes on the psychoanalytical investigation of manic depressive insanity and allied conditions. In: *Selected Papers of Karl Abraham.* London: Hogarth Press.

Alexander, F. 1948. *Fundamentals of Psychoanalysis.* New York: Norton.

———. 1950. *Psychosomatic Medicine.* New York: Norton.

———. 1956. Two forms of regression and their therapeutic implications. *Psa. Q.* 25:178–196.

———. et al. 1934. The influences of psychological factors upon gastrointestinal disturbances: A symposium. *Psa. Q.* 3:501.

———, French, T. M., et al., eds. 1948. *Studies in Psychosomatic Medicine.* New York: Ronald Press.

Anthony, E. J. 1964. Panel on child analysis at different developmental stages. *J. Amer. Psa. Assn.* 12:86–99.

Arlow, J. A. 1969a. Fantasy, memory and reality testing. *Psa. Q.* 38:28–52.

———. 1969b. Unconscious fantasy and disturbances of conscious experience. *Psa. Q.* 38:1–28.

Arnstein, R. 1979. The adolescent identity crisis revisited. *Adol. Psychiatry* 7: 71–84.

Bacon, C. L. 1948. Typical personality trends and conflicts in cases of gastric disturbances. In: *Studies in Psychosomatic Medicine,* ed. F. Alexander et al. New York: Ronald Press.

———. 1956. The role of aggression in the asthmatic attack. *Psa. Q.* 25:309.

———, Renneker, R., & Cutler, M. 1952. A psychosomatic survey of cancer of the breast. *Psychosom. Med.* 14:453.

Balint, M. 1955. Friendly expanses—horrid empty spaces. *Internat. J. Psa.* 36: 225–241.

Benedek, T. 1938. Adaptation to reality in early infancy. *Psa. Q.* 7:200–215.

———. 1949. The psychosomatic implications of the primary unit: mother-child. *Amer. J. Orthopsychiat.* 19:642–654.

———. 1956. Psychobiological aspects of mothering. *Amer. J. Orthopsychiat.* 26: 272–278.

———. 1959. Parenthood as a developmental phase. *J. Amer. Psa. Assn.* 7:389–417.

Beres, D. 1957. Communication and the creative process. *J. Amer. Psa. Assn.* 5:408–423.

———. 1960. Psychoanalytic psychology of imagination. *J. Amer. Psa. Assn.* 8:252–269.

———. 1962. The unconscious fantasy. *Psa. Q.* 31:309–328.

Bergman, P. & Escalona, S. 1949. Unusual sensitivities in very young children. *Psa. Study of the Child* 3/4:333–352. New York: International Universities Press.

Bettelheim, B. 1964. *The Empty Fortress: Infantile Autism and the Birth of the Self.* New York: Free Press.

Bibring, E. 1937. Symposium on the theory of the therapeutic results of psychoanalysis. *Int. J. Psa.* 18:170–189.

Bleger, J. 1967. *Simbiosis y ambigüedad.* Buenos Aires: Paidos.

Blos, P. 1962. *On Adolescence.* New York: Free Press.

Bonaparte, M. 1940. Time and the unconscious. *Int. J. Psa.* 21:427–468.

————, et al., eds. 1954. *Origins of Psycho-Analysis: Letters to Wilhelm Fliess, Drafts and Notes, 1887–1902.* Trans. by E. Mosbacher and J. Strachey. New York: Basic Books.

Borowitz, G. M. 1967a. The capacity to masturbate alone in adolescence. Paper presented to the Society for Adolescent Psychiatry, Chicago, Ill.

————. 1967b. Premature sexual stimulation: developmental aspects. Paper presented to the Illinois Psychiatric Society, 1966, and to the Jewish Hospital, St. Louis, Mo.

————, & Giovacchini, P. L. 1966. Workshop on the psychotherapy of adolescents. *Society for Adolescent Psychiatry Bull.* 1:4–6.

Bowlby, J. 1951. Maternal care and mental health. *World Health Organization 2.*

————. 1958. The nature of the child's tie to his mother. *Internat. J. Psa.* 39:350–373.

————. 1960a. Grief and mourning in infancy. *Psa. Study of the Child* 15:9–52. New York: International Universities Press.

————. 1960b. Separation anxiety. *Internat. J. Psa.* 41:89–114.

Boyer, L. B. 1956. On maternal overstimulation and ego defects. *Psa. Study of the Child* 11:236–256. New York: International Universities Press.

————. 1961a. Provisional evaluation of psychoanalysis with few parameters in the treatment of schizophrenia. *Internat. J. Psa.* 42:389–403.

————. 1961b. Psychoanalytic treatment of schizophrenia. *Int. J. Psa.* 42:389–404.

———— & Giovacchini, P. L. 1967. *Psychoanalytic Treatment of Schizophrenic and Characterological Disorders.* New York: Aronson.

Brain, R. 1940. *Diseases of the Nervous System.* London: Oxford Unversity Press.

Breuer, J. & Freud, S. 1895. Studies on hysteria. *Standard Ed.* 2:1–307. London: Hogarth Press, 1955.

Brodey, W. M. 1965. On the dynamics of narcissism: I. Externalization and early ego development. *Psa. Study of the Child* 20:165–193. New York: International Universities Press.

Bronowski, J. 1958. The creative process. *Scientific Amer.* 199:59–65.

Bruch, H. 1962. Falsification of bodily needs and body image in schizophrenia. *Arch. Gen. Psychiatry* 6:18–24.

Bush, M. 1969. Psychoanalysis and scientific creativity. *J. Amer. Psa. Assn.* 17:136–190.

Cannon, W. B. 1932. *The Wisdom of the Body.* New York: Norton.

Cohn, F. S. 1957. Time and the ego. *Psa. Q.* 26:168–189.

Colby, K. M. 1955. *Energy and Structure in Psychoanalysis.* New York: Ronald Press.

DeBary, A. 1879. *Die Erscheinung der Symbiose.* Strasbourg: Trubner.

DeLevita, D. J. 1965. *The Concept of Identity.* New York: Ronald Press.

Deutsch, F. 1953. *The Psychosomatic Concept in Psychoanalysis.* New York: International Universities Press.

Deutsch, H. 1942. Some forms of emotional disturbances and their relationship to schizophrenia. *Psa. Q.* 11:301-321.

Edelheit, H. 1969. Speech and psychic structure: the vocal-auditory organization of the ego. *J. Amer. Psa. Assoc.* 17:381-412.

Eissler, K. 1951. Remarks on the psychoanalysis of schizophrenics. *Int. J. Psa.* 32:139-156.

———. 1952. Time experience and the mechanism of isolation. *Psa. Rev.* 39: 1-22.

———. 1953a. The effect of the structure of the ego on psychoanalytic technique. *J. Amer. Psa. Assn.* 1:104-143.

———. 1953b. Notes upon the emotionality of a schizophrenic patient. *Psa. Study of the Child* 8:199-251. New York: International Universities Press.

———. 1958a. Goethe and science: A contribution to the psychology of Goethe's psychosis. In: *Psychoanalysis and the Social Sciences,* 5, ed. W. Muensterberger & S. Axelrad. New York: International Universities Press, pp. 51-98.

———. 1958b. Notes on problems of technique in the psychoanalytic treatment of adolescents. *Psa. Study of the Child* 13:223-254. New York: International Universities Press.

———. 1960. On isolation. *Psa. Study of the Child* 14. New York: International Universities Press.

Ekstein, R. 1966. *Children of Time and Space, of Action and Impulse.* New York: Appleton-Century-Crofts.

Engel, G. 1954. Selection of clinical material in psychosomatic medicine. *Psychosom. Med.* 16:368.

———. 1968. Follow-up on Monica. Paper read before the Chicago Psychoanalytic Society, Oct. 22.

——— & Reichsman, I. 1956. Spontaneous and experimentally induced depressions in an infant with gastric fistula. *J. Amer. Psa. Assn.* 4:428-452.

Erikson, E. H. 1956. The problem of ego identity. *J. Amer. Psa. Assn.* 4:56-121.

———. 1959. *Identity and the Life Cycle.* New York: International Universities Press.

Fairbairn, W. R. D. 1954. A revised psychopathology of the psychoses and psychoneuroses. In: *An Object Relations Theory of the Personality.* New York: Basic Books.

Fechner, G. T. 1873. *Einige Ideen zu Schöpfungs und Entwickelungsgeschichte der Organismen.* Leipzig: von Breitkopf und Haertel.

Federn, P. 1928. Narcissism in the structure of the ego. *Internat. J. Psa.* 9.

———. 1952. *Ego Psychology and the Psychoses.* New York: Basic Books.

Fenichel, O. 1941. The ego and the affects. *Psa. Rev.* 28:47-60.

———. 1945. *The Psychoanalytic Theory of Neurosis.* New York: Norton.

Ferenczi, S. 1909. Introjection and transference. In: *First Contributions to Psychoanalysis*. London: Hogarth Press, 1952.

——. 1924. Sensations of giddiness at the end of the psychoanalytic session. In: *Further Contributions to the Theory and Technique of Psychoanalysis*. New York: Basic Books, 1952.

——. 1926. *Sunday Neuroses*. London: Institute of Psychoanalysis and Hogarth Press.

—— & Rank, O. 1924. *The Development of Psychoanalysis*. Baltimore: Williams & Williams.

Fisher, R., ed. 1967. Interdisciplinary perspectives of time. *Annals N.Y. Acad. Sci.* 138.

Fleming, J., & Altschul, S. 1963. Activation of mourning and growth by psychoanalysis. *Int. J. Psa.* 44.

Frazer, J. R., ed. 1966. *The Voices of Time*. New York: Braziller.

French, T. M. 1929. Psychogenic material related to the function of the semicircular canals. *Internat. J. Psa.* 10.

——. 1939. Psychogenic factors in asthma. *Amer. J. Psychiatry* 96:87.

——. 1954. *The Integration of Behavior: The Integrative Process in Dreams*, 2. Chicago: University of Chicago Press.

Freud, A. 1938. *The Ego and the Mechanisms of Defense*. New York: International Universities Press.

——. 1946. *The Psychoanalytic Treatment of Children*. London: Imago Publishing Company.

——. 1949. Aggression in relation to emotional development. *Psa. Study of the Child* 3/4:37–47. New York: International Universities Press.

——. 1965. *Normality and Pathology in Childhood*. New York: International Universities Press.

Freud, S. 1896. Further remarks on the neuro-psychoses of defense. *Standard Ed.* 3. London: Hogarth Press, 1967.

——. 1898. Sexuality in the aetiology of the neuroses. *Standard Ed.* 3. London: Hogarth Press, 1967.

——. 1900. The interpretation of dreams. *Standard Ed.* 4 & 5. London: Hogarth Press, 1953.

——. 1905a. Fragment of an analysis of a case of hysteria. *Standard Ed.* 7. London: Hogarth Press, 1953.

——. 1905b. Three essays on the theory of sexuality. *Standard Ed.* 7. London: Hogarth Press, 1953.

——. 1909. Notes upon a case of obsessional neurosis. *Standard Ed.* 10. London: Hogarth Press, 1955.

——. 1911a. Formulations on the two principles of mental functioning. *Standard Ed.* 12. London: Hogarth Press, 1958.

——. 1911b. Psycho-analytic notes on an autobiographical account of a case of paranoia (Dementia paranoides). *Standard Ed.* 12. London: Hogarth Press, 1958.

——. 1912a. The dynamics of transference. *Standard Ed.* 12. London: Hogarth Press, 1958.

——. 1912b. Recommendations to physicians practicing psycho-analysis. *Standard Ed.* 12. London: Hogarth Press, 1958.

——. 1913. On beginning the treatment. *Standard Ed.* 12. London: Hogarth Press, 1958.

——. 1914a. On narcissism. *Standard Ed.* 14. London: Hogarth Press, 1957.

——. 1914b. Remembering, repeating and working through. *Standard Ed.* 12: 145–157. London: Hogarth Press, 1958.

——. 1915b. The unconscious. *Standard Ed.* 14:159–215. London: Hogarth Press, 1957.

——. 1915b. The unconscious. *Standard Ed.* 14:158–215. London: Hogarth Press, 1957.

——. 1916–1917. *Introductory Lectures on Psychoanalysis. Standard Ed.* 16. London: Hogarth Press, 1963.

——. 1918. The history of an infantile neurosis. *Standard Ed.* 17. London: Hogarth Press, 1955.

——. 1920. Beyond the pleasure principle. *Standard Ed.* 18. London: Hogarth Press, 1955.

——. 1921. Group psychology and the analysis of the ego. *Standard Ed.* 18:12–66. London: Hogarth Press, 1955.

——. 1923. The ego and the id. *Standard Ed.* 19:12–66. London: Hogarth Press, 1961.

——. 1924a. Neurosis and psychosis. *Standard Ed.* 19. London: Hogarth Press, 1961.

——. 1924b. The loss of reality in neurosis and psychosis. *Standard Ed.* 19. London: Hogarth Press, 1961.

——. 1926a. Inhibitions, symptoms and anxiety. *Standard Ed.* 20:87–174. London: Hogarth Press, 1959.

——. 1926b. The problem of anxiety. *Standard Ed.* 20. London: Hogarth Press, 1959.

——. 1937. Analysis terminable and interminable. *Standard Ed.* 23:209–255. London: Hogarth Press, 1964.

Fuchs, S. H. 1937. On introjection. *Int. J. Psa.* 18.

Geleerd, E. R. 1956. Clinical contribution to the problem of the early mother-child relationship. *Psa. Study of the Child* 11:336–351. New York: International Universities Press.

Gerard, R. 1955. The biological roots of psychiatry. *Amer. J. Psychiatry* 112:81.

Ghiselin, B. 1952. *The Creative Process.* New York: Mentor Books.

Gifford, S. 1960. Sleep, time and the early ego. *J. Amer. Psa. Assoc.* 8:5–42.

Gill, M. 1963. Topography and systems in psychoanalytic theory. *Psychol. Issues* 3.

Giovacchini, P. L. 1956. Coexisting organ neurosis: a clinical study. *Psychosom. Med.* 18:84.

——. 1959. On gadgets. *Psa. Q.* 28:330–341.

——. 1960. On scientific creativity. *J. Amer. Psa. Assn.* 8(3):407–426.

——. 1961. Ego adaptation and cultural variables. *Arch. Gen. Psychiatry* 5:37–45.

———. 1966a. Discussion: The psychoanalytic situation. In: *Psychoanalysis in the Americas,* ed. R. Litman. New York: International Universities Press, pp. 112–118.

———. 1966b. Workshop on structural theory. *Bull. Chicago Psa. Soc.* 2:3–4.

———. 1969. Aggression: Adaptive and disruptive aspects. *Bull. Philadelphia Assn. Psa.* 19:79–86.

———. 1972. *Tactics and Techniques in Psychoanalytic Therapy,* 1. New York: Aronson.

Gitelson, M. 1958a. On ego distortion. *Internat. J. Psa.* 39:245–257.

———. 1958b. Panel discussion: Neurotic ego distortion. *Internat. J. Psa.* 39:243–275.

———. 1962. The first phase of psychoanalysis. *Internat. J. Psa.* 43.

Glover, E. 1930. Grades of ego differentiation. *Internat. J. Psa.* 11:1–12.

Greenacre, P. 1945. The biological economy of birth. *Psa. Study of the Child* 1:31. New York: International Universities Press.

———. 1947. Vision, headache and the halo. *Psa. Q.* 177–194.

———. 1950. The prepuberty trauma in girls. *Psa. Q.* 19:298–317.

———. 1956. Experiences of awe in childhood. *Psa. Study of the Child* 11:9–30. New York: International Universities Press.

———. 1957. The childhood of the artist. *Psa. Study of the Child* 12:47–72. New York: International Universities Press.

———. 1958. The family romance of the artist. *Psa. Study of the Child* 13. New York: International Universities Press.

Greene, W. A., Jr., Young, L. E., & Swisher, S. N. 1956. Psychological factors and reticuloendothelial disease. II. Observations of a group of women with lymphomas and leukemia. *Psychosom. Med.* 18:284.

Greenson, R. 1958. On screen defenses, screen hunger and screen identity. *J. Amer. Psa. Assoc.* 6:242–262.

———. 1965. The working alliance and the transference neurosis. *Psa. Q.* 34:155–181.

———. 1969. *The Technique and Practice of Psychoanalysis.* New York: International Universities Press.

Grinker, R. R. 1953. Some current trends and hypotheses of psychosomatic research. In: *The Psychosomatic Concept in Psychoanalysis,* ed. F. Deutsch. New York: International Universities Press.

———. 1963. A dynamic study of the "homoclite." In: *Science and Psychoanalysis,* ed. J. H. Masserman. New York: Grune & Stratton.

———, Werble, B., & Drye, R. C. 1968. *The Borderline Syndrome.* New York: Basic Books.

Hartmann, H. 1939. *Ego Psychology and the Problem of Adaptation.* New York: International Universities Press, 1958.

———. 1946. The mutual influences in the development of the ego and the id. *Psa. Study of the Child* 2. New York: International Universities Press.

———. 1950. Comments on the psychoanalytic theory of the ego. *Psa. Study of the Child* 5:74–96. New York: International Universities Press.

———. 1952. The mutual influences in the development of ego and id. *Psa. Study of the Child* 7:9–30. New York: International Universities Press.

———. 1955. Notes on the theory of sublimation. *Psa. Study of the Child* 10:9–29. New York: International Universities Press.

———. 1956. Ego psychology and the problems of adaptation. In: *Organization and Pathology of Thought*, ed. D. Rapaport. New York: Columbia University Press.

——— & Kris, E. 1945. The genetic approach in psychoanalysis. *Psa. Study of the Child* 1:11–30. New York: International Universities Press.

———, ———, & Loewenstein, M. 1949. Notes on the theory of aggression. *Psa. Study of the Child* 3/4:9–36. New York: International Universities Press.

Hayman, A. 1965. Verbalization and identity. *Int. J. Psa.* 46:455–466.

Heilbrunn, G. 1967. How "cool" is the beatnik? *Psa. Forum* 2:31–55.

Heimann, P. 1942. A contribution to the problem of sublimation and its relation to internalization. *Internat. J. Psa.* 23:8–17.

Herrick, E. J. 1956. *The Evolution of Human Nature*. Austin: University of Texas Press.

Isaacs, S. 1952. The nature and function of phantasy. In *Developments in Psychoanalysis*, ed. Miklein et al. London: Hogarth Press.

Jacobson, E. 1954. The self and the object world. *Psa. Study of the Child* 9:75–127. New York: International Universities Press.

———. 1959. Depersonalization. *J. Amer. Psa. Assn.* 7:591–610.

———. 1964. *The Self and the Object World*. New York: International Universities Press.

James, M. 1960. Premature ego development: some observations on disturbances in the first three months of life. *Int. J. Psa.* 41:288–294.

Johnson, A. M. 1949. Sanction for superego lacunae of adolescents. In *Searchlights on Delinquency*, ed. K. Eissler. New York: International Universities Press.

——— & Szurek, S. A. 1952. The genesis of antisocial acting out in children and adults. *Psa. Q.* 3:323.

Jones, E. 1953. *The Life and Works of Sigmund Freud,* 1. New York: Basic Books.

Kalina, E. 1969. El proceso analitico de un adolescente con un estado "como si." Paper presented to the Argentinian Analytic Association, November.

Kanzer, M. 1955. The reality testing of the scientist. *Psychoanal. Rev.* 42:412–419.

———. 1967. Discussion of Ego Regression by P. Giovacchini, American Psychoanalytic Association, Spring meeting, Detroit.

Kernberg, Otto. 1969. The treatment of patients with borderline personality organization. *Int. J. Psa.* 49:600–620.

———. 1975. *Borderline Conditions and Pathological Narcissism*. New York: Aronson.

Khan, M. M. R. 1960a. Clinical aspects of the schizoid personality: affects and technique. *Int. J. Psa.* 41:430–437.

————.1960b. Regression and integration in the analytic setting. *Int. J. Psa.* 41:130–146.

————. 1964. Ego distortion, cumulative trauma, and the role of reconstruction in the analytic situation. *Internat. J. Psa.* 45:272–279.

Klein, M. 1929. Infantile anxiety situations reflected in a work of art. *Internat. J. Psa.* 10:436–444.

————. 1932. *The Psycho-Analysis of Children*. London: Hogarth Press, 1937.

————. 1935. A contribution to the psychogenesis of manic-depressive states. In: *Contributions to Psycho-Analysis 1921–1945*. London: Hogarth Press, 1948.

————. 1946. Notes on some schizoid mechanisms. In: *Developments in Psychoanalysis*, ed. J. Riviere. London: Hogarth Press, 1948.

————. 1948. *Contributions to Psycho-Analysis 1921–1945*. London: Hogarth Press.

————. 1958. On the development of mental functioning. *Internat. J. Psa.* 39:84–90.

Knight, R. 1953. Borderline patients. *Bull. Menninger Clinic* 19:1–12.

Kris, E. 1936. The psychology of caricature. *Internat. J. Psa.* 17:285–303.

————. 1950a. Notes on the development and on some current problems of psychoanalytic child psychology. *Psa. Study of the Child 5*. New York: International Universities Press.

————. 1950b. On preconscious mental processes. *Psa. Q.* 19:540–556.

————. 1951. Ego psychology and interpretation in psychoanalytic therapy. *Psa. Q.* 20:15–30.

————. 1952. *Psychoanalytic Explorations in Art*. New York: International Universities Press.

————. 1955. Neutralization and sublimation: Observations on young children. *Psa. Study of the Child* 10:30–46. New York: International Universities Press.

Landauer, K. 1938. Affects, passions and temperament. *Int. J. Psa.* 19:388–415.

Langer, S. 1942. *Philosophy in a New Key*. New York: New American Library.

Laughlin, H. P. 1954. King David's anger. *Psa. Q.* 23.

LeShan, L. & Reznikoff, M. 1960. A psychological factor apparently associated with neoplastic disease. *J. Abnorm. & Social Psychol.* 60:439.

Lee, H. B. 1940. A theory concerning free creation in the inventive arts. *Psychiatry* 3:229–293.

————. 1947. On the aesthetic states of the mind. *Psychiatry* 10:281–306.

Lewin, B. 1946. Sleep, the mouth and the dream screen. *Psa. Q.* 15:419–433.

————. 1950. *The Psychoanalysis of Elation*. New York: Norton.

Lewin, K. 1951. Intention, will and need. In: *Organization and Pathology of Thought*, ed. D. Rapaport. New York: Columbia University Press.

Liberman, D. 1957. Interpretación correlativa entre relato y repetición. *Rev. Psicoanál.* 14:55–62.

————. 1966. *La Comunicación en Terapeutica Psicoanalitica*. Buenos Aires: Eudelia.

Lichtenstein, H. 1961. Identity and sexuality: a study of their interrelationship in man. *J. Amer. Psa. Assoc.* 9:179–260.

———. 1964. The role of narcissism in the emergence and maintenance of primary identity. *Int. J. Psa.* 45:49–56.

———. 1965. Towards a metapsychological definition of the concept of self. *Int. J. Psa.* 46:117–128.

———. 1970. Changing implications of the concept of psychosexual development: an inquiry concerning the validity of classical psychoanalytic assumptions concerning sexuality. *J. Amer. Psa. Assoc.* 18:300–318.

Lindon, J. A., ed. 1967. Panel on regression. *Psa. Forum* 2:295–317.

Little, M. 1958. On delusional transference. *Internat. J. Psa.* 39:134–138.

———. 1966. Transference in borderline states. *Internat. J. Psa.* 47:476–485.

Loewald, H. 1960. On the therapeutic action of psycho-analysis. *Internat. J. Psa.* 41:16–33.

———. 1962. The superego and the ego-ideal. *Internat. J. Psa.* 43:264–268.

———. 1972. Panel: The experience of time. *J. Amer. Psa. Assn.* 20:456–483.

Loewenstein, R. 1956. Some remarks on the role of the speech in psychoanalytic technique. *Int. J. Psa.* 37:460–467.

Lorand, S. & Schneer, H., eds. 1962. *Adolescents: Psychoanalytic Approach to Problems and Therapy.* New York: Harper & Row.

Mahler, M. 1952. On child psychosis and schizophrenia: Autistic and symbiotic infantile psychoses. *Psa. Study of the Child* 7:286–305. New York: International Universities Press.

——— & Elkisch, P. 1953. Some observations of disturbances of the ego in a case of infantile psychosis. *Psa. Study of the Child* 8:252–261. New York: International Universities Press.

Margolin, S. 1953. Genetic and dynamic psychophysiological determinants of pathophysiological processes. In: *The Psychosomatic Concept in Psychoanalysis,* ed. F. Deutsch. New York: International Universities Press.

Marmor, J. 1955. Orality in the hysterical personality. *J. Amer. Psa. Assn.* 3.

Menaker, E. 1956. A note on some biological parallels between certain innate animal behavior and moral masochism. *Psa. Rev.* 43:31–41.

Menninger, K. 1954. Psychological aspects of the organism under stress. Parts 1 and 2. *J. Amer. Psa. Assn.* 2:67, 280.

Mirsky, I. A. 1953. Psychoanalysis and the biological sciences. In *Twenty Years of Psychoanalysis.* New York: Norton.

Mittelmann, B. 1944. Complementary neurotic reactions in intimate relationships. *Psa. Q.* 13:479.

Modell, A. 1963. Primitive object relationships and the predisposition to schizophrenia. *Int. J. Psa.* 44:282–293.

Moran, M. 1956. Some emotional responses of patients' husbands to the psychotherapeutic course as indicated in interviews with the psychiatric caseworker. *Amer. J. Orthopsychiat.* 24:317–325.

Mosse, E. P. 1954. The handling of relatives in the psychoanalytic situation. *Psa. Rev.* 41.

Muslin, H. & Pieper, W. 1962. Separation experience and cancer of the breast. *Psychosomatics* 11:230.

Nacht, S. 1962. The curative factors in psycho-analysis. *Int. J. Psa.* 43.

Oberndorf, C. P. 1938. Psychoanalysis of married couples. *Psa. Rev.* 25:453.
Offer, D. & Sabshin, M. 1966. *Normality.* New York: Basic Books.
Orgel, S. 1965. On time and timelessness. *J. Amer. Psa. Assoc.* 13:102–121.

Panel on Isolation. 1959. Reported by H. F. Marasse. *J. Amer. Psa. Assn.* 7:163–172.
Piaget, J. 1951. *Play, Dreams and Imitation.* New York: Norton.
———. 1952. *The Moral Judgment of the Child.* Glencoe, Ill.: Free Press.
———. 1966. Time perception in children. In: *The Voices of Time,* ed. J. F. Frazer. New York: Braziller.
Poincaré, J. H. 1952. *Science and Method.* New York: Dover.
Pollock, G. H. 1964. On symbiosis and symbiotic neurosis. *Internat. J. Psa.* 45:1–31.
Pressman, M. 1969. The cognitive function of the ego in psychoanalysis. *Int. J. Psa.* 50:187–196.
Provence, S. & Ritvo, S. 1961. Effects of deprivation on institutionalized infants. *Psa. Study of the Child* 16:189–205. New York: International Universities Press.
Pupin, M. I. 1925. *From Immigrant to Inventor.* New York: Scribner's.

Rado, S. 1928. The problem of melancholia. *Internat. J. Psa.* 9:4–20.
Rangell, L. 1959. The nature of conversion. *J. Amer. Psa. Assn.* 7.
Rank, O. 1932. *Art and Artist.* New York: Knopf.
Rapaport, D. 1956. Toward a theory of thinking. In: *Organization and Pathology of Thought.* New York: Columbia University Press, pp. 689–731.
———. 1966. The structure of psychoanalytic theory. *Psychol. Issues.*
——— & Gill, M. 1959. The points of view and assumptions of metapsychology. *Int. J. Psa.* 40:153–163.
Reich, A. 1953. Narcissistic object choice in women. *J. Amer. Psa. Assoc.* 1:218–238.
Reisen, A. H. 1947. The development of visual perception in man and chimpanzee. *Science* 106:6–20.
Renneker, R. et al. 1963. Psychoanalytic exploration of emotional correlates of cancer of the breast. *Psychosom. Med.* 25:106.
Roe, A. 1953. *The Making of a Scientist.* New York: Dodd, Mead.
Róheim, G. 1947. *Psychoanalysis and the Social Sciences.* New York: International Universities Press.
Rosen, V. H. 1953. On mathematical "illumination" and the mathematical thought process. *Psa. Study of the Child* 8:127–154. New York: International Universities Press.
———. 1955. Strephosymbolia: an intrasystemic disturbance of the synthetic function of the ego. *Psa. Study of the Child* 10:83–99. New York: International Universities Press.
———. 1958. Abstract thinking and object relations. With special reference to the

use of abstraction as a regressive defense in highly gifted individuals. *J. Amer. Psa. Assn.* 6:653–661.

———. 1960. Imagination in the analytic process. *J. Amer. Psa. Assn.* 8:229–251.

———. 1961. The relevance of "style" to certain aspects of defense and the synthetic function of the ego. *Internat. J. Psa.* 42:447–457.

Ross, N. 1967. The "as if" concept. *J. Amer. Psa. Assoc.* 15:58–83.

Sachs, H. 1942. *The Creative Unconscious.* Cambridge, Mass.: Sci-Art.

——— & Joffe, W. 1963. The ego ideal and the ideal self. *Psa. Study of the Child* 18: 139–158. New York: International Universities Press.

——— & Rosenblatt, B. 1962. The concept of the representational world. *Psa. Study of the Child* 17:128–145. New York: International Universities Press.

Sanford, B. 1957. Some notes on a dying patient. *Internat. J. Psa.* 38:158.

———. 1966. A patient and her cats. *Psa. Forum* 1:170–176.

Saul, L. 1939. Hostility in cases of essential hypertension. *Psychosom. Med.* 1:153.

Schafer, R. 1960. The loving and beloved superego in Freud's structural theory. *Psa. Study of the Child* 15:163–188. New York: International Universities Press.

Schmale, A. N. 1958. Relationships of separation and depression to disease. *Psychosom. Med.* 20:259.

Schur, M. 1955. Comments on the metapsychology of somatization. *Psa. Study of the Child* 10:119–165. New York: International Universities Press.

———. 1958. The ego and the id in anxiety. *Psa. Study of the Child* 13:190–223. New York: International Universities Press.

Schwartz, J. & Semrad, E. 1951. Psychosomatic disorders in psychoses. *Psychosom. Med.* 13:314.

Searles, H. F. 1961a. The evolution of the mother transference in psychotherapy with the schizophrenic patient. In *Collected Papers on Schizophrenia and Related Subjects.* New York: International Universities Press, 1965.

———. 1961b. Phases of patient-therapist interaction in the psychotherapy of chronic schizophrenia. *Br. J. Med. Psychol.* 34:169–193.

———. 1963. Transference psychosis in the psychotherapy of chronic schizophrenia. *Int. J. Psa.* 44:654–716.

———. 1965. *Collected Papers on Schizophrenia and Related Subjects.* New York: International Universities Press.

Sechehaye, M. A. 1951. *Symbiotic Realization.* New York: International Universities Press.

Segal, H. 1967. Melanie Klein's technique. *Psa. Forum* 2:197–241.

Seitz, P. F. D. 1963. Representation of structures in the concrete imagery of dreams. Paper presented before the Chicago Psychoanalytic Society, January 22.

Sharfstein, B. 1978. Adolescents and philosophers: A word in favor of both. *Adol. Psychiatry* 6:51–58.

Sharpe, E. F. 1930. Certain aspects of sublimation and delusion. *Internat. J. Psa.* 11:12–23.

———. 1935. Similar and divergent unconscious determinants underlying the sublimations of pure art and pure science. *Internat. J. Psa.* 16:186–202.

Siegman, A. J. 1954. Emotionality: A hysterical character defense. *Psa. Q.* 23:339.

Silber, E. 1962. The analyst's participation in the treatment of an adolescent. *Psychiat.* 25.

Silverman, S. 1959. The role of the aggressive drives in the conversion process. In: *On the Mysterious Leap from the Mind to the Body,* ed. F. Deutsch. New York: International Universities Press.

Spitz, R. A. 1945. Hospitalism: An inquiry into the genesis of psychiatric conditions in early childhood. *Psa. Study of the Child* 1. New York: International Universities Press.

————. 1951. The psychogenic diseases in infancy: An attempt at their etiologic classification. *Psa. Study of the Child* 6:255–275. New York: International Universities Press.

————. 1956a. Countertransference. *J. Amer. Psa. Assn.* 4.

————. 1956b. Transference: The analytic setting and its prototype. *Internat. J. Psa.* 37:380–385.

————. 1957. *No and Yes.* New York: International Universities Press.

————. 1959. *A Genetic Field Theory of Ego Formation.* New York: International Universities Press.

————. 1965. *The First Year of Life.* New York: International Universities Press.

Stein, M. 1953. Creativity and culture. *J. Psychol.* 32:311–322.

Stekel, W. 1920. Poetry and neurosis. *Psa. Rev.* 10:73–96.

Sterba, R. 1934. The fate of the ego in analytic therapy. *Internat. J. Psa.* 15:117–126.

Stone, L. 1963. *The Psychoanalytic Situation.* New York: International Universities Press.

Strachey, J. 1934. The nature of the therapeutic action of psychoanalysis. *Internat. J. Psa.* 15:127–159.

Strauss, E. W. 1967. An existential approach to time. In: *Interdisciplinary perspectives of time,* ed. R. Fisher. *Annals N.Y. Acad. Sci.* 138.

Waelder, R., et al. 1958. Neurotic ego distortion. *Int. J. Psa.* 39.

Weiss, E. 1950. *Principles of Psychodynamics.* New York: Grune and Stratton.

Weiss, S. 1963. Parameters in child analysis. Paper presented before the American Psychoanalytic Association fall meeting, New York.

Winnicott, D. W. 1947. Hate in the countertransference. In: *Collected Papers,* 1958a.

————. 1949. Mind and its relation to the psyche-soma. In: *Collected Papers,* 1958a.

————. 1952. Psychoses and child care. In: *Collected Papers,* 1958a.

————. 1953. Transitional objects and transitional phenomena. In: *Collected Papers,* 1958a.

————. 1955. Metapsychological and clinical aspects of regression within the psycho-analytic set-up. In: *Collected Papers,* 1958a.

————. 1958a. *Collected Papers: Through Pediatrics to Psycho-analysis.* New York: Basic Books.

————. 1958b. The capacity to be alone. *Internat. J. Psa.* 39:416–440.

————. 1963. Psychotherapy of character disorders. In: *The Maturational Processes and the Facilitating Environment.* New York: International Universities Press, 1965.

————. 1965. *The Maturational Processes and the Facilitating Environment.* New York: International Universities Press.

Zeigarnek, B. 1927. Das behalten erledigter und unerledigter handlung. *Psychologische Forschung* 9:1–85.

Zetzel, E. 1949. Anxiety and the capacity to bear it. *Int. J. Psa.* 30:1–12.

————. 1956. Current concepts of transference. *J. Amer. Psa. Assn.* 1:526–537.

Zilboorg, G. 1933. Anxiety without affect. *Psa. Q.* 2:48–67.

INDEX